THE Chicago Tribune

GOOD EATING COOKBOOK

EDITED BY
CAROL MIGHTON HADDIX

CB

CONTEMPORARY BOOKS

Library of Congress Cataloging-in-Publication Data

The Chicago Tribune good eating cookbook / edited by Carol Mighton Haddix.
     p.   cm.
   ISBN 0-8092-9975-5
    1. Cookery.   I. Mighton Haddix, Carol.   II. *Chicago Tribune*.
TX714.C475   2000
641.5—dc21   00-29473

Interior design by Hespenheide Design

Published by Contemporary Books
A division of NTC/Contemporary Publishing Group, Inc.
4255 West Touhy Avenue, Lincolnwood (Chicago), Illinois 60712-1975 U.S.A.
Copyright © 2001 by the Chicago Tribune Company
All rights reserved. No part of this book may be reproduced, stored in a retrieval
system, or transmitted in any form or by any means, electronic, mechanical,
photocopying, recording, or otherwise, without the prior written permission of
NTC/Contemporary Publishing Group, Inc.
Printed in the United States of America
International Standard Book Number: 0-8092-9975-5

01 02 03 04 05 06 QK 18 17 16 15 14 13 12 11 10 9 8 7 6 5 4 3 2 1

CONTENTS

~ ACKNOWLEDGMENTS ~

WE WOULD LIKE to thank the many people who have made this book possible. We appreciate the support and encouragement of *Tribune* vice president and editor Howard Tyner, managing editor Ann Marie Lipinski, associate editor of operations Joe Leonard, deputy managing editor of features Gerould Kern, and special features editor Janet Franz.

The "Good Eating" staff provided the introductions to the recipes as well as general support: thanks go to Andy Badeker, Kristin Eddy, Renée Enna, and William Rice.

For recipe testing and food styling, Alicia Tessling, Joan Moravek, and Dianne Hugh deserve credit. For the beautiful photographs, kudos go to Bob Fila, James F. Quinn, and Bill Hogan and to the photo lab staff for tracking down photos.

Staff members of the *Chicago Tribune*'s Editorial Information Center combed the archives for recipes and photographs, and Rosemary Johnson ably tracked down recipe permissions. Nutritional analysis was provided by registered dietitians Jodie Shield and Mary Mullen.

And special appreciation goes to all of the cooks, chefs, restaurateurs, authors, and readers who have contributed recipes through the years to the *Chicago Tribune*. Without them, there would be no "Good Eating" section and no cookbook.

INTRODUCTION

When an earlier version of these recipes was published in 1989, the world seemed less connected and less rushed than today. In ten years, the pace of life has shifted into overdrive, leaving the dinner table by the roadside—or maybe just relegated to the backseat. Some of the changes in the last decade are striking:

∾ We want faster food. A typical dinner used to take an hour to cook; now we aim for ten minutes.

∾ "Low in fat" is a mantra. Our obsession with cutting out fat in recipes has grown, though signs of a backlash hover on the food fringes (desserts, for example, are our most requested recipes).

∾ Simple recipes are saved. Those with fewer than five ingredients are hits.

∾ Fewer families eat together. Meals are grabbed rather than savored.

∾ From-scratch recipes are as rare as line-hung laundry. Cans, bottles, and frozen packages ease the way to mealtime now. Convenience items line our cupboards and freezers. Say hello to instant polenta, rice in a bowl, premarinated meats, and ready-to-heat roasts.

∾ Takeout is taking over. And more foods are delivered from restaurants than ever before.

∾ *Web food* has nothing to do with ducks' feet. The Internet now provides us with an overabundance of instant recipes and information. It can calculate the nutrition content of your favorite recipes or find you a quick weeknight menu. The number of on-line food shoppers is growing faster than that of supermarket customers.

∾ Ethnic-inspired recipes and foods are becoming mainstream. Thai coconut milk, lemon grass, Japanese sushi, Indian frozen entrees, and

Mexican chilies are found in most urban supermarkets and are making inroads elsewhere.

∾ Cookbooks have become late-night reading. People buy them to read and enjoy vicariously; few use them for actually cooking.

The *Tribune* food staff's challenge in this changing world is to address these changes, ease mealtime burdens, and provide help in the kitchen, from sharing tested recipes or shopping advice to reporting the latest nutrition news. But most of all we want to bring readers proven recipes that taste great. We've been working to that end for years.

The *Tribune* test kitchen dates back to 1948, though it has appeared in many guises and locations. It is now located on the fourth floor of Tribune Tower, where we test five hundred to seven hundred recipes each year. The photography studio, where the photos in this book were created, is conveniently located next to the kitchen.

Through weekly tastings we choose the recipes that will appear in "Good Eating," "Home & Garden," and the *Tribune Magazine*. When tasting them, we all ask ourselves one major question: "Would I make this recipe at home?"

In putting this book together, we tried to tell the story behind the recipes. Some come from local or national chefs, some from our readers, some from new cookbooks. The rest we have developed in the test kitchen.

For this edition, we have replaced some of the more dated recipes with 250 new ones to better match today's cooking styles. We have also updated some of the older recipes, cutting down on fat in some, simplifying directions in others. We've added nutrition information to every recipe in response to reader requests.

The recipes include a good number of comfort foods such as macaroni and cheese, smothered pork chops, and pumpkin pie. But you'll also find a quick ten-minute pasta and an exotic Vietnamese salad. Many regional classics from a series of articles we called "American Originals" also appear: Mangrove Mama's Key Lime Pie, Carolina Pork Barbecue, and Indiana-Style Persimmon Pudding, for example.

Cooking is creative and fun. And yet many have lost sight of the joy cooking can bring. Our constant rushing to meet the deadlines of our busy lives has nothing to do with nurturing. Hopefully, some of the recipes in this book will inspire you to take up a wooden spoon again and cook.

Carol Mighton Haddix
Food Editor
Chicago Tribune

❧ TWENTY-FIVE ❧
SUGGESTED MENUS

Winter

FESTIVE NEW YEAR'S BRUNCH

Bubbling Passion (see Note, page 49)
Lobster Margarita (page 12)
Egg Crepes with Red Bell Peppers and Mushrooms (page 61)
Spinach Salad with Orange-Chipotle Dressing (page 350)
Macadamia Nut Tart (page 458)

LOW-FAT SUPPER

Chicken with Potato "Skin" (page 263)
Sesame, Broccoli, and Cauliflower Salad (page 356)
Mixed Seed Crisp Bread (page 421)
Pineapple-Ginger Sorbet (page 471)
Chardonnay

WINTER IN THE TROPICS

Lemon Raita Dip (page 6)
Pita or nan bread
Jerk Pork Tenderloin (page 238)
Jasmine Rice with Red Pepper and Cumin–Spiced Shallots (page 124)
Tropical Bean Salad (page 359)
Frozen Mango Whip (page 473)
Indian Spiced Tea (page 39)

HEARTY BREAKFAST

Orange-pineapple juice
Oven French Toast (page 64)
Spicy Mixed Sausage Grill (page 74)
Spiced Applesauce (page 479)

VALENTINE'S DAY DINNER

Champagne
Oysters with Endive and Cream (page 14)
Steak Diane (page 213)
Oprah's Potatoes (page 322)
Balsamic-Glazed Carrots (page 313)
Warm, Soft Chocolate Cake (page 434)

ST. PATRICK'S DAY CELEBRATION

Salmon over Sweet Onions and Cabbage with Light Cream Sauce (page 184)
Buttered New Potatoes and Peas with Watercress (page 326)
Irish Soda Bread (page 408)
Lemon Shortbread Cookies (page 481)
Irish ale

Spring

EASTER BRUNCH

Citrus Spritzer (page 36)
Alsatian Onion Tart (page 27)
Ham with Peanut-Chili Glaze (glaze, page 245)
Asparagus with Lemon Butter (page 300)
Hot Cross Buns (page 407)
White Chocolate Coconut Cake (page 435)

"FAST" FOOD FEAST

Angel Hair with Garlic and Arugula (page 116)
Peas with Purple Basil and Shallots (page 332)
Focaccia
Kiwi and Strawberry Compote with Ginger-Mint Syrup (page 475)
Ginger-Peach Tea (page 38)

SPRING LUNCHEON

Rhubarb Lemonade Punch (page 34)
Sweet-Hot Monte Cristo Sandwiches (page 138)
Tropical Fruit Platter with Honey-Lime Dressing (page 362)
Java Brownies (page 498)

MEMORIAL DAY PICNIC

Sparkling Orange-Mint Juleps (page 35)
Quinoa with Chicken (page 131)
Zucchini or Green Beans in Fresh Tarragon Marinade (page 338)
Jalapeño Corn Muffins (page 411)
Buttermilk Lemon Cake (page 423)

FAMILY WEEKEND LUNCH

Quick Creole Gumbo (page 84)
Cheddar-Onion Corn Muffins (page 411)
Chocolate Peanut Butter Cookies (page 495)
Milk

FUSION FARE

Vegetarian Stir-Fry with Pan-Seared Tofu in Citrus-Soy Broth (page 339)
Swordfish with Fusion Barbecue Sauce (sauce, page 256)
Asian Pesto with Noodles (page 121)
Sassy Slaw (page 365)
Ginger Peach Pie (page 451)
Riesling

Summer

GRILLING PARTY

Hot Goat Cheese and Herbed Tomato Sauce Dip (page 6)
French bread croutons
Grilled Butterflied Leg of Lamb with Herb Marinade (page 253)
Green Beans with Garlic Almonds (page 303)
Orzo with Browned Onions and Basil (page 123)
Tangy Lemon-Plum Tart (page 457)
Sangria or merlot

TWENTY-MINUTE MEAL

Veal Scallops with Sage and Capers (page 227)
Mustardy Green Beans (page 302)
Balsamic-Dressed Mixed Green Salad (page 344)
Breadsticks
Blueberry–Passion Fruit Compote (page 474)
Sauvignon blanc

TRATTORIA DINNER PARTY

Tomato and Basil Tart (page 26)
Roasted Vegetable Risotto (page 126)
Seared Pepper-Crusted Tuna with Tomatoes and Balsamic Glaze (page 174)
Arugula and Fennel Salad (page 352)
Fresh Figs and Raspberries with Cream (page 476)
Pinot grigio
Espresso

THAI SAMPLER

Thai Pork Satay with Peanut Sauce and Cucumbers (page 16)
Thai Whole Fried Red Snapper (page 167)
Chicken Curry with Bamboo Shoots (page 272)
Basil Fried Rice (page 125)
Honeydew Melon Sorbet (page 470)
Gewürztraminer

BACKYARD BASH

Coyote's Ultimate Margarita (page 44)
Spicy Bean Dip (page 5) with tortilla chips
Chicago-Style Barbecued Ribs (page 245)
Garlic Potato Salad (page 369)
Santa Fe Vegetable Salad with Lime Cream Dressing (page 355)
Triple-Berry Lattice Pie (page 446)
Vanilla ice cream

Autumn

PASTA PARTY

White Bean and Black Truffle Soup (page 93)
Caesar Salad (page 346)
Fiesta Spaghetti Sauce and Meatballs (page 106)
Country Parmesan Herb Bread (page 389)
Mama T.'s Italian Cheesecake (page 441)
Barbaresco or Chianti

QUICK WEEKNIGHT MEAL

Strip Steaks with Shallot-Pepper Relish (page 210)
Gorgonzola-Cheese Baked Potatoes (page 326)
Mixed Greens with Spiced Almonds and Chutney Dressing (page 343)
Coffee ice cream
Chocolate Cognac Sauce (page 479)
Cabernet sauvignon

FRENCH BISTRO SUPPER

Duck Liver Pâté (page 15)
French bread
Blackbird's Fish Soup (page 78)
Lyonnaise Salad (page 348)
Crème Caramel (page 465)
Sancerre

PIZZA PIZZAZZ

Romaine with Creamy Black Peppercorn Dressing (dressing, page 384)
Chicago-Style Stuffed Pizza (page 158)
Pear Lemon Ice (page 472)
Zinfandel

THANKSGIVING FEAST

Peppered Sweet Potato–Sage Bisque (page 102)
Turkey with Herbed Cornbread Stuffing and Pan Gravy (page 281)
    or Stuffed Turkey Breast (page 284)
Marbled Mashed Potatoes (page 323)
Smoky Brussels Sprouts (page 308)
Steamed Butternut Squash with Gingerroot (page 335)
Holiday Cranberry Salad (page 359)
Ginger Apple Pie (page 448)
Bourbon-Pecan-Pumpkin Pudding (page 462)
Riesling and/or zinfandel

HANUKKAH CELEBRATION

Curried Sweet Potato Latkes (page 329)
Roast Brisket with Barbecue Sauce (page 219)
Sweet-and-Sour Red Cabbage (page 309)
Braised Artichoke Hearts with Arugula and Fava Beans (page 298)
Sour Cherry Rugelach (page 492)
Kosher wine

CHRISTMAS DINNER

Swedish Glogg (page 47)
Smoked Trout Mousse (page 10)
Curried Cream of Acorn Squash Soup (page 101)
Herb-Crusted Pork Loin Roast (page 240)
Oprah's Potatoes (page 322)
Green Beans with Garlic Almonds (page 303)
Beet and Mâche Salad with Walnuts (page 352)
Mary Meade's White Fruitcake (page 437)
Sweet Potato Pie (page 453)
Burgundy

NEW YEAR'S EVE PARTY

Sparkling Apricot Punch (page 48)
Creole Pecans (page 1)
Cheddar Cheese Wafers (page 3)
Spicy Mustard Beef Tenderloin with Oven-Roasted Potatoes (page 215)
Carrot and Red Pepper Puree (page 312)
Black-Eyed Peas (page 306)
Pecan Meringue Cake (page 428)
Bordeaux

ABOUT THE RECIPES' NUTRITION INFORMATION

BECAUSE OF VARIATIONS in ingredients and measurements, the numbers at the end of each recipe are approximations. This is especially true for dishes that involve marinades; in most cases we have assumed that one-fourth of marinade ingredients end up in the finished dish.

When a recipe gives a range in the amount of an ingredient, the smaller amount is used.

Analyses do not include optional ingredients, garnishes, fat used to grease pans, or suggested accompaniments unless specific amounts are given.

Salt is figured only if a recipe calls for a specific amount. Salt added to cooking water is not included. Broth or stock is considered to be the salted variety unless otherwise specified.

APPETIZERS

Creole Pecans

PREPARATION TIME: 5 minutes
COOKING TIME: 5 minutes
YIELD: 12 ¼-cup servings

THE COOKS OF New Orleans are masters of seasoning. Here's a deceptively simple recipe that offers proof of their skill as interpreted by our test kitchen.

1 teaspoon ground red pepper
1 teaspoon dried leaf thyme
½ teaspoon onion powder
½ teaspoon salt

½ teaspoon freshly ground black pepper
¼ teaspoon garlic powder
3 tablespoons unsalted butter
3 cups pecan halves *or* cashews

1. Stir together red pepper, thyme, onion powder, salt, black pepper, and garlic powder in a small bowl.
2. Melt butter in a large skillet over medium heat. Stir in nuts. Cook, stirring often, over medium heat until nuts are lightly toasted, about 3 minutes. Add spice mixture; toss to coat well.
3. Cool on a baking sheet set on a wire rack.

NUTRITION INFORMATION PER SERVING:

207 calories	21 g fat	3.3 g saturated fat
87% calories from fat	8 mg cholesterol	98 mg sodium
5 g carbohydrate	2.2 g protein	2.2 g fiber

Indian-Style Nuts

PREPARATION TIME: 15 minutes
COOKING TIME: 5 minutes
YIELD: 20 ¼-cup servings

THERE'S NOTHING NEW about nuts as a party snack, but your guests will do a double take when they taste nuts with the lively spice coating this recipe provides. Will they come back for more? You bet.

1 cup dry-roasted unsalted cashews *or* macadamia nuts	1 tablespoon curry powder
	¾ teaspoon ground cumin
1 cup dry-roasted unsalted peanuts	¾ teaspoon ground coriander
1 cup halved Brazil nuts *or* walnuts	¼ teaspoon ground red pepper
1 cup hazelnuts	¼ teaspoon salt
1 cup dark raisins	6 tablespoons unsalted butter

1. Combine cashews, peanuts, Brazil nuts, hazelnuts, and raisins in a large bowl. Stir together curry, cumin, coriander, red pepper, and salt in a small bowl.

2. Melt butter in a large skillet. Add nuts and spice mixture; toss well to coat. Cook, stirring often, over medium heat until nuts are lightly toasted, about 3 minutes. Cool on a baking sheet set on a wire rack.

NUTRITION INFORMATION PER SERVING:

229 calories	19 g fat	6 g saturated fat
72% calories from fat	9 mg cholesterol	34 mg sodium
12 g carbohydrate	5 g protein	2.4 g fiber

Sesame Pita Chips

PREPARATION TIME: 15 minutes
COOKING TIME: 15 minutes
YIELD: 6 4-chip servings

TRANSFORM PITA BREAD into a crisp, crunchy snack simply by brushing pieces of it with butter and baking them until crisp. Serve the pita chips with vegetable dips or eggplant spread.

3 pita pockets	1 tablespoon sesame seeds
½ cup (1 stick) butter, melted	Salt, garlic salt, *or* onion salt

1. Heat oven to 350°F. Cut each pita pocket into quarters. Split each quarter in half. Brush insides of slices with butter.

2. Put slices in a single layer on a baking sheet buttered side up. Sprinkle with sesame seeds. Bake until crisp and golden, about 15 minutes. Season with salt to taste.

NUTRITION INFORMATION PER SERVING:

227 calories	16 g fat	10 g saturated fat
65% calories from fat	17 mg cholesterol	317 mg sodium
17 g carbohydrate	3 g protein	0.8 g fiber

Cheddar Cheese Wafers

PREPARATION TIME: 20 minutes
CHILLING TIME: 1 hour
BAKING TIME: 10 to 12 minutes
YIELD: About 5 dozen wafers

USE GOOD, SHARP cheddar cheese, such as a New York Herkimer, for these delicious and crispy crackers. They're like nuts—you can't stop eating them.

2 cups all-purpose flour	⅔ cup chilled unsalted butter *or*
1 teaspoon salt	margarine
¼ teaspoon dried dill weed	¾ cup grated cheddar cheese
¼ teaspoon ground red pepper	4 to 5 tablespoons ice water
⅛ teaspoon freshly ground black	
pepper	

1. Combine flour, salt, dill weed, red pepper, and black pepper in a large bowl. Cut in butter using a pastry blender or 2 knives until mixture forms coarse crumbs. Stir in cheese. Gradually add ice water 1 tablespoon at a time. Toss with a fork until dough gathers into a ball. Roll dough into a log about 1½ inches in diameter. Refrigerate wrapped in waxed paper until firm, about 1 hour.

2. Heat oven to 400°F. Cut log into ¼-inch-thick slices and place slices on ungreased baking sheets. Bake until wafers are crisp and bottoms are golden, 10 to 12 minutes. Cool on a wire rack. Store in a covered tin.

NUTRITION INFORMATION PER WAFER:

39 calories	2.5 g fat	1.6 g saturated fat
59% calories from fat	7 mg cholesterol	48 mg sodium
3.2 g carbohydrate	0.8 g protein	0.1 g fiber

Fresh Tomatillo Salsa

PREPARATION TIME: 15 minutes

YIELD: 6 ¼-cup servings

THE TOMATILLO, A small green fruit encased in a papery husk, is the base of this salsa. Tomatillos are often labeled "green tomatoes," but they are related to the gooseberry, not the tomato. For the freshest taste, prepare the salsa just before serving it with your favorite tortilla chips.

8 tomatillos, husks removed	1 medium-sized white onion,
2 cloves garlic	chopped
½ teaspoon salt	1 serrano chili, seeded and chopped
	½ cup cilantro leaves

1. Heat water to boil in a large saucepan over high heat. Add tomatillos; boil 1 minute. Drain; rinse in cold water.

2. Grind garlic with salt in a food processor fitted with a metal blade or in a *molcajete* (Mexican mortar and pestle). Do not puree. Add onion, serrano, chili and cilantro; pulse or crush slightly. Add tomatillos a few at a time, pulsing or crushing slightly after each. Taste and adjust seasonings.

NUTRITION INFORMATION PER SERVING:

20 calories	0.4 g fat	0.1 g saturated fat
15% calories from fat	0 mg cholesterol	197 mg sodium
4.1 g carbohydrate	0.7 g protein	1 g fiber

Guacamole with Tomatoes

PREPARATION TIME: 15 minutes

YIELD: 6 servings

THE BEST WAY to achieve an appealing texture for guacamole is also the simplest: make it by hand. An ordinary fork will do the job. Haas avocados (they have a black-green skin with a pebbly surface) work well, but you can use other varieties too.

3 green onions, white part only,	1 small ripe tomato, peeled, seeded,
chopped	and diced
2 serrano chilies *or* jalapeños,	1 tablespoon finely chopped cilantro
seeded and minced	¼ teaspoon coarse salt
	2 ripe avocados, preferably Haas

1. Combine green onion, serrano chilies, tomato, cilantro, and salt in a small bowl. Mash mixture gently with a fork to release the juices of the tomato.

2. Cut each avocado in half; discard pit. Scrape the flesh from the shell into another bowl using a large spoon. Mash avocado with fork until chunky. Add the avocado to the vegetable mixture. Mix well. Taste and adjust seasoning.

NUTRITION INFORMATION PER SERVING:

117 calories	10 g fat	1.6 g saturated fat
73% calories from fat	0 mg cholesterol	107 mg sodium
7.1 g carbohydrate	1.8 g protein	3.8 g fiber

Spicy Bean Dip

PREPARATION TIME: 10 minutes

COOKING TIME: 5 minutes

YIELD: 8 ¼-cup servings

WHY GO OUT and buy bean dip in those little pull-top tin cans when it is so simple to make? Making it is also less costly. This dip is best served warm and with sturdy tortilla chips.

2 tablespoons vegetable oil
1 large yellow onion, minced
1 large clove garlic, minced
1 15-ounce can pinto beans, undrained

¾ cup shredded Monterey Jack cheese with jalapeños
Hot pepper sauce
Diced avocado
Tortilla chips
Salsa

1. Heat oil in a medium-sized saucepan over medium heat. Add onion and garlic. Cook, stirring often, until tender and lightly browned, about 5 minutes.

2. Puree beans with liquid in a food processor fitted with a metal blade or in a blender. Stir into onion mixture. Stir in cheese and hot pepper sauce to taste.

3. Heat dip over low heat just until hot and most of cheese is melted. Garnish with avocado. Serve with tortilla chips and salsa.

✻ NOTE: *To make in advance, complete through step 2 and refrigerate.*

NUTRITION INFORMATION PER SERVING:

124 calories	7 g fat	2.5 g saturated fat
51% calories from fat	9 mg cholesterol	160 mg sodium
10 g carbohydrate	6 g protein	3.2 g fiber

Lemon Raita Dip

PREPARATION TIME: 10 minutes
YIELD: 4 servings

TRADITIONALLY, THIS REFRESHING dip would be served with an Indian bread, such as nan. You may use pita bread instead. For best flavor, warm the bread over a gas burner before serving. This dip also works well with vegetable dippers. For *raita*, use whole-milk yogurt for the best texture.

½ small cucumber, peeled, seeded, and grated
½ cup plain whole-milk yogurt
Zest of ½ lemon, grated

1 tablespoon fresh lemon juice
¼ teaspoon ground cumin
¼ teaspoon ground coriander
⅛ teaspoon salt

1. Put cucumber in a double thickness of strong paper towels or cheesecloth; squeeze gently to remove excess moisture.

2. Combine cucumber, yogurt, lemon zest, lemon juice, cumin, coriander, and salt in a medium-sized bowl; mix well.

NUTRITION INFORMATION PER SERVING:

25 calories	1 g fat	0.7 g saturated fat
34% calories from fat	4 mg cholesterol	90 mg sodium
3.2 g carbohydrate	1.4 g protein	0.6 g fiber

Hot Goat Cheese and Herbed Tomato Sauce Dip

PREPARATION TIME: 30 minutes
CHILLING TIME: 3 hours
COOKING TIME: 1 hour
YIELD: 6 servings

THIS RECIPE FOR goat cheese dip comes from Chicago's Café Ba-Ba-Reeba! which serves an array of Spanish tapas. Garlic-flavored bread slices are a natural to serve with this flavorful dip.

Cheese Spread
6 ounces mild French goat cheese, such as Montrachet
6 ounces domestic *or* French goat cheese

2 tablespoons fresh rosemary leaves, minced
1 tablespoon fresh thyme leaves, minced
⅛ teaspoon white pepper

Tomato Sauce

2 tablespoons olive oil
½ onion, diced
½ small fresh fennel bulb, chopped
    (see Note)
1 small carrot, diced
5 cloves garlic, crushed
1 15-ounce can plum tomatoes,
    drained and diced

1 tablespoon tomato paste
2 teaspoons dried basil
1 teaspoon sugar
Salt
Freshly ground black pepper
6 tablespoons coarse bread crumbs
Black olives, preferably niçoise
Garlic bread slices

1. To make cheese spread, combine French goat cheese, domestic goat cheese, rosemary, thyme, and white pepper in a large bowl. Mix until smooth. Scrape onto waxed paper or aluminum foil; roll into a log shape. Refrigerate 3 to 12 hours.

2. To make tomato sauce, heat olive oil in a large saucepan over medium heat. Add onion, fennel, carrot, and garlic. Cook vegetables until soft, about 15 minutes. Stir in tomatoes, tomato paste, basil, sugar, salt, and black pepper. Simmer uncovered 35 minutes. Transfer sauce to a food processor fitted with a metal blade or to a blender. Process until almost smooth.

3. Heat oven to 500°F. Put about ½ cup of the tomato sauce into the bottom of 6 5½-inch gratin or other shallow oven-safe dishes. Top each with one-sixth of the goat cheese log. Sprinkle each with 1 tablespoon bread crumbs.

4. Bake until warm but cheese has not yet melted, 5 to 10 minutes. Garnish with olives. Serve with garlic bread for dipping.

❧ NOTE: *You may substitute ½ cup diced celery and ½ teaspoon fennel seeds for the fresh fennel bulb in the tomato sauce.*

NUTRITION INFORMATION PER SERVING:

258 calories
59% calories from fat
14 g carbohydrate

17 g fat
26 mg cholesterol
13 g protein

9 g saturated fat
398 mg sodium
2.3 g fiber

Baked Marinated Goat Cheese with Croutons and Olives

PREPARATION TIME: 25 minutes
DRAINING TIME: 12 hours or more
MARINATING TIME: 1 week
COOKING TIME: 8 minutes
YIELD: 4 servings

ODESSA PIPER, CHEF-OWNER of L'Etoile restaurant in Madison, Wisconsin, creates a weekly menu that expresses a special kinship between the restaurant and the exceptional local farmers market held across the street. Among the vendors there is Fantome Farm, which produces the goat cheese used by Piper in this hot appetizer.

1 pound fresh goat cheese	4 teaspoons dried basil
1 tablespoon kosher salt	4 teaspoons dried oregano
2 cups extra-virgin olive oil	12 ⅓-inch-thick slices French bread
8 large cloves garlic, minced	Salt
8 bay leaves	24 black brine-cured olives, pitted
4 teaspoons dried rosemary	and chopped fine

1. Divide cheese into 4 portions. Gently form each into a ball. Roll balls in kosher salt. Wrap balls in cheesecloth, tying them with string. Suspend cheese by the string from a knife set across a large bowl. Let cheese drain for 12 hours at room temperature. For firmer cheese, keep cheese suspended for another 24 hours in the refrigerator.

2. Mix olive oil, garlic, bay leaves, rosemary, basil, and oregano in a glass bowl or jar. Add unwrapped cheese; cover. Marinate 1 week to 1 month in refrigerator.

3. Heat oven to 300°F. Arrange bread slices in a single layer on a cookie sheet. Brush slices lightly with some of the marinade. Sprinkle them with salt. Bake croutons until crisp and golden, about 20 minutes; cool.

4. Heat oven to 425°F. Remove cheese from marinade. Put each in a baking or soufflé dish. Drizzle 2 tablespoons of the marinade over each. Bake until oil bubbles, about 8 minutes. Sprinkle with olives. Place each dish on a salad plate along with croutons.

❧ NOTE: *You may make the croutons 1 day ahead and store them in an airtight container at room temperature.*

NUTRITION INFORMATION PER SERVING:

830 calories	68 g fat	30 g saturated fat
74% calories from fat	90 mg cholesterol	1,105 mg sodium
27 g carbohydrate	28 g protein	1.3 g fiber

Salmon Mousse Toast Cups

PREPARATION TIME: 20 minutes
COOKING TIME: 12 minutes
YIELD: 12 servings

THESE ARE EASY, but your guests will think they took hours. White, egg, or sour-dough bread works well. This recipe was developed in the *Tribune* test kitchen to go with a story on toast by staff writer Bob Condor.

12 slices bread, crusts removed
¼ cup (½ stick) unsalted butter, melted
1 pound skinless salmon fillet, cooked and cooled
½ cup whipping cream
2 green onions, chopped

2 tablespoons chopped fresh dill
1 tablespoon fresh lemon juice
½ teaspoon grated lemon zest
Salt
Freshly ground black pepper
Dill sprigs, optional

1. Heat oven to 375°F. Brush both sides of bread slices with butter. Gently push slices into the cups of a muffin tin with the centers of the slices on the bottom and the four corners facing up, creating points (the slices may slightly overlap on themselves). Bake until lightly browned, 12 to 14 minutes. Cool toast cups 10 minutes in tins; transfer to a cooling rack.

2. Place half of the salmon in a food processor fitted with a metal blade. Add whipping cream, green onion, chopped dill, lemon juice, and lemon zest. Add salt and black pepper to taste. Process until smooth; spoon into a medium-sized bowl. Flake reserved salmon; stir into mousse. Chill until ready to serve. Spoon mousse into toast cups; garnish with dill sprigs if desired.

NUTRITION INFORMATION PER SERVING:

200 calories	11 g fat	5 g saturated fat
50% calories from fat	46 mg cholesterol	165 mg sodium
15 g carbohydrate	10 g protein	0.7 g fiber

Smoked Trout Mousse

PREPARATION TIME: 15 minutes

YIELD: 12 2-tablespoon servings

"THESE DAYS TROUT appears to be swimming in a stream that runs between the fashionable and the forgotten," William Rice wrote in the "Good Eating" section in 1998. His article pointed out trout's finer points, making it deserving of more attention. It's mild tasting, versatile, simple to cook, and reasonably priced. Underlining trout's versatility, this recipe uses the smoked version to make an excellent appetizer. Serve this mousse on crackers, pumpernickel bread, or toast rounds.

1 smoked trout, deboned, skinned, and flaked	½ cup sour cream *or* crème fraîche (see Index)
1 shallot, minced	¼ teaspoon white pepper
2 tablespoons shredded fresh horseradish	⅛ teaspoon salt
	⅛ teaspoon ground red pepper
	¼ cup chopped fresh dill weed

1. Combine trout, shallot, horseradish, sour cream, white pepper, salt, and red pepper in a medium-sized bowl; mix well. For a smoother spread, use a food processor instead of a mixer.
2. Refrigerate until ready to serve.
3. Stir in dill just before serving.

NUTRITION INFORMATION PER SERVING:

60 calories	3.4 g fat	1.6 g saturated fat
54% calories from fat	20 mg cholesterol	430 mg sodium
1 g carbohydrate	6 g protein	0 g fiber

Shrimp Remoulade

PREPARATION TIME: 10 minutes

YIELD: 8 servings

HERE'S A RECIPE that's pure Louisiana: shrimp from the Gulf accented with a creamy dressing from the French settlers. This is but one version of the elegant seafood appetizer famous in New Orleans and perfect for hot weather. This shrimp remoulade was developed in the *Tribune* test kitchen.

1½ cups mayonnaise	2 tablespoons Dijon mustard

2 tablespoons capers
1 tablespoon fresh lemon juice
¾ teaspoon paprika
¼ teaspoon hot pepper sauce
¼ teaspoon ground red pepper
2 pounds medium-sized peeled and
    deveined cooked shrimp

Boston lettuce leaves, optional
3 hard-cooked eggs, peeled and
    halved, optional
6 cherry tomatoes, halved, optional
Parsley sprigs, optional

1. Combine mayonnaise, mustard, capers, lemon juice, paprika, hot pepper sauce, and red pepper in a large bowl; mix well. Stir in shrimp to coat.

2. Place lettuce if desired on a serving platter. Top with shrimp remoulade. Garnish with egg, tomato, and parsley if desired. Serve at room temperature or cover and chill in refrigerator 30 minutes.

NUTRITION INFORMATION PER SERVING:

415 calories	34 g fat	9 g saturated fat
74% calories from fat	235 mg cholesterol	365 mg sodium
0 g carbohydrate	24 g protein	0 g fiber

Shrimp Skewers with Almond Pesto

PREPARATION TIME: 25 minutes
MARINATING TIME: 30 minutes
COOKING TIME: 4 minutes
YIELD: 24 servings

CHEF WOLFGANG PUCK of Spago restaurants in Chicago and Beverly Hills sponsors yearly Oscar parties for winners and presenters. He serves signature appetizers such as his famous pizzas and this simple grilled shrimp.

24 large shrimp (about ¾ pound),
    peeled and deveined

Marinade
¼ cup olive oil
½ teaspoon salt
½ teaspoon white pepper
¼ cup chopped fresh basil leaves
3 cloves garlic, minced

Pesto
5 cloves garlic
1 cup fresh parsley leaves
1 cup fresh basil leaves
1 tablespoon finely ground almonds
¾ cup olive oil
2 tablespoons lemon juice
1 teaspoon white pepper
½ teaspoon salt

➤

1. Straighten each shrimp; insert skewers through lengthwise. Arrange on a large platter or baking pan. To make marinade, combine olive oil, salt, white pepper, basil, and garlic in a small bowl; mix well. Pour over shrimp, turning to coat well. Marinate in the refrigerator 30 minutes. Soak 24 6-inch bamboo skewers in water at least 1 hour.

2. To make pesto, drop the 5 cloves garlic into boiling water; cook 30 seconds. Drain; run under cold running water to stop cooking. Dry cloves; mince. Combine garlic, parsley, basil, almonds, and a little of the oil in a blender or in a food processor fitted with a metal blade; puree. Slowly pour remaining oil through the feed tube with the motor running. Process until smooth. Season with lemon juice, white pepper, and salt. Put into a small serving bowl; set aside.

3. Prepare grill or heat broiler. Arrange skewers of shrimp on grill or under broiler, being careful that bare ends of skewers are not near the flame. Grill or cook about 2 minutes per side or just until shrimp turn pink. Do not overcook.

4. Place dipping sauce in the center of a serving platter. Arrange skewers around sauce; serve hot.

NUTRITION INFORMATION PER SERVING:

79 calories	8 g fat	1 g saturated fat
85% calories from fat	20 mg cholesterol	85 mg sodium
0.6 g carbohydrate	2 g protein	0.2 g fiber

Lobster Margarita

PREPARATION TIME: 45 minutes

COOKING TIME: 30 minutes

YIELD: 6 servings

ADAPTED FROM A recipe Patrick Concannon prepares at his family's restaurant, Don Juan, this is a prime example of the whimsy that often permeates fusion creations. Taking the margarita cocktail as an inspiration and using tender American lobster, crème fraîche, and black caviar, the chef makes a savory seafood cocktail with a south of the border accent.

2 1½-pound Maine lobsters	½ cup sugar
½ cup water	Zest and juice of 2 lemons

Zest and juice of 2 limes	Salt
½ cup extra-virgin olive oil	Freshly ground black pepper
¼ cup chopped cilantro	1 cup crème fraîche (see Note)
1 shallot, chopped	½ cup mayonnaise
2 tablespoons tequila	Black caviar

1. Heat 2 quarts heavily salted water to boil in a large pot over high heat. Drop lobsters into water. Cook 10 to 12 minutes; plunge immediately into ice water to stop cooking. Cool completely. Remove meat from tail and claws; rinse under cold water and pat dry. Cut into medium-sized chunks. Set aside in refrigerator.

2. Put water, sugar, lemon zest, lime zest, half of the lemon juice, and half of the lime juice in a small saucepan. Heat to boil over medium-high heat. Cook until syrupy but not caramelized and reduced to about ¼ cup, about 20 minutes. Cool syrup completely in refrigerator.

3. Toss lobster meat, reserved lemon and lime juice, olive oil, cilantro, shallot, and tequila together in a medium-sized bowl. Season with salt and pepper. Marinate 10 to 15 minutes; drain.

4. Whip crème fraîche to the consistency of whipped cream. Fold in half of the cooled syrup. (Syrup must be completely cool to prevent loss of volume.) Fold in remaining syrup. Gently fold in mayonnaise. Season with salt and black pepper to taste.

5. Place generous dollops of crème fraîche mixture in the bottom of 6 margarita glasses. Top with lobster. Garnish with caviar.

❉ NOTE: *Crème fraîche can be found in specialty stores and some supermarkets such as Treasure Island. Substitute whipping cream, or make your own crème fraîche: Combine 1 cup whipping cream with 2 tablespoons buttermilk; stir well. Pour into a glass container and cover. Let sit at room temperature 8 to 24 hours. It can be refrigerated for 10 days.*

NUTRITION INFORMATION PER SERVING:

519 calories	47 g fat	13 g saturated fat
78% calories from fat	74 mg cholesterol	188 mg sodium
25 g carbohydrate	6 g protein	1.1 g fiber

Oysters with Endive and Cream

PREPARATION TIME: 45 minutes
COOKING TIME: 30 minutes
YIELD: 12 servings

THE HIGHLY ACCLAIMED restaurant Tallgrass, located in Lockport, Illinois, sometimes serves this elegant oyster dish as first course. The oysters, poached in their own liquid, are topped with a cream-endive mixture.

3 heads Belgian endive
Juice of 1 lemon
Pinch salt
36 oysters in the shell
1 small shallot, minced
1 cup whipping cream

1½ cups (3 sticks) unsalted butter, softened
Freshly ground white pepper
1 ripe tomato, peeled, seeded, and diced

1. Cut endive into ½-inch-thick slices. Put into a saucepan with 1 cup water, lemon juice, and salt. Heat to simmer. Cook, stirring occasionally, until endive is very tender, 15 to 20 minutes. Drain endive. Puree in a food processor or blender; set aside.

2. Heat oven to 200°F. Carefully shuck oysters over a bowl, saving their liquid. Put oysters into a separate bowl. Reserve the deeper half of each oyster shell; discard the shallow halves. Rinse reserved shells. Arrange shells on a baking sheet and warm in the oven.

3. Heat reserved oyster liquid to simmer in a medium-sized heavy-bottomed saucepan. Gently poach oysters in this liquid 1 minute. Remove oysters with a slotted spoon; keep warm.

4. Add shallot to oyster liquid; boil gently until liquid is reduced to a glaze. Stir in whipping cream and pureed endive. Boil gently until reduced and thickened enough to coat the back of a spoon. Cool 3 to 5 minutes. Vigorously whisk in butter 1 tablespoon at a time over very low heat until incorporated and frothy. Do not boil. Add white pepper to taste.

5. Put oysters into warmed shells. Spoon warm sauce over all. Garnish with tomato.

NUTRITION INFORMATION PER SERVING:

339 calories	32 g fat	20 g saturated fat
85% calories from fat	133 mg cholesterol	205 mg sodium
6 g carbohydrate	7 g protein	1 g fiber

Onion-Cabbage Strudel (page 24)

Photo by Bob Fila

Cheese-Stuffed Phyllo (page 22)

Shrimp Skewers with Almond Pesto (page 11)

Photo by Bob Fila

Caipirinha (page 45)

Chocolate Soda Deluxe (page 33)

Indian Spiced Tea (page 39)

Mary Meade's Eggnog (page 46)

Photo by Bob Fila

Tangerine Tea (page 38)

Ginger-Pecan Pancakes (page 68)

Baked Apple Pancake (page 68)

Mexican Omelet with Avocado Topping (page 55)

Oven French Toast (page 64)

Photo by Bob Fila

Quick Creole Gumbo (page 84)

Photo by James F. Quinn

Chard and White Bean Soup (page 94)

Photo by Bob Fila

Peppered Sweet Potato–Sage Bisque (page 102)

Photo by Bob Fila

Curried Lentil and Brown Rice Soup (page 95)

Duck Liver Pâté

PREPARATION TIME: 45 minutes
COOKING TIME: 30 minutes
CHILLING TIME: 3 hours
YIELD: 8 servings

THE LATE LESLEE Reis served this luscious duck liver pâté at her Café Provençal restaurant in Evanston, Illinois. Home cooks may not be able to purchase duck livers, but you can freeze livers from about five ducks until you have a total of one pound. Or, for faster results, simply substitute fresh chicken livers.

1¼ cups (2½ sticks) unsalted
    butter, softened
1 small onion, chopped fine
1 clove garlic, minced
1 small tart apple, peeled and
    grated coarse
1 pound duck *or* chicken livers,
    trimmed of membrane and fat

¼ cup port wine
1 tablespoon brandy
¼ cup whipping cream
Fresh lemon juice
Salt
Freshly ground black pepper
Homemade melba toast, toast
    points, *or* French bread

1. Melt ½ stick butter in a medium-sized skillet over medium-low heat. Add onion and garlic; cook, stirring often, until soft and golden, about 15 minutes. Add apple; cook 2 minutes. Add livers. Cook on medium heat, tossing, until livers are cooked but still pink inside, 3 to 4 minutes. Transfer mixture to a food processor fitted with a metal blade or to a blender.

2. Add port and brandy to skillet; raise heat. Stir and scrape up any brown bits sticking to bottom of skillet. Add them to food processor along with whipping cream. Pulse until mixture is smooth (for blender, process in 2 batches). Push mixture through a fine-mesh sieve; let cool.

3. Return strained liver mixture to the food processor. Add the reserved 1 cup butter by tablespoons with machine running until all butter is incorporated. Season to taste with lemon juice, salt, and black pepper.

4. Spoon pâté into ramekins or a 3-cup terrine. Cover with plastic wrap; refrigerate until firm, about 3 hours. Serve with homemade melba toast, toast points, or French bread.

NUTRITION INFORMATION PER SERVING:

377 calories	34 g fat	20 g saturated fat
82% calories from fat	380 mg cholesterol	87 mg sodium
5 g carbohydrate	11 g protein	0.4 g fiber

Thai Pork Satay with Peanut Sauce and Cucumbers

PREPARATION TIME: 1 hour
MARINATING TIME: 1 hour
COOKING TIME: 10 minutes
YIELD: 8 to 10 servings

THIS CLASSIC THAI appetizer for pork on skewers is from Saard Kongsuwan at Roong-Petch Restaurant in Chicago. For home cooks, praise from family and friends should more than justify the extra effort of making the sauce and cucumber salad that are served with the pork. Thai ingredients, including the gingerlike root *galangal*, are available at Thai and some Asian markets.

10 black peppercorns
1 teaspoon whole coriander seeds
½ teaspoon ground cumin
¾ teaspoon salt
6 tablespoons water
½ white onion, diced
7 cloves garlic, halved
2 stalks fresh lemongrass, sliced thin (see Index)
2 slices *galangal*, minced, optional
2 pounds pork tenderloin, trimmed
2 teaspoons fish sauce (*nam pla*)
½ teaspoon turmeric

Peanut Sauce
1 cup sweetened coconut milk
⅓ cup creamy peanut butter
⅓ cup water
1 tablespoon packed dark brown sugar
½ teaspoon ground red pepper
Pinch salt

Sweet-Sour Cucumbers
¾ cup sugar
½ cup water
½ cup distilled white vinegar
⅛ teaspoon salt
1 large cucumber, ends trimmed, peeled
2 jalapeños, sliced thin
Vegetable oil
Milk

1. Put peppercorns, coriander seeds, cumin, and ¼ teaspoon of the salt into a mortar. Grind with a pestle, an electric spice grinder, or a coffee grinder until almost a powder. Put into a blender. Add water, onion, garlic, lemongrass, and *galangal*. Process until mixture forms a smooth, thick paste.

2. Cut pork crosswise into ¼-inch-thick slices. Pound slices between two sheets of waxed paper until they are ⅛ inch thick. Cut slices in half. Put pork slices into a large bowl. Add fish sauce, turmeric, and remaining ½ teaspoon salt. Add 5 tablespoons of the garlic-onion mixture. Mix well to coat all slices. Cover; refrigerate 1 hour. (Set remaining garlic-onion mixture aside.)

3. Soak wooden or bamboo skewers in water at least 30 minutes; drain. To make peanut sauce, put coconut milk, peanut butter, and water into a small saucepan. Heat to simmer over low heat, stirring constantly. Cook, stirring frequently, until oil rises to surface. Stir in brown sugar, red pepper, and salt. Taste and adjust seasonings. Set aside.

4. To make sweet-sour cucumbers, heat sugar, water, vinegar, and salt to boil in a small saucepan over medium-high heat. Remove from heat; cool. Cut cucumber lengthwise into quarters and cut quarters into ⅛-inch-thick slices. Put cucumber, reserved garlic-onion mixture, and cooled vinegar mixture in a large bowl; mix well. Top with jalapeños. Set aside.

5. Prepare grill or heat broiler. Thread pork onto skewers. Grill or broil 6 inches from heat source, brushing with vegetable oil and a little milk to prevent drying, 2 minutes. Turn; cook second side 2 minutes. Serve hot with peanut sauce for dipping. Pass sweet-sour cucumbers.

NUTRITION INFORMATION PER SERVING:

237 calories	8 g fat	3.7 g saturated fat
30% calories from fat	54 mg cholesterol	278 mg sodium
21 g carbohydrate	21 g protein	1 g fiber

Pot Stickers with Spicy Dipping Sauce

PREPARATION TIME: 1 hour
STANDING TIME: 1 hour
COOKING TIME: 10 minutes
YIELD: 24 pot stickers

YOU DON'T HAVE to go to a Chinatown restaurant to find pot stickers, those delicious pan-fried dumplings. Make them in your kitchen. A food processor makes short work of preparing the dough. For even quicker preparation, purchase pot sticker wrappers at Asian markets.

Dough
2 cups all-purpose flour
¼ teaspoon salt
⅔ cup warm water

Spicy Dipping Sauce
2 cups chicken broth
½ cup chopped green onion

2 tablespoons tamari (soy sauce)
1 tablespoon minced garlic
2 teaspoons sugar
2 teaspoons grated gingerroot
1 teaspoon crushed red pepper flakes
1 teaspoon chopped cilantro

►

Filling

4 dried Chinese black mushrooms
½ pound ground pork
1 cup finely shredded cabbage
1 large egg, beaten
4 green onions, minced
2 tablespoons dry sherry
1 ¼-inch-thick piece gingerroot,
    peeled and minced
1 teaspoon soy sauce

1 teaspoon Asian sesame oil
1 teaspoon oyster sauce
1 small clove garlic, minced
¼ teaspoon freshly ground white
    pepper
Flour for rolling dough

Cooking

4 tablespoons vegetable oil
½ cup hot water

1. To make dough, put flour and salt into a food processor fitted with a metal blade. Process until mixed. With machine running, add water in a slow, steady stream until dough forms a loose ball. Lightly flour the work surface. Knead dough about 30 seconds. Wrap in plastic wrap; let rest 1 hour.

2. To make spicy dipping sauce, combine chicken broth, green onion, tamari, garlic, sugar, gingerroot, red pepper flakes, and cilantro in a medium-sized bowl. Set aside.

3. To make filling, soak mushrooms in hot water to cover in a small bowl until soft, about 20 minutes. Drain; discard stems. Chop caps fine. Stir together mushroom, ground pork, cabbage, egg, green onion, sherry, gingerroot, soy sauce, sesame oil, oyster sauce, garlic, and white pepper in a medium-sized bowl.

4. Divide dough in half; wrap one half in plastic. Set aside. Divide the remaining dough into 12 equal-sized pieces. Roll each piece on a lightly floured surface into a 3-inch circle with its center slightly thicker than its edges. Put about 2 teaspoons of the filling onto each dough circle. Fold dough circles in half, making half-moon shapes. Crimp and pleat edges of dough together, making crescent shapes. Let pot stickers sit on the floured surface; cover loosely with waxed paper. Repeat with remaining dough and filling.

5. To cook pot stickers, heat a large, heavy skillet over medium heat until hot. Pour 2 tablespoons of the oil into the skillet. Arrange pot stickers flat side down in the oil. Fry until bottoms are lightly golden, about 2 minutes. Pour in hot water. Cover; cook 5 minutes. Drain excess liquid. Add remaining 2 tablespoons oil to the skillet. Fry until bottoms are crisp-golden, about 3 minutes. Serve with spicy dipping sauce.

NUTRITION INFORMATION PER POT STICKER (WITHOUT SAUCE):

86 calories	4.2 g fat	0.9 g saturated fat
44% calories from fat	15 mg cholesterol	49 mg sodium
9 g carbohydrate	3.2 g protein	0.5 g fiber

Latin Meat Turnovers

PREPARATION TIME: 45 minutes
CHILLING TIME: 4 hours
BAKING TIME: 25 minutes
YIELD: 16 servings

IT ISN'T A quick recipe, but the Latin-style taste combination of meat with almonds, raisins, and spices wrapped in a flaky cream cheese pastry is worth the effort.

Cheese Dough
1 cup (2 sticks) unsalted butter, softened
8 ounces cream cheese, softened
¼ teaspoon salt
2 cups flour

Filling
½ pound ground beef round
4 green onions, minced
2 cloves garlic, minced
¼ cup slivered almonds
¼ cup raisins
½ teaspoon dried oregano
¼ teaspoon dried marjoram
¼ teaspoon freshly ground black pepper
¼ teaspoon salt
⅛ teaspoon cinnamon
Pinch ground red pepper
1 egg yolk
1 tablespoon whipping cream *or* milk

1. To make cheese dough, beat butter, cream cheese, and salt in the bowl of an electric mixer until smooth. Stir in flour by hand to form a stiff dough. Gather dough into ball. Wrap in plastic wrap; refrigerate 4 to 24 hours.

2. To make filling, combine ground beef, onions, and garlic in a large skillet. Cook over medium heat, stirring often, until beef is no longer pink. Remove from heat; drain fat. Add almonds, raisins, oregano, marjoram, black pepper, salt, cinnamon, and red pepper. Mix well. Taste and adjust seasonings.

3. Heat oven to 350°F. Mix egg yolk with whipping cream in a small bowl. Lightly flour the work surface. Roll dough into a rectangle about ⅛ inch thick. Cut dough into 3 ½-inch circles. Place about 1 teaspoon of meat mixture in the center of each circle. Moisten the edge of the circle with egg yolk mixture. Fold over; press edge firmly to enclose filling. Repeat with remaining dough circles and filling.

4. Put filled turnovers onto a baking sheet. Brush tops with egg yolk mixture. Bake until golden brown, about 25 minutes. Serve hot.

NUTRITION INFORMATION PER SERVING:

265 calories	20 g fat	11 g saturated fat
67% calories from fat	71 mg cholesterol	128 mg sodium
15 g carbohydrate	7 g protein	1 g fiber

Samosas with Cilantro-Mint Chutney

PREPARATION TIME: 1½ hours
CHILLING TIME: 1 hour
COOKING TIME: 40 minutes
YIELD: 24 servings

SAMOSAS, SMALL FILLED pastries, may be the most popular appetizer in Chicago's Indian restaurants. This recipe calls for potatoes, peas, and chilies, plus a cilantro-mint chutney on the side.

Dough
2 cups all-purpose flour plus more
  for kneading
6 tablespoons vegetable oil
1 teaspoon salt
½ cup water

Chutney
1 bunch cilantro
16 to 18 fresh mint sprigs
¼ cup water
3 tablespoons lemon juice
2 tablespoons dry-roasted peanuts
6 small green chilies, seeded
1 teaspoon cumin seeds
½ teaspoon salt

Filling
¼ cup vegetable shortening *or*
  vegetable oil
2 teaspoons cumin seeds
2 teaspoons fennel seeds
2 jalapeños *or* serrano chilies,
  seeded and minced
6 medium-sized potatoes, boiled,
  peeled, and cut into ¼-inch
  cubes
½ cup shelled fresh *or* thawed
  frozen peas
4 teaspoons ground coriander
2 teaspoons curry powder
2 teaspoons lemon juice
1 teaspoon salt
Vegetable oil

1. To make dough, combine flour, oil, and salt in a large bowl. Add water slowly, tossing with a fork. Lightly flour the work surface. Turn dough out onto the surface; knead to a hard dough. Knead with oiled hands an additional 10 minutes. Cover dough with plastic wrap; refrigerate at least 1 hour.

2. To make chutney, combine cilantro, mint, water, lemon juice, peanuts, chilies, cumin seeds, and salt in a blender or food processor. Process until smooth.

3. To make filling, heat shortening in a large skillet over medium heat 2 minutes. Add cumin, fennel, and jalapeños; cook 1 minute. Stir in potatoes and peas; cook, stirring often, until mixture looks dry, about 10 minutes. Remove from heat; stir in coriander, curry powder, lemon juice, and salt.

4. Knead dough 1 minute; divide in half. Cut each half into 12 equal-sized pieces. Roll each piece into a ball. Work with 1 piece of dough at a time on a lightly floured surface; keep remaining dough covered. Roll dough piece out into a 7-inch circle. Cut circle in half (each semicircle will make 1 *samosa*).

Form a cone out of each semicircle: moisten half of the straight edge with water. Fold dry half of straight edge so it overlaps the moistened portion by ¼ inch. Press overlapped edges securely together to seal.

Drop about 1 teaspoon of the filling into cone. Moisten the open end of the cone and pinch shut, closing cone in a triangular shape; press tightly to seal. Repeat with remaining dough and filling.

5. Heat oil in a deep saucepan to 350°F. Add 8 to 10 *samosas*; fry, turning occasionally, until evenly browned and flaky, about 10 minutes. Remove with a slotted spoon. Drain on paper towels. Repeat with remaining *samosas*. Serve with mint chutney.

☙ NOTE: Samosas *can be shaped several hours ahead of time; keep them loosely covered in the refrigerator. Let* samosas *come to room temperature 30 minutes before frying. Chutney can be stored in the refrigerator up to 3 weeks.*

NUTRITION INFORMATION PER SERVING:

173 calories	11 g fat	1.7 g saturated fat
54% calories from fat	0 mg cholesterol	258 mg sodium
18 g carbohydrate	2.6 g protein	1.7 g fiber

Cheese-Stuffed Phyllo (Peynirli Börek)

PREPARATION TIME: 30 minutes
SOAKING TIME: Overnight
COOKING TIME: 40 minutes
YIELD: 50 pastries

TURKISH COOKING HAS changed very little over the centuries. What makes it attractive today is the pleasure of its simplicity. "Good Eating" writer Kristin Eddy developed this recipe for *börek*, phyllo rolls filled with cheese.

½ pound feta cheese
2 large eggs
1 cup (4 ounces) shredded
    mozzarella cheese
½ cup chopped parsley
¼ cup chopped fresh dill

¼ teaspoon grated nutmeg
1 1-pound box frozen phyllo pastry
    sheets, thawed
½ cup (1 stick) unsalted butter,
    melted

1. Heat oven to 350°F. Place feta in a bowl with enough cool water to cover; refrigerate overnight to remove excess saltiness. Drain.

2. Stir together feta, eggs, mozzarella, parsley, dill, and nutmeg with fork in a medium bowl.

3. Place phyllo sheets on a cutting board and cut in half. Cover sheets with a damp towel when not using. Take 1 half sheet phyllo and brush with melted butter. Place 1 tablespoon cheese filling at bottom edge and form mixture lengthwise into a cigar shape. Fold bottom edge over filling. Fold in sides and roll pastry into a tube. Brush edges with melted butter; press lightly to seal. Set aside. Continue with remaining pastry and filling.

4. Brush tops of rolls with butter; bake rolls until golden and crisp, about 40 minutes. Serve hot.

NUTRITION INFORMATION PER PASTRY:

65 calories	4 g fat	2.4 g saturated fat
55% calories from fat	19 mg cholesterol	110 mg sodium
5 g carbohydrate	2.3 g protein	0.3 g fiber

Springtime Strudel with Morels

PREPARATION TIME: 45 minutes
COOKING TIME: 18 minutes
YIELD: 16 slices

THIS PERFECT APPETIZER for a spring dinner party was developed in the *Tribune* test kitchen in 1998 to accompany a story by Kristin Eddy on morels and an attempt to grow them commercially in Alabama.

½ cup (1 stick) unsalted butter, melted

3 green onions, minced

1 clove garlic, minced

1 tablespoon minced fresh thyme leaves

1 pound morel mushrooms, chopped

2 teaspoons all-purpose flour

2 tablespoons dry white wine

1 tablespoon soy sauce

½ teaspoon salt

8 sheets phyllo

½ cup dry bread crumbs

5 fresh thyme sprigs

1. Heat oven to 350°F. Heat ¼ cup of the butter in a large skillet over medium-high heat. Add onions, garlic, and thyme. Cook until onions soften, about 3 minutes. Stir in morels; cook, stirring frequently, 5 minutes. Sprinkle with flour; cook, stirring constantly, 1 minute. Add wine, soy sauce, and salt. Cook until mixture has thickened, stirring constantly, about 5 minutes. Set aside.

2. Remove phyllo from package; immediately cover with plastic wrap. Keep dough sheets covered at all times. Place 1 sheet of the phyllo on a flat surface. Quickly brush with melted butter, starting with edges. Sprinkle with 1 tablespoon of the bread crumbs. Place second sheet on top of first; brush with butter. Sprinkle with bread crumbs. Repeat with remaining sheets, but do not sprinkle the last sheet with crumbs.

3. Spread morel mixture over phyllo to within ½ inch of the edges. Roll up lengthwise, jelly roll style. Bake seam-side down on a greased baking sheet until golden brown, about 15 minutes. Slice with a serrated knife.

NUTRITION INFORMATION PER SLICE:

100 calories

59% calories from fat

9 g carbohydrate

7 g fat

15 mg cholesterol

1.9 g protein

3.7 g saturated fat

215 mg sodium

0.6 g fiber

Onion-Cabbage Strudel

PREPARATION TIME: 35 minutes
COOKING TIME: 40 minutes
YIELD: 6 servings

CABBAGE IS AN international comfort food. This appetizer of savory strudel has its roots in Central Europe. It also makes a fine meatless entree for three or four diners. Serve it with an Alsatian Riesling.

1 tablespoon olive oil	¼ teaspoon freshly ground black pepper
1 large onion, chopped coarse	
1 large clove garlic, minced	1 large egg
1 small head green cabbage, shredded	1 tablespoon whipping cream
	5 sheets phyllo
1 tablespoon stone-ground mustard with horseradish	¼ cup (½ stick) butter, melted
	¼ cup bread crumbs
2 teaspoons caraway seeds	1 large egg white
½ teaspoon salt	1 teaspoon water

1. Heat oven to 350°F. Heat oil in a large skillet over medium heat. Add onion and garlic. Cook, stirring often, until onion is very soft and golden, about 8 minutes.

2. Add cabbage to skillet a handful at a time, stirring frequently, until cabbage has wilted, about 10 minutes. Remove from heat; stir in mustard, caraway, salt, and pepper. Add egg and cream; stir well.

3. Place 1 sheet of the phyllo on the work surface with short sides at top and bottom. Keep rest of phyllo sheets covered with a slightly damp towel while working. Brush sheet with some of the butter. Sprinkle with 1 tablespoon of the bread crumbs. Place next sheet on top of first. Repeat process until you've used 4 sheets. Top with last phyllo sheet. Put cabbage mixture on lower third of sheets, about 4 inches from sides. Fold long edges over to cover part of filling. Fold short edge over filling; roll up, forming a square package.

4. Brush top of package with remaining butter, making sure to seal edge. Decorate top with additional phyllo if desired. Beat egg white with water. Brush pastry with egg white mixture. Place on greased cookie sheet. Bake until golden brown, about 40 minutes. Let stand 5 minutes before slicing.

NUTRITION INFORMATION PER SERVING:

240 calories	13 g fat	6 g saturated fat
49% calories from fat	60 mg cholesterol	485 mg sodium
24 g carbohydrate	6 g protein	4.9 g fiber

Vegetable and Shrimp Tempura

PREPARATION TIME: 20 minutes
COOKING TIME: 2 minutes per batch
YIELD: 4 servings

To HELP READERS overcome the fear of frying in a large quantity of oil, writer Kristin Eddy compiled tips and several tempting recipes, including this one created by chef Leo San Pedro of the former Won Ton Club restaurant in Chicago.

Peanut oil
1 cup plus 2 tablespoons ice water
1 large egg
1½ cups all-purpose flour
16 large shrimp, peeled and deveined, with tails left on

12 to 16 broccoli florets, slightly cooked
1 sweet potato, peeled and sliced about ⅛ inch thick
1 onion, sliced into thin rings

1. Pour oil to depth of at least 2 inches in a wok or deep pan. Heat over medium-high heat to 350°F.
2. Combine ice water and egg in a small bowl; mix well. Sift 1 cup of the flour into the egg mixture. Mix gently with a fork; do not use a whisk or overbeat.
3. Dust shrimp and vegetables lightly with remaining flour. Dip 2 to 3 pieces into batter at a time. Do not crowd pan. Fry in hot oil until golden, not browned, 1 to 2 minutes. Drain; repeat with remaining shrimp and vegetables.

NUTRITION INFORMATION PER SERVING:

223 calories	15 g fat	2.6 g saturated fat
58% calories from fat	50 mg cholesterol	46 mg sodium
18 g carbohydrate	6 g protein	1.7 g fiber

Asparagus Tempura

PREPARATION TIME: 10 minutes
CHILLING TIME: 1 hour
COOKING TIME: 10 minutes
YIELD: 8 servings

NUMEROUS RAW VEGETABLES can be dipped into tempura batter and fried, but fresh asparagus prepared in this manner is especially good.

Dipping Sauce
2 tablespoons soy sauce
2 tablespoons water

1½ teaspoons *mirin* (see Note)
½ teaspoon sugar

►

Tempura
2 cups ice water
1⅔ cups all-purpose flour
1 large egg yolk

⅛ teaspoon baking soda
3 cups vegetable oil
2 pounds thin asparagus, trimmed
    and chilled

1. To make dipping sauce, combine soy sauce, water, *mirin*, and sugar in a small bowl.

2. To make tempura, combine ice water, flour, egg yolk, and baking soda in a medium-sized bowl; whisk until smooth. Cover and refrigerate until thoroughly chilled, about 1 hour.

3. Heat oil in a wok or deep saucepan to 375°F. Dip asparagus into batter; drain excess. Deep-fry in batches until golden brown, 1 to 2 minutes. Remove from oil with a slotted spoon. Drain on paper towels. Serve immediately with dipping sauce.

❧ NOTE: Mirin *is a sweet rice wine. You can find* mirin *in the Asian aisle of most supermarkets.*

NUTRITION INFORMATION PER SERVING:

375 calories	29 g fat	2 g saturated fat
70% calories from fat	25 mg cholesterol	280 mg sodium
25 g carbohydrate	6 g protein	3 g fiber

Tomato and Basil Tart

PREPARATION TIME: 30 minutes

COOKING TIME: 35 minutes

YIELD: 8 servings

A COMBINATION OF simple flavors creates an elegant appetizer in New York chef Jean-Georges Vongerichten's tomato and basil tart that was featured in a "Practical Cook" column.

4 sheets phyllo
2 tablespoons extra-virgin olive oil
3 medium-sized tomatoes
½ teaspoon chopped green chili
    pepper
½ teaspoon minced garlic
½ teaspoon minced fresh thyme
    leaves

Salt
Freshly ground black pepper
Sugar
2 tablespoons fresh basil leaves,
    cut into thin ribbons
1 tablespoon freshly grated
    Parmesan cheese

1. Place the oven rack in the lowest position. Heat oven to 400°F.

2. Stack the phyllo sheets together. Brush the top sheet with olive oil. Cut out a 10-inch circle. Place the circle on a nonstick baking sheet. Bake until golden, about 5 minutes. Turn; bake for 3 more minutes. Set aside.

3. Bring water to a boil in a large saucepan. Plunge tomatoes into boiling water for 5 to 15 seconds. Drain. When tomatoes are just cool enough to touch, remove skins. Cut in half horizontally; squeeze gently to remove excess water and seeds. Dice tomatoes.

4. Combine tomatoes, chili, garlic, thyme, and 1 tablespoon of olive oil in an ovenproof skillet. Season with salt, pepper, and sugar to taste. Bake, stirring occasionally, until tomatoes begin to turn brown and caramelize, about 20 minutes. Set aside.

5. Just before serving, spread the tomatoes over the oiled surface of the phyllo tart. Top with basil, Parmesan, and the remaining olive oil. Bake to melt cheese, about 5 minutes. Cut in wedges to serve.

NUTRITION INFORMATION PER SERVING:

65 calories	4.2 g fat	0.7 g saturated fat
56% calories from fat	0.6 mg cholesterol	53 mg sodium
6 g carbohydrate	1.3 g protein	0.7 g fiber

Alsatian Onion Tart

PREPARATION TIME: 30 minutes
CHILLING TIME: 30 minutes
COOKING TIME: 45 minutes
YIELD: 6 servings

FOR AN ARTICLE on the wines of Alsace, William Rice asked chef Jean Joho of Chicago's Everest restaurant to re-create classic recipes from his native Alsatian cuisine, among them this onion tart. A perfect appetizer for a New Year's Eve party or for anytime, especially when served with a glass of chilled Alsace muscat or sylvaner, it became one of the year's top recipes.

Pastry
1½ cups all-purpose flour
½ teaspoon salt

½ cup (1 stick) chilled unsalted
   butter, cut in chunks
2 to 3 tablespoons cold water

►

Filling
2 tablespoons vegetable oil
3 medium-sized yellow onions
    (about 1 pound), peeled and
    sliced thin
⅔ cup whole milk
⅔ cup whipping cream
¼ cup all-purpose flour
2 egg yolks
¼ teaspoon salt
Freshly ground black pepper
Nutmeg

1. Heat oven to 350°F. To make pastry, combine in a food processor or by hand flour, salt, and butter until mixture is the consistency of coarse bread crumbs. Add cold water to make a dough. Cover with plastic wrap; refrigerate 30 minutes.

2. Roll out dough into a 12-inch circle. Fit dough into a 10-inch tart pan with a removable bottom, cutting off any dough that comes above the sides of the pan. Bake until crust begins to color, about 20 minutes. Remove to a wire rack. Reduce oven temperature to 325°F.

3. Heat oil in a large skillet. Add onions; cook over low heat until onions are soft and golden, 15 to 20 minutes. Spread cooked onions in bottom of tart shell. Combine milk, whipping cream, flour, egg yolks, and salt in the bowl of a food processor or blender. Add black pepper and nutmeg to taste. Blend until mixture is smooth; pour over onions.

4. Place tart on a baking sheet. Bake until filling is set and a wooden pick inserted in the center comes out clean, about 25 minutes. Cool on a rack. Remove tart and bottom from tart pan before cutting tart into pieces. Serve at room temperature.

NUTRITION INFORMATION PER SERVING:

463 calories	33 g fat	17 g saturated fat
63% calories from fat	152 mg cholesterol	224 mg sodium
36 g carbohydrate	7 g protein	2.4 g fiber

Ratatouille Terrine

PREPARATION TIME: 45 minutes
COOKING TIME: 50 minutes
YIELD: 12 servings

IN 1997, WILLIAM Rice chronicled the participation of Chicago chef Steven Chiappetti in the prestigious Bocuse d'Or cooking competition in Lyons, France. Chiappetti failed to win, but he brought home the recipe for this colorful mix of sliced vegetables baked in a loaf pan that he cooked for the judges. It makes a fine appetizer. Try it plain or with a tomato sauce, either homemade or purchased.

4 red bell peppers	3 large eggs
1 large eggplant	1 cup whipping cream
5 small zucchini	3 sprigs fresh basil, chopped
Salt	½ teaspoon salt
2 tablespoons corn oil or more as needed	¼ teaspoon ground black pepper
	Tomato sauce, optional

1. Heat oven to 400°F. Roast red peppers in oven until charred on all sides, turning occasionally, 20 to 30 minutes. Remove peppers from the oven; place in a paper or plastic bag. Let stand 5 minutes. Reduce oven temperature to 350°F. Remove skin from peppers; cut into 2″ × 4″ rectangles.

2. Slice eggplant and zucchini into 2″ × 4″ × ¼″ slices. Salt lightly; set aside 10 minutes. Pat dry with paper towels. Heat oil in a large skillet. Cook peppers, eggplant, and zucchini in batches until cooked through, about 5 minutes per batch.

3. Whisk together eggs and whipping cream in a medium-sized bowl; stir in basil, salt, and pepper. Layer one-fourth of the vegetables in a greased 9″ × 5″ terrine or loaf pan. Top with one-third of the egg mixture. Continue layering, ending with vegetables.

4. Bake until a wooden pick inserted in the center comes out clean, 50 to 60 minutes. Let stand 10 minutes before unmolding. Heat tomato sauce if desired. Slice terrine. Spoon sauce onto warmed plates; top with terrine slices. Serve warm.

NUTRITION INFORMATION PER SERVING:

132 calories	11 g fat	5 g saturated fat
73% calories from fat	80 mg cholesterol	122 mg sodium
6 g carbohydrate	2.9 g protein	2 g fiber

Mushrooms with Ancho Chilies

PREPARATION TIME: 30 minutes
SOAKING TIME: 30 minutes
COOKING TIME: 20 minutes
YIELD: 16 servings

THE LATE CHEF-RESTAURATEUR Leslee Reis, who was noted for culinary innovation at her restaurant Café Provençal in Evanston, Illinois, paired dried ancho chilies with mushrooms for a hearty appetizer that can be served year-round.

2 ounces dried mushrooms, such as cèpe *or* porcini (see Note)
3 cups hot water
3 dried ancho chilies
½ cup olive oil
2 jalapeños, seeded and minced, optional
4 ounces pancetta, sliced and cut into strips (see Note)

2 cloves garlic, minced
2 pounds fresh button mushrooms, halved *or* quartered if large
1 to 2 tablespoons fresh lemon juice
Salt
Freshly ground black pepper
¼ cup minced fresh parsley

1. Soak dried mushrooms in hot water until softened, about 30 minutes. Strain; reserve liquid and mushrooms separately. Slit ancho chilies open; remove stems and seeds. Cut chilies into ¼-inch-wide strips.

2. Heat oil in a large heavy-bottomed skillet over high heat until hot but not smoking. Add mushrooms, ancho chilies, and jalapeños. Cook, stirring often, 1 minute. Reduce heat to medium; add pancetta. Cook, stirring often, until pancetta begins to brown, 2 to 3 minutes.

3. Add garlic. Cook, stirring often, until garlic begins to turn golden, about 2 minutes. Stir in reserved mushroom liquid. Heat to boil; boil until liquid reduces to a glaze, 5 to 10 minutes.

4. Stir in fresh mushrooms, lemon juice, salt, and black pepper. Cook, stirring often, over medium heat until most of the moisture has evaporated, about 5 minutes. Remove from heat; cool. Sprinkle with parsley. Serve at room temperature.

❧ NOTE: *Mushrooms are extremely porous, like a sponge. Unless they're very dirty, wipe them clean with a damp paper towel and not under running water.*

❧ NOTE: *Dried cèpe and porcino mushrooms are available at gourmet food shops. Other dried mushrooms, such as chanterelle or shiitake, may be substituted. Pancetta, unsmoked Italian bacon, is available at Italian markets. Salt pork or lightly smoked bacon may be substituted.*

NUTRITION INFORMATION PER SERVING:

106 calories	8 g fat	1.4 g saturated fat
67% calories from fat	2 mg cholesterol	43 mg sodium
7 g carbohydrate	2.6 g protein	1.9 g fiber

Prosciutto-Wrapped Green Beans

PREPARATION TIME: 20 minutes
COOKING TIME: 6 minutes
CHILLING TIME: 10 minutes
YIELD: 12 servings

TENDER GREEN BEANS, marinated in olive oil and lemon juice, are wrapped in a piece of prosciutto or ham for a light appetizer. To save on preparation time, have the prosciutto sliced by the butcher.

1 pound fresh green beans, ends trimmed
3 tablespoons olive oil
2 tablespoons fresh lemon juice
¼ teaspoon salt
¼ teaspoon freshly ground black pepper plus more as needed
18 thin slices prosciutto *or* smoked ham
2 lemons, cut into wedges

1. Bring a large pot of water to boil. Add beans; boil uncovered until beans are bright green and crisp-tender, about 6 minutes. Drain; rinse under cold water to stop cooking.

2. Stir together oil, lemon juice, salt, and black pepper in a large bowl. Add beans; toss to coat. Refrigerate, stirring occasionally, 10 minutes.

3. Drain beans; reserve marinade. Cut prosciutto slices in half crosswise. Wrap several beans in each piece of prosciutto. Arrange on a platter. Drizzle with reserved marinade; sprinkle with black pepper. Garnish with lemon wedges.

NUTRITION INFORMATION PER SERVING:

57 calories	4.1 g fat	0.5 g saturated fat
62% calories from fat	3.9 mg cholesterol	163 mg sodium
3.4 g carbohydrate	2.3 g protein	1.2 g fiber

BEVERAGES

Chocolate Soda Deluxe

PREPARATION TIME: 8 minutes

YIELD: 1 serving

INSPIRED BY THE chocolate soda at the Ghirardelli Café in Chicago, the *Tribune* test kitchen staff came up with its own version, one that adults as well as children will appreciate.

¼ cup whipping cream
1½ teaspoons sugar
½ cup milk
¼ cup chocolate syrup

2 cups chocolate *or* vanilla ice cream
⅓ cup club soda
Maraschino cherry, optional
Chopped nuts, optional

1. Beat whipping cream and sugar together in the bowl of an electric mixer until stiff peaks form. Set aside.

2. Stir together milk and syrup in the bottom of a large glass. Add two-thirds of the ice cream, pushing it down into the milk mixture. Pour in club soda. Add one-half of the whipped cream, then the remaining ice cream, and then the remaining whipped cream. Top with maraschino cherry and nuts if desired.

NUTRITION INFORMATION PER SERVING:

1,065 calories	54 g fat	34 g saturated fat
44% calories from fat	180 mg cholesterol	340 mg sodium
136 g carbohydrate	17 g protein	5.2 g fiber

Frothy Lemon Cooler

PREPARATION TIME: 10 minutes

YIELD: 4 servings

LEMONADE TURNS INTO something thicker and cooler when a blender becomes involved. This drink is an icy way to beat summertime heat.

5 large lemons	2 cups crushed ice
2 cups ice water	½ cup sugar

1. Cut lemons crosswise in half. Squeeze lemon juice through a sieve into a glass measure. This should yield about 1 cup juice. Put half of the lemon juice, 1 cup of the ice water, 1 cup of the ice, and ¼ cup of the sugar into a blender. Process on high speed until frothy.

2. Pour into a tall, chilled pitcher. Repeat with remaining ingredients.

NUTRITION INFORMATION PER SERVING:

112 calories	0 g fat	0 g saturated fat
0% calories from fat	0 mg cholesterol	5 mg sodium
30 g carbohydrate	0.2 g protein	0.2 g fiber

Rhubarb Lemonade Punch

PREPARATION TIME: 10 minutes

COOKING TIME: 20 minutes

CHILLING TIME: 2 hours

YIELD: 12 servings

READER JEAN E. Reeb of Woodstock, Illinois, contributed this unusual nonalcoholic fruit punch in 1986. For best results, chill the base mixture several hours. Add the lemon-lime soda just before serving. Sparkling water or club soda can be substituted for the lemon-lime soda for a less sweet punch.

4 to 5 cups fresh *or* frozen diced rhubarb	¼ to ½ cup sugar
1 6-ounce can frozen lemonade concentrate	Ice
	1 16-ounce bottle chilled lemon-lime carbonated soda
3 cups water	

1. Put rhubarb, lemonade concentrate, water, and sugar into a large nonreactive saucepan. Heat to simmer over medium-high heat. Reduce heat to low. Cover; cook until rhubarb is very soft, about 20 minutes. Press mixture through a fine-mesh sieve into a pitcher. Discard pulp. Refrigerate until chilled, at least 2 hours.

2. Pour rhubarb mixture over ice in a small punch bowl. Slowly pour in lemon-lime soda. Serve immediately.

NUTRITION INFORMATION PER SERVING:

65 calories	0.1 g fat	0 g saturated fat
1% calories from fat	0 mg cholesterol	8 mg sodium
17 g carbohydrate	0.4 g protein	0.8 g fiber

Sparkling Orange-Mint Juleps

PREPARATION TIME: 15 minutes
STANDING TIME: Overnight
YIELD: 6 servings

A DRINK DOESN'T have to contain alcohol to have some spirit. These nonalcoholic mint juleps are flavored with fresh orange juice as well as fresh mint for a refreshing summer pick-me-up.

¾ cup fresh orange juice	Crushed ice
¾ cup sugar	1 32-ounce bottle club soda
½ cup water	Mint sprigs
3 cups lightly packed fresh mint leaves	

1. Heat orange juice, sugar, and water in a small saucepan over medium heat. Cook, stirring often, until sugar dissolves, about 5 minutes. Cool completely. Put mint leaves in a large bowl or jar with a tight-fitting lid. Pour orange juice mixture over leaves. Cover; refrigerate overnight or up to 24 hours.

2. Strain orange juice mixture. Fill 6 10-ounce glasses with crushed ice. Stir in ¼ cup of the orange mixture and ½ cup of the club soda in each glass. Garnish each glass with a mint sprig.

NUTRITION INFORMATION PER SERVING:

118 calories	0.2 g fat	0 g saturated fat
2% calories from fat	0 mg cholesterol	33 mg sodium
29 g carbohydrate	0.9 g protein	0.1 g fiber

Citrus Spritzer

PREPARATION TIME: 10 minutes
YIELD: 4 servings

HERE'S A REFRESHING cocktail to serve at summer parties. The alcohol is optional.

1 cup orange juice
1 cup unsweetened pineapple juice
Juice of 1 lemon
Juice of 1 lime
1⅓ cups chilled club soda *or*
    carbonated mineral water

½ cup vodka, optional
Crushed ice
Maraschino cherries
Lemon slices

Mix orange juice, pineapple juice, lemon juice, lime juice, club soda, and vodka if desired in a tall pitcher. Serve over crushed ice in 4 tall glasses. Garnish with cherries and lemon slices.

NUTRITION INFORMATION PER SERVING (WITHOUT VODKA):

70 calories	0.2 g fat	0 g saturated fat
2% calories from fat	0 mg cholesterol	20 mg sodium
18 g carbohydrate	0.8 g protein	0.4 g fiber

Mango Lassi

PREPARATION TIME: 10 minutes
YIELD: 2 servings

THE SPICY FLAVORS of Indian cuisine meet their delicious match in the *lassi*, a cold, sweet, and frothy yogurt-based drink that is often flavored with mint, cumin, fruit juice, or any number of ingredients. This recipe uses mango and comes from Udupi Palace restaurant in Chicago.

1 mango, peeled, pitted, and sliced
2 cups plain nonfat yogurt
¼ cup sugar

4 teaspoons honey
1 teaspoon rose water
Ice cubes

Puree mango, yogurt, sugar, honey, and rose water in a blender or a food processor fitted with a metal blade until smooth. Serve over a few ice cubes.

NUTRITION INFORMATION PER SERVING:

345 calories	0.7 g fat	0.4 g saturated fat
2% calories from fat	4 mg cholesterol	190 mg sodium
73 g carbohydrate	16 g protein	1.9 g fiber

Cranberry Nog

PREPARATION TIME: 15 minutes

COOKING TIME: 15 minutes

CHILLING TIME: 2 hours

YIELD: 12 servings

MAKING EGGNOG FROM scratch is neither difficult nor particularly time-consuming. A basic eggnog requires only three ingredients: eggs, cream or milk, and sugar. For those who find traditional eggnog too rich, this nonalcoholic version reduces the milk and adds the fruit flavor—and Christmas color—of cranberry.

6 large eggs, lightly beaten
1 cup cold milk
1 cup confectioners' sugar

2 cups chilled cranberry juice cocktail
2 cups chilled whipping cream
Ground nutmeg, optional

1. Combine eggs, milk, and sugar in a medium-sized saucepan. Cook over medium-low heat, stirring often, until mixture thickens and temperature reads 160°F on an instant-reading thermometer, about 15 minutes. Refrigerate until chilled, 2 to 12 hours.

2. Stir in cranberry juice cocktail and whipping cream. Sprinkle each serving with nutmeg if desired.

❧ NOTE: *You may store the nog covered in the refrigerator for 1 day before serving if desired.*

NUTRITION INFORMATION PER SERVING:

245 calories	18 g fat	10 g saturated fat
63% calories from fat	160 mg cholesterol	55 mg sodium
18 g carbohydrate	4.6 g protein	0 g fiber

Ginger-Peach Tea

PREPARATION TIME: 5 minutes
STEEPING TIME: 45 minutes
YIELD: 2 servings

WHAT'S MORE REFRESHING than a tall glass of iced tea on a warm summer day? How about one with the fruity flavor of peach nectar and some extra zing from fresh ginger? This recipe was featured in a "Drink!" column. Mint sprigs and lemon wedges are traditional accompaniments to iced tea. Lime also works. Another idea is to freeze leftover tea in ice cube trays and use those cubes to ice your tea the next time.

2 cups boiling water
4 bags black tea
6 thin slices gingerroot

2 cups peach nectar
Ice

Pour boiling water over tea bags and ginger in a heavy glass pitcher. Steep unrefrigerated until tea comes to room temperature. Add peach nectar. Fill a tall glass with ice; add tea-nectar mixture.

NUTRITION INFORMATION PER SERVING:

135 calories
0% calories from fat
35 g carbohydrate

0 g fat
0 mg cholesterol
1 g protein

0 g saturated fat
25 mg sodium
1.6 g fiber

Tangerine Tea

PREPARATION TIME: 5 minutes
COOKING TIME: 5 minutes
STEEPING TIME: 5 minutes
YIELD: 4 servings

SPICE AND CITRUS make an extra-refreshing, reviving hot tea. Or, chill it for a special iced tea.

2 cups cold water
1½ cups fresh tangerine juice *or* orange juice
¼ cup sugar

¼ teaspoon cinnamon
⅛ teaspoon ground cloves
2 bags black tea

1. Heat water to boil in a medium-sized nonreactive saucepan over high heat. Stir in tangerine juice, sugar, cinnamon, and cloves. Reduce heat to medium; heat to boil. Cook, stirring frequently, until sugar is dissolved, about 5 minutes. Remove from heat.

2. Add tea bags. Cover; steep 5 minutes. Serve hot or chill and serve over ice.

NUTRITION INFORMATION PER SERVING:

90 calories	0.2 g fat	0 g saturated fat
2% calories from fat	0 mg cholesterol	5 mg sodium
22 g carbohydrate	0.5 g protein	0.3 g fiber

Indian Spiced Tea

PREPARATION TIME: 5 minutes
STEEPING TIME: 4 minutes
YIELD: 6 servings

WHEN YOU'RE LOOKING for something different in your cup of tea, try this delightful variation. Serve it to company or enjoy it after an Indian meal to refresh the palate.

6 tablespoons Darjeeling tea	2 to 3 whole cloves
4 to 5 green cardamom pods	6 cups boiling water
½-inch piece cinnamon stick, broken up	Half-and-half, optional
	Sugar, optional

1. Heat a teapot. Add tea, cardamom, cinnamon, and cloves. Pour in boiling water. Cover; steep 4 minutes.

2. Strain tea into cups. Serve with half-and-half and sugar if desired.

NUTRITION INFORMATION PER SERVING:

4 calories	0.1 g fat	0 g saturated fat
17% calories from fat	0 mg cholesterol	9 mg sodium
0.1 g carbohydrate	0.7 g protein	0 g fiber

Rum Risk Punch

PREPARATION TIME: 15 minutes

YIELD: 30 servings

A BARTENDER AT the now defunct City Tavern restaurant created the lively combination of fruity flavors that will make this punch a hit at parties year-round.

4 cups chilled amber *or* gold rum
4 cups chilled cranberry juice
  cocktail
4 cups chilled pineapple juice
4 cups chilled orange juice

1 cup chilled lemon sour mix
6 tablespoons orange-flavored
  liqueur
Ice cubes

Mix rum, cranberry juice cocktail, pineapple juice, orange juice, lemon sour mix, and orange-flavored liqueur in a punch bowl. Mix well. Serve over ice cubes.

NUTRITION INFORMATION PER SERVING:

150 calories	0.2 g fat	0 g saturated fat
1% calories from fat	0 mg cholesterol	10 mg sodium
17 g carbohydrate	0.4 g protein	0.4 g fiber

Papaya Daiquiri

PREPARATION TIME: 15 minutes

YIELD: 2 servings

THE DAIQUIRI, NAMED for a town in Cuba, is one of the world's most versatile cocktails. This version features the tropical flavor of papaya. When buying papayas look for vivid yellow and orange fruit that yields slightly to the touch. Peaches or strawberries can be used in this recipe too.

1 large papaya, peeled, seeded, and
  cubed
⅓ cup light rum
3 tablespoons confectioners' sugar

2 tablespoons fresh lime juice
1 cup crushed ice
Lime slices

1. Put papaya, rum, confectioners' sugar, and lime juice into a blender. Process until smooth. Add crushed ice; blend until frothy. Pour into 2 glasses. Garnish with lime slices.

● VARIATIONS: *To make a peach daiquiri, substitute 2 cups diced, peeled peaches for the papaya and ¼ cup dark rum for the light rum.*

To make a slushy strawberry daiquiri, substitute 4 cups partly frozen hulled, halved strawberries for the papaya. Omit ice.

NUTRITION INFORMATION PER SERVING:

235 calories	0.3 g fat	0.1 g saturated fat
1% calories from fat	0 mg cholesterol	8 mg sodium
35 g carbohydrate	1.5 g protein	4.1 g fiber

Blue Hawaii

PREPARATION TIME: 5 minutes

YIELD: 2 servings

FOR A COVER story on the retro appeal of all things Polynesian, writer Renée Enna included this potent tropical drink. It uses two kinds of rum and blue curaçao, an orange-flavored liqueur, and comes from Stanley Sacharski, co-owner of Hala Kahiki, a Polynesian-themed bar in River Grove, Illinois.

1 cup crushed ice	¼ cup sweet-and-sour mix
½ cup blue curaçao	2 tablespoons sugar
⅓ cup dark rum	Pineapple chunks
¼ cup light rum	Maraschino cherries
¼ cup orange juice	

Combine crushed ice, blue curaçao, dark rum, light rum, orange juice, sweet-and-sour mix, and sugar in a blender. Blend until smooth. Pour into 2 highball glasses. Garnish each with pineapple and cherries on a swizzle stick.

NUTRITION INFORMATION PER SERVING:

375 calories	0.1 g fat	0 g saturated fat
0% calories from fat	10 mg cholesterol	16 mg sodium
39 g carbohydrate	0.2 g protein	0 g fiber

Mango Madness

PREPARATION TIME: 15 minutes

YIELD: 6 servings

FOOD AND WINE columnist William Rice included this mango libation in a Sunday magazine article on fruity blender drinks. When making a tropical blender drink, feel free to veer from the recipe and add sugar or citrus juice if the fruit is too sweet or too tart. And use lots of ice. If you can't find fresh mangoes for this cocktail, mango pulp is available canned at many Asian food markets.

1 ripe mango, peeled, seeded, and chopped, *or* 1 cup canned mango pulp
¾ cup light rum *or* tequila
½ cup orange juice
2 tablespoons fresh lemon juice
2 tablespoons fresh lime juice
1 tablespoon sugar
8 ice cubes, or more as needed
6 strips lime zest

1. Combine mango, rum, orange juice, lemon juice, lime juice, sugar, and ice cubes in a blender. Add extra ice cubes as needed to bring liquid level to 30 ounces. Blend until smooth.

2. Serve in 6 martini glasses. Garnish each drink with a strip of lime zest.

NUTRITION INFORMATION PER SERVING:

116 calories
1% calories from fat
11 g carbohydrate
0.1 g fat
0 mg cholesterol
0.4 g protein
0 g saturated fat
2 mg sodium
0.7 g fiber

Cajun Martini

PREPARATION TIME: 5 minutes

CHILLING TIME: 8 to 16 hours

YIELD: 15 servings

WHEN CAJUN CHEF Paul Prudhomme first told us about his Cajun martini, we thought it would be too wicked to enjoy. Surprisingly, the piquantness of the hot pepper adds flavor to the vodka or gin without making it too hot to drink. Served very cold with crisp crackers or salted nuts, it's a drink that won't last long.

1 jalapeño
1 unopened fifth of gin *or* vodka
Dry vermouth
Ice
Pickled green tomatoes, okra, *or* eggplant, optional

1. Slice jalapeño lengthwise without cutting through stem. Open bottle of gin or vodka. Put jalapeño in bottle. Fill remaining air space with vermouth. Recap bottle; refrigerate 8 to 16 hours.

2. Remove jalapeño. Fill a pitcher with ice and pour in martini. Strain into 15 serving glasses. Garnish with pickled vegetables on toothpicks if desired.

✱ NOTE: *After removing the jalapeño from the bottle, be sure to store the bottle in the refrigerator until you're ready to use it.*

NUTRITION INFORMATION PER SERVING:

130 calories	0 g fat	0 g saturated fat
0% calories from fat	0 mg cholesterol	1 mg sodium
0.2 g carbohydrate	0 g protein	0 g fiber

Passion Fruit Margaritas

PREPARATION TIME: 5 minutes

YIELD: 4 servings

MARGARITAS GET DRESSED up with the sweet, rich flavor of passion fruit in this recipe from a "Fast Food" column. Because fresh passion fruit is rarely available, this concoction uses frozen juice concentrate, such as Welch's.

1½ cups margarita mix	¼ cup fresh lime juice
1 cup gold tequila	Ice cubes
½ cup frozen passion fruit juice concentrate	Lime wedges
¼ cup Triple Sec	Salt

1. Combine margarita mix, tequila, passion fruit juice concentrate, Triple Sec, and lime juice in a blender; fill the blender container with ice cubes. Blend on high speed until smooth and slushy.

2. Run one of the lime wedges around the rims of 4 glasses; dip rims in salt. Garnish margaritas with lime wedges.

NUTRITION INFORMATION PER SERVING:

275 calories	0 g fat	0 g saturated fat
0% calories from fat	0 mg cholesterol	65 mg sodium
30 g carbohydrate	0.2 g protein	0.1 g fiber

Coyote's Ultima Margarita

PREPARATION TIME: 10 minutes

YIELD: 1 serving

CAN YOU HAVE too many margarita recipes? We think not. Writer Kristin Eddy, during her travels for a food story on the Southwest, procured this potent formula from the famous Coyote Café in Santa Fe.

2 lime wedges	1 tablespoon superfine sugar
Salt for glass	1 teaspoon Cointreau
3 tablespoons silver tequila	Ice cubes
3 tablespoons fresh lime juice	

1. Run one of the lime wedges around the rim of a chilled margarita or other serving glass; dip rim in salt.

2. Fill a cocktail shaker with tequila, lime juice, sugar, Cointreau, and ice cubes. Squeeze in juice of lime wedge used for glass. Shake until foam forms on top of mixture, at least 30 seconds.

3. Pour into a blender; blend at low speed a few seconds, until ice is cracked but not slushy. Strain margarita into serving glass; garnish with remaining lime wedge.

NUTRITION INFORMATION PER SERVING:

150 calories	0 g fat	0 g saturated fat
0% calories from fat	0 mg cholesterol	1 mg sodium
14 g carbohydrate	0 g protein	0 g fiber

Sake-Pineapple Punch

PREPARATION TIME: 10 minutes

CHILLING TIME: 4 hours

YIELD: 12 servings

THIS DELICIOUSLY REFRESHING cocktail goes well with almost any Asian appetizer. It comes from Shilla, a Korean restaurant in Chicago.

9 cups chilled unsweetened pineapple juice	¾ cup peach-flavored brandy
1½ cups light rum	Ice cubes
¾ cup sake	Orange slices
	Maraschino cherries

1. Combine pineapple juice, rum, sake, and brandy in a large pitcher. Refrigerate until very cold, at least 4 hours or overnight.

2. Pour punch into 12 tall glasses filled with ice cubes. Garnish with orange slices and maraschino cherries.

NUTRITION INFORMATION PER SERVING:

230 calories	0.2 g fat	0 g saturated fat
1% calories from fat	0 mg cholesterol	2 mg sodium
27 g carbohydrate	0.7 g protein	0.4 g fiber

Caipirinha

PREPARATION TIME: 10 minutes

YIELD: 4 servings

THE *CAIPIRINHA* (PRONOUNCED ky-ee-pea-REEN-hya) is one of Brazil's unofficial national drinks. Made from *cachaca* (KAH-sha-sa)—a liquor distilled from sugar cane juice—and lime simple syrup, it packs a potent punch. This version is adapted from a recipe at Nacional 27 restaurant in Chicago.

¾ cup sugar	Granulated sugar
¾ cup water	4 limes, cut in wedges
Zest of 2 limes	1 cup *cachaca*
Fresh lime juice	Crushed ice

1. Heat sugar and water in a small, heavy saucepan over medium heat. Cook, stirring occasionally, until sugar is completely dissolved, about 10 minutes. Add lime zest. Cover; refrigerate syrup until chilled, at least 1 hour. Strain.

2. Moisten the rims of 4 tall tumblers with lime juice; dip rims in sugar.

3. Divide lime wedges and sugar syrup among glasses. Press limes using a pestle to release juice and oils in skin. Divide *cachaca* among glasses. Fill glasses with crushed ice. Stir and serve.

NUTRITION INFORMATION PER SERVING:

375 calories	0.2 g fat	0 g saturated fat
1% calories from fat	0 mg cholesterol	5.2 mg sodium
67 g carbohydrate	0.3 g protein	0.3 g fiber

Pisco Sour

PREPARATION TIME: 5 minutes
YIELD: 2 servings

COOL DRINKS WITH roots in Latin America are the perfect antidote to summer's tropical temperatures, wrote Judy Hevrdejs in a 1999 article on Latin drinks. Among the most famous is the *pisco* sour, which blends *pisco* brandy—an aged brandy made from grapes—and fresh lime juice. This recipe comes from Rinconcito Sudamericano and is that Chicago restaurant's most popular alcoholic drink.

1 cup ice
6 tablespoons *pisco* brandy
4 tablespoons fresh lime juice

2 tablespoons sugar
1 egg white, optional
Cinnamon

Puree ice, *pisco* brandy, lime juice, sugar, and egg white if desired in a blender. Pour into 2 glasses. Lightly sprinkle tops with cinnamon.

NUTRITIONAL INFORMATION PER SERVING (WITHOUT EGG WHITE):

170 calories	0 g fat	0 g saturated fat
0% calories from fat	0 mg cholesterol	0 mg sodium
15 g carbohydrate	0.1 g protein	0.1 g fiber

Mary Meade's Eggnog

PREPARATION TIME: 15 minutes
COOKING TIME: 20 minutes
CHILLING TIME: 2 hours
YIELD: 20 servings

RUTH ELLEN CHURCH, the *Tribune*'s food editor in the 1950s and 1960s, wrote many cookbooks under the name of Mary Meade (like Betty Crocker, a mythical personality). This recipe appeared in the 1955 book *Mary Meade's Kitchen Companion* and countless times in the pages of the newspaper. We've updated the recipe by cooking the eggs first to eliminate any food bacteria that may be present. You may store the eggnog covered in the refrigerator for one day before serving if desired.

6 large eggs, lightly beaten
6 cups milk
1 cup sugar
3 cups whipping cream *or*
   half-and-half

1 cup rum
1 cup orange-flavored brandy
½ cup Cognac *or* brandy
Freshly ground nutmeg

1. Combine eggs, milk, and sugar in a large saucepan. Cook over medium-low heat, stirring often, until mixture thickens and temperature reads 160°F on an instant-reading thermometer, about 20 minutes. Refrigerate until chilled, 2 to 12 hours.

2. Stir in whipping cream, rum, orange-flavored brandy, and Cognac. Sprinkle each serving with nutmeg.

NUTRITION INFORMATION PER SERVING:

295 calories	16 g fat	9.6 g saturated fat
48% calories from fat	120 mg cholesterol	70 mg sodium
15 g carbohydrate	5 g protein	0 g fiber

Swedish Glogg

PREPARATION TIME: 10 minutes

COOKING TIME: 15 minutes

YIELD: 16 1-cup servings

READER VIOLA HAGSTROM shared her delicious recipe for Swedish glogg in 1998. In Sweden, it's traditional to serve this spiced, warm drink during the holidays. But don't let the sweetness fool you: this version is quite potent and capable of fighting off the bitterest winter chill. The recipe can be cut in half.

4 cups water	10 whole cloves
¾ cup sugar	1 cinnamon stick
⅓ cup raisins	1 3-inch piece orange zest
⅓ cup slivered almonds	8 cups port wine
10 cardamom seeds	4 cups whiskey

1. Combine water, sugar, raisins, almonds, cardamom seeds, cloves, cinnamon stick, and orange zest in a Dutch oven or large saucepan. Heat to boil over medium-high heat. Reduce heat to medium-low; simmer 15 minutes.

2. Add port wine and whiskey; heat to boil. Serve warm.

NUTRITION INFORMATION PER SERVING:

275 calories	1 g fat	0.1 g saturated fat
4% calories from fat	0 mg cholesterol	9 mg sodium
15 g carbohydrate	0.8 g protein	0.4 g fiber

Sparkling Apricot Punch

PREPARATION TIME: 10 minutes
FREEZING TIME: Overnight
YIELD: 20 ½-cup servings

A VIVID CENTERPIECE for a Yuletide gathering comes from the celebrated restaurant for celebrities The Pump Room, in the Omni Ambassador East Hotel in Chicago.

Ice Ring
3 cups ginger ale
3 cups cranberry juice cocktail
Fresh cranberries

Punch
1 14-ounce can chilled apricot
   nectar
2 cups chilled cranberry juice
   cocktail
¾ cup Grand Marnier *or* other
   orange-flavored liqueur
2 750-milliliter bottles chilled
   Spanish *or* other sparkling wine
Orange slices
Lemon slices
Mint sprigs

1. To make ice ring, fill an 8-cup ring mold or any holiday mold with ginger ale and cranberry juice. Sprinkle very liberally with fresh cranberries; freeze overnight.

2. To make punch, mix apricot nectar, cranberry juice cocktail, and orange-flavored liqueur in a punch bowl. Unmold ice ring; place in center of punch. Add sparkling wine.

3. Serve in chilled champagne glasses; garnish with orange slices, lemon slices, and mint sprigs.

❧ NOTE: *Champagne or sparkling wine is a wonderful aperitif all by itself, and that's how the very best should be served. But moderately priced bubbly can be dressed up to suit any mood or occasion. Here are several fruitful additions to consider:*
Summer Bliss: Float a wedge of poached fresh peach in a glass of rosé champagne or
   sparkling wine.
Berry Bubbly: Put 1 teaspoon berry-flavored liqueur into the bottom of a champagne
   glass. Fill glass with brut, or extra-dry, champagne or sparkling wine. Garnish with
   any kind of berry, such as strawberry, blueberry, raspberry, or black raspberry.
Orange Kiss: Put 1 tablespoon orange-flavored brandy or liqueur into the bottom of a
   champagne glass. Add 2 teaspoons brandy. Fill the glass with brut champagne or
   sparkling wine. Garnish with an orange twist.
Lemon Fizz: Fill a stemmed dessert glass with lemon ice or lemon sorbet. Pour several
   tablespoons of brut champagne or sparkling wine over the top. Garnish with a mint
   sprig.

Classic Mimosa: Mix equal parts brut champagne or sparkling wine and orange juice.

Kir Royale: Put a teaspoon of crème de cassis (black currant liqueur) into the bottom of a champagne glass. Fill the glass with brut champagne or sparkling wine.

Bubbling Passion: Put 3 tablespoons passion fruit liqueur into the bottom of a champagne glass. Fill the glass with brut champagne or sparkling wine. Garnish with a lemon twist.

NUTRITION INFORMATION PER SERVING:

150 calories	0.1 g fat	0 g saturated fat
1% calories from fat	0 mg cholesterol	10 mg sodium
27 g carbohydrate	0.2 g protein	0.2 g fiber

BREAKFAST AND EGGS

Make-Ahead Poached Eggs

PREPARATION TIME: 5 minutes
COOKING TIME: 3 to 4 minutes
YIELD: 6 servings

POACHED EGGS ARE simple to prepare once you master the technique of slipping the eggs into the simmering water. Practice on the family before making them for company. This recipe allows you to prepare the eggs several hours in advance of serving. To serve, simply reheat the eggs in a bowl of hot water.

Cold water
2 tablespoons white vinegar

12 large eggs

1. Set a large bowl of cold water near the stove top. Heat 3 quarts water and vinegar to boil in a large, high-sided skillet over high heat; reduce heat to simmer.

2. Break 1 egg at a time into a small bowl. Hold the bowl as close to the water surface as possible; let egg slip out into the water. Immediately push the egg white over the yolk with a large spoon. Repeat with remaining eggs. Poach until whites are set and yolks are still soft, 3 to 4 minutes.

3. Carefully remove eggs from the water with a slotted spoon; put them into the cold water. Lift eggs 1 at a time from the water when cool; trim uneven edges with scissors. Return to cold water.

4. To serve, put eggs into a large bowl of hot, not boiling, water. Let stand until heated, about 1 minute. Remove with a slotted spoon; drain on paper towels.

NUTRITION INFORMATION PER SERVING:

150 calories	10 g fat	3.1 g saturated fat
62% calories from fat	425 mg cholesterol	126 mg sodium
1.5 g carbohydrate	13 g protein	0 g fiber

Creole Poached Eggs on Toast

PREPARATION TIME: 15 minutes
COOKING TIME: 10 minutes
YIELD: 4 servings

NEW ORLEANS, THE nation's quintessential brunch spot, offers plenty of inspiration for a Mother's Day morning meal. A classic egg breakfast is jazzed up here with spices and a colorful topping of chopped bell pepper. Look for Creole seasoning blend in the spice aisle of the supermarket.

1 tablespoon unsalted butter	Ground red pepper
½ red bell pepper, diced fine	1 tablespoon orange juice
½ green bell pepper, diced fine	4 cups water
1 small onion, diced fine	1 tablespoon vinegar
2 to 3 teaspoons Creole seasoning blend	4 large eggs
	4 thick slices French bread, toasted
⅛ teaspoon salt	Minced fresh chives, optional

1. Melt half of the butter in a medium-sized nonstick skillet over medium-high heat. Add red bell pepper, green bell pepper, onion, Creole seasoning blend, salt, and ground red pepper; cook, stirring often, until vegetables are tender and begin to brown at edges, about 4 minutes. Stir in remaining butter and orange juice. Remove from heat; keep warm.

2. Heat water and vinegar to a boil in a saucepan over high heat; reduce heat to simmer. Break 1 egg at a time into a small bowl. Hold bowl as close to water surface as possible; let egg slip out into the water. Immediately push the egg white over the yolk with a large spoon. Repeat with remaining eggs. Poach until whites are set and yolks are still soft, 3 to 4 minutes.

3. Carefully remove the eggs from the water with a slotted spoon; drain. Place on top of toast. Spoon vegetable mixture over eggs; sprinkle with chives if desired.

NUTRITION INFORMATION PER SERVING:

210 calories	9 g fat	4 g saturated fat
40% calories from fat	220 mg cholesterol	305 mg sodium
20 g carbohydrate	10 g protein	1 g fiber

Scrambled Eggs with Chorizo
(Huevos con Chorizo)

PREPARATION TIME: 10 minutes
COOKING TIME: 5 minutes
YIELD: 4 servings

WRITER JUDY HEVRDEJS contributed this recipe for the classic Mexican combination of spicy chorizo and eggs. Chorizo is a Mexican sausage with a unique flavor found in Mexican food stores and other specialty stores.

¼ pound chorizo, casing removed
2 tablespoons butter
6 large eggs, lightly beaten

Salt
Freshly ground black pepper
Minced cilantro, optional

1. Crumble chorizo into a medium-sized skillet. Cook over low heat until dry and crumbly. Drain liquid.

2. Melt butter in a medium-sized skillet over medium heat. Add eggs; cook, stirring constantly. Stir in chorizo when eggs are half cooked. Finish cooking eggs. Season with salt and pepper to taste. Sprinkle with cilantro if desired.

NUTRITION INFORMATION PER SERVING:

292 calories	24 g fat	10 g saturated fat
75% calories from fat	359 mg cholesterol	503 mg sodium
1.5 g carbohydrate	16 g protein	0 g fiber

Scrambled Eggs with Smoked Salmon
and Chive Cheese

PREPARATION TIME: 15 minutes
COOKING TIME: 5 minutes
YIELD: 4 servings

THIS BRUNCH DISH, developed for a story on quick Mother's Day meals, would be nice any weekend of the year. Be sure to use good-quality smoked salmon.

6 large eggs
4 large egg whites
Freshly ground black pepper
2 teaspoons unsalted butter
1 to 2 ounces smoked salmon,
    cut in strips

1½ ounces cream cheese with
    chives
1 tablespoon snipped fresh chives,
    optional

►

1. Whisk together eggs, egg whites, and black pepper.

2. Melt butter in a large nonstick skillet over medium-high heat. Add eggs; cook, stirring, until softly scrambled. Fold in salmon, cream cheese in small bits, and chives just before eggs are fully cooked.

NUTRITION INFORMATION PER SERVING:

250 calories	18 g fat	7 g saturated fat
68% calories from fat	550 mg cholesterol	430 mg sodium
1.8 g carbohydrate	18 g protein	0 g fiber

Santa Fe Scrambled Eggs

PREPARATION TIME: 10 minutes
COOKING TIME: 5 minutes
YIELD: 4 servings

A VISIT TO the spice drawer gives the all-American breakfast of sausage and eggs a Southwestern accent in this recipe from a "Fast Food" column. The scrambled eggs get a little extra panache from an unlikely ingredient: corn tortilla chips folded in as a nod to a popular New Mexican breakfast dish called *migas*.

4 large eggs	2 teaspoons unsalted butter
4 large egg whites	2 green onions, sliced thin
½ cup coarsely crumbled tortilla chips	1 jalapeño, seeded and minced
Salt	¼ cup minced cilantro
Freshly ground black pepper	Salsa, optional

1. Whisk together eggs and egg whites in a medium-sized bowl. Add tortilla chips, salt, and black pepper; set aside.

2. Melt butter in a medium-sized nonstick skillet over medium heat. Add green onions and jalapeño; cook, stirring constantly, until slightly softened, 45 seconds. Add egg mixture; sprinkle with cilantro. Cook, stirring to scramble eggs, over medium heat until set. Serve with salsa if desired.

NUTRITION INFORMATION PER SERVING:

130 calories	8 g fat	2.9 g saturated fat
54% calories from fat	215 mg cholesterol	145 mg sodium
4.6 g carbohydrate	10 g protein	0.6 g fiber

Farmer's Omelet

PREPARATION TIME: 20 minutes
COOKING TIME: 30 minutes
YIELD: 8 servings

FOR A STORY about kielbasa, that garlicky Polish sausage, the *Tribune* test kitchen staff developed this excellent quick brunch or supper dish.

½ pound smoked Polish sausage,
   cut into ½-inch slices
1 tablespoon butter
1 large potato, cooked and diced
1 small onion, diced

1 small green bell pepper, seeded
   and diced
¼ pound mushrooms, sliced
8 large eggs, beaten well
¼ teaspoon salt
Freshly ground black pepper

1. Heat oven to 350°F. Cook sausage over medium heat in a 10-inch cast-iron or ovenproof skillet, stirring until browned, 2 to 3 minutes. Remove with a slotted spoon to a bowl.

2. Melt butter in the skillet. Add potato. Cook, stirring, until browned, 5 to 7 minutes. Remove with a slotted spoon; add to sausage in the bowl. Put onion, green bell pepper, and mushrooms in skillet. Cook, stirring, until soft, about 5 minutes. Add sausage and potato to skillet; cook, stirring, 1 minute.

3. Add beaten eggs, salt, and black pepper to taste to skillet. Do not stir. Bake in the oven until puffed and firm, 15 to 20 minutes.

NUTRITION INFORMATION PER SERVING:

200 calories	15 g fat	5 g saturated fat
66% calories from fat	235 mg cholesterol	400 mg sodium
6 g carbohydrate	11 g protein	0.7 g fiber

Mexican Omelet with Avocado Topping

PREPARATION TIME: 10 minutes
COOKING TIME: 5 minutes
YIELD: 2 servings

SALSA, EITHER BOTTLED or homemade, is the key to this zesty omelet that is suitable for either brunch or a fast vegetarian dinner. Toasted flour tortillas, Mexican rice, or refried beans and a tossed salad make traditional accompaniments.

1 avocado, peeled, pitted,
   and diced

2 tablespoons plain yogurt *or*
   sour cream

➤

1 tablespoon minced cilantro

1 teaspoon lemon juice

4 large eggs, lightly beaten

2 tablespoons water

2 tablespoons butter

½ cup medium *or* hot

   chunky-style salsa

1.   Mix avocado, yogurt, cilantro, and lemon juice in a small bowl. Whisk eggs and water in a separate small bowl.

2.   Heat butter in a 10-inch skillet. Add egg mixture. Cook, stirring lightly with a fork, until mixture begins to set on bottom. Cook without stirring until set. Spoon salsa down the middle of the omelet. Loosen edges with a spatula. Tip pan so the omelet rolls into itself when you lift the top edge with a spatula. Tilt the pan until it's nearly vertical; continue rolling the omelet onto plate. Top with avocado mixture.

NUTRITION INFORMATION PER SERVING:

442 calories	37 g fat	13 g saturated fat
73% calories from fat	457 mg cholesterol	546 mg sodium
14 g carbohydrate	16 g protein	6 g fiber

Morel and Asparagus Omelet

PREPARATION TIME: 15 minutes

COOKING TIME: 15 minutes

YIELD: 2 servings

MORELS, THOSE HIGHLY prized wild mushrooms, have a certain mystique about them, so the combination of morels and asparagus makes this a very elegant omelet for a spring brunch.

8 fresh morels (see Note)

6 asparagus spears

2 tablespoons shredded Swiss

   cheese

4 large eggs

2 tablespoons water

Freshly ground black pepper

2 teaspoons unsalted butter

Salt

1.   Soak fresh morels in lightly salted warm water about 5 minutes.

2.   Snap off ends of asparagus spears. Lightly peel stalks. Heat 2 inches of water to boil in a large skillet; add asparagus. Cook until crisp-tender, about 2 minutes. Drain well; chop stalks. Set tips aside for garnish.

3. Mix morels, diced asparagus stalks, and Swiss cheese in a small bowl. To make each omelet, beat 2 eggs, 1 tablespoon water, and black pepper in a medium-sized bowl until combined.

4. Heat a 9-inch omelet pan or nonstick skillet over medium-high heat until hot. Add 1 teaspoon of the butter; swirl the pan until butter is melted. Pour in egg mixture; stir gently with a fork until eggs begin to set. Stop stirring; cook until almost set. Spread half of the morel mixture and salt over omelet. Loosen the edges with a spatula. Tip the pan so the omelet rolls when you lift the top edge with the spatula. Tilt the pan until it's nearly vertical; continue rolling the omelet onto a plate. Repeat for the second omelet. Garnish each with reserved asparagus tips.

❧ NOTE: *If fresh morels are unavailable, substitute dried morels. Soak dried morels in very hot water to cover until they are softened, about 20 minutes, and then drain. Use soaking water for flavoring soups and sauces.*

NUTRITION INFORMATION PER SERVING:

248 calories	16 g fat	7 g saturated fat
58% calories from fat	442 mg cholesterol	150 mg sodium
9 g carbohydrate	18 g protein	2.3 g fiber

Potato and Pepper Frittata

PREPARATION TIME: 15 minutes
COOKING TIME: 11 minutes
YIELD: 6 servings

A FRITTATA IS an Italian omelet. This one, chock full of potatoes, peppers, and green onions, may be served for brunch, but it is also hearty enough for a light supper or vegetarian entree.

2 tablespoons butter	6 green onions, sliced
4 small red potatoes, cooked and cut into ½-inch chunks	8 large eggs, lightly beaten
1 red bell pepper, seeded and diced	½ teaspoon salt
1 green bell pepper, seeded and diced	¼ teaspoon freshly ground black pepper
	¼ teaspoon cayenne pepper

1. Heat oven to 375°F. Melt 1 tablespoon of the butter in a 10-inch ovenproof skillet over low heat. Add potatoes, red bell pepper, green bell pepper, and onions. Sauté vegetables until potatoes are browned and cooked through. Remove with a slotted spoon to a bowl.

➤

2. Mix eggs, salt, black pepper, and cayenne pepper in a large bowl. Add sautéed vegetables; stir to mix.

3. Heat remaining 1 tablespoon butter in the same skillet over low heat. Pour in egg mixture. Cook until light brown on the bottom, 2 to 3 minutes. Bake until eggs are set, 8 to 10 minutes.

4. Loosen the edges; slide frittata onto a plate. Serve hot, or cool to room temperature and serve. Cut into 6 wedges.

NUTRITION INFORMATION PER SERVING:

201 calories	11 g fat	4.5 g saturated fat
47% calories from fat	294 mg cholesterol	325 mg sodium
16 g carbohydrate	10 g protein	2.4 g fiber

Crab Egg Foo Young

PREPARATION TIME: 20 minutes

SOAKING TIME: 30 minutes

COOKING TIME: 5 minutes

YIELD: 4 servings

HERE'S A DISH developed by former columnist Beverly Dillon that will put some zip in your mealtime. The two accompanying sauces may be made in advance, stored in jars with tightly fitting lids, and refrigerated for up to two days. Let them come to room temperature before serving.

Ginger Sauce

¼ cup soy sauce

1 tablespoon dry sherry

1 tablespoon light brown sugar

1 tablespoon grated gingerroot

½ teaspoon white wine vinegar

Hot Mustard Sauce

2 tablespoons dry mustard

Dash Asian sesame oil (see Note)

Warm water as needed

Egg Foo Young

6 to 8 dried black Chinese mushrooms

3 large eggs

1 6½-ounce can lump crabmeat, drained and flaked

1 cup fresh bean sprouts, rinsed and drained

1 8-ounce can water chestnuts, drained and chopped coarse

2 green onions, chopped

2 tablespoons soy sauce

1 tablespoon chopped cilantro

1 clove garlic, minced

2 to 3 tablespoons vegetable oil

1. To make ginger sauce, stir together soy sauce, sherry, brown sugar, ginger-root, and white wine vinegar in a small bowl. To make hot mustard sauce, stir together dry mustard, sesame oil, and water to moisten in another small bowl. Set sauces aside.

2. To make egg foo young, soak mushrooms in hot water to cover until soft, about 30 minutes. Squeeze out as much water as possible. Remove and discard stems. Dice mushroom caps. Lightly beat eggs in a medium-sized bowl. Stir in crabmeat, bean sprouts, water chestnuts, onions, soy sauce, cilantro, and garlic.

3. Heat 2 tablespoons of the oil in a large skillet over medium heat. Fill a ¼-cup measure with egg mixture. Gently pour into the skillet; press to flatten slightly with a spatula. Cook until bottom is almost set, 1 to 2 minutes. Turn; cook until bottom is golden yet still a bit moist, about 1 minute. Arrange on a platter; cover lightly with aluminum foil to keep warm. Continue cooking until you use all of the egg mixture. Serve with ginger and mustard sauces.

❧ NOTE: *Many recipes call for dashes or pinches of ingredients. What's the difference between them? Generally a dash refers to a liquid ingredient and a pinch refers to dry ingredients such as spices. The amounts called for in the recipe are too small to measure in ordinary measuring spoons. If you could measure a dash or pinch, it would probably be less than ⅛ teaspoon.*

Some old-fashioned recipes often use the word scant. *A scant tablespoon means one that is not filled totally to the top of the measuring spoon's bowl.*

NUTRITION INFORMATION PER SERVING:

259 calories	13 g fat	2.2 g saturated fat
44% calories from fat	187 mg cholesterol	1,708 mg sodium
21 g carbohydrate	16 g protein	4.5 g fiber

Ham and Eggs Basque Style

PREPARATION TIME: 30 minutes
STANDING TIME: 5 minutes
COOKING TIME: 25 minutes
YIELD: 2 servings

FOR A VALENTINE'S Day story on perfect partners, William Rice developed this recipe for ham and eggs dressed up for a brunch table or as the first course in a celebratory dinner for two. The famous red, white, and green vegetable combination (tomato, onion, and green bell pepper) of Basque cooking provides lively flavor and color. If you use a conventional oven instead of a microwave, heat the casserole dish in a 350°F oven for about 10 minutes.

4 large eggs
1 tablespoon olive oil
1 small onion, sliced thin
½ red *or* green bell pepper, sliced thin
1 small clove garlic, minced
¼ teaspoon dried Italian seasoning

½ teaspoon Hungarian hot *or* other paprika
2 tablespoons dry vermouth *or* dry white wine
1 ripe tomato, chopped
Salt
Freshly ground black pepper
3 ounces smoked ham, julienned

1.   Place eggs in a small saucepan; cover with cold water. Heat just to boil over medium-low heat. Turn off heat; leave eggs in the water 10 minutes. Drain. Cover with cold water; let stand 5 minutes. Drain and peel. Cut each egg crosswise into 6 slices; set aside.

2.   Heat olive oil in a medium-sized skillet over medium-low heat. Add onion and bell pepper; cook until soft and on the verge of browning, about 6 to 7 minutes. Add garlic, Italian seasoning, and paprika. Stir 30 seconds. Add vermouth; heat to boil. Cook until liquid is reduced to a syrup, about 1 minute. Add tomato, salt, and black pepper. Cover; cook on medium-low heat 10 minutes. Uncover; cook to reduce liquid to a syrup, about 1 minute. Set aside.

3.   Line the bottom of a small, microwave-proof 1-quart casserole dish with half of the ham. Top with egg slices. Scatter the remaining ham over the egg slices. Spread onion mixture over the top. Heat covered casserole dish in a microwave oven on medium (50 percent) power until warm but not bubbling hot, about 5 minutes.

NUTRITION INFORMATION PER SERVING:

345 calories	24 g fat	3 g saturated fat
57% calories from fat	450 mg cholesterol	535 mg sodium
9 g carbohydrate	23 g protein	0 g fiber

Egg Crepes with Red Bell Peppers and Mushrooms

PREPARATION TIME: 45 minutes
COOKING TIME: 30 minutes
YIELD: 4 servings

THIS DISH, CREATED by Beverly Dillon, uses roasted red bell peppers as a hearty sauce for mushroom-filled egg crepes. The crepes may be served any time you entertain: brunch, supper, or as a first course for a formal dinner. The most time-consuming part of this recipe is roasting the red bell peppers, but you may prepare them in advance and refrigerate them for several days.

Roasted Red Bell Pepper Sauce
5 medium-sized red bell peppers
1 cup whipping cream
2 tablespoons fresh lemon juice
1 tablespoon minced fresh tarragon
    or ½ teaspoon dried
½ teaspoon salt
¼ teaspoon freshly ground black
    pepper
Dash hot pepper sauce

Mushroom Filling
2 tablespoons butter
2 tablespoons olive oil

1½ pounds mixed fresh
    mushrooms, such as button,
    oyster, and shiitake
½ shallot, minced, *or* 1 green
    onion, sliced thin

Egg Crepes
8 large eggs, lightly beaten
6 tablespoons water
½ teaspoon salt
½ teaspoon freshly ground black
    pepper
2 tablespoons butter, or more as
    needed
Fresh tarragon sprigs

1. To make roasted red bell pepper sauce, heat broiler. Put red bell peppers in the broiler pan. Broil 4 to 6 inches from heat source, turning often until skins are blistered and charred. Place in a paper or plastic bag; let stand until cool. Discard stems and seeds. Peel away charred skin. Cut into ¼-inch-wide strips.

2. Put 1 cup of the roasted red bell pepper and whipping cream, lemon juice, tarragon, salt, black pepper, and hot pepper sauce into a food processor fitted with a metal blade. Process until smooth. Transfer to a saucepan; cook over medium heat until warm.

3. To make mushroom filling, melt butter with oil over medium-high heat in a large, heavy skillet. Add mushrooms and shallots. Cook, stirring occasionally, over medium heat until mushrooms give up liquid and are lightly browned. Add remaining red bell pepper and heat through. Remove from heat and set aside.

►

4. To make egg crepes, put eggs, water, salt, and black pepper into a medium-sized bowl. Whisk to blend. Melt 1 teaspoon of the butter in an 8-inch nonstick crepe pan or skillet over low heat. Add ¼ cup of the crepe mixture to the pan. Cook until set, about 1 minute. Carefully lift edge of crepe, turn, and cook other side 30 seconds. Continue until you've used all of the remaining butter and crepe mixture. Stack crepes between sheets of waxed paper. Loosely cover crepes with aluminum foil to keep warm.

5. Spoon roasted red bell pepper sauce onto bottom of 4 serving plates. Tip plates to spread sauce. Put some of the mushroom filling in the center of each crepe; fold crepes into quarters. Place 2 filled crepes on top of sauce on each plate. Top with additional mushroom mixture. Garnish with tarragon sprigs.

NUTRITION INFORMATION PER SERVING:

609 calories	51 g fat	25 g saturated fat
73% calories from fat	538 mg cholesterol	859 mg sodium
24 g carbohydrate	20 g protein	5 g fiber

Cheddar Cheese Soufflé

PREPARATION TIME: 20 minutes

COOKING TIME: 40 minutes

YIELD: 6 servings

THIS SOUFFLÉ MAKES a rich and satisfying main course or brunch entree. For variety try substituting an aged Swiss, Comte, or Havarti cheese for the cheddar.

¼ cup butter	5 large egg yolks
¼ cup all-purpose flour	½ pound sharp cheddar cheese,
1 teaspoon dry mustard	shredded (about 2 cups)
½ teaspoon salt	7 large egg whites
Pinch cayenne pepper	½ teaspoon cream of tartar
1 cup hot milk	

1. Melt butter in a small saucepan; blend in flour. Cook, stirring, 1 minute. Stir in mustard, salt, and cayenne pepper. Gradually add hot milk; cook, stirring, until thickened and smooth. Cool mixture.

2. Heat oven to 375°F. Beat egg yolks in the large bowl of an electric mixer until thick and lemon-colored. Gradually beat in hot milk mixture; stir in cheddar cheese.

3. Beat egg whites in the medium-sized bowl of an electric mixer until foamy. Gradually beat in cream of tartar; beat until stiff but not dry. Gently fold egg whites into cheese mixture.

4. Spoon into an ungreased 1½-quart soufflé dish. With a teaspoon, draw a circle around the top of the soufflé mixture 1 inch from edge. Bake until puffed and golden, about 35 minutes.

NUTRITION INFORMATION PER SERVING:

395 calories	31 g fat	15 g saturated fat
70% calories from fat	489 mg cholesterol	615 mg sodium
9 g carbohydrate	21 g protein	0.2 g fiber

French Toast, Three Ways

PREPARATION TIME: 15 minutes
COOKING TIME: 6 minutes per batch
YIELD: 6 2-slice servings

DEVELOPED IN THE *Tribune* test kitchen, this recipe comes from a story on the joy of toast. As writer Bob Condor put it, "Like a good neighbor or cheerful coworker, toast can make life richer without much fanfare." This French toast is better if made with dense, slightly stale bread.

6 large eggs	4 tablespoons butter, or more as
1 cup whipping cream *or*	needed
half-and-half	12 slices French, white, *or* other
1 tablespoon sugar	bread
2 teaspoons vanilla extract	Maple syrup *or* confectioners' sugar
2 teaspoons cinnamon	Fresh fruit

1. Whisk together eggs and whipping cream. Add sugar, vanilla extract, and cinnamon; whisk until well combined. Pour mixture into a pie plate or shallow bowl.

2. Melt 2 tablespoons of the butter in a heavy skillet over medium heat. Dip each bread slice into egg mixture, turning once. Place 2 to 4 of the bread slices in the skillet without overlapping. Fry until golden brown, about 3 minutes. Turn; cook until other sides are golden. Remove slices to a warm plate; keep warm. Repeat with remaining bread slices, adding butter as needed.

3. Top French toast slices with syrup or confectioners' sugar. Garnish with fresh fruit.

➤

❧ VARIATIONS: *Rum French Toast: Replace vanilla extract with 1 to 2 teaspoons rum and decrease cinnamon to 1 teaspoon.*

Orange French Toast: Decrease vanilla extract and cinnamon to 1 teaspoon each. Add 2 teaspoons fresh orange juice and 1 teaspoon grated orange zest.

NUTRITION INFORMATION PER SERVING (BASIC RECIPE):

430 calories	29 g fat	16 g saturated fat
60% calories from fat	290 mg cholesterol	420 mg sodium
31 g carbohydrate	12 g protein	1.9 g fiber

Oven French Toast

PREPARATION TIME: 15 minutes
CHILLING TIME: Overnight
BAKING TIME: 45 to 50 minutes
YIELD: 6 servings

FRENCH TOAST IS usually a stand-and-serve-from-the-stove dish: the cook stands and everyone else sits and eats. The following recipe remedies that situation. You make this French toast casserole the night before, then just pop it in the oven to bake while you're reading the morning paper.

Butter	1 tablespoon vanilla extract
1 8-ounce loaf French bread, cut into 1-inch-thick slices	1 teaspoon cinnamon
	¾ teaspoon salt
8 large eggs	2 tablespoons butter, cut into small
3 cups milk	pieces
4 teaspoons sugar	Maple syrup *or* honey

1. Generously butter a 13″ × 9″ baking dish. Arrange bread slices in dish.
2. Whisk together eggs, milk, sugar, vanilla, cinnamon, and salt in a large bowl. Pour over bread slices. Cover with aluminum foil; refrigerate overnight.
3. Heat oven to 350°F. Remove the baking dish from the refrigerator; uncover. Dot top with 2 tablespoons butter pieces. Bake uncovered until puffed and golden, 45 to 50 minutes. Let stand 5 minutes before serving. Cut in squares; serve with maple syrup or honey.

❧ VARIATION: *Try using half-and-half instead of milk for a richer version. Instead of vanilla extract, use rum or rum extract.*

NUTRITION INFORMATION PER SERVING:

314 calories	14 g fat	6.1 g saturated fat
40% calories from fat	303 mg cholesterol	705 mg sodium
29 g carbohydrate	15 g protein	1.1 g fiber

Orange-Maple Butter

PREPARATION TIME: 5 minutes

YIELD: 4 1-tablespoon servings

A SMALL AMOUNT of heat from the ground red pepper makes this breakfast spread complex and interesting. Try it on white or wheat bread, pancakes, or waffles.

¼ cup (½ stick) unsalted butter, softened

1 tablespoon plus 1½ teaspoons pure maple syrup

½ teaspoon finely grated orange zest

Pinch ground red pepper

Stir together butter, maple syrup, orange zest, and ground red pepper in a small bowl.

NUTRITION INFORMATION PER SERVING:

120 calories	12 g fat	7 g saturated fat
83% calories from fat	30 mg cholesterol	2 mg sodium
5 g carbohydrate	0.1 g protein	0 g fiber

Maple-Glazed Pears

PREPARATION TIME: 15 minutes

COOKING TIME: 5 minutes

YIELD: 4 servings

FRESH PEARS SWEETLY scented with cinnamon, orange, and maple make a stylish topping for pancakes.

2 tablespoons unsalted butter

1 ripe pear, peeled, cored, and sliced thin

¼ teaspoon cinnamon

½ cup pure maple syrup

1 tablespoon orange marmalade

1 teaspoon vanilla extract

➤

1. Melt butter in a large nonstick skillet over high heat. Add pear slices. Cook, stirring frequently, until edges begin to brown, 2 to 3 minutes. Sprinkle with cinnamon; cook 1 minute.

2. Add maple syrup, marmalade, and vanilla; cook over high heat 1 minute to thicken slightly. Serve hot.

NUTRITION INFORMATION PER SERVING:

195 calories	6 g fat	3.6 g saturated fat
27% calories from fat	15 mg cholesterol	7 mg sodium
37 g carbohydrate	0.3 g protein	1 g fiber

Foolproof Pancakes

PREPARATION TIME: 5 minutes
COOKING TIME: 3 minutes per batch, 12 minutes
YIELD: 10 3-inch pancakes

IN AN ATTEMPT to revive Americans' commitment to homemade flapjacks by finding the perfect recipe, we borrowed this great version from Chicago chef Ina Pinkney.

1 cup all-purpose flour	½ teaspoon salt
¾ cup buttermilk	1 large egg
¼ cup whole milk	2 tablespoons unsalted butter,
1 teaspoon sugar	melted
½ teaspoon baking soda	Vegetable oil for cooking

1. Combine flour, buttermilk, milk, sugar, baking soda, salt, eggs, and butter in a mixing bowl; whisk lightly. It's fine if there are small lumps and streaks.

2. Heat 2 teaspoons of the vegetable oil in a 10-inch skillet over high heat. Wipe away excess oil with a paper towel, leaving a thin film on entire surface. Reduce heat to medium-high. Add ¼ cup batter for each of 3 pancakes. Cook until there are bubbles at edges, about 1½ minutes. Turn with a spatula; cook until browned, about 1 minute. Repeat with remaining batter, cooking pancakes in batches of 3, adding more oil as necessary.

❧ VARIATIONS: *Whole Wheat Pancakes: Decrease flour to ¾ cup and add ¼ cup whole wheat flour.*

Blueberry Pancakes: Fold ¾ cup blueberries into batter.

Banana Pancakes: Slice 1 ripe banana into batter.

Pecan Pancakes: Add ⅔ cup chopped, toasted pecans to the batter.

NUTRITION INFORMATION PER PANCAKE (BASIC RECIPE):

85 calories	3.3 g fat	1.8 g saturated fat
35% calories from fat	30 mg cholesterol	210 mg sodium
11 g carbohydrate	2.8 g protein	0.3 g fiber

German Puffed Pancake

PREPARATION TIME: 5 minutes
COOKING TIME: 25 minutes
YIELD: 4 servings

SIMPLE PREPARATIONS AND presentations are the key to getting brunch on the table quickly. Here an oven-baked pancake brings a breakfast favorite to the table without the endless small batches and pancake flipping that traditional skillet pancakes require. This pancake goes well with cooked fruit; try it with a mixture of strawberries and peaches. For a sweeter pancake, add one teaspoon sugar and one-half teaspoon vanilla extract.

2 tablespoons unsalted butter	¼ teaspoon salt
2 large eggs	Freshly grated nutmeg
½ cup all-purpose flour	Confectioners' sugar
½ cup whole milk	Lemon wedges

1. Heat oven to 425°F. Place butter in a 9-inch pie plate; put pan in the oven to melt butter.

2. Whisk eggs in a medium-sized bowl. Add flour, milk, salt, and nutmeg to taste; stir to combine. Pour batter into the hot pie plate.

3. Bake until pancake is puffed and golden, 20 minutes. Sift confectioners' sugar over top; serve hot, with lemon wedges.

NUTRITION INFORMATION PER SERVING:

164 calories	9 g fat	5 g saturated fat
85% calories from fat	130 mg cholesterol	180 mg sodium
14 g carbohydrate	6 g protein	0.4 g fiber

Ginger-Pecan Pancakes

PREPARATION TIME: 10 minutes
COOKING TIME: 2 minutes per batch
YIELD: 4 servings

THE TIMELESS APPEAL of a pancake breakfast gets a speedy update with a doctored box mix, pecans, and fresh ginger. This recipe is from our "Fast Food" column.

1 cup buttermilk pancake mix	¼ cup toasted chopped pecans
1 ¼-inch piece gingerroot, peeled and minced	½ teaspoon freshly grated nutmeg
	Butter *or* vegetable oil

1. Mix pancake batter according to package directions. Heat oven to 200°F.
2. Combine pancake batter, gingerroot, pecans, and nutmeg in a medium-sized bowl; mix lightly.
3. Heat a thin film of butter or oil in a large nonstick skillet or griddle over medium heat. Pour about 3 tablespoons of the batter per pancake into the pan. Cook until bubbly on top; turn and cook other side until golden brown, about 2 minutes total per batch. Keep warm in oven while cooking remaining batter.

NUTRITION INFORMATION PER SERVING:

165 calories	8 g fat	0.4 g saturated fat
42% calories from fat	12 mg cholesterol	345 mg sodium
22 g carbohydrate	3 g protein	0.6 g fiber

Baked Apple Pancake

PREPARATION TIME: 30 minutes
COOKING TIME: 20 to 30 minutes
YIELD: 2 servings

THE BATTER FOR this pancake is similar to that of a Yorkshire pudding or a popover. It puffs up very high in the oven and then deflates quickly when removed. The juice from the apples, butter, and sugar combine to form a syrup in the bottom of the pan, so no other syrup is needed when serving. A cast-iron, enameled cast-iron, or heavy anodized aluminum skillet is required to produce crispy edges and a golden brown bottom. A nonstick skillet will do, but the edges of the pancake won't crisp as nicely.

2 Granny Smith apples, peeled, cored, and sliced thin	½ cup granulated sugar
	½ cup packed light brown sugar

2 teaspoons cinnamon

1 cup milk

4 large eggs

1 cup all-purpose flour

Pinch salt

¼ cup (½ stick) unsalted butter

1. Heat oven to 425°F. Toss together apples, granulated sugar, brown sugar, and cinnamon in a medium-sized bowl.

2. Put milk and eggs into a blender or into a food processor fitted with a metal blade. Process until well mixed. Add flour and salt. Process until smooth.

3. Lightly oil an oven-safe, 10-inch cast-iron or enameled cast-iron skillet. Melt butter in skillet over medium heat. Add apple mixture. Cook, stirring often, until sugars have melted and apples are well coated, about 5 minutes.

4. Gently pour batter over apples. Bake until pancake is puffed, its edges are golden, and apples are tender, 20 to 30 minutes. Cut into wedges to serve.

NUTRITION INFORMATION PER SERVING:

1,108 calories	36 g fat	19 g saturated fat
29% calories from fat	496 mg cholesterol	519 mg sodium
177 g carbohydrate	24 g protein	6 g fiber

Pumpkin Flapjacks with Cider-Walnut Syrup

PREPARATION TIME: 35 minutes

COOKING TIME: 20 minutes

YIELD: 8 servings

THESE HEARTY PANCAKES, developed in the *Tribune* test kitchen, are packed with flavor from canned pumpkin and spices. Serve them with maple syrup or an easy-to-make cider-walnut syrup.

Cider-Walnut Syrup

2 cups packed light brown sugar

1 cup unsweetened apple cider *or* apple juice

½ cup coarsely chopped walnuts

¼ teaspoon cinnamon

Flapjacks

1½ cups whole wheat flour

1½ cups all-purpose flour

1 cup old-fashioned rolled oats

2 tablespoons sugar

1 tablespoon baking powder

2 teaspoons baking soda

1 teaspoon salt

1 teaspoon cinnamon

½ teaspoon ground ginger

½ teaspoon ground nutmeg

¾ cup (1½ sticks) chilled unsalted butter, cut into small pieces, plus more for cooking

▶

4 large eggs, separated	½ cup canned solid-pack pumpkin
1 quart buttermilk	

1.   To make cider-walnut syrup, heat brown sugar, apple cider, walnuts, and cinnamon in a medium-sized saucepan to boil over medium-high heat, stirring occasionally; boil 3 minutes. Remove from heat and keep warm.

2.   To make flapjacks, put whole wheat flour, all-purpose flour, oats, sugar, baking powder, baking soda, salt, cinnamon, ginger, and nutmeg in a food processor fitted with a metal blade. Process until blended. Add butter; pulse until mixture resembles coarse crumbs.

3.   Beat egg whites in the bowl of an electric mixer until soft peaks form. Beat egg yolks, buttermilk, and pumpkin in a separate bowl of the electric mixer until smooth. Stir in flour mixture by hand just until blended. Fold in beaten egg whites.

4.   Heat a large griddle or 2 skillets until hot. Melt some butter on the griddle. Spoon batter onto the griddle in several places, making 3-inch round pancakes. Cook until bubbles appear uniformly across top. Turn; cook second side until golden, about 2 minutes total. Repeat, using more butter as needed. Serve with warm syrup.

NUTRITION INFORMATION PER SERVING:

729 calories	27 g fat	13 g saturated fat
32% calories from fat	157 mg cholesterol	1,012 mg sodium
9 g carbohydrate	21 g protein	6 g fiber

Chocolate Waffles with Poached Strawberries

PREPARATION TIME: 25 minutes

STANDING TIME: 30 minutes

COOKING TIME: 20 minutes

YIELD: 6 servings

CHOCOLATE WAFFLES? MICHAEL Foley, chef-owner of Printer's Row restaurant in Chicago, shared this unusual recipe that works as a dessert or a brunch dish. The waffles are delicious, especially topped with the warm, sweetened strawberries.

Strawberries	2 cups water
2½ pints fresh strawberries, hulled	1 vanilla bean *or* ½ teaspoon
1¾ cups sugar	vanilla extract
Juice of 1 small lemon	

Waffles
1¼ cups all-purpose flour
½ cup unsweetened cocoa powder
¼ cup sugar
1 teaspoon baking powder
½ teaspoon baking soda

½ teaspoon salt
3 large eggs, separated
1¾ cups milk
¼ cup (½ stick) butter, melted
Whipped cream, optional
Mint sprigs, optional

1. To make strawberries, toss together strawberries, 1 cup of the sugar, and lemon juice. Let sit about 30 minutes. Heat remaining ¾ cup sugar, water, and vanilla bean in a large saucepan over medium heat. Cook, stirring often, until sugar dissolves. Add strawberries. Heat to simmer; reduce heat to low. Cook until almost tender, 1 to 3 minutes. Cool slightly.

2. To make waffles, lightly brush waffle iron grids with vegetable oil. Close waffle iron; heat according to manufacturer's directions. Stir together flour, cocoa, sugar, baking powder, baking soda, and salt in a medium-sized bowl. Whisk in egg yolks and milk.

3. Beat egg whites in the bowl of an electric mixer until stiff but not dry. Fold into batter. Fold in melted butter. Bake waffle batter in batches according to manufacturer's directions.

4. Serve waffles hot, topped with warm poached strawberries. Garnish with whipped cream and mint sprigs.

NUTRITION INFORMATION PER SERVING:

555 calories	13 g fat	7 g saturated fat
21% calories from fat	132 mg cholesterol	532 mg sodium
105 g carbohydrate	11 g protein	6 g fiber

Baked Peppered Bacon

PREPARATION TIME: 5 minutes
COOKING TIME: 12 to 15 minutes
YIELD: 4 servings

As PART OF an easy brunch menu, consider baking the bacon instead of frying it. It's a strategy that renders the job practically effortless. A little seasoning turns it into guest fare.

8 strips bacon
¼ cup packed light brown sugar

¼ to 1 teaspoon ground red pepper

►

1. Heat oven to 350°F. Line a jelly roll pan with aluminum foil; place a wire rack inside pan.

2. Arrange bacon on the rack. Bake 10 minutes. Stir together brown sugar and red pepper to taste; sprinkle over bacon (some may fall into the pan). Bake until bacon is browned and cooked as desired, 2 to 5 minutes.

NUTRITION INFORMATION PER SERVING:

270 calories	19 g fat	7 g saturated fat
63% calories from fat	35 mg cholesterol	615 mg sodium
14 g carbohydrate	12 g protein	0 g fiber

Maple-Glazed Smoked Pork

COOKING TIME: 5 minutes

PREPARATION TIME: 5 minutes

YIELD: 4 servings

FOR A STORY on easy weekend breakfasts, writer Pat Dailey proposed making subtly smoked pork sweetened with a hint of maple syrup as a lean alternative to bacon. You may use Canadian bacon if smoked pork chops are unavailable.

1 tablespoon unsalted butter	2 teaspoons bourbon, optional
2 tablespoons pure maple syrup	4 chops (2 ounces each) boneless
1 teaspoon Dijon mustard	smoked pork
⅛ teaspoon ground red pepper	

1. Melt butter in a 10-inch nonstick skillet over medium-high heat. Add maple syrup, mustard, and red pepper. Mix well; cook several seconds until bubbly. Stir in bourbon if desired.

2. Add pork slices. Cook, turning several times, until meat is deeply glazed, 4 to 5 minutes.

NUTRITION INFORMATION PER SERVING:

150 calories	7 g fat	3 g saturated fat
40% calories from fat	35 mg cholesterol	180 mg sodium
7 g carbohydrate	15 g protein	0 g fiber

Herbed Breakfast Sausage

PREPARATION TIME: 10 minutes
COOKING TIME: 15 minutes
YIELD: 4 servings

HERE IS A make-it-yourself breakfast sausage that will stand out on a brunch menu. The fresh basil gives the sausage a wonderful scent and flavor, but many other fresh herbs will work just fine. Experiment to find your favorite, or prepare several different versions for everyone to sample.

1 pound ground pork
½ pound ground veal
1½ teaspoons minced fresh basil

½ teaspoon freshly ground black pepper
½ teaspoon rubbed sage
¼ teaspoon salt

1. Stir together pork, veal, basil, black pepper, sage, and salt in a large bowl. Shape sausage into patties about 2½ inches in diameter.

2. Cook in a nonstick skillet until golden on all sides and cooked through, 10 to 15 minutes. Drain on a paper towel.

NUTRITION INFORMATION PER SERVING:

298 calories
60% calories from fat
0.2 g carbohydrate

19 g fat
110 mg cholesterol
29 g protein

7 g saturated fat
232 mg sodium
0.1 g fiber

Chicken and Apple Sausage

PREPARATION TIME: 15 minutes
COOKING TIME: 5 minutes
YIELD: 8 patties

THIS HOMEMADE SAUSAGE is great when teamed with muffins and eggs. It's not a bad dinner entree, either. If you prepare it ahead, cover tightly and refrigerate overnight.

2 large whole skinless, boneless
    chicken breasts, well chilled
2 ounces pork fat, well chilled
½ Granny Smith apple, peeled
1 small shallot, peeled
4 fresh sage leaves

1 tablespoon light brown sugar
½ teaspoon salt
Freshly grated nutmeg
All-purpose flour
1 tablespoon butter
1 tablespoon vegetable oil

➤

1. Trim fat from chicken; cut chicken into 1-inch chunks. Cut pork fat into 1-inch chunks. Cut apple into 1-inch chunks.

2. Mince shallot and sage leaves in a food processor. Add chicken and pork fat; pulse the processor until meat is chopped coarse. Add apple, brown sugar, salt, and nutmeg; pulse until the mixture is finely and uniformly ground but not pureed.

3. Flour your hands and shape mixture into eight patties. Melt butter with oil in a large skillet over medium heat. Add patties; cook, turning once, until browned and cooked through, about 5 minutes.

NUTRITION INFORMATION PER PATTY:

150 calories	12 g fat	4.5 g saturated fat
73% calories from fat	30 mg cholesterol	180 mg sodium
3 g carbohydrate	7 g protein	0.2 g fiber

Spicy Mixed Sausage Grill

PREPARATION TIME: 5 minutes

COOKING TIME: 7 minutes

YIELD: 4 servings

GIVE BRUNCH SOME extra pizzazz with a sweet-and-sour glaze brushed over two types of grilled sausage. Andouille sausage is a spicy Cajun pork sausage; look for it in most supermarkets.

2 teaspoons unsalted butter	1 tablespoon brown sugar
2 andouille sausages, split lengthwise	1 tablespoon cider vinegar
	½ teaspoon hot pepper sauce
2 chicken sausages, split lengthwise	

1. Melt butter in a large nonstick skillet over medium heat. Add andouille sausages and chicken sausages. Cook, turning several times, until browned at the edges and heated through, about 5 minutes.

2. Mix brown sugar, cider vinegar, and hot pepper sauce to taste, stirring until sugar dissolves. Add syrup to the pan; increase heat to high. Cook until syrup lightly coats sausage, about 1 minute.

NUTRITION INFORMATION PER SERVING:

190 calories	16 g fat	6 g saturated fat
73% calories from fat	40 mg cholesterol	560 mg sodium
4 g carbohydrate	9 g protein	0 g fiber

SOUPS AND STOCKS

Basic Beef or Veal Stock

PREPARATION TIME: 20 minutes
COOKING TIME: 3 to 4 hours
YIELD: 10 cups

WHEN MAKING STOCK, you should use this recipe as an outline, filling in with what you have on hand. Leaving out the leek or adding an extra carrot won't ruin the brew. Store this broth in the refrigerator up to one week or freeze up to several months.

1 onion	3 to 6 ribs celery, chopped
2 to 3 whole cloves	2 carrots, chopped
4 to 6 pounds beef *or* veal bones (especially marrow and knuckle bones) with beef *or* veal scraps (see Note)	1 leek, chopped
	1 tomato, chopped
	8 black peppercorns
	1 bay leaf
5 quarts water	Parsley sprigs

1. Stick cloves into onion. Put beef or veal bones, water, celery, carrots, onion, leek, tomato, peppercorns, bay leaf, and parsley into a large stockpot. Heat to boil over medium-high heat; reduce heat to low. Skim surface. Simmer partly covered, skimming surface occasionally, until liquid is reduced by half, 3 to 4 hours.

2. Strain broth through a fine-mesh sieve. Cool; refrigerate covered until chilled. Remove solidified fat from surface.

➤

❧ NOTE: *For a darker brown beef or veal stock, heat oven to 400°F. Put bones in a single layer in a roasting pan. Roast bones, turning often, until dark brown but not burned. Proceed with the recipe as directed.*

NUTRITION INFORMATION PER CUP:

35 calories	0.5 g fat	0.1 g saturated fat
12% calories from fat	1 mg cholesterol	640 mg sodium
6.4 g carbohydrate	1.6 g protein	1.2 g fiber

Rich Chicken Broth

PREPARATION TIME: 20 minutes

COOKING TIME: 2 hours

YIELD: 6 cups

IN A PINCH, you can use beef, chicken, ham, or vegetable broth concentrate to enhance your soups and sauces, but remember there is no substitute for a broth you make yourself. Cubes and concentrates have a lot of salt to boost their meager flavors. For even richer broth, use a whole fryer chicken; save the meat for later casseroles or soup. Store this broth in the refrigerator up to one week or freeze up to three months.

4 to 5 pounds chicken parts, such as backs, wings, and necks (avoid liver)	1 carrot, halved
	1 white onion, quartered
	1 leek, halved
3 quarts water	4 parsley sprigs
2 ribs celery, halved	8 black peppercorns

1. Put chicken parts, water, celery, carrot, onion, leek, parsley, and peppercorns into a Dutch oven or small stockpot. Heat to boil over medium-high heat; reduce heat to medium-low. Simmer partly covered, skimming surface occasionally, until liquid is reduced by half, about 2 hours.

2. Strain broth through a fine-mesh sieve and cool. Refrigerate covered until chilled. Remove solidified fat from surface.

NUTRITION INFORMATION PER CUP:

11 calories	0.7 g fat	0.2 g saturated fat
49% calories from fat	1 mg cholesterol	635 mg sodium
1.1 g carbohydrate	0.5 g protein	0.1 g fiber

Turkey Broth

PREPARATION TIME: 15 minutes
COOKING TIME: 2½ hours
YIELD: About 3 cups

THIS BROTH MAKES a good base for a gravy that will hold together the Thanksgiving feast of turkey, potatoes, and dressing. You may prepare the broth the day before, when the oven is free. Store this broth in the refrigerator up to three days or freeze up to two months.

1 onion, chopped	Turkey neck and giblets
1 rib celery, chopped	1 quart water
1 carrot, chopped	¼ cup parsley sprigs

1. Heat oven to 350°F. Place onion, celery, carrot, turkey neck, and giblets in a small roasting pan. Bake, turning often, until browned on all sides, about 1 hour. Transfer to a medium-sized saucepan.

2. Place roasting pan with juices directly on the stove burner. Cook over high heat until juices sizzle. Add 1 cup of the water; heat to boil, scraping all brown bits from the bottom of the pan. Pour liquid into the saucepan with giblet mixture. Add remaining 3 cups water and parsley to giblet mixture.

3. Heat to boil over high heat. Reduce heat to medium; simmer partly covered 1½ hours. Strain broth through a fine-mesh sieve into storage containers. Cool. Cover and refrigerate. Remove solidified fat from surface.

NUTRITION INFORMATION PER CUP:

12 calories	0.8 g fat	0.3 g saturated fat
55% calories from fat	2 mg cholesterol	735 mg sodium
0.8 g carbohydrate	0.6 g protein	0 g fiber

Fish Broth

PREPARATION TIME: 20 minutes
COOKING TIME: 30 to 40 minutes
YIELD: About 6 cups

USE FISH BROTH or stock for fish or seafood dishes only unless a recipe specifically calls for it. Store this broth in the refrigerator up to two days or freeze up to one month.

2 tablespoons butter *or* vegetable oil	1 onion, chopped
2 ribs celery, chopped	1 carrot, chopped

►

3 pounds fish heads, bones, and
    tails (see Note)

2 quarts water

¼ cup dry white wine

2 tablespoons fresh lemon juice *or*
    white vinegar

6 black peppercorns

2 whole cloves

1 bay leaf

1 teaspoon dried leaf thyme

1.   Melt butter in the bottom of a stockpot over medium-high heat. Add celery, onion, and carrot; cook, stirring frequently, until onion is translucent, about 3 minutes. Add fish parts, water, white wine, lemon juice, peppercorns, cloves, bay leaf, and thyme. Heat to boil; reduce heat to medium-low. Simmer uncovered, skimming surface occasionally, for 30 minutes. (Longer cooking will impart a bitter flavor.)

2.   Strain broth through a fine-mesh sieve into storage containers. Cool; refrigerate covered until chilled. Remove solidified fat from surface.

❧ NOTE: *Fish heads and tails often are available at supermarket fish counters, but some stores now charge for them. Bones from halibut, cod, pike, and sea bass make an exceptionally tasty stock. Avoid using strong, oily, or fatty fish such as buffalo fish, mackerel, mullet, and salmon.*

NUTRITION INFORMATION PER SERVING:

38 calories	1.4 g fat	0.4 g saturated fat
36% calories from fat	0 mg cholesterol	755 mg sodium
1 g carbohydrate	4.7 g protein	0 g fiber

Blackbird's Fish Soup

PREPARATION TIME: 45 minutes
COOKING TIME: 1 hour 10 minutes
YIELD: 8 servings

IN 1998, *TRIBUNE* food and wine columnist William Rice profiled Paul Kahan, chef-partner of Blackbird restaurant in Chicago. "I cook the way I like to eat," Kahan told Rice. "I like a combination of clean, contrasting flavors that work well together." This soup blends many intriguing elements to accomplish Kahan's goal. It starts with a fumet (foo-MAY), which is a concentrated stock made from fish. Serve this soup with crusty bread and a dry white wine, such as Sancerre, or beer.

Fumet
1 tablespoon butter

1½ pounds white-fleshed fish bones,
    rinsed and chopped coarse

¼ cup dry white wine

10 black peppercorns

8 cups water

2 medium-sized carrots, peeled and chopped

2 ribs celery, chopped

1 small fennel bulb, chopped

1 onion, chopped

1 bay leaf

Soup

2 tablespoons olive oil

5 cloves garlic, sliced thin

1 pound small red potatoes, cut in ¼-inch rounds

1 onion, peeled and sliced thin

1 16-ounce can plum tomatoes in juice, drained and chopped coarse

1 tablespoon Pernod *or* another anise-flavored liqueur

Pinch saffron

Salt

Freshly ground black pepper

1 pound black mussels, scrubbed and debearded

1 pound white-fleshed fish, such as whitefish, pike, *or* bass, cut in ½-inch cubes

2 teaspoons chopped fresh parsley

2 teaspoons chopped fresh thyme

1. To make fumet, melt butter in a heavy-bottomed Dutch oven. Add fish bones; cook, stirring occasionally, over medium heat, 5 minutes. Add wine; simmer until almost evaporated. Add peppercorns, water, carrots, celery, fennel, onion, and bay leaf. Heat to boil; skim surface. Simmer partially covered, 30 minutes. Strain through a fine-mesh sieve. Discard solids; refrigerate fumet.

2. To make soup, heat olive oil in a Dutch oven over medium-high heat. Add garlic, potatoes, and onion. Cover; cook until onion has wilted, 8 minutes. Stir in tomatoes, Pernod, and saffron. Cook uncovered until pan is almost dry, about 10 minutes.

3. Add fumet and salt and pepper to taste; heat to boil over medium-high heat. Reduce heat to medium-low. Simmer until potatoes are tender, about 10 minutes.

4. Add mussels, fish, parsley, and thyme. Cook, stirring occasionally, until mussels open and fish flakes easily, 5 to 8 minutes.

❧ NOTE: *You may prepare recipe ahead through step 3. Refrigerate it several hours or overnight, and then reheat it.*

NUTRITION INFORMATION PER SERVING:

200 calories	9 g fat	2 g saturated fat
41% calories from fat	45 mg cholesterol	220 mg sodium
13 g carbohydrate	16 g protein	1.9 g fiber

Thai Fish Soup with Seared Black Bass

PREPARATION TIME: 40 minutes
COOKING TIME: About 1 hour
YIELD: 4 servings

WHAT IS FUSION cooking? "It can be anything, although the word is most often associated with Asian spices and seasonings," Austrian-born and French-trained chef Wolfgang Puck told William Rice in a 1998 story about the trendy technique that melds different cuisines. Puck shared this soup recipe from his Spago Chicago restaurant; it combines European ingredients such as olive oil, fennel, and tomato paste with Asian lemongrass and coconut milk.

½ cup plus 2 teaspoons olive oil
20 cloves garlic, chopped
2 leeks, 1 chopped, 1 julienned
2 small fennel bulbs, 1 chopped,
    1 julienned
2 stalks lemongrass, each cut into
    quarters (see Index)
1 3-inch-long piece gingerroot,
    peeled and chopped coarse
4 cups fish broth, homemade
    preferred
2 ripe tomatoes, chopped
¼ cup tomato paste

½ bunch basil (about 1 ounce)
1 teaspoon fennel seed
⅛ teaspoon saffron threads
⅛ teaspoon ground red pepper
½ cup unsweetened coconut milk
1 tablespoon fresh lemon juice
Salt
Freshly ground black pepper
1 carrot, peeled and julienned
½ cup snow peas, julienned
4 3-ounce fillets black bass, skin on
    and lightly scored
4 sprigs cilantro

1. Heat ½ cup of the olive oil in a large stockpot over low heat. Add garlic, chopped leek, chopped fennel, lemongrass, and gingerroot. Cook, stirring frequently, about 5 minutes. Add broth, tomatoes, tomato paste, basil, fennel seed, saffron, and ground red pepper. Reduce heat to low; simmer uncovered 45 minutes.

2. Remove the pot from the heat; discard lemongrass. Blend soup in batches in a food processor fitted with a metal blade or in a blender. Strain into a clean saucepan. Add coconut milk; heat to boil. Simmer 5 minutes. Season with lemon juice and salt and black pepper to taste.

3. Heat 1 teaspoon of the olive oil in a medium-sized skillet over medium heat. Add julienned leek; cook for 3 minutes. Add julienned fennel; cook for 3 minutes. Add carrot; cook for 3 minutes. Finally, add snow peas. Cook until snow peas are crisp-tender; set vegetables aside.

4. Heat remaining 1 teaspoon oil in another skillet; cook fish fillets skin side down until medium rare 4 to 5 minutes or to desired doneness. Ladle soup into 4 bowls. Place one quarter of vegetables in the center of each bowl; top each with 1 fillet. Garnish with cilantro.

NUTRITION INFORMATION PER SERVING:

555 calories	40 g fat	10 g saturated fat
63% calories from fat	45 mg cholesterol	905 mg sodium
30 g carbohydrate	23 g protein	7.6 g fiber

Bookbinder Red Snapper Soup

PREPARATION TIME: 40 minutes

COOKING TIME: 25 minutes

YIELD: 8 servings

WHEN A READER wrote the *Tribune* requesting the Drake Hotel's recipe for its Bookbinder Red Snapper Soup, former test kitchen director Alicia Tessling forwarded the request to executive chef Leo Waldmeier, who generously obliged. The hotel's Cape Cod Room has been serving this soup since it opened for the 1933 World's Fair in Chicago. The Drake's recipe was adapted from the snapper soup from Bookbinders restaurant in Philadelphia, with a few changes. The Philadelphia recipe called for turtle; the Cape Cod Room uses red snapper.

Soup Base

2 tablespoons olive oil

2 carrots, chopped

2 ribs celery, chopped

2 cloves garlic, chopped

1 onion, chopped

½ red bell pepper, chopped

½ green bell pepper, chopped

12 white *or* black peppercorns, crushed

1 bay leaf

3 tablespoons tomato paste

2 teaspoons chopped fresh thyme

2 teaspoons chopped fresh rosemary

2 teaspoons chopped cilantro

8 cups vegetable broth

3 tablespoons unsalted butter

2 tablespoons all-purpose flour

1 tablespoon cornstarch

Salt

Red Snapper

2 small onions, chopped fine

3 ribs celery, chopped fine

1 to 2 fillets red snapper (10 ounces)

¼ cup sherry, optional

►

1. To make soup base, heat olive oil in a Dutch oven over medium heat. Add carrots, celery, garlic, onion, red bell pepper, and green bell pepper; cook, stirring frequently, about 4 minutes. Stir in peppercorns, bay leaf, tomato paste, thyme, rosemary, and cilantro. Cook 2 minutes. Add 7 cups of the vegetable broth; heat to boil.

2. Melt butter in a small saucepan; add flour and cornstarch. Cook, stirring constantly, 4 to 5 minutes. Slowly whisk in remaining 1 cup broth until mixture is smooth. Add mixture to soup base; cover and simmer over medium-low heat 20 minutes. Taste and adjust seasonings. Strain through a fine-mesh sieve or cheesecloth; discard solids. Return broth to pot.

3. To make snapper, heat water to boil in a medium-sized saucepan over medium-high heat. Add onions and celery; blanch until soft, about 3 minutes. Remove with a slotted spoon and add to broth. Boil fish in the same water until cooked through. Remove fish from water; flake very finely with a fork. Stir snapper and sherry, if desired, into soup base; heat through.

NUTRITION INFORMATION PER SERVING:

165 calories	9 g fat	3.3 g saturated fat
50% calories from fat	29 mg cholesterol	1,075 mg sodium
8 g carbohydrate	13 g protein	0.7 g fiber

Bouillabaisse

PREPARATION TIME: 1 hour
COOKING TIME: 40 minutes
YIELD: 6 servings

WHEN THE MAGICAL word *bouillabaisse* is pronounced on the French Riviera, wrote William Rice in his Sunday *Tribune Magazine* column, the waiter soon brings a copious quantity of rich, robust fish stew. While no one can quite agree on the true bouillabaisse recipe, this version, from the now defunct Le Perroquet restaurant, contains an ample supply of rouille, a spicy mayonnaise-like condiment. To make bouillabaisse ahead, proceed through step 2 of recipe. Refrigerate it covered up to two days.

Bouquet Garni	1 tablespoon minced fresh thyme
6 sprigs parsley	*or* 1 teaspoon dried
3 bay leaves	⅛ teaspoon saffron threads
1 tablespoon minced fresh tarragon	
or 1 teaspoon dried	

Broth

¼ cup olive oil

2 ribs celery, diced

1 large peeled carrot, diced

1 large onion, diced

1 leek, white part only, diced

1 large head garlic, unpeeled, cut in half

2 cups dry white wine

1 cup brandy

8 cups fish broth

1 28-ounce can Italian-style plum tomatoes, drained and chopped coarse

1 tablespoon tomato paste

Salt

Freshly ground white pepper

Fish (see sidebar on page 84)

24 mussels, scrubbed and debearded

1 pound halibut steak *or* monkfish fillet, cubed

24 medium-sized shrimp, peeled and deveined

24 sea scallops

12 thin slices French bread, optional

1 cup rouille, optional (see Note)

1. To make bouquet garni, tie parsley, bay leaves, tarragon, thyme, and saffron in cheesecloth. Set aside. To make broth, heat olive oil in a Dutch oven over medium heat. Add celery, carrot, onion, leek, and garlic; reduce heat to low. Cook partially covered until tender, about 20 minutes. Add wine and brandy. Heat to boil over medium heat; boil until liquid is reduced by half.

2. Add bouquet garni to pot along with fish broth, tomatoes, and tomato paste. Stir well. Simmer over low heat 25 minutes. Add salt and white pepper. Strain through a fine-mesh sieve; discard solids.

3. Pour broth back into the Dutch oven. Heat to boil over medium heat. Add mussels; cover pan. Simmer 3 minutes. Add halibut. Simmer covered 2 minutes; add shrimp and scallops. Cook uncovered until shrimp and scallops are just firm, about 3 minutes. Remove from heat.

4. Divide fish and shellfish among 6 bowls. Spoon hot broth over each portion. Serve with French bread and rouille if desired.

❧ NOTE: *To make rouille, put ¼ cup chopped pimiento and ¼ cup chopped, cooked potato in a food processor fitted with a metal blade or in a blender. Add 4 cloves garlic and ½ teaspoon ground red pepper. Process until well mixed. Add ⅓ cup olive oil in a slow, steady stream with motor running until smooth and thickened. Add 3 tablespoons warm fish broth and salt and additional ground red pepper to taste. Makes about 1 cup.*

NUTRITION INFORMATION PER SERVING (WITHOUT ROUILLE):

390 calories	22 g fat	3.7 g saturated fat
54% calories from fat	95 mg cholesterol	1,495 mg sodium
10 g carbohydrate	34 g protein	1.4 g fiber

Buying and Cooking Shellfish

Mussels in the shell, like clams and oysters, are sold alive. Tap the shells. If they close tightly, you know they are still alive and fresh. Store them up to 2 days in the refrigerator in an uncovered bowl so they can breathe.

Before cooking shellfish, scrub the shells well with a stiff brush and then rinse. Mussels will need to be debearded: Pull off the stringy growth from the bottom of the shell. Cook them (steaming is the most popular method) only until their shells open, about 5 minutes. Otherwise, you risk overcooking them and making them tough. Discard any shells that do not open.

Quick Creole Gumbo

PREPARATION TIME: 15 minutes
COOKING TIME: 10 minutes
YIELD: 4 servings

GUMBO—THAT THICK, complex soup so closely associated with New Orleans—brings many influences to the table, including African, French, and Caribbean. It is notoriously time-consuming, so "Fast Food" columnist Pat Dailey created a quick version that's tailor-made for busy schedules. What it lacks in authenticity it compensates for in ease and appeal.

1 tablespoon olive oil *or* vegetable oil	½ cup instant rice
1 medium-sized onion, diced	1 to 2 teaspoons Creole seasoning blend
1 small red bell pepper, diced	¼ teaspoon ground red pepper
1 small green bell pepper, diced	¼ teaspoon freshly ground black pepper
4 ounces chicken andouille sausage, sliced	Salt
1 14½-ounce can diced tomatoes	½ pound frozen medium-sized cooked shrimp
2 14½-ounce cans chicken broth	

1. Heat olive oil in a large saucepan over medium-high heat. Add onion, red bell pepper, green bell pepper, and sausage. Cook, stirring often, until sausage begins to brown, 4 to 5 minutes.

2. Add tomatoes with their liquid, broth, rice, and Creole seasoning and red pepper, black pepper, and salt to taste. Heat to boil; reduce heat. Simmer 2 minutes; add shrimp. Simmer 3 more minutes. Taste and adjust seasonings; serve.

NUTRITION INFORMATION PER SERVING:

295 calories	12 g fat	2.9 g saturated fat
39% calories from fat	135 mg cholesterol	1,500 mg sodium
20 g carbohydrate	24 g protein	2.4 g fiber

Duck and Sausage Gumbo

PREPARATION TIME: 1 hour

COOKING TIME: 1¼ hours

YIELD: 8 servings

GUMBOS DON'T GET much richer than this one, but the taste is worth the indulgence. Duck and andouille sausage add flavor and texture to this main course soupstew created by former *Tribune* test kitchen director JeanMarie Brownson.

⅔ cup vegetable oil

2 ducks (about 4 pounds each) *or* 2 small chickens, quartered

⅔ cup all-purpose flour

1 pound andouille sausage *or* smoked Polish sausage, cut into ¼-inch-thick slices

2 medium-sized yellow onions, chopped

6 ribs celery, chopped

9 green onions, chopped

1 small green bell pepper, seeded and chopped

¼ cup chopped fresh parsley

5 large cloves garlic, minced

8 cups chicken broth

3 bay leaves, crumbled

2½ teaspoons salt

1 teaspoon dried thyme

1 teaspoon freshly ground black pepper

¼ teaspoon ground red pepper

2½ to 3 tablespoons filé powder (see Note)

Cooked rice

Hot pepper sauce

1. Heat oil in a heavy Dutch oven over medium heat. Add duck quarters in a single layer. Cook until brown on all sides. Remove duck and set aside.

2. Add flour to hot oil; stir until smooth. Cook, stirring constantly, over medium-high heat, until roux is the color of cinnamon, about 12 minutes. Remove from heat.

3. Stir in sausage, yellow onions, celery, green onions, green pepper, parsley, and garlic. Cook, stirring frequently, over medium heat until vegetables are crisp-tender, about 10 minutes.

►

4. Stir in ½ cup of the chicken broth, scraping up browned bits from bottom of pan. Stir in browned duck quarters, bay leaves, salt, thyme, black pepper, and red pepper. Stir in remaining 7½ cups broth. Heat to boil over medium heat. Skim to surface. Reduce heat to low; simmer uncovered until duck is tender, 30 to 40 minutes. Taste and adjust seasonings. Remove duck quarters from gumbo. Cool.

5. Skim surface of gumbo. Remove skin and bones from duck; discard. Cut meat into thin shreds. Reheat gumbo; add duck meat. Heat to boil. Remove from heat; let simmer die down. Stir in filé powder. Let stand 5 minutes. Serve in 8 soup bowls over rice. Pass hot pepper sauce.

❧ NOTE: *An important ingredient in Creole cooking, filé powder is made from the ground, dried leaves of sassafras trees. It helps thicken stews and adds an earthy herbal flavor. Filé powder can be found in the spice section of most grocery stores and in specialty shops.*

❧ NOTE: *To make gumbo ahead, proceed through step 4 of recipe. Refrigerate duck and gumbo in separate containers. When you're ready to serve gumbo, remove solidified fat from surface and continue following recipe directions.*

NUTRITION INFORMATION PER SERVING:

600 calories	40 g fat	8.7 g saturated fat
60% calories from fat	175 mg cholesterol	1,900 mg sodium
18 g carbohydrate	41 g protein	3.2 g fiber

Mulligatawny with Lentils

PREPARATION TIME: 30 minutes
COOKING TIME: 2 hours 10 minutes
YIELD: 8 servings

MULLIGATAWNY IS A classic Indian chicken and lentil soup. Translated, *mulligatawny* means "pepper water." This recipe comes from Klay Oven Restaurant in Chicago, which specializes in the Moghlai cooking of the Punjab region in northern India—a cuisine that downplays the hot pepper seasonings prevalent in the south. Garam masala is a popular Indian blend of ground spices; many variations abound. Look for it in specialty or Indian food stores.

1 16-ounce package dried lentils, rinsed and picked over	5 cups water
	¼ cup (½ stick) unsalted butter

1 onion, chopped

2 cloves garlic, minced

1 ½-inch piece gingerroot, peeled and minced

¼ cup minced fresh mint leaves

2 tablespoons garam masala

1 tablespoon freshly ground black pepper

1 teaspoon salt

½ teaspoon ground cumin

8 cups chicken broth

1 cup cubed cooked chicken

2 teaspoons minced cilantro

1. Place lentils in a large saucepan; cover with water. Heat to boil over high heat. Cover; reduce heat to medium-low. Cook until soft, about 2 hours, adding extra water as needed. Transfer contents of pan in batches to a blender or a food processor fitted with a metal blade; puree. Set aside.

2. Melt butter in a large saucepan over medium heat. Add onion, garlic, gingerroot, mint, garam masala, black pepper, salt, and cumin. Cook until garlic begins to brown, about 2 minutes. Stir in lentil puree, chicken broth, and chicken. Heat to simmer; cook 5 minutes. Stir in cilantro.

NUTRITION INFORMATION PER SERVING:

320 calories	10 g fat	4.7 g saturated fat
28% calories from fat	30 mg cholesterol	1,090 mg sodium
34 g carbohydrate	24 g protein	13 g fiber

Chicken and Avocado Soup

PREPARATION TIME: 30 minutes

COOKING TIME: 25 minutes

YIELD: 6 servings

SIMPLE, MEXICAN-STYLE chicken soup is thick with chunks of avocado and cheese. Serve it with toasted warm tortillas and a tossed salad for a casual lunch or supper.

5 cups chicken broth

1 whole chicken breast, split

6 fresh cilantro sprigs

¼ teaspoon crushed red pepper flakes

2 ripe avocados, seeded, peeled, and sliced

1 6-ounce package Chihuahua *or* brick cheese, cubed

Thin slices lime

➤

1.　Heat broth to simmer in a large saucepan over medium heat. Add chicken breast; simmer over low heat until chicken is opaque, 15 to 20 minutes. Remove chicken from broth. Remove and discard skin and bones. Tear meat into thin shreds.

2.　Put chicken, cilantro, and red pepper flakes in broth. Heat to simmer over low heat. Add avocados and Chihuahua cheese. Garnish with lime slices.

NUTRITION INFORMATION PER SERVING:

295 calories	21 g fat	7.6 g saturated fat
63% calories from fat	55 mg cholesterol	850 mg sodium
7.4 g carbohydrate	20 g protein	3.4 g fiber

Turkey Soup with Angel Hair Pasta

PREPARATION TIME: 45 minutes

COOKING TIME: 2 hours

YIELD: 6 servings

THE PROBLEM OF using Thanksgiving leftovers is an annual one, but this method for getting the most from the turkey carcass is an elegant end for the old bird. It is best looking when the broth is clear, so try to skim the broth as it cooks. You may substitute three pounds chicken bones, such as necks, backs, and wings for the turkey carcass and four cups diced skinless, boneless chicken for the turkey meat.

Bouquet Garni
2 bay leaves
1 sprig parsley
12 black peppercorns
¼ teaspoon dried leaf thyme

Soup
1 cooked turkey carcass
1 cup dry sherry *or* dry white wine
3 quarts turkey *or* chicken broth
1 large leek, trimmed, halved
　　lengthwise, and sliced

1 medium-sized onion, chopped
4 cups diced skinless, boneless
　　cooked turkey
2 medium-sized carrots, peeled
　　and sliced
1 ½-inch-thick piece gingerroot,
　　peeled and minced
1 teaspoon soy sauce
Salt
¼ pound dried angel hair pasta
2 cups shredded fresh spinach

1. To make bouquet garni, tie bay leaves, parsley, black peppercorns, and dried leaf thyme in a double thickness of cheesecloth. Set aside. To make soup, heat oven to 350°F. Cut turkey carcass into pieces. Put into roasting pan. Bake until browned, about 30 minutes. Transfer bones to a large Dutch oven. Pour sherry into roasting pan. Heat sherry in roasting pan to boil over medium heat, scraping up browned bits from the bottom of the pan. Add sherry to bones in Dutch oven.

2. Add broth, leek, onion, and bouquet garni to bones. Heat to boil; reduce heat. Simmer partially covered skimming surface occasionally, 1 hour.

3. Remove and discard bouquet garni. Remove bones, reserving any meat on bones. Add meat to soup. Add diced turkey, carrots, gingerroot, and soy sauce. Cook until carrots are crisp-tender, about 10 minutes. Taste and adjust seasonings, adding salt to taste.

4. Add pasta noodles and spinach to soup. Cook just until pasta is al dente and spinach wilts, about 3 minutes.

NUTRITION INFORMATION PER SERVING:

265 calories	6.4 g fat	2 g saturated fat
22% calories from fat	75 mg cholesterol	1,080 mg sodium
18 g carbohydrate	32 g protein	2 g fiber

Hungarian Steak Soup

PREPARATION TIME: 20 minutes

COOKING TIME: 40 minutes

YIELD: 6 servings

WILLIAM RICE HERALDED the return of steak in a 1997 *Tribune Magazine* column: "A steak dinner doesn't have to be a larger-than-life feast to be enjoyable and satisfying. At home it can be a normal family meal . . . with the meat served in portions that fit easily within the dietary guidelines." This soup, made in a pressure cooker, fits the bill. The recipe is adapted from Rice's *Steak Lover's Cookbook*.

2 tablespoons vegetable oil	1 medium-sized sweet onion
1½ pounds ¾-inch-thick boneless beef round steak, excess fat removed, cut into ¾-inch cubes	1 green bell pepper, seeded
	1 red bell pepper, seeded
	1 teaspoon sweet paprika

➤

1 teaspoon hot paprika	2 bay leaves
¼ teaspoon freshly ground black pepper	2 cloves garlic, minced
	2 teaspoons tomato paste
½ teaspoon caraway seeds, briefly toasted	Salt
6 cups beef broth	6 ounces wide egg noodles
	Sour cream

1. Heat oil in an uncovered pressure cooker or stockpot over medium-high heat. Add half the meat; brown on all sides, about 4 minutes. Transfer to a bowl with a slotted spoon. Repeat with remaining meat.

2. Chop the onion in half; set one half aside. Coarsely chop one half and put in the pressure cooker. Repeat with green bell pepper and red bell pepper. Cook, stirring frequently, until vegetables soften, 4 to 5 minutes. Add sweet paprika, hot paprika, black pepper, and caraway to vegetables in pressure cooker; stir 1 minute. Pour in beef broth. Add bay leaves, garlic, tomato paste, and steak.

3. Cover and seal pressure cooker. Heat to full pressure over high heat. Regulate heat to maintain steady pressure; cook 20 minutes. (In a conventional pot, simmer meat partly covered 1 hour.) Release pressure and uncover. Meat should be cooked through and tender. If not, recover pot, regain full pressure, and cook 5 minutes longer.

4. Pour soup through a colander into a bowl. Return meat cubes to pot; discard vegetables. Slice reserved half onion thin; add to pot. Cut reserved half green bell pepper and red bell pepper into ¼-inch strips; add to pot. Return broth to pot. Heat to boil over high heat; turn heat to low. Simmer until vegetables are just tender, 7 to 8 minutes.

5. Meanwhile, heat water to boil in a large saucepan. Add salt and egg noodles; cook until just tender, about 5 minutes. Drain noodles. Put ½ cup of the cooked noodles into each of 6 soup plates. Ladle hot soup over noodles. Pass sour cream.

NUTRITION INFORMATION PER SERVING:

315 calories	10 g fat	2.5 g saturated fat
30% calories from fat	95 mg cholesterol	840 mg sodium
20 g carbohydrate	33 g protein	1.6 g fiber

Speedier Goulash Soup

PREPARATION TIME: 30 minutes
MICROWAVE COOKING TIME: 1 hour
STANDING TIME: 10 minutes
YIELD: 6 servings

THICK, HEARTY, AND old-fashioned, this goulash soup is cooked in a microwave oven, cutting the cooking time in half. To ensure tender meat, set the microwave at medium power. Use canned broth if you must, but if you just happen to have home-made stock, you will see how much better your soup can be.

2 tablespoons butter
2 large onions, chopped
1 clove garlic, minced
1 pound boneless beef chuck, cut into ½-inch cubes
¼ cup all-purpose flour
3 cups beef broth
1 tablespoon tomato paste
1 tablespoon sweet Hungarian paprika
¾ teaspoon caraway seeds
½ teaspoon ground ginger

¼ teaspoon ground red pepper
3 medium-sized red potatoes, cubed
2 carrots, peeled and diced
1 green bell pepper, seeded and diced
1 tomato, peeled, seeded, and chopped
Salt
Freshly ground black pepper
Sour cream

1. Microwave butter in a 3-quart microwave-safe bowl on high (100 percent power) until melted, about 30 seconds. Stir in onions and garlic. Microwave on high until onions are soft, about 2 minutes. Toss beef cubes with flour. Add to onion mixture; microwave on high, stirring, until beef is no longer pink, about 5 minutes.

2. Stir in broth, tomato paste, paprika, caraway, ginger, and red pepper. Microwave covered on medium (50 percent power), stirring often, until beef is almost tender, 20 to 30 minutes.

3. Stir in potatoes and carrots. Microwave on medium until potatoes are fork-tender, 10 to 15 minutes. Stir in green pepper and tomato. Microwave on medium until green pepper is crisp-tender, 5 to 10 minutes. Let stand 10 minutes. Add salt and black pepper. Serve with dollop of sour cream.

NUTRITION INFORMATION PER SERVING:

355 calories	18 g fat	7.9 g saturated fat
46% calories from fat	60 mg cholesterol	500 mg sodium
30 g carbohydrate	19 g protein	4 g fiber

Lithuanian Beet Soup

PREPARATION TIME: 40 minutes
COOKING TIME: 1 hour
YIELD: 6 servings

THIS LITHUANIAN SOUP is a cousin to the more robust borscht favored in other parts of that area of the world. The dried mushrooms are a traditional Lithuanian touch.

1 ounce dried mushrooms, such as cèpe, porcini, *or* shiitake (see Index)
¼ cup hot water
4 to 6 medium-sized beets, cleaned, greens trimmed slightly

1 tablespoon unsalted butter
1 medium-sized onion, sliced thin
1 teaspoon sugar
3 cups beef, veal, *or* chicken broth
1 to 2 tablespoons fresh lemon juice
Salt
Freshly ground black pepper

1. Soak mushrooms in hot water until soft; reserve soaking liquid. Put beets in a large saucepan with water to cover. Cover; heat to boil over high heat. Reduce heat to low. Cook until fork-tender, 20 to 30 minutes. Strain beets, reserving beets and 2 cups of the cooking liquid separately. Cool, trim, and cut beets into ½-inch cubes.

2. Melt butter in a 4-quart saucepan over medium heat. Add onion; cook until tender, about 2 minutes. Add beets and sugar to pan. Cook until sugar is melted and vegetables are glazed, 3 to 5 minutes. Add broth, reserved liquid, and mushrooms with soaking liquid. Simmer over low heat until flavors are blended, about 20 minutes. Add lemon juice and salt and pepper to taste.

✷ NOTE: *To remove beet stains from your hands, rub your damp hands together with salt. To keep beets from bleeding and losing their color, cook them whole with a small portion of their stems still attached.*

NUTRITION INFORMATION PER SERVING:

95 calories	2.5 g fat	1.4 g saturated fat
21% calories from fat	5 mg cholesterol	475 mg sodium
17 g carbohydrate	3.8 g protein	3 g fiber

White Bean and Black Truffle Soup

PREPARATION TIME: 45 minutes
COOKING TIME: 1 hour 30 minutes
YIELD: 8 servings

IN A 1998 profile of prominent chefs in Chicago, *Tribune* food and wine columnist William Rice talked to Patrick Robertson of one sixtyblue restaurant. "Contemporary cooking involves honesty," Robertson said. "Not only do you have to know proper cooking techniques and pay attention to detail, you have to respect the flavors of foods and avoid clutter and complication." Although truffles add a wonderful fall touch to this bean soup from Robertson, you can eliminate them if cost is a factor. The soup is delicious even without them. (Recipe may be done ahead through step 2. Reheat before continuing.)

2 tablespoons plus ½ cup olive oil
1 medium-sized carrot, chopped coarse
1 large rib celery, chopped coarse
1 small onion, chopped coarse
2 cloves garlic, peeled
1 clove garlic, chopped
1¾ cups dried white beans, such as Great Northern, rinsed and soaked overnight
1 bay leaf, broken in half

5 teaspoons chopped fresh rosemary
5 16-ounce cans chicken broth *or* 10 cups homemade chicken stock
½ cup grated Parmesan cheese
2 ounces (about 8) fresh *or* canned black truffles, sliced, optional
3 tablespoons truffle juice (from canned truffles), optional
½ teaspoon salt
Freshly ground black pepper

1. Heat 2 tablespoons of the olive oil in a casserole or large saucepan. Add carrot, celery, onion, and 2 cloves garlic. Cook, stirring often, until vegetables soften, about 5 minutes. Add beans, bay leaf, and rosemary; stir to mix. Add broth; simmer partly covered until beans are tender, 1 to 1¼ hours.

2. Remove soup from heat; remove bay leaf pieces. Allow soup to cool slightly; puree in batches in a food processor fitted with a metal blade or in a blender until smooth.

3. Add Parmesan, chopped garlic, and remaining olive oil and truffle slices if desired through feed tube with motor running; puree until almost smooth.

4. Return soup to saucepan. Heat, adding water if too thick. Add truffle juice if using, salt, and black pepper to taste.

NUTRITION INFORMATION PER SERVING:

350 calories	21 g fat	4 g saturated fat
53% calories from fat	5 mg cholesterol	1,175 mg sodium
25 g carbohydrate	17 g protein	8 g fiber

Chard and White Bean Soup

PREPARATION TIME: 20 minutes
COOKING TIME: 20 minutes
YIELD: 4 servings

WHEN CHILLY WINDS begin to blow, can anything be more comforting than a meal centered on a steaming bowl of hearty homemade soup? This recipe, from a "Fast Food" column, stars chard and white beans, and it's as easy as it is delicious. Serve it with rustic cheese toasts, a simple salad, and a glass of pinot grigio.

2 strips smoked bacon, diced fine
1 medium-sized onion, diced
1 clove garlic, minced
¼ teaspoon freshly grated nutmeg
⅛ teaspoon red pepper flakes
3 16-ounce cans low-sodium
    chicken broth
1 15-ounce can small white beans,
    rinsed and drained

1 small bunch red *or* white Swiss
    chard
¼ cup tiny dried pasta, such as
    pastina *or ancini de pepe*
5 to 6 large fresh sage leaves,
    minced
2 teaspoons extra-virgin olive oil

1. Combine bacon, onion, garlic, nutmeg, and red pepper flakes in a 4-quart saucepan. Cook over medium heat, stirring frequently, until onion is softened, 4 to 5 minutes.

2. Add chicken broth and white beans. Increase heat to high; cook until mixture comes to boil.

3. Cut chard stems into ¾-inch slices. Cut leaves in half lengthwise, stack, and cut crosswise into 1-inch ribbons.

4. Add chard stems and pasta when soup boils. Reduce heat to medium-low; simmer 7 minutes. Add chard leaves; simmer until wilted, 3 to 4 minutes. Add sage; remove from heat. Ladle soup into 4 bowls and drizzle with olive oil.

NUTRITION INFORMATION PER SERVING:

280 calories	7 g fat	2 g saturated fat
22% calories from fat	7 mg cholesterol	815 mg sodium
36 g carbohydrate	19 g protein	7 g fiber

Curried Lentil and Brown Rice Soup

PREPARATION TIME: 10 minutes
COOKING TIME: 30 minutes
YIELD: 4 servings

"FAST FOOD" COLUMNIST Pat Dailey created this Indian soup, inspired by one served at Tabla restaurant in New York. There it is made with brown basmati rice and garnished with fried curry leaves.

2 tablespoons unsalted butter
1 large onion, chopped
2 carrots, sliced
1 ½-inch piece gingerroot, minced
2 teaspoons hot curry powder
½ teaspoon cumin seed
1 10-ounce can diced tomatoes with
    chilies

5 cups vegetable *or* chicken broth
⅔ cup lentils, preferably small
    French lentils
⅓ cup instant brown rice
½ cup minced cilantro
3 tablespoons minced fresh mint

1. Melt butter in a 4-quart saucepan over medium-high heat. Add onion, carrots, and gingerroot; cook, stirring frequently, until vegetables begin to brown at edges, about 4 minutes. Stir in curry powder and cumin seed; cook 30 seconds.

2. Add tomatoes, broth, lentils, and rice. Cover; heat to boil. Cook until lentils are tender, 20 to 25 minutes. Remove from heat; stir in cilantro and mint.

NUTRITION INFORMATION PER SERVING:

255 calories	8 g fat	3.7 g saturated fat
26% calories from fat	15 mg cholesterol	1,560 mg sodium
39 g carbohydrate	12 g protein	10 g fiber

Salpicón Lentil Soup

PREPARATION TIME: 25 minutes
COOKING TIME: 45 to 50 minutes
YIELD: 8 servings

MAKING RESTAURANT FOOD seem home-cooked comes naturally to Priscila Satkoff, the talented chef-owner of Salpicón, a contemporary Mexican restaurant in Chicago. Satkoff was never formally trained; her cooking is based on the grounding provided by her mother. Satkoff shared this recipe with William Rice for the Sunday *Tribune Magazine*. It's a traditional soup of her mother. *Pasilla* chilies and *queso añejo* are available in Latin markets and some specialty food stores.

4 cups water	¾ pound plum tomatoes
1½ teaspoons salt	4 cups water
½ pound lentils	1 small onion, quartered
½ pineapple, peeled, cored, and cut into ¾-inch-thick slices	1 clove garlic
	1½ teaspoons vegetable oil
2 *pasilla* chilies *or* other large, dried chilies, seeded	2 ounces *queso añejo* (Mexican dry cheese), grated

1. Heat 4 cups water to boil in a large saucepan over high heat. Add 1 teaspoon of the salt. Stir in lentils; cook until softened, 20 to 30 minutes. Let cool. Puree lentils with cooking water in batches in a blender or a food processor fitted with a metal blade. Set puree aside.

2. Prepare grill or heat broiler. Grill or broil pineapple until slices begin to brown, about 2 minutes per side. Cut into small pieces; set aside. Place small dry skillet over medium-high heat. Add *pasilla* chilies; toast briefly until crisp, about 20 seconds per side. Let cool. Crumble chilies into a small bowl. Set aside.

3. Put tomatoes into a medium-sized saucepan; cover with 4 cups water. Heat to boil over high heat. Reduce heat to simmer; cook 10 minutes. Let cool. Transfer tomatoes and cooking water to a blender. Add onion and garlic; puree until smooth. Strain through a fine-mesh sieve; discard solids.

4. Heat oil in a large saucepan over medium-high heat. Add tomato puree; heat to boil. Reduce heat to medium-low; simmer until thickened, about 8 minutes. Stir in lentil puree. Increase heat to high. Add remaining ½ teaspoon salt; simmer 5 minutes.

5. Pour 1 cup of soup into each of 8 soup bowls. Garnish with pineapple pieces, crumbled *pasilla*, and *queso añejo*.

NUTRITION INFORMATION PER SERVING:

160 calories	3.2 g fat	1.3 g saturated fat
17% calories from fat	5 mg cholesterol	525 mg sodium
26 g carbohydrate	8.6 g protein	7.7 g fiber

Creamy Split Pea Soup

PREPARATION TIME: 30 minutes
COOKING TIME: 2¼ hours
YIELD: 8 servings

CREAMY SPLIT PEA soup, created by former *Tribune* test kitchen director JeanMarie Brownson, is a five-star production that features a humble ham bone. The added fennel gives the soup a special touch. Do not add any salt, as the ham will do that adequately.

Soup
2 tablespoons butter
2 small leeks, split lengthwise, rinsed, and chopped
2 medium-sized carrots, peeled and chopped
1 medium-sized onion, chopped
½ cup minced fresh fennel bulb *or* celery
2 large cloves garlic, minced
8 cups chicken broth
1 pound dried green split peas
1 ham bone with some meat *or* 2 ham hocks (about 1½ pounds)

Bouquet Garni (see Note)
3 bay leaves
½ teaspoon dried leaf thyme
½ teaspoon dried marjoram
4 parsley sprigs
10 black peppercorns

1 10-ounce package frozen peas, optional

Croutons
1 tablespoon vegetable oil, or more as needed
4 cups large day-old French bread cubes
Whipping cream, optional

►

1. To make soup, heat butter in a 6-quart Dutch oven over medium heat until hot. Add leeks, carrots, onion, fennel, and garlic. Cook, stirring often, until vegetables are limp, about 10 minutes. Stir in broth, split peas, and ham bone. To make bouquet garni, put bay leaves, dried leaf thyme, dried marjoram, parsley, and peppercorns on a double thickness of cheesecloth. Bring up ends of cheesecloth and tie securely with kitchen string. Add bouquet garni to soup. Simmer uncovered over low heat, stirring occasionally, until peas are very tender, about 2 hours.

2. Remove and discard bouquet garni. Remove ham bone to a cutting board. Add frozen peas to soup if desired; stir until peas thaw. Puree soup in batches in a blender or in a food processor fitted with a metal blade. Return soup to the Dutch oven.

3. Remove any meat from bones; chop. Add to soup. Reheat soup. Add additional broth if soup is too thick.

4. To make croutons, heat oil in a large skillet over medium heat. Add bread cubes; cook, stirring frequently, until crisp and golden on all sides, adding additional oil as needed. Drain on paper towels. Ladle soup into 8 bowls. Drizzle a little whipping cream into the center of the soup, if desired. Sprinkle with croutons.

❧ NOTE: *We tie up dried herbs in cheesecloth in what the French call a* bouquet garni. *This makes it easy to retrieve the herbs out of any soup or stew.*

NUTRITION INFORMATION PER SERVING:

395 calories	11 g fat	3.9 g saturated fat
24% calories from fat	25 mg cholesterol	1,040 mg sodium
51 g carbohydrate	24 g protein	14 g fiber

Chickpea and Garlic Soup

PREPARATION TIME: 10 minutes

COOKING TIME: 15 minutes

YIELD: 4 servings

TIME-PRESSED COOKS don't always have the luxury of preparing dinner from scratch. But there are wholesome alternatives, courtesy of convenience foods. This quick recipe from a "Fast Food" column starts with canned chickpeas for a healthful soup. Serve it with sandwiches for a hearty meal.

1 tablespoon olive oil	Pinch crushed red pepper flakes
1 large garlic clove, minced	1 small rib celery, chopped fine

½ small red bell pepper, chopped
fine

1 16-ounce can chickpeas (garbanzo
beans), drained

1½ cups low-sodium chicken broth

¾ cup spicy *or* regular tomato juice

Salt

1. Heat oil in a medium-sized saucepan. Add garlic and red pepper flakes. Cook gently, stirring, until garlic is fragrant, 2 minutes. Add celery and bell pepper; cook, stirring, until vegetables begin to soften, 3 minutes.

2. Add drained chickpeas, chicken broth, and tomato juice. Cover; heat to boil. Reduce heat to low; simmer gently until vegetables are soft, 10 minutes. Transfer soup to a blender; puree. Add salt to taste.

NUTRITION INFORMATION PER SERVING:

155 calories	6 g fat	0.8 g saturated fat
34% calories from fat	1 mg cholesterol	450 mg sodium
21 g carbohydrate	6 g protein	6 g fiber

Green Pea and Mint Soup

PREPARATION TIME: 15 minutes

COOKING TIME: 18 minutes

YIELD: 4 servings

WHEN SOUPS ARE made from scratch, they tend to be time-consuming to prepare. Searching for shortcuts, William Rice found some appealing vegetable combinations in the frozen foods section of his neighborhood supermarket. This spring soup uses canned broth and a bag of frozen peas with pearl onions. But Rice added this caveat: should you choose to make it with fresh vegetables and homemade broth, he would not be offended.

1 tablespoon butter

1 medium-sized potato, peeled and
cut in ½-inch dice

1 10-ounce package frozen green
peas and pearl onions

¼ to ½ teaspoon sugar

1 16-ounce can chicken broth

2 tablespoons shredded fresh mint
leaves

½ cup whipping cream

Salt

White pepper

Hot pepper sauce

Packaged small, plain croutons,
optional

Mint sprigs

►

1. Melt butter in a medium-sized saucepan over medium heat. Add potato; cook 5 minutes. Add peas and onions; cook until vegetables are heated through, about 4 minutes. Taste a pea; depending on its sweetness, add ¼ to ½ teaspoon sugar. Stir in broth and shredded mint leaves. Heat to simmer; cook until potato is very tender, about 10 minutes.

2. Puree mixture, working in batches if necessary, in a blender or in a food processor fitted with a metal blade until smooth. Return soup to saucepan; add cream. Heat to simmer; season with salt, white pepper, and hot pepper sauce to taste. Serve in 4 soup bowls; top with croutons if desired and mint sprigs.

NUTRITION INFORMATION PER SERVING:

230 calories	15 g fat	9 g saturated fat
57% calories from fat	50 mg cholesterol	735 mg sodium
18 g carbohydrate	6.8 g protein	3.8 g fiber

Cream of Cauliflower Soup

PREPARATION TIME: 15 minutes
COOKING TIME: 20 minutes
YIELD: 4 servings

MANY PEOPLE DISLIKE cauliflower, but this quick soup, based on a classic recipe, may change their minds. Try it on cauliflower haters you know. This soup is also delicious served cold.

1 head cauliflower, broken into florets	¼ teaspoon salt
4 cups chicken broth	⅛ teaspoon freshly ground white pepper
4 slices bread, crusts removed and chopped	2 tomatoes peeled, seeded, diced, and drained
1½ cups half-and-half *or* milk	2 tablespoons minced fresh dill
2 tablespoons dry white wine	

1. Cook cauliflower and broth covered in a large saucepan over medium heat until cauliflower is very soft, about 20 minutes. Puree in batches in a food processor fitted with a metal blade or in a blender. Return puree to saucepan.

2. Soak bread in half-and-half in a small bowl. Puree in the food processor or blender; stir into soup. Cook soup, stirring often, over low heat until heated through. Stir in wine, salt, and white pepper. Taste and adjust seasonings. Ladle soup into 4 serving bowls. Top each with a spoonful of tomatoes; sprinkle with dill.

NUTRITION INFORMATION PER SERVING:

310 calories	14 g fat	7.4 g saturated fat
38% calories from fat	35 mg cholesterol	1,190 mg sodium
35 g carbohydrate	16 g protein	7.4 g fiber

Curried Cream of Acorn Squash Soup

PREPARATION TIME: 40 minutes

COOKING TIME: 2 hours

YIELD: 6 servings

SIMPLE ACORN SQUASH is seasoned with the exotic overtones of curry, apple, and smoked ham in this soup. It is perfect for making after Thanksgiving when there's plenty of turkey bones to use for a broth. To prepare broth ahead, proceed with recipe through step 4. Refrigerate broth covered up to several days and then continue with recipe.

6 small acorn squash	¾ teaspoon curry powder
4 tablespoons butter	½ teaspoon dried chervil
2 leeks, white part only, chopped coarse	¼ teaspoon freshly ground black pepper
1 medium-sized carrot, peeled and diced	2 cups half-and-half
5 cups chicken *or* turkey broth	2 teaspoons fresh lemon juice
2 small ham hocks	Salt
1 medium-sized apple, peeled, cored, and diced	1½ cups bread cubes
1 bay leaf	¾ cup shredded Gruyère *or* Swiss cheese

1. Cut a small slice from the top of each squash; remove seeds with a spoon. Scoop out flesh with a melon baller, leaving ½-inch-thick wall around shell. Put flesh into a measuring cup. Cut a small slice off bottom of each squash so it stands upright. Reserve shells in a 13″ × 9″ baking pan.

▶

2. Melt 2 tablespoons of the butter in a nonreactive Dutch oven over medium heat. Add leeks and carrot. Cook, stirring often, until soft, about 5 minutes. Stir in squash flesh, broth, ham hocks, apple, bay leaf, curry powder, chervil, and pepper. Heat to boil; reduce heat to low. Simmer uncovered, stirring often, until squash is very tender, about 1 hour.

3. Remove ham hocks to a small bowl; reserve. Remove and discard bay leaf. Transfer solids in pan using slotted spoon to a blender or a food processor fitted with a metal blade, leaving broth in pan. Add half-and-half to squash mixture in blender or food processor; process until smooth. Set aside.

4. Heat broth in pan to simmer over medium heat. Simmer uncovered until mixture reduces to 2 cups. Stir squash mixture into broth.

5. Remove and dice meat from ham hocks; stir into soup. Reheat soup; add lemon juice and salt to taste.

6. Heat remaining 2 tablespoons butter in a large nonstick skillet. Add bread cubes; sauté until golden. Remove from heat. Heat broiler. Ladle soup into reserved squash shells. Sprinkle bread cubes over top and the cheese. Broil until cheese browns, about 2 minutes.

NUTRITION INFORMATION PER SERVING:

550 calories	28 g fat	15 g saturated fat
43% calories from fat	85 mg cholesterol	920 mg sodium
61 g carbohydrate	21 g protein	8 g fiber

Peppered Sweet Potato–Sage Bisque

PREPARATION TIME: 5 minutes

COOKING TIME: 15 minutes

YIELD: 4 servings

TURKEY ISN'T THE only Thanksgiving leftover. This easy soup, from a November 1998 "Fast Food" column, puts post–Turkey Day sweet potatoes to use, teaming them with fragrant sage. It's so quick and so good that you can make it any time of year. Plus you can make it several days in advance and refrigerate it.

1 tablespoon unsalted butter	1 small clove garlic, minced
1 onion, sliced paper-thin	2 16-ounce cans reduced-sodium chicken broth

1 40-ounce can sweet potatoes,
  drained, *or* 2 cups mashed
  baked sweet potatoes
6 large fresh sage leaves

1 teaspoon freshly ground black
  pepper
¼ teaspoon salt
⅓ cup whipping cream *or* milk,
  optional

1. Melt butter in a large pan. Add onion and garlic; cook over medium heat until soft, 5 minutes. Add broth and sweet potatoes. Cover; heat to boil. Reduce heat; simmer 8 to 10 minutes.

2. Transfer to a blender; add sage, black pepper, and salt. Blend until smooth. Blend in cream or milk if desired. Serve hot.

NUTRITION INFORMATION PER SERVING:

350 calories	6 g fat	3 g saturated fat
14% calories from fat	13 mg cholesterol	325 mg sodium
70 g carbohydrate	9 g protein	8 g fiber

Melon Citrus Soup

PREPARATION TIME: 25 minutes
COOKING TIME: 8 minutes
CHILLING TIME: 4 hours
YIELD: 6 servings

DOES ANYTHING SUMMON summer more quickly than a juicy, ripe watermelon? This recipe, featured in a tribute to the melons of summer, puts watermelon to use in a rich, sweet dessert soup. By reducing the sugar somewhat, you could also serve it as a first course. It was developed in the *Tribune* test kitchen.

1 cup water
⅓ cup sugar
Zest and juice of 2 limes
½ medium-sized seedless
  watermelon, rind removed and
  diced (about 6 cups)

1 cup half-and-half *or* whipping
  cream
1 tablespoon coarsely chopped
  mint, optional

➤

1. Heat water and sugar in a small, heavy saucepan over low heat until sugar completely dissolves and mixture is clear, about 8 minutes. Pour into a small bowl. Refrigerate covered until chilled, at least 2 hours or up to 1 week.

2. Combine syrup, lime juice, and 4 cups of the watermelon in a food processor fitted with a metal blade or in a blender in two batches if necessary. Pour mixture through a fine-mesh sieve; discard solids. Stir in lime zest, cover, and chill at least 2 hours.

3. Finely dice remaining watermelon; evenly divide it among 6 bowls, mounding melon in the centers. Stir half-and-half into soup; ladle soup into bowls. Sprinkle with mint if desired.

NUTRITION INFORMATION PER SERVING:

150 calories	5.3 g fat	3 g saturated fat
30% calories from fat	15 mg cholesterol	20 mg sodium
26 g carbohydrate	23 g protein	1.3 g fiber

PASTA, RICE, AND OTHER GRAINS

Homemade Noodles

PREPARATION TIME: 45 minutes
RESTING TIME: 30 minutes
COOKING TIME: 3 minutes
YIELD: 6 servings

MAKING NOODLES FROM scratch not only is satisfying but results in more flavorful pasta. Guests or family are sure to appreciate your efforts. This basic recipe uses eggs in the dough, which makes the noodles even richer.

4 cups sifted all-purpose flour	4 large eggs
1 teaspoon salt	2 tablespoons plus 1½ teaspoons olive oil

1. Combine flour and salt in the bowl of an electric mixer. Make a well in the center; pour eggs and oil into well. Gradually draw flour from the edges of the bowl into the egg mixture to form a stiff dough using a dough hook on a mixer at low speed or a large wooden spoon. Lightly flour the work surface. Knead dough until very smooth and elastic, about 10 minutes. Cover with plastic wrap; let rest 30 minutes.

2. Divide dough into quarters; cover 3 of the quarters. Put 1 quarter through the rollers of a pasta machine according to manufacturer's directions. Or roll dough out on a lightly floured surface with a rolling pin into a very thin sheet.

3. Cut dough in the thinnest cutter portion of the pasta machine, or use a sharp knife to cut dough into very thin strands for linguini or noodles. Let noodles dry on flour-dusted baking sheet while rolling and cutting remaining dough.

➤

4. Bring a large pot of salted water to boil. Cook noodles until al dente (tender but still firm), 1 to 3 minutes. Drain; serve immediately.

❧ NOTE: *Cut noodles can be dried overnight. Turn them occasionally. Store them in an airtight jar up to several days. Cook as directed.*

NUTRITION INFORMATION PER SERVING:

400 calories	10 g fat	2 g saturated fat
22% calories from fat	140 mg cholesterol	430 mg sodium
64 g carbohydrate	13 g protein	2.3 g fiber

Fiesta Spaghetti Sauce and Meatballs

PREPARATION TIME: 1½ hours
COOKING TIME: 3 to 6 hours
YIELD: 12 servings

DURING THE 1985 Fiesta Italiana celebration in Chicago, Geri DeStefano won the spaghetti sauce contest with this recipe. She serves the sauce over cooked spaghetti or cheese ravioli. This spaghetti sauce can be frozen for up to two months.

Meatballs
2 pounds ground beef chuck
4 large eggs
1 medium-sized white onion, chopped fine
3 green onions, minced
½ cup chopped fresh parsley
½ cup shredded fontinella cheese
¾ cup fine, dry, seasoned bread crumbs
½ teaspoon seasoned salt
½ teaspoon garlic powder
½ teaspoon salt-free herb and spice mixture
¼ teaspoon freshly ground black pepper

Sauce
½ cup extra-virgin olive oil
2 medium-sized white onions, chopped
6 green onions, minced
1 green bell pepper, seeded and chopped
5 cloves garlic, minced
1½ pounds Italian sausage, removed from casings and crumbled

<table>
<tr><td>1 pound beef tenderloin, cut in
   strips</td><td>½ cup shredded fontinella cheese</td></tr>
</table>

1 pound beef tenderloin, cut in strips	½ cup shredded fontinella cheese
1 pound pork shoulder steaks, cut in strips	1 teaspoon dried oregano
2 15-ounce cans Italian-style tomato sauce	1 teaspoon dried basil
1 28-ounce can tomato puree	1 teaspoon Italian seasoning
1 28-ounce can plum tomatoes	1 teaspoon salt-free herb and spice mixture
1 12-ounce can tomato paste	½ teaspoon garlic powder
½ cup chopped fresh parsley	½ teaspoon freshly ground black pepper
	1 bay leaf

1. To make meatballs, combine beef, eggs, white onion, green onions, parsley, cheese, bread crumbs, seasoned salt, garlic powder, spice mixture, and black pepper in a large bowl until well mixed. Shape into 2-inch meatballs.

2. To make sauce, heat olive oil in a heavy-bottomed Dutch oven over medium-high heat. Add white onions, green onions, bell pepper, and garlic. Cook, stirring often, until crisp-tender, about 2 minutes.

3. Add meatballs in a single layer to onion mixture. Cook over medium heat, turning occasionally, until brown on all sides, about 10 minutes. Remove meatballs to a large bowl; set aside in refrigerator.

4. Add sausage, beef strips, and pork strips to the Dutch oven in a single layer. Cook over medium heat until brown on all sides, 15 to 20 minutes. Set aside in refrigerator.

5. Stir tomato sauce, tomato puree, plum tomatoes, tomato paste, parsley, cheese, oregano, basil, Italian seasoning, spice mixture, garlic powder, pepper, and bay leaf into onion mixture. Cover; simmer over low heat 2 hours, stirring often to prevent scorching. Taste sauce during cooking and adjust seasonings. Discard bay leaf. Add meatballs, sausage, beef strips, and pork strips; heat 10 minutes; and serve.

NUTRITION INFORMATION PER SERVING:

635 calories	37 g fat	12 g saturated fat
52% calories from fat	200 mg cholesterol	1,610 mg sodium
31 g carbohydrate	46 g protein	6 g fiber

Light and Easy Lasagna

PREPARATION TIME: 45 minutes
COOKING TIME: 3 hours
YIELD: 12 servings

JEANNE JONES, IN her popular "Cook It Light" column, adapts readers' recipes to be lower in fat, cholesterol, and sodium. Her healthful, meatless lasagna has a winning flavor.

3 medium-sized onions, chopped	½ teaspoon freshly ground black
3 cloves garlic, minced	pepper
2 28-ounce cans plum tomatoes,	8 ounces lasagna noodles
undrained	Oil for baking dish
2 12-ounce cans tomato paste	1 pound part-skim ricotta cheese
1 cup chopped fresh parsley	½ pound part-skim mozzarella
2 teaspoons dried oregano	cheese
½ teaspoon dried leaf thyme	2 ounces Parmesan cheese, grated
½ teaspoon dried marjoram	

1. Put onions and garlic in a large saucepan. Cook, covered, over low heat until tender, adding a little water if necessary to prevent scorching. Add tomatoes, tomato paste, parsley, oregano, thyme, marjoram, and pepper. Simmer covered, stirring occasionally, about 2 hours.

2. Cook lasagna noodles in boiling water until al dente, about 12 minutes. Drain in colander; rinse with cold water. Drain well.

3. Heat oven to 350°F. Lightly oil 13″ × 9″ baking dish. Cover bottom with one-fourth of the sauce. Add a layer of lasagna noodles. Top with one-third of the ricotta cheese and one-third of the mozzarella. Sprinkle with one-fourth of the Parmesan cheese. Cover with one-fourth of the sauce. Repeat procedure 2 more times. Sprinkle remaining Parmesan cheese on top.

4. Bake until sauce is bubbly and cheese is melted, about 45 minutes. Let stand 10 minutes before serving.

NUTRITION INFORMATION PER SERVING:

275 calories	9 g fat	5 g saturated fat
27% calories from fat	25 mg cholesterol	885 mg sodium
35 g carbohydrate	17 g protein	5 g fiber

Squash and Sweet Potato Lasagna with Pumpkin Seeds and Prosciutto

PREPARATION TIME: 35 minutes

COOKING TIME: 1 hour 20 minutes

STANDING TIME: 10 minutes

YIELD: 8 servings

THE PUMPKIN SEEDS give this dish a delightful crunch, and the squash and ham give it richness. This is definitely a dish for a special occasion. It was developed in the *Tribune* test kitchen for a story on using seeds in cooking.

Lasagna

1 medium-sized acorn squash, seeded and cooked *or* 1 16-ounce can solid pumpkin

3 sweet potatoes, cooked and peeled

4 ounces prosciutto *or* ham, chopped

¼ cup grated Parmesan cheese

2 tablespoons unsalted butter, melted

1 tablespoon chopped fresh sage

½ teaspoon salt

¼ teaspoon freshly ground black pepper

1 16-ounce box lasagna noodles, cooked according to package directions

Sauce

½ cup (1 stick) unsalted butter

3 ounces prosciutto *or* ham, julienned

¼ cup roasted, salted pumpkin seeds

1 tablespoon chopped fresh sage

Freshly ground black pepper

Parmesan cheese cut into shavings with a vegetable peeler

1. To make the lasagna, heat the oven to 375°F. Scoop the flesh out of the squash shell; place in large bowl. Add sweet potatoes; mash with a potato masher until smooth. Stir in prosciutto, 2 tablespoons of the Parmesan, butter, sage, salt, and black pepper. Set aside.

2. Grease a 13″ × 9″ baking pan. Line the bottom of pan with a single, slightly overlapping layer of noodles. Spread one-half of the squash mixture over the noodles. Repeat with remaining noodles and filling, finishing with noodles on top. Sprinkle remaining 2 tablespoons Parmesan over the top. Cover with aluminum foil; bake until heated through, about 35 minutes. Remove from the oven; let stand 10 minutes before cutting.

3. To make the sauce, melt butter in a small, heavy skillet over medium-high heat. Stir in prosciutto, pumpkin seeds, sage, and black pepper. Cook until butter starts to brown, about 8 minutes.

➤

4. Cut lasagna into 8 squares. Place on serving plates. Top with sauce and Parmesan shavings.

NUTRITION INFORMATION PER SERVING:

425 calories	16 g fat	7 g saturated fat
34% calories from fat	45 mg cholesterol	670 mg sodium
55 g carbohydrate	17 g protein	5 g fiber

Fettuccine with Asparagus, Ham, and Herbed Cheese

PREPARATION TIME: 20 minutes

COOKING TIME: 15 minutes

YIELD: 4 servings

LEFTOVER EASTER HAM can provoke a range of emotions, from plain boredom to downright dread. It shouldn't, though. Here it becomes a satisfying main course pasta. We toss fettuccine noodles with spring vegetables (you may have some of these left over, too) and gloss them with a light, herbed cheese sauce.

½ pound fettuccine	1 4.4-ounce package boursin *or*
1 tablespoon olive oil	other garlic-herb cheese
½ pound asparagus, trimmed and	1 cup reduced-sodium chicken *or*
cut diagonally into 1-inch pieces	vegetable broth
1 small red bell pepper, diced fine	2 cups diced cooked ham
1 small yellow bell pepper, diced	1 teaspoon minced fresh tarragon
fine	Salt
	Freshly ground black pepper

1. Cook fettuccine according to package directions; drain well. Heat oil in a large skillet over high heat. Add asparagus; cook 2 minutes. Stir in red bell pepper and yellow bell pepper; cook until vegetables are tender and begin to brown at edges, 4 to 5 minutes.

2. Stir cheese and broth together in a small bowl until smooth. Add cheese mixture, drained pasta, and ham to vegetables in the skillet. Cook over low heat until mixture is heated through. Add tarragon and salt and pepper to taste.

NUTRITION INFORMATION PER SERVING:

440 calories	18 g fat	7 g saturated fat
36% calories from fat	80 mg cholesterol	375 mg sodium
37 g carbohydrate	34 g protein	4 g fiber

Fettuccine with Wild Mushrooms

PREPARATION TIME: 20 minutes
COOKING TIME: 10 minutes
YIELD: 6 servings

YOU MAY USE any fresh wild mushrooms in this recipe, if you're lucky enough to find them. Supermarkets sell cultivated versions of many formerly wild types. You may use fresh or dried pasta, but the fresh will absorb the sauce better. You may add one to two cups chopped or shredded cooked poultry to the sauce. Serve this dish with a barbaresco or another rich red Italian wine.

½ pound wild mushrooms, such as oyster *and/or* shiitake	1 14-ounce can plum tomatoes, drained and chopped
3 tablespoons butter	1 clove garlic, minced
2 slices bacon, diced	Freshly ground black pepper
1 medium-sized carrot, peeled and diced	1 cup beef broth
1 medium-sized onion, sliced thin	1 pound fettuccine, preferably fresh
1 rib celery, diced	Freshly grated Parmesan cheese
	Salt

1. Wipe mushrooms clean with damp paper towels; chop coarse. Heat 2 tablespoons of the butter in a large skillet over medium-high heat; add bacon. Cook, turning occasionally, until bacon is cooked but not crisp.

2. Add carrot, onion, and celery. Cover; cook over low heat until vegetables are soft, 5 to 7 minutes. Increase heat to medium. Add mushrooms. Cook, stirring often, until mushrooms begin to give off liquid, about 2 minutes. Add tomatoes and garlic and black pepper to taste. Cook 1 minute; stir in beef broth. Heat to boil; reduce heat to low. Cover; cook 15 minutes.

3. Bring a large pot of salted water to boil. Cook fettuccine until al dente, about 3 minutes for fresh and 10 to 12 minutes for dried. Put remaining 1 tablespoon butter in a large bowl. Drain pasta; toss with butter. Add half of the sauce. Add Parmesan. Toss to mix; add salt and black pepper to taste. Divide among 6 warm bowls. Spoon remaining sauce over pasta. Pass additional Parmesan at table.

NUTRITION INFORMATION PER SERVING:

330 calories	11 g fat	5 g saturated fat
28% calories from fat	20 mg cholesterol	535 mg sodium
50 g carbohydrate	12 g protein	4 g fiber

Pasta with Broccoli, Cheese, and Bacon

PREPARATION TIME: 15 minutes

COOKING TIME: 15 minutes

YIELD: 4 servings

SEVEN SIMPLE INGREDIENTS are combined in this hearty, comforting dish from a "Fast Food" column. It can be a main course or side dish. You can use almost any small pasta, such as pastina, orzo, small shells, or even elbow macaroni.

8 ounces pastina, orzo, *or* other small pasta

1 large head fresh broccoli

¼ cup (½ stick) unsalted butter

½ pound bacon, cooked and crumbled

¾ cup freshly grated Parmesan cheese

Salt

Freshly ground black pepper

1. Bring a medium-sized pot of water to boil. Cook pasta according to package directions. Drain and set aside. Meanwhile, trim tough ends from broccoli stalks. Separate florets from stalks. Lightly peel stalks; slice into ½-inch pieces. Bring a large saucepan of water to boil. Cook broccoli until crisp-tender, 3 to 5 minutes. Drain well.

2. Melt butter in a large skillet over medium heat. Stir in broccoli, bacon, pasta, and Parmesan; heat through. Add salt and pepper to taste.

NUTRITION INFORMATION PER SERVING:

520 calories	27 g fat	14 g saturated fat
47% calories from fat	60 mg cholesterol	665 mg sodium
46 g carbohydrate	22 g protein	3 g fiber

Pasta with Broccoli Raab and Bell Peppers

PREPARATION TIME: 10 minutes

COOKING TIME: 15 minutes

YIELD: 3 servings

IN THE FOLLOWING recipe, pasta and vegetables are cooked together, eliminating a pan and a step. *Broccoli raab* is also spelled "rabe" and "rape" or, in Italian, *rapini*. If grilled or roasted bell peppers are not available at the supermarket, roast them at home. Or, stir-fry them in a small amount of hot oil before adding them to the pasta mixture.

½ pound small pasta shapes, such as *orrechiette or* small shells

1 pound broccoli raab, trimmed and cut in 1-inch lengths

2 roasted red *and/or* yellow bell
   peppers, diced
1 small clove garlic, minced fine
2 tablespoons extra-virgin olive oil

Salt
Crushed red pepper flakes
Freshly ground black pepper
⅓ cup Parmesan cheese, grated

1. Heat a large saucepan of salted water to boil over high heat; add pasta. About 5 minutes before it is cooked al dente, add broccoli raab and stir well. Continue cooking until pasta and broccoli raab are tender, 4 to 6 minutes.

2. Combine bell peppers, garlic, and oil and salt, red pepper flakes, and black pepper to taste in a serving bowl.

3. Drain pasta and broccoli raab, shaking colander to remove as much water as possible. Add to bell pepper mixture; toss to combine. Lightly mix in cheese; taste and adjust seasoning.

NUTRITION INFORMATION PER SERVING:

485 calories	14 g fat	3.6 g saturated fat
25% calories from fat	9 mg cholesterol	235 mg sodium
73 g carbohydrate	19 g protein	4.4 g fiber

Linguine with Bay Scallops, Goat Cheese, and Red Bell Pepper

PREPARATION TIME: 15 minutes
COOKING TIME: 10 minutes
YIELD: 2 servings

THIS RECIPE COMES from Ann Topham of Fantome Farm in Ridgeway, Wisconsin, where she raises goats and makes goat cheese.

½ pound fresh linguine
3 tablespoons butter
1 leek, chopped
1 red bell pepper, seeded and sliced
   thin
8 ounces bay scallops

4 ounces goat cheese
1 to 2 tablespoons whipping cream
Salt
Freshly ground black pepper
Ground red pepper
Chopped fresh parsley

1. Cook linguine according to package directions; drain. Meanwhile, melt 2 tablespoons of the butter in a large skillet over medium-high heat. Add leek and red bell pepper; cook, stirring often, until tender, 3 to 4 minutes.

➤

2. Stir in scallops and remaining 1 tablespoon butter. Cook, stirring frequently, over medium heat until scallops are opaque, about 1 minute. Stir in goat cheese and whipping cream until blended; heat through. Season with salt, black pepper, and ground red pepper to taste.

3. Toss scallop mixture with hot, drained pasta. Sprinkle with parsley.

NUTRITION INFORMATION PER SERVING:

850 calories	43 g fat	25 g saturated fat
45% calories from fat	135 mg cholesterol	1,145 mg sodium
76 g carbohydrate	43 g protein	5 g fiber

Creamy Corned Beef Pasta

PREPARATION TIME: 40 minutes
COOKING TIME: 20 minutes
YIELD: 4 servings

THIS DISH WAS created in the *Tribune* test kitchen to use up St. Patrick's Day leftovers. It was voted one of the *Tribune*'s ten best recipes of 1985. You may vary the basic recipe by using cooked turkey or chicken in place of the corned beef.

1 8-ounce box small shell-shaped
    pasta
1 tablespoon olive oil
2 tablespoons butter
2 medium-sized leeks, white part
    only, chopped
2 cups whipping cream *or* milk
2 cups cubed cooked corned beef

⅛ teaspoon ground nutmeg
¼ teaspoon salt
¼ teaspoon freshly ground black
    pepper
1 tablespoon freshly grated
    Parmesan cheese
1 tablespoon chopped fresh parsley

1. Bring a large pot of water to boil. Cook pasta according to package directions; drain. Toss with oil and put on a serving platter. Cover to keep warm.

2. Melt butter in a large saucepan over medium-high heat. Add leeks; cook until wilted, 3 to 4 minutes. Stir in whipping cream. Heat to boil; cook until thickened and reduced to 1½ cups, about 15 minutes. Add corned beef, nutmeg, salt, and black pepper. Cook until heated through, about 1 minute. Pour corned beef mixture over pasta; sprinkle with Parmesan and parsley.

NUTRITION INFORMATION PER SERVING:

865 calories	65 g fat	36 g saturated fat
67% calories from fat	240 mg cholesterol	985 mg sodium
43 g carbohydrate	29 g protein	2 g fiber

Beef and Bell Peppers on Vermicelli

PREPARATION TIME: 30 minutes

COOKING TIME: 10 minutes

YIELD: 4 servings

HERE IS A quickly prepared main course from the *Tribune* test kitchen—about forty minutes from start to finish. Pale noodles, tender beef, and flavorings are complemented by the visual appeal of tricolored bell pepper chunks.

1 pound boneless beef sirloin	1 large yellow bell pepper, seeded
1 cup beef broth	8 ounces vermicelli *or* fettuccine
3 tablespoons soy sauce	2 tablespoons peanut oil
2 tablespoons red wine	1 small yellow onion, sliced thin
2 tablespoons cornstarch	2 green onions, sliced
2 teaspoons Asian sesame oil	1 ½-inch-thick piece gingerroot,
¼ teaspoon crushed red pepper	peeled and minced
flakes	2 large cloves garlic, minced
1 large green bell pepper, seeded	Salt
1 large red bell pepper, seeded	Freshly ground black pepper

1. Cut beef into very thin slices.

2. Stir together broth, soy sauce, wine, cornstarch, sesame oil, and red pepper flakes in a small bowl. Cut green bell pepper, red bell pepper, and yellow bell pepper into 1-inch chunks.

3. Cook vermicelli according to package directions until al dente. Drain; toss with 1 tablespoon of the peanut oil; keep warm.

4. Heat remaining 1 tablespoon peanut oil in a wok or large skillet over high heat. Add yellow onion, green onions, gingerroot, and garlic. Cook, stirring constantly, 1 minute.

►

5. Add meat. Cook, stirring constantly, 1 minute. Add bell pepper chunks; cook until vegetables are crisp-tender, about 2 minutes. Stir broth mixture well and add to meat mixture. Cook, stirring constantly, until thickened, about 2 minutes. Add salt and black pepper to taste.

6. Put vermicelli on a platter. Spoon meat mixture on top.

❧ NOTE: *To help with slicing, place meat in freezer until it's partly frozen, about 15 minutes.*

NUTRITION INFORMATION PER SERVING:

545 calories	17 g fat	4.4 g saturated fat
29% calories from fat	75 mg cholesterol	1,030 mg sodium
59 g carbohydrate	36 g protein	4.8 g fiber

Angel Hair with Garlic and Arugula

PREPARATION TIME: 10 minutes

COOKING TIME: 7 minutes

YIELD: 4 servings

USING ANGEL HAIR strands, also known as capellini, is a smart choice for hurried cooks. Once added to boiling water, angel hair cooks in less than 2 minutes. Because it is so fine, angel hair is best matched with lighter sauces. This one is ideal. As a bonus, the sauce is cooked in the same pan used to cook the pasta, making this a one-pot meal. Arugula, also called rocket, is a salad green. The deep-green leaves have a peppery bite that softens when cooked.

12 ounces angel hair pasta	¼ teaspoon crushed red pepper
Salt	flakes
2 cloves garlic, sliced paper-thin	3 cups finely minced arugula leaves
1 tablespoon extra-virgin olive oil	½ cup whipping cream
	Grated pecorino cheese

1. Bring a pot of water to boil. Cook pasta in boiling salted water just until al dente, 1 to 2 minutes. Drain and set aside.

2. Combine garlic, oil, and red pepper flakes in the same pan. Cook over low heat until garlic is fragrant and tender, 4 to 5 minutes, taking care not to let garlic brown. Add arugula and whipping cream; cook to thicken slightly, 1 minute. Toss in pasta and salt to taste.

3. Divide among 4 pasta bowls and sprinkle pecorino over top.

NUTRITION INFORMATION PER SERVING:

385 calories	16 g fat	7 g saturated fat
37% calories from fat	40 mg cholesterol	305 mg sodium
50 g carbohydrate	12 g protein	2 g fiber

Penne with Turkey, Bacon, and Camembert

PREPARATION TIME: 15 minutes

COOKING TIME: 12 minutes

YIELD: 4 servings

LEFTOVER TURKEY, AMONG the most versatile meats, can be used as the starting point for stir-fries, casseroles, soups, and pasta dishes. Here, it finds its way into a creamy but not too rich pasta enlivened with bacon, fresh basil, and a bit of cheese. It was developed for a "Fast Food" column and takes only twelve minutes to cook.

8 ounces penne pasta	2 ounces Camembert cheese, cut in
1 medium-sized onion, diced	small bits
2 strips bacon, diced	2 tablespoons whipping cream
1¼ cups diced cooked turkey	2 tablespoons minced fresh basil
⅔ cup turkey broth *or*	¼ teaspoon salt
reduced-sodium chicken broth	Freshly ground black pepper

1. Cook penne according to package directions. Drain and set aside. Meanwhile, cook onion and bacon in a medium-sized saucepan over medium-high heat, stirring often, until bacon is browned, about 4 minutes. Add turkey; cook 1 minute.

2. Reduce heat to medium; add turkey broth and Camembert. Cook just until cheese melts. Stir in pasta, whipping cream, and basil and salt and black pepper to taste.

NUTRITION INFORMATION PER SERVING:

335 calories	12 g fat	6 g saturated fat
34% calories from fat	35 mg cholesterol	300 mg sodium
40 g carbohydrate	16 g protein	2.3 g fiber

Shells with Fennel, Leek, and Sausage Ragù

PREPARATION TIME: 20 minutes

COOKING TIME: 25 minutes

YIELD: 2 servings

THOUGH RED SAUCE still leads the way as the standard pasta topper, there are other ways to extend the noodle's timeless appeal. Here, lower-fat turkey sausage is simmered with leeks and fresh fennel for a simple topping that's ideal for pasta shells.

6 ounces (2 cups) medium-sized shell pasta

1 teaspoon olive oil

6 ounces Italian turkey sausage, casing removed

1 medium-sized leek, trimmed and sliced

½ medium-sized fennel bulb, diced

½ cup reduced-sodium chicken broth

Pinch red pepper flakes

⅓ cup half-and-half *or* milk

Salt

Freshly ground black pepper

2 tablespoons minced fresh basil

Grated Parmesan cheese

1. Cook pasta according to package directions. Meanwhile, heat oil in a large skillet over medium heat. Crumble sausage into pan; cook until no longer pink, about 5 minutes. Add leek and fennel; cook, stirring often, until vegetables begin to soften, 4 minutes. Add broth and red pepper flakes; simmer until vegetables are almost tender, 5 minutes.

2. Add half-and-half and increase heat to high. Cook until mixture thickens slightly, 3 minutes. Add salt and black pepper to taste.

3. Drain pasta thoroughly. Add pasta and basil to sauce mixture; toss to coat. Divide between 2 bowls; serve with Parmesan.

NUTRITION INFORMATION PER SERVING:

675 calories	23 g fat	8 g saturated fat
30% calories from fat	90 mg cholesterol	665 mg sodium
84 g carbohydrate	34 g protein	6 g fiber

Real McCoy Macaroni and Cheese

PREPARATION TIME: 10 minutes
COOKING TIME: 55 minutes
YIELD: 4 servings

DESIRE FOR A really good macaroni and cheese, the pasta tender and the cheese sauce bubbling and tangy, prompted experimentation in the *Tribune* test kitchen. Here is the result. This recipe can be made the day before serving. Prepare the recipe up to the baking step, but do not add cracker crumbs. Refrigerate covered. Remove from refrigerator and allow the macaroni and cheese to sit 15 minutes before baking as directed.

1 7-ounce package elbow macaroni
¼ cup (½ stick) plus 2 tablespoons butter
¼ cup all-purpose flour
½ teaspoon salt
½ teaspoon paprika
½ teaspoon dried mustard
Freshly ground black pepper
2 cups milk
2 cups (8 ounces) shredded sharp cheddar cheese
½ cup crushed saltine crackers

1. Cook macaroni according to package directions; drain. Meanwhile, heat oven to 350°F. Melt ¼ cup of the butter in a large saucepan over medium heat. Add flour, salt, paprika, and mustard and black pepper to taste; stir well. Cook 1 minute. Stir in milk. Reduce heat to low; cook, stirring constantly, until thickened, about 15 minutes.

2. Remove from heat; stir in macaroni and cheddar. Stir until cheese is melted. Spoon into a 2-quart casserole. Cover; bake 20 minutes. Melt remaining 2 tablespoons butter in a small skillet; stir in crushed crackers. Remove the cover from the casserole; sprinkle macaroni with cracker crumbs. Bake uncovered until top is golden and mixture is bubbly, about 20 minutes.

NUTRITION INFORMATION PER SERVING:

715 calories	41 g fat	25 g saturated fat
52% calories from fat	115 mg cholesterol	1,075 mg sodium
59 g carbohydrate	27 g protein	2.4 g fiber

Special Pesto with Pasta

PREPARATION TIME: 10 minutes
YIELD: 6 servings

PESTO, A BLEND of basil, garlic, olive oil, pine nuts, and Parmesan cheese, is a classic Italian sauce that should be part of any good cook's repertoire. This version, rich with pine nuts and the addition of butter, will not disappoint you.

1 16-ounce box spaghetti *or* other pasta
4 cups chopped fresh basil leaves
3 cloves garlic, quartered
Juice of ¼ lemon
1 cup olive oil
¾ cup pine nuts

⅔ cup finely grated Parmesan cheese
¼ cup (½ stick) unsalted butter
⅓ cup finely grated Romano cheese
Freshly ground black pepper

1. Cook pasta according to package directions. Drain and set aside.
2. Meanwhile, put basil, garlic, lemon juice, olive oil, pine nuts, Parmesan, butter, Romano, and black pepper to taste into a food processor fitted with a metal blade. Process until chopped fine but not pureed.
3. Serve over hot pasta.

❧ NOTE: *Here are some suggested uses for pesto:*
Stir it into hot soup.
Substitute it for mayonnaise in chicken salad or on sandwiches.
Serve it on grilled meats and hamburgers.
Stuff it into broiled mushroom caps or cherry tomatoes.

NUTRITION INFORMATION PER SERVING:

860 calories	59 g fat	14 g saturated fat
61% calories from fat	35 mg cholesterol	275 mg sodium
64 g carbohydrate	21 g protein	5 g fiber

Asian Pesto with Noodles

PREPARATION TIME: 20 minutes
COOKING TIME: 4 minutes
YIELD: 5 servings

IN A STORY on Chinese New Year, columnist William Rice included this intriguing recipe from Asian food consultant Bruce Cost. Although it borrows from the Italian concept of pesto, this is definitely an all-Asian dish. Try using Asian basil and mint in this recipe. Look for them in Thai or Vietnamese food markets.

½ cup packed fresh basil
¼ cup packed fresh mint
¼ cup packed cilantro
½ cup peanut oil
½ cup raw *or* dry roasted skinless peanuts (see Note)
2 small fresh green chilies, seeded

1 2-inch-long piece gingerroot, peeled and chopped coarse
4 cloves garlic
3 tablespoons fresh lemon juice
1 teaspoon sugar
½ teaspoon salt
15 ounces fresh Chinese wheat flour noodles

1. Combine basil, mint, and cilantro in a small bowl; set aside. Heat oil in a small skillet; add peanuts. Fry until lightly browned, about 10 seconds. Drain, reserving oil.

2. Put peanuts in a food processor fitted with a metal blade or in a blender. Puree until a rough paste forms. Add chilies, gingerroot, and garlic through the feed tube with the motor running. Add herb mixture and a little of the reserved oil. Add lemon juice, sugar, and salt. Process until herbs are minced fine. Add remaining reserved oil with the motor running; process until blended.

3. Heat a large pot of water to boil over high heat; add noodles. Cook until soft, about 4 minutes. Drain. Add pesto; toss lightly to mix.

❧ NOTE: *Raw peanuts can be purchased in bulk food stores, specialty stores, and some health food stores.*

NUTRITION INFORMATION PER SERVING:

550 calories	31 g fat	5 g saturated fat
50% calories from fat	65 mg cholesterol	260 mg sodium
56 g carbohydrate	15 g protein	5 g fiber

Big Bowl's Blazing Rice Noodles

PREPARATION TIME: 35 minutes

COOKING TIME: 10 minutes

YIELD: 2 servings

INTEREST HAS SURGED in noodle dishes from China, Japan, and Southeast Asia. Inexpensive noodle shops and stir-fry bars have sprung up everywhere, and home cooks are developing a taste for these dishes. Asian ingredients and cookbooks are relatively easy to find for those who want to re-create them at home. This recipe comes from Big Bowl, a Chicago restaurant. Adjust the level of spicy heat to your taste by using more or less of the jalapeño.

2 teaspoons dark soy sauce

1 teaspoon cornstarch

½ teaspoon Asian sesame oil plus more for garnish

¼ teaspoon salt

5 ounces slightly frozen beef flank steak, sliced thin

2 tablespoons oyster sauce

2 tablespoons light soy sauce

1 tablespoon red wine vinegar

1½ teaspoons sugar

3 green onions

6 tablespoons peanut *or* vegetable oil

15 ounces fresh rice noodles, sliced into 4-inch widths

½ to 1 jalapeño, cut into strips

2 cloves garlic, minced

1 1-inch piece gingerroot, peeled and minced

1½ teaspoons canned salted black beans

½ red bell pepper, cut into strips

2 baby bok choy, each sliced lengthwise into quarters

¾ cup chicken broth, preferably homemade

Freshly ground black pepper

1. Combine 1 teaspoon of the dark soy sauce, cornstarch, ½ teaspoon sesame oil, and salt in a medium-sized bowl. Add beef; stir to coat. Set aside. Combine remaining 1 teaspoon dark soy sauce, oyster sauce, light soy sauce, vinegar, and sugar in a separate bowl. Mix; set aside.

2. Cut the white part of the green onions into 2-inch lengths; set aside. Slice the green part of green onions; set aside. Heat 3 tablespoons of the oil in a wok or skillet until hot but not smoking. Add beef; cook, stirring, until meat begins to change color, about 1 minute. Remove; drain well.

3. Clean wok or skillet; heat until very hot. Heat remaining 3 tablespoons oil. Add noodles; toss to coat. Cook, stirring frequently, until noodles brown slightly, 2 minutes. Stir in jalapeño, garlic, gingerroot, and black beans. Cook until fragrant, about 2 minutes.

4. Add bell pepper, white portion of green onions, and bok choy. Cook, stirring constantly, until heated through, 1 to 2 minutes. Return beef to wok; stir to reheat. Stir in oyster sauce mixture. Add broth; stir over high heat until most of the liquid has evaporated. Transfer to a platter. To garnish, sprinkle with green portion of green onions, more of the sesame oil, and black pepper to taste.

NUTRITION INFORMATION PER SERVING:

985 calories	49 g fat	10 g saturated fat
45% calories from fat	36 mg cholesterol	1,980 mg sodium
110 g carbohydrate	25 g protein	3 g fiber

Orzo with Browned Onions and Basil

PREPARATION TIME: 5 minutes
COOKING TIME: 10 minutes
YIELD: 4 servings

To MAKE THIS orzo dish, cook the onions in the same pan as the pasta for a one-pot preparation or in a separate pan to speed preparation. The basic orzo recipe can be varied many ways, so it makes sense to make a double batch and have the extra on hand. Roasted vegetables, especially zucchini and eggplant, are excellent additions.

1 tablespoon olive oil	½ teaspoon salt
1 dried red pepper *or* pinch crushed red pepper flakes	1 cup dried orzo pasta
	2 tablespoons whipping cream
1 large sweet onion, diced fine	1 tablespoon minced fresh basil

1. Heat oil and red pepper in a medium-sized skillet over high heat. When hot, add onion; cook, stirring, until golden, 8 to 10 minutes. Stir in salt.

2. Cook pasta according to package directions; drain well. Add pasta to onions; stir in whipping cream and basil. Taste and adjust salt.

NUTRITION INFORMATION PER SERVING:

245 calories	7 g fat	2.3 g saturated fat
26% calories from fat	10 mg cholesterol	300 mg sodium
39 g carbohydrate	7 g protein	1.7 g fiber

Jasmine Rice with Red Pepper and Cumin–Spiced Shallots

PREPARATION TIME: 10 minutes

COOKING TIME: 20 minutes

YIELD: 4 servings

THIS PEPPERY RICE dish would go well with Asian-flavored pork entrees or even grilled chicken.

1 tablespoon peanut *or* vegetable oil
½ teaspoon ground cumin
⅛ teaspoon ground red pepper
3 large shallots, sliced thin
1 cup uncooked jasmine rice
1 16-ounce can reduced-sodium chicken broth
1 tablespoon seasoned rice vinegar
¼ teaspoon salt

1. Heat oil in a medium-sized saucepan over high heat. Stir in cumin and red pepper to taste. Separate shallots into rings; add to pan. Cook, stirring constantly, until shallots begin to soften, 2 to 3 minutes. Remove from pan; set aside.

2. Add rice to the same saucepan. Cook, stirring constantly, 30 seconds. Add chicken broth. Cover; heat to boil. Reduce heat to low; simmer until liquid is absorbed, 15 to 17 minutes. Turn off heat; let stand 5 minutes. Add shallots, vinegar, and salt; toss.

NUTRITION INFORMATION PER SERVING:

240 calories	4.7 g fat	1.2 g saturated fat
18% calories from fat	2 mg cholesterol	55 mg sodium
44 g carbohydrate	6 g protein	1.1 g fiber

Ham and Sausage Jambalaya

PREPARATION TIME: 45 minutes

COOKING TIME: 1¾ hours

YIELD: 12 servings

SPICY, EASY JAMBALAYA is a one-pot meal that can serve a crowd. The trick lies in cooking the fat-and-flour mixture, or roux, to a dark, flavorful state without burning it. You can prepare this dish in advance and refrigerate it up to two days or freeze it up to one month.

¼ cup vegetable oil
¼ cup all-purpose flour
7 large onions, chopped coarse
1 large green bell pepper, seeded and chopped
3 ribs celery, chopped

3 cloves garlic, minced

¼ cup chopped fresh parsley

3 pounds diced smoked ham

1 pound hot sausage, such as andouille *or* kielbasa, sliced

4½ cups chicken broth

2 teaspoons freshly ground black pepper

½ teaspoon salt

¼ teaspoon ground red pepper

3 cups long-grain rice

Minced fresh parsley

Hot pepper sauce

1. Heat oil in an 8-quart cast-iron or enameled cast-iron Dutch oven. Add flour; cook, stirring constantly, over medium heat until flour is the color of cinnamon, about 10 minutes. Add onions. Cook, stirring often, over low heat until tender, about 15 minutes. Add bell pepper, celery, garlic, and parsley; cook 2 minutes. Stir in ham and sausage. Cover; cook 15 minutes.

2. Add broth, black pepper, salt, and red pepper. Cover; simmer 30 minutes. Stir in rice; heat to boil, stirring occasionally. Reduce heat. Cover; simmer until rice is tender, 30 to 45 minutes. Sprinkle with parsley. Pass hot pepper sauce.

NUTRITION INFORMATION PER SERVING:

530 calories	20 g fat	6 g saturated fat
34% calories from fat	80 mg cholesterol	2,185 mg sodium
55 g carbohydrate	31 g protein	2.6 g fiber

Basil Fried Rice (Khao Phad Kraprao)

PREPARATION TIME: 20 minutes

COOKING TIME: 10 minutes

YIELD: 4 servings

THIS SPICY RICE recipe is from Arun's, a luxury-class Thai restaurant in Chicago. Serve it as a side dish for grilled meats or as a light supper dish.

3 tablespoons vegetable oil

1 clove garlic, minced

1 to 2 serrano chilies, seeded and minced

3 tablespoons ground *or* minced chicken (about ½ chicken breast)

3 peeled, deveined shrimp, chopped coarse

1 tablespoon plus 1½ teaspoons fish sauce (*nam pla*)

1 teaspoon sugar

1 cup jasmine *or* long-grain rice, cooked

10 to 15 fresh holy basil (*kraprao*) *or* sweet basil leaves

10 to 12 sprigs cilantro

1 lime, cut in 6 wedges

►

1. Heat 2 tablespoons of the oil in a wok or large skillet over medium heat. Add garlic; cook, stirring constantly, until golden, 2 to 3 minutes.

2. Add serranos; cook 15 seconds. Add chicken; cook, stirring constantly and breaking up chicken. Add shrimp; cook 1 minute. Add fish sauce and sugar. Stir well.

3. Add rice; cook, stirring constantly, until all ingredients are well mixed. Add remaining 1 tablespoon oil and basil; cook until basil softens, about 30 seconds. Transfer to a platter. Garnish with cilantro and lime wedges. Squeeze lime onto rice before eating.

NUTRITION INFORMATION PER SERVING:

310 calories	11 g fat	1.6 g saturated fat
33% calories from fat	19 mg cholesterol	545 mg sodium
44 g carbohydrate	8 g protein	0.7 g fiber

Roasted Vegetable Risotto

PREPARATION TIME: 20 minutes
COOKING TIME: 1 hour 10 minutes
YIELD: 4 servings

THIS VEGETARIAN RISOTTO, developed in the *Tribune* test kitchen, depends on a good homemade vegetable stock. Chicken broth would make an acceptable substitute for nonvegetarians.

1 butternut squash (2 to 3 pounds), halved and seeded	1 bunch green onions, trimmed
2 large red bell peppers, halved and seeded	¼ to ½ pound assorted fresh mushrooms
1 head garlic, cloves separated, unpeeled	2 quarts vegetable stock
6 shallots, unpeeled	3 cups arborio *or* short-grain rice
½ cup vegetable oil	½ cup white wine
	Salt
	Freshly ground black pepper

1. Heat oven to 350°F. Place squash, bell peppers, garlic cloves, and shallots in a large roasting pan. Pour 6 tablespoons of the oil over vegetables; toss to coat all surfaces. Turn squash and bell peppers cut side down in the pan; bake 30 minutes.

2. Remove pan from the oven; add green onions and mushrooms to pan; stir until coated with oil. Roast 15 minutes longer; cool. Remove peel from squash; cut squash and bell peppers into medium-sized chunks. Squeeze garlic and shallots pulp from peels; chop. Slice green onions. Set vegetables aside.

3. Heat vegetable stock through; set aside. Heat remaining oil in a heavy saucepan or Dutch oven over medium-high heat. Add rice; stir to coat with oil. Add wine; cook until wine is mostly absorbed, 3 to 5 minutes. Stir in vegetable stock 1 cup at a time, allowing rice to absorb each addition. Cook just until the rice is cooked through, about 20 minutes.

4. Stir in vegetables. Season with salt and black pepper to taste. Cover; let stand 1 or 2 minutes before serving.

NUTRITION INFORMATION PER SERVING:

945 calories	28 g fat	4 g saturated fat
27% calories from fat	0 mg cholesterol	25 mg sodium
158 g carbohydrate	14 g protein	15 g fiber

Making Basic Vegetable Stock

To make a basic vegetable stock, use 2 ½ quarts cold water, 2 carrots, 1 onion, 2 ribs celery, 1 bunch green onions, 4 cloves garlic, 8 branches parsley, 6 sprigs thyme, and 2 bay leaves. Cook 45 minutes.

If you're preparing just a small amount, such as 2 quarts, a large, heavy-bottomed Dutch oven may be adequate for holding all the ingredients and liquid. Otherwise, consider investing in a real stockpot, made of fairly lightweight metal in the diameter of a regular pot but with high sides, that holds 10 to 40 quarts.

Avoid strong-tasting vegetables such as broccoli, brussels sprouts, turnips, and rutabagas.

Ingredients for quick-cooking vegetable stocks should be chopped or broken into small pieces.

Give extra color to a stock by browning onion halves in a dry pan before adding them to the stock; by cooking vegetables in a little oil before adding them to the stock; or by including a tomato along with the other vegetables.

It's not necessary to peel vegetables before adding them to the water for stock because they will be strained out later. But be sure to rinse or scrub the vegetables thoroughly to remove dirt.

Start the stock with cold water and heat it to a boil. Reduce heat to a simmer for the remaining cooking time; ingredients should not cook too quickly.

Vegetable stocks will not need to be skimmed unless they give off a lot of dirt. Allow the foam to mass and then carefully remove it with a large, shallow spoon.

When the stock has finished cooking, remove large ingredients with a slotted spoon or tongs. Pour the remaining stock through a colander lined with cheesecloth or through a fine-mesh sieve.

➤

Let the stock cool to just above room temperature, then cover and refrigerate it. The stock will taste better the second day.

Stock can be thoroughly heated and used immediately or simmered about 2 more hours to reduce and concentrate the flavor. Store unused stock in airtight containers in the refrigerator for several days or freeze them for several months. Concentrated stock can be frozen in ice cube trays for times when a small amount is called for. Once they're frozen, transfer the stock cubes to a freezer bag. Thaw the stock in the refrigerator, and then make sure the liquid comes to a boil or is well-cooked in a recipe before consuming.

Indian-Spiced Rice Pilaf

PREPARATION TIME: 5 minutes

COOKING TIME: 15 minutes

YIELD: 4 servings

RICE IS A great accompaniment to a multitude of dishes. When plain steamed rice seems too, well, plain, you can add some dash in the form of warm spices without increasing your kitchen time.

1 cup basmati *or* Texmati rice	¼ teaspoon ground red pepper
2 cups reduced-sodium chicken broth *or* water	1 bay leaf
½ teaspoon ground cumin	¼ teaspoon salt
¼ teaspoon ground cardamom, optional	1 tablespoon minced fresh mint

1. Combine rice, chicken broth, cumin, cardamom if desired, red pepper, and bay leaf in a medium-sized saucepan.

2. Heat to boil. Cover; reduce heat. Simmer gently until liquid is absorbed, 15 minutes. Remove bay leaf. Stir in salt and mint with a fork.

NUTRITION INFORMATION PER SERVING:

195 calories	0.7 g fat	0.2 g saturated fat
3% calories from fat	0 mg cholesterol	370 mg sodium
42 g carbohydrate	5 g protein	0.6 g fiber

Wild Rice and Barley Pilaf

PREPARATION TIME: 10 minutes
COOKING TIME: 1 hour
YIELD: 6 servings

THIS WONDERFUL PILAF was featured in a story about the wild rice harvest in Minnesota. Fall holiday meals would benefit from its presence, as would any dinner featuring duck or game.

¼ cup (½ stick) unsalted butter
½ cup chopped pecans
1 medium-sized onion, diced
½ teaspoon dried leaf thyme

1 cup wild rice
¼ cup pearl barley
4 cups beef broth
½ cup minced parsley

1. Melt butter in a large skillet. Add pecans; cook, stirring, until fragrant and toasted, about 2 minutes. Remove pecans with a slotted spoon; set aside.

2. Add onion and thyme to pan. Reduce heat to medium; cook until onion begins to soften, 3 to 4 minutes. Stir in wild rice and barley; cook 1 minute longer. Add beef broth; cover. Simmer until grains are tender and almost all of the liquid has cooked away, about 50 minutes. Remove from heat. Add pecans and parsley.

NUTRITION INFORMATION PER SERVING:

280 calories	15 g fat	6 g saturated fat
47% calories from fat	20 mg cholesterol	530 mg sodium
39 g carbohydrate	8 g protein	4.3 g fiber

Couscous with Vegetables and Harissa Sauce

PREPARATION TIME: 20 minutes
COOKING TIME: 12 minutes
YIELD: 4 servings

COUSCOUS IS A semolina pasta in the shape of small beads or tiny grains. Tossed with fresh vegetables and garbanzo beans it becomes a meatless main course. *Harissa* is a powerfully hot condiment popular in Morocco. Though the couscous is fine without it, a judicious amount of *harissa* adds an authentic touch.

Harissa Sauce
1 clove garlic

4 habanero chilies
1 teaspoon grated orange zest

▶

¼ cup olive oil
1 tablespoon fresh lemon juice
¼ teaspoon salt
⅛ teaspoon caraway seeds

Couscous
¾ cup chicken broth
1 cup couscous
¼ cup dried currants
¼ cup olive oil
¼ cup pine nuts
1 zucchini, diced
1 red bell pepper, diced
½ teaspoon ground cumin

⅛ teaspoon cinnamon
¼ teaspoon salt
4 green onions, sliced
1 15-ounce can chickpeas (garbanzo beans), rinsed and drained
½ cup frozen peas, thawed
1 habanero chili, seeded and minced
¼ cup minced fresh herbs, preferably a mix of cilantro, mint, and parsley
3 to 4 tablespoons fresh lemon juice

1. To make *harissa* sauce, mince garlic in a food processor or blender. Add habanero chilies and orange zest. Process until minced. Add olive oil, lemon juice, salt, and caraway; mix 30 seconds. Set aside.

2. To make couscous, heat broth to boil. Combine couscous and currants in a large bowl. Pour boiling broth over couscous mixture; cover. Let stand 10 minutes. Fluff with a fork to separate grains.

3. Heat 1 tablespoon of the oil in a large skillet. Add pine nuts; cook, stirring often, until lightly browned, 2 to 3 minutes. Remove with a slotted spoon; set aside.

4. Add 1 tablespoon of the oil to the skillet. Add zucchini, bell pepper, cumin, cinnamon, and salt. Cook over high heat until vegetables begin to soften, about 4 minutes. Add green onions, chickpeas, peas, and habanero chili. Cook until heated through, 2 minutes. Remove from heat.

5. Transfer contents of skillet to couscous mixture. Add herb mixture, remaining oil, lemon juice, and reserved pine nuts. Toss lightly. Taste and adjust seasonings. Serve hot or at room temperature, passing *harissa* sauce separately.

NUTRITION INFORMATION PER SERVING:

640 calories	34 g fat	4.6 g saturated fat
46% calories from fat	0 mg cholesterol	785 mg sodium
71 g carbohydrate	16 g protein	10 g fiber

Spicy Herbed Couscous

PREPARATION TIME: 5 minutes
STANDING TIME: 15 minutes
YIELD: 4 servings

HERE'S A GOOD side dish to go with the grilled foods of summer. Although couscous is usually softened with boiling liquids, any temperature gets the job done. Using room-temperature vegetable juice eliminates a step and cleaning a pan, although the couscous will take about twice as long to soften.

1 cup couscous
1¼ cups spicy vegetable juice, such as Spicy Hot V8 *or* Bloody Mary mix
1 teaspoon ground cumin

1 tablespoon seasoned rice vinegar
1 tablespoon olive oil
¼ teaspoon salt
Freshly ground black pepper
¼ cup minced cilantro

1. Put couscous in a medium-sized bowl. Add vegetable juice and cumin; stir to moisten couscous. Cover; let stand 15 minutes to soften.

2. Add vinegar, oil, salt, and black pepper to taste. Add cilantro just before serving.

NUTRITION INFORMATION PER SERVING:

215 calories	3.7 g fat	0.5 g saturated fat
16% calories from fat	0 mg cholesterol	340 mg sodium
38 g carbohydrate	6 g protein	3.1 g fiber

Quinoa with Chicken

PREPARATION TIME: 20 minutes
COOKING TIME: 5 minutes
YIELD: 4 servings

QUINOA, A STAPLE in some South American countries, is a protein-rich grain available at many natural foods stores. This recipe makes an excellent light main course. It is also delicious served cold or at room temperature for a picnic or casual supper.

2 cups quinoa, rinsed well
3 tablespoons olive oil

1 red bell pepper, seeded and diced
2 green onions, chopped

➤

1 clove garlic, minced

1 15½-ounce can red kidney beans, drained

1 4-ounce can chopped green chilies, drained

2 cups skinless, boneless cooked chicken, diced

3 tablespoons fresh lemon juice

2 tablespoons minced fresh parsley

½ teaspoon salt

½ teaspoon freshly ground black pepper

¼ teaspoon ground cumin

¼ teaspoon ground coriander

1. Cook quinoa according to package directions. Drain well and set aside. Meanwhile, heat 1 tablespoon of the oil in a large skillet over high heat. Add bell pepper, green onions, and garlic. Cook, stirring frequently, until vegetables are crisp-tender, 2 to 3 minutes.

2. Stir in quinoa, kidney beans, chilies, and chicken. Cook, stirring frequently, until heated through. Stir in remaining 2 tablespoons oil, lemon juice, parsley, salt, pepper, cumin, and coriander. Serve hot or at room temperature.

NUTRITION INFORMATION PER SERVING:

685 calories	21 g fat	3 g saturated fat
27% calories from fat	60 mg cholesterol	830 mg sodium
85 g carbohydrate	42 g protein	15 g fiber

Polenta with Gorgonzola

PREPARATION TIME: 5 minutes

COOKING TIME: 5 to 7 minutes

YIELD: 2 servings

POLENTA, THE SOFTLY cooked Italian cornmeal, goes nicely with a grilled steak or any roasted meat. Here, it is lightly flavored with pungent but creamy Gorgonzola cheese. If you don't like blue cheeses, consider substituting a soft, creamy cheese flavored with herbs or truffles.

1½ cups water

¼ teaspoon salt

½ cup instant *or* quick-cooking polenta

2 teaspoons olive oil

½ ounce crumbled Gorgonzola cheese

Freshly ground black pepper

1. Heat water and salt to boil in a medium saucepan. Slowly whisk in polenta. Reduce heat to medium-low; cook, stirring often, until thickened, 5 to 7 minutes.

2. Add oil, Gorgonzola, and black pepper; stir briefly. Remove from heat. Taste and adjust seasoning; serve hot.

NUTRITION INFORMATION PER SERVING:

240 calories	10 g fat	3 g saturated fat
38% calories from fat	10 mg cholesterol	790 mg sodium
31 g carbohydrate	7 g protein	2.7 g fiber

SANDWICHES AND PIZZAS

Wheatberry Veggie Burger

PREPARATION TIME: 20 minutes
SOAKING TIME: 4 hours
COOKING TIME: 6 minutes
YIELD: 8 burgers

THIS MEATLESS "BURGER," developed in the *Tribune* test kitchen, has a hearty, pleasant flavor and chewy texture from the grains. Feel free to jazz it up further with cheese and onions. Wheatberries and flaxseed can be found in the health food sections of many grocery stores, at health food stores, or at bulk food stores.

1½ cups wheatberries
¼ cup ground flaxseed
½ cup brown rice
1 yellow onion, diced
1 large egg, lightly beaten
1 cup fresh whole wheat bread
    crumbs
⅓ cup peanut butter

3 tablespoons olive oil
3 tablespoons soy sauce
1½ teaspoons dried sage
½ teaspoon salt
¼ cup vegetable oil
Hamburger buns
Ketchup
Mustard

1. Soak wheatberries in cold water to cover at least 4 hours; drain well. Soak flaxseed 1 hour in 2 tablespoons water.

2. Cook brown rice according to package directions. Cool and set aside. Meanwhile, stir together wheatberries, flaxseed, rice, and onion in a medium-sized bowl. Combine egg, bread crumbs, peanut butter, oil, soy sauce, sage, and salt in a separate bowl; add to wheatberry mixture. Mix well. Form into 8 patties.

➤

3. Heat vegetable oil in a large skillet over medium heat. Cook patties until cooked through, turning once, about 3 minutes per side. Serve on buns with ketchup and mustard.

NUTRITION INFORMATION PER BURGER:

555 calories	24 g fat	4 g saturated fat
37% calories from fat	25 mg cholesterol	950 mg sodium
73 g carbohydrate	16 g protein	9 g fiber

Avocadowiches

PREPARATION TIME: 30 minutes

HEATING TIME: 10 minutes

YIELD: 4 servings

THE *TRIBUNE* TEST kitchen created this unusually fine sandwich that uses pita bread stuffed with a mashed avocado salad.

1 large, ripe avocado, peeled and pitted	1 small tomato, peeled, seeded, and chopped
1 tablespoon lemon juice	½ cup shredded cheddar cheese
1 2¼-ounce can sliced black olives, drained	Garlic salt
4 green onions, sliced thin	Hot pepper sauce
2 ribs celery, diced	4 rounds pita bread, halved
2 hard-cooked eggs, peeled and chopped	3 cups shredded iceberg lettuce

1. Mash avocado and lemon juice in a large bowl with a fork until well blended. Stir in olives, onions, celery, eggs, tomato, and cheese. Season with garlic salt and hot pepper sauce to taste. Cover; refrigerate (up to 2 hours).

2. Heat oven to 350°F. Wrap pita in aluminum foil; bake until hot, about 10 minutes. Evenly divide lettuce and avocado mixture among pita halves.

NUTRITION INFORMATION PER SERVING:

390 calories	19 g fat	5 g saturated fat
43% calories from fat	120 mg cholesterol	600 mg sodium
43 g carbohydrate	14 g protein	5 g fiber

Tex-Mex Egg Salad

COOKING TIME: 5 minutes
PREPARATION TIME: 15 minutes
YIELD: 4 servings

THOSE WHO MONITOR their cholesterol intake should take note of the egg option in this egg salad recipe from a story by Pat Dailey. Instead of using all whole eggs, try using more egg whites than yolks. All of the cholesterol in eggs is found in the yolks, while the whites are a good source of protein. You can use any proportion, from all whites to an equal balance of yolks and whites. Serve this on lettuce leaves, toast, or wrapped in a corn or flour tortilla. The salad can be served immediately or refrigerated overnight.

6 hard-cooked eggs *or*
   8 hard-cooked egg whites plus
   2 hard-cooked whole eggs
2 green onions, sliced thin
1 jalapeño *or* serrano chili, seeded
   and minced

¼ cup minced cilantro leaves
½ small red bell pepper, diced fine
¼ cup mayonnaise
1 tablespoon salsa
¼ teaspoon ground cumin

1. Peel eggs; mash coarsely with fork.
2. Add green onions, jalapeño, cilantro, bell pepper, mayonnaise, salsa, and cumin; mix well.

NUTRITION INFORMATION PER SERVING:

170 calories	13 g fat	3 g saturated fat
67% calories from fat	325 mg cholesterol	220 mg sodium
4.4 g carbohydrate	10 g protein	0.7 g fiber

Grilled Ham and Cheese Sandwich (Croque Monsieur)

PREPARATION TIME: 10 minutes
COOKING TIME: 5 minutes
YIELD: 2 servings

CROQUE MEANS "CRUNCH" in French, and crunchy the *croque monsieur* is. The sandwich can be found in two versions: *croque monsieur* and *croque madame*. The masculine version is the original. The *croque madame* is a lighter adaptation that leaves out the prosciutto completely or at least reduces the amount.

4 thick slices French bread
2 tablespoons butter, softened

►

8 slices Swiss *or* Gruyère cheese
  (about 4 ounces)
6 very thin slices prosciutto
  (about 2 ounces)
Dijon mustard
1 large egg

3 tablespoons milk
2 tablespoons butter
1 tablespoon vegetable oil
Tomato wedges
Cornichon pickles

1. Spread bread slices generously on one side with softened butter. Top 1 slice on buttered side with 2 slices of the cheese. Top cheese with 3 slices of the prosciutto. Spread prosciutto very lightly with mustard. Top with 2 slices of the cheese. Put second slice of bread buttered side down on top to form a sandwich. Repeat for second sandwich.

2. Whisk egg and milk together in a pie plate. Heat a large skillet over medium heat until hot. Add 2 tablespoons butter and oil to skillet; heat until butter is melted. Dip sandwiches in egg mixture; turn to coat. Let excess drain. Put sandwiches in skillet; reduce heat to low. Cook, turning once and flattening slightly with spatula, until golden brown on both sides and cheese is warm and slightly melted. Remove to plates; serve with extra mustard, tomato wedges, and pickles.

NUTRITION INFORMATION PER SERVING:

775 calories	61 g fat	32 g saturated fat
71% calories from fat	230 mg cholesterol	1,240 mg sodium
27 g carbohydrate	30 g protein	1.5 g fiber

Sweet-Hot Monte Cristo Sandwiches

PREPARATION TIME: 10 minutes

COOKING TIME: 5 minutes

YIELD: 4 servings

THIS REWORKED CLASSIC was a winning recipe in the Jones Dairy Farm annual Best Recipes of America's Bed and Breakfast Inns roundup. It comes from the Shore House at Lake Tahoe in Tahoe Vista, California. Sturdy and filling, the sandwiches need little more to round out the menu than a beverage and fresh fruit.

2 to 4 teaspoons sweet-hot mustard
8 slices sourdough *or* other bread
4 slices Muenster cheese (about
  ¾ ounce each)
6 slices Canadian bacon *or* lean
  ham rounds

8 to 12 thin apple slices
1 large egg, lightly beaten
2 tablespoons low-fat milk
1 tablespoon unsalted butter
2 to 3 tablespoons maple syrup
Confectioners' sugar

1. Spread mustard evenly over 1 side of 4 bread slices. Layer each slice with cheese, Canadian bacon, apple slices, and remaining bread slice. Beat egg and milk in a pie plate. Dip each sandwich in egg mixture, soaking until bread is moistened.

2. Melt butter in a large nonstick skillet over medium heat. Add sandwiches; cook, turning once, until golden and thoroughly heated. Cut into halves or quarters; drizzle lightly with maple syrup. Dust with confectioners' sugar.

NUTRITION INFORMATION PER SERVING:

370 calories	15 g fat	8 g saturated fat
37% calories from fat	100 mg cholesterol	1,035 mg sodium
38 g carbohydrate	20 g protein	2.3 g fiber

Aged Gouda and Chicken Grilled Cheese Sandwich

PREPARATION TIME: 5 minutes

COOKING TIME: 1 to 2 minutes

YIELD: 1 serving

OPEN-FACE CHEESE SANDWICHES—heated under the broiler to melt the central ingredient—are a favorite snack or lunch centerpiece. William Rice came up with this tasty combo for the Sunday *Chicago Tribune Magazine*.

1 ½-inch-thick slice rye bread
1½ teaspoons mustard
2 slices cooked chicken *or* turkey
    breast (about 3 ounces total),
    cut about ⅛ inch thick

1 teaspoon finely chopped slivered
    almonds, plus more for garnish
1 ounce aged *or* smoked Gouda
    cheese, sliced about ⅛ inch
    thick

1. Heat the broiler or a toaster oven. Lightly toast the bread on both sides. Spread mustard over one side of the bread. Place chicken on mustard, leaving a border. Sprinkle almonds over chicken. Cover chicken with Gouda.

2. Broil sandwich until chicken is heated through and cheese has melted and begins to brown. If desired, garnish with additional slivered almonds.

NUTRITION INFORMATION PER SERVING:

310 calories	14 g fat	7 g saturated fat
41% calories from fat	70 mg cholesterol	535 mg sodium
17 g carbohydrate	28 g protein	2.5 g fiber

Grilled Goat Cheese and Bacon Sandwich

PREPARATION TIME: 10 minutes
COOKING TIME: 3 minutes
YIELD: 2 servings

WILLIAM RICE DECIDED to doll up that old standby, the grilled cheese sandwich. Among his inventions was this simple one featuring goat cheese and crumbled bacon. No need to stop there, Rice advises, "Devise your own combinations such as cheddar flavored with horseradish, chipotle peppers, or other flavorful ingredients; or Brie with pepper or herbs."

1 individual French bread roll
   (about 7 inches long)
1 tablespoon olive oil
½ cup goat cheese, softened

2 strips bacon, cooked and
   crumbled
4 teaspoons medium-hot salsa

1. Heat the broiler. Cut roll in half lengthwise. Sprinkle olive oil evenly over each half. Combine goat cheese and bacon in a small bowl. Spread mixture evenly over each half. Spoon salsa on top.

2. Place bread in a broiler-safe baking pan. Broil until cheese is hot and begins to brown, about 3 minutes.

NUTRITION INFORMATION PER SERVING:

390 calories	30 g fat	13 g saturated fat
69% calories from fat	45 mg cholesterol	675 mg sodium
11 g carbohydrate	19 g protein	0.8 g fiber

Toasted Cheddar, Bacon, and Tomato Sandwiches

PREPARATION TIME: 20 minutes
COOKING TIME: 4 minutes
YIELD: 4 servings

EVERYONE HAS AN idea of what makes a perfect toasted cheese sandwich. The *Tribune* test kitchen came up with this formula to take advantage of some aged Wisconsin cheddar.

8 slices ½-inch-thick crusty,
   whole-grain *or* sourdough bread
Prepared honey mustard, optional
Fresh oregano leaves, optional

8 ounces bacon, cooked and drained
1 large tomato, sliced ¼ inch thick
8 ounces sharp cheddar cheese,
   sliced ⅛ inch thick

1. Heat oven to 350°F. Place bread slices on a baking sheet. Spread with mustard and dot with oregano leaves if desired. Top with bacon, tomato, and cheese.

2. Cook on top rack of oven until cheese is thoroughly melted, 4 to 5 minutes.

NUTRITION INFORMATION PER SERVING:

475 calories	30 g fat	16 g saturated fat
23% calories from fat	75 mg cholesterol	910 mg sodium
27 g carbohydrate	25 g protein	3.8 g fiber

Double-T BLT

PREPARATION TIME: 20 minutes

COOKING TIME: 10 minutes

YIELD: 4 servings

THIS YUMMY SANDWICH is doubly blessed with tomatoes: the fresh slices and the oven-dried tomatoes chopped into the mayonnaise. It was developed in the *Tribune* test kitchen.

½ cup mayonnaise

¼ cup finely chopped oven-dried tomatoes (see Note)

¼ cup chopped fresh basil *or* cilantro

Pinch ground red pepper *or* dash hot pepper sauce

12 thick slices smoked bacon

8 slices sesame semolina *or* other firm bread

4 leaves lettuce, such as leaf *or* Bibb

2 large tomatoes, sliced thin

8 fresh basil leaves *or* cilantro sprigs

1. Mix mayonnaise, dried tomatoes, chopped basil, and ground red pepper in a small bowl.

2. Cook bacon in a large skillet or on a foil-lined baking sheet in a 375°F oven until crisp. Drain well.

3. Spread mayonnaise mixture over one side of each bread slice. Top four of the slices with a lettuce leaf; divide tomato slices over lettuce. Top lettuce with 3 strips of bacon and 2 basil leaves. Cover each with 1 slice bread.

❧ NOTE: *To make oven-dried tomatoes, heat oven to 200°F. Cut 2 pints cherry tomatoes in half vertically (through the stem end). Lightly oil a foil-lined baking sheet. Place tomatoes on sheet cut side up in a single layer. Sprinkle lightly with salt. Put baking sheet into the middle of the oven and check occasionally until tomatoes are dried as*

➤

desired, usually about 6 hours for cherry tomatoes, 8 hours for small plum tomatoes, and up to 12 hours for round tomatoes. Cool and pack in a covered container and refrigerate up to 1 week or freeze up to several months.

NUTRITION INFORMATION PER SERVING:

740 calories	53 g fat	15 g saturated fat
65% calories from fat	70 mg cholesterol	1,470 mg sodium
40 g carbohydrate	25 g protein	3 g fiber

Chicken and Feta Sandwiches on Tomato Focaccia

PREPARATION TIME: 15 minutes

YIELD: 4 servings

COOKED CHICKEN BREASTS can come from leftovers, rotisserie chicken, or roasted chicken breasts from the meat case. Find pizzalike loaves of focaccia at most supermarkets. Or use any type of bread.

½ of a 1-pound loaf tomato focaccia

¼ cup regular *or* reduced-calorie mayonnaise

1 tablespoon fresh lemon juice

Pinch ground red pepper *or* crushed red pepper flakes

4 Boston *or* leaf lettuce leaves

4 large fresh basil leaves

8 ounces sliced cooked chicken breast

¼ cup crumbled feta cheese (1 ounce)

1. Cut focaccia into 4 wedges; carefully split each wedge in half horizontally.

2. Mix together mayonnaise, lemon juice, and red pepper; spread on bottom half of bread wedges. Layer each with lettuce, basil leaves, chicken, and feta cheese. Replace top of bread.

NUTRITION INFORMATION PER SERVING:

370 calories	18 g fat	4.7 g saturated fat
43% calories from fat	65 mg cholesterol	425 mg sodium
26 g carbohydrate	23 g protein	1.2 g fiber

Steak and Cheese Sandwiches

PREPARATION TIME: 15 minutes
MARINATING TIME: 8 to 12 hours
COOKING TIME: 5 minutes
YIELD: 6 servings

A PHILADELPHIA-STYLE CHEESE steak sandwich is difficult to find in Chicago. To help the situation, former test kitchen cook Beverly Dillon created this recipe.

½ cup cider vinegar
½ cup Italian salad dressing
1 clove garlic, minced
1 bay leaf
4 tablespoons vegetable oil
1 tablespoon soy sauce
¼ teaspoon freshly ground black pepper

1½ pounds beef flank steak
2 onions, sliced and separated into rings
2 green bell peppers, seeded and cut into ½-inch strips
6 French-style rolls
6 slices provolone cheese

1. Combine vinegar, salad dressing, garlic, bay leaf, 2 tablespoons of the oil, soy sauce, and black pepper in a large food storage bag. Add steak; seal. Turn so steak is covered with marinade. Refrigerate 8 to 12 hours.

2. Heat remaining 2 tablespoons oil in a large skillet over medium-high heat. Add onions and bell peppers; cook until crisp-tender. Remove with a slotted spoon to a small bowl; set aside.

3. Heat oven to 200°F. Cut rolls lengthwise; wrap in foil and place in oven until warmed through.

4. Remove steak from marinade; drain. Cut steak against the grain into ⅛-inch-thick strips. Add to skillet; cook, stirring often, over medium heat until rare, 1 to 2 minutes per side. Unwrap rolls. Divide steak slices evenly and place on bottom halves of rolls. Spread bell pepper mixture evenly over meat; cover each with slice of cheese.

5. Put rolls into the oven to melt cheese. Cover top with remaining half of roll. Brush the cut roll with some of the pan juices if desired.

NUTRITION INFORMATION PER SERVING:

470 calories	26 g fat	8 g saturated fat
50% calories from fat	70 mg cholesterol	580 mg sodium
27 g carbohydrate	32 g protein	2.6 g fiber

Open-Face Corned Beef and Cheese Sandwiches with Pickled Onions

PREPARATION TIME: 10 minutes

COOKING TIME: 3 minutes

YIELD: 4 servings

TRADITION DEMANDS THAT corned beef be part of the St. Patrick's Day feast. If it doesn't arrive in the form of a boiled dinner complete with cabbage, potatoes, and carrots, sandwiches are more than adequate as a time-wise substitute. Here the warm, open-face sandwiches are topped with mild, green-veined Derby sage cheese—an apt tribute to the holiday. Derby sage, an English cheese, is available at some large supermarkets as well as cheese and specialty shops. You may use other cheese instead. The pickled onions can be made several days ahead, covered, and refrigerated until ready to use.

½ onion, sliced paper-thin

2 tablespoons cider vinegar

2 tablespoons water

2 tablespoons sugar

Pinch crushed red pepper flakes

4 slices Irish soda bread *or* French bread

Mayonnaise

Spicy mustard

6 ounces thinly sliced lean corned beef

4 ounces Derby sage cheese, sliced thin

1. Combine onion, vinegar, water, sugar, and red pepper flakes in a small bowl.

2. Heat broiler. Drain onions. To assemble sandwiches, spread thin layers of mayonnaise and mustard on bread slices; top with a portion of drained onions. Top with corned beef and cheese.

3. Broil 6 to 8 inches from heat until sandwiches are heated through and cheese is melted, about 3 minutes.

NUTRITION INFORMATION PER SERVING:

435 calories	22 g fat	10 g saturated fat
44% calories from fat	80 mg cholesterol	865 mg sodium
43 g carbohydrate	20 g protein	1.9 g fiber

Chicken and Arugula Sandwiches with Tomato Pesto

PREPARATION TIME: 15 minutes
YIELD: 8 servings

ALTHOUGH THE RECIPE is written for small sandwiches, these flavorful ingredients can easily be adjusted for full-sized offerings if you prefer. Select an interesting and complementary bread or roll. Asiago cheese rolls are an excellent choice. Sun-dried tomato pesto is available at many supermarkets. Sun-dried tomato tapenade or basil pesto also can be used.

8 dinner rolls (1½ ounces each), halved
¼ cup light *or* regular mayonnaise
3 tablespoons sun-dried tomato pesto
24 arugula leaves

8 thin slices Vidalia onion
3 skinless, boneless cooked chicken breast halves, sliced diagonally
Salt
Freshly ground black pepper

1. Spread one half of each roll with mayonnaise and the other with tomato pesto.
2. Top bottom halves with arugula, onion, and chicken. Season chicken with salt and black pepper; add top halves of rolls.

NUTRITION INFORMATION PER SERVING:

185 calories	7 g fat	1.8 g saturated fat
36% calories from fat	30 mg cholesterol	250 mg sodium
17 g carbohydrate	14 g protein	1.2 g fiber

Chicken Sandwiches with Lemon-Basil Mayonnaise

PREPARATION TIME: 15 minutes
COOKING TIME: 4 minutes
CHILLING TIME: About 2 hours
YIELD: 4 servings

FORMER COLUMNIST BEVERLY Dillon developed this sandwich as the perfect choice for a picnic at the Ravinia Park summer concerts in Highland Park, Illinois. You might even strain the broth and save it for soup or other uses.

Lemon-Basil Mayonnaise
½ cup mayonnaise
1 tablespoon fresh lemon juice

2 tablespoons loosely packed fresh basil leaves
1 clove garlic, minced

➤

⅛ teaspoon salt
⅛ teaspoon freshly ground black
    pepper

Sandwiches
2 16-ounce cans chicken broth
¼ cup fresh lemon juice
¼ cup white wine
2 bay leaves
3 basil leaves
1 teaspoon dried tarragon

1 teaspoon salt
½ teaspoon freshly ground black
    pepper
¼ teaspoon crushed red pepper
    flakes
4 boneless chicken breast halves
4 croissants *or* French rolls, split
1 small head leaf lettuce
1 large ripe tomato, sliced thin

1. To make lemon-basil mayonnaise, combine mayonnaise, lemon juice, basil, garlic, salt, and black pepper in a small bowl. Cover; refrigerate until ready to use.

2. To make sandwiches, put broth, lemon juice, white wine, bay leaves, basil, tarragon, salt, black pepper, and red pepper flakes in a large nonreactive saucepan. Heat to boil over high heat. Add chicken breasts; be sure liquid covers chicken. Reduce heat to low; cover and simmer 4 minutes. Remove pan from heat. Keep chicken covered; let cool in broth.

3. Remove chicken from broth. Remove skin from chicken and discard. Slice meat thin; set aside.

4. Spread cut side of each croissant with lemon-basil mayonnaise. Arrange sliced chicken, lettuce, and sliced tomatoes evenly on croissants.

NUTRITION INFORMATION PER SERVING:

610 calories	37 g fat	12 g saturated fat
55% calories from fat	135 mg cholesterol	725 mg sodium
33 g carbohydrate	35 g protein	5 g fiber

Smoked Turkey and Chili Mayonnaise Smørrebrød

PREPARATION TIME: 25 minutes
YIELD: 6 servings

CULTURAL VARIATIONS ON the sandwich abound. Many of them do without the second slice of bread, such as the open-face sandwiches that the Danish call *smørrebrød*. The following small sandwiches would be ideal on any party buffet table.

¼ cup mayonnaise
½ teaspoon ground cumin
½ teaspoon chili powder

½ teaspoon tomato paste *or*
    1 teaspoon ketchup
¼ teaspoon cider vinegar

1 small clove garlic, minced, *or*
    ⅛ teaspoon garlic powder
Pinch ground red pepper
6 thin slices firm white bread
6 teaspoons unsalted butter,
    softened

6 ounces thinly sliced smoked
    turkey breast
6 slices ripe tomato
12 slices sweet pickle *or* 6 pickled
    okra, halved lengthwise

1.   Mix mayonnaise, cumin, chili powder, tomato paste, vinegar, garlic, and red pepper in a small bowl.

2.   Spread each bread slice with 1 teaspoon butter. Top each with 1 ounce smoked turkey, folding it to fit. Top each with 1 slice tomato and a dollop of chili mayonnaise. Top with pickle slices or okra halves. Cut sandwiches into wedges if desired.

NUTRITION INFORMATION PER SERVING:

230 calories	13 g fat	4.1 g saturated fat
51% calories from fat	29 mg cholesterol	540 mg sodium
20 g carbohydrate	8 g protein	1 g fiber

Taos Turkey Burgers

PREPARATION TIME: 15 minutes
COOKING TIME: 8 to 10 minutes
YIELD: 4 servings

THE FOURTH OF July means many things, fireworks and parades, stars and stripes—and celebrations. And certainly it means food, a great menu of summery tastes. Burgers are traditional, though in this rendition they take on new twists. Lean ground turkey replaces the beef, and a host of sassy Southwestern seasonings brings extra kick. For cool refreshment, try a big pitcher of Passion Fruit Margaritas (see Index) with the burgers.

1 pound ground turkey
1 serrano chili, seeded and minced
¼ cup green (tomatillo) salsa
¼ cup minced cilantro
3 tablespoons whipping cream
Salt

Freshly ground black pepper
4 hamburger buns
Cilantro leaves
Lettuce leaves
Sliced tomato
Sliced red onion

►

1. Prepare grill. Combine turkey, serrano, salsa, minced cilantro, and whipping cream and salt and pepper to taste in a mixing bowl; mix gently to combine. Shape into four patties.

2. Grill over medium fire until cooked through, 8 to 10 minutes, turning once. Add buns to grill during last minute to toast.

3. Place patties on bottom halves of buns; sprinkle with cilantro leaves. Add lettuce, tomato, and onion. Top with bun.

NUTRITION INFORMATION PER SERVING:

360 calories	17 g fat	6 g saturated fat
44% calories from fat	100 mg cholesterol	375 mg sodium
23 g carbohydrate	26 g protein	1.5 g fiber

Turkey Burgers with Chili-Bean Salsa

PREPARATION TIME: 10 minutes

COOKING TIME: 10 minutes

YIELD: 4 servings

SERIOUS BURGERS DON'T have to be beefy. This one is made of ground turkey and some sassy seasonings that get further support from a chili-bean salsa. Leave the seeds in the minced jalapeño or serrano chili if desired.

1 pound ground turkey breast	Ground red pepper
1 jalapeño *or* serrano chili, seeded and minced	1 14-ounce jar salsa plus more for serving
¾ cup minced cilantro	1 15½-ounce can hot chili beans, drained
⅓ cup finely shredded cheddar cheese	2 teaspoons chili powder
2 tablespoons half-and-half *or* whipping cream	Toasted rolls
½ teaspoon ground cumin	Lettuce leaves
Salt	Sliced red onion
	Sliced tomatoes

1. Combine turkey, jalapeño, ½ cup of the cilantro, cheddar, half-and-half, and cumin and salt and red pepper to taste in a bowl; mix to combine. Shape into 4 patties.

2. Prepare charcoal grill or heat a cast-iron griddle. Cook burgers, turning once, until no longer pink in the middle, 8 to 10 minutes.

3. Combine salsa, beans, and chili powder in a microwave-proof bowl; heat through. Stir in remaining ¼ cup cilantro.

4. Serve burgers on rolls with lettuce, onion, and tomatoes. Top with more salsa or serve on the side.

NUTRITION INFORMATION PER SERVING:

340 calories	15 g fat	6 g saturated fat
36% calories from fat	105 mg cholesterol	755 mg sodium
28 g carbohydrate	30 g protein	8 g fiber

Hamburgers with Green Peppercorns

PREPARATION TIME: 15 minutes
COOKING TIME: 10 minutes
YIELD: 4 servings

GREEN PEPPERCORNS AND freshly cracked black peppercorns combine to make a distinctively spicy burger in this recipe created by former test kitchen director JeanMarie Brownson. Pour a zinfandel wine with them.

2 pounds ground beef round	⅓ cup dry bread crumbs
2 small cloves garlic, minced	½ teaspoon freshly crushed black
¼ cup drained green peppercorns	peppercorns
1 large egg, beaten	¼ teaspoon ground nutmeg
1 tablespoon brandy	4 hamburger buns, split
1 tablespoon Dijon mustard	4 thick slices ripe tomato

1. Prepare charcoal grill or heat broiler. Stir together beef, garlic, green peppercorns, egg, brandy, Dijon, bread crumbs, black peppercorns, and nutmeg in a large bowl. Shape into 4 patties.

2. Grill or broil hamburgers 6 inches from heat source, turning once, until medium or desired doneness, 6 to 10 minutes. Serve on buns with tomato slices.

NUTRITION INFORMATION PER SERVING:

690 calories	36 g fat	13 g saturated fat
48% calories from fat	215 mg cholesterol	975 mg sodium
31 g carbohydrate	56 g protein	2.5 g fiber

Muffulettas

PREPARATION TIME: 20 minutes
CHILLING TIME: 8 to 12 hours
YIELD: 2 servings

THE SECRET TO this muffuletta (a layered sandwich on round Italian bread that is popular in New Orleans) is to make the olive oil dressing the night before and let the flavors marinate. The mixture will keep at least two weeks in the refrigerator.

6 tablespoons extra-virgin olive oil
¼ cup red wine vinegar
2 cloves garlic, minced fine
2 tablespoons finely chopped celery
2 tablespoons finely chopped pitted green olives
1 tablespoon finely chopped red onion
1 tablespoon finely chopped green *or* red bell pepper
1 tablespoon fresh lemon juice
¼ teaspoon dried leaf thyme
¼ teaspoon freshly ground black pepper
¼ teaspoon crushed fennel seeds
⅛ teaspoon ground red pepper
2 muffulettas *or* round Italian rolls
6 slices mortadella
6 slices capicola sausage
6 slices aged Swiss cheese
6 slices provolone cheese
2 large leaves leaf lettuce
10 *or* 12 thin red onion rings
8 slices tomato

1. Whisk together oil, vinegar, garlic, celery, olives, chopped onion, bell pepper, lemon juice, thyme, black pepper, crushed fennel, and red pepper in a small bowl. Cover; refrigerate 8 to 12 hours.

2. Slice rolls in half horizontally with a serrated knife. On the bottom of each roll layer 3 slices mortadella, 3 slices capicola, 3 slices Swiss cheese, 3 slices provolone, 1 lettuce leaf, 5 to 6 red onion rings, and 4 slices tomato.

3. Spoon 5 tablespoons of olive mixture over tomato slices on each sandwich. Cover with tops of rolls.

NUTRITION INFORMATION PER SERVING:

1,015 calories	73 g fat	31 g saturated fat
64% calories from fat	135 mg cholesterol	1,775 mg sodium
47 g carbohydrate	45 g protein	5 g fiber

Shrimp Poor Boys

PREPARATION TIME: 45 minutes
COOKING TIME: 5 minutes
YIELD: 6 servings

SPICY SHRIMP SANDWICHES with a chili sauce are the perfect main course for a casual company lunch or supper.

Sauce
¾ cup chili sauce *or* ketchup
1 tablespoon orange marmalade
1 tablespoon brown mustard *or* Dijon mustard
½ teaspoon Worcestershire sauce
2 to 3 drops hot pepper sauce

Sandwiches
6 rectangular sandwich rolls
2 large eggs
1 cup milk
1¾ cups all-purpose flour
¼ cup yellow cornmeal
1 tablespoon baking powder
1 teaspoon salt

1 teaspoon freshly ground black pepper
1 teaspoon ground red pepper
1 teaspoon paprika
1 teaspoon garlic powder
1 teaspoon onion powder
1 teaspoon dried oregano
½ teaspoon dried leaf thyme
¼ teaspoon dry mustard
16 ounces frozen small shrimp, thawed
1 cup peanut oil
3 tablespoons butter
1 head leaf lettuce, cored, washed, and dried

1. To make sauce, mix chili sauce, marmalade, mustard, Worcestershire sauce, and hot pepper sauce in a small bowl.

2. To make sandwiches, split rolls three-fourths of the way through; remove some of the bread from each side to make more room for filling.

3. Whisk eggs and milk in a small bowl until well mixed. Stir together flour, cornmeal, baking powder, salt, black pepper, red pepper, paprika, garlic powder, onion powder, oregano, thyme, and dry mustard in a large bowl until well mixed. Add shrimp; toss to coat. Transfer shrimp to a sieve or strainer; shake off excess flour mixture over the bowl.

4. Add shrimp to milk mixture. Turn to moisten all sides of shrimp. Drain liquid. Return shrimp to flour mixture. Toss with fingertips to coat again in flour mixture.

►

5. Heat oil and butter in a large skillet until temperature reads 300°F on an instant-reading thermometer. Add a few shrimp, shaking off any excess flour. Cook, turning often, until golden, about 1 minute. Remove with a slotted spoon. Drain on paper towels. Repeat until all shrimp are cooked.

6. Line rolls with lettuce. Divide shrimp evenly among rolls. Spoon on sauce.

NUTRITION INFORMATION PER SERVING:

715 calories	22 g fat	7 g saturated fat
27% calories from fat	160 mg cholesterol	1,360 mg sodium
100 g carbohydrate	30 g protein	6 g fiber

Italian Beef Sandwiches

PREPARATION TIME: 20 minutes

COOKING TIME: 50 minutes

YIELD: 8 servings

CHICAGOANS LOVE THEIR beef, especially in the following sandwich. Italian beef was developed in Chicago as an Italian twist to a French dip, and it's the city's answer to a Philly cheese steak sandwich. Though we've provided a recipe, Italian beef, like a Chicago-style hot dog, is best enjoyed straight off the waxed paper from a reliable neighborhood stand. An electric knife comes in handy here for slicing the meat paper-thin.

1 teaspoon crushed red pepper flakes	½ teaspoon salt
1 teaspoon garlic powder	1 small beef sirloin tip roast (about 2½ pounds)
1 teaspoon dried basil	1 cup cold water
1 teaspoon dried oregano	8 soft Italian rolls, warmed
1 teaspoon freshly ground black pepper	Pickled hot sport peppers *or* sliced green bell peppers

1. Heat oven to 450°F. Combine red pepper flakes, garlic powder, basil, oregano, black pepper, and salt in a small dish; rub half over all surfaces of meat, working some of it under the fat layer. Put meat in a shallow pan just large enough to hold it. Roast 15 minutes. Reduce oven temperature to 350°F; roast 20 minutes.

2. Remove pan from oven; add cold water to bottom of pan. Let stand several minutes until fat has solidified; remove and discard fat. Add remaining seasoning mixture to pan juices. Return meat to oven; continue roasting until cooked as desired, preferably rare (130°F on an instant-reading thermometer), 15 to 20 minutes. Remove to cutting board; let cool 20 minutes.

3. Slice meat in paper-thin slices. Heat pan juices if necessary; spoon over split rolls. Add meat and peppers to each split roll.

NUTRITION INFORMATION PER SERVING:

335 calories	10 g fat	4.4 g saturated fat
26% calories from fat	90 mg cholesterol	475 mg sodium
25 g carbohydrate	36 g protein	1.3 g fiber

Texas-Style Barbecue Sandwiches

PREPARATION TIME: 45 minutes
COOKING TIME: 3 hours
YIELD: 8 servings

BARBECUED SANDWICHES ARE a tradition across the South, where they're not just an entree—they're an event. This recipe is unusual in that it combines beef and pork. Try it for your next Super Bowl party. The cooking can be done up to three days in advance.

2 tablespoons all-purpost flour
2 tablespoons chili powder
1 teaspoon ground coriander
1 teaspoon ground cumin
1 teaspoon dried oregano
1 teaspoon paprika
1 teaspoon salt
1 teaspoon black pepper
1 lean beef chuck roast (about 2 pounds), cut in 1-inch pieces
1 large pork tenderloin (about 1¼ pounds), cut in 1-inch pieces
3 tablespoons vegetable oil

3 carrots, chopped
2 green bell peppers, seeded and chopped
2 cloves garlic, minced
1 large onion, chopped
1 28-ounce can crushed tomatoes in puree
1 13¾-ounce can beef broth
½ cup packed light brown sugar
½ cup ketchup
¼ cup minced cilantro *or* fresh parsley
8 hamburger buns, split and toasted

►

1. Mix flour, chili powder, coriander, cumin, oregano, paprika, salt, and black pepper in a large plastic food storage bag. Add beef and pork; seal bag. Shake to coat with seasoning.

2. Heat 1½ tablespoons of the oil in a 6-quart heavy saucepan or Dutch oven. Cook meat in batches over medium heat until well browned on all sides, using remaining oil if necessary. Set meat aside.

3. Add carrots, bell peppers, garlic, and onion to the same saucepan. Cook, stirring, over medium-high heat until onions soften, 6 to 8 minutes. Scrape up browned bits from bottom of pan.

4. Return meat to pan; add tomatoes, beef broth, brown sugar, and ketchup; heat to boil. Reduce heat; cover. Simmer gently, stirring occasionally, until meat begins to fall apart, about 1½ hours. Uncover; simmer until juices are thickened, about 1 hour longer.

5. Press meat to break it into shreds using the back of a wooden spoon or 2 large forks. Add cilantro. Serve on hamburger buns.

NUTRITION INFORMATION PER SERVING:

680 calories	32 g fat	11 g saturated fat
42% calories from fat	120 mg cholesterol	1,145 mg sodium
56 g carbohydrate	44 g protein	6 g fiber

Chicago-Style Hot Dog

PREPARATION TIME: 5 minutes
COOKING TIME: 5 minutes
YIELD: 1 serving

THE WELL-DRESSED CHICAGO red hot typically starts with a Vienna Sausage Company hot dog. All-beef, it has a natural casing that makes it snap when you take a bite. It's steamed over water (unless you've ordered a "char-dog") and cradled in a steamed poppy seed bun. Bright yellow mustard, never the dark stuff, is applied. Purists do not allow ketchup. Some vendors use celery salt, though some South Siders say celery salt is a North Side frippery. The proper pickle relish is an unnaturally vivid green. Here is what it takes to make one great Chicago-style hot dog.

1 all-beef hot dog in natural casing	1 tablespoon green pickle relish
1 poppy seed hot dog bun	1 tablespoon chopped onion
1 teaspoon yellow prepared mustard	3 sport peppers
	3 tomato wedges
Celery salt, optional	1 wedge kosher dill pickle

1. Place hot dog in steamer rack over boiling water; steam, covered, until hot, about 4 minutes. Add bun; steam 1 minute.

2. Place hot dog in bun. Top with mustard, celery salt if desired, pickle relish, onion, peppers, tomatoes, and pickle.

NUTRITION INFORMATION PER SERVING:

365 calories	20 g fat	8 g saturated fat
49% calories from fat	35 mg cholesterol	1,360 mg sodium
35 g carbohydrate	13 g protein	4.3 g fiber

Reuben Hot Dogs

PREPARATION TIME: 10 minutes
COOKING TIME: 1 to 2 minutes
YIELD: 8 servings

SAUERKRAUT IS THE key element here, providing the juicy tang that defines a Reuben sandwich or hot dog.

8 hot dogs	Dash hot pepper sauce
1 small onion, chopped	Salt
1 cup mayonnaise	Freshly ground pepper
3 tablespoons chili sauce	8 hot dog buns
1 teaspoon hickory-flavored barbecue sauce	1 16-ounce can sauerkraut, drained and rinsed
1 teaspoon Worcestershire sauce	½ pound sliced Swiss cheese

1. Cook hot dogs according to package directions. Meanwhile, heat broiler. Stir together onion, mayonnaise, chili sauce, barbecue sauce, and Worcestershire in a small bowl; season with salt and pepper to taste.

2. Put hot dogs on buns; spread sauce over. Top with sauerkraut and Swiss cheese. Broil until cheese melts, 1 to 2 minutes.

NUTRITION INFORMATION PER SERVING:

620 calories	49 g fat	17 g saturated fat
71% calories from fat	85 mg cholesterol	1,385 mg sodium
27 g carbohydrate	19 g protein	1.2 g fiber

Chicken Caesar Wrap

PREPARATION TIME: 20 minutes
YIELD: 2 servings

THIS ROLLED-UP SANDWICH calls for whole wheat tortillas, but any flexible bread wrapper will do the job. Consider *lefse*, nan, Syrian bread, or the ever useful pita rounds.

2 skinless, boneless cooked chicken
   breast halves, cut in strips
4 cups torn romaine lettuce
2 large plum tomatoes, diced
¼ cup bottled Caesar salad
   dressing plus more for serving

2 whole wheat *or* regular flour
   tortillas (about 10 inches in
   diameter)
¼ cup (1 ounce) shaved *or* grated
   Parmesan cheese
¼ teaspoon salt
¼ teaspoon freshly ground black
   pepper

1. Place chicken strips in a medium-sized bowl; season with salt and pepper. Add lettuce, tomatoes, and ¼ cup of the dressing. Toss to combine.

2. Divide chicken mixture between tortillas, placing filling on bottom quarter. Add Parmesan, salt, and black pepper. Fold the bottom edge up over filling; fold the two sides in toward the center, overlapping slightly. Serve with additional Caesar salad dressing.

NUTRITION INFORMATION PER SERVING:

580 calories	23 g fat	6 g saturated fat
37% calories from fat	105 mg cholesterol	1,375 mg sodium
47 g carbohydrate	44 g protein	5 g fiber

Paella Wrap

PREPARATION TIME: 20 minutes

COOKING TIME: 25 minutes

YIELD: 6 servings

WRAPS ARE GIVING traditional sandwiches a run for their money in the food-on-the-go sweepstakes. Anything that's flat and foldable, from tortillas, pita bread, rice papers, won ton skins, phyllo, *lefse*, even lettuce leaves, is being rolled around fillings equally diverse. Toast Restaurant in Chicago stuffs flour tortillas with a golden paella of shrimp, chicken, and sausage.

1 6-ounce box saffron rice

1 tablespoon olive oil

Ground red pepper

2 skinless, boneless cooked chicken breast halves, cut in strips

1 pound chicken sausage, cooked and sliced

10 medium-sized peeled and deveined cooked shrimp, split in half

4 plum tomatoes, diced

½ cup chopped cilantro, optional

½ cup mayonnaise

1 tablespoon fresh lemon juice

1 clove garlic, minced

6 flour tortillas (about 8 inches in diameter)

1. Cook rice according to package directions using 1 tablespoon olive oil in place of butter called for. Add ground red pepper to taste; cool to room temperature.

2. Combine rice, chicken, sausage, shrimp, and tomatoes and cilantro if desired in a medium-sized bowl. Toss well. Taste and add more ground red pepper if desired. Stir together mayonnaise, lemon juice, and garlic in another small bowl.

3. Warm tortillas if desired. Divide chicken mixture among tortillas, spooning it into bottom quarter. Top with lemon mayonnaise. Fold bottom edge over chicken mixture, and then fold the two sides in toward the center, overlapping slightly to close.

NUTRITION INFORMATION PER SERVING:

640 calories	35 g fat	8 g saturated fat
50% calories from fat	135 mg cholesterol	1,515 mg sodium
51 g carbohydrate	28 g protein	3 g fiber

Chicago-Style Stuffed Pizza

PREPARATION TIME: 45 minutes
COOKING TIME: 45 minutes
YIELD: 6 servings

ANOTHER CHICAGO WONDER, stuffed pizza, comes with the cheesy filling hidden inside a double layer of crust topped with tomato sauce. This version was developed by the *Tribune* test kitchen using Giordano's stuffed pizza as inspiration.

Crust
1 package active dry yeast
1¼ cups warm water (105 to 115°F)
1 tablespoon vegetable shortening, melted
2 tablespoons sugar
1 teaspoon salt
4¼ to 4½ cups all-purpose flour
Vegetable oil

Filling
1 10-ounce package mozzarella cheese, sliced thin
1½ pounds mild Italian sausage, casing removed

1 tablespoon vegetable oil
1 medium-sized onion, chopped
1 medium-sized green bell pepper, seeded
½ teaspoon salt
¼ pound fresh mushrooms, sliced

Topping
1 28-ounce can plum tomatoes, drained and chopped
½ teaspoon Italian seasoning
¼ teaspoon fennel seed
⅓ cup freshly grated Parmesan cheese

1. To make crust, dissolve yeast in warm water in a large bowl; let stand until bubbly. Add shortening, sugar, and salt. Stir in 2 cups of the flour. Stir in additional flour to form a soft dough. Turn dough onto a lightly floured surface; knead, working in more flour as needed until smooth and elastic, 8 to 10 minutes.

2. Divide dough into thirds. Set one-third aside, covered. Roll two-thirds of the dough together into a 14-inch circle. Lightly oil a 12-inch round pizza pan. Press dough circle evenly over bottom and up sides of pan.

3. To make filling, heat oven to 425°F. Layer half of mozzarella slices over crust. Crumble sausage onto mozzarella. Heat oil in a small skillet over medium-high heat. Add onion and green pepper; cook, stirring often, until tender. Add salt to onion mixture; sprinkle over sausage. Top with remaining mozzarella cheese and mushrooms.

4. To make topping, cook tomatoes, Italian seasoning, and fennel in a medium-sized saucepan over medium heat 10 minutes, breaking up tomatoes with a wooden spoon. Roll out remaining one-third of dough on a lightly floured surface to form a 12-inch circle. Set over filling in pan. Crimp edges of top and bottom crust together to seal well. Pierce top crust with a fork to allow steam to escape.

5. Spread tomato sauce topping over top. Sprinkle with Parmesan cheese. Bake until crust is golden, 45 minutes. Let pizza stand 10 minutes before serving.

NUTRITION INFORMATION PER SERVING:

785 calories	34 g fat	16 g saturated fat
39% calories from fat	85 mg cholesterol	1,725 mg sodium
84 g carbohydrate	36 g protein	5 g fiber

Chicago-Style Stuffed Spinach Pizza

PREPARATION TIME: 1 hour

RISING TIME: 1 hour

COOKING TIME: 1 hour

YIELD: 6 servings

FOR A SATISFYING vegetarian meal-in-one, try this spinach and mushroom–stuffed pizza, developed in the *Tribune*'s test kitchen.

Crust
2 packages active dry yeast
1 tablespoon sugar
2 cups warm water (105 to 115°F)
⅓ cup vegetable oil
4 to 6 cups all-purpose flour

Sauce
2 tablespoons olive oil
1 clove garlic, minced
1 28-ounce can crushed tomatoes
   in puree
2 teaspoons dried oregano
1½ teaspoons dried basil
¼ teaspoon salt
¼ teaspoon freshly ground black
   pepper

➤

Filling

3 10-ounce packages frozen chopped spinach, thawed and well drained

2½ cups shredded mozzarella cheese

8 ounces fresh mushrooms, sliced, optional

½ cup freshly grated Parmesan cheese

½ cup freshly grated Romano cheese

2 cloves garlic, minced

2 tablespoons olive oil

1 teaspoon dried basil

¼ teaspoon salt

¼ teaspoon freshly ground black pepper

1. To make crust, dissolve yeast and sugar in water in a large bowl; let stand until bubbly. Stir in oil. Stir in 4 cups of the flour until smooth. Add additional flour as needed to form a stiff dough. Lightly flour the work surface. Knead dough until smooth and elastic, 7 to 10 minutes. Put into a greased bowl. Turn to coat top. Let rise covered in a warm place until doubled, about 1 hour.

2. To make sauce, heat oil in a large saucepan over medium-high heat. Add garlic; cook 2 minutes. Stir in tomatoes, oregano, basil, salt, and pepper. Simmer until very thick, about 30 minutes.

3. To make filling, mix spinach, mozzarella, mushrooms, Parmesan, Romano, garlic, olive oil, basil, salt, and pepper in a large bowl.

4. Heat oven to 450°F. Punch down dough; let rest 10 minutes. Lightly oil a 12-inch pizza pan (at least 2 inches deep). Roll two-thirds of dough into a 16-inch circle. Fit into pan; let sides overhang.

5. Put spinach mixture into center of dough; smooth evenly over surface. Roll remaining dough on a lightly floured surface to a 12-inch circle. Place over filling. Crimp edges; cut excess dough at edges so bottom dough is level with top crust. Pour sauce over dough to cover. Bake until crust is golden, 20 to 40 minutes. Let stand 10 minutes before serving.

NUTRITION INFORMATION PER SERVING:

790 calories	38 g fat	12 g saturated fat
42% calories from fat	50 mg cholesterol	885 mg sodium
86 g carbohydrate	31 g protein	10 g fiber

Chicago-Style Thin-Crust Sausage Pizza

PREPARATION TIME: 25 minutes
COOKING TIME: 30 minutes
YIELD: 6 servings

FOR THOSE WHO like it thin, the *Tribune* test kitchen developed this recipe, using the pizza from Chicago's trusty Home-Run Inn as a model.

Crust
1 package active dry yeast
¾ cup warm water (105 to 115°F)
1½ teaspoons vegetable shortening, melted
1 tablespoon sugar
½ teaspoon salt
2 to 2½ cups all-purpose flour
Vegetable oil

Topping
½ pound mild Italian sausage, casing removed
1 medium-sized onion, chopped
1 medium-sized green bell pepper, seeded and chopped
1 8-ounce can pizza sauce
1 10-ounce package mozzarella cheese, sliced thin
⅓ cup freshly grated Parmesan cheese
¼ pound fresh mushrooms, sliced

1. To make crust, dissolve yeast in water in a large bowl; add shortening, sugar, and salt. Stir in 1 cup of the flour. Gradually stir in remaining flour to form a soft dough. Lightly flour a board. Turn dough out onto the board; knead until smooth and elastic, 7 to 10 minutes.

2. Heat oven to 425°F. Lightly oil a 14-inch pizza pan (at least ¾ inch deep). Roll dough to form a 16-inch circle. Fit into pizza pan. Crimp edges to form a slight rim.

3. To make topping, crumble sausage into a medium-sized skillet. Cook over low heat until cooked through, about 10 minutes. Remove sausage with a slotted spoon; set aside. Cook onion and pepper in the same skillet over medium-high heat until tender, about 5 minutes.

4. Spread pizza sauce over dough. Top with onion mixture, sausage, and mozzarella cheese. Sprinkle with Parmesan cheese and mushrooms. Bake until crust is golden, about 15 minutes.

NUTRITION INFORMATION PER SERVING:

425 calories	19 g fat	10 g saturated fat
40% calories from fat	55 mg cholesterol	725 mg sodium
42 g carbohydrate	21 g protein	2.9 g fiber

Prosciutto and Goat Cheese Pizzas

PREPARATION TIME: 30 minutes
RISING TIME: 1 hour
COOKING TIME: 10 to 14 minutes
YIELD: 3 8-inch pizzas

SOMETIMES THE TRICK to a good pizza is to let your imagination run wild, as in this prosciutto and goat cheese version. You can use prepared crusts from the supermarket if time is scarce.

Dough
1 package active dry yeast
1¼ cups warm water (105 to 115°F)
1½ teaspoons sugar
2 teaspoons olive oil
1½ teaspoons salt
3 to 4 cups all-purpose flour

Toppings
3 ounces prosciutto, julienned
1 tablespoon olive oil
3 ounces sliced mozzarella cheese

3 medium-sized tomatoes, seeded and diced
1 teaspoon coarse salt, preferably kosher
1 medium-sized red onion, julienned
1 medium-sized red bell pepper, seeded and julienned
6 ounces goat cheese, crumbled
6 fresh basil leaves

1.   To make dough, stir together yeast, ¼ cup of the water, and sugar in a large bowl; let stand until bubbly. Add oil and salt; stir well. Add 1 cup flour; stir until smooth. Stir in remaining 1 cup water. Add remaining flour 1 cup at a time, stirring until a dough forms. Flour the work surface. Turn dough out onto the surface; knead until smooth and elastic, about 10 minutes. Grease a bowl. Put dough into the bowl; turn once to coat top. Let rise covered in a warm place until doubled in size, about 1 hour.

2.   Heat oven to 475°F. Divide dough into three equal portions; pat or roll into 8-inch circles. Lightly grease 3 baking sheets. Place dough circles on the baking sheets. Toss julienned prosciutto with olive oil. Top dough circles each with (in this order) one-third of the mozzarella, tomatoes, salt, onion, bell pepper, prosciutto, and goat cheese. Bake until cheese has melted and crust browns around edges, 10 to 12 minutes. Top with basil leaves.

NUTRITION INFORMATION PER PIZZA:

1,015 calories	44 g fat	22 g saturated fat
40% calories from fat	80 mg cholesterol	2,565 mg sodium
108 g carbohydrate	43 g protein	6 g fiber

SEAFOOD

Grilled Cod with Moroccan-Spiced Tomato Relish

PREPARATION TIME: 15 minutes
COOKING TIME: 8 to 10 minutes
YIELD: 4 servings

THE MILD TASTE of cod is ideally suited to this preparation, although you can use other types of fish in its place. Consider walleye, sea bass, or halibut. Serve this summery dish with a white sangría.

4 cod fillets (about 6 ounces each)
3 tablespoons olive oil
Salt
Freshly ground black pepper
½ teaspoon ground cumin
½ teaspoon ground coriander

⅛ teaspoon ground red pepper
1 large clove garlic, minced
3 medium-sized tomatoes, seeded
   and diced
2 tablespoons orange juice
½ teaspoon salt

1. Prepare grill or heat broiler. Brush fillets with 1 tablespoon of the oil; season with salt and black pepper to taste. Grill or broil fish until done, 8 to 10 minutes. Heat remaining 2 tablespoons oil in a small skillet over high heat. Add cumin, coriander, and red pepper; cook until fragrant, 45 seconds. Add garlic; cook, stirring constantly, 15 seconds.

2. Transfer spice mixture to a medium-sized bowl. Add tomatoes, orange juice, and salt to taste. Stir gently to combine. Top hot fish with tomato mixture.

NUTRITION INFORMATION PER SERVING:

200 calories
50% calories from fat
6 g carbohydrate

11 g fat
45 mg cholesterol
19 g protein

1.6 g saturated fat
360 mg sodium
1 g fiber

Poached Halibut with Ginger-Sesame Glaze

PREPARATION TIME: 10 minutes

COOKING TIME: 10 minutes

YIELD: 4 servings

POACHING IS AN excellent way to prepare fish. Columnist Pat Dailey described it as "simple, quick and forgiving" in a "Fast Food" column. After poaching, the fish is topped with a wonderful Asian glaze. Salmon fillets, scrod, and walleye also are good choices for this simple preparation. Serve it with a crisp sauvignon blanc from California or New Zealand.

4 cups water

1 cup dry white wine *or* dry vermouth

2 tablespoons white wine vinegar

2 to 3 branches fresh herbs, such as parsley and thyme

Salt

Freshly ground black pepper

4 halibut fillets (5 to 6 ounces each)

1 tablespoon Asian flavored oil (such as lemongrass) *or* peanut oil

1 teaspoon sesame oil

1 clove garlic, minced

1 ¾-inch piece fresh gingerroot, minced

½ teaspoon reduced-sodium *or* regular soy sauce

½ teaspoon sesame seeds

3 tablespoons seasoned rice vinegar

1. To poach fish, combine water, wine, vinegar, herb branches, and salt and pepper to taste in a large shallow pan or skillet. Heat to boil over medium-high heat; cook 2 minutes. Reduce heat to low.

2. Add fish. Simmer gently, turning fish once with a large metal spatula, until opaque in the center, 8 to 10 minutes. Remove from poaching liquid and transfer to 4 serving plates. Discard poaching liquid.

3. Heat oils in the same pan over medium-high heat. Add garlic and gingerroot; stir-fry until fragrant, 45 to 60 seconds. Add soy sauce and sesame seeds. Stir well; pour in vinegar. Swirl sauce in pan briefly; spoon sauce over fish.

NUTRITION INFORMATION PER SERVING:

281 calories	22 g fat	5 g saturated fat
73% calories from fat	59 mg cholesterol	128 mg sodium
0.4 g carbohydrate	19 g protein	0.03 g fiber

Grilled Halibut with Mustard Cream Sauce

PREPARATION TIME: 20 minutes

GRILLING TIME: 6 to 10 minutes

YIELD: 4 servings

THIS RECIPE WAS created by the late Chicago chef Dennis Terczak, who prepared the simple but elegant dish for a U.S. Culinary Olympics fundraiser dinner in Geneva, Illinois. The fish also can be cooked under a broiler.

½ cup dry white wine

¾ cup whipping cream

1 to 2 tablespoons Dijon mustard

Salt

Freshly ground pepper

20 asparagus spears, trimmed

2 tablespoons vegetable oil

4 halibut fillets (6 to 8 ounces each)

1. Prepare grill. Heat wine to boil in a small saucepan over medium heat. Boil until reduced by half, about 10 minutes. Add whipping cream; heat to boil. Simmer 2 minutes; remove from heat. Whisk in mustard and salt and pepper to taste.

2. Place asparagus spears in steamer rack over boiling water; steam 5 minutes. Keep warm.

3. Brush one side of each fillet with oil; sprinkle with salt. Grill 6 inches from heat source 3 to 4 minutes; turn. Grill until fish barely flakes with fork, about 3 to 6 more minutes.

4. Put just enough sauce onto each serving plate to cover bottom. Arrange fish and asparagus on top of sauce.

NUTRITION INFORMATION PER SERVING:

526 calories

77% calories from fat

4.9 g carbohydrate

46 g fat

132 mg cholesterol

15 g protein

17 g saturated fat

244 mg sodium

1.3 g fiber

Red Snapper Firepot

PREPARATION TIME: 40 minutes
MARINATING TIME: 30 minutes
COOKING TIME: 40 minutes
YIELD: 6 servings

YOUNGHEE NA OF Chicago wowed the judges with this dramatic dish, then stood surprised as she was awarded first place in the 1985 *Tribune* Seafood Recipe Contest.

Meat
½ pound beef flank steak

Marinade
3 tablespoons soy sauce
2 teaspoons Asian sesame oil
2 teaspoons toasted sesame seeds
   (see Index)
1 green onion, minced
2 cloves garlic, minced
⅛ teaspoon sugar

Sauce
¼ cup soy sauce
2 tablespoons water
2 tablespoons rice vinegar
1 tablespoon dry sherry
1 tablespoon Asian sesame oil
1 tablespoon toasted sesame seeds

2 green onions, minced
2 cloves garlic, minced
1 teaspoon salt
½ teaspoon sugar
½ teaspoon crushed red pepper
   flakes

Firepot
8 large shrimp, peeled and
   deveined
½ pound fresh tofu, cut into
   2″ × 2″ × ⅔″ pieces
1 pound red snapper fillets, cut into
   2-inch pieces
12 large fresh clams, cleaned
1 small carrot, peeled and sliced
   thin, cooked until crisp-tender
6 green onions, cut diagonally into
   2-inch pieces

1. Cut steak lengthwise in half. Cut each half crosswise into strips as thin as possible, ⅜ inch thick at most. To make marinade, mix soy sauce, sesame oil, sesame seeds, onions, garlic, and sugar in a shallow bowl. Add meat; toss to coat well. Marinate at least 30 minutes.

2. To make sauce, mix soy sauce, water, vinegar, sherry, sesame oil, sesame seeds, onions, garlic, salt, sugar, and red pepper flakes in a small bowl; stir until salt and sugar are dissolved. Divide evenly into 6 small individual bowls. Set aside.

3. Heat a large, deep skillet or wok over medium heat. Coat lightly with vegetable oil if necessary. Add marinated beef; stir-fry until no longer pink. Add 3 cups water; heat to boil. Reduce heat to medium-low. Simmer covered 30 minutes.

4. Add shrimp, tofu, snapper, clams, and carrot, arranging ingredients snugly in groups. The liquid should barely cover the ingredients at this point; if not, add more water. Heat to boil. Adjust heat to medium-high; cook uncovered until fish flakes easily and clams have opened slightly, 5 to 7 minutes.

5. Add green onions, making room for them between ingredients; cook 30 seconds. Serve in 6 wide soup bowls. Pass sauce.

NUTRITION INFORMATION PER SERVING:

273 calories	11 g fat	2.6 g saturated fat
36% calories from fat	79 mg cholesterol	1,304 mg sodium
7.5 g carbohydrate	35 g protein	1.8 g fiber

Thai Whole Fried Red Snapper

PREPARATION TIME: 30 minutes

COOKING TIME: 20 minutes

YIELD: 2 servings

A RECIPE FOR delicious fried whole red snapper came from Chanpen Ratana, owner of the Thai Room restaurant in Chicago. She prefers to fry the whole fish in a deep fryer or deep kettle in a basket to keep the fish from falling apart. After frying, the oil can be strained and stored in an airtight container to use for cooking other fish.

¼ cup dried Chinese black mushrooms, sliced	2 tablespoons cold water
	4 green onions, sliced thin
1 whole (1–1½ pounds) red snapper, cleaned	1 small onion, chopped
	1 small carrot, peeled and slivered
Vegetable oil	½ jalapeño, seeded and slivered
2 tablespoons vegetable oil	¾ cup chicken *or* pork broth
2 cloves garlic, minced	2 tablespoons fish sauce (*nam pla*)
2 ounces ground pork	2 tablespoons sugar
1 1-inch-thick piece gingerroot, peeled and slivered	1 tablespoon soy sauce
	1 tablespoon brown bean sauce
1½ teaspoons cornstarch	

1. Soak mushrooms in hot water for 30 minutes. Meanwhile, score both sides of fish about ½ inch deep in a crisscross pattern with a sharp knife. Heat enough vegetable oil in a Dutch oven or deep fryer to 375°F to completely cover fish. Fry whole fish, turning occasionally, until skin is very crisp and golden brown, 10 to 15 minutes. Warm a platter. Drain fish on paper towels; put on the platter.

➤

2. Heat 2 tablespoons oil in a wok or large skillet over medium-high heat. Add garlic; cook, stirring often, until golden, about 4 minutes. Stir in pork, gingerroot, and mushrooms. Cook, stirring occasionally, until pork is no longer pink.

3. Dissolve cornstarch in cold water. Stir in onions, carrot, jalapeño, broth, fish sauce, sugar, soy sauce, bean sauce, and cornstarch mixture to pork mixture in skillet. Cook until vegetables are crisp-tender, 2 minutes. Pour over fish; serve.

NUTRITION INFORMATION PER SERVING:

317 calories	11 g fat	2.2 g saturated fat
31% calories from fat	23 mg cholesterol	2,816 mg sodium
36 g carbohydrate	19 g protein	5 g fiber

Grilled Fillet of Catfish with Dijon Mustard

PREPARATION TIME: 10 minutes
STANDING TIME: 30 minutes
GRILLING TIME: 6 minutes
YIELD: 4 servings

CATFISH IS CATCHING on because of its mild, white flesh. Instead of frying it in the Southern tradition, coat it with mustard and grill it. Using fruitwood or hickory chips will give it a lovely smoky flavor.

Fruitwood *or* hickory chips, optional	Salt
4 catfish fillets	Freshly ground black pepper
3 tablespoons Dijon mustard	Vegetable oil

1. Prepare grill. Soak wood chips in water at least 20 minutes. Brush each side of catfish fillet with ¾ tablespoon mustard. Let stand 30 minutes. Season with salt and pepper to taste.

2. Sprinkle wood chips over coals if desired; brush grill rack and grill basket lightly with oil. Put fish in the grill basket; grill 6 inches from coals 3 minutes. Turn; grill until fish almost flakes, 3 to 5 minutes.

NUTRITION INFORMATION PER SERVING:

213 calories	12 g fat	2.7 g saturated fat
52% calories from fat	69 mg cholesterol	362 mg sodium
1.3 g carbohydrate	24 g protein	0.1 g fiber

Cornmeal-Fried Catfish with Barbecue Sauce

PREPARATION TIME: 25 minutes
COOKING TIME: 10 minutes
FRYING TIME: 5 minutes per batch
YIELD: 6 servings

BEVERLY DILLON CREATED this recipe in the test kitchen for down-home catfish complete with a tangy homemade barbecue sauce. She served it with sweet potato hush puppies. A cold beer is the best liquid chaser for a fish fry. Sauce can be stored in the refrigerator up to two weeks.

Barbecue Sauce
½ cup ketchup
½ cup chili sauce
1 tablespoon orange juice
1 tablespoon yellow *or* Dijon
   mustard
1 tablespoon packed brown sugar
2 teaspoons lemon juice
2 teaspoons Worcestershire sauce
1½ teaspoons chili powder
¼ teaspoon ground red pepper
¼ teaspoon freshly ground black
   pepper

Catfish
2 large eggs
1 cup buttermilk
2 cups stone-ground yellow
   cornmeal
2 cups all-purpose flour
2½ teaspoons salt
1½ teaspoons paprika
1½ teaspoons onion powder
1 teaspoon ground red pepper
1 teaspoon freshly ground black
   pepper
1 teaspoon dry mustard
Vegetable oil
3 pounds catfish fillets

1. To make barbecue sauce, combine ketchup, chili sauce, orange juice, mustard, brown sugar, lemon juice, Worcestershire sauce, chili powder, ground red pepper, and black pepper in a small nonreactive saucepan. Heat to simmer over medium heat, stirring occasionally. Reduce heat to low; simmer 10 minutes.

2. To make catfish, beat eggs and buttermilk in a pie plate. Combine cornmeal, flour, salt, paprika, onion powder, red pepper, black pepper, and dry mustard in a second pie plate.

3. Pour oil to depth of about 2½ inches in a deep fryer or Dutch oven. Heat oil to 350°F. Dip catfish fillets into buttermilk mixture. Allow excess to drip off. Coat fillets in cornmeal mixture, pressing it firmly into fish; gently shake off any excess.

➤

4. Fry fish a few at a time until golden brown and crisp, about 5 minutes. Remove with a slotted spoon. Drain on paper towels; keep warm while frying remaining fish. Serve with barbecue sauce.

NUTRITION INFORMATION PER SERVING:

554 calories	30 g fat	6 g saturated fat
48% calories from fat	144 mg cholesterol	1,174 mg sodium
36 g carbohydrate	36 g protein	3.1 g fiber

Uptown Fish

PREPARATION TIME: 30 minutes
MARINATING TIME: 30 minutes
COOKING TIME: 10 minutes
YIELD: 4 servings

"EXCITING," AND "THE best aroma—you could smell this across the room," the judges said of the following Asian curry that William H. Schmit III of Chicago submitted and cooked in the test kitchen to win first place in the 1984 *Tribune* Seafood Recipe Contest. Schmit likes to serve this over rice pilaf flavored with saffron. Lemongrass, chili paste, fish sauce, and unsweetened coconut milk are available at most Asian or Thai grocery stores.

3 green onions	1 ½-inch-thick piece gingerroot, julienned
½ pound catfish, swordfish, *or* whitefish fillets, skinned, deboned, and cut in small pieces	⅛ teaspoon saffron threads
	1 tablespoon fish sauce (*nam pla*)
½ pound fresh shrimp, shelled and deveined	1 tablespoon Asian chili paste
	2 tablespoons peanut oil
2 stalks lemongrass, sliced thin (see Note)	1 medium-sized onion, minced
	½ cup unsweetened coconut milk
	1 small bunch cilantro, chopped

1. Cut tops off green onions and chop; set aside. Slice white part of green onions. Combine catfish, shrimp, the white part of the green onion, lemongrass, gingerroot, saffron, fish sauce, and chili paste in a large nonreactive bowl. Mix well. Cover; refrigerate 20 to 30 minutes.

2. Heat oil in a large skillet over high heat; reduce heat to low. Add minced onion; sauté slowly until transparent. Add fish mixture. Increase heat to medium; sauté until shrimp start to curl and just turn pink, about 2 minutes.

3. Add coconut milk; heat, stirring often, almost to a boil. Reduce heat; simmer 2 minutes. Sprinkle with cilantro and green onion tops.

❧ NOTE: *When preparing lemongrass for use in recipes, use only the inner portion of the stalk. The outside layers are too tough and dry to be edible. If you can't find lemongrass, substitute grated lemon zest, about ½ teaspoon for each stalk called for in the recipe.*

NUTRITION INFORMATION PER SERVING:

177 calories	9 g fat	1.8 g saturated fat
47% calories from fat	96 mg cholesterol	646 mg sodium
5.3 g carbohydrate	18 g protein	0.8 g fiber

Sea Bass with Buttered Hazelnuts

PREPARATION TIME: 20 minutes
COOKING TIME: 10 minutes
YIELD: 4 servings

DEVELOPED IN THE *Tribune* test kitchen, this recipe accompanied a story we called "Butter, Come Back." At the risk of being politically incorrect, we urged the return of the purest, sweetest, most indulgent ingredient on earth.

2 pounds sea bass *or* other white fish fillets, skin on	½ cup all-purpose flour
Salt	½ cup (1 stick) unsalted butter
Freshly ground black pepper	½ cup coarsely chopped hazelnuts
½ cup milk	Juice of 1 lemon
1 large egg	1 tablespoon chopped fresh parsley

1. Season fillets with salt and pepper to taste. Stir together milk and egg in a shallow bowl. Put flour on a plate. Dip fillets into milk mixture; place in flour to coat. Shake off any extra flour.

2. Heat butter in a large skillet over medium heat. Add fillets; cook 3 minutes. Turn; cook until fish is golden brown and flakes with a fork, about 4 minutes, depending on the thickness of fish.

▶

3. Remove fillets from pan; keep warm. Add hazelnuts to the same skillet. Cook, stirring constantly, until lightly browned, about 3 minutes. Stir in lemon juice and parsley. Taste and adjust salt and pepper; pour hazelnut mixture over fish.

NUTRITION INFORMATION PER SERVING:

533 calories	37 g fat	16 g saturated fat
62% calories from fat	171 mg cholesterol	153 mg sodium
10 g carbohydrate	40 g protein	1.2 g fiber

Sea Bass Provençale

PREPARATION TIME: 10 minutes
MICROWAVE COOKING TIME: 6 to 6½ minutes
YIELD: 4 servings

OLIVE OIL—a monounsaturated fat that is believed to help reduce cholesterol—is added to this light microwave recipe for flavor. You can eliminate the olive oil if you like. Serve it with steamed or sautéed fennel on the side.

1 16-ounce can plum tomatoes, drained and chopped	⅛ teaspoon salt
1 green bell pepper, seeded and julienned	⅛ teaspoon freshly ground black pepper
1 small onion, sliced ⅛ inch thick	4 sea bass fillets (about 1 pound total)
2 cloves garlic, minced	¼ teaspoon cornstarch
1 tablespoon olive oil	1 tablespoon cold water
¼ teaspoon dried oregano	¼ cup sliced black olives
¼ teaspoon sugar	

1. Mix tomatoes, green pepper, onion, garlic, olive oil, oregano, sugar, salt, and pepper in a 2-quart microwave-safe casserole. Cover tightly with plastic wrap, turning back a small corner to vent. Microwave on high (100 percent power) 2 minutes.

2. Push vegetables to the side in the casserole. Arrange fish in the casserole skin side down with the thickest portion to outside. If one end of a fillet is thin, tuck it under the meatier portion of the fillet. Spoon vegetables over fish. Cover tightly with plastic wrap, venting corner.

3. Microwave on high until fish is opaque and barely flakes with a fork, 3½ to 4 minutes. Drain juices into a 1-cup microwave-safe glass measure. Cover fish; set aside.

4. Dissolve cornstarch in cold water. Stir cornstarch mixture into juices. Microwave on high until sauce boils and thickens, about 30 seconds. Stir well. Pour sauce over fish and vegetables. Sprinkle with olives.

NUTRITION INFORMATION PER SERVING:

177 calories	7 g fat	1 g saturated fat
34% calories from fat	40 mg cholesterol	363 mg sodium
10 g carbohydrate	20 g protein	2 g fiber

Swordfish with Spicy Basil Butter

PREPARATION TIME: 15 minutes

GRILLING TIME: 10 minutes

YIELD: 4 servings

SWORDFISH IS SUCCESSFUL on the grill because of the meaty texture of the fish. For added flavor, this quick recipe adds jalapeño, garlic, and basil in a butter topping. For less saturated fat, you can substitute olive oil for the butter and make a sauce to pour over the fish.

¼ cup (½ stick) unsalted butter, softened
½ small onion, chopped
1 small clove garlic, minced
1 ⅛-inch-thick piece gingerroot, peeled and minced

¼ jalapeño, seeded and minced
1 tablespoon chopped fresh basil
4 swordfish fillets (about 8 ounces each)

1. Prepare charcoal grill or heat broiler. Put butter into the small bowl of an electric mixer. Beat until fluffy, about 2 minutes. Add onion, garlic, gingerroot, jalapeño, and basil. Mix well; refrigerate until needed.

2. Grill or broil fish 6 inches from heat source, until fish is opaque and begins to flake with a fork, 7 to 10 minutes. Put fish onto 4 serving plates; dollop with flavored butter.

NUTRITION INFORMATION PER SERVING:

295 calories	18 g fat	9 g saturated fat
55% calories from fat	92 mg cholesterol	141 mg sodium
1.3 g carbohydrate	31 g protein	0.2 g fiber

Seared Pepper-Crusted Tuna with Tomatoes and Balsamic Glaze

PREPARATION TIME: 10 minutes

COOKING TIME: 10 minutes

YIELD: 4 servings

SUMMER FOOD IS all about ease and freshness. This tuna recipe from a "Fast Food" column is quick to prepare. It is best when summer tomatoes are at their ripest. Serve it hot or at room temperature.

⅓ cup balsamic vinegar	2 tablespoons olive oil
1 branch fresh rosemary	½ lemon
Coarsely crushed black pepper	1 large tomato, diced
4 fillets fresh tuna (about 5 ounces each)	Salt

1. Boil vinegar with half of the rosemary branch until vinegar is reduced by half, about 3 minutes. Set aside. Press a light coating of pepper onto both sides of tuna fillets.

2. Heat 1 tablespoon of the oil in a large nonstick skillet over high heat. Add tuna; sear well on both sides. Continue cooking to desired doneness, 3 to 5 minutes. Squeeze lemon over fish; remove from heat.

3. Mince remaining rosemary. Toss with tomato; add remaining 1 tablespoon oil and salt and more black pepper to taste. Place tuna on 4 serving plates. Spoon tomatoes over each fillet; drizzle lightly with vinegar glaze.

NUTRITION INFORMATION PER SERVING:

208 calories	8 g fat	1.3 g saturated fat
36% calories from fat	57 mg cholesterol	54 mg sodium
6 g carbohydrate	27 g protein	0.5 g fiber

Melon Citrus Soup (page 103)

Angel Hair with Garlic and Arugula (page 116)

Fettuccine with Asparagus, Ham, and Herbed Cheese (page 110)

Couscous with Vegetables and Harissa Sauce (page 129)

Real McCoy Macaroni and Cheese (page 119)

Grilled Goat Cheese and Bacon Sandwich (page 140)

Photo by Bill Hogan

Photo by Bob Fila

Double-T BLT (page 141)

Chicken and Arugula Sandwiches with Tomato Pesto (page 145)

Paella Wrap (page 157)

Taos Turkey Burgers (page 147)

Photo by James F. Quinn

Grilled Cod with Moroccan-Spiced Tomato Relish (page 163)

Brazilian Seafood Stew (page 206)

Salmon over Sweet Onions and Cabbage
with Light Cream Sauce (page 184)

Photo by Bob Fila

Photo by Bob Fila

Tuna with a Black Sesame Crust (page 177)

Bourbon-Cued Shrimp (page 194)

Photo by James F. Quinn

Garlicky Clams in Paprika Dunking Broth (page 204)

Tuna Souvlaki

PREPARATION TIME: 25 minutes
MARINATING TIME: 2 hours
COOKING TIME: 8 minutes
YIELD: 4 servings

PAPAGUS RESTAURANT IN Chicago has updated a variety of classic Greek recipes. Here is its version of souvlaki, which uses tuna or swordfish threaded on skewers with vegetables. Rice flavored with balsamic vinegar and tomatoes makes a fine accompaniment.

4 tuna steaks *or* swordfish pieces (about 6 ounces each), cut in 1-inch chunks
1 red onion, cut in 1-inch chunks
1 large green bell pepper, seeded and cut in 2″ × ½″ pieces
4 plum tomatoes, quartered

Marinade
2 tablespoons finely minced red onion

2 tablespoons white wine
2 tablespoons fresh lemon juice
1 teaspoon olive oil
½ teaspoon minced garlic
½ teaspoon dried oregano
½ teaspoon salt
½ teaspoon crushed black pepper
¼ bay leaf, crushed fine

1. Skewer tuna chunks, red onion, bell pepper, and tomatoes on 9-inch-long bamboo or other skewers. Arrange skewers in a glass baking dish.

2. To make marinade, mix onion, wine, lemon juice, olive oil, garlic, oregano, salt, black pepper, and bay leaf in a small bowl. Pour over prepared skewers. Cover with plastic wrap; marinate in the refrigerator 2 to 8 hours, turning often.

3. Prepare grill or broiler. Place skewers about 6 inches from heat source; cook, turning once, brushing with marinade occasionally, until fish is just cooked through, 8 minutes. Serve hot.

NUTRITION INFORMATION PER SERVING:

189 calories	2 g fat	0.6 g saturated fat
10% calories from fat	68 mg cholesterol	134 mg sodium
8 g carbohydrate	33 g protein	2 g fiber

Tuna Fillets Creole

PREPARATION TIME: 30 minutes

COOKING TIME: 20 minutes

YIELD: 2 servings

BROILED FRESH TUNA sprinkled with herbs and spices is presented on a creamy mustard and horseradish sauce, then topped with chopped avocado. The idea, and the skills needed to cook it up in the *Tribune* test kitchen, earned Dorothy DeVries-Wolf of Palatine, Illinois, third place in the *Tribune's* 1986 Seafood Recipe Contest. Swordfish or halibut may be used in place of tuna.

1¼ cups fish stock *or* chicken broth	Salt
½ cup whipping cream *or* half-and-half	Freshly ground black pepper
	Fresh lemon juice
2 tablespoons Dijon mustard	Minced fresh thyme
1½ teaspoons prepared horseradish	Chopped fresh parsley
1 teaspoon ketchup	1 avocado, peeled and chopped
Vegetable oil	Fresh lime juice
2 fresh tuna fillets (about 6 ounces each)	

1. Put fish stock in a small nonreactive saucepan. Heat to boil over medium heat until reduced by half, about 10 minutes. Add cream. Boil until thick enough to coat the back of a spoon, about 5 minutes. Stir in mustard, horseradish, and ketchup. Keep warm.

2. Heat broiler. Lightly oil broiler pan. Lightly oil fish; sprinkle lightly with salt, pepper, lemon juice, thyme, and parsley. Broil 6 inches from heat source until an instant-reading thermometer registers about 130°F and fish barely flakes with a fork, 5 to 6 minutes.

3. Sprinkle avocado with lime juice. Place 2 tablespoons of the sauce in a small bowl; add avocado. Stir lightly. Divide remainder of sauce between 2 serving plates. Put fish on top of sauce; top with avocado mixture.

NUTRITION INFORMATION PER SERVING:

583 calories	43 g fat	17 g saturated fat
65% calories from fat	149 mg cholesterol	978 mg sodium
13 g carbohydrate	39 g protein	5.4 g fiber

Tuna with a Black Sesame Crust and Mixed Greens

PREPARATION TIME: 15 minutes

COOKING TIME: 7 minutes

YIELD: 4 servings

TUNA, WHICH THESE days is often served rare to raw, particularly benefits from the crunch and delicate flavor of sesame seeds. They turned up as a crust on a fillet of tuna at Chicago's Bongo Room restaurant.

Lemon Dressing
2 tablespoons fresh lemon juice
2 teaspoons chopped shallot
2 teaspoons chopped chives
2 teaspoons chopped green onion
¼ cup extra-virgin olive oil
¼ teaspoon salt
¼ teaspoon sugar
Freshly ground black pepper

Tuna and Greens
4 fillets center-cut ahi tuna (about
    4 ounces each)
½ teaspoon salt
Freshly ground black pepper
1 tablespoon vegetable oil
¼ cup black sesame seeds
Mixed salad greens

1. To make dressing, combine lemon juice, shallot, chives, and green onion in a small bowl. Whisk in oil in a very slow stream. Season with salt, sugar, and black pepper to taste. Set aside.

2. To make tuna, season fillets with salt and pepper; lightly coat with oil. Put sesame seeds on a plate. Coat top and bottom of fillets with seeds. Heat a large, dry skillet over high heat. Add fillets; cook about 3 minutes. Turn; cook until desired doneness, about 3 to 4 minutes for rare.

3. Divide mixed greens among 4 plates. Top each with 1 tuna fillet. Drizzle with lemon dressing.

NUTRITION INFORMATION PER SERVING:

284 calories	20 g fat	3 g saturated fat
64% calories from fat	39 mg cholesterol	469 mg sodium
5 g carbohydrate	20 g protein	3 g fiber

Grilled Trout with Chayote Slaw

PREPARATION TIME: 40 minutes
COOKING TIME: 6 minutes
YIELD: 4 servings

THIS SUMMER DISH is from the Biloxi Grill in Wauconda, Illinois. Both the sauce and the slaw can be made a day ahead if you like. Chayote, a green squash, and jicama, a crisp root vegetable, can be found in most supermarkets or Hispanic markets.

Slaw
1 ¼-inch piece gingerroot, peeled and minced
1 small clove garlic, minced
¼ cup mayonnaise
¼ teaspoon fresh lemon juice
⅛ teaspoon celery salt
⅛ teaspoon salt
2 carrots, peeled and julienned
1 chayote, peeled and julienned
½ small jicama, peeled and julienned
½ cup shredded red cabbage
½ cup julienned red bell pepper

Sauce
2 teaspoons roasted garlic puree (see Note)
1 ½-inch piece gingerroot, peeled and minced
½ cup mayonnaise
1 teaspoon soy sauce
¾ teaspoon fresh lemon juice
½ teaspoon sesame oil

Trout
4 fillets rainbow trout (8 ounces each), boned
1 tablespoon olive oil
¼ cup black sesame seeds *and/or* toasted white sesame seeds

1. To make slaw, stir together gingerroot, garlic, mayonnaise, lemon juice, celery salt, and salt in a small bowl. Set dressing aside (or refrigerate covered if not using immediately). Combine carrots, chayote, jicama, red cabbage, and bell pepper in a large bowl. Add dressing. Toss until vegetables are coated. Set aside or refrigerate covered if not using immediately.

2. To make sauce, mix roasted garlic, gingerroot, mayonnaise, soy sauce, lemon juice, and sesame oil in a bowl. Set aside.

3. To make trout, prepare grill or heat broiler. Coat fillets (and grill basket if using) lightly with olive oil. Grill in a grill basket or broil until firm and cooked through, about 5 to 6 minutes.

4. Make a bed of slaw on each of 4 serving plates. Place trout fillets on plates. Cover fillet with sauce; sprinkle with sesame seeds.

❧ NOTE: *To make a roasted garlic puree, remove as much of the papery wrap on a bulb of garlic as possible, leaving the cloves intact. Cut off the top of the bulb and sprinkle with olive oil. Wrap bulb in aluminum foil and bake in a 350°F oven until soft, 35 to 45 minutes depending on size of garlic bulb. Allow to cool slightly; squeeze pulp from bulb.*

Or, for a faster method, use roasted garlic paste found in a tube. It is available in most supermarkets. If you make the sauce ahead, cover and refrigerate until you're ready to use it.

NUTRITION INFORMATION PER SERVING:

638 calories	49 g fat	9 g saturated fat
69% calories from fat	123 mg cholesterol	524 mg sodium
15 g carbohydrate	34 g protein	7 g fiber

Pan-Roasted Stuffed Trout with Watercress Sauce

PREPARATION TIME: 30 minutes

COOKING TIME: 15 minutes

YIELD: 6 servings

IN THE KITCHEN, fresh trout's versatility is uncontested, though it hasn't won any popularity contests in recent years. For a story that we hoped would rectify that situation, chef Steve Permaul, then of Park Avenue Café, teamed cornbread-stuffed trout with a fresh watercress sauce.

Watercress Sauce
1 bunch watercress, washed and dried, large stems removed
1 teaspoon green peppercorns in brine
2 tablespoons chicken broth *or* water
2 teaspoons olive oil
Salt
Freshly ground black pepper

Stuffing and Trout
1 tablespoon butter

1 shallot, minced
¼ red *or* orange bell pepper, seeded and diced
2 cups dry cornbread cubes
¼ cup warm chicken broth *or* water
1 large egg
¼ cup diced cooked shrimp
1 tablespoon chopped parsley
¼ teaspoon salt plus more for seasoning flour
Freshly ground black pepper

➤

Hot pepper sauce

12 trout fillets, skin on

⅓ cup all-purpose flour

3 tablespoons vegetable oil

1. To make watercress sauce, fill a medium-sized saucepan half full with water; heat to boil. Fill a medium-sized bowl halfway with water and ice. Cook watercress in boiling water 30 seconds; drain. Immediately plunge into cold water to stop cooking. Drain. Combine watercress, green peppercorns, broth, olive oil, and salt and pepper to taste in a blender or in a food processor fitted with a metal blade. Puree; strain through a fine-mesh sieve. Add salt and pepper to taste. Set aside.

2. To make stuffing and trout, melt butter in a small skillet over medium heat. Add shallot and bell pepper; cook until soft, 2 to 3 minutes. Transfer to a medium-sized bowl. Add cornbread, broth, and egg to bowl; stir until combined. Stir in shrimp, parsley, salt, and pepper and hot pepper sauce to taste. Set aside to cool.

3. Heat oven to 375°F. Lay 6 fillets on the work surface. Spread stuffing evenly over each, ¼ to ½ inch. Cover each with one of the remaining fillets. Secure with a wooden pick if needed.

4. Season flour to taste with salt and black pepper. Dust exterior of fillets with seasoned flour. Heat oil in a heavy-bottomed, oven-proof skillet. Add fillets; cook until skin is crisp and caramelized, about 2 minutes. Turn each so caramelized side is up. Bake in oven until cooked through, 10 to 12 minutes. Place stuffed trouts in the center of plates; drizzle with sauce.

NUTRITION INFORMATION PER SERVING:

474 calories	21 g fat	5 g saturated fat
40% calories from fat	140 mg cholesterol	597 mg sodium
33 g carbohydrate	37 g protein	1.6 g fiber

Port Washington Fried Smelt

PREPARATION TIME: 20 minutes

COOKING TIME: 3 minutes per batch

YIELD: 6 servings

PORT WASHINGTON, WISCONSIN, is proud home of the World's Largest Smelt Fry, an annual event held at the local American Legion Post to honor the spring smelt season on Lake Michigan. The batter used to coat the fish for the Port Washington fry is a closely held secret. But a few details slipped out, and we grabbed them.

1⅓ cups all-purpose flour

1¼ to 1½ cups water or more as needed

1 cup beer
20 unsalted saltine crackers,
    crushed fine
½ cup yellow cornmeal

1 48-ounce bottle peanut *or*
    vegetable oil
2 pounds cleaned fresh smelt

1. Whisk together flour, 1¼ cups water, and beer in a large bowl until smooth. Add more water if needed to make a thin batter. Combine crackers and cornmeal in a pie plate.

2. Heat oven to 200°F. Heat oil in a heavy, deep saucepan over medium-high heat till temperature reads 375°F on an instant-reading thermometer.

3. Dip smelt a few at a time into beer batter, allowing excess to drip off; roll lightly in cracker mixture. Add smelt to hot oil in batches. Cook, turning occasionally, until crisp and browned on all sides, about 3 minutes. Remove with a slotted spoon; drain on paper towels. Keep fried smelt warm in oven while frying remaining smelt. Serve hot.

NUTRITION INFORMATION PER SERVING:

377 calories	16 g fat	2.5 g saturated fat
40% calories from fat	88 mg cholesterol	280 mg sodium
28 g carbohydrate	26 g protein	1.4 g fiber

Spicy Fried Smelt

PREPARATION TIME: 15 minutes
MARINATING TIME: 1 to 2 hours
COOKING TIME: 10 minutes
YIELD: 4 servings

JOHN HUSAR'S FAVORITE way of eating Lake Michigan smelt called for hot and spicy tomato juice cocktail. "Some people use beer, or even lemon-lime soda," said Husar, the *Tribune*'s late outdoors writer. "If you don't like the tomato juice flavor, you can soak the fish in cocktail mix for Bloody Marys. The result is super."

1½ pounds cleaned fresh smelt
1 cup hot and spicy tomato juice
    cocktail
1¼ cups buttermilk baking mix
¼ teaspoon salt

¼ teaspoon freshly ground black
    pepper
⅛ teaspoon garlic powder
Vegetable oil
¼ cup grated Parmesan cheese

➤

1. Put smelt in a large nonreactive bowl or in a plastic food storage bag. Pour tomato juice over smelt. Refrigerate covered or sealed 1 to 2 hours.

2. Stir together baking mix, salt, pepper, and garlic powder in a pie plate. Pour oil to depth of 1 inch in a large skillet. Heat until temperature reads 350°F on an instant-reading thermometer.

3. Heat oven to 200°F. Remove smelt from tomato juice; dredge in flour mixture. Fry in hot oil, turning occasionally, until crisp and golden, 3 to 4 minutes. Remove with a slotted spoon; drain on paper towels. Keep fried smelt warm in the oven while frying remaining smelt. Sprinkle with Parmesan cheese.

NUTRITION INFORMATION PER SERVING:

386 calories	22 g fat	4.6 g saturated fat
52% calories from fat	108 mg cholesterol	617 mg sodium
15 g carbohydrate	31 g protein	0.5 g fiber

Whitefish with Golden Tomato Butter Sauce

PREPARATION TIME: 25 minutes

COOKING TIME: 15 minutes

YIELD: 6 servings

FROM THE HEART of the Midwest comes this Great Lakes whitefish with golden tomato butter sauce, a tasty summer entree featured at Harlan (Pete) Peterson's Tapawingo restaurant in Ellsworth in northern Michigan. Out of season, use canned Italian plum tomatoes or red cherry tomatoes in place of golden tomatoes. Team the fish with new potatoes, assorted miniature vegetables, and a crisp chardonnay. To speed the process, cook the fish in two skillets at the same time.

1½ cups chopped golden tomatoes
¼ cup white wine vinegar
¼ cup fresh lemon juice plus more as needed
1 shallot, minced
¾ to 1 cup (1½ to 2 sticks) chilled unsalted butter, cut in ½-inch pieces
Salt
Freshly ground white pepper

Sugar
½ cup all-purpose flour
6 fresh whitefish fillets (8 to 10 ounces each) trimmed, pin bones removed
3 tablespoons olive oil
Golden cherry *or* pear tomatoes, optional
Snipped chives, optional
Minced red bell pepper, optional

1. Heat chopped golden tomatoes to boil in a small nonreactive saucepan. Simmer gently until reduced to ½ cup. Push pulp through a fine-mesh sieve. Reserve.

2. Heat vinegar, lemon juice, and shallot to boil in a separate nonreactive saucepan over medium heat. Cook until reduced to 2 tablespoons. Stir in tomato pulp.

3. Remove saucepan from heat; immediately beat in chilled butter one piece at a time until sauce is smooth and creamy. Season with salt, pepper, sugar, and additional lemon juice to taste. Do not allow sauce to boil; keep warm.

4. Spread flour on a large plate. Stir in salt and pepper to taste. Lightly coat fish fillets.

5. Heat oil in a large skillet over medium heat. Add fish in a single layer, skin side up. Cook 3 minutes. Turn; cook just until flesh is opaque and barely flakes with a fork, 3 to 4 minutes. Repeat with remaining fish, adding additional oil as needed.

6. Spoon tomato sauce onto 6 dinner plates. Put fillets on plates; garnish with cherry tomatoes, chives, and red pepper if desired.

NUTRITION INFORMATION PER SERVING:

604 calories	44 g fat	17 g saturated fat
65% calories from fat	202 mg cholesterol	131 mg sodium
6.5 g carbohydrate	46 g protein	0.5 g fiber

Skate Wing with Brown Butter and Oyster Mushrooms

PREPARATION TIME: 35 minutes
COOKING TIME: 22 minutes
YIELD: 6 servings

HALIBUT OR OTHER firm fish can be substituted for skate, if you wish, in this recipe adapted from John Bubala of Thyme restaurant. Bubala shared his recipe for a story on up-and-coming chefs in Chicago's West Loop neighborhood.

1¼ cups (2½ sticks) unsalted butter
2 tablespoons chopped fresh thyme
2 tablespoons fresh lemon juice
6 bone-in skate wing fillets
    (6 ounces each), washed and
    patted dry
½ teaspoon salt
Freshly ground black pepper

4 shallots, minced
3 cloves garlic, minced
8 ounces oyster *or* other wild
    mushrooms
24 medium-sized caper berries *or*
    3 tablespoons capers
Fresh chive strips

►

1. Heat oven to 400°F. Melt ¾ cup of the butter in a skillet over medium-high heat until butter begins to turn brown, about 10 minutes. Remove from heat, stir in thyme and lemon juice; set aside.

2. Season skate with salt and pepper to taste. Melt ¼ cup of the butter in a large oven-proof skillet (or divide between two smaller skillets) over medium heat. Add skate. Transfer skillet to oven; bake until fillets are lightly brown and cooked through, 10 to 12 minutes.

3. Melt remaining ¼ cup butter in a medium-sized skillet over medium heat. Add shallots, garlic, and mushrooms; cook until softened, about 5 minutes. Add caper berries; heat through 3 to 4 minutes. Reheat reserved browned butter mixture from step 1.

4. Place fillets on 6 plates. Spoon mushroom mixture and browned butter mixture equally over each fillet. Garnish with chives.

NUTRITION INFORMATION PER SERVING:

653 calories	60 g fat	29 g saturated fat
82% calories from fat	174 mg cholesterol	495 mg sodium
5 g carbohydrate	25 g protein	0.8 g fiber

Salmon over Sweet Onions and Cabbage with Light Cream Sauce

PREPARATION TIME: 30 minutes
COOKING TIME: 30 minutes
YIELD: 6 servings

FRESH SALMON FROM Ireland's icy streams can be some of the best in the world. This tender, poached salmon is a natural over a bed of sweet onions and cabbage. Developed by columnist Beverly Dillon as an alternative to corned beef one St. Patrick's Day, it was voted one of that year's ten best recipes by the food staff.

Bouquet Garni	1 bay leaf
2 sprigs fresh parsley	1 clove garlic, minced
2 teaspoons dried leaf thyme	6 whole black peppercorns

Cabbage

1 medium-sized head cabbage,
    cored and chopped coarse
1 large sweet onion, chopped
    coarse
2 8-ounce bottles clam juice
1 cup dry white wine

Fish

1 large fresh salmon fillet (about
    2 pounds)

4 tablespoons butter
Salt
Fresh ground black pepper

Sauce

2 cups whipping cream *or*
    half-and-half
1 tablespoon chopped fresh parsley
¼ teaspoon salt
¼ teaspoon freshly ground black
    pepper

1. To make bouquet garni, wrap parsley, thyme, bay leaf, garlic, and pepper-corns in cheesecloth. Tie the ends with string. Set aside.

2. To make cabbage, spread cabbage, onion, clam juice, wine, and bouquet garni in the bottom of a heavy-duty roasting pan that is large enough so salmon can lie flat. Cover the pan with a lid or with heavy-duty aluminum foil. Heat to boil on the stove; reduce heat to medium. Simmer until cabbage is crisp-tender, 4 to 5 minutes.

3. Lay salmon skin side down over cabbage mixture. Lightly salt and pepper salmon. Cover. Simmer over medium heat until fish is opaque and flakes easily with the tip of a small knife, about 10 minutes per inch thickness of fish.

4. Carefully remove salmon with a spatula to a serving platter. Discard bouquet garni. Strain cabbage mixture over a saucepan, reserving liquid. Return cabbage to the baking pan; add butter and salt and pepper to taste. Toss to mix. Spoon cabbage around salmon on the serving platter. Cover loosely with plastic wrap to keep it warm.

5. To make sauce, heat reserved strained liquid in the saucepan to boil. Reduce to ½ cup liquid, about 8 minutes. Stir in whipping cream. Return to boil. Cook until reduced and thickened slightly, 5 to 6 minutes. Remove from heat. Add parsley, salt, and pepper. Spoon some sauce over fish. Pass remaining sauce in a small bowl.

NUTRITION INFORMATION PER SERVING:

624 calories	49 g fat	25 g saturated fat
70% calories from fat	220 mg cholesterol	302 mg sodium
13 g carbohydrate	33 g protein	4.6 g fiber

Salmon in Pinot Noir Marinade

PREPARATION TIME: 20 minutes

MARINATING TIME: 30 minutes

COOKING TIME: About 7 minutes

YIELD: 2 servings

MARINATING MEAT, POULTRY, and fish before grilling is a tried-and-true technique for adding flavor and preventing foods from drying out. At Chicago's Harvest on Huron restaurant, chef Allen Sternweiler's marinade for salmon and red meats uses no oil at all, relying on pinot noir and herbs for flavor.

1 cup pinot noir	1 teaspoon peppercorns
2 shallots, peeled and sliced	2 salmon fillets
2 sprigs fresh thyme, chopped	2 tablespoons unsalted butter
1 tablespoon sugar	

1. Combine wine, shallots, thyme, sugar, and peppercorns in a nonreactive bowl. Pour over salmon fillets in a flat dish or in a plastic food storage bag. Cover or seal; refrigerate, turning several times, 30 minutes to 1 hour.

2. Heat oven to 350°F. Butter a baking dish big enough to hold fillets in one layer. Remove fillets from marinade; pat dry. Melt butter in a large skillet over high heat. Add fillets; sear, turning once, about 30 seconds per side. Bake in buttered baking dish until just cooked through, about 4 minutes.

❧ VARIATION: *After removing fish, add the leftover marinade to the hot skillet. Heat to boil; cook until reduced by two-thirds. Strain. Drizzle over fillets before serving.*

NUTRITION INFORMATION PER SERVING:

370 calories	24 g fat	9 g saturated fat
60% calories from fat	133 mg cholesterol	80 mg sodium
2.6 g carbohydrate	32 g protein	0.1 g fiber

Using Marinades

Always marinate food in nonreactive containers. Shallow glass or ceramic dishes or heavy self-sealing plastic bags are perfect.

Always refrigerate marinating food, covered.

Turn food frequently while marinating.

To avoid food poisoning, do not reuse marinades. Don't use leftover uncooked marinade as a sauce without first boiling it for at least 3 minutes to destroy any bacteria that may be present.

Do not overmarinate delicate foods such as seafood (no longer than 1 hour, and shrimp no longer than 30 minutes), boneless chicken breast and smaller cuts of veal and pork (no longer than 2 hours), and veal and pork (no longer than 4 hours). The acid in the marinade will break down the surface tissues. You may marinate larger cuts of beef, pork, lamb, venison, buffalo, and duck for 24 hours.

Slow-Baked Salmon with Cumin-Cayenne Dust

PREPARATION TIME: 10 minutes
COOKING TIME: 35 minutes
YIELD: 4 servings

SALMON IS NOT the first foodstuff that comes to mind when you're planning a menu for Cinco de Mayo, the Mexican holiday. But the rich fish takes well to a festive dusting of cumin and cayenne before baking in a very slow oven. Cooked this way, the fish is extraordinarily moist and succulent. For even cooking, select boneless fillets of equal size. Other types of fish can be substituted, such as sea bass or halibut.

2 cups kosher salt
1 teaspoon ground cumin
½ teaspoon light brown sugar

¼ teaspoon ground red pepper
4 salmon fillets (5 to 6 ounces each)

1. Spread salt in a shallow roasting pan just large enough to hold salmon. Put in oven; heat oven to 350°F. Combine cumin, brown sugar, and red pepper. Sprinkle over salmon, gently patting onto surface.
2. Reduce oven temperature to 225°F. Carefully arrange salmon over salt, placing salmon skin side down. Bake until just cooked in center, 25 to 30 minutes. Remove from salt bed with a spatula; carefully remove skin.

NUTRITION INFORMATION PER SERVING:

255 calories	13 g fat	2.3 g saturated fat
47% calories from fat	100 mg cholesterol	75 mg sodium
0.9 g carbohydrate	32 g protein	0.3 g fiber

Hoisin Sesame Salmon

PREPARATION TIME: 20 minutes

COOKING TIME: 12 minutes

YIELD: 4 servings

"IT'S TIME TO separate the good fats from the bad," wrote health and fitness writer Bob Condor in a "Good Eating" cover story. He went on to explain where to find the good fats that are beneficial to health: in foods such as avocados, olives, olive oil, nuts, seeds, tuna, sardines, and salmon. Alicia Tessling created this Asian-style recipe to go with the story. Look for Chinese hoisin sauce and sesame oil in the ethnic aisle of most supermarkets.

1 8-ounce package *udon* noodles	1 tablespoon canola oil
1 ½-inch piece gingerroot, minced	3 green onions, minced
¼ cup hoisin sauce	2 teaspoons sesame oil
4 skinless salmon fillets	¼ teaspoon salt
¼ cup sesame seeds	Freshly ground black pepper

1.   Cook *udon* noodles according to package directions; drain. Keep warm. Stir together gingerroot and hoisin sauce in a small bowl. Reserve 1 tablespoon of the mixture in another small bowl. Brush sauce over salmon fillets. Coat each fillet with sesame seeds.

2.   Heat canola oil in a large, heavy skillet over medium heat. Add fillets; cook, turning once, until seeds are browned and fish is cooked through, about 6 minutes per side.

3.   Toss noodles, reserved hoisin sauce, green onions, sesame oil, salt, and pepper to taste in a large bowl. Divide noodles among 4 plates; top each with a fillet.

NUTRITION INFORMATION PER SERVING:

545 calories	20 g fat	2.5 g saturated fat
34% calories from fat	85 mg cholesterol	555 mg sodium
51 g carbohydrate	38 g protein	6.9 g fiber

Braised Spring Salmon with Leek, Asparagus, and Morel Ragout

PREPARATION TIME: 40 minutes
COOKING TIME: 30 minutes
YIELD: 4 servings

UNLIKE SOME OTHER high-end mushrooms, such as shiitake and portobello, morels have been notoriously difficult to cultivate. But Terry Farms was one of the first companies to grow morels commercially, so we profiled the farm and gathered recipes, including this elegant spring dish from chef Mark Baker of Seasons restaurant in Chicago's Four Seasons Hotel.

Ragout
1 16-ounce can chicken broth
1 pound asparagus, cut diagonally
    into 1-inch pieces
2 tablespoons butter
4 ounces morel mushrooms, sliced
1 leek, sliced thin
1¼ cups white wine
3 large fresh basil leaves, chopped
Zest of ½ lemon
¼ teaspoon salt
Freshly ground black pepper

Salmon
2 tablespoons extra-virgin olive oil
4 salmon fillets (6 ounces each)
3 tablespoons chopped fresh chives
3 tablespoons chopped fresh thyme
½ teaspoon salt
Freshly ground black pepper
2 cups white wine
2 cups water
2 bay leaves

1. To make ragout, heat chicken broth in a small saucepan; simmer to reduce to ¼ cup. Set aside. Heat water in a large skillet to boil. Add asparagus; cook 1 minute. Drain. Melt 1 tablespoon of the butter in the same skillet over medium heat. Stir in asparagus, morels, and leek; cook 4 minutes. Add wine to reduced chicken broth; pour into skillet. Stir in basil, lemon zest, salt, and pepper to taste. Cook until sauce has thickened slightly and vegetables are tender, about 15 minutes. Stir in remaining 1 tablespoon butter. Keep warm.

➤

2. Meanwhile, to make salmon, heat oil in a large, heavy skillet over high heat. Season fillets with two tablespoons of the chives and 2 tablespoons of the thyme, salt, and black pepper to taste. Place fillets in skillet flesh side down; cook on high until lightly browned, about 2 minutes. Add white wine and water to cover fillets. Add bay leaves and remaining 1 tablespoon chives and 1 tablespoon thyme. Heat to slow boil over medium heat; reduce heat. Simmer gently 12 minutes. Place fillets on 4 individual plates; top with ragout.

NUTRITION INFORMATION PER SERVING:

462 calories	27 g fat	7 g saturated fat
52% calories from fat	117 mg cholesterol	1,387 mg sodium
10 g carbohydrate	38 g protein	2.5 g fiber

More on Morels

To handle morels and most wild mushrooms:

> *Keep morels refrigerated until you're ready to use them. Morels should keep about 3 days.*

> *Wild morel mushrooms are likely to hide a fair amount of dirt and small bugs in their honeycomblike heads. Rinse them in cold water and pat them dry. Don't soak them for too long; it will diminish their flavor.*

> *Morels should always be cooked; eating them raw is not recommended.*

> *Don't overpower morels' gentle flavor. French cooks combine them with cream sauces or with white wine, broths, and butter. You can stuff the caps with pureed cheese.*

Terry Farms sells the fresh cultivated morel mushrooms only to restaurants and through wholesale companies. Mail-order sources for morels include Earthy Delights in Michigan. Prices and minimum orders vary with availability. Call 800-367-4709.

Coho Berteau

PREPARATION TIME: 20 minutes
COOKING TIME: 10 minutes
YIELD: 4 servings

TERRY ROY OF Chicago walked away with the first-place prize (a trip to France to study French cooking) in the 1986 *Tribune* Seafood Recipe Contest. Her winning recipe? An elegantly simple treatment for coho salmon. Whole baby coho salmon or rainbow trout may be used instead of fillets; cooking time will be slightly longer.

1 avocado, peeled and chopped fine	2 tablespoons vegetable oil
1 roasted red bell pepper (see Index), peeled, seeded, and julienned	1 pound baby coho fillets
	6 pea pods, julienned
Juice of ½ lemon	Seasoned salt
⅓ cup butter	Freshly ground pepper

1. Heat avocado, bell pepper, lemon juice, and butter in a small saucepan over medium-low heat until barely warm.

2. Heat oil in a large skillet over medium-high heat; add salmon and pea pods. Cook until fish almost flakes, about 2 minutes per side. Remove to a serving platter. Season with salt and pepper. Spoon avocado mixture over fish.

NUTRITION INFORMATION PER SERVING:

423 calories	34 g fat	13 g saturated fat
71% calories from fat	94 mg cholesterol	218 mg sodium
6.6 g carbohydrate	24 g protein	3.3 g fiber

Stir-Fried Shrimp on Rice

PREPARATION TIME: 15 minutes
COOKING TIME: 15 minutes
YIELD: 4 servings

THE *TRIBUNE* TEST kitchen developed this stir-fry recipe for cooks who are in a hurry. The cooking time is only fifteen minutes and the vegetables and shrimp can be prepared ahead.

1 tablespoon vegetable oil	1 ¾-inch-thick piece gingerroot, peeled and minced
4 green onions, sliced	

➤

1 clove garlic, sliced
1 6-ounce box frozen snow pea
    pods, thawed
1 small zucchini, sliced
1 small yellow squash, sliced
1 small red bell pepper, seeded and
    diced

1 pound medium-sized shrimp,
    peeled and deveined
1 to 2 tablespoons soy sauce
1 to 2 teaspoons Asian sesame oil
Cooked rice
Cilantro sprigs

1. Heat oil in a large skillet over medium heat. Add green onions, gingerroot, and garlic. Cook, stirring constantly, 1 minute.

2. Add pea pods, zucchini, squash, and bell pepper. Cook, stirring constantly, over medium-high heat until vegetables are crisp-tender, 2 to 4 minutes. Add shrimp; cook just until shrimp turn pink, 2 minutes.

3. Stir in soy sauce and sesame oil. Serve over cooked rice; garnish with cilantro.

NUTRITION INFORMATION PER SERVING:

173 calories	5.8 g fat	0.9 g saturated fat
30% calories from fat	161 mg cholesterol	443 mg sodium
10 g carbohydrate	20 g protein	3.8 g fiber

Garlic Prawns (Goong Kratiam Prik-Thai)

PREPARATION TIME: 10 minutes

COOKING TIME: 10 minutes

YIELD: 4 servings

ONLY A FEW ingredients are listed in this recipe from Arun's restaurant in Chicago, but don't let that fool you. The fish sauce and garlic add up to plenty of flavor for the shrimp.

¼ cup vegetable oil
3 cloves garlic, minced
1 pound prawns *or* large shrimp,
    peeled with tails left on and
    deveined

2 tablespoons fish sauce
    (*nam pla*)
½ teaspoon minced cilantro
¼ teaspoon freshly ground black
    pepper
¼ teaspoon white pepper

1. Heat oil in a large skillet over medium heat. Add garlic; cook and stir until garlic is translucent, 2 to 3 minutes.

2. Stir in shrimp, fish sauce, cilantro, black pepper, and white pepper. Cook over medium heat, stirring often, until shrimp is opaque, about 3 minutes.

NUTRITION INFORMATION PER SERVING:

196 calories	14 g fat	2 g saturated fat
66% calories from fat	135 mg cholesterol	850 mg sodium
1.3 g carbohydrate	15 g protein	0.1 g fiber

Shrimp de Jonghe

PREPARATION TIME: 30 minutes
COOKING TIME: 15 minutes
YIELD: 4 servings

SHRIMP DE JONGHE, a Chicago classic, has endured Prohibition police raids—which closed Henri de Jonghe's Monroe Street hotel and restaurant where the dish was created around the turn of the century—and modern low-fat eating trends. This simple-to-make recipe is a close approximation of the great-tasting original.

1½ quarts (6 cups) water	2 tablespoons dry sherry *or* white
½ small onion, sliced	wine
1 rib celery, halved	1½ cups coarse French bread
3 black peppercorns	crumbs
1 bay leaf	1 small shallot, minced
¼ teaspoon salt	2 cloves garlic, minced
1½ pounds large shrimp in shell	2 tablespoons minced fresh parsley
½ cup (1 stick) unsalted butter,	½ teaspoon sweet paprika
melted	⅛ teaspoon ground red pepper

1. Put water, onion, celery, peppercorns, bay leaf, and salt into large saucepan. Heat to boil over high heat. Add shrimp; cover and return to boil. Drain immediately.

2. Peel shrimp; put into large bowl. Add half of the melted butter and sherry. Toss to mix.

3. Heat oven to 400°F. Combine remaining melted butter and bread crumbs in small bowl. Stir in shallot, garlic, parsley, paprika, and red pepper.

►

4. Spoon half of the shrimp mixture into a buttered 1½-quart baking dish. Top with half of bread crumbs. Top with remaining shrimp mixture. Finish with remaining bread crumbs. Bake until crumbs are lightly browned, about 10 minutes.

NUTRITION INFORMATION PER SERVING:

472 calories	26 g fat	15 g saturated fat
50% calories from fat	264 mg cholesterol	586 mg sodium
31 g carbohydrate	27 g protein	1.2 g fiber

Bourbon-Cued Shrimp

PREPARATION TIME: 10 minutes

GRILLING TIME: 6 to 10 minutes

MARINATING TIME: 15 minutes

YIELD: 4 servings

FOR A CONTEST sponsored by Jim Beam, cooks were asked to come up with spirited renditions of grill fare. The winning recipe from Rick Szekely of Milwaukee flaunts great taste and summer style. It's a simple shrimp dish that cooks in just 6 minutes.

½ cup olive oil	1½ teaspoons dried basil
¼ cup bourbon	¼ teaspoon hot red pepper sauce
3 tablespoons chili sauce	1 clove garlic, minced
1 tablespoon Worcestershire sauce	¼ teaspoon salt
1½ teaspoons Bavarian mustard	1¼ pounds peeled shrimp
1½ teaspoons prepared horseradish	

1. Prepare grill or heat broiler. Combine olive oil, bourbon, chili sauce, Worcestershire sauce, Bavarian mustard, horseradish, basil, hot pepper sauce, garlic, and salt in a small bowl. Pour over shrimp in a medium-sized bowl; stir to coat. Let stand 15 minutes.

2. Thread shrimp on skewers. Cook over medium-hot coals or under broiler 4 minutes. Turn; cook until pink, 2 to 5 minutes.

NUTRITION INFORMATION PER SERVING:

154 calories	8 g fat	1.1 g saturated fat
46% calories from fat	168 mg cholesterol	247 mg sodium
0.4 g carbohydrate	18 g protein	0.04 g fiber

Kerala-Style Shrimp

PREPARATION TIME: 30 minutes
COOKING TIME: 15 minutes
YIELD: 4 servings

In December, the *Tribune* food staff picks their favorite printed recipes of the year. It's a chance to look back and remember the great recipes out of the hundreds they've tasted in the test kitchen. Freelance writer Colleen Taylor Sen included this curry recipe in a story about Kerala, in southwest India, in 1993. It was so simple and delicious that it easily made it to the best of the year list. Serve this with cooked basmati rice. Curry leaves are available in Asian markets.

1 tablespoon vegetable oil
2 small onions, sliced thin
2 teaspoons minced garlic
2 teaspoons grated gingerroot
2 teaspoons ground coriander
½ teaspoon cayenne pepper
½ teaspoon turmeric
1 14-ounce can diced tomatoes

1 14-ounce can unsweetened
   coconut milk
12 curry leaves, optional
2 pounds large shrimp, peeled and
   deveined
¼ teaspoon salt
Handful cilantro leaves, stems
   removed and chopped coarse
3 green chilies, sliced lengthwise

1. Heat oil in a large, deep skillet over medium heat. Add onions; cook, stirring, until transparent, about 4 minutes. Add garlic and gingerroot; cook, stirring, 1 minute. Stir in coriander, cayenne, and turmeric.

2. Drain about half of the juice from the tomatoes. Add tomatoes to onion mixture; cook, stirring, 2 minutes. Reduce heat to low; add coconut milk and curry leaves. Simmer 5 minutes. Add shrimp; heat to boil, reduce heat to low. Simmer until shrimp are cooked, about 3 minutes. Add salt. Garnish with cilantro and chilies.

NUTRITION INFORMATION PER SERVING:

219 calories	5 g fat	0.8 g saturated fat
23% calories from fat	269 mg cholesterol	673 mg sodium
10 g carbohydrate	31 g protein	1.4 g fiber

Chipotle Shrimp with Corn Cakes

PREPARATION TIME: 30 minutes
COOKING TIME: 8 minutes
YIELD: 6 servings

AN INVENTIVE USE of corn and chilies is this short stack of griddled corn cakes spread with a pureed chili butter and seasoned shrimp. It's from chef Jeff Drew of Coyote Café in Santa Fe, New Mexico. This also would make a fine brunch dish along with an avocado salad.

3 tablespoons unsalted butter
1½ pounds medium-sized shrimp, peeled and deveined (see Note)
½ cup (1 stick) unsalted butter, softened
3 canned chipotle chilies

Corn Cakes
¾ cup all-purpose flour
½ cup coarse cornmeal
½ teaspoon baking powder
½ teaspoon baking soda

1 teaspoon salt
1 teaspoon sugar
1¼ cups buttermilk plus more as needed
2 tablespoons melted butter
1 large egg, beaten
Kernels of 2 ears fresh corn
2 green onions, chopped

Garnish
2 green onions, chopped
1 cup salsa

1. Melt 3 tablespoons butter in a large skillet over low heat. Add shrimp; cook, stirring occasionally, until cooked through, about 4 minutes. Puree ½ cup butter and chilies in a food processor fitted with a metal blade or in a blender until smooth; set aside.

2. To make corn cakes, mix together flour, cornmeal, baking powder, baking soda, salt, and sugar in a medium-sized bowl. Whisk 1¼ cups buttermilk and melted butter together in another bowl; whisk in egg. Add liquid ingredients to dry; mix thoroughly. Puree ½ cup of the corn kernels in a food processor fitted with a metal blade or mash with the back of a spoon. Stir pureed corn, whole kernels, and green onions into batter. Add additional buttermilk if necessary to thin mixture.

3. Ladle corn batter onto a nonstick griddle or skillet over medium heat to form 3-inch cakes. Cook until golden brown on both sides, turning once, about 2 minutes per side.

4. Place 3 corn cakes on each serving plate. Divide shrimp among cakes; spread liberally with chipotle butter. Sprinkle with chopped green onions; serve salsa on side.

❧ NOTE: *Instead of cooking shrimp in a skillet, you can grill them. If so, omit the 3 tablespoons butter.*

NUTRITION INFORMATION PER SERVING:

472 calories	28 g fat	16 g saturated fat
53% calories from fat	266 mg cholesterol	841 mg sodium
32 g carbohydrate	24 g protein	2.2 g fiber

Sautéed Lobster with Couscous, Pancetta, and Tarragon

PREPARATION TIME: 30 minutes

COOKING TIME: 30 minutes

YIELD: 4 servings

THOUGH MANY DINERS prefer their lobster simply served with melted butter, this dish may change their minds. Adapted from an elegant entree served at Bacchanalia restaurant in Atlanta, this recipe teams the rich crustacean with couscous.

1 cup couscous	¼ pound pancetta, diced
2 live lobsters, about 1 pound each	1 tablespoon chopped fresh
1 tablespoon olive oil	tarragon
2 shallots, peeled and chopped	Salt
2 cups chicken broth	Freshly ground black pepper

1. Heat oven to 350°F. Place couscous on a jelly roll pan; toast until golden brown, about 10 minutes.

2. Fill a large pot or Dutch oven half full with water. Heat to boil over high heat. Add lobsters; cook 3½ minutes. Remove from water; let cool. Remove lobster meat from the shells; dice.

3. Heat olive oil in a heavy-bottomed saucepan. Add the shallots; cook until soft, about 4 minutes. Stir in the toasted couscous and the chicken broth; heat to a boil. Remove from the heat and cover. Let stand until the broth is absorbed and couscous is puffed, about 5 minutes.

➤

4. Heat a large skillet over medium heat; add the pancetta. Cook over low heat until the pancetta is almost crisp, about 5 minutes. Drain the fat, if desired. Add the lobster meat; toss and cook 2 minutes. Add tarragon; toss and cook 5 minutes. Stir in couscous; season with salt and pepper to taste.

NUTRITION INFORMATION PER SERVING:

291 calories	9 g fat	2.4 g saturated fat
29% calories from fat	21 mg cholesterol	611 mg sodium
36 g carbohydrate	15 g protein	2.2 g fiber

Lobster Salad with Avocado Mayonnaise

PREPARATION TIME: 30 minutes

COOKING TIME: 6 minutes

YIELD: 2 servings

FOR A VALENTINE'S Day entree, Fresh Start Bakery and Catering in Flossmoor, Illinois, shared this lobster salad recipe. A generous serving of gently simmered lobster tail with a dollop of avocado mayonnaise and a raspberry vinaigrette make an indulgent main course. Pour equally indulgent champagne for the perfect accompaniment.

Lobster
1¼ cups dry white wine
¼ cup raspberry-flavored liqueur
¼ cup water
1 leek, white part only, julienned
Juice of 1 lemon
1 large *or* 2 small lobster tails

Vinaigrette
⅔ cup walnut oil *or* vegetable oil
⅓ cup raspberry vinegar
¼ cup raspberry puree (see Note)
1 tablespoon sugar
¼ teaspoon white pepper

Salad
4 cups torn assorted salad greens
1 ripe avocado, peeled, pitted, and sliced
1 large grapefruit, peeled and sectioned
¼ cup shredded radicchio *or* red cabbage

Avocado Mayonnaise
½ ripe avocado, peeled
¼ cup mayonnaise
Salt
Freshly ground black pepper

1. To make lobster, put white wine, raspberry-flavored liqueur, water, leek, and lemon juice into a medium-sized saucepan. Heat to simmer over medium-high heat. Add lobster tails; return to simmer. Simmer until lobster is pink and meat is opaque, 4 to 6 minutes, depending on size. Drain; cool lobster. Remove meat from shells and slice into rounds.

2. To make vinaigrette, put walnut oil, vinegar, raspberry puree, sugar, and white pepper into a glass jar with a tight-fitting lid. Shake well.

3. To make salad, arrange salad greens on 2 serving plates. Arrange lobster rounds, avocado slices, and grapefruit sections over greens. Put a small pile of shredded radicchio in the center of salad.

4. To make avocado mayonnaise, mash avocado and mayonnaise in a small bowl. Stir in salt and pepper to taste.

5. Serve salad with a dollop of avocado mayonnaise in the middle. Drizzle with some of the raspberry vinaigrette. Pass remaining vinaigrette.

❧ NOTE: *To make raspberry puree, push ½ cup fresh or frozen raspberries through a fine-mesh sieve to extract the seeds.*

NUTRITION INFORMATION PER SERVING:

1,226 calories	119 g fat	14 g saturated fat
84% calories from fat	52 mg cholesterol	375 mg sodium
35 g carbohydrate	15 g protein	11 g fiber

Scallops in Tomato Butter Sauce

PREPARATION TIME: 30 minutes
COOKING TIME: About 2 hours
YIELD: 4 to 6 servings

WITH ITS TANGY tomato beurre blanc enhancing fresh scallops, this recipe won Susan M. Swett, of Glencoe, Illinois, second place in the 1984 *Tribune* "Food Guide" Seafood Recipe Contest. The judges particularly liked the taste and aroma from the garlic and tarragon vinegar and the perfectly textured sauce that just clings to the scallops. Serve with French bread to sop up the extra sauce. (Sauce may be made ahead through step 2. Refrigerate it covered a few days or freeze it up to six months.)

1 28-ounce can whole tomatoes	4 cloves garlic, peeled
8 shallots, peeled	6 sprigs fresh tarragon

➤

1 cup dry white wine

¼ cup white wine tarragon vinegar

1¾ teaspoons kosher salt

1 teaspoon sugar

½ teaspoon freshly ground black
   pepper

1 cup (2 sticks) unsalted butter,
   softened

1½ pounds bay *or* sea scallops,
   rinsed and patted dry

Chopped parsley

1. Combine tomatoes, shallots, garlic, tarragon, wine, vinegar, salt, sugar, and black pepper in a 2- to 2½-quart heavy nonreactive saucepan. Heat to boil over medium heat; reduce heat to low. Boil gently uncovered, stirring often, until thick and most of the liquid has evaporated, about 20 minutes.

2. Push mixture through a fine-mesh sieve into a 2-cup glass measure. Push through as much of the solids as possible to yield about 1¾ cups. (If you have more than 1¾ cups, return mixture to the saucepan and simmer until it's reduced to that amount.) Remove from heat.

3. Put ¼ cup of the sauce and ¼ cup of the butter in a large skillet; set aside.

4. Put remaining 1½ cups sauce in a small saucepan; heat to boil over medium-high heat. Reduce heat to low; cook, stirring often, until it's the consistency of tomato paste, about 1 hour. Watch carefully because sauce burns easily.

5. Vigorously beat in remaining 12 tablespoons butter 1 tablespoon at a time, removing pan from heat whenever butter appears to be melting rather than thickening or foaming. Remove from heat when butter is incorporated and sauce is thick and foamy.

6. Heat the skillet with reserved butter and sauce over high heat to boil. Add scallops; cook, stirring frequently, until scallops are opaque and tender, 2 to 5 minutes, depending on size. Do not overcook. Divide scallops evenly among serving plates using a slotted spoon to drain off liquid. Put a heaping tablespoon of sauce over scallops; sprinkle with parsley.

NUTRITION INFORMATION PER SERVING:

373 calories	33 g fat	19 g saturated fat
77% calories from fat	101 mg cholesterol	960 mg sodium
11 g carbohydrate	22 g protein	1.6 g fiber

Scallops with Lemon, Tarragon, and Tomatoes

PREPARATION TIME: 10 minutes
COOKING TIME: 6 minutes
YIELD: 4 servings

DESPITE ITS REPUTATION, French cookery doesn't have to be elaborate. Simple preparations are among the best that the cuisine has to offer, a point confirmed by this Easter dish from a "Fast Food" column. Seasonal asparagus is a good accompaniment, and for wine, try a Loire Valley Sancerre.

1 tablespoon extra-virgin olive oil
1 clove garlic, minced
1 pound bay scallops
¼ teaspoon salt
Freshly ground black pepper

1 tablespoon fresh lemon juice
3 tablespoons whipping cream
8 teardrop *or* cherry tomatoes, quartered
2 teaspoons minced fresh tarragon

1. Heat oil in a large skillet over low heat. Add garlic; cook until garlic begins to soften but does not brown, 2 minutes.

2. Increase heat to high; add scallops, salt, and black pepper to taste. Cook, stirring constantly, until scallops are cooked through, 1 to 2 minutes. Sprinkle with lemon juice; cook briefly.

3. Remove scallops with a slotted spoon. Add cream and tomatoes to liquid in pan; boil until tomatoes are warmed through and liquid has thickened slightly, 1 minute. Return scallops to pan; add tarragon. Cook 10 seconds. Taste and adjust seasoning.

NUTRITION INFORMATION PER SERVING:

140 calories	10 g fat	3 g saturated fat
61% calories from fat	33 mg cholesterol	385 mg sodium
3.8 g carbohydrate	10 g protein	0.4 g fiber

Pumpkin Seed–Dusted Scallops with Spaghetti Squash

PREPARATION TIME: 25 minutes
COOKING TIME: 40 minutes
YIELD: 4 servings

SEEDS OF ALL kinds add a concentrated burst of flavor and the faintest bit of oil to food. "No wonder more chefs are using seeds such as sesame, sunflower, or pumpkin in their cooking," wrote Kristin Eddy in an article about the trend. She included this wonderful scallop dish with pumpkin seeds that was then on the menu at the Blackhawk Lodge in Chicago. (You can cook the seeds in the oil the day before and then refrigerate them. Leaving seeds in the oil longer will give them a stronger flavor.)

½ cup extra-virgin olive oil
1 cup plus 2 tablespoons toasted pumpkin seeds
1 small spaghetti squash
¼ cup boursin *or* other creamy herb cheese
2 tablespoons grated Parmesan cheese

½ teaspoon salt
¼ cup fresh bread crumbs
Freshly ground black pepper
1½ pounds sea scallops, trimmed
2 tablespoons unsalted butter
2 large shallots, minced
1 tablespoon white wine

1. Heat olive oil and 2 tablespoons of the pumpkin seeds in a small saucepan over low heat; cook 30 minutes. Pour mixture into blender; blend until smooth. Strain and set aside.

2. Heat oven to 350°F. Cut squash in half lengthwise; remove seeds. Place squash in a baking pan cut side down. Pierce skin with a fork; bake until tender, 30 to 40 minutes. Remove flesh with a fork, shredding it into fine strands, into a medium-sized bowl. Add boursin, Parmesan, and salt; stir well. Keep warm.

3. Put remaining 1 cup pumpkin seeds, bread crumbs, and pepper to taste in a food processor fitted with a metal blade. Pulse until fine crumbs form; place on a plate. Coat scallops in seed mixture. Set aside.

4. Melt butter in a large skillet over medium heat. Add shallots; cook 1 minute. Stir in wine; cook until almost evaporated, about 1 minute. Add scallops; cook until golden brown on one side, about 2 minutes. Turn; cook until opaque inside, about 2 minutes, depending on size of scallops. Remove from pan.

5. Place squash mixture on 4 individual plates; top with scallops. Drizzle each with some of the pumpkin seed oil.

NUTRITION INFORMATION PER SERVING:

624 calories	48 g fat	13 g saturated fat
67% calories from fat	5 mg cholesterol	810 mg sodium
19 g carbohydrate	34 g protein	4.4 g fiber

Seed Sense

Look for various seeds at natural food and ethnic markets. Because the seeds contain oil, which gives them their flavor, they are perishable and should be purchased at stores that have a high product turnover. Store seeds in the freezer to prevent rancidity if buying in bulk, or buy small quantities.

In cooking, the flavor of seeds is brought out best when they are toasted. Simply shake raw, hulled seeds in a dry skillet over low heat until they color slightly. Be careful not to let the seeds burn.

The oil in seeds also will add fat to dishes, from 5 grams of fat per tablespoon of sesame seeds to 14 grams per tablespoon of sunflower seeds.

Mussels with Marinara Sauce

PREPARATION TIME: 45 minutes
COOKING TIME: 25 minutes
YIELD: 4 servings

INSPIRED BY THE herby, aromatic version of this dish at Italian restaurants, this recipe treats fresh mussels to a simmered marinara sauce. Serve the mussels over cooked pasta if desired. For a more formal presentation, remove mussels from shells before adding them to the sauce.

4 pounds fresh mussels, scrubbed
   and debearded
½ cup water
½ cup white wine
¼ cup olive oil

2 onions, chopped
3 cloves garlic, minced
1 28-ounce can Italian-style plum
   tomatoes with basil

▶

1 green bell pepper, seeded and
  diced

2 whole green hot finger peppers

¼ teaspoon dried basil

¼ teaspoon dried oregano

⅛ teaspoon sugar

⅛ teaspoon salt

⅛ teaspoon freshly ground black
  pepper

½ pound fresh mushrooms, sliced

3 tablespoons minced fresh Italian
  flat-leaf parsley

1. Scrub mussels clean under running water, using a stiff-bristle brush. Cut off stringy beard from shells with a knife or scissors. Put into a Dutch oven; add water and wine. Set aside.

2. Heat oil in a large skillet over medium-high heat until hot. Add onions and garlic; cook, stirring often, until golden brown, about 5 minutes. Stir in tomatoes, green pepper, whole finger peppers, basil, oregano, sugar, salt, and black pepper. Simmer, stirring often and breaking up tomatoes, 15 minutes.

3. Heat pan of mussels over high heat to boil. Cover pan tightly; cook just until mussels open slightly, 3 to 4 minutes. Do not overcook. Strain over a bowl to catch cooking liquid. Stir ½ cup of the cooking liquid and mushrooms into tomato sauce. Taste and adjust seasonings. Sprinkle with parsley.

4. Stir mussels into sauce. Serve with lots of napkins and eat with fingers, breaking open mussels and using shell to scoop up sauce.

NUTRITION INFORMATION PER SERVING:

366 calories	16 g fat	2.4 g saturated fat
36% calories from fat	13 mg cholesterol	1,319 mg sodium
47 g carbohydrate	15 g protein	10 g fiber

Garlicky Clams in Paprika Dunking Broth

PREPARATION TIME: 20 minutes

COOKING TIME: 5 minutes

YIELD: 6 servings

THE FOLLOWING RECIPE was developed in the *Tribune* test kitchen for a story that featured the many kinds of paprika. Spanish paprika is particularly prized by chefs for its robust flavor, but any kind of paprika, hot or sweet, will work well for this recipe.

2 tablespoons olive oil

1 medium onion, chopped fine

5 cloves garlic, chopped fine

3 pounds Manila clams *or* small
   littlenecks in shells, well rinsed
¾ cup dry white wine
1 cup fish *or* chicken broth
½ cup water

2 teaspoons Spanish paprika
5 sprigs parsley, chopped
2 teaspoons fresh lemon juice
Salt to taste
Crusty bread for serving

1. Heat oil in large skillet over high heat until very hot. Add onion; cook 2 minutes. Add garlic; cook 1 minute. Add clams and wine. Cook wine to reduce slightly, about 1 minute. Add broth, water, and paprika; cook until clams open. (Discard any clams that don't open.)

2. Add parsley, lemon juice, and salt. Divide clams into six bowls; pour broth over each. Serve with crusty bread for dipping.

NUTRITION INFORMATION PER SERVING:

145 calories	6 g fat	1 g saturated fat
37% calories from fat	40 mg cholesterol	190 mg sodium
6 g carbohydrate	16 g protein	0.6 g fiber

Soft-Shell Crabs with Walnut-Tarragon Vermicelli

PREPARATION TIME: 20 minutes
COOKING TIME: 10 minutes
YIELD: 2 servings

THIS TEST KITCHEN recipe combines sauteed soft-shell crabs served on a bed of vermicelli and toasted walnuts. It's rich and oh-so-satisfying.

¼ pound vermicelli noodles
6 tablespoons butter
⅓ cup coarsely chopped walnuts
¼ cup finely chopped fresh parsley,
   plus more for garnish
1 teaspoon dried tarragon
¼ cup all-purpose flour

¼ teaspoon salt
¼ teaspoon freshly ground black
   pepper
4 soft-shelled crabs, cleaned and
   rinsed
1 tablespoon fresh lemon juice
Lemon wedges

1. Cook vermicelli according to package directions until al dente. Drain. Melt 2 tablespoons of the butter in a large skillet over medium heat. Add walnuts; cook until lightly browned, about 1 minute. Add parsley and tarragon; toss to mix. Cook 1 minute. Add vermicelli; toss to mix. Keep warm.

►

2. Combine flour, salt, and pepper on a large, shallow plate. Dredge crabs lightly in flour mixture; shake off excess. Heat 4 tablespoons of the remaining butter in the same skillet until hot. Add crabs in a single layer. Cook over medium-high heat, turning occasionally, until crispy and browned, about 5 minutes. Sprinkle with lemon juice.

3. Divide vermicelli between 2 dinner plates. Top each with two crabs. Garnish with lemon wedges and parsley.

NUTRITION INFORMATION PER SERVING:

723 calories	48 g fat	23 g saturated fat
58% calories from fat	98 mg cholesterol	664 mg sodium
61 g carbohydrate	16 g protein	6 g fiber

Brazilian Seafood Stew (Mocqueca)

PREPARATION TIME: 35 minutes

COOKING TIME: 1 hour

YIELD: 12 servings

THIS SEAFOOD STEW comes from Brazil via the now-closed Chicago restaurant Rhumba. "It's a perfect main course for holiday entertaining," wrote William Rice in a December column. Serve the stew with cooked rice and slabs of corn bread or French bread. Recipe may be done ahead through step 2. Reheat to simmer before continuing.

8 cups water
4 pounds mussels, scrubbed and
   debearded
2 tablespoons olive oil
1 small Spanish onion, diced
2 small jalapeños, diced
10 cloves garlic, minced
1 16-ounce can pureed tomatoes
2 cups dry white wine

2 bay leaves
1½ cups coarsely chopped cilantro
⅛ teaspoon crushed saffron
   threads
Salt
Freshly ground black pepper
3 pounds assorted fish and
   shellfish, such as shrimp, squid,
   cod, snapper, and sea bass

1. Heat 8 cups water to boil in a Dutch oven. Add mussels. Cover; cook only until mussels have opened, 3 to 5 minutes. Drain broth through a sieve lined with cheesecloth into a large bowl. Shell mussels if desired; reserve. Return broth to pot; reduce to 6 cups over high heat. Reserve.

2. Heat oil in a separate saucepan over medium-high heat. Add onion, jalapeños, and garlic; cook, stirring occasionally, until soft, about 10 minutes. Add tomatoes; cook, stirring occasionally, until reduced by half. Add wine, reserved mussel broth, bay leaves, 1 cup cilantro, and saffron. Heat to boil; reduce heat to medium-low. Simmer 20 minutes. Season with salt and pepper to taste.

3. Add fish to stew; cook 5 minutes. Add shellfish; cook 3 minutes. Add mussels; heat through. Taste and adjust seasoning. Garnish with remaining ½ cup cilantro.

❧ NOTE: *To reduce the heat of chili peppers, such as jalapeños, remove and discard the seeds and veins.*

NUTRITION INFORMATION PER SERVING:

254 calories	6 g fat	1.3 g saturated fat
23% calories from fat	112 mg cholesterol	616 mg sodium
11 g carbohydrate	35 g protein	1.1 g fiber

MEAT

Grilled Porterhouse with Arugula

PREPARATION TIME: 5 minutes
COOKING TIME: About 14 minutes
STANDING TIME: 5 minutes
YIELD: 4 servings

CHEF JOE DECKER of the Wildfire restaurants in Chicago and Oak Brook says he frequently experiments with grilled dishes at home and at the restaurant. Here's his simple recipe for home-grilled steak.

1 beef porterhouse steak (about
   2 pounds)
3 cloves garlic, minced
2 teaspoons olive oil
12 black peppercorns, crushed
   (see Note)

2 teaspoons chopped fresh
   rosemary
Kosher salt
1 bunch (3 ounces) arugula
Lemon wedges

1. Prepare grill. Rub steak on both sides with garlic and olive oil. Season with black pepper to taste, rosemary, and salt to taste.
2. Grill steak to desired doneness, 7 to 8 minutes per side for medium rare. Remove from heat; cover and let rest, 5 minutes. Arrange arugula in a bed on a platter.
3. Carve steak against the grain. Place on bed of arugula and squeeze lemon over entire dish.

►

❧ NOTE: *Crushing peppercorns at home will add a fresher flavor to dishes than will using commercial crushed pepper. Simply place whole peppercorns on a paper towel on a cutting board and crush them with a heavy pan. Don't grind them into powder.*

NUTRITIONAL INFORMATION PER SERVING:

390 calories	22 g fat	7 g saturated fat
51% calories from fat	115 mg cholesterol	120 mg sodium
1.8 g carbohydrate	44 g protein	0.5 g fiber

Strip Steaks with Shallot-Pepper Relish

PREPARATION TIME: 20 minutes

COOKING TIME: 15 minutes

YIELD: 4 servings

"FAST FOOD" COLUMNIST Pat Dailey created this steak recipe for Father's Day. She did not specify, however, whether dad is meant to cook the steak as well as eat it.

4 beef strip steaks (6 to 8 ounces each)	1 red bell pepper, seeded and diced fine
2 tablespoons plus 1½ teaspoons extra-virgin olive oil	1 teaspoon dried basil
Coarsely crushed black pepper	1 teaspoon balsamic vinegar
¼ pound shallots, diced fine	2 tablespoons half-and-half *or* whipping cream
	¼ teaspoon salt

1. Prepare grill or heat broiler. Rub steaks with 2 tablespoons of the oil. Sprinkle with pepper. Set aside.

2. Heat remaining 1½ teaspoons oil in a heavy, medium-sized nonstick skillet over high heat. Add shallots and bell pepper. Cook, stirring frequently, until vegetables are tender and begin to brown at edges, 5 to 7 minutes. Add basil and vinegar. Reduce heat to medium; cook 1 minute. Stir in half-and-half; remove from heat. Season with salt and more black pepper to taste.

3. Grill or broil steak until cooked as desired, 6 to 7 minutes per side; sprinkle lightly with salt. Spoon several tablespoons relish over steaks.

NUTRITION INFORMATION PER SERVING:

310 calories	18 g fat	6 g saturated fat
53% calories from fat	75 mg cholesterol	220 mg sodium
7 g carbohydrate	29 g protein	1 g fiber

Japanese Beef with Soy Dipping Sauce

PREPARATION TIME: 25 minutes
MARINATING TIME: 30 minutes
COOKING TIME: 5 minutes
YIELD: 2 main course or 8 appetizer servings

THIS RECIPE, FROM the former Japanese restaurant Suntory in Chicago, offers contrasts in texture and temperature. This may be served as a summertime main course or a cocktail party hors d'oeuvre at any time of year. Daikon (Japanese radish) and wasabi (Japanese horseradish) powder are available at most Asian markets.

Marinade
2 tablespoons soy sauce
2 tablespoons rice vinegar
2 tablespoons sake
2 beef tenderloin filet steaks (each
    2 inches thick)
1 small daikon, peeled

3 tablespoons wasabi powder
Warm water

Dipping Sauce
3 tablespoons soy sauce
2 tablespoons sake
¼ teaspoon sugar
3 green onions, chopped fine

1. To make marinade, stir together soy sauce, rice vinegar, and sake in a small nonreactive bowl or large plastic food storage bag. Add steaks; cover bowl or seal bag. Marinate in refrigerator 30 minutes.

2. Cut daikon into very fine shreds with a grater or in a food processor fitted with a shredder blade. Mix wasabi powder with just enough warm water to make a thick paste. Arrange daikon and wasabi on serving plates.

3. To make dipping sauce, stir together soy sauce, sake, and sugar in a small bowl.

4. Heat broiler. Remove steaks from marinade; place on broiler pan. Broil 4 inches from heat source, turning once, 5 minutes. Do not overcook. Center of steaks should be very rare.

5. To serve, cut steaks into very thin slices. Arrange slices on serving plates. Sprinkle slices with green onion. Serve immediately with dipping sauce.

NUTRITION INFORMATION PER 1 MAIN-COURSE SERVING:

607 calories	38 g fat	15 g saturated fat
57% calories from fat	141 mg cholesterol	1,949 mg sodium
14 g carbohydrate	46 g protein	3.6 g fiber

Steak with Pepper (Filet au Poivre)

PREPARATION TIME: 10 minutes
COOKING TIME: 8 to 10 minutes
YIELD: 2 servings

COGNAC HAS A place in the kitchen as well as in the liquor cabinet. Less elegant, less expensive brandies are more economical for quantity cooking. But Cognac provides a haunting aroma and distinctive flavor nuance to this simple steak recipe from columnist William Rice. He suggests serving the steak with homemade french fries and a hearty red wine.

1½ tablespoons black peppercorns, crushed
2 beef tenderloin filet steaks (about 5 ounces each), room temperature
2 tablespoons vegetable oil

1 tablespoon butter
Salt
2 tablespoons Cognac
⅓ cup crème fraîche (see Index) *or* whipping cream
Watercress sprigs

1. Put crushed peppercorns onto a plate. Press filets into peppercorns, turning to coat both sides. Let stand 30 minutes.

2. Heat oil and butter in a heavy skillet over medium-high heat. Add filets when butter just begins to sizzle. Cook until crisp and dark brown on one side, about 5 minutes; turn. Salt filets. Cook, basting with pan juices, until still rare in center, about 4 more minutes.

3. Remove pan from heat; remove filets. Pour off grease in pan. Return steaks to pan. Put pan over medium heat; add Cognac. Carefully ignite Cognac with a long match. Gently shake pan over heat until flame dies. Transfer steaks to 2 plates or a platter. Keep warm.

4. Add crème fraîche to pan; heat to simmer over medium heat. Scrape browned bits from bottom of pan. Cook until reduced and slightly thickened, about 2 minutes. Taste and adjust seasoning. Pour sauce over filets; garnish with watercress.

NUTRITION INFORMATION PER SERVING:

638 calories	57 g fat	24 g saturated fat
80% calories from fat	155 mg cholesterol	142 mg sodium
4.4 g carbohydrate	28 g protein	1.3 g fiber

Steak Diane

PREPARATION TIME: 25 minutes
COOKING TIME: 10 minutes
YIELD: 2 servings

THE CONTINENTAL CLASSIC Steak Diane, as done by Hans Lautenbacher at Fond de la Tour restaurant in Oak Brook, Illinois, was included in a Valentine's Day cooking story by William Rice.

2 beef filets mignons (6 ounces each), cut in half crosswise
2 tablespoons Dijon mustard
4 teaspoons unsalted butter
3 large shallots, chopped fine
8 ounces thinly sliced mushroom caps
2 tablespoons brandy, Cognac preferred

1 bay leaf
½ cup red wine
¼ cup red wine vinegar
1 teaspoon chopped fresh thyme *or* parsley
Salt
Freshly ground black pepper

1. Coat filets with mustard. Melt 2 teaspoons of the butter in a large heavy skillet over medium-high heat. Add filets; cook until browned, 1 to 2 minutes per side. Stir in shallots and mushrooms. Cook, stirring often, until vegetables soften, 2 minutes.

2. Heat brandy in a small saucepan over medium heat about 30 seconds. Light with a long match; pour over meat. Gently shake skillet until flames die.

3. Cook filets to desired doneness. Remove to 2 plates; keep warm. Add bay leaf, wine, vinegar, and thyme and salt and pepper to taste to skillet. Heat to simmer over medium heat; cook until slightly thickened. Taste and adjust seasoning. Whisk in remaining butter until melted. Pour sauce over filets.

❧ NOTE: *Flaming alcohol need not be dangerous, especially if you follow these tips:*

- ∾ *Pour alcohol into a pan placed well away from the source of heat.*
- ∾ *Heat the alcohol before attempting to flame it.*
- ∾ *Light warm alcohol with a long kitchen match or a match held by tongs.*
- ∾ *Avert your face at the moment of igniting the alcohol.*
- ∾ *Be careful not to spill or splash the flaming alcohol.*
- ∾ *Flames burn blue and may be difficult to see in some dishes. Look from the side to check for flames.*

►

     ∾ *Once burning alcohol has been added to food, shake the pan or dish gently to burn off as much alcohol as possible.*

     ∾ *Remember, every kitchen should be equipped with a fire extinguisher.*

NUTRITION INFORMATION PER SERVING:

425 calories	22 g fat	10 g saturated fat
48% calories from fat	125 mg cholesterol	470 mg sodium
14 g carbohydrate	40 g protein	1.8 g fiber

Beef Barbecued Korean Style (Bul Goki)

PREPARATION TIME: 20 minutes

MARINATING TIME: 30 minutes

GRILLING TIME: 5 minutes

YIELD: 6 servings

SUGAR AND SPICE make a very nice treat in this recipe for Korean-style barbecue from Shilla restaurant in Chicago. To complete the menu, start with a noodle soup, grill some eggplant or zucchini to go with the beef, and offer fresh fruit and cookies for dessert. Hot bean paste can be purchased at Asian food markets.

6 beef rib-eye steaks (about 6 ounces each)	6 teaspoons sugar
6 small cloves garlic, minced	Freshly ground black pepper
6 tablespoons water	Lettuce leaves
6 tablespoons Asian sesame oil	Cooked rice
6 tablespoons soy sauce	Hot bean paste

1. Freeze meat until partly solid for easiest slicing, about 1 hour. Slice meat into thin strips large enough not to fall through grill or broiler pan grate.

2. Stir together garlic, water, sesame oil, soy sauce, sugar, and black pepper to taste in a nonreactive bowl or food storage bag. Add beef strips; cover or seal. Marinate, turning occasionally, about 30 minutes.

3. Prepare hibachi or grill or heat broiler. Drain marinade off beef. Grill or broil beef about 4 inches from heat source, turning once, until meat just begins to crisp yet remains juicy and pink inside, depending on thickness of meat, usually 2 to 4 minutes.

4. Immediately remove meat from grill to a large platter. Serve with lettuce leaves and rice. Drizzle meat with hot bean paste or additional soy sauce if desired.

❧ VARIATIONS: *For kalbi, Korean barbecued short ribs, substitute 2 ¼ pounds boneless beef short ribs. Save bones for another use. Cut meat into 1-inch cubes. Marinate as directed in step 2, but increase marinating time to 1 to 2 hours. Cook as directed in steps 3, 4, and 5. Grilling time will be slightly longer, but take care to keep meat slightly pink in the center to prevent toughening.*

NUTRITION INFORMATION PER SERVING:

434 calories	28 g fat	7.9 g saturated fat
60% calories from fat	101 mg cholesterol	1,117 mg sodium
7 g carbohydrate	36 g protein	0.1 g fiber

Spicy Mustard Beef Tenderloin
with Oven-Roasted Potatoes

PREPARATION TIME: 45 minutes
COOKING TIME: 45 to 50 minutes
YIELD: 6 servings

AN IMAGINATIVELY SEASONED roast can be the centerpiece of a special occasion meal. Serve it with smoked salmon to start and a watercress salad on the side. Châteauneuf-du-Pape or another Rhône red wine will not be overwhelmed by the peppercorns and mustard. You may store the spice mixture from step 1 of the recipe in a covered jar up to one week. You may prepare steak through step 3, refrigerate it covered up to one day, and then proceed.

1 teaspoon black peppercorns
1 teaspoon whole allspice
1 teaspoon sage leaves
1 teaspoon dried leaf thyme
1 teaspoon salt
2 tablespoons Dijon mustard
2 teaspoons green peppercorns,
    drained and mashed
1 trimmed beef tenderloin (about
    3 pounds)

1 to 2 thin pieces of beef fat (about
    ½ pound) to cover tenderloin
4 bay leaves
18 small red potatoes, peeled and
    halved
3 tablespoons butter, softened
2 to 3 tablespoons vegetable oil
½ cup dry red wine

1. Grind spices in a spice grinder, coffee mill, small food processor, or blender until finely ground.

➤

2. Stir together mustard and green peppercorns in a small bowl. Make a lengthwise cut down the center of tenderloin, cutting through two-thirds of tenderloin, using a very sharp knife. Lay tenderloin open like a book. Flatten slightly with a meat pounder.

3. Spread mustard mixture on cut side of meat. Sprinkle 1 teaspoon of the spice mixture over mustard. Roll meat back to its original shape. Lay beef fat over meat; top with bay leaves. Tie meat securely in several places with kitchen string to form a compact shape. Let stand at room temperature 1 hour before roasting.

4. Heat a large pot of water to boil; add potatoes. Cook 5 minutes; drain well. Pat dry.

5. Heat oven to 425°F. Rub outside of roast with softened butter. Press remaining spice mixture into butter. Put roast into roasting pan. Rub potatoes with oil and place around roast in the pan.

6. Roast, basting potatoes occasionally with pan juices, 6 to 8 minutes per pound for rare, or until a meat thermometer registers 130°F. Transfer meat and potatoes to a serving platter; let stand 10 minutes.

7. Set roasting pan over medium heat. Pour wine into pan juices. Cook, stirring frequently, scraping up browned bits from bottom of pan, until mixture boils. Remove from heat; skim off fat. Pour into a serving dish. Remove string and fat from tenderloin; slice meat thin. Pass pan juices.

NUTRITION INFORMATION PER SERVING:

528 calories	28 g fat	10 g saturated fat
48% calories from fat	157 mg cholesterol	682 mg sodium
16 g carbohydrate	51 g protein	2.7 g fiber

Goose Island's Beer-Braised Short Ribs

PREPARATION TIME: 30 minutes

COOKING TIME: 2½ to 3 hours

YIELD: 4 servings

As the number of intriguing beers in America increased, it became inevitable that chefs, borrowing from German and Belgian models, would start experimenting with them. For those not used to the concept, it may help to think of beer as a flavored liquid, just as wine and stock are flavored liquids. This recipe comes from a Chicago restaurant and brewery.

8 beef short ribs	1 cup all-purpose flour

Salt

Freshly ground black pepper

½ cup vegetable oil

2 tablespoons unsalted butter

4 large onions, chopped

4 cloves garlic, peeled and sliced

48 ounces (6 cups) brown ale

3 sprigs fresh thyme

2 bay leaves

2 tablespoons tomato paste

1½ quarts chicken *or* beef broth

Freshly grated horseradish,
    optional

1. Pat ribs dry with paper towels. Put flour on a plate or in a shallow soup dish; season generously with salt and pepper. Coat ribs in seasoned flour; set aside.

2. Heat oil in a large skillet over medium-high heat until hot. Cook ribs in batches, browning all sides, about 10 minutes per batch.

3. Transfer ribs to a Dutch oven or a large, heavy-bottomed pot. Pour off fat from skillet. Add butter, onions, and garlic to skillet; cook until softened, about 4 minutes. Spoon onion mixture over ribs.

4. Pour beer over ribs and onions; heat to boil. Lower heat; simmer uncovered until beer is reduced by one-third, about 45 minutes. Add thyme, bay leaves, tomato paste, and broth. Cover; simmer until meat is tender, 1½ to 2 hours, stirring occasionally.

5. Remove ribs to a serving platter or bowl; keep warm. Remove and discard thyme and bay leaf. Pass broth and onions through a food mill into a saucepan, or puree onions with a little broth in a food processor and transfer to a saucepan. Skim fat from sauce. Heat to boil; cook to thicken slightly. Taste and adjust seasoning. Spoon sauce onto 4 plates. Top with ribs. Pass horseradish at the table if desired.

NUTRITION INFORMATION PER SERVING:

660 calories	39 g fat	12 g saturated fat
53% calories from fat	100 mg cholesterol	1,150 mg sodium
29 g carbohydrate	48 g protein	3 g fiber

Mexican-Style Pot Roast with Vegetables

PREPARATION TIME: 30 minutes

MARINATING TIME: 8 hours to 12 hours

COOKING TIME: 2½ hours

YIELD: 8 servings

BEVERLY DILLON'S MEXICAN pot roast became one of the *Tribune*'s ten favorite recipes of 1985. The chilies are not difficult to work with once they have been softened. They provide more flavor than heat. Marinating the meat with this pasty coating adds incredible flavor. The chayote is a West Indian squash, also known as a mirliton.

4 dried *pasilla* chilies	¼ cup vegetable oil
4 dried ancho chilies	1 28-ounce can plum tomatoes,
4 cloves garlic	undrained
¼ cup vegetable oil	1 13¾-ounce can beef broth
3 tablespoons fresh lime juice	1 pound carrots, peeled and halved
1 teaspoon ground cumin	6 to 8 small yellow onions
½ teaspoon salt	8 medium-sized red potatoes,
4 pounds beef chuck top blade	halved
pot roast	2 chayotes *or* zucchini, quartered

1. Soak chilies in hot water to cover until softened, about 20 minutes. Drain. Remove and discard veins and seeds.

2. Drop garlic into a food processor fitted with a metal blade or into a blender with machine running. Process until minced. Add drained chilies, oil, lime juice, cumin, and salt. Process to a smooth paste.

3. Spread paste over all sides of pot roast. Refrigerate covered in a shallow nonreactive pan or in a sealed plastic food storage bag 8 to 12 hours.

4. Heat oven to 350°F. Heat oil in a large Dutch oven. Add roast with marinade; cook until browned on both sides. Stir in undrained tomatoes and broth. Heat to simmer; break up tomatoes. Bake covered, adding more broth or water as needed, 2 hours.

5. Add carrots, onions, potatoes, and squash. Bake covered until meat and vegetables are fork-tender, about 30 minutes.

6. Remove meat and vegetables with a slotted spoon to a serving platter. Skim fat from pan juices. Pour pan juices over meat and vegetables. Thinly slice meat to serve.

NUTRITION INFORMATION PER SERVING:

550 calories	23 g fat	4.9 g saturated fat
38% calories from fat	102 mg cholesterol	554 mg sodium
47 g carbohydrate	40 g protein	9 g fiber

Roast Brisket with Barbecue Sauce

PREPARATION TIME: 30 minutes
COOKING TIME: 3½ to 4 hours
YIELD: 10 servings

IN 1984, READER Joyce Klein won the *Tribune*'s Jewish Mother Cooking Contest and had her brisket selected as one of the year's ten best recipes. She said, "I could never serve eight to ten people on this recipe; we loved it so much, four people ate the whole thing."

1 beef brisket (about 4 pounds)
2 cloves garlic, minced
3 large onions, quartered
1 green bell pepper, seeded and cut
    into 1½-inch squares
4 potatoes, peeled and halved
4 large carrots, cut into 1½-inch
    pieces

1½ to 2 cups water
¾ cup barbecue sauce
¾ cup chili sauce
Salt
Freshly ground black pepper

1. Heat oven to 425°F. Rub brisket with garlic. Put into roasting pan fat side up, leaving enough room around meat for carrots and potatoes. Bake uncovered until top is browned, about 30 minutes.

2. Add onions and bell pepper to pan; bake until onion edges start to turn brown. Add ½ of the cup water if they're too brown. Turn meat over; bake until second side is browned, about 20 minutes.

3. Add potatoes, carrots, 1½ cups water, barbecue sauce, and chili sauce. Bake uncovered, basting frequently, 2 hours. Reduce oven temperature to 350°F; cover. Bake until meat is fork-tender, 40 to 60 minutes.

4. Put meat on a serving plate; surround with potatoes and vegetables. Season with salt and pepper to taste. Pass pan juices.

NUTRITION INFORMATION PER SERVING:

564 calories	39 g fat	17 g saturated fat
62% calories from fat	110 mg cholesterol	245 mg sodium
23 g carbohydrate	30 g protein	3 g fiber

Basic Corned Beef

PREPARATION TIME: 10 minutes
COOKING TIME: 3 hours
YIELD: 8 servings

THIS EASY PREPARATION came from the late Peter Kump who wrote the "Practical Cook" column. Serve the corned beef with vegetables for dinner or with rye bread and mustard or horseradish for sandwiches.

1 corned beef (4 to 6 pounds), preferably brisket
2 teaspoons black peppercorns
2 cloves garlic, unpeeled
1 onion, quartered
1 bay leaf

1. Put corned beef, peppercorns, garlic, onion, and bay leaf in a Dutch oven. Add cold water to cover by 2 to 3 inches. Heat to boil over high heat; reduce heat to low. Simmer until fork pierces meat easily, about 3 hours.

2. Allow corned beef to sit on a cutting board at least 10 minutes before carving; slice meat thin.

⬥ NOTE: *When making corned beef and cabbage (or other vegetables, such as carrots, onions, turnips, or potatoes), it is better to boil or steam the vegetables in a separate pot and combine them later on a platter. Cooking them with the meat will result in greasy vegetables.*

NUTRITION INFORMATION PER SERVING:

457 calories
68% calories from fat
2.1 g carbohydrate
34 g fat
122 mg cholesterol
34 g protein
11 g saturated fat
277 mg sodium
0.4 g fiber

Corned Beef Hash

PREPARATION TIME: 20 minutes
COOKING TIME: 30 to 35 minutes
YIELD: 4 servings

THIS WAS A Recipe of the Week in March 1980. The meat cake will break up when you turn it. Just pat it back into shape.

3 to 3½ cups finely chopped cooked corned beef
1 pound potatoes, peeled, diced, and cooked

½ cup chopped onion

¼ teaspoon ground nutmeg

⅛ teaspoon freshly ground black
  pepper

2 tablespoons butter *or* margarine

¼ cup whipping cream *or*
  half-and-half

1. Mix corned beef, potatoes, onion, nutmeg, and black pepper in a large bowl.

2. Melt butter in a large skillet over medium-high heat. Pat corned beef mixture evenly over the bottom of the pan. Press down firmly. Pour whipping cream evenly over mixture. Cook until golden brown on bottom, 15 to 20 minutes.

3. Turn browned portions over with a pancake turner. Cook until golden brown on bottom, about 15 more minutes.

NUTRITION INFORMATION PER SERVING:

458 calories	27 g fat	14 g saturated fat
54% calories from fat	126 mg cholesterol	1,125 mg sodium
22 g carbohydrate	31 g protein	2.1 g fiber

Sweet-and-Sour Meat Loaf

PREPARATION TIME: 25 minutes
COOKING TIME: 1 hour 25 minutes
YIELD: 8 servings

THIS INNOVATIVE RECIPE for meat loaf came from reader Jeff Winter of Skokie, Illinois. He glazes the loaf with a sweet-and-sour glaze and serves it with an Asian flavored sauce. Try this over cooked noodles or rice.

Meat Loaf

2 tablespoons olive oil

1 rib celery, chopped

1 onion, chopped

2 pounds ground beef *and/or* veal

3 large eggs

1 cup dried bread crumbs

½ cup ketchup

1 tablespoon Worcestershire sauce

1 teaspoon ground cumin

Glaze

2 tablespoons honey

2 tablespoons ketchup

2 tablespoons soy sauce

Sauce

1 tablespoon cornstarch

1 cup water

1 tablespoon olive oil

1 small onion, chopped

3 cloves garlic, minced

2 tablespoons molasses

2 tablespoons soy sauce

Salt

Freshly ground black pepper

►

1. Heat oven to 350°F. To make meat loaf, heat oil in a medium-sized skillet over medium heat. Add celery and onion; cook until translucent, 4 to 5 minutes. Combine meat, eggs, bread crumbs, ketchup, Worcestershire, cumin, onion, and celery in a large bowl. Mix until completely combined. Put meat mixture into a 9″ × 5″ loaf pan.

2. To make glaze, stir together honey, ketchup, and soy sauce in a small bowl. Brush the top of meat loaf with glaze. Bake until an instant-reading thermometer reads 170°F, about 1 hour 20 minutes, brushing occasionally with glaze. Let stand 15 minutes before slicing.

3. To make sauce, dissolve cornstarch in water. Heat oil in a small skillet. Add onion and garlic; cook until softened, about 3 minutes. Stir in molasses and soy sauce, and salt and pepper to taste. Add cornstarch mixture; stir well. Heat to boil, stirring constantly, until thickened. Serve over sliced meat loaf.

NUTRITION INFORMATION PER SERVING:

444 calories	24 g fat	8 g saturated fat
48% calories from fat	161 mg cholesterol	978 mg sodium
28 g carbohydrate	30 g protein	1.2 g fiber

Beef and Pork Meat Loaf with Red Bell Pepper Sauce

PREPARATION TIME: 35 minutes

BAKING TIME: 1½ hours

YIELD: 6 servings

FOOD EDITOR CAROL Mighton Haddix explained in late 1989 how the *Tribune*'s top ten recipes of that year were chosen. "We tested more than 1,200 dishes, from readers, chefs, cookbooks, nutritionists, and famous personalities. And we developed quite a few ourselves in the *Tribune*'s fourth floor test kitchen. Our criteria for whether a recipe passes the test or not are simple: Does it taste good and would I make this recipe in my own home?" This is one of the recipes selected that year.

1½ pounds beef ground chuck	2 eggs
¾ pound ground pork	3 tablespoons tomato paste
1 large white potato, peeled and grated	½ cup whipping cream *or* half-and-half
1 onion, minced	1½ tablespoons fresh thyme leaves *or* ½ teaspoon dried leaf thyme
1 large clove garlic, minced	

1¼ teaspoons salt

½ teaspoon freshly ground black
pepper

1 bay leaf

6 slices bacon

Red Bell Pepper Sauce

3 roasted medium-sized red bell
peppers (see Index)

2 tablespoons olive oil

1 teaspoon lemon juice

¼ teaspoon salt

⅛ teaspoon cayenne pepper

1. Heat oven to 350°F. Combine ground beef and ground pork in a large bowl. Add potato, onion, garlic, eggs, tomato paste, cream, thyme, salt, and pepper to meat. Mix well with your hands.

2. Put mixture in a 2-quart loaf pan, terrine, or other baking dish. Pat down to make sure meat is packed well with no air pockets. Put bay leaf on top. Cover loaf with bacon. Bake 1½ hours or until juices run clear. Cool at least 15 minutes.

3. To make red bell pepper sauce, puree bell peppers in a food processor or blender. Stir in olive oil, lemon juice, salt, and cayenne.

4. Drain fat or juices from meat loaf pan. To remove meat loaf from pan, invert it onto a serving platter. Cut meat loaf into ½-inch-thick slices. Top each slice with 1 spoonful of red bell pepper sauce.

NUTRITION INFORMATION PER SERVING:

614 calories	43 g fat	18 g saturated fat
64% calories from fat	233 mg cholesterol	987 mg sodium
11 g carbohydrate	45 g protein	1.4 g fiber

Cajun Meat Loaf

PREPARATION TIME: 1 hour
COOKING TIME: About 1 hour
YIELD: 6 servings

WHEN THE *TRIBUNE* kitchen tested recipes from *Chef Paul Prudhomme's Louisiana Kitchen* cookbook in 1984, tasters fell in love with his meat loaf recipe. The king of Cajun cooks, Prudhomme is a master at combining flavors, so follow the seasoning quantities exactly. Mashed potatoes belong on the plate with this meat loaf. You won't need a sauce.

Seasoning Mix

2 whole bay leaves

1 tablespoon salt

1 teaspoon ground red pepper

➤

1 teaspoon freshly ground black
  pepper
½ teaspoon white pepper
½ teaspoon ground cumin
½ teaspoon ground nutmeg

Meat Loaf
¼ cup (½ stick) unsalted butter
1 onion, chopped fine
2 ribs celery, chopped fine
½ green bell pepper, seeded and
  chopped fine

4 green onions, chopped fine
2 cloves garlic, minced
1 tablespoon hot pepper sauce
1 tablespoon Worcestershire sauce
½ cup evaporated milk
½ cup ketchup
1½ pounds ground beef round
½ pound ground pork
2 large eggs, lightly beaten
1 cup dry bread crumbs

1. To make seasoning mix, combine bay leaves, salt, ground red pepper, black pepper, white pepper, cumin, and nutmeg in a small bowl; set aside.

2. To make meat loaf, melt butter in a 1-quart saucepan over medium heat. Add onion, celery, green pepper, green onions, garlic, hot pepper sauce, Worcestershire sauce, and seasoning mix. Cook, stirring occasionally and scraping pan bottom well, until mixture starts sticking excessively, about 6 minutes.

3. Stir in milk and ketchup. Continue cooking 2 minutes, stirring occasionally. Remove from heat; cool to room temperature. Remove bay leaves.

4. Heat oven to 350°F. Put ground beef and pork in an ungreased 13″ × 9″ baking pan. Add eggs, cooked vegetable mixture, and bread crumbs. Mix by hand until thoroughly combined.

5. Shape mixture into a loaf about 12″ × 6″ × 1½″ and place in center of pan. Bake uncovered 25 minutes. Increase oven temperature to 400°F; continue cooking until cooked through, about 35 minutes.

NUTRITION INFORMATION PER SERVING:

556 calories	32 g fat	14 g saturated fat
53% calories from fat	199 mg cholesterol	1,737 mg sodium
27 g carbohydrate	39 g protein	2.3 g fiber

Hodgepodge Chili

PREPARATION TIME: 35 minutes
COOKING TIME: 3 hours
YIELD: 10 1-cup servings

IN PREPARING FOR an October 1998 story about chili contests, the "Good Eating" section ran some winning recipes. But we also came up with one of our own: staff members described their ideas of what makes a perfect chili, and test kitchen director Alicia Tessling combined those ideas to create this recipe—a milder, bean-filled, Midwest-style chili. It's appropriately called Hodgepodge Chili.

1 tablespoon vegetable oil
1 pound Italian sausage
1 pound ground beef
1 large onion, chopped
1 green bell pepper, seeded and
   chopped
4 cloves garlic, minced
2 jalapeños, chopped
1 tablespoon chili powder
1 tablespoon cumin seeds
¾ teaspoon salt
1 15-ounce can kidney beans
1 15-ounce can Great Northern
   beans, undrained

1 28-ounce can chopped tomatoes,
   undrained
1 16-ounce can chicken broth
1 6-ounce can tomato paste
¼ cup chopped cilantro
¼ cup chopped parsley
Shredded cheddar cheese, optional
Chopped red onion, optional
Sliced jalapeño, optional
Chopped tomato, optional
Sliced green onion, optional
Chopped avocado, optional
Sliced black olives, optional

1. Heat oil in a Dutch oven over medium heat. Remove sausage from casing; add sausage and beef to oil. Cook until browned. Stir in onion, bell pepper, garlic, jalapeños, chili powder, cumin seed, and salt. Cook, stirring often, until onion softens, about 4 minutes.

2. Add beans, tomatoes, broth, tomato paste, cilantro, and parsley. Stir to combine. Cook partly covered until flavors have blended, about 3 hours. Taste and adjust seasonings. Serve with toppings on the side if desired.

NUTRITION INFORMATION PER SERVING:

310 calories	13 g fat	4.8 g saturated fat
37% calories from fat	45 mg cholesterol	960 mg sodium
28 g carbohydrate	28 g protein	7 g fiber

Veal Scaloppine with Fresh Tomato Relish

PREPARATION TIME: 20 minutes

COOKING TIME: 3 minutes

YIELD: 4 servings

THOUGH VEAL IS expensive, a pound of the boneless meat will feed four and it makes a light presentation that is ideal for a spring or summer dinner for company. Usually, the butcher will slice and pound the veal to order. Serve this veal with a green vegetable such as zucchini, cut in chunks and sautéed, and a light red wine such as valpolicella.

1 ripe tomato, seeded and chopped

1 tablespoon capers

4 ounces fresh mozzarella cheese, cubed

3 tablespoons olive oil

2 teaspoons balsamic vinegar

½ teaspoon freshly ground black pepper, plus more for seasoning flour and veal

¼ teaspoon salt plus more for seasoning flour and veal

2 large eggs

1 cup all-purpose flour

1 cup dry bread crumbs

1 pound veal scallops, pounded ⅛ inch thick

2 teaspoons unsalted butter

1. Combine chopped tomato, capers, mozzarella, 1 tablespoon of the olive oil, balsamic vinegar, ½ teaspoon pepper, and ¼ teaspoon salt in a small bowl. Stir well; set aside.

2. Beat eggs in a shallow bowl until yolks and whites are combined. Put flour on a plate; season generously with salt and pepper. Put bread crumbs on another plate.

3. Coat each veal scallop with flour, then with egg, then with bread crumbs. Place on a baking sheet.

4. Divide butter and the 2 tablespoons remaining oil between 2 skillets; heat over medium-high heat until butter stops bubbling. Add veal; cook until well browned on one side, about 2 minutes. Turn; season cooked side with salt and pepper. Cook until second side is brown, 1 to 2 minutes.

5. Blot veal with a paper towel to remove excess oil. Transfer to plates; top with tomato relish.

NUTRITION INFORMATION PER SERVING:

465 calories

46% calories from fat

24 g carbohydrate

24 g fat

175 mg cholesterol

37 g protein

8 g saturated fat

455 mg sodium

1.3 g fiber

Veal Scallops with Sage and Capers

PREPARATION TIME: 5 minutes
COOKING TIME: 4 minutes
YIELD: 2 servings

HERE IS A fast and piquant Italian preparation for veal. If you don't have a 12-inch skillet, cook the veal in two batches (or in two skillets) so the pan isn't crowded.

1 tablespoon extra-virgin olive oil
2 large cloves garlic, halved
2 veal scallops (4 ounces each),
   pounded to ⅛ inch thick
¼ cup dry vermouth
2 tablespoons whipping cream *or*
   half-and-half

1 tablespoon drained capers
1 teaspoon dried sage
½ teaspoon balsamic vinegar
Salt
Freshly ground black pepper

1. Heat oil and garlic in a 12-inch nonstick skillet over high heat. Cook, stirring often, until garlic begins to color. Remove garlic with a slotted spoon; discard.

2. Add veal to pan; cook, turning once, until lightly browned at edges, 1 to 2 minutes per side. Transfer to 2 plates; keep warm.

3. Add vermouth, cream, capers, sage, and vinegar and salt and pepper to taste to pan; cook over high heat until slightly thickened, 1 to 2 minutes. Pour over veal.

NUTRITION INFORMATION PER SERVING:

371 calories	28 g fat	10 g saturated fat
68% calories from fat	125 mg cholesterol	235 mg sodium
1.8 g carbohydrate	27 g protein	0.2 g fiber

Sliced Veal with Anchovy Sauce (Vitello Tonnato)

PREPARATION TIME: 15 minutes
COOKING TIME: 10 minutes
YIELD: 6 servings

HERE IS CHICAGO chef Jennifer Newbury's version of the Italian classic *vitello tonnato*. It's fun to see how many diners will guess that the base of the creamy, delicious sauce is tuna fish. An Italian white wine such as Gavi will match well with this fish and meat combination.

1 7-ounce can albacore tuna packed
   in water, drained

5 anchovy fillets, rinsed and
   drained

►

½ cup mayonnaise
½ cup extra-virgin olive oil
½ cup whipping cream
¼ cup water
1 tablespoon plus 2 teaspoons
    drained capers

6 thin veal cutlets
Salt
Freshly ground black pepper
2 tablespoons butter
Arugula *or* green lettuce

1. Puree tuna, anchovies, mayonnaise, oil, whipping cream, water, and capers in a blender until almost smooth.

2. Season veal cutlets with salt and pepper. Heat butter in a large skillet over medium-high heat. Add veal in a single layer; cook until brown on both sides, about 2 minutes. Remove to a serving plate; repeat with remaining veal.

3. Cover veal with tuna sauce; garnish with arugula. Serve warm or at room temperature.

NUTRITION INFORMATION PER SERVING:

690 calories	60 g fat	18 g saturated fat
78% calories from fat	166 mg cholesterol	544 mg sodium
1.1 g carbohydrate	37 g protein	0 g fiber

Veal Tarragon Stew with Tiny Dumplings

PREPARATION TIME: 30 minutes
COOKING TIME: 1 hour 10 minutes
YIELD: 8 servings

THE BAKERY RESTAURANT in Chicago served thousands of customers during its long run. This veal tarragon stew with dumplings is just an example of the hearty, satisfying fare enjoyed there. Barbara Kuck, once the Bakery's chef-director, says the recipe originally comes from Transylvania and has an "intriguing taste" from the tarragon, bay leaf, and vinegar.

Dumplings
4 slices dried white bread,
    preferably crusty French, *or*
    2 dried hard rolls
1 cup veal stock *or* chicken broth
1 tablespoon butter
½ small onion, minced
3 slices bacon, cooked and
    crumbled

2 large egg whites, lightly beaten
2 tablespoons sour cream
½ teaspoon salt
¼ teaspoon freshly ground white
    pepper
½ cup all-purpose flour
1 tablespoon minced fresh Italian
    flat-leaf parsley

Stew

¼ cup (½ stick) butter

2 onions, chopped

1 clove garlic

2 teaspoons salt

2 pounds boneless lean veal, cut into 1-inch cubes

1 cup dry white wine

⅓ cup distilled white vinegar

3 tablespoons chopped fresh Italian flat-leaf parsley

2 teaspoons dried tarragon

2 teaspoons sugar

1 bay leaf

½ pound mushrooms, sliced

1½ cups milk

¼ cup all-purpose flour

Salt

Freshly ground white pepper

1 cup sour cream

1. To make dumplings, heat oven to 300°F. Cut bread into ¼-inch cubes; toast in oven until crisp and golden. Heat veal stock in a small saucepan over medium heat. Put bread cubes in a large bowl. Pour hot veal stock over bread; let stand until cool and well soaked.

2. Melt butter in a small skillet over medium heat. Add onion; cook until soft, about 5 minutes. Add bacon, egg whites, sour cream, salt, and white pepper to bread cubes. Stir in flour and parsley. Let stand 30 minutes.

3. Bring salted water to a simmer in a large saucepan over high heat. Form dough into balls about ¾ inch in diameter with wet hands. Ease dumplings into simmering water. Simmer dumplings until they are tender and rise to the surface, about 10 minutes. Keep warm in cooking liquid until just before serving.

4. To make stew, melt butter in a Dutch oven over medium heat. Add onions; cook, stirring often, until soft, about 5 minutes. Mash together garlic and salt with the flat surface of a chef's knife until a paste forms. Add to onions. Stir in veal, white wine, vinegar, 2 tablespoons of the parsley, tarragon, sugar, and bay leaf. Cook covered over medium heat until veal is tender, 30 to 40 minutes.

5. Add mushrooms; cook 3 minutes. Mix milk and flour until smooth in a separate bowl. Stir mixture into veal; heat through until thickened. Taste and adjust seasonings. Stir in sour cream and remaining 1 tablespoon parsley just before serving. Heat until warm; do not boil or sauce will curdle. Serve with dumplings on top.

NUTRITION INFORMATION PER SERVING:

492 calories	30 g fat	15 g saturated fat
56% calories from fat	131 mg cholesterol	1,218 mg sodium
25 g carbohydrate	29 g protein	1.7 g fiber

Braised Veal Shanks (Osso Buco)

PREPARATION TIME: 30 minutes

COOKING TIME: 2 hours

YIELD: 4 servings

A PERFECT WINTER meal, osso buco needs only a crusty Italian bread and a salad to be complete. Serve with a full-bodied Chianti Classico.

½ cup all-purpose flour

2 teaspoons salt

¼ teaspoon freshly ground black pepper

4 pounds veal shanks, cut in 3-inch-long pieces

⅓ cup olive oil

2 large carrots, peeled and diced

2 onions, minced

1 rib celery, diced

3 cloves garlic, minced

1 16-ounce can whole tomatoes, chopped

½ cup dry red wine

1 13¾-ounce can beef broth

1 teaspoon dried basil

¼ teaspoon dried rosemary

¼ teaspoon dried leaf thyme

1 bay leaf

2 tablespoons minced fresh parsley

2 teaspoons finely grated lemon zest

1. Stir together flour, salt, and pepper in a medium-sized bowl. Coat veal with flour mixture. Heat oil in a large Dutch oven over medium-high heat. Add veal in a single layer. Cook, turning occasionally, until browned on all sides. Remove to a platter.

2. Add carrots, onions, celery, and two-thirds of the minced garlic to pan. Cook, stirring often, until onions are golden, 5 to 8 minutes. Add tomatoes and wine. Heat to a boil; reduce heat to medium-low. Cook until liquid is reduced by half. Stir in broth, basil, rosemary, thyme, and bay leaf.

3. Return veal to the pan. Heat to simmer. Cover; simmer until veal is tender but not falling off bones, 1½ to 2 hours. Remove bay leaf.

4. Stir together remaining garlic, parsley, and lemon zest. Sprinkle over all. Simmer covered 5 minutes. Serve in 4 wide soup bowls, spooning pan juices over veal.

NUTRITION INFORMATION PER SERVING:

640 calories	31 g fat	7 g saturated fat
44% calories from fat	240 mg cholesterol	1,275 mg sodium
23 g carbohydrate	66 g protein	4.6 g fiber

Braised Veal Shanks with Vegetables and Penne

PREPARATION TIME: 30 minutes
COOKING TIME: 2 hours
YIELD: 6 servings

COLUMNIST ABBY MANDEL offered an October entertaining menu in 1992 featuring a veal shank dish that you can make in advance and refrigerate for a day or two or even freeze. It was included in that year's best recipes selection. You can make this dish two days ahead through step 4 of recipe and refrigerate or freeze it. When ready to serve, thaw if frozen. Reheat it covered, in a 300°F oven until hot, about 30 minutes, adding remaining stock or broth as needed.

Veal Shanks
3 tablespoons all-purpose flour
¾ teaspoon dried leaf thyme
¾ teaspoon dried marjoram
¾ teaspoon salt
Freshly ground black pepper
6 sliced veal shanks with bone (about 1½ inches thick, 8 ounces each)
1½ tablespoons olive oil

Vegetables
1½ tablespoons olive oil
3 large cloves garlic, minced

1 large leek, trimmed, split lengthwise, and cut into thin slices
6 small carrots, cut into 1-inch diagonal slices
1 large bulb fennel, cut into ⅓-inch dice
8 medium-sized mushrooms, trimmed and quartered
1 to 1¾ cups chicken stock *or* broth
¾ cup dry white wine
2 tablespoons tomato paste
4 ounces penne pasta
Minced parsley, optional

1. Heat oven to 375°F. To make veal shanks, combine flour, herbs, salt, and pepper to taste in a large plastic food storage bag. Add shanks in batches; shake to coat evenly. Shake off excess flour into a large, shallow baking dish. Sprinkle excess flour from plastic bag into a dish.

2. Heat oil in a 12-inch nonstick skillet over medium-high heat. Add veal shanks; brown both sides, about 6 minutes total. Transfer shanks to a baking dish, arranging them in a single layer.

3. To make vegetables, add oil to the same skillet. When oil is hot, add garlic, leek, carrots, fennel, and mushrooms. Cook, stirring often, over medium-high heat uncovered until leeks are limp, about 4 minutes. Transfer to the baking dish, arranging vegetables around shanks. Add 1 cup chicken broth, ¾ cup dry white wine, and tomato paste to skillet. Heat to boil. Pour over vegetables and meat. Cover baking dish with foil.

►

4. Bake until meat is fork-tender, almost falling off the bones, 1½ to 2 hours, turning meat halfway through cooking. Add remaining broth only as needed to keep meat and vegetables from drying out.

5. Meanwhile, cook penne according to package directions. Add penne to veal and mix with pan juices. There should be some excess pan juices on bottom of pan; if not, add remaining stock or water. Bake until hot, about 5 minutes. Taste and adjust seasoning. Divide evenly among 6 shallow soup or pasta dishes, arranging vegetables and penne attractively. Sprinkle with parsley if desired. Serve hot.

NUTRITION INFORMATION PER SERVING:

489 calories	15 g fat	3 g saturated fat
28% calories from fat	214 mg cholesterol	637 mg sodium
27 g carbohydrate	59 g protein	4 g fiber

Cumin-Rubbed Grilled Pork Chops

PREPARATION TIME: 5 minutes

COOKING TIME: 10 minutes

MARINATING TIME: Up to 6 hours

YIELD: 4 servings

BURGERS, STEAKS, AND chicken aren't the only candidates for the quick cooking an outdoor grill affords, according to "Fast Food" columnist Pat Dailey. Butterflied, center-cut pork chops, briefly marinated with brown sugar, vinegar, and spices, get a further boost from being seared over an open fire.

2 tablespoons packed brown sugar
1 tablespoon plus 2 teaspoons cider
  vinegar
2 teaspoons ground cumin

½ teaspoon ground red pepper
4 butterflied center-cut pork loin
  chops (4 to 5 ounces each)

1. Prepare grill or heat broiler. Combine sugar, vinegar, cumin, and red pepper in a small bowl; mix well.

2. Put pork chops in a large plastic food storage bag or glass baking dish. Pour cumin mixture over; turn meat to coat. Seal bag or cover dish; marinate at least 10 minutes or as long as 6 hours.

3. Remove meat from marinade. Grill or broil, turning once, until cooked through, 8 to 10 minutes. Move to a cooler part of the grill if the sugar in the rub starts to burn.

NUTRITION INFORMATION PER SERVING:

170 calories	6 g fat	1.9 g saturated fat
32% calories from fat	80 mg cholesterol	50 mg sodium
1.4 g carbohydrate	26 g protein	0 g fiber

Smoked Pork Chops with Shallot-Mustard Sauce

PREPARATION TIME: 10 minutes
COOKING TIME: 10 minutes
YIELD: 4 servings

THE RELENTLESS CALL for easy, quick-cooking ingredients has prompted several stores to add smoked pork chops to their meat cases. In one "Fast Food" column, they were paired with a shallot-mustard sauce. Serve these with sauerkraut and a Riesling or gewürztraminer.

1 tablespoon unsalted butter	½ teaspoon dried leaf thyme
4 smoked pork chops	2 tablespoons whipping cream
3 large shallots, sliced thin	Salt
⅔ cup low-sodium chicken broth	Freshly ground black pepper
1 tablespoon horseradish mustard	
or country-style mustard	

1. Melt half of the butter in a large skillet over medium-high heat. Add pork chops; cook, turning several times, until browned and heated through, 4 to 5 minutes. Remove from pan; keep warm.

2. Melt remaining butter in the same pan. Add shallots; cook, stirring often, until lightly browned at edges, 2 minutes. Add chicken broth, mustard, and thyme; stir to dissolve mustard. Heat to boil; cook 1 minute. Add cream; boil 30 seconds. Remove from heat. Pour over pork chops.

NUTRITION INFORMATION PER SERVING:

417 calories	33 g fat	14 g saturated fat
71% calories from fat	111 mg cholesterol	147 mg sodium
4.2 g carbohydrate	26 g protein	0.3 g fiber

Smoky Paprika Pork

PREPARATION TIME: 20 minutes
MARINATING TIME: 48 hours
COOKING TIME: 6 minutes
YIELD: 6 servings

THIS RECIPE, WHICH accompanied a cover story on paprika, is adapted from a recipe by François Sanchez, chef-owner of Mesón Sabika in Naperville, Illinois. The paprika marinade also works well on chicken, shrimp, or firm fish fillets, but the marinating time should be only one hour. Look for smoked paprika in specialty stores or spice stores. Hungarian or American paprika can be substituted.

½ cup plus 1 tablespoon olive oil
½ cup sherry vinegar
5 whole cloves
2 cloves garlic, minced
1 tablespoon fresh marjoram, chopped

1½ teaspoons smoked paprika
Zest and juice of 1 lemon
Salt
Freshly ground black pepper
2 pounds pork tenderloin

1. Put ½ cup of the olive oil, vinegar, cloves, garlic, marjoram, paprika, lemon zest, and lemon juice and salt and pepper to taste into a plastic food storage bag. Add pork; seal. Marinate in refrigerator, turning a few times, about 48 hours.

2. Remove meat from marinade. Slice into medallions. Heat remaining olive oil in a skillet; cook pork medallions 2 minutes. Turn; cook through, about 3 minutes.

NUTRITION INFORMATION PER SERVING:

205 calories
34% calories from fat
0.3 g carbohydrate

7 g fat
90 mg cholesterol
32 g protein

2.2 g saturated fat
64 mg sodium
0.1 g fiber

Pork and Sauerkraut

PREPARATION TIME: 20 minutes
COOKING TIME: 40 to 45 minutes
YIELD: 4 servings

COLUMINIST JEANNE JONES makes this cold-weather dish a day ahead of time and reheats it just before serving to allow the flavors to "marry" and become even more intense. Serve with rye bread and a bottle of Alsatian Riesling, if you like.

4 slices low-sodium bacon, chopped coarse
1 onion, chopped
1 16-ounce can sauerkraut, rinsed and drained
2 tablespoons packed light brown sugar
4 1-inch-thick smoked pork loin chops
2 potatoes, peeled and quartered
2 tart apples, peeled and sliced
1 16-ounce can fat-free, low-sodium chicken broth

Bouquet Garni
10 juniper berries, optional
6 whole peppercorns
2 whole cloves
1 parsley sprig
1 bay leaf

1. Heat a large pot or Dutch oven over medium-low heat. Add bacon and onion. Cook, stirring occasionally, until onion is soft and bacon is crisp, 10 to 12 minutes. Stir in sauerkraut and brown sugar. Add pork chops, potatoes, and apples. Pour broth over mixture.

2. To make bouquet garni, tie juniper berries, peppercorns, cloves, parsley, and bay leaf in cheesecloth or put in a tea ball; add to pot. Heat to boil over medium-high heat. Reduce heat to low; cook covered until potatoes are tender, about 30 minutes.

3. Remove bouquet garni; discard. Transfer sauerkraut, potatoes, and apples to a large platter using a slotted spoon. Arrange pork chops around edge.

NUTRITION INFORMATION PER SERVING:

473 calories	15 g fat	6 g saturated fat
28% calories from fat	125 mg cholesterol	992 mg sodium
37 g carbohydrate	51 g protein	6 g fiber

Smothered and Covered Chops

PREPARATION TIME: 20 minutes
COOKING TIME: 40 minutes
YIELD: 4 servings

THIS RECIPE FOR smothered pork chops was adapted from one by actress Vivica Fox, who was part of the cast of the family film *Soul Food*, filmed in Chicago in 1996.

2 tablespoons butter
1 onion, chopped
1 green bell pepper, chopped
4 ounces mushrooms, sliced thin
1 clove garlic, minced
½ cup milk
1 large egg
¼ cup plus 2 tablespoons
    all-purpose flour

½ teaspoon seasoning salt
¼ teaspoon freshly ground black
    pepper
4 large pork chops
2 tablespoons peanut *or* vegetable
    oil
1½ cups chicken broth *or* water

1. Melt butter in a large skillet over medium-high heat. Add onion, bell pepper, mushrooms, and garlic. Cook until onion is soft, about 3 minutes. Remove vegetables to a bowl; set aside.

2. Whisk together milk and egg in a medium-sized bowl. Combine ¼ cup of the flour, seasoning salt, and pepper, in a plastic food storage bag. Dip one chop into milk mixture. Place chop in bag with flour mixture; seal. Shake to coat. Repeat with remaining chops.

3. Heat oil in the same skillet over high heat. Add chops; cook until browned on both sides, about 5 minutes. Remove and set aside. Stir remaining 2 tablespoons flour into oil in the skillet. Cook, stirring, until mixture begins to brown, 3 to 4 minutes. Whisk in broth. Heat to boil, stirring; reduce heat to medium-low.

4. Add onion mixture; simmer 15 minutes. Add more broth or water to thin to desired consistency. Add chops; cook until tender and no longer pink, 10 to 15 minutes. Taste and adjust seasoning.

NUTRITION INFORMATION PER SERVING:

515 calories	27 g fat	10 g saturated fat
47% calories from fat	190 mg cholesterol	585 mg sodium
17 g carbohydrate	50 g protein	1.8 g fiber

Grilled Pork Tenderloin with Garlic, Thyme, and Fennel

PREPARATION TIME: 20 minutes

MARINATING TIME: 24 hours

COOKING TIME: 15 to 20 minutes

YIELD: 6 servings

PORK TENDERLOIN LENDS itself to some unusual flavorings. Here, vodka, thyme, and fennel seed are used in a grilled dish from Gabriel Viti of Gabriel's Restaurant in Highwood, Illinois.

10 cloves garlic, minced

4 sprigs fresh thyme *or*

   1 tablespoon dried

½ cup toasted fennel seeds, ground (see Note)

3 pork tenderloins (8 to 10 ounces each)

¾ cup vodka

½ cup olive oil

1.   Combine garlic, thyme, and ground fennel in a small bowl; rub thoroughly over tenderloins.

2.   Place tenderloins in a plastic food storage bag. Carefully pour vodka and oil over meat; seal bag. Refrigerate 24 hours, turning several times.

3.   Prepare grill. Heat oven to 375°F. Remove meat from marinade. Grill tenderloins until just cooked through, about 12 minutes. Let stand 10 minutes before slicing.

❧ NOTE: *To toast fennel, heat a small skillet over medium-low heat. Add fennel; cook, stirring frequently, until golden, about 8 minutes. Grind toasted seeds in a food mill, a small food processor fitted with a metal blade, or a coffee grinder.*

❧ VARIATION: *Meat also can be cooked in a large skillet in 1 tablespoon hot oil. Transfer meat to 350°F oven; bake until a meat thermometer reads 170°F, about 12 minutes.*

NUTRITION INFORMATION PER SERVING:

195 calories	8 g fat	1.8 g saturated fat
35% calories from fat	65 mg cholesterol	55 mg sodium
6 g carbohydrate	25 g protein	3.5 g fiber

Jerk Pork Tenderloin

PREPARATION TIME: 25 minutes
MARINATING TIME: 3 hours
COOKING TIME: 23 minutes
YIELD: 6 servings

N. N. SMOKEHOUSE OWNER Larry Tucker, profiled in a story about the black chefs of Chicago, often cooks with a Caribbean accent. Here he uses hot peppers, sugar, and plenty of spice to create smoking-hot jerk pork. The best beverage accompaniment is cold beer or a combination of fruit juice and tonic water.

3 to 4 habanero chilies, seeded and minced
4 cloves garlic, minced
2 shallots, chopped, *or* 4 green onions, chopped
1 2-inch-thick piece gingerroot, peeled and minced
1 sprig fresh thyme, chopped
¼ cup packed brown sugar
4 teaspoons ground allspice
4 teaspoons chili powder

2 teaspoons cinnamon
2 teaspoons nutmeg
Freshly ground black pepper
⅔ cup peanut oil
¼ cup fresh lime juice
⅔ cup soy *and/or* Worcestershire sauce
4 pork tenderloins (about 12 ounces each)
1 cup chicken broth

1. Combine habanero chilies, garlic, shallots, gingerroot, thyme, brown sugar, allspice, chili powder, cinnamon, nutmeg, and black pepper to taste in a medium-sized bowl. Stir until well combined. Stir in oil, lime juice, and soy and/or Worcestershire sauce. Place tenderloins in a large plastic food storage bag or a large bowl; add marinade, reserving ¼ cup. Seal or cover marinated pork; refrigerate 3 to 4 hours.

2. Heat broiler. Remove tenderloins from marinade; place on roasting pan. Broil, turning once, 15 to 18 minutes for medium doneness. Remove pork from pan; set on a cutting board. Cover loosely with aluminum foil. Let rest 10 minutes.

3. Remove fat from surface of pan drippings. Add ⅓ cup of the broth; cook, scraping the bottom of the pan to loosen browned bits. Combine pan drippings, ¼ cup reserved marinade, and remaining ⅔ cup chicken broth in a medium-sized saucepan. Heat to boil, stirring frequently. Reduce heat to medium-low; simmer 8 to 10 minutes. Strain sauce and discard solids; taste and adjust seasoning.

4. Slice tenderloins on the diagonal into ½-inch slices. Pour some of the sauce on each plate; place pork slices on top of sauce. Pass remaining sauce.

NUTRITION INFORMATION PER SERVING:

330 calories	12 g fat	3.5 g saturated fat
34% calories from fat	135 mg cholesterol	500 mg sodium
3.2 g carbohydrate	49 g protein	0.3 g fiber

Plum-Glazed Pork Roast

PREPARATION TIME: 20 minutes
COOKING TIME: 2 hours
YIELD: 8 servings

ASIAN-STYLE COOKING is unbeatable when it comes to combining fruit and pork. Serve this roast with white rice and a fruit-friendly green vegetable such as brussels sprouts.

1 pork top loin rolled roast *or* shoulder blade (3 to 4 pounds)	¼ cup rice wine *or* dry sherry
1 17-ounce can whole red plums, pitted	¼ cup soy sauce
1 clove garlic, minced	1 tablespoon chopped crystallized ginger
½ cup orange marmalade	Slivered green onions
	Orange slices

1. Heat oven to 350°F. Place roast on a rack set in a roasting pan. Roast 1½ hours.

2. Meanwhile, put undrained plums, garlic, marmalade, wine, soy sauce, and ginger in a small saucepan. Cook uncovered over low heat until thickened, about 10 minutes. Set aside.

3. Brush glaze over roast. Cook, brushing every 10 minutes, until a meat thermometer registers 160°F, about 30 minutes. Remove roast to a serving platter. Let stand 15 minutes before carving. Garnish each serving with green onions and orange slices. Pass any remaining plum glaze.

NUTRITION INFORMATION PER SERVING:

507 calories	31 g fat	12 g saturated fat
56% calories from fat	119 mg cholesterol	565 mg sodium
25 g carbohydrate	31 g protein	0.6 g fiber

Herb-Crusted Pork Loin Roast

PREPARATION TIME: 15 minutes
MARINATING TIME: 8 to 12 hours
COOKING TIME: 1½ hours
YIELD: 8 servings

WRITER PAT DAILEY created a special June menu to celebrate the Expo '92 celebration and the Olympic Games being held in Spain that year. The following pork dish was later voted one of the year's best dishes.

1 boneless pork loin roast (about 3 pounds), rolled and tied
1 clove garlic, halved
1 tablespoon dried rosemary
1 tablespoon dried leaf thyme
1 tablespoon coarse-ground black pepper

1 teaspoon salt
1 tablespoon sherry wine vinegar
1 teaspoon honey
½ teaspoon salt
Freshly ground black pepper

1. Wipe pork roast dry with a paper towel. Rub cut side of garlic all over meat; discard garlic. Combine herbs, pepper, and salt in a small dish. Press herb mixture all over roast; wrap tightly in plastic wrap. Refrigerate 8 to 12 hours.

2. Heat oven to 400°F. Put roast in a heavy, shallow roasting pan. Cook 1 hour. Reduce heat in oven to 350°F. Cook until internal temperature of meat registers 160°F on a meat thermometer, about 30 minutes. Remove meat from pan; cover with foil.

3. Skim fat from pan drippings; place pan over high heat. Add vinegar; stir up any browned bits from pan. Add honey and any drippings that have accumulated from the meat. Boil 1 minute. Add salt and pepper to taste. Cut meat into thin slices; pass sauce separately.

NUTRITION INFORMATION PER SERVING:

274 calories	13 g fat	4.5 g saturated fat
42% calories from fat	103 mg cholesterol	366 mg sodium
1.9 g carbohydrate	37 g protein	0.6 g fiber

Carolina Pork Barbecue

PREPARATION TIME: 30 minutes
COOKING TIME: 8 hours
YIELD: 6 servings

ASSISTANT "GOOD EATING" editor Andy Badeker toured North Carolina to find a true barbecued pork preparation. His article was part of the award-winning *Tribune* series on regional foods called "American Originals." The two-kettle grill method is adapted from one in Bob Garner's *North Carolina Barbecue*.

1 fresh shoulder picnic ham *or* pork Boston butt roast (6 to 7 pounds)	Lexington-style "dip" *or* mustard barbecue sauce (see Note)
Salt	Coleslaw, optional
	Warm sandwich buns

1. Salt meat; let stand 30 minutes. Meanwhile, light 5 pounds of briquettes in a charcoal grill. Let heat until they're covered in ash, 30 to 45 minutes. Move all but 6 or 7 briquettes into 2 piles on the sides of the kettle. Arrange remaining 6 or 7 briquettes in a circle. Place 2 hickory chunks on each pile. Replace grate. Set meat directly over the circle of coals fat side up. (The fat under the skin will melt and baste the meat.) Cover the grill; leave the vent open.

2. Light 12 more briquettes in an auxiliary grill. When they're covered in ash, 30 to 45 minutes, add 6 to each existing pile in the first grill. (If you position the grate on the kettle just right, you can put briquettes through the spaces under the wire handles without having to remove the grate.) Top briquette piles with fresh hickory chips. Continue adding 6 fully lighted (ash-covered) briquettes from the auxiliary grill and 2 hickory chips to each side of grill every 30 to 45 minutes.

3. After about 6 hours, turn meat fat side down. (If meat is browning too much, cut down the additional briquettes to 4 or 5 per side.) Cook 2 more hours until exposed meat is a deep reddish brown.

4. Move meat to a cutting board. Remove skin in one piece with a gentle tug. Scrape or cut away any fat with a knife. The remaining lean meat should be tender enough to be easily pulled from the bones. Pile meat on the cutting board; chop to the consistency you like. Splash it with the sauce of your choice. Serve meat on buns topped with coleslaw if desired.

❧ NOTE: *A thin sauce like Lexington-style "dip" is often served on the side in western North Carolina restaurants. Mix 3 cups cider vinegar with ⅔ cup brown or white sugar, ½ cup ketchup, 2 tablespoons hot pepper sauce, 2 teaspoons Kitchen Bouquet, 1 teaspoon salt, 1 teaspoon freshly ground black pepper, 1 teaspoon Worcestershire sauce,*

▶

and 1 teaspoon onion powder in a large nonreactive saucepan. Stir over medium heat until sugar melts, about 8 minutes. Let stand several hours in a tightly sealed container. Makes about 4½ cups.

Mustard barbecue sauce, adapted from a recipe by David Koelling, chef at Biloxi Grill in Wauconda, Illinois, is a hallmark of much South Carolina barbecue. Mix 1 cup yellow prepared mustard, 1 cup water, ½ cup brown sugar, ½ cup Dijon mustard, ½ cup cider vinegar, 2 teaspoons salt, 1 teaspoon ground red pepper, 1 teaspoon paprika, and 1 teaspoon dried leaf thyme in a medium-sized saucepan over medium-high heat. Heat to boil. Simmer, stirring frequently, 3 minutes. Remove from heat; cool to room temperature.

NUTRITION INFORMATION PER SERVING (WITHOUT SAUCE):

716 calories	51 g fat	18 g saturated fat
65% calories from fat	237 mg cholesterol	192 mg sodium
0 g carbohydrate	61 g protein	0 g fiber

Down-Home Barbecued Pork with Good-Old-Boy Sauce

PREPARATION TIME: 15 minutes

COOKING TIME: 2 hours

YIELD: 8 servings

CHICAGOAN LAMAR BRANTLEY'S "down-home" pork received a one-word review: "Yum!" Depending on where down-home is, cooks will slice the pork very thin and serve it with sauce on the side, chop it on a wooden cutting board with a knife, or use a fork to pull the tender meat into shreds. In any event, it usually winds up on a plate with cornbread and greens or between two slices of supermarket white bread. You can refrigerate extra sauce up to three weeks.

1 pork shoulder blade roast (about 4 pounds)	2 tablespoons Liquid Smoke
2 small lemons	1½ teaspoons freshly ground black pepper
2 cups natural apple cider vinegar	1½ teaspoons ground red pepper
1 14-ounce bottle ketchup	1½ teaspoons salt
½ cup Worcestershire sauce	1½ teaspoons sugar
½ cup prepared mustard	¾ teaspoon ground cumin
½ cup (1 stick) butter *or* margarine	¾ teaspoon dried oregano

1. Prepare grill for indirect heat. Place drip pan in the center. Put roast on the grill rack over the drip pan. Cover; grill, maintaining grill temperature at about 325°F, until a meat thermometer registers 160°F, about 2 hours.

2. Meanwhile, cut ends off lemons; cut lemons into ¼-inch slices. Remove seeds. Combine lemon slices with vinegar, ketchup, Worcestershire, mustard, butter, Liquid Smoke, peppers, salt, sugar, cumin, and oregano in a medium-sized nonreactive saucepan. Cook over medium-low heat until pulp is cooked from lemon rinds, about 1 hour. Remove rinds; put in a blender or in a food processor fitted with a metal blade with a little of the sauce. Puree until smooth; return to saucepan. Cook until heated through, about 2 minutes. Set aside.

3. Let meat cool 15 minutes; trim off fat. Slice, chop, or shred meat. Toss meat with hot barbecue sauce to taste.

NUTRITION INFORMATION PER SERVING:

544 calories	38 g fat	17 g saturated fat
61% calories from fat	138 mg cholesterol	1,587 mg sodium
25 g carbohydrate	30 g protein	2.7 g fiber

Roast Ham with Pickled Ginger Hoisin Glaze

PREPARATION TIME: 5 minutes
COOKING TIME: 1 hour
STANDING TIME: 1 hour
YIELD: 18 servings

AN ASIAN FORMULA for glazing ham was incorporated into a 1999 "Good Eating" story by Kristin Eddy on preparing Easter ham. Hoisin sauce, pickled ginger, and the spice star anise can be found in the Asian section of most grocery stores.

½ cup hoisin sauce
2 tablespoons minced pickled
   ginger
1 fully cooked ham half (about
   9 pounds)

Star anise, optional
Star fruit (carambola), sliced thin,
   optional

1. Stir together hoisin and pickled ginger in a small bowl. Let stand 1 hour to blend flavors.

►

2. Heat oven to 325°F. Trim fat on ham to ½ inch. Place ham fat side up in a roasting pan lined with foil. Roast ham 10 minutes per pound or until a meat thermometer inserted in the thickest part reads 130°F, about 1½ hours.

3. Remove ham; score top of ham in a crisscross pattern. Brush ham with glaze. Roast 10 minutes. Garnish top of ham with star anise and star fruit slices. Roast 10 minutes. Remove from oven; brush with glaze. Let stand 20 minutes before carving.

NUTRITION INFORMATION PER SERVING:

331 calories	22 g fat	8 g saturated fat
61% calories from fat	80 mg cholesterol	1,687 mg sodium
3.4 g carbohydrate	28 g protein	0.3 g fiber

How to Top a Ham with Style

Reduce apple cider over medium heat until syrupy; stir in dried cherries.

Glaze with ground cumin and bottled pomegranate molasses from a Middle Eastern market.

Mix toasted bread crumbs and crushed, toasted almonds with honey and orange marmalade for a sweet and crunchy spread.

Sweeten your favorite barbecue sauce with brown sugar and brush it over the ham; top with slow-cooked onion rings.

Melt sugar with lemon juice for a thin glaze; spice it up with a little ground red pepper.

Combine Chinese plum sauce with hot mustard to spread over ham; garnish with sliced plums.

Peanut-Chili Glaze

PREPARATION TIME: 5 minutes
STANDING TIME: 1 hour
YIELD: About ⅔ cup

LOOKING FOR AN alternative to the usual garnishes, writer Kristin Eddy used Asian condiments to give an Easter ham a new coat for a "Good Eating" cover story. This glaze also works well on poultry. Thai peanut sauce can be found in the Asian section of most supermarkets.

½ cup Thai peanut sauce

2 tablespoons Thai *or* Chinese chili puree with garlic

1. Stir together peanut sauce and chili puree in a small bowl. Let stand 1 hour to blend flavors.
2. Use glaze to brush a ham or roast poultry during the last 30 minutes of cooking time.

NUTRITION INFORMATION PER TABLESPOON OF SAUCE:

36 calories	2.9 g fat	0.6 g saturated fat
67% calories from fat	0 mg cholesterol	147 mg sodium
1.7 g carbohydrate	1.4 g protein	0.4 g fiber

Chicago-Style Barbecued Ribs

PREPARATION TIME: 30 minutes
CHILLING TIME: 2 hours
COOKING TIME: 1 hour
YIELD: 4 servings

PROFESSIONAL RIB MASTER Leon Finney has a wide reputation for his great ribs. While the recipe for the sauce slathered on the ribs at the Leon Finney's Bar-B-Q restaurants in Chicago is a trade secret, the *Tribune* test kitchen created a similar recipe in 1982. This sauce will keep two to three weeks in the refrigerator.

4 slabs pork baby back ribs (4 to 6 pounds total)

Seasoned salt for ribs, plus ½ teaspoon more

►

1 cup ketchup

½ cup plus 1 tablespoon cider
vinegar

⅓ cup packed dark brown sugar

2 tablespoons plus 2 teaspoons
Worcestershire sauce

2 tablespoons cornstarch

2 teaspoons steak sauce

½ teaspoon hickory-smoked salt

Hot pepper sauce

1. Generously sprinkle ribs on both sides with seasoned salt. Refrigerate 2 to 12 hours. Remove from refrigerator 30 minutes before cooking; let ribs come to room temperature.

2. Mix ketchup, vinegar, brown sugar, Worcestershire, cornstarch, steak sauce, hickory salt, hot pepper sauce to taste, and ½ teaspoon seasoned salt, in a medium-sized nonreactive saucepan. Heat to boil over medium-high heat. Reduce heat to medium-low; cook uncovered 30 minutes. Taste and adjust seasonings.

3. Prepare grill. Soak hickory wood chips in water to cover at least 20 minutes. Put ribs on the grill rack at least 8 inches from heat. Cover; grill until ribs are golden on both sides. Add a handful of drained hickory chips periodically to grill to maintain a steady amount of hickory smoke.

4. Continue grilling until ribs are tender, 30 to 40 minutes. Baste one side heavily with sauce; grill until sauce bubbles. Turn; baste second side with sauce. Grill until sauce bubbles. Remove to a serving platter.

❧ NOTE: *For the best results with ribs, cook them with only a moderate amount of charcoal so the grill is not too hot. The longer the ribs take to cook, the better the smoke flavor will permeate the meat. Do not allow ribs to char.*

NUTRITION INFORMATION PER SERVING:

1,031 calories	67 g fat	24 g saturated fat
58% calories from fat	265 mg cholesterol	1,668 mg sodium
42 g carbohydrate	65 g protein	0.9 g fiber

Ground Pork and Chorizo Enchiladas

PREPARATION TIME: 40 minutes
COOKING TIME: 55 minutes
YIELD: 4 servings

CHORIZO, A SPICY Mexican sausage that can be found in most Hispanic markets and some supermarkets, is combined with ground pork in this lively ground meat combo. You can prepare these enchiladas one day ahead through step 2 of recipe. Refrigerate until you're ready to serve.

⅔ pound lean ground pork
⅓ pound chorizo, chopped
⅓ cup chopped onion
¾ cup buttermilk
¾ teaspoon vinegar
1 large bay leaf
½ teaspoon salt
2 cloves garlic, minced
2 medium tomatoes, peeled,
    seeded, and chopped
2 teaspoons ground cumin

1½ teaspoons dried oregano
¼ teaspoon crushed red pepper
    flakes
1 cup tomato sauce
1 cup salsa
1 to 2 teaspoons sugar
8 6-inch corn tortillas
5 ounces Chihuahua cheese,
    shredded
¼ cup chopped cilantro

1. Cook pork, chorizo, and onions in a large skillet over medium-low heat, stirring to break up meat, until browned, about 7 minutes. Drain off fat. Add buttermilk, vinegar, bay leaf, salt, and half of the garlic. Cook over medium heat until buttermilk is nearly evaporated, about 15 minutes.

2. Add tomatoes, cumin, oregano, and pepper flakes. Cook 5 minutes; remove bay leaf. Allow mixture to cool; skim fat.

3. Heat tomato sauce, salsa, sugar, and remaining garlic in a medium-sized skillet. Cook over medium heat until sauce thickens, 10 to 15 minutes. Place a small amount of sauce on the bottom of a 13″ × 9″ baking pan. Set aside.

►

4. Heat oven to 200°F. Wrap tortillas in foil; place in oven to soften, about 5 minutes. Remove tortillas; increase heat in oven to 350°F. Place each tortilla on a flat surface and top with ⅓ cup of the meat mixture. Roll or fold tortilla to encase filling. Place filled tortillas in a row in baking pan. Spoon remaining sauce over. Cover pan; bake until heated through, about 15 minutes. Sprinkle with Chihuahua cheese and chopped cilantro.

NUTRITION INFORMATION PER SERVING:

661 calories	38 g fat	17 g saturated fat
51% calories from fat	122 mg cholesterol	1,802 mg sodium
45 g carbohydrate	37 g protein	7 g fiber

Lamb Chops with Bourbon and Rosemary

PREPARATION TIME: 15 minutes

MARINATING TIME: 3 to 4 hours

COOKING TIME: 7 minutes

YIELD: 2 servings

LAMB SHOULDER CHOPS, sometimes called "blade" or "arm," are wonderfully flavorful and considerably less expensive than rib and leg cuts. The meat is chewier, but since the chewing releases the meat's enticing flavor, patience pays off. With the lamb, food and wine columnist William Rice recommends serving a hearty wine such as zinfandel and a potato salad flavored with the same ingredients used in the marinade.

4 shoulder lamb chops (about ¾-inch thick), fat trimmed	1½ teaspoons chopped fresh rosemary leaves
3 cloves garlic, minced	½ teaspoon salt
2 tablespoons bourbon	½ teaspoon freshly ground black pepper
2 tablespoons lemon juice	¼ cup olive oil plus more for oiling skillet
2 teaspoons Dijon mustard	

1. Place chops in a large plastic food storage bag. Combine garlic, bourbon, lemon juice, mustard, rosemary, salt, and pepper in a small bowl; stir well. Slowly whisk in oil. Pour marinade over chops. Seal bag; marinate in refrigerator 3 to 4 hours, turning occasionally.

2. Prepare grill or lightly oil a cast-iron skillet large enough to hold chops in a single layer. Remove chops from marinade; pat dry. Grill or cook in pan, turning once, about 7 minutes for medium rare.

NUTRITION INFORMATION PER SERVING:

937 calories	71 g fat	28 g saturated fat
69% calories from fat	276 mg cholesterol	390 mg sodium
1 g carbohydrate	70 g protein	0.1 g fiber

Roast Rack of Lamb

PREPARATION TIME: 10 minutes

COOKING TIME: 30 minutes

YIELD: 2 servings

THIS IS THE perfect entree for a romantic dinner for two—if both partners like garlic. Otherwise, note that parsley effectively counters the lingering taste of garlic; use some sprigs for garnish and feel free to nibble the leaves. Crisp green beans and roast or mashed potatoes are traditional accompaniments. If the coating becomes dark brown during cooking, cover it with a piece of foil. If you are splurging, open a bottle of Bordeaux.

½ cup fresh bread crumbs	2 teaspoons dried basil
1 green onion, minced	2 teaspoons dried chervil
1 clove garlic, minced	3 tablespoons olive oil
1 tablespoon fresh parsley	1 rack of lamb (about 1 pound)

1. Mix bread crumbs, onion, garlic, parsley, basil, and chervil in a small bowl. Add enough oil to make a damp mixture that clings together.

2. Heat oven to 400°F. Spread crumb mixture over the top of lamb. Place lamb on a rack set in a roasting pan.

3. Roast until meat thermometer registers 130°F for rare, 13 to 15 minutes per pound. Let stand 10 minutes before carving.

NUTRITION INFORMATION PER SERVING:

655 calories	53 g fat	16 g saturated fat
70% calories from fat	140 mg cholesterol	165 mg sodium
8.4 g carbohydrate	36 g protein	1.3 g fiber

Seven-Spice Rack of Lamb

PREPARATION TIME: 35 minutes
COOKING TIME: 1 hour 25 minutes
YIELD: 2 servings

JEAN-GEORGES VONGERICHTEN, creator of Vong, a French-Thai fusion restaurant that opened a Chicago branch in 1999, provided the "Good Eating" section with this recipe for rack of lamb. "Once Americans start to taste food made well with a variety of spices, they are hooked," the chef said. "With spice, we can create cravings." There will be extra spice mixture left after you make this recipe. Store it in an airtight container for later use. Also try it with poultry. When buying the rack of lamb, ask your butcher for additional lamb bones for the sauce.

1 whole clove	1 small onion, chopped
1 stick cinnamon	1 small carrot, peeled and chopped
1 tablespoon cardamom pods	1 rib celery, chopped
1 tablespoon sesame seeds	1½ cups water or more as needed
1 tablespoon fenugreek	1 rack of lamb (7 *or* 8 chops, about
1 tablespoon ground cumin	1 pound)
1 tablespoon ground mace	Salt
1½ teaspoons crushed red pepper flakes	1 tablespoon butter
1½ teaspoons grated nutmeg	1 cucumber, peeled, seeded, and sliced
Additional lamb bones and trimmings for sauce	¼ pound French *or* other green beans, blanched and drained

1. Combine clove, cinnamon, cardamom, sesame seeds, fenugreek, cumin, mace, red pepper flakes, and nutmeg in a large skillet; heat over low heat until fragrant, about 8 minutes. Do not allow spice mixture to singe or burn. Grind to medium-fine in a spice mill or small food processor.

2. Brown lamb trimmings and bones with onion, carrot, and celery in a medium-sized saucepan over medium heat. Add 1 teaspoon of the spice mix; cover with at least 1½ cups water. Simmer uncovered 45 minutes; strain. Return strained sauce to pan. Heat to reduce liquid to ⅔ cup, about 15 minutes.

3. Heat oven to 425°F. Season lamb with 1 tablespoon of the spice mixture and salt. Place in a large, heavy oven-safe skillet; sear meat over medium-high heat. Transfer to oven; cook 15 to 17 minutes for medium rare. Melt butter in a medium-sized skillet over medium heat. Add cucumber and beans; cook, stirring often, until crisp-tender, 5 to 7 minutes. Reheat sauce.

4. Make a bed of vegetables in center of each plate. Slice the rack of lamb into individual chops. Arrange chops on top of vegetables. Pour sauce around outside of vegetables.

NUTRITION INFORMATION PER SERVING:

700 calories	46 g fat	21 g saturated fat
58% calories from fat	190 mg cholesterol	210 mg sodium
25 g carbohydrate	50 g protein	8 g fiber

Roast Rack of Lamb with Figs and Herbs

PREPARATION/STANDING TIME: 45 minutes

COOKING TIME: 45 minutes

YIELD: 4 servings

BLACKBIRD CHEF PAUL Kahan, one of several young Chicago chefs making waves along West Randolph Street, looks to country French cooking for inspiration and seeks to modernize old favorites, as he does here. This fall recipe can be simplified by serving the lamb with the sauce only or the compote only, if you wish. Ask the butcher to remove the cap on the racks of lambs and "french" the bones. You may prepare recipe ahead through step 3.

Lamb
2 racks of lamb
1 tablespoon extra-virgin olive oil
2 tablespoons herbes de Provence
2 tablespoons coarsely ground
    black pepper
½ teaspoon salt
2 tablespoons vegetable oil

Sauce
2 large ripe black figs, Mission
    preferred, cut into quarters
1 16-ounce can chicken broth *or* 2
    cups homemade veal *or* chicken
    stock
1 sprig fresh thyme

1 sprig fresh rosemary
1 tablespoon honey
¼ teaspoon salt
Freshly ground black pepper

Fig Compote
6 large ripe black figs, stems
    removed, cut into ½-inch cubes
1 jalapeño, seeded and chopped
    fine
Juice of 1 lime
2 tablespoons extra-virgin olive oil
1 tablespoon finely chopped fresh
    mint
¼ teaspoon salt
Freshly ground black pepper

►

1. Coat lamb with olive oil; rub with herbes de Provence and pepper. Set aside 30 minutes to 1 hour.

2. To make sauce, place quartered figs, broth, thyme, and rosemary in a medium-sized saucepan. Heat to boil over medium heat; cook until reduced by half, about 30 minutes. Stir in honey; simmer until dissolved. Pour through a fine-mesh sieve, pushing fig pulp through with the back of a spoon. Return liquid to the pan; season with salt and black pepper to taste. Set aside.

3. To make compote, stir together all ingredients in a medium-sized bowl. Set aside.

4. Heat oven to 500°F. Season racks with ½ teaspoon salt. Heat vegetable oil in an oven-safe skillet large enough to hold both racks over medium-high heat; brown lamb on all sides. Transfer skillet to oven; roast until a meat thermometer reads 155°F, 12 to 15 minutes. Remove pan from oven, transfer racks to platter; cover loosely with aluminum foil.

5. Pour all but 1 teaspoon of the oil and drippings from skillet. Add reserved sauce; cook over medium heat, stirring, until thickened. Season with salt and pepper to taste. Add water or broth if it's too thick.

6. Slice racks into 2-bone chops. Divide chops among 4 plates; pour ¼ cup sauce over each portion. Top with fig compote.

❧ NOTE: *Herbes de Provence is a fragrant blend of herbs from the Provence region of France. Typically it includes a mix of basil, fennel seeds, lavender, marjoram, rosemary, sage, summer savory, and thyme. Look for it in the spice aisle of some supermarkets and in specialty food shops.*

NUTRITION INFORMATION PER SERVING:

430 calories	24 g fat	7 g saturated fat
49% calories from fat	80 mg cholesterol	1,050 mg sodium
28 g carbohydrate	28 g protein	4.3 g fiber

Grilled Butterflied Leg of Lamb with Herb Marinade

PREPARATION TIME: 20 minutes
MARINATING TIME: 8 to 12 hours
GRILLING TIME: About 1 hour
YIELD: 8 servings

CHICAGO HERB EXPERT Jim Haring offered this recipe for easy-to-carve, flavorful lamb. Most butchers will bone and butterfly the leg of lamb for you with some advance notice. Because the meat is uneven in thickness, you will be able to offer a choice of rare, medium, and well-done lamb. In summertime, wrap potatoes, onions, and summer squash in foil and cook them on the grill as well. Serve this with a California merlot or cabernet.

1 cup dry red wine
1 cup olive oil
12 sprigs thyme, chopped coarse
6 sprigs rosemary, chopped coarse
3 cloves garlic, minced
1 large sprig sage, chopped coarse
1 teaspoon coarsely ground black pepper
½ teaspoon salt
1 leg of lamb, boned and butterflied (about 6 pounds)

1. Stir together wine, oil, thyme, rosemary, garlic, sage, pepper, and salt in a large, shallow nonreactive bowl or large plastic food storage bag. Add lamb; turn to coat thoroughly with marinade. Cover or seal; refrigerate overnight, turning lamb at least once.

2. Prepare grill for indirect heat. Remove lamb from marinade; reserve marinade. Put lamb on a grill rack over a drip pan. Cover; grill, turning once, until meat thermometer registers 130°F for rare, 13 to 15 minutes per pound. Brush frequently with reserved marinade. Maintain grill temperature at about 350°F.

3. Let meat stand on serving platter 10 minutes; temperature will rise about 10 degrees. Serve very thinly sliced.

❧ NOTE: *Lamb can be cooked in the oven at 350°F. Remove lamb from marinade; set on a rack in a roasting pan. Cook until meat thermometer registers 130°F for rare, 13 to 15 minutes per pound. Brush frequently with reserved marinade.*

NUTRITION INFORMATION PER SERVING:

711 calories	46 g fat	10 g saturated fat
60% calories from fat	218 mg cholesterol	312 mg sodium
0.7 g carbohydrate	69 g protein	.09 g fiber

Moroccan Lamb Pie

PREPARATION TIME: 1 hour
CHILLING TIME: 2 hours
COOKING TIME: 2 hours 15 minutes
YIELD: 10 servings

EASY TO TRANSPORT in its baking pan, this savory pie can be an exotic treat at a picnic. Beverly Dillon created it for a candlelight supper at Ravinia Park, the open-air amphitheater that is the Chicago Symphony Orchestra's summer home. Phyllo is available in many supermarket frozen food sections or at Greek and Middle Eastern food markets. You may make the recipe ahead through step 2 and freeze it. To freeze, spoon meat filling into a freezer bag. Squeeze out any excess air; seal shut. Meat mixture may be frozen up to one month. To assemble after freezing, defrost and heat just so juices are easier to extract.

Meat Filling
3 pounds boneless lamb shoulder *or* leg of lamb, cut into ½-inch cubes
3 onions, diced
2 cloves garlic, minced
1 stick cinnamon
2 16-ounce cans whole tomatoes, undrained, chopped
3 tablespoons butter
3 tablespoons olive oil
2 tablespoons tomato paste
1 teaspoon ground ginger
1 teaspoon salt
1 teaspoon freshly ground black pepper
½ teaspoon loosely packed saffron threads *or* ⅛ teaspoon saffron powder
¼ cup honey
1 teaspoon ground cinnamon
¼ cup fine homemade bread crumbs

Dough
1 1-pound box frozen phyllo, thawed
1½ cups (3 sticks) unsalted butter, melted

1. To make filling, stir together lamb, onions, garlic, cinnamon stick, tomatoes, butter, oil, tomato paste, ginger, salt, pepper, and saffron in a 6-quart Dutch oven with a tight-fitting lid. Add enough water to cover mixture. Heat to boil over medium-high heat. Reduce heat to medium-low; simmer covered until meat is very tender, 1 to 1½ hours. Stir mixture several times during cooking. Remove from heat. Transfer meat with a slotted spoon to a platter. Discard cinnamon stick.

2. Return pan with juices to medium-high heat. Cook, stirring often, until broth is thick and reduced to 2 cups. Stir in honey and ground cinnamon. Remove from heat. Stir meat back into reduced liquid. Refrigerate to cool.

3. Put meat filling in a strainer over a bowl to drain all juices. Press meat with back of spoon to squeeze out as much of the juice as possible, about 2 cups. (Reserve meat juices for couscous salad or other use.) Spoon meat into bowl; stir in bread crumbs.

4. Heat oven to 375°F. Butter a 13″ × 9″ baking pan; place 1 sheet of phyllo on the bottom of the pan. Keep remaining phyllo covered with a towel. Brush lightly with melted butter. Repeat layering until there are 10 layers. Tuck in any excess phyllo. Spread meat mixture evenly over phyllo layers in pan. Stack another 10 sheets of buttered phyllo on top.

5. Bake 15 minutes. Reduce oven temperature to 350°F. Bake until phyllo is crisp and golden, about 30 minutes. Cool 15 minutes before cutting into squares. Serve warm or at room temperature.

NUTRITION INFORMATION PER SERVING:

765 calories	57 g fat	28 g saturated fat
66% calories from fat	169 mg cholesterol	719 mg sodium
40 g carbohydrate	26 g protein	2.8 g fiber

Spiced Rabbit with Salsa-Flavored Sauce

PREPARATION TIME: 40 minutes
MARINATING TIME: 8 to 12 hours
COOKING TIME: 50 minutes
YIELD: 4 servings

CHEF AYDIN DINCER, a culinary innovator, developed this recipe while he was chef of the former Star Top Café. It represents the trend toward reintroducing game, once a Midwestern staple, on restaurant menus. The chef calls this "a very hearty, cold-weather dish" and serves it with cracked wheat or brown rice. This recipe also works well with one chicken in place of the rabbit.

¼ cup chopped fresh parsley
2 tablespoons lemon juice
1 clove garlic, minced
¾ teaspoon salt
½ teaspoon ground red pepper
¼ teaspoon ground cumin
2 rabbits, cut into serving pieces

1 14½-ounce can stewed tomatoes, undrained
1 onion, chopped
1 small green bell pepper, seeded and chopped
2 jalapeños, seeded and minced
¼ teaspoon salt

►

¼ teaspoon dried oregano
Freshly ground black pepper
Vinegar
Flour
Vegetable *or* olive oil

2 cups chicken broth
¾ cup dry white wine
1 cup whipping cream *or*
   half-and-half

1. Stir together parsley, lemon juice, garlic, salt, red pepper, and cumin in a small bowl; rub into each rabbit piece. Place rabbit in a plastic food storage bag; seal. Refrigerate 8 to 12 hours.

2. Combine tomatoes, onion, bell pepper, jalapeños, salt, oregano, and black pepper and vinegar to taste in a medium-sized bowl. Taste and adjust seasonings. Let stand at least 1 hour before serving.

3. Heat oven to 375°F. Coat rabbit pieces in flour; shake off excess. Heat ¼ inch of oil in a large skillet over high heat. Add rabbit pieces in a single layer. Cook until golden brown on all sides. Drain on a paper towel. Put rabbit in a single layer in a roasting pan. Bake until juices run clear, about 20 minutes.

4. Heat chicken broth and wine in a medium-sized saucepan to boil; reduce to about one-quarter of original amount. Add cream; boil gently until reduced enough to lightly coat the back of a spoon. Add salsa to taste, about ¼ cup. (Refrigerate remaining salsa for a later use.) Serve rabbit with sauce.

NUTRITION INFORMATION PER SERVING:

795 calories	44 g fat	20 g saturated fat
51% calories from fat	295 mg cholesterol	1,345 mg sodium
15 g carbohydrate	82 g protein	2.2 g fiber

Fusion Barbecue Sauce

PREPARATION TIME: 5 minutes

STANDING TIME: 1 hour

YIELD: About 20 1-tablespoon servings

CHEF ALLEN STERNWEILER at Harvest on Huron uses grated gingerroot to give an Asian accent to all-American barbecue sauce. Use this quick sauce on swordfish, chicken, pork, lamb roasts, or ribs.

1 1½-inch-thick piece gingerroot,
   peeled and minced
1 cup plain (not smoke-flavored)
   barbecue sauce

2 tablespoons honey
1 tablespoon vanilla extract

1. Stir together gingerroot, barbecue sauce, honey, and vanilla in a small bowl until thoroughly combined. Let stand at room temperature at least 1 hour.

2. Brush sauce on meat of your choice during its final minutes of cooking.

NUTRITION INFORMATION PER SERVING:

18 calories	0.2 g fat	.04 g saturated fat
11% calories from fat	0 mg cholesterol	102 mg sodium
3.5 g carbohydrate	0.2 g protein	0.2 g fiber

White Wine Marinade

PREPARATION TIME: 10 minutes
COOKING TIME: 5 minutes
YIELD: 2½ cups

ALTHOUGH MARINADES WON'T tenderize truly tough cuts of meat, they will add flavor to everything from duck to buffalo, as freelance writer Nancy Ross Ryan showed in a "Good Eating" story. Use this recipe from John Birdsall, chef at Rita's Catering in Chicago, for up to three pounds of chicken, duck, pork, seafood (especially shrimp and salmon steaks), or vegetables. You may make this marinade in advance through step 1 and refrigerate it covered.

2 cups dry white wine (chardonnay, sauvignon blanc, *or* Riesling)	4 cloves garlic, minced
	4 sprigs fresh thyme *or* 3 teaspoons dried leaf thyme
2 tablespoons champagne vinegar	6 juniper berries, crushed
½ cup extra-virgin olive oil	1 teaspoon salt
½ ounce dried mushrooms (porcino *or* Chinese black), chopped	Freshly ground black pepper
	1½ teaspoons grated orange zest

1. Combine wine, vinegar, oil, mushrooms, garlic, thyme, juniper berries, salt, and black pepper to taste in a small nonreactive saucepan. Heat to boil over medium heat. Cool to room temperature.

2. Add orange zest to marinade. Combine marinade and meat in a covered, nonreactive container or plastic food storage bag. Cover or seal; refrigerate. Marinate pork and duck up to 4 hours, chicken up to 2 hours, and seafood and vegetables for less than 1 hour, turning frequently.

➤

❧ VARIATIONS: *Omit juniper berries and add ¼ cup Dijon mustard. Or substitute rosemary for thyme.*

❧ NOTE: *We have not calculated nutrition information since the amount of marinade absorbed by the meat is minimal.*

Cool It!

Below are conservative suggestions for cold storage times for a few selected foods. Frozen food can be stored for up to one year, but the quality begins to deteriorate after the times listed here.

For food storage questions, call the USDA *Meat and Poultry Hotline, 800-535-4555.*

Refrigerator storage		Freezer storage	
Berries	3 days	Butter	6 to 9 months
Butter	2 to 3 weeks	Poultry	12 months
Citrus fruit	2 weeks	Cookie dough	3 months
Deli meats	5 days	Dark fish	2 to 3 months
Eggs	1 month	White fish	6 months
Greens	5 days	Fruit juice concentrate	12 months
Margarine	1 month	Ground meat	2 to 3 months
Milk	1 week	Ice cream	2 months
Red meat	2 to 3 days	Pie dough	4 to 6 months
Root vegetables	2 weeks	Roasts	6 months
Salad dressing	3 months	Unfrosted cakes	2 to 4 months
Seafood	2 days	Vegetables	8 months
Sliced and cream cheeses	2 weeks		

Source: USDA *(U.S. Department of Agriculture)*

POULTRY

Roast Chicken with Lemon and Rosemary

PREPARATION TIME: 35 minutes
COOKING TIME: 1 hour 30 minutes
YIELD: 6 servings

A SIMPLE ROASTED chicken gets a big flavor boost from lemon and rosemary in this recipe developed by JeanMarie Brownson in the test kitchen. If you happen to find fresh rosemary in the market, try substituting it for the dried version.

1 roasting chicken (about 5½ pounds)	2½ teaspoons dried rosemary leaves
Salt	1 tablespoon vegetable oil
Freshly ground black pepper	3 tablespoons olive oil
1 lemon	½ cup chicken broth
3 large cloves garlic, halved	⅓ cup dry white wine
3 sprigs fresh parsley	3 tablespoons unsalted butter
	Chopped parsley

1. Rinse chicken under cold water; pat dry. Sprinkle cavity with salt and pepper to taste. Juice the lemon, grate its zest, and reserve its shells. Put lemon shells, garlic, half of the lemon zest, parsley, and 1 teaspoon of the rosemary into cavity of chicken.

2. Heat oven to 375°F. Gently lift skin from breasts, thighs, and back of chicken by slipping fingers between skin and meat. Put the remaining lemon zest and 1½ teaspoons rosemary between skin and meat.

3. Brush vegetable oil over the bottom of a heavy roasting pan. Put chicken in pan; brush generously on all sides with olive oil. Sprinkle with black pepper.

➤

4. Roast chicken, basting occasionally with pan juices and chicken broth, until temperature of thigh registers 170°F on a meat thermometer and juices run clear, about 1 hour 20 minutes. Transfer to a platter; let rest, loosely tented with aluminum foil. (Temperature will rise about 10°F.)

5. Skim fat from pan juices. Put roasting pan over medium heat; stir in remaining chicken broth and wine. Simmer, scraping up browned bits from bottom of pan, until liquid reduces to about ½ cup. Stir in 3 tablespoons lemon juice. Vigorously whisk in butter. Taste and adjust seasonings. Stir in parsley.

NUTRITION INFORMATION PER SERVING:

602 calories	42 g fat	13 g saturated fat
63% calories from fat	179 mg cholesterol	224 mg sodium
2.1 g carbohydrate	52 g protein	0.5 g fiber

Clay-Pot Chicken with Forty Cloves of Garlic

PREPARATION TIME: 20 minutes
COOKING TIME: About 1¼ hours
YIELD: 4 servings

FORMER *TRIBUNE* COLUMNIST Lee Thompson wrote an ode to the clay pot in one memorable article. According to Thompson, the clay pot makes possible cooking at high temperatures without burning the food within, and it gives foods an extra depth of flavor. This classic French dish is a perfect selection for clay-pot cookery. After roasting the chicken, don't throw away the garlic; squeeze it from the skins and spread it on French bread.

1 roasting chicken (3½ to 4 pounds)	1 teaspoon ground rosemary
Juice of ½ lemon	Salt
3 tablespoons butter, softened	Freshly ground black pepper
1 teaspoon rubbed sage	3 to 4 heads garlic (40 cloves),
1 teaspoon dried leaf thyme	cloves separated, unpeeled

1. Soak the clay pot and lid in lukewarm water at least 15 minutes. Drain. Put chicken into the clay pot. Pour lemon juice into body cavity. Rub chicken with butter, sage, thyme, rosemary, salt and pepper to taste. Distribute garlic cloves around and over chicken.

2. Cover; place in a cold oven. Set oven temperature to 425°F. Bake 50 minutes from time oven reaches temperature. Remove clay pot lid. Baste chicken with juices. Increase oven temperature to 450°F. Bake uncovered until breast skin is golden and thigh juices run clear when tested with a fork, 10 to 15 more minutes.

❧ NOTE: *While the clay pot yields the best results, this recipe can be prepared in a Dutch oven. To do so, omit the soaking step. Follow the remaining directions, except place chicken in a 4-quart Dutch oven and pour 2½ cups chicken broth or water over chicken. Bake covered in a 350°F oven until thigh juices run clear, about 1 hour. Raise oven temperature to 400°F; bake until skin becomes crisp, about 15 minutes. After cooking, remove chicken and garlic cloves to a platter; keep warm. Simmer pan juices over medium heat until reduced by one-third; season to taste with salt and pepper.*

NUTRITION INFORMATION PER SERVING:

585 calories	36 g fat	13 g saturated fat
57% calories from fat	180 mg cholesterol	245 mg sodium
11 g carbohydrate	51 g protein	1 g fiber

Roasted Garlic–Stuffed Chicken Breasts with Tomato-Caper Sauce

PREPARATION TIME: 30 minutes
COOKING TIME: 1½ hours
YIELD: 4 servings

Is AMISH CHICKEN better than supermarket brands? A *Tribune* tasting discerned little difference between them. But many chefs prefer the taste of the birds, which are usually raised free-range. This flavorful dish is from a recipe by Christopher Koetke, former chef at Les Nomades and a Kendall College culinary instructor. You may prepare the chicken breasts ahead through step 2 and refrigerate up to one day.

20 cloves garlic, peeled
½ cup olive oil, or more as needed
4 boneless chicken breast halves
1 onion, chopped fine
3 cloves garlic, minced
3 tomatoes, peeled, seeded, and
    chopped

1 teaspoon herbes de Provence (see
    Index)
Salt
Freshly ground black pepper
½ cup chicken broth
¼ cup white wine
3 tablespoons capers

▶

1. Heat oven to 350°F. Place garlic cloves in a small oven-proof skillet; add olive oil to cover garlic. Heat to a simmer over medium-high heat. Bake covered until garlic is lightly browned, about 20 minutes. Cool garlic; reserve oil. Mash cooked garlic in a small bowl with 1 teaspoon of the reserved oil until a smooth paste forms.

2. Cut a pocket in the side of each chicken breast; stuff with mashed garlic.

3. Heat 2 tablespoons of the reserved oil in a medium-sized skillet over medium-high heat. Add onion; cook until translucent, about 3 minutes. Add minced garlic; cook 1 minute. Stir in tomatoes, herbes de Provence, and salt and pepper to taste. Cook 5 minutes. Add broth; simmer over low heat 15 minutes.

4. Heat oven to 400°F. Heat 2 tablespoons of the reserved oil in a medium-sized oven-proof skillet over medium-high heat. Add chicken breasts; cook until browned on both sides. Place skillet with chicken breasts skin side up in oven. Bake until chicken is no longer pink in center, 8 to 10 minutes.

5. Remove chicken from pan; keep warm. Add wine to pan; heat to a boil over medium-high heat, scraping the bottom of the pan to remove any browned pieces. Add wine and capers to tomato sauce; cook 15 minutes to reduce and thicken sauce. Pour over chicken breasts.

NUTRITION INFORMATION PER SERVING:

441 calories	31 g fat	4.6 g saturated fat
62% calories from fat	73 mg cholesterol	364 mg sodium
13 g carbohydrate	30 g protein	2.2 g fiber

Chicken Stuffed with Pistachios and Currants

PREPARATION TIME: 30 minutes

COOKING TIME: 20 minutes

YIELD: 4 servings

"THIS IS A very seasonal cuisine," said Robert Stern, who was quoted in a story about Turkish cooking. "People here only cook with the best of the best. If it's not the right time of year for plums or nectarines or melons, they don't eat it." Stern, chef at Ciragan Palace Hotel, Istanbul, shared this recipe for one of his specialties.

Warm water	1 tomato, seeded and chopped
⅓ cup dried currants	¾ cup chopped pistachio nuts
4 skinless, boneless chicken breast halves	1 tablespoon chopped fresh dill
	Salt

Freshly ground black pepper
2 teaspoons vegetable oil
3 tablespoons unsalted butter
1 large yellow onion, chopped fine
2 cloves garlic, minced

1 10-ounce bag fresh spinach leaves, washed, trimmed, and chopped
1 cup whipping cream *or* half-and-half

1. Soak currants in warm water until soft; drain. Meanwhile, heat oven to 375°F. Slice a pocket horizontally down the length of each chicken breast. Combine tomato, pistachios, currants, dill, and salt and pepper to taste; stuff mixture in chicken breasts. Brush chicken with oil; place in a baking pan. Bake 20 to 25 minutes.

2. Melt butter in a large skillet over medium heat; cook onion and garlic until golden, about 8 minutes. Add spinach; cook 1 minute. Stir in cream.

3. Slice each chicken breast into 4 pieces. Place some of the spinach sauce on each of 4 plates; top with chicken slices and additional sauce.

NUTRITION INFORMATION PER SERVING:

625 calories	48 g fat	22 g saturated fat
67% calories from fat	175 mg cholesterol	155 mg sodium
17 g carbohydrate	36 g protein	6 g fiber

Chicken with Potato "Skin"

PREPARATION TIME: 20 minutes
COOKING TIME: 25 minutes
YIELD: 4 servings

COOKBOOK AUTHOR JANE Freiman Schanberg met one New Year's diet resolution with the following low-calorie entree of chicken breasts and potatoes. It's only 232 calories per portion, and it is quick and easy with the help of the food processor.

¼ cup firmly packed fresh parsley leaves
1 large clove garlic
¼ cup Dijon mustard
1 medium-sized baking potato, peeled and cut into large chunks

Cold water
1½ teaspoons olive oil
2 whole chicken breasts, skinned, split, rinsed, and patted dry
Freshly ground black pepper

►

1. Process parsley in a food processor fitted with a metal blade. Add garlic through the feed tube with the motor running. Add mustard; process 10 seconds. Transfer mixture to a small bowl; set aside.

2. Shred potato in the food processor fitted with a medium shredding blade. Put potato shreds in a bowl of cold water; let stand 5 minutes. Rinse; drain thoroughly. Pat potato shreds dry with paper towels. Dry bowl. Put potato shreds back into bowl; toss thoroughly with oil.

3. Heat oven to 375°F. Brush chicken pieces with one-quarter of the mustard mixture. Put chicken bone side down onto a jelly roll pan. Top each chicken piece with one-quarter of the potato shreds, spreading shreds into a thin, even layer to replace chicken skin. Sprinkle lightly with black pepper.

4. Bake until chicken juices run clear when you pierce the chicken and a meat thermometer reads 170°F, about 20 minutes. Set oven to broil; broil until potatoes are crisp, about 5 minutes.

NUTRITION INFORMATION PER SERVING:

214 calories	6 g fat	1.2 g saturated fat
26% calories from fat	73 mg cholesterol	447 mg sodium
11 g carbohydrate	29 g protein	0.9 g fiber

Chicken Vesuvio

PREPARATION TIME: 25 minutes

COOKING TIME: 1 hour

YIELD: 4 servings

CHICKEN VESUVIO IS a true Chicago original—served in almost all the Italian restaurants in town. It's fried and then baked with plenty of garlic, white wine, olive oil, and potatoes. The following *Tribune* test kitchen version reduces the amount of olive oil traditionally used, for a less greasy dish.

⅓ cup flour	1 broiler/fryer chicken (about 3
1½ teaspoons dried basil	pounds), cut into pieces
¾ teaspoon dried leaf oregano	½ cup olive oil
½ teaspoon salt	3 baking potatoes, cut into
¼ teaspoon dried leaf thyme	lengthwise wedges
¼ teaspoon freshly ground pepper	3 cloves garlic, minced
⅛ teaspoon dried rosemary	3 tablespoons minced fresh parsley
⅛ teaspoon rubbed sage	¾ cup dry white wine

1. Mix flour, basil, oregano, salt, thyme, pepper, rosemary, and sage in a shallow dish. Dredge chicken in flour mixture. Shake off excess.

2. Heat oil in a 12-inch cast-iron or other oven-safe skillet over medium-high heat until hot. Add chicken pieces in single layer. Fry, turning occasionally, until light brown on all sides, about 15 minutes. Remove and place on paper towels. Repeat until all pieces are fried.

3. Add potato wedges to same skillet. Fry, turning occasionally, until light brown on all sides, about 15 minutes. Remove and place on paper towels.

4. Heat oven to 375°F. Pour off all but 2 tablespoons of the fat from skillet. Put chicken and potatoes back into skillet. Sprinkle with garlic and parsley. Pour wine over all.

5. Bake, uncovered, until potatoes are fork-tender, thigh juices run clear, and thermometer reads 170°F, 20 to 25 minutes. Let stand 5 minutes before serving. Serve with pan juices.

NUTRITION INFORMATION PER SERVING:

724 calories	37 g fat	8 g saturated fat
47% calories from fat	134 mg cholesterol	434 mg sodium
48 g carbohydrate	47 g protein	4.5 g fiber

Grilled Lemon Chicken with Tomato-Feta Relish

PREPARATION TIME: 20 minutes

COOKING TIME: 10 minutes

YIELD: 4 servings

THIS CHICKEN IS seasoned lightly and quickly, sidestepping lengthy marinating. A fresh, vibrant tomato relish tops it off. The relish is versatile—use it on pasta, grilled fish, bruschetta, and veal chops as well. You may also broil chicken or cook it in a cast-iron, ridged grill pan.

2 tablespoons olive oil	Crushed red pepper flakes
2 tablespoons fresh lemon juice	4 skinless, boneless chicken breast
1 teaspoon Worcestershire sauce	halves
1 teaspoon Dijon mustard	Salt

▶

Relish
2 large tomatoes, preferably 1 red
    and 1 yellow, cored and diced
2 tablespoons olive oil
2 teaspoons red wine vinegar
Salt

Freshly ground black pepper
4 large basil leaves, minced
4 sage leaves, minced
1 ounce (¼ cup) crumbled feta
    cheese

1. Prepare grill. Combine oil, lemon juice, Worcestershire sauce, mustard, and red pepper flakes in a small dish; mix well.

2. Put chicken breasts in a glass pie plate; pour marinade over, turning breasts once to coat both sides. Let stand 10 minutes.

3. Grill over medium-hot coals, turning once, until chicken is white but still juicy in the center, 8 to 10 minutes. Season lightly with salt.

4. Combine tomatoes, oil, vinegar, and salt and black pepper to taste. Add basil, sage, and feta cheese. Taste and adjust seasoning. Serve chicken hot or at room temperature with tomato relish spooned on top.

NUTRITION INFORMATION PER SERVING:

261 calories	14 g fat	3.5 g saturated fat
48% calories from fat	81 mg cholesterol	188 mg sodium
4.9 g carbohydrate	29 g protein	1.1 g fiber

Greek-Style Grilled Chicken

PREPARATION TIME: 10 minutes
MARINATING TIME: 8 to 12 hours
COOKING TIME: 45 minutes
YIELD: 6 servings

CHICAGOAN STEVE COTSIRILOS likes to grill chicken and add a Greek flavor. Plenty of lemon and oregano are the secrets to his flavorful entree that was described in one Memorial Day article.

2 whole broiler/fryer chickens
    (about 2 pounds each), rinsed
    and patted dry
2 tablespoons dried oregano
4 teaspoons freshly ground black
    pepper

1 teaspoon garlic powder
1 teaspoon salt
Juice of 4 lemons
6 tablespoons vegetable oil
2 tablespoons olive oil

1. Cut chickens in half. Stir together oregano, pepper, garlic powder, and salt in a small bowl.

2. Rub oregano mixture onto chicken. Combine lemon juice, vegetable oil, and olive oil in a large plastic food storage bag or in a nonreactive bowl. Add chicken; turn to coat. Seal bag or cover bowl. Refrigerate, turning chicken occasionally, 8 to 12 hours.

3. Prepare grill. Remove chicken from marinade; arrange on the grill rack. Cover; grill, turning and basting with marinade every 5 to 10 minutes, until juices run clear and a meat thermometer reads 170°F, about 45 minutes.

NUTRITION INFORMATION PER SERVING:

395 calories	38 g fat	6.5 g saturated fat
59% calories from fat	119 mg cholesterol	503 mg sodium
1.5 g carbohydrate	38 g protein	0.6 g fiber

Soul-Style Smothered Chicken and Dressing

PREPARATION TIME: 30 minutes

COOKING TIME: 40 minutes

YIELD: 6 servings

"EVERYBODY'S GRANDMA WAS a good cook," said Helen Anglin, owner of the South Side's Soul Queen restaurant, in a story about Chicago's soul food scene, "and everybody's grandma made their recipes in a different way." This recipe is adapted from Anglin's book, *Mama Was Together: The Soul Queen Cookbook*.

Dressing
½ cup (1 stick) plus 1 tablespoon
  unsalted butter, melted
1 onion, chopped
1 rib celery, chopped
½ green bell pepper, seeded and
  chopped
½ cup yellow cornmeal
½ cup all-purpose flour
1 tablespoon poultry seasoning
1 teaspoon salt
½ teaspoon baking soda
½ cup buttermilk
2 large eggs, lightly beaten

Chicken
1 cup plus 2 tablespoons
  all-purpose flour
2 tablespoons salt
1 tablespoon freshly ground black
  pepper
1 broiler/fryer chicken (about 2
  pounds), cut up
½ cup shortening *or* vegetable oil
1 cup chicken broth

►

1.   Heat oven to 400°F. To make dressing, melt 1 tablespoon of the butter in a small skillet over medium heat. Add onion, celery, and bell pepper; cook until softened, about 3 minutes.

2.   Mix cornmeal, flour, poultry seasoning, salt, and baking soda in a medium-sized bowl. Add buttermilk, melted butter, and eggs; stir to mix. Stir in onion mixture. Pour into a 2-quart greased casserole. Bake until a wooden pick inserted in the center comes out clean, 25 to 30 minutes. Keep warm.

3.   To make chicken, put 1 cup of the flour, salt, and pepper in a medium-sized paper bag. Add 1 piece chicken; shake to coat. Continue with all pieces. Melt shortening in a large skillet. Add chicken in a single layer. Cook in batches until browned, about 3 minutes per side. Remove chicken; drain on paper towel.

4.   Drain off all but 2 tablespoons of the shortening in the skillet. Reheat shortening, scraping up browned bits from the bottom. Whisk in remaining 2 tablespoons flour. Add broth; heat to boil. Reduce heat. Cook, stirring constantly, until mixture thickens. Add salt and pepper to taste.

5.   Return chicken to skillet. Cover; simmer until chicken registers 170°F on a meat thermometer when measured at thickest part of thigh, about 20 minutes. Serve chicken with dressing.

NUTRITION INFORMATION PER SERVING:

693 calories	48 g fat	19 g saturated fat
62% calories from fat	178 mg cholesterol	3,061 mg sodium
39 g carbohydrate	27 g protein	2.6 g fiber

Stir-Fry of Chicken, Carrots, and Asparagus

PREPARATION TIME: 20 minutes

COOKING TIME: 6 minutes

YIELD: 2 servings

COLUMNIST PAT DAILEY included this simple stir-fry recipe in one of her "Fast Food" menus. For best results, have everything ready before you start to cook. You don't need a wok; a large nonstick skillet works very well. Just make sure not to overcrowd the pan or the food will steam rather than sear.

1 tablespoon dry sherry	2 teaspoons teriyaki sauce
1 tablespoon seasoned rice vinegar	2 teaspoons peanut *or* vegetable oil
2 teaspoons hoisin sauce	½ to 1 teaspoon Asian sesame oil

2 large carrots, peeled and sliced
  thin diagonally
1 small onion, cut in 1-inch dice
8 asparagus spears, trimmed, cut
  diagonally into 1-inch pieces
1 ½-inch piece gingerroot, peeled
  and minced

1 clove garlic, minced
5 to 6 ounces skinless, boneless
  cooked chicken breast strips
Crushed red pepper flakes
Minced cilantro

1. Stir together sherry, vinegar, hoisin sauce, and teriyaki sauce in a small bowl; set aside. Heat peanut oil and sesame oil in a large nonstick skillet or wok. Add carrots and onion; stir-fry over high heat until softened and browned at edges, 2 to 3 minutes. Add asparagus, gingerroot, and garlic; cook until vegetables are crisp-tender, about 2 minutes.

2. Add chicken; toss to mix. Add sherry mixture to pan; cook until sauce coats chicken and vegetables. Remove from heat; add red pepper flakes and cilantro to taste.

NUTRITION INFORMATION PER SERVING:

225 calories	10 g fat	2 g saturated fat
29% calories from fat	45 mg cholesterol	380 mg sodium
16 g carbohydrate	18 g protein	3.8 g fiber

Paprika Chicken Kabobs with Sour Cream Dipping Sauce

PREPARATION TIME: 20 minutes
MARINATING TIME: 2 hours
COOKING TIME: 10 minutes
YIELD: 4 servings

PAPRIKA IS ONE of the forgotten spices. Often used merely as a garnish, its flavor has gone largely unnoticed in American cooking. But the spice comes in many types, including an intriguing smoky paprika from Spain, which we featured in one cover story. This dish is delicious with any kind of paprika. It comes from Foods from Spain, a trade organization based in New York City.

¼ cup vegetable oil
1 onion, chopped
2 cloves garlic, minced

1 tablespoon tomato paste
1 tablespoon tarragon vinegar *or*
  red wine vinegar

➤

1 teaspoon salt
1 teaspoon sweet paprika
1 teaspoon hot paprika
1 pound skinless, boneless chicken breasts, cut into 1½-inch cubes
1 large red bell pepper, seeded and cut into 1-inch pieces

Dipping Sauce
1 cup chicken broth
¾ cup sour cream
1 teaspoon fresh lemon juice
¼ teaspoon salt
Sweet and hot paprika

1. Heat oil in a medium-sized saucepan over medium heat. Add onion; cook 5 minutes. Remove from heat, transfer to a large bowl to cool. Stir in garlic, tomato paste, vinegar, salt, sweet paprika, and hot paprika. Add chicken; toss to coat. Cover; marinate refrigerated 2 hours.

2. Soak 8 wooden skewers in water 1 hour, or use metal skewers. Prepare grill or broiler. Arrange cubes of chicken and bell peppers on metal skewers or wooden skewers. Grill or broil, turning as chicken browns, about 10 minutes.

3. To make dipping sauce, place chicken broth in a small, heavy pan. Heat to boil over high heat. Reduce heat to medium; simmer until broth has reduced to ¼ cup. Mix reduced broth, sour cream, lemon juice, and salt in a bowl. Sprinkle with sweet and hot paprika for garnish. Serve with chicken skewers.

NUTRITION INFORMATION PER SERVING:

265 calories	16 g fat	7 g saturated fat
53% calories from fat	180 mg cholesterol	575 mg sodium
5.4 g carbohydrate	26 g protein	1 g fiber

Sources for Paprika

American paprika is sold in supermarkets. European and other specialty stores often sell sweet and hot Hungarian paprikas and occasionally Spanish paprika. Smoked Spanish paprika from La Vera is available at the Spice House in Evanston, Illinois, for $1.09 per ounce. Call 847-328-3711.

Also, a 2.47-ounce can costs $3 to $4 (plus shipping) from the following:

The Spanish Table in Seattle, 206-682-2827.

Fine Products of Spain, at www.tienda.com, or by mail order, 888-472-1022.

Formaggio Kitchen, Cambridge, Massachusetts, 888-212-3224.

Williams-Sonoma Food, 800-699-2297. (It is called "smoked pimiento powder" in the catalog.)

Cumin-Rubbed Grilled Pork Chops (page 232)

Photo by Bob Fila

Photo by James F. Quinn

Hodgepodge Chili (*page 225*)

Veal Scaloppine with Fresh Tomato Relish (*page 226*)

Photo by Bob Fila

Turkey with Herbed Corn Bread Stuffing (page 281)

Pork and Sauerkraut (page 235)

Photo by Bob Fila

*Chicken and Spinach Ragout with
Horseradish–Mashed Potato Crust (page 278)*

Sausage-Sage Stuffing (page 292)

Photo by Bob Fila

Vegetarian Stir-Fry with Pan-Seared
Tofu in Citrus-Soy Broth (page 339)

Curried Sweet Potato Latkes (page 329)

Photo by Bob Fila

Barbecued Lima Beans (page 305)

Photo by Bob Fila

Michael Altenberg's Fingerling Potatoes (page 325)

Photo by Bob Fila

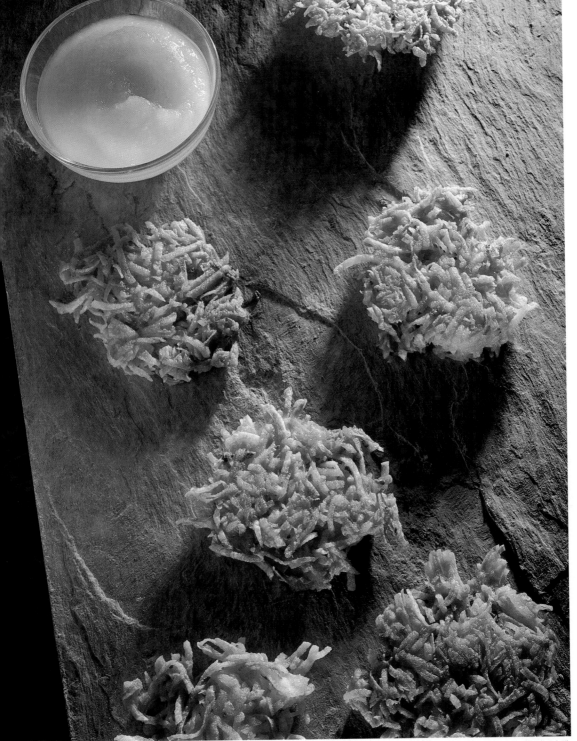

Marjorie Biederman's Latkes (page 328)

Photo by Bob Fila

Corn Custard Cups (page 318)

Photo by Bob Fila

Bean and Squash Coconut Milk Stew (page 303)

Black-Eyed Peas (page 306)

Photo by Bob Fila

Autumn Squash Stuffed with Carrot Couscous (page 336)

Chicken, Okra, and Onion Curry
with Cilantro Chutney

PREPARATION TIME: 30 minutes
COOKING TIME: 15 minutes
YIELD: 4 servings

FROZEN OKRA, BELL peppers, and a little bit of coconut milk turn boneless chicken breasts into an Indian-style curry. For an alternative serving idea, slice the chicken breasts after they're cooked and fold the chicken and vegetables as well as the pilaf into warmed nan or pita bread. The chutney can be refrigerated up to two days.

Chutney
1½ cups cilantro leaves
2 tablespoons fresh mint leaves
⅓ cup water
3 jalapeños, seeded
1 1-inch piece gingerroot, peeled
1 tablespoon fresh lime juice

Curry
2 tablespoons vegetable oil
2 to 3 teaspoons curry powder
¼ teaspoon ground red pepper
1 slice gingerroot, minced
6 small onions, peeled and
    quartered lengthwise

1 large red bell pepper, cut in
    1-inch squares
2 hot green chilies, seeded and
    sliced
1 10-ounce box frozen okra,
    thawed, *or* 8 ounces fresh okra,
    trimmed
4 skinless, boneless chicken breast
    halves
3 tablespoons canned coconut
    milk, light *or* regular
¼ cup minced cilantro
¼ teaspoon salt

1. To make chutney, combine cilantro, mint, water, jalapeños, gingerroot, and lime juice in a blender; blend to a fine texture.

2. To make curry, heat 1 tablespoon of the oil in a large nonstick skillet over high heat. Stir in curry powder and ground red pepper; cook several seconds. Add gingerroot; cook until fragrant, 30 seconds. Add onions, bell pepper, and chilies; cook, stirring often, until onions are soft and brown, 7 to 8 minutes. Add okra. Remove from heat. Set mixture aside in a small bowl.

3. Heat remaining 1 tablespoon oil in the same pan over medium heat. Add chicken breasts; cover. Cook, turning occasionally, until no longer pink, 6 to 8 minutes. Return vegetable mixture to pan. Add coconut milk, cilantro, and salt. Cook to heat through, 1 minute. Serve curry with chutney.

►

NUTRITION INFORMATION PER SERVING:

325 calories	13 g fat	4 g saturated fat
35% calories from fat	73 mg cholesterol	232 mg sodium
23 g carbohydrate	31 g protein	5.7 g fiber

Chicken Curry with Bamboo Shoots (Kang Kai Nor Mai)

PREPARATION TIME: 30 minutes

COOKING TIME: 12 minutes

YIELD: 6 servings

ARUN'S, A THAI restaurant in Chicago, contributed this classic recipe for a story on the basics of Thai cuisine. Homemade red curry paste adds the kick to this soup-stew main course. Use leftover red curry paste in soups or stews. You may refrigerate extra red curry paste covered up to several weeks.

Red Curry Paste

7 to 10 small dried red chilies

¼ cup warm water

2 tablespoons chopped lemongrass (see Index)

½ shallot, chopped

3 cloves garlic, minced

1 ⅓-inch-thick piece gingerroot, minced

1 tablespoon dried shrimp paste (*kapi*)

1 teaspoon salt

½ teaspoon dried citrus rind

Chicken

2 tablespoons corn oil

1 pound skinless, boneless chicken breast strips

2 tablespoons fish sauce (*nam pla*)

1 8-ounce can thinly sliced bamboo shoots, drained

2 cups canned unsweetened coconut milk

½ jalapeño, seeded and shredded

½ cup fresh basil leaves

Cooked white rice

1. To make red curry paste, remove stems and seeds from chilies (or keep the seeds for a hotter curry paste). Put chilies, water, lemongrass, shallot, garlic, gingerroot, dried shrimp paste, salt, and citrus rind into a food processor fitted with a metal blade or in a blender. Process, scraping down sides of container occasionally, until smooth paste forms.

2. Heat oil in a large skillet over medium heat until hot. Add 2 tablespoons of the curry paste; cook, stirring constantly, about 4 minutes.

3. To make chicken, stir in chicken and fish sauce; cook, stirring often, until chicken turns opaque, about 4 minutes. Add bamboo shoots and coconut milk; heat to boil. Add jalapeño and basil leaves. Simmer 2 minutes. Serve with cooked rice.

NUTRITION INFORMATION PER SERVING:

405 calories	27 g fat	15 g saturated fat
55% calories from fat	42 mg cholesterol	1,144 mg sodium
26 g carbohydrate	23 g protein	15 g fiber

Balanced Chicken Tetrazzini

PREPARATION TIME: 45 minutes

COOKING TIME: 45 minutes

YIELD: 8 servings

"Cook It Light" columnist Jeanne Jones took the classic tetrazzini recipe and turned it into a lighter, more healthful version for one of her columns in 1995. We voted it one of the ten best recipes of that year.

1 12-ounce package yolkless egg
  noodles
Nonstick cooking spray
4 teaspoons corn-oil margarine
3 tablespoons dry white wine
1 pound (about 6 cups)
  mushrooms, sliced
1½ cups defatted reduced-sodium
  chicken broth
1 cup nonfat milk
¼ cup unbleached all-purpose
  flour
1 tablespoon minced fresh thyme

1 tablespoon minced fresh tarragon
½ teaspoon salt
¼ teaspoon freshly ground black
  pepper
¼ cup light sour cream
¼ cup minced fresh parsley
1¼ pounds skinless, boneless
  chicken breasts, poached (see
  Note) and cut into bite-sized
  pieces (about 3 cups)
3 to 4 tablespoons shredded
  Parmesan cheese, optional

1. Cook egg noodles according to package directions. Drain and set aside. Heat oven to 375°F. Spray a 13″ × 9″ baking dish with nonstick cooking spray; set aside.

2. Heat 1 teaspoon of the margarine and the wine over medium heat. Add mushrooms; cook until soft, about 5 minutes. Strain liquid into a small bowl; reserve liquid and mushrooms separately.

➤

3. Using a wire whisk, mix chicken broth, milk, and flour in a medium-sized saucepan until smooth. Stir in reserved mushroom liquid and remaining 3 teaspoons of margarine; set over medium heat. Cook, stirring with a wooden spoon, until thickened and boiling, about 10 minutes. Stir in thyme, tarragon, salt, and pepper. Taste and adjust seasonings. Remove sauce from heat. Blend in sour cream and 2 tablespoons of the parsley.

4. Combine noodles, chicken, reserved mushrooms, and sauce. Pour into prepared dish. Sprinkle with Parmesan if desired. Bake until bubbly hot and top is starting to brown, about 20 minutes. Sprinkle with remaining 2 tablespoons parsley.

❧ NOTE: *To poach chicken, put chicken in a single layer in a large skillet. Add water to cover. Heat to a simmer; cover and simmer 6 minutes. Remove from heat and allow to cool in the liquid.*

NUTRITION INFORMATION PER SERVING:

295 calories	6 g fat	1.6 g saturated fat
17% calories from fat	43 mg cholesterol	248 mg sodium
37 g carbohydrate	23 g protein	2.3 g fiber

Old-Fashioned Chicken Pot Pie

PREPARATION TIME: 30 minutes

COOKING TIME: 50 to 55 minutes

YIELD: 8 servings

"WE ARE TIRED of frozen food, dinner out of a box, meals from a package. No matter how many ways food companies devise to sell us home-style food, nothing beats the real McCoy," wrote Kristin Eddy for a winter cover story. She proceeded to include the following recipe, developed in the *Tribune* test kitchen.

Filling

1 13¾-ounce can chicken broth	1 onion, chopped
1 cup cold water	1 rib celery, chopped
⅓ cup flour	1 carrot, peeled and chopped
1½ teaspoons salt	1 9-ounce package frozen peas
Freshly ground black pepper	1 8¾-ounce can corn, drained
1 tablespoon vegetable oil	3 cups shredded cooked chicken *or* turkey (see Note)

Crust

1¼ cups flour	½ cup shortening
½ teaspoon salt	2 to 3 tablespoons ice water
¼ teaspoon baking powder	1 large egg
	1 tablespoon water

1. Heat oven to 400°F. For filling, heat broth in a large saucepan over medium-high heat. Combine water, flour, salt, and pepper in a small bowl; stir until smooth. Add flour mixture to broth. Cook, stirring constantly, until thickened, 10 to 12 minutes.

2. Heat oil in a small skillet over medium heat. Add onion, celery, and carrot. Cook, stirring frequently, until vegetables are tender, 4 to 5 minutes. Stir in peas and corn. Stir vegetables and chicken into sauce; mix well. Spoon mixture into 2-quart casserole dish; set aside.

3. For crust, combine flour, salt, and baking powder in a medium bowl. Cut in shortening with pastry blender or two knives until size of peas. Add ice water, 1 tablespoon at a time, stirring until ball forms. Roll out on lightly floured surface to ⅛ inch thick. Place over chicken mixture. Cut hole in top of crust for steam to escape. Mix egg and water; brush crust with egg mixture.

4. Bake until crust is golden and filling is bubbly, about 35 minutes. Let stand 10 minutes before serving.

✒ NOTE: *This is a fine use for leftover cooked chicken or turkey. Or buy cooked rotisserie chicken at the supermarket for an even easier preparation. If you have prepared pastry dough in your freezer, the preparation is a snap.*

✒ NOTE: *If a decorative top is desired, use a small portion of the dough to roll out and use to cut out leaves or other patterns. Lay on top of crust before brushing with egg mixture.*

NUTRITION INFORMATION PER SERVING:

420 calories	23 g fat	5.8 g saturated fat
50% calories from fat	73 mg cholesterol	914 mg sodium
32 g carbohydrate	21 g protein	3.4 g fiber

Lighter Chicken Pie

PREPARATION TIME: 40 minutes
COOKING TIME: 40 minutes
YIELD: 8 servings

JEANNE JONES LIGHTENED up a reader's recipe for chicken pot pie in her "Cook It Light" column. She wrote, "This is a delicious, down-home recipe that takes time to make but is well worth it."

Filling
2½ pounds chicken breast tenders
3 carrots, peeled and diced
3 tablespoons butter
2 onions, peeled and chopped
¾ cup all-purpose flour
¾ teaspoon salt
¾ teaspoon paprika
2 16-ounce cans chicken broth
1 cup fresh shelled peas *or*
    1 10-ounce package frozen peas,
    thawed

½ cup chopped parsley
1 teaspoon Worcestershire sauce

Pastry
1 cup low-fat biscuit mix
2 tablespoons butter, softened
¼ teaspoon freshly ground black
    pepper
⅔ cup nonfat milk
¼ cup nonfat egg substitute
1 tablespoon fresh lemon juice

1. Heat oven to 375°F. To make filling, bring a large skillet of water to boil. Place chicken in skillet; simmer until cooked through, 5 to 7 minutes. Drain; cool slightly. Cut into bite-sized pieces; set aside.

2. Bring a medium-sized saucepan of water to boil. Add carrots; cook 4 minutes. Drain; set aside. Melt butter in a large skillet or Dutch oven over medium heat. Add onions; cook until transparent, about 3 minutes. Add flour; cook over medium heat, stirring constantly, 3 minutes. Add salt and paprika. Mix well. Gradually add broth, stirring constantly. Cook, stirring, until thickened, about 4 minutes. Add chicken, carrots, peas, parsley, and Worcestershire sauce. Mix well. Transfer to a 3-quart casserole or 13″ × 9″ baking pan.

3. To make pastry, place biscuit mix, butter, and pepper in a medium-sized bowl. Mix with a fork until butter is well combined. Stir in milk, egg substitute, and lemon juice. Pour egg mixture over the top of filling, spreading it evenly. Bake until top is golden brown, 40 minutes.

NUTRITION INFORMATION PER SERVING:

450 calories	17 g fat	7 g saturated fat
35% calories from fat	105 mg cholesterol	1,010 mg sodium
33 g carbohydrate	39 g protein	3.8 g fiber

Quick Chicken Enchiladas

PREPARATION TIME: 25 minutes
MICROWAVE COOKING TIME: 15 minutes
YIELD: 2 servings

WITH THE USE of the microwave oven, chicken enchiladas can be prepared more easily than in the conventional manner. The fresh green sauce, made with cilantro, brings a lively flavor to the dish.

2 small onions, chopped	1 clove garlic, minced
2 tablespoons vegetable oil	1½ cups shredded, cooked chicken
2 tablespoons all-purpose flour	2 fresh *or* canned green chilies,
2 cups shredded lettuce	chopped
¼ cup minced fresh parsley	4 corn tortillas
¼ cup water	Vegetable oil
1 tablespoon minced cilantro	Sour cream
Salt	Tomato wedges
Hot pepper sauce	Chopped green onions

1. Put half of the chopped onion and 1 tablespoon of the oil into a 1-quart microwave-safe bowl. Microwave on high (100 percent power) until onion is soft, about 1 minute. Stir in flour; microwave on high for 1 minute. Stir in lettuce, parsley, and water; microwave on high for 6 minutes. Puree in a blender or in a food processor; add an additional 1 to 2 tablespoons of water if necessary for a medium-thick sauce. Add cilantro, salt, and hot pepper sauce.

2. Put garlic, remaining onion, and 1 tablespoon of the oil into a 2-quart microwave-safe bowl. Microwave on high until soft, about 2 minutes. Stir in chicken, chilies, and half of the green sauce; add salt to taste.

3. Brush each tortilla lightly with oil. Put tortillas into an 8-inch round microwave-safe baking dish. Microwave covered on high until warm and soft, about 1 minute.

4. Spoon one-fourth of the chicken mixture down the center of each tortilla. Roll up; arrange enchiladas on a microwave-safe platter or serving dish. Top with remaining green sauce. Put a dollop of sour cream in center of each tortilla. Microwave on high until hot, 2 to 4 minutes. Garnish with tomatoes and green onions.

NUTRITION INFORMATION PER SERVING:

531 calories	24 g fat	4 g saturated fat
39% calories from fat	88 mg cholesterol	190 mg sodium
44 g carbohydrate	38 g protein	6 g fiber

Chicken and Spinach Ragout with Horseradish–Mashed Potato Crust

PREPARATION TIME: 35 minutes

COOKING TIME: 1 hour 10 minutes

YIELD: 8 servings

"MAYBE IT'S TIME to try some new heat with four versatile seasonings that normally don't get a second look," wrote Kristin Eddy in her story that profiled the spicy condiments horseradish, mustard, wasabi, and peppercorns. This recipe, developed in the *Tribune* test kitchen, uses horseradish.

Chicken Ragout

1 tablespoon vegetable oil

1 large onion, sliced

½ pound shiitake mushrooms, sliced

2 pounds skinless, boneless chicken breast strips

1½ teaspoons salt

Freshly ground black pepper

1 cup chicken broth

2 tablespoons all-purpose flour

2 tomatoes, seeded and diced

1 10-ounce bag fresh spinach, stems removed, rinsed, and drained well

Mashed Potatoes

2½ pounds (about 4 large) russet potatoes, peeled and cut into cubes

½ cup freshly grated horseradish root

¼ cup milk

¼ cup sour cream

4 tablespoons plus 2 tablespoons melted unsalted butter

Salt

Freshly ground black pepper

1. To make chicken ragout, heat oven to 350°F. Heat oil in a Dutch oven over medium heat; cook onion until soft. Add mushrooms, chicken strips, salt, and pepper to taste. Cook 2 minutes or until chicken is golden and mushrooms are soft. Stir together chicken broth and flour until flour is dissolved. Add flour mixture, tomatoes, and spinach to pot. Cook 2 minutes uncovered; set aside. Keep warm.

2. To make potatoes, boil potatoes in water to cover until soft, about 10 minutes. Drain; mash together potatoes, horseradish, milk, sour cream, 4 tablespoons of the butter, and salt and black pepper to taste.

3. Put chicken ragout in a 2½-quart casserole dish; place dish on a baking sheet to catch drips. Mound mashed potatoes over chicken; drizzle with 2 tablespoons melted butter. Cover with foil; bake 45 minutes. Uncover; bake 10 minutes or until top is browned. Serve hot.

NUTRITION INFORMATION PER SERVING:

400 calories	15 g fat	7.5 g saturated fat
34% calories from fat	90 mg cholesterol	637 mg sodium
38 g carbohydrate	29 g protein	3.9 g fiber

Grilled Rock Cornish Game Hens with Italian Sausage Stuffing

PREPARATION TIME: 30 minutes
COOKING TIME: 1 hour 20 minutes
YIELD: 8 servings

ROCK CORNISH GAME hens get an Italian touch in this recipe from former test kitchen cook Beverly Dillon. It is perfect for outdoor grilling. Serve it with a simple pasta salad and Chianti.

5 tablespoons olive oil
¾ pound mild Italian sausage, casings removed
¾ pound hot Italian sausage, casings removed
1 onion, chopped
2 ribs celery, chopped
1 clove garlic, minced
2 slices toasted white bread, cut into ¼-inch cubes
1 large egg, lightly beaten
½ cup freshly grated Parmesan cheese
2 tablespoons minced fresh parsley
1 teaspoon dried oregano
½ teaspoon dried rubbed sage
½ teaspoon dried rosemary
½ teaspoon salt
½ teaspoon freshly ground black pepper
8 Rock Cornish game hens (about 1 pound each)
Parsley sprigs

1. Heat 1 tablespoon of the oil in a large skillet over medium heat. Add sausages, onion, celery, and garlic. Cook, chopping sausage up during cooking, until browned, about 20 minutes. Transfer sausage to a large bowl with a slotted spoon. Add bread cubes, egg, cheese, minced parsley, oregano, sage, rosemary, salt, and pepper. Mix well. Cool.

2. Stuff hens with cooled stuffing. Truss openings with kitchen twine. Tuck wings underneath and tie legs together. Rub skin with some of the remaining oil.

3. Prepare grill. Arrange hens on a grill rack 6 to 8 inches from coals. Cover; grill, basting often with oil, until thigh juices run clear when pierced and a meat thermometer reads 170°F, 40 to 50 minutes. Let stand on platter 10 minutes before slicing. Garnish with parsley.

►

❧ NOTE: *To cook in oven, heat oven to 400°F. Put hens in a shallow roasting pan breast side up. Rub well with oil; cover with foil. Roast covered 30 minutes. Uncover and roast, basting often with pan drippings, until golden and thigh juices run clear when pierced and a meat thermometer reads 170°F, about 20 more minutes.*

NUTRITION INFORMATION PER SERVING:

1,008 calories	64 g fat	18 g saturated fat
58% calories from fat	333 mg cholesterol	1,672 mg sodium
6.6 g carbohydrate	96 g protein	0.8 g fiber

Cornish Game Hen with Sautéed Morels, Spinach, and White Truffle Oil

PREPARATION TIME: 35 minutes

COOKING TIME: 1 hour 15 minutes

YIELD: 2 servings

TERRY FARMS, A Minnesota-based company, has been successfully cultivating and selling about 1,000 pounds of morel mushrooms a week at an indoor farm in Alabama. In a story about the farm, we included this recipe from Charles Warshawsky of Earth restaurant in Chicago. Dried mushrooms can be used in place of fresh. Simply soak them in hot water for 30 minutes first. Look for white truffle oil in specialty food stores.

1 Cornish game hen, halved	½ pound morel mushrooms,
½ teaspoon salt	halved (see Index)
Freshly ground black pepper	4 cups fresh spinach, washed,
¼ cup (½ stick) butter	stems removed
1 shallot, minced	2 teaspoons white truffle oil *or*
2 cloves garlic, minced	mushroom-flavored olive oil,
	optional

1. Heat oven to 375°F. Place Cornish game hen halves in a baking dish; season with ¼ teaspoon of the salt and black pepper to taste. Bake until cooked through, about 1 hour.

2. Melt butter in a large skillet over medium heat. Add shallot and garlic; cook, stirring frequently, until softened, about 3 minutes. Stir in mushrooms. Cook, stirring frequently, until mushrooms are almost tender, about 5 minutes. Add spinach; cook until spinach is wilted, about 2 to 3 minutes.

3. Place half of spinach mixture on 1 side of each of 2 plates. Place Cornish hen halves next to spinach mixture. Drizzle spinach and hen halves with truffle oil if desired.

NUTRITION INFORMATION PER SERVING:

660 calories	49 g fat	21 g saturated fat
67% calories from fat	195 mg cholesterol	1,115 mg sodium
10 g carbohydrate	46 g protein	3.1 g fiber

Turkey with Herbed Corn Bread Stuffing and Pan Gravy

PREPARATION TIME: 1 hour
COOKING TIME: 3 hours 15 minutes
YIELD: 16 servings

FOR THANKSGIVING ONE year, the late caterer Marion Mandeltort of Lincolnshire, Illinois, shared her recipes for a heartland dinner, including the following roast turkey. Both the corn bread for the stuffing and the turkey broth for the gravy can be made a day ahead of time.

Stuffing
1 9-inch loaf corn bread
1½ cups cubed, toasted white bread
¾ cup minced parsley
½ cup (1 stick) unsalted butter *or* margarine
4 ribs celery, chopped coarse
2 onions, chopped coarse
2 teaspoons salt
2 teaspoons freshly ground black pepper
1 tablespoon sage
1 tablespoon rosemary
1 tablespoon thyme
2 large eggs, lightly beaten
1 cup turkey *or* chicken broth
1 cup coarsely chopped walnuts
1 10-ounce box frozen corn kernels, thawed

Turkey
1 fresh turkey (about 16 pounds)
Salt
¾ cup (1½ sticks) unsalted butter *or* margarine
1 tablespoon dried rosemary
1 tablespoon rubbed sage
1 tablespoon dried leaf thyme
1 tablespoon paprika
1 tablespoon minced fresh parsley
1 tablespoon minced garlic
1 teaspoon freshly ground black pepper

Pan Gravy
2 tablespoons all-purpose flour
2 tablespoons butter
2¼ cups turkey *or* chicken broth

➤

1. To make stuffing, crumble corn bread into a large bowl; add bread cubes and parsley. Toss. Melt butter in a large skillet. Add celery, onions, salt, pepper, sage, rosemary, and thyme. Sauté until celery and onions are slightly wilted but not browned, about 8 minutes. Remove from heat. Combine beaten eggs with 1 cup turkey broth in a small bowl; pour over corn bread mixture. Add walnuts and corn kernels; toss lightly. Cool 15 minutes.

2. To make turkey, heat oven to 475°F. Rinse turkey under cold water; pat dry. Rub inside of turkey with salt. Spoon stuffing into cavity and neck end of bird loosely to fill. Do not pack tight (stuffing will expand). Truss openings with kitchen string. Tuck wings underneath; tie legs together. Melt butter in a small saucepan. Add rosemary, sage, thyme, paprika, parsley, garlic, and black pepper. Simmer over low heat 5 minutes. Cool.

3. Oil a rack. Put turkey on the oiled rack set in a roasting pan. Rub outside of turkey with butter mixture. Roast uncovered 45 minutes. Reduce oven temperature to 400°F; loosely tent turkey with aluminum foil. Continue to roast, basting occasionally with pan juices, until a meat thermometer inserted in thigh registers 170°F, about 2½ hours. Let stand on a carving board covered loosely with foil at least 15 minutes. Remove stuffing from cavity; place in a serving bowl.

4. To make gravy, mix flour and butter until blended to a paste. Skim fat from surface of pan juices in roasting pan. Pour turkey broth into roasting pan; heat over medium heat to boil, scraping up browned bits from bottom of pan. Gradually whisk in flour paste. Cook, whisking, until thickened. Reduce heat; simmer 5 minutes. Taste and adjust seasonings. Strain if desired. Serve with turkey and stuffing.

NUTRITION INFORMATION PER SERVING:

800 calories	44 g fat	18 g saturated fat
50% calories from fat	290 mg cholesterol	835 mg sodium
20 g carbohydrate	77 g protein	2.4 g fiber

Sweet-Spiced Turkey Breast with Onions and Raisins

PREPARATION TIME: 25 minutes

COOKING TIME: 35 minutes

YIELD: 8 servings

IN JUNE OF 1991, Abby Mandel wrote about a Mexican-inspired party featuring light and appealing summer fare. Her sweet-spiced turkey main course is excellent served hot, at room temperature, or chilled. You can prepare turkey breast ahead through step 1; put it in a sealed large plastic food storage bag and refrigerate.

3 large cloves garlic, minced

2 large green onions, minced

1 tablespoon safflower oil

1½ teaspoons salt

1 teaspoon cinnamon

1 teaspoon allspice

1 teaspoon coarsely crushed pepper

1 large skinless, boneless turkey breast (about 2¼ pounds)

2 large Spanish onions (about 1 pound total), sliced thin

½ cup golden raisins

2 tablespoons cider vinegar

1 tablespoon minced cilantro

1. Heat oven to 500°F. Mix garlic, green onions, oil, 1¼ teaspoons of the salt, cinnamon, allspice, and pepper in a small dish. Rinse turkey breast; pat dry with paper toweling. Rub paste evenly onto entire surface of turkey.

2. Separate onion slices into rings. Put onions and raisins in the center of a piece of heavy-duty aluminum foil large enough to enclose turkey. Sprinkle vinegar over. Place turkey breast on top of onions and raisins. Wrap turkey airtight in foil, leaving a small amount of air space between foil and breast. Place turkey foil pack on a baking sheet.

3. Roast until an instant-reading thermometer inserted through the foil and halfway through thickest portion of the breast registers 160°F, 30 to 35 minutes. Remove turkey from oven.

4. Carefully open foil. Let rest 10 to 20 minutes; move turkey to a cutting board. Slice into thin diagonal slices. Arrange slices on a platter. Spoon juices and onions over. Sprinkle lightly with ¼ teaspoon salt and minced cilantro. Serve hot, at room temperature, or chilled.

NUTRITION INFORMATION PER SERVING:

295 calories

11% calories from fat

19 g carbohydrate

3.6 g fat

123 mg cholesterol

46 g protein

0.6 g saturated fat

567 mg sodium

2 g fiber

Stuffed Turkey Breast

PREPARATION TIME: 30 minutes

COOKING TIME: 2 hours

YIELD: 10 servings

AN ELEGANT WAY to serve turkey is to stuff a turkey breast with sausage and vegetables. The *Tribune* test kitchen came up with this ideal entree for smaller dinner parties that won't put a dent in the budget.

½ pound bulk pork sausage, crumbled

2 zucchini, shredded and patted dry

1 apple, cored and chopped fine

1 large red onion, chopped

2 large eggs

3 cups coarse, dry bread crumbs

¼ cup brandy

3 tablespoons chicken broth

3 tablespoons minced fresh parsley

1 tablespoon finely grated lemon zest

½ teaspoon rubbed sage

½ teaspoon salt

¼ teaspoon freshly ground black pepper

1 whole boneless turkey breast (about 5 pounds)

1 tablespoon butter, melted

1. Cook sausage in a medium-sized skillet over medium heat until brown; drain fat. Put sausage into a large bowl; stir in zucchini, apple, onion, eggs, bread crumbs, brandy, broth, parsley, lemon zest, sage, salt, and pepper. Taste and adjust seasonings.

2. Heat oven to 350°F. Put turkey breast skin side down onto work surface. Pound turkey breast slightly with a meat mallet. Sprinkle with salt and pepper. Spread stuffing over breast, leaving a 1½-inch border on all sides. Roll up jelly roll fashion. Tie securely in several places with string to completely enclose stuffing.

3. Oil a rack. Put turkey breast onto the oiled rack set in a roasting pan. Brush with butter. Roast until thermometer inserted in center of stuffing registers 160°F, about 1 hour 45 minutes. Let stand 10 minutes before slicing. (Temperature will rise about 10 degrees.) Serve hot.

NUTRITION INFORMATION PER SERVING:

536 calories	21 g fat	6.4 g saturated fat
36% calories from fat	174 mg cholesterol	681 mg sodium
28 g carbohydrate	56 g protein	1.6 g fiber

Easy Moroccan Turkey Pie

PREPARATION TIME: 25 minutes
COOKING TIME: 1 hour
YIELD: 6 servings

AH, TURKEY LEFTOVERS. Some think they're better than the original roast bird. Here's a novel finale for leftovers, from the *Tribune* test kitchen. It's reason enough to invite the relatives back again after the holiday. Commercial puff pastry, found in the freezer case at the supermarket, takes the place of the traditional phyllo dough.

3 tablespoons butter	½ pound whole blanched almonds
3 tablespoons olive oil	¼ cup confectioners' sugar
1 large onion, minced	1 teaspoon cinnamon
3 cloves garlic, minced	8 large eggs, lightly beaten
2 cinnamon sticks	1½ pounds cubed cooked turkey
1 cup minced fresh parsley	(about 4 cups)
2 tablespoons minced cilantro	2 tablespoons fresh lemon juice
¾ teaspoon ground ginger	1 17¼-ounce package frozen puff
¼ teaspoon freshly ground black	pastry sheets, thawed
pepper	2 teaspoons butter, melted
¼ teaspoon turmeric	Cinnamon
¼ cup vegetable oil	Confectioners' sugar

1.   Heat butter and olive oil in a medium-sized Dutch oven over medium heat. Add onion and garlic; cook, stirring often, until tender, about 2 minutes. Stir in cinnamon sticks, parsley, cilantro, ginger, pepper, and turmeric. Cook, stirring occasionally, 15 minutes. Remove and discard cinnamon sticks.

2.   Heat vegetable oil in a medium-sized skillet over medium heat. Add almonds; cook, stirring often, until golden, about 5 minutes. Drain almonds on paper towels. Cool; chop coarse. Toss together almonds, confectioners' sugar, and cinnamon in a medium-sized bowl.

3.   Pour eggs over onion mixture. Cook, stirring frequently, over low heat until mixture is thick and fairly dry. Stir in turkey and lemon juice. Taste and adjust seasoning.

4.   Heat oven to 350°F. Line a deep 10-inch pie plate with half of the puff pastry; trim and flute the edge. Put turkey mixture into the pastry-lined pie plate using a slotted spoon. Sprinkle with almond mixture. Top with remaining half of puff pastry; crimp edges together. Brush with melted butter.

►

5. Bake until pastry is golden and puffed, about 35 minutes. Cool on a wire rack 10 minutes. Sprinkle cinnamon and confectioners' sugar in a decorative pattern over top. Serve warm.

NUTRITION INFORMATION PER SERVING:

1,166 calories	85 g fat	20 g saturated fat
65% calories from fat	374 mg cholesterol	439 mg sodium
54 g carbohydrate	50 g protein	4.8 g fiber

Turkey-Pork Meat Loaf with Carrots and Spinach

PREPARATION TIME: 25 minutes

COOKING TIME: 1 hour 15 minutes

YIELD: 8 servings

THE COMBINATION OF ground turkey and pork makes a lighter-than-usual meat loaf. With the increase in ground meat selections in the supermarket, it is easier to mix and match them. Ground meats still remain the bargains of the meat case.

1½ pounds ground turkey	1 teaspoon salt
1 pound pork sausage	1 teaspoon dried thyme
1 onion, chopped fine	1 teaspoon dried marjoram
1 clove garlic, minced	¾ teaspoon black pepper
2 large carrots, peeled and chopped	½ cup dry bread crumbs
1 10-ounce package frozen chopped spinach, thawed and squeezed dry	2 large eggs

1. Heat oven to 350°F. Combine turkey, pork sausage, onion, garlic, carrots, and spinach in a large bowl. Add salt, thyme, marjoram, and pepper. Mix well. Add bread crumbs and eggs; mix thoroughly. Pack meat loaf mixture into a 9″ × 5″ loaf pan, rounding the top slightly.

2. Bake until meat registers 160°F on a thermometer, about 1 hour 15 minutes. Drain off fat. Cool on a rack, turn onto a cutting board, cut into 8 slices, and serve hot or cold.

NUTRITION INFORMATION PER SERVING:

304 calories	20 g fat	6.5 g saturated fat
60% calories from fat	121 mg cholesterol	838 mg sodium
11 g carbohydrate	20 g protein	2.2 g fiber

Safety First

Ground meat presents more of a safety concern than other meats. Bacteria that may be present on the meat's surface can be blended throughout by grinding. To counter the bacteria threat, buy the freshest possible ground meat and cook it thoroughly.

Here are other tips from meat safety experts:

Completely defrost frozen patties in the refrigerator. A partly frozen burger may look done on the outside but may not have reached the recommended internal temperature of 160°F.

Cook ground meat thoroughly. That means until it is no longer pink in the middle (but it still can be juicy). This effectively kills any bacteria present.

After handling raw ground meat, wash hands and utensils with hot, soapy water.

Don't put cooked burgers on the same platter used to transport them when they were raw. Likewise, don't use the same utensils on cooked meat that were used on raw.

Smothered Turkey Wings

PREPARATION TIME: 30 minutes
COOKING TIME: 2 hours 15 minutes
YIELD: 6 servings

CHEF JOHN MEYER of B.J.'s Market & Bakery on Chicago's South Side shared his delicious turkey wings recipe for a story profiling black chefs in Chicago.

Wings
6 turkey wings
1 tablespoon vegetable oil
1 tablespoon salt
1 teaspoon freshly ground black
   pepper
1 teaspoon garlic powder
1 teaspoon poultry seasoning
½ teaspoon onion powder

Sauce
½ cup (1 stick) butter
2 ribs celery, chopped
½ medium onion, chopped
1 teaspoon dried leaf thyme
1 teaspoon freshly ground black
   pepper
7 tablespoons all-purpose flour
6 cups turkey *or* chicken broth
2 cups milk

▶

1.   To make wings, heat oven to 350°F. Brush wings with vegetable oil; place in a large roasting pan. Stir together salt, pepper, garlic powder, poultry seasoning, and onion powder in a medium-sized bowl; sprinkle over turkey wings. Bake until browned, 45 to 60 minutes.

2.   To make sauce, melt butter in a large heavy saucepan or Dutch oven. Add celery and onion; cook over medium-low heat until soft but not browned, about 5 minutes. Stir in thyme and pepper; cook 1 minute. Add flour; cook, stirring constantly, until light brown, about 5 minutes. Slowly whisk in broth.

3.   Heat liquid to a boil; reduce heat. Simmer uncovered 20 minutes. Strain sauce through a sieve; return to the saucepan. Slowly whisk in milk. Stir constantly until sauce returns to a simmer. Pour sauce over turkey wings; cover. Cook until tender, about 1 hour.

NUTRITION INFORMATION PER SERVING:

805 calories	48 g fat	19 g saturated fat
55% calories from fat	240 mg cholesterol	2,305 mg sodium
15 g carbohydrate	74 g protein	1 g fiber

Duck Breast with Mixed Greens and Hazelnut Dressing

PREPARATION TIME: 45 minutes

COOKING TIME: 10 minutes

YIELD: 4 servings

THE CHEFS AT the former Les Plumes restaurant in Chicago prepared this appetizer salad that's really large enough for an entree. However you serve it, the duck is superb with its dressing of sherry wine vinegar and hazelnut oil.

Salad Cups

4 large *or* 8 medium-sized
   radicchio leaves

1 cup torn Boston lettuce

1 cup torn radicchio

1 cup torn curly endive

1 cup julienned mushrooms

1 cup sliced Belgian endive

¼ pound very thin green beans,
   cooked, drained, and chilled

4 tablespoons hazelnut oil

2 tablespoons sherry wine vinegar

1 cup toasted blanched hazelnuts
   (see Note)

Salt

Freshly ground black pepper

Duck

4 boneless duck breast halves

1 cup chicken *or* duck broth

1. To make salad cups, rinse and refrigerate radicchio leaves. Mix lettuce, torn radicchio, curly endive, mushrooms, Belgian endive, and green beans in a large bowl. Add 3 tablespoons of the hazelnut oil, 1 tablespoon of the vinegar, and hazelnuts, and salt and pepper to taste. Toss to mix.

2. To make duck, heat oven to 550°F. Rinse duck under cold water; pat dry. Heat a large oven-safe skillet over medium heat until hot. Add duck skin side down. Cook until golden brown, about 5 minutes. Drain off some of the fat from the skillet. Roast in the oven until medium rare, about 5 minutes. Remove duck to a plate; keep warm.

3. Pour off all fat from skillet. Add remaining 1 tablespoon vinegar. Cook; stirring often, while scraping up browned bits from the bottom of the pan. Add chicken broth; cook, stirring often, until stock is reduced by half. Remove from heat; stir in remaining 1 tablespoon hazelnut oil.

4. Strain sauce through a fine-mesh sieve. Cut duck breast lengthwise into thin slices. Pour some of the sauce onto 4 serving plates. Arrange duck slices on plates. Put 1 large radicchio leaf or 2 medium-sized leaves onto the edge of each plate, forming a cup. Fill cup with salad mixture.

☛ NOTE: *To toast hazelnuts, heat a large skillet over medium heat. Add hazelnuts. Cook, stirring often, until fragrant, about 5 minutes.*

NUTRITION INFORMATION PER SERVING:

490 calories	42 g fat	4.5 g saturated fat
74% calories from fat	82 mg cholesterol	256 mg sodium
11 g carbohydrate	22 g protein	4.5 g fiber

Duck Breast with Green Olive Relish

PREPARATION TIME: 40 minutes
MARINATING TIME: 30 minutes
COOKING TIME: 5 minutes
YIELD: 2 servings

OPPOSITES ATTRACT, IN literature, in life, and on the dinner plate. Duck, for instance, a dark and dense meat with a thick layer of fleecy fat and rich flavor, matches very well with briny, brawny, and slightly bitter olives in this treat from a "Good Eating" Valentine's Day story. Serve the duck with a Spanish wine such as rioja.

3 tablespoons extra-virgin olive oil	Freshly ground black pepper
2 duck breast halves, skin removed, fat trimmed	4 sprigs plus ¼ teaspoon chopped fresh thyme

►

12 imported green olives, pitted and chopped coarse	1 rib celery, chopped
2 green onions, chopped	1 clove garlic, chopped
1 peeled and chopped carrot	2 teaspoons red wine vinegar
	Salt

1. Rub 1 tablespoon of the olive oil over the surface of duck; sprinkle liberally with pepper. Place each breast half over 2 sprigs of thyme in a small dish. Cover with plastic wrap; marinate 30 minutes in refrigerator.

2. Combine olives, green onions, carrot, celery, garlic, chopped thyme leaves, remaining 2 tablespoons oil, and vinegar in a food processor fitted with a metal blade. Process until ingredients are minced. Taste and adjust seasoning. Transfer to a serving dish; set aside.

3. Heat a small nonstick skillet over medium-high heat until hot. Add duck breasts; cook 2½ minutes. Turn; cook until medium rare, about 2½ minutes. Transfer to a cutting board; let rest 3 to 5 minutes.

4. Carve each duck breast half crosswise into 6 slices; divide between 2 plates. Season with salt and pepper. Pass olive relish at table.

NUTRITION INFORMATION PER SERVING:

601 calories	43 g fat	8 g saturated fat
65% calories from fat	231 mg cholesterol	658 mg sodium
9 g carbohydrate	43 g protein	2 g fiber

Duck Breasts with Berry Sauce

PREPARATION TIME: 40 minutes

COOKING TIME: 12 minutes

YIELD: 8 servings

THIS RECIPE IS from André and Ariane Daguin, a French father-and-daughter team who visited Chicago for a special all-duck meal at Bistro 110. If you don't have Armagnac on hand, just add more port to the recipe.

1 pound mixed fresh berries, such as raspberries, boysenberries, and blackberries	2 whole duck breasts (about 1 pound each), halved
¾ cup port	Salt
⅓ cup Armagnac	Freshly ground black pepper
	½ cup water

1. Combine ¾ pound of the berries, port, and Armagnac in a heavy saucepan. Heat to boil; simmer 15 minutes, stirring occasionally, or until mixture is reduced by half. Pour through a fine-mesh sieve, pressing on fruit. Reserve fruit puree.

2. Trim excess fat from breasts. Score skin side of each duck breast with a knife, making small diamonds without cutting into meat. Sprinkle both sides with salt and pepper.

3. Heat two dry, heavy skillets until very hot. Place 2 breast halves in each pan skin sides down. Cook 8 minutes. Turn; lower heat to medium. Cook 4 minutes. Put all breasts in one pan. Keep warm.

4. Pour fat from empty pan; add water. Heat to boil, scraping bottom to loosen any browned bits. Stir in reserved fruit puree. Heat to boil over high heat. Continue cooking until reduced by half. Add remaining berries to sauce; cook only long enough to heat.

5. Warm 8 serving plates. Carve breast halves diagonally into thin slices. Position meat on warmed serving plates. Pour any duck juices into sauce; stir. Spoon over meat.

NUTRITION INFORMATION PER SERVING:

170 calories	5 g fat	1.5 g saturated fat
28% calories from fat	85 mg cholesterol	65 mg sodium
7 g carbohydrate	23 g protein	3.9 g fiber

Grilled Quail and Polenta

PREPARATION TIME: 20 minutes
CHILLING/MARINATING TIME: 24 hours
COOKING TIME: 30 minutes
YIELD: 4 servings

ELEGANT GRILLED QUAIL is served on a bed of shaped polenta in this recipe from Chicago chef Tony Mantuano, who often serves the quail with grilled Italian sausage on the side. Chicken broth or stock, instead of water, helps polenta keep its shape.

4 cloves garlic, minced
1 cup loosely packed flat-leaf
   Italian parsley, chopped
¼ cup olive oil
1 tablespoon juniper berries,
   crushed
4 quail, rinsed and patted dry

Grilled Polenta
2½ cups chicken stock *or* broth
1 cup fine yellow cornmeal
¼ teaspoon salt
⅛ teaspoon freshly ground white
   pepper
Vegetable oil

▶

1. Put garlic, parsley, oil, and juniper berries into a large plastic food storage bag or a shallow nonreactive bowl. Add quail; turn to coat with marinade. Refrigerate, turning occasionally, up to 24 hours.

2. To make polenta, heat broth to simmer in a large saucepan over medium-high heat. Slowly whisk in cornmeal, salt, and pepper. Reduce heat to low. Simmer, stirring constantly, until mixture is very thick and smooth, about 20 minutes. Butter a baking sheet. Pour mixture while still warm onto the baking sheet in a ¾-inch layer. Smooth with a rubber spatula. Cool in refrigerator until firm, 3 to 4 hours.

3. Bring quail to room temperature. Prepare grill. Cut polenta into desired shapes with cookie cutters. Brush grill rack with oil. Dip one side of polenta in oil; place it oiled side down onto the grill. Grill, turning once, until heated through and slightly crisp on both sides, about 3 minutes. Remove to a platter; keep warm in the oven.

4. Remove quail from marinade, scraping off excess. Grill quail, turning often, until breast meat is still slightly pink, 8 to 12 minutes. Serve with grilled polenta.

NUTRITION INFORMATION PER SERVING:

508 calories	26 g fat	6.6 g saturated fat
47% calories from fat	135 mg cholesterol	669 mg sodium
29 g carbohydrate	39 g protein	2.7 g fiber

Sausage-Sage Stuffing

PREPARATION TIME: 45 minutes
DRYING TIME: 8 to 12 hours
COOKING TIME: 45 minutes
YIELD: 18 cups, enough to stuff 1 20-pound bird

FORMER STAFF WRITER Barbara Sullivan contributed this recipe for her favorite stuffing for one of our Thanksgiving sections. It is sinfully rich and wonderful. To dry bread quicker, warm bread chunks in a 200°F oven, stirring often, until dry, 45 to 60 minutes.

4 16-ounce loaves sliced white bread, torn into chunks
2 pounds sliced bacon
2 pounds bulk pork sausage with sage

2 onions, diced
4 ribs celery, diced
½ cup (1 stick) unsalted butter
3½ to 4 cups chicken *or* turkey broth

| 2 tablespoons plus 1½ teaspoons poultry seasoning | 1 teaspoon freshly ground black pepper |
| ¼ cup rubbed sage | ½ teaspoon salt |

1. Spread bread pieces out on baking sheets; let stand uncovered on counter overnight to dry out bread slightly.

2. Chop bacon. Cook bacon, sausage, onions, and celery in a large deep skillet over medium heat, stirring often, until bacon and sausage are thoroughly browned, 30 minutes. Drain off fat occasionally during cooking. Cool mixture slightly; drain off all fat. Transfer mixture to a very large bowl using a slotted spoon. Do not wash skillet.

3. Melt butter in the same skillet over medium heat; stir in 1 cup of the broth. Heat to simmer while scraping up browned bits from bottom of pan; cool slightly.

4. Add bread, poultry seasoning, sage, pepper, and salt to bacon mixture. Pour some of the broth mixture over bread mixture; toss to mix. Gradually stir in some of the remaining broth to desired consistency.

5. Taste and adjust seasonings. Use to stuff poultry or butter a baking dish. Spoon stuffing into the baking dish; bake covered at 350°F until heated through, about 30 minutes. Uncover; bake until top is crisp, about 30 minutes.

NUTRITION INFORMATION PER CUP:

511 calories	25 g fat	10 g saturated fat
43% calories from fat	51 mg cholesterol	1,235 mg sodium
53 g carbohydrate	20 g protein	2.6 g fiber

Apple–Corn Bread Stuffing

PREPARATION TIME: 30 minutes

COOKING TIME: About 1 hour

YIELD: 10 ½-cup servings, enough to stuff 1 12-pound turkey

CORN BREAD ADDS a sweetness to any stuffing. Mix it with white bread or let it stand on its own. Food editor Carol Mighton Haddix uses it mixed with apples and pecans for a Thanksgiving turkey or any type of poultry. The recipe can be doubled for large birds. You may bake and dry the corn bread as in step 1 one day ahead.

| 1 8-ounce box corn bread mix | ⅓ cup milk |
| 2 large eggs | 1 cup pecan halves |

▶

3 tablespoons butter

2 medium-sized tart apples, such
as Granny Smith

2 ribs celery, diced

1 small onion, chopped fine

¼ cup chicken broth

¼ cup (½ stick) melted butter

½ teaspoon salt

¼ teaspoon poultry seasoning

¼ teaspoon freshly ground black
pepper

1. Prepare corn bread according to package directions, using 1 of the eggs and ⅓ cup milk. Bake according to directions. Set corn bread aside to dry out.

2. Heat oven to 400°F. Put pecans into a shallow baking pan. Dot with 3 tablespoons butter. Bake, stirring often, until light brown and fragrant, about 10 minutes. Turn nuts out onto paper towels. Cool completely; chop coarse.

3. Core and chop apples. Mix apples, celery, onion, and pecans in a large bowl. Crumble in all of the dry corn bread. Toss lightly. Beat remaining 1 egg with broth, melted butter, salt, poultry seasoning, and black pepper. Gradually pour over corn bread mixture while tossing, just until moist. Use to stuff poultry. Or butter a baking dish. Spoon stuffing into baking dish; bake covered at 350°F until heated through, about 30 minutes. Uncover; bake until top is crisp, about 30 minutes.

NUTRITION INFORMATION PER SERVING:

274 calories	19 g fat	7 g saturated fat
62% calories from fat	65 mg cholesterol	494 mg sodium
23 g carbohydrate	4.4 g protein	3.1 g fiber

Savory Apple Brown Betty

PREPARATION TIME: 25 minutes

COOKING TIME: 10 minutes

YIELD: 8 servings

WHEN SUSAN GOSS and her husband, Drew, opened Zinfandel restaurant in Chicago, she says she began a crusade to "celebrate American food and encourage a resurgence of small-scale American farmers," a crusade that continues years later. This is her version of corn bread stuffing for poultry or roast pork, but it's cooked separately from the meat.

6 tablespoons unsalted butter

3 large unpeeled apples, cored

3 medium-sized yellow onions,
chopped

1 1-inch-thick piece gingerroot,
   peeled and minced
3 tablespoons fresh thyme leaves *or*
   1 teaspoon dried leaf thyme
1½ teaspoons ground black pepper

¾ teaspoon salt
¼ cup apple brandy *or* cider
3 cups diced corn bread made
   without sugar

1. Melt butter in a large skillet over medium-high heat. Add apples and onions; cook until onion is soft and translucent, 5 to 6 minutes.

2. Add gingerroot, thyme, pepper, and salt; mix well. Stir in brandy. Increase heat to high; cook, stirring constantly, until sizzling stops, 4 to 5 minutes.

3. Remove from heat. Stir in corn bread; mix well. Serve with meat or poultry of your choice.

NUTRITION INFORMATION PER SERVING:

235 calories	12 g fat	6 g saturated fat
44% calories from fat	41 mg cholesterol	442 mg sodium
31 g carbohydrate	2.9 g protein	3.7 g fiber

VEGETABLES

Artichokes with Hollandaise Sauce

PREPARATION TIME: 20 minutes
COOKING TIME: 30 to 40 minutes
YIELD: 4 servings

AT FIRST GLANCE, a fresh artichoke appears to be a cooking challenge. But you can cook artichokes like an expert in any of three ways: boiling, steaming, or microwaving.

Artichokes	*Hollandaise Sauce*
4 medium-sized artichokes	4 large egg yolks
Vegetable oil	½ cup (1 stick) unsalted butter,
Lemon juice	softened and cut into thirds
Salt	2 to 3 teaspoons fresh lemon juice
	Salt
	Freshly ground white pepper

1. Trim artichoke stems off at the base so artichokes sit level. Pull off small lower leaves. Cut off top quarter of each artichoke. Trim off tips of outer leaves.
2. Cook artichokes using one of the following methods:
   a. To boil artichokes, place them in a saucepan just large enough to hold artichokes upright. Fill pan with 3 inches of water. Add 1 tablespoon olive oil, 1 tablespoon lemon juice, and ¼ teaspoon salt. Cover pan; heat to boil over high heat. Reduce heat; simmer until fork-tender and any leaf near the center pulls out easily, 30 to 40 minutes. Set artichokes upside down to drain.
   b. To steam artichokes, place artichokes on a rack over about 1½ inches boiling water. Drizzle lemon juice over the top of each artichoke; sprinkle with salt. Cover; steam until fork-tender and any leaf near the center pulls out easily, 30 to 40 minutes.

➤

c. To microwave artichokes, invert 1 artichoke in a deep, 1-quart microwave-safe cup or bowl; add 3 tablespoons water, 1 teaspoon oil, 1 teaspoon lemon juice, and salt to taste. Cover with heavy-duty plastic wrap; pierce wrap with a fork to allow steam to escape. Microwave on high (100 percent power) until any leaf near the center pulls out easily, 6 to 8 minutes. Let stand 5 minutes.

3. To make hollandaise sauce, put egg yolks and one-third of the butter in the top of a double boiler. Bring water to simmer in the bottom of the double boiler. (Water in the bottom of the double boiler should not touch the top pan.) Cook egg mixture over simmering water, stirring vigorously until butter melts. Add second third of the butter; continue stirring vigorously. Sauce should be somewhat runny. As butter melts and mixture thickens, add remaining one-third of the butter, stirring constantly. Sauce will be thick and fluffy. Remove sauce from the double boiler. Stir rapidly using a wooden spoon, 2 minutes. Season with lemon juice and salt and pepper to taste. Return to the double boiler; stir constantly until heated through, about 2 minutes. (Do not let sauce boil at any time. If sauce curdles, immediately stir in 1 to 2 tablespoons boiling water and mix well. If necessary, keep warm in an insulated bottle.)

NUTRITION INFORMATION PER SERVING:

324 calories	28 g fat	16 g saturated fat
75% calories from fat	275 mg cholesterol	131 mg sodium
14 g carbohydrate	7 g protein	7 g fiber

Braised Artichoke Hearts
with Arugula and Fava Beans

PREPARATION TIME: 35 minutes

COOKING TIME: 40 minutes

YIELD: 4 servings

THIS RECIPE FROM an article by William Rice on Passover dishes made by Chicago chefs is adapted from one by Geoff Felsenthal, then executive chef at Avanzare. Sephardic Jews eat beans; Ashkenazic Jews do not and should omit the favas. You may prepare this recipe ahead through step 4.

3 artichokes *or* 1 10-ounce package frozen artichoke hearts, thawed	3 lemons 1 cup water

¾ cup olive oil

4 sprigs Italian flat-leaf parsley

1 pound fava beans, shelled, *or*
    8 ounces frozen lima beans,
    thawed

¾ teaspoon salt

2 shallots, chopped fine

Freshly ground black pepper

6 ounces arugula, washed, dried,
    large stems removed

2 tablespoons chopped Italian
    flat-leaf parsley

3 ounces pecorino Romano cheese

1. Trim off stems, leaves, and fuzzy choke of artichokes, leaving only soft inner heart (reserve leaves for another use). Cut one of the lemons in half; rub exterior of each artichoke heart. Squeeze juice from remaining lemon half into a medium-sized bowl of cold water; add artichokes. Set aside.

2. Heat oven to 375°F. Juice one more of the lemons. Combine 1 cup water, ¼ cup of the olive oil, parsley sprigs, and juice of 1 lemon in a small bowl; mix well. Drain artichokes. Place in a small roasting pan; pour olive oil mixture over. Cover with foil; bake until tender, about 40 minutes. Remove from oven; cool in broth. Cut each artichoke heart into quarters. (If using frozen artichoke hearts, bake until tender, 15 to 20 minutes.)

3. Heat water to boil in a medium-sized saucepan over high heat. Add fava beans and ½ teaspoon of the salt. Cook until just tender, about 2 minutes. Drain; cool in cold water. Drain again; remove skin from beans.

4. Juice the 1 remaining lemon. Combine lemon juice, shallots, remaining ¼ teaspoon salt, and black pepper to taste; whisk in remaining ½ cup olive oil.

5. Combine artichokes, fava beans, and arugula in a large bowl. Toss with dressing and chopped parsley. Arrange salad on 4 plates. Cut cheese into thin slices using a vegetable peeler. Top salads with slices of cheese.

NUTRITION INFORMATION PER SERVING:

450 calories	34 g fat	8 g saturated fat
68% calories from fat	17 mg cholesterol	965 mg sodium
25 g carbohydrate	17 g protein	8 g fiber

Asparagus with Lemon Butter

PREPARATION TIME: 15 minutes

COOKING TIME: 5 minutes

YIELD: 4 servings

ASPARAGUS DRESSED IN lemon juice makes an elegant side dish for a spring weekend brunch.

Salt

1¼ pounds fresh asparagus, cut into 1-inch pieces

2 teaspoons butter

2 teaspoons seasoned rice vinegar

1 teaspoon minced lemon zest

1. Heat salted water to a boil in a large saucepan. Add asparagus; cook just until tender, about 5 minutes, depending on size. Drain well, shaking to remove all water.

2. Transfer to a serving bowl; lightly toss with butter, vinegar, lemon zest, and salt to taste.

NUTRITION INFORMATION PER SERVING:

49 calories

37% calories from fat

6 g carbohydrate

2.3 g fat

5 mg cholesterol

3.4 g protein

1.3 g saturated fat

34 mg sodium

2.2 g fiber

Asparagus with Tomato-Ginger Chutney

PREPARATION TIME: 25 minutes

COOKING TIME: 10 minutes

YIELD: 4 servings

THIS DELICATE SIDE dish is from the former Eurasia restaurant in Chicago. It steams asparagus until crisp-tender, then tops it with a thick, aromatic chutney in an example of East-meets-West cuisine.

2 tablespoons sugar

2 tablespoons water

1 small onion, chopped fine

½ jalapeño, minced

4 cloves garlic, minced

2 tablespoons white wine vinegar

2 medium-sized tomatoes, peeled, seeded, and chopped

1 teaspoon chopped cilantro

⅛ teaspoon ground cardamom

⅛ teaspoon turmeric

⅛ teaspoon cinnamon

1 pound fresh asparagus, trimmed and peeled

1. To make chutney, heat sugar and water in a medium-sized saucepan over medium-high heat. Cook, stirring frequently, until amber in color. Add onion, jalapeño, and one-fourth of the minced garlic; cook, stirring constantly, 1 minute. Add vinegar. Reduce heat to low; cook 2 minutes. Add tomatoes; cook 5 minutes. Stir in remaining garlic, cilantro, cardamom, turmeric, and cinnamon. Simmer 2 minutes; remove from heat.

2. Bring water to a boil. Place asparagus in steamer rack over boiling water and steam until crisp-tender, 2 to 4 minutes. Place on a serving platter; pour warm chutney over asparagus.

NUTRITION INFORMATION PER SERVING:

64 calories	0.4 g fat	0.1 g saturated fat
6% calories from fat	0 mg cholesterol	14 mg sodium
14 g carbohydrate	2.4 g protein	2 g fiber

Roasted Asparagus with Bacon-Shallot Vinaigrette

PREPARATION TIME: 20 minutes

COOKING TIME: 10 minutes

YIELD: 10 servings

THIS ASPARAGUS RECIPE was developed for an Easter menu; it's a perfect side dish for ham. You may cook the asparagus as in step 1 several hours ahead and serve it at room temperature.

3 pounds slender asparagus	2 large shallots, minced
1 tablespoon olive oil	¼ cup extra-virgin olive oil
¼ teaspoon salt	4 teaspoons fresh lemon juice
	2 teaspoons balsamic vinegar
Dressing	1 teaspoon Dijon mustard
4 slices smoked bacon	¼ teaspoon salt
½ cup chopped cilantro	Freshly ground black pepper

1. Heat oven to 500°F. Trim ends of asparagus. Toss spears with olive oil. Arrange in a single layer on a jelly roll pan; sprinkle with salt. Bake until tender and browned, about 10 minutes, turning asparagus once.

2. To make dressing, cook bacon until crisp; drain well. Crumble into a small bowl. Add cilantro; mix well.

►

3. Whisk together shallots, olive oil, lemon juice, vinegar, mustard, salt, and pepper to taste. Arrange asparagus on a platter. Drizzle with dressing; sprinkle bacon mixture over the top.

NUTRITION INFORMATION PER SERVING:

140 calories	11 g fat	2.3 g saturated fat
65% calories from fat	7 mg cholesterol	255 mg sodium
7 g carbohydrate	6 g protein	3 g fiber

Mustardy Green Beans

PREPARATION TIME: 5 minutes

COOKING TIME: 7 minutes

YIELD: 4 servings

GREEN BEANS GET some zip in this recipe from a dash of mustard. Serve the beans with roast chicken or duck.

1 pound green beans, trimmed	Salt
1 tablespoon olive oil	Freshly ground black pepper
½ teaspoon Dijon mustard	

1. Bring water to a boil. Cook beans until crisp-tender, 5 to 7 minutes. Drain.

2. Heat oil in the same pan. Stir in mustard and salt and pepper to taste. Add beans; toss to coat. Serve warm.

NUTRITION INFORMATION PER SERVING:

85 calories	4 g fat	1 g saturated fat
46% calories from fat	0 mg cholesterol	19 mg sodium
8 g carbohydrate	2 g protein	3 g fiber

Green Beans with Garlic Almonds

PREPARATION TIME: 15 minutes
COOKING TIME: 10 minutes
YIELD: 6 servings

BUTTER AND ALMONDS pick up a mild garlic flavor and then are stirred into crisp-tender green beans in the following quick recipe.

1½ pounds fresh green beans, ends trimmed
¼ cup (½ stick) butter
1 clove garlic, minced

⅓ cup slivered almonds
2 tablespoons lemon juice
Salt

1. Heat 3 quarts water to boil in a large saucepan. Add beans; cook uncovered until crisp-tender, 6 to 8 minutes. Drain; rinse under cold water to stop cooking.

2. Melt butter in a large saucepan over medium heat. Add garlic. Cook, stirring often, until soft, about 2 minutes. Stir in almonds. Cook until almonds are light brown, about 2 minutes. Stir in beans, lemon juice, and salt to taste. Cook, stirring often, just until hot.

NUTRITION INFORMATION PER SERVING:

136 calories	11 g fat	5 g saturated fat
66% calories from fat	21 mg cholesterol	81 mg sodium
9 g carbohydrate	3.1 g protein	4 g fiber

Bean and Squash Coconut Milk Stew (Ginataan Sitawa Kalabasa)

PREPARATION TIME: 40 minutes
COOKING TIME: 1 hour
YIELD: 4 servings

A STORY ON the little-known cuisine of the Philippines featured this recipe, adapted from the Fish Pond restaurant in Chicago. The gingerroot and coconut milk in this dish reflect the influence of Southeast Asia on Filipino cooking.

1 tablespoon butter
1 small onion, chopped
1 1-inch piece gingerroot, minced

1 clove garlic, minced
8 ounces shrimp, peeled and deveined

►

1 14-ounce can coconut milk
1 acorn squash, skin removed and
    cut in ½-inch cubes

8 ounces green beans *or* long beans,
    cut in 3-inch pieces
Salt
Freshly ground black pepper

1. Melt butter in a large skillet or wok over medium heat. Add onion, ginger-root, and garlic. Cook, stirring frequently, until onion is softened, about 5 minutes.
2. Stir in shrimp. Cook, stirring often, until pink and cooked through, 2 to 3 minutes. Remove shrimp; set aside. Add coconut milk to skillet; simmer 30 minutes.
3. Stir in squash and beans. Cook, stirring often, until tender, about 20 minutes. Return shrimp to skillet. Heat through. Season with salt and pepper to taste.

NUTRITION INFORMATION PER SERVING:

320 calories	25 g fat	21 g saturated fat
65% calories from fat	90 mg cholesterol	140 mg sodium
13 g carbohydrate	17 g protein	6 g fiber

Back-of-the-Stove Baked Beans

PREPARATION TIME: 5 minutes
COOKING TIME: 1 hour
YIELD: 6 servings

ONE OF THE pleasures of making baked beans from scratch is the aroma that sweetens up the whole kitchen. It's not necessary to start with dried beans set to soak for hours. Buy good-quality canned white beans, such as imported Italian cannellini beans, to make preparation easier.

5 strips bacon
1 large onion, diced
2 16-ounce cans white beans,
    rinsed and drained
1 cup chicken broth
½ cup molasses

¼ cup tomato paste
¼ cup brown sugar
1½ teaspoons dry mustard
½ teaspoon salt
½ teaspoon ground black pepper

1. Cook bacon over low heat in a heavy-bottomed saucepan until crisp. Remove bacon to paper towels to drain. Pour off all but 1 tablespoon fat from pan. Raise heat to medium; add onion. Cook until soft and golden, about 2 minutes.

2. Add beans, broth, molasses, tomato paste, brown sugar, mustard, salt, and pepper. Stir until beans are coated and sauce is blended. Cover; cook over low heat 45 minutes. Crumble cooked bacon; stir bacon into beans before serving.

NUTRITION INFORMATION PER SERVING:

392 calories	9 g fat	3 g saturated fat
20% calories from fat	14 mg cholesterol	693 mg sodium
62 g carbohydrate	17 g protein	14 g fiber

Barbecued Lima Beans

PREPARATION TIME: 25 minutes

SOAKING TIME: 8 to 12 hours

COOKING TIME: 2 hours

YIELD: 10 servings

LIMA BEANS GET a barbecue-style punch in this recipe from reader Arlene Chisholm of Inverness, Illinois. If you like beans less sweet, go ahead and reduce the sugar.

1 pound dried small white lima beans	1 large onion, chopped
	1 green bell pepper, chopped
½ pound bacon *or* salt pork, chopped, cooked crisp, and drained	1 cup packed brown sugar
	¼ cup ketchup
	1 tablespoon dry mustard
1 14½-ounce can tomato soup	1 tablespoon Worcestershire sauce

1. Wash beans; sort. Soak beans in water to cover in a large bowl 8 to 12 hours. Transfer beans and soaking water to a large saucepan. Heat to boil over medium-high heat. Reduce heat to medium-low; simmer 1 hour. Drain.

2. Heat oven to 350°F. Combine beans, bacon, tomato soup, onion, bell pepper, brown sugar, ketchup, mustard, and Worcestershire sauce in a large bowl; mix well. Transfer mixture to a 13″ × 9″ inch baking pan. Bake until hot and bubbly, about 1 hour.

NUTRITION INFORMATION PER SERVING:

285 calories	5 g fat	1.5 g saturated fat
15% calories from fat	6 mg cholesterol	730 mg sodium
52 g carbohydrate	11 g protein	7 g fiber

Black-Eyed Peas

PREPARATION TIME: 25 minutes

SOAKING TIME: 8 to 12 hours

COOKING TIME: 1 hour

YIELD: 8 servings

A NUMBER OF Chicago restaurants carry on the Southern tradition of soul food cooking. This recipe from Wishbone restaurant is a comforting example.

4 cups dried black-eyed peas
1 tablespoon vegetable oil
2 onions, minced
1 rib celery, minced
1 carrot, minced
6 cups water

2 cloves garlic, minced
1 tomato, chopped
2 tablespoons brown sugar
1 teaspoon salt
1 teaspoon ground black pepper
Hot pepper sauce

1. Soak black-eyed peas in water to cover 8 to 12 hours; drain. Heat oil in a heavy stockpot or Dutch oven over medium heat. Add onions, celery, and carrot; cook until onions are tender, about 5 minutes.

2. Add water, black-eyed peas, garlic, tomato, brown sugar, salt, and pepper. Heat to boil, stirring occasionally. Reduce heat; simmer 45 minutes. Add water if mixture begins to dry out. Beans should be soft but not mushy. Taste and adjust seasoning. Serve with hot sauce.

NUTRITION INFORMATION PER SERVING:

275 calories
9% calories from fat
48 g carbohydrate

3 g fat
0 mg cholesterol
17 g protein

1 g saturated fat
1,763 mg sodium
9 g fiber

Horseradish and Beet Relish
(Hrin)

PREPARATION TIME: 35 minutes
COOKING TIME: 15 minutes
YIELD: 4 cups

COLORFUL FOODS ARE a hallmark of the Russian Orthodox Easter feast, as in this relish/side dish from Olga Kiewetz-Rue, a member of Chicago's Holy Trinity Russian Orthodox Cathedral parish. Serve this pungent treat with roast lamb or poultry. Store it in a tightly covered container in the refrigerator.

6 cups water
6 large beets, trimmed
1 horseradish root

¼ cup sugar
¼ cup white vinegar
½ teaspoon salt

1. Place water and beets in a large saucepan. Heat to boil over medium-high heat. Reduce heat; simmer until beets are almost tender, 15 to 20 minutes. Drain beets; set aside to cool.

2. Peel cooled beets. Coarsely grate beets and horseradish root into a large bowl. Stir in sugar and vinegar. Add salt. Taste and adjust seasoning.

NUTRITION INFORMATION PER TABLESPOON:

5 calories	0 g fat	0 g saturated fat
1% calories from fat	0 mg cholesterol	22 mg sodium
1.2 g carbohydrate	0.1 g protein	0.1 g fiber

Colorful Broccoli Stir-Fry

PREPARATION TIME: 30 minutes
COOKING TIME: 10 minutes
YIELD: 4 servings

BROCCOLI STIR-FRIED with onion, garlic, gingerroot, bell peppers, pea pods, and water chestnuts makes a light vegetarian entree or a colorful side dish. Serve this dish over cooked brown rice or toss it with cooked shell-shaped pasta noodles. Or, stir in 1 pound peeled and deveined cooked shrimp.

1 bunch broccoli (about 1½ pounds)

3 tablespoons peanut oil
½ small red onion, diced

►

1 ¾-inch-thick piece gingerroot,
  peeled and minced
2 cloves garlic, minced
1 yellow *or* green bell pepper,
  seeded and diced
1 red bell pepper, seeded and diced
1 6-ounce package frozen snow pea
  pods, thawed

1 6-ounce can sliced water
  chestnuts
¼ cup teriyaki sauce
¼ cup dry sherry
2 tablespoons soy sauce
1 tablespoon sesame seeds

1. Cut broccoli florets from stalks; lightly peel stalks. Cut stalks into ¼-inch-thick slices. Separate florets into equal-sized pieces.

2. Heat a large skillet over high heat until hot. Add oil; heat until hot. Add onion, gingerroot, and garlic. Cook, stirring constantly, until golden, about 2 minutes. Stir in broccoli pieces, yellow or green bell pepper, and red bell pepper. Cook, stirring constantly, until crisp-tender, about 3 minutes. Stir in snow pea pods, water chestnuts, teriyaki sauce, sherry, soy sauce, and sesame seeds. Cook; stirring constantly, until broccoli is tender, about 3 minutes.

NUTRITION INFORMATION PER SERVING:

225 calories	12 g fat	2.1 g saturated fat
45% calories from fat	0 mg cholesterol	1,231 mg sodium
24 g carbohydrate	8 g protein	8 g fiber

Smoky Brussels Sprouts

PREPARATION TIME: 20 minutes
COOKING TIME: 15 minutes
YIELD: 4 servings

HUMBLE BRUSSELS SPROUTS are anything but mundane when paired with hickory-smoked bacon, shallots, and almonds. For the best results, select fresh, firm brussels sprouts and remove the cores with the tip of a paring knife before cooking.

2 cups brussels sprouts, trimmed
Kosher salt
1 tablespoon butter
3 tablespoons sliced almonds

4 slices hickory-smoked bacon,
  diced
2 shallots, minced
Freshly ground black pepper
Ground nutmeg

1. Carefully cut out core from brussels sprouts with a small paring knife. Bring a large saucepan of water to boil; salt. Cook sprouts until crisp-tender, about 8 minutes. Drain; rinse under cold water to stop cooking.

2. Melt butter in a small nonstick skillet. Add almonds; cook, stirring constantly, until lightly toasted, about 2 minutes. Remove almonds from pan to stop cooking.

3. Heat a large skillet until hot. Add bacon; cook, stirring often, until almost crisp, about 3 minutes. Stir in shallots; cook 1 minute. Add brussels sprouts and salt, black pepper, and nutmeg to taste. Cook, stirring occasionally, until sprouts are heated through. Place in a serving bowl; sprinkle almonds over all.

NUTRITION INFORMATION PER SERVING:

188 calories	15 g fat	5 g saturated fat
69% calories from fat	24 mg cholesterol	346 mg sodium
7 g carbohydrate	8 g protein	2.3 g fiber

Sweet-and-Sour Red Cabbage

PREPARATION TIME: 20 minutes

COOKING TIME: 35 minutes

YIELD: 6 servings

DARK BROWN SUGAR provides the sweet and white vinegar the sour for this treatment of red cabbage. Serve it with roast pork or game.

4 slices bacon, chopped	1 teaspoon caraway seeds
1 onion, minced	½ teaspoon salt
1 small clove garlic, minced	⅛ teaspoon freshly ground black
¼ cup distilled white vinegar	pepper
3 tablespoons packed dark brown	1 medium-sized red cabbage (about
sugar	2 pounds), shredded
2 teaspoons Dijon mustard	½ cup beef broth

1. Fry bacon in a large, nonreactive Dutch oven over low heat until crisp, about 5 minutes. Add onion and garlic; cook over low heat until onion is soft, about 8 minutes.

2. Stir in vinegar, brown sugar, mustard, caraway seeds, salt, and pepper. Add cabbage, tossing to coat evenly. Cover; cook over medium-low heat, stirring occasionally, 15 minutes.

➤

3. Add beef broth; cook uncovered, stirring frequently, until cabbage is tender, about 5 minutes. Taste and adjust seasonings.

NUTRITION INFORMATION PER SERVING:

153 calories	7 g fat	2.3 g saturated fat
39% calories from fat	11 mg cholesterol	525 mg sodium
18 g carbohydrate	7 g protein	4 g fiber

Sauerkraut with Dried Cherries

PREPARATION TIME: 5 minutes

COOKING TIME: 6 minutes

YIELD: 4 servings

GIVE TRADITIONAL SAUERKRAUT a lift with bits of dried cherries. The sweetness from the sugar and dried fruit goes well with pork or poultry. Dried cherries are available at some supermarkets and specialty stores. You may substitute other dried fruit such as cranberries or apples.

1 1-pound package refrigerated sauerkraut	2 teaspoons brown sugar
	Salt
¼ cup white wine	Coarsely crushed black pepper
2 tablespoons minced dried cherries	2 tablespoons unsalted butter
	2 tablespoons sour cream
1 tablespoon red wine vinegar	

1. Put sauerkraut in a colander; rinse under cold water. Drain.

2. Combine sauerkraut, wine, cherries, vinegar, sugar, and salt and pepper to taste in a medium-sized nonaluminum saucepan. Cook over medium heat until most of wine has evaporated, 4 to 5 minutes. Stir in butter and sour cream; heat through. Remove from heat; adjust seasoning.

NUTRITION INFORMATION PER SERVING:

111 calories	8 g fat	5 g saturated fat
60% calories from fat	19 mg cholesterol	816 mg sodium
10 g carbohydrate	1.4 g protein	4 g fiber

Colcannon

PREPARATION TIME: 5 minutes
COOKING TIME: 25 minutes
YIELD: 4 servings

IT WOULDN'T BE a Saint Patrick's Day celebration without corned beef. The most traditional vegetable to go with it? This delicious mixture of cabbage and potatoes. But don't save it just for March 17; it's a fine side dish for any winter feast.

12 to 14 ounces tiny red potatoes, scrubbed
½ pound green cabbage, trimmed and cut into ¾-inch-wide ribbons

5 tablespoons whipping cream
1½ teaspoons prepared horseradish
2 green onions, sliced thin
Salt
Freshly ground black pepper

1. Put potatoes in a large saucepan of water to cover; add salt. Heat to boil over medium-high heat; cook until potatoes are tender, 20 to 25 minutes. About 5 minutes before potatoes are cooked, add cabbage to pan. Cook until tender.

2. Drain well. Return to pan; briefly place over low heat to dry. Remove from heat; add whipping cream, horseradish, green onions, and salt and pepper to taste. Coarsely mash potato mixture with a potato masher.

NUTRITION INFORMATION PER SERVING:

140 calories	7 g fat	4.3 g saturated fat
42% calories from fat	25 mg cholesterol	30 mg sodium
19 g carbohydrate	3 g protein	3 g fiber

Carrot and Red Pepper Puree

PREPARATION TIME: 45 minutes
COOKING TIME: 10 minutes
YIELD: 4 servings

STAFF WRITER RICHARD Longworth's story on vegetable purees showed them to be a colorful and elegant accompaniment to any meal, not to mention a wonderful opportunity to mix and match flavors. Make the purees ahead and keep them warm, or reheat them in a double boiler. Serve this puree with roasted poultry or grilled fish; it also can add color and taste to mashed potatoes.

5 carrots, peeled and chopped	2 teaspoons butter, melted
2 roasted red bell peppers, peeled, seeded, and chopped (see Note)	¼ teaspoon ground mace
	¼ teaspoon salt

1. Steam or boil carrots in water until tender, about 10 minutes. Drain well.
2. Puree carrots with roasted red bell peppers in a food processor fitted with a metal blade. Add butter, mace, and salt; process until smooth.

❧ NOTE: *To roast fresh bell peppers, hold them with a fork over a gas flame to blacken skin on all sides. Place peppers in a bowl; cover with plastic wrap until cool. Remove skins, seeds, and cores.*

Or place bell peppers on a baking sheet in a 500°F oven. Roast, turning occasionally, until blackened on all sides, 20 to 25 minutes. Place peppers in a paper bag; close and let steam 10 minutes. Remove skins, seeds, and cores. You may substitute bottled roasted bell peppers if you like.

NUTRITION INFORMATION PER SERVING:

70 calories	2.2 g fat	1.3 g saturated fat
26% calories from fat	5 mg cholesterol	195 mg sodium
13 g carbohydrate	2 g protein	4 g fiber

Balsamic-Glazed Carrots

PREPARATION TIME: 5 minutes
COOKING TIME: 6 minutes
YIELD: 4 servings

A TOUCH OF balsamic vinegar turns ordinary carrots into a sweet-sour sensation. Using a bag of ready-to-cook vegetables speeds the preparation time considerably. This recipe is from a "Fast Food" column.

1 1-pound bag baby-cut carrots
⅔ cup reduced-sodium vegetable
   or chicken broth
2 teaspoons extra-virgin olive oil

2 teaspoons balsamic vinegar
Pinch sugar
Salt
Freshly ground black pepper

1. Combine carrots and broth in a 1- to 1½-quart saucepan (pan must be small enough so that broth covers carrots). Heat to boil. Cook uncovered over high heat until almost all broth has cooked away, about 4 minutes.

2. Add oil, vinegar, sugar, and salt and pepper to taste. Cook, stirring constantly over medium heat, until carrots are glazed, 1 to 2 minutes.

NUTRITION INFORMATION PER SERVING:

70 calories	3 g fat	0.4 saturated fat
38% calories from fat	1 mg cholesterol	58 mg sodium
10 g carbohydrate	2 g protein	2 g fiber

Steamed Cauliflower with Red Bell Pepper Sauce

PREPARATION TIME: 20 minutes
MICROWAVE COOKING TIME: 15 minutes
YIELD: 6 servings

WITH A MICROWAVE oven and a food processor, you can produce this dramatically colored—and healthful—dish in 35 minutes.

Cauliflower
1 head cauliflower (about 2
   pounds)
3 tablespoons water

Sauce
1 tablespoon olive oil
1 small white onion, chopped
1 rib celery, diced

►

1 small clove garlic, minced
2 roasted red bell peppers, peeled
    and seeded (see Index)
2 tomatoes, peeled, seeded, and
    chopped

¼ teaspoon dried leaf thyme
Salt
Freshly ground black pepper
Minced fresh parsley

1. Separate cauliflower into 2-inch florets, discarding center core.
2. Put florets into a 2-quart microwave-safe baking dish. Add water. Cover with plastic wrap vented at one corner. Microwave on high (100 percent power), stirring occasionally, until almost fork-tender, 4 to 6 minutes. Let stand covered, 5 minutes.
3. To make sauce, put oil into a 1½-quart microwave-safe casserole. Microwave uncovered on high until hot, 45 seconds to 1 minute. Stir in onion, celery, and garlic. Microwave uncovered on high, stirring once, until crisp-tender, about 2 minutes.
4. Stir in bell peppers, tomatoes, and thyme. Microwave covered on high until very tender, 4 to 5 minutes. Puree in a blender or in a food processor fitted with a metal blade. Season with salt and black pepper to taste. Ladle sauce onto a serving plate. Top with cauliflower florets. Garnish with parsley.

NUTRITION INFORMATION PER SERVING:

60 calories	3 g fat	0.4 g saturated fat
35% calories from fat	0 mg cholesterol	29 mg sodium
9 g carbohydrate	2.1 g protein	3 g fiber

Cauliflower with Leeks and Sun-Dried Tomatoes

PREPARATION TIME: 10 minutes

COOKING TIME: 10 minutes

YIELD: 4 servings

CAULIFLOWER MIXED WITH tangy sun-dried tomatoes and the mild onion flavor of leeks makes a side dish with color and character.

½ medium-sized head cauliflower,
    broken into florets
1 tablespoon unsalted butter
2 small leeks, trimmed and cut in
    ½-inch slices

3 to 4 oil-packed sun-dried
    tomatoes, patted dry and
    minced
Salt
Freshly ground black pepper

1. Bring a large pot of water to boil. Cook cauliflower until tender, 7 to 8 minutes. Drain; set aside.

2. Melt butter in the same pot over medium-high heat. Add leeks and tomatoes. Cook, stirring often, until leeks begin to soften, 2 minutes. Add cauliflower and salt and pepper to taste. Gently toss.

NUTRITION INFORMATION PER SERVING:

79 calories	4 g fat	2 g saturated fat
37% calories from fat	8 mg cholesterol	32 mg sodium
12 g carbohydrate	2 g protein	2.4 g fiber

Swiss Chard with Tomatoes

PREPARATION TIME: 20 minutes

COOKING TIME: 6 minutes

YIELD: 4 servings

SWISS CHARD IS a seldom used vegetable, but it makes a wonderful accompaniment for chicken. This recipe combines the chard with fresh tomatoes and garlic for a hearty side dish.

1 pound red *or* green Swiss chard
3 tablespoons olive oil
½ cup soft bread crumbs
1 large clove garlic, minced

2 small tomatoes, seeded and diced
¼ teaspoon salt
Crushed red pepper flakes

1. Trim coarse leaves and thick center ribs from chard. Cut tender stems and leaves into ½-inch slices.

2. Heat 1 tablespoon of the oil in a large skillet. Add bread crumbs; cook, stirring often, until crisp and golden. Remove from skillet; set aside.

3. Cool skillet slightly. Add remaining oil and garlic. Cook, stirring, 2 minutes. Add chard; cook until wilted, 1 to 2 minutes. Add tomatoes, salt, and red pepper flakes to taste. Remove from heat. Sprinkle bread crumbs over top.

NUTRITION INFORMATION PER SERVING:

135 calories	11 g fat	2 g saturated fat
67% calories from fat	0.2 mg cholesterol	400 mg sodium
9 g carbohydrate	8 g protein	2.3 g fiber

Collard Greens

PREPARATION TIME: 25 minutes
COOKING TIME: 2 to 3 hours
YIELD: 6 servings

FILMMAKER GEORGE TILLMAN made family meals the star attraction in his 1997 movie *Soul Food*, which was filmed in and around Chicago. This recipe comes from Tillman and his mother.

3 bunches collard greens, washed
and cut into ¼-inch strips
2 ham hocks

1 teaspoon salt
1 to 2 jalapeños, chopped fine

1. Heat a large pot of water to a boil over high heat. Add collards; boil 10 minutes. Drain; refill pot with fresh water.
2. Add ham hocks and salt. Heat to boil; reduce heat to medium. Simmer until greens and ham hocks are tender, 2 to 3 hours. Add jalapeños during last 15 minutes of cooking. Drain; season to taste.

NUTRITION INFORMATION PER SERVING:

104 calories	4.3 g fat	1.4 g saturated fat
35% calories from fat	18 mg cholesterol	470 mg sodium
11 g carbohydrate	7 g protein	5 g fiber

Bacon-Fried Corn

PREPARATION TIME: 20 minutes
COOKING TIME: 15 minutes
YIELD: 4 servings

WHEN MARCIA LYTHCOTT, a *Tribune* editor, cooked up this family favorite in the *Tribune* test kitchen, the smoky, rich corn disappeared faster than a double-layer chocolate cake.

9 strips bacon, diced
1 large onion, chopped
4 cups fresh corn kernels
1 red bell pepper, seeded and
chopped

2 tablespoons minced fresh parsley
1 tablespoon milk
Salt
Freshly ground black pepper

1. Cook bacon in a large skillet over medium heat until bacon is crisp, about 5 minutes. Remove bacon with a slotted spoon to paper towels to drain. Reserve fat in skillet.

2. Add onion to bacon fat; cook, stirring often, until crisp-tender, about 4 minutes. Add corn and bell pepper. Cook, stirring often, until corn is crisp-tender, about 5 minutes. Stir in parsley and milk and salt and pepper to taste. Garnish with bacon pieces.

NUTRITION INFORMATION PER SERVING:

402 calories	23 g fat	8 g saturated fat
50% calories from fat	37 mg cholesterol	715 mg sodium
34 g carbohydrate	19 g protein	5 g fiber

Jalapeño Corn Pudding

PREPARATION TIME: 20 minutes

BAKING TIME: 40 to 45 minutes

YIELD: 6 servings

THIS RICH, SOFT pudding, featuring a combination of corn and jalapeños, makes a nice side dish for roast or grilled pork. Accompanied by a salad, it could be a main course for brunch.

6 large eggs, beaten
¼ green bell pepper, seeded and
    chopped fine
3 green onions, chopped fine
1 to 2 jalapeños, seeded and
    minced

2 16-ounce cans cream-style corn
1 pound shredded cheddar cheese
2 tablespoons all-purpose flour
¼ teaspoon salt

1. Heat oven to 350°F. Stir together eggs, bell pepper, green onions, and jalapeños in a large bowl. Add corn, cheese, flour, and salt. Mix to blend.

2. Grease a 13″ × 9″ baking pan. Bring a larger pan of water to boil. Pour corn mixture into the baking pan. Place the baking pan in the boiling water. Bake until center is almost firm, 40 to 45 minutes. Cool on a wire rack 10 minutes.

NUTRITION INFORMATION PER SERVING:

501 calories	31 g fat	18 g saturated fat
54% calories from fat	292 mg cholesterol	1,061 mg sodium
32 g carbohydrate	28 g protein	3.2 g fiber

Corn Custard Cups

PREPARATION TIME: 30 minutes
COOKING TIME: 20 minutes
YIELD: 12 servings

CHICAGO RESTAURATEUR STEVEN Chiappetti was the American finalist at the Bocuse D'Or cooking competition in Lyons, France, in 1997. He didn't get to take home the gold, but you can, with these custards of golden corn, an elegant side dish for a party.

2 teaspoons olive oil	¼ teaspoon ground black pepper
¾ cup frozen corn kernels, thawed	1 cup whipping cream
1 shallot, minced	3 large eggs
2 teaspoons chopped fresh thyme	1 5.3-ounce jar pickled baby corn,
½ teaspoon salt	drained

1. Heat oven to 350°F. Heat olive oil in a medium-sized skillet over medium heat. Add corn and shallot; cook until tender, about 3 minutes. Stir in thyme, salt, and pepper. Set mixture aside.

2. Place whipping cream and eggs in a blender. Blend at high speed until well combined. Add corn mixture; blend slightly until corn is chopped coarse.

3. Cut 12 baby corn pieces in half lengthwise. Cut each half into thirds horizontally. Grease 12 muffin cups. Line each muffin cup with 6 pieces of baby corn. Pour equal amounts of corn mixture into each cup. Bake until a wooden pick inserted in the center comes out clean, about 20 to 25 minutes. Let cool slightly; carefully unmold onto 12 dinner plates. Serve warm.

NUTRITION INFORMATION PER SERVING:

114 calories	10 g fat	5 g saturated fat
73% calories from fat	80 mg cholesterol	147 mg sodium
5 g carbohydrate	3 g protein	1 g fiber

Southwestern Succotash

PREPARATION TIME: 20 minutes
STANDING TIME: 6 to 12 hours
COOKING TIME: 2½ hours
YIELD: 4 servings

A TRIP TO New Mexico uncovered some of the Southwest's finest regional foods, such as this savory bean and corn recipe, adapted from one by chef David Sellers at Santacafé in Santa Fe. He uses heirloom beans, such as Anasazi, black turtle, or Jacob's cattle beans, but any dried bean will work fine. Look for heirloom beans in specialty food shops.

1⅓ cups mixed heirloom beans *or* other dried beans
1 red bell pepper, seeded and chopped
1 red onion, chopped
3 cups fresh *or* thawed frozen corn kernels
1 cup chopped cilantro
2 cloves garlic, minced
¼ cup vegetable oil
2 tablespoons fresh lime juice
2 teaspoons honey
1 to 2 teaspoons crushed red pepper flakes
¼ teaspoon salt
¼ teaspoon freshly ground black pepper

1. Put beans in a large bowl; add enough water to cover tops of beans by several inches. Let stand covered 6 to 12 hours.

2. Drain beans. Put beans into a Dutch oven; add 4 cups fresh water. Heat to boil over medium-high heat. Reduce heat; simmer covered until beans are tender, about 2½ hours. Drain.

3. Combine warm cooked beans, bell pepper, onion, corn, and cilantro in a medium-sized bowl.

4. Whisk together garlic, oil, lime juice, honey, red pepper flakes, salt, and black pepper in a small bowl. Pour dressing over bean mixture; toss to coat. Serve slightly warm or at room temperature.

NUTRITION INFORMATION PER SERVING:

475 calories	16 g fat	2.2 g saturated fat
28% calories from fat	0 mg cholesterol	415 mg sodium
74 g carbohydrate	17 g protein	19 g fiber

Baked Whole Garlic

PREPARATION TIME: 10 minutes
BAKING TIME: 35 minutes
YIELD: 10 servings

BAKING GIVES GARLIC a full yet mild flavor. Vary the recipe to better suit the food it accompanies by using the same broth flavor as the meat you are serving.

10 whole heads garlic	⅓ cup olive oil
1 cup beef, chicken, pork, *or* lamb broth	Salt
	Freshly ground black pepper

1. Heat oven to 350°F. Peel away as much of the papery outer skin of garlic heads as possible but leave individual cloves still covered. Put garlic in a single layer in a shallow, nonreactive baking pan.
2. Pour broth over all. Drizzle with oil; sprinkle with salt and pepper to taste. Bake partly covered, basting frequently, until heads are soft to the touch, 35 to 45 minutes, depending on size. Remove cover during last 10 minutes to allow skins to turn golden.
3. To serve, squeeze pulp out of skins onto toasted bread or roasted meats such as beef, chicken, pork, or lamb.

NUTRITION INFORMATION PER SERVING:

17 calories	1.4 g fat	0.2 g saturated fat
72% calories from fat	0 mg cholesterol	10 mg sodium
1 g carbohydrate	0.2 g protein	0.1 g fiber

Crispy Light Onion Rings

PREPARATION TIME: 25 minutes
COOKING TIME: 10 minutes
YIELD: 6 servings

DEEP-FRYING ONION rings in two stages makes them easy to prepare ahead for entertaining. Though not cooked in a loaf shape, your guests will enjoy these fried onion rings similar to those found in many restaurants.

Vegetable oil for deep-frying	1½ cups all-purpose flour
6 yellow onions, cut very thin and separated into rings	Salt
	Freshly ground red pepper

1. Pour oil to a depth of 3 inches in a deep-fryer, wok, or deep heavy saucepan. Heat oil to 375°F.

2. Toss onion rings lightly in flour; shake off excess. Deep-fry a few at a time in oil until very light gold color, about 1 minute. Do not overbrown. Remove with a slotted spoon to paper towels. Repeat with remaining onion rings. Let cool completely. Cover with foil to keep up to several hours.

3. Strain oil back into the clean pan when you're ready to serve the onion rings; heat to 365°F, using a deep-frying thermometer. Deep-fry onions until golden in color. Drain on paper towels. Sprinkle with salt and red pepper to taste.

NUTRITION INFORMATION PER SERVING:

240 calories	18 g fat	3 g saturated fat
68% calories from fat	0 mg cholesterol	5 mg sodium
17 g carbohydrate	2 g protein	2 g fiber

Fried Onion–Ginger Chutney

PREPARATION TIME: 20 minutes
COOKING TIME: 15 minutes
YIELD: 32 1-tablespoon servings

MOST CHUTNEY RECIPES use fruit as the base. Chuck Allen of Dana Point, California, suggested an alternative, made with fried onions, for the "You're the Cook" column. It's a lighter chutney than many and a fine match for Indian food or grilled beef or pork. You may refrigerate the chutney for up to a week.

2 tablespoons olive oil	2 tablespoons molasses
2 white onions, cut into thin slices	2 tablespoons cider vinegar
2 tablespoons minced gingerroot	2 whole star anise, crushed
1 tablespoon minced garlic	1 tablespoon curry powder
2 tablespoons orange juice	¼ teaspoon ground mace

1. Heat oil in a large skillet over medium-high heat. Add onions; cook, stirring often, until browned, 10 to 12 minutes. Add gingerroot and garlic; cook 1 minute.

2. Add orange juice, molasses, vinegar, star anise, curry powder, and mace; cook over low heat, stirring occasionally, until flavors are blended, 3 to 4 minutes. Serve at room temperature.

NUTRITION INFORMATION PER SERVING:

14 calories	1 g fat	0.1 g saturated fat
46% calories from fat	0 mg cholesterol	1 mg sodium
2 g carbohydrate	0.2 g protein	0.2 g fiber

Oprah's Potatoes

PREPARATION TIME: 10 minutes
COOKING TIME: 25 minutes
YIELD: 14 servings

LUMPS ARE PART of the tradition of television talk show host Oprah Winfrey's horseradish-flavored mashed potatoes. Once on the menu of the now defunct The Eccentric restaurant, these potatoes were described by columnist William Rice as "the stuff of legends." Look for horseradish sauce in the condiment aisle of most supermarkets.

2½ pounds red potatoes
2½ pounds Idaho potatoes
1¼ cups (2½ sticks) butter, cut in pieces
1 to 1¼ cups bottled horseradish sauce

1½ cups whipping cream *or* whole milk
½ teaspoon salt
Freshly ground black pepper
Chopped parsley, optional

1. Wash red potatoes and Idaho potatoes well, leaving skins on; cut in half. Transfer to a large pot; cover with water. Heat water to boil; lower heat to simmer. Cook until potatoes are tender, about 25 minutes.

2. Drain potatoes well; return them to the pot. Do not peel them. Add butter. Mash slightly by hand. Add horseradish sauce, whipping cream, salt, and black pepper to taste. Mash until texture is creamy but still slightly lumpy. Garnish with parsley.

NUTRITION INFORMATION PER SERVING:

410 calories
63% calories from fat
34 g carbohydrate

29 g fat
86 mg cholesterol
4.2 g protein

18 g saturated fat
317 mg sodium
3.2 g fiber

Santa Fe Mashed Potatoes

PREPARATION TIME: 20 minutes
COOKING TIME: 30 minutes
YIELD: 10 servings

FOR A STORY on lighter versions of meat and potatoes, writer Pat Dailey created these mashed potatoes with a Southwestern twist.

1½ pounds Idaho potatoes

1½ pounds red potatoes

4 tablespoons unsalted butter
1 onion, diced fine
1 teaspoon cumin seeds
1 Anaheim *or* poblano chili,
    roasted and diced
⅓ cup sour cream

½ cup milk
1 tablespoon barbecue sauce
½ teaspoon salt
Freshly ground black pepper
⅓ cup chopped cilantro

1. Cut unpeeled potatoes into chunks. Put into a large pan of salted water. Heat to boil; cook until tender, 20 to 25 minutes. Drain thoroughly; return potatoes to the pan. Cook over medium heat about 30 seconds to dry out.

2. Melt 1 tablespoon of the butter in a skillet over high heat. Add onion and cumin seeds. Cook, stirring often, until onion is browned, 6 to 8 minutes. Add roasted chili. Remove from heat; set aside.

3. Mash potatoes with a potato masher. Add remaining 3 tablespoons butter and sour cream; mix well. Add milk and barbecue sauce; mix well. Mix in onion mixture, salt, black pepper to taste, and cilantro.

NUTRITION INFORMATION PER SERVING:

192 calories	7 g fat	4.1 g saturated fat
31% calories from fat	18 mg cholesterol	150 mg sodium
30 g carbohydrate	4 g protein	3 g fiber

Marbled Mashed Potatoes

PREPARATION TIME: 30 minutes
COOKING TIME: 1 hour 10 minutes
YIELD: 8 servings

JEANMARIE BROWNSON, FORMER *Tribune* test kitchen director, elevated potatoes from ordinary fare to the center of attention when she swirled together orange sweet potatoes and white potatoes in a baking dish. This dish freezes well, making it perfect for hectic holiday entertaining.

1½ pounds medium-sized red
    potatoes, halved
3 large sweet potatoes, quartered
¼ cup (½ stick) butter
4 large shallots, minced

1 cup sour cream
1 cup whipping cream, whipped
½ teaspoon salt
¼ teaspoon white pepper
⅛ teaspoon freshly ground nutmeg

►

Topping
½ cup fresh homemade bread
  crumbs

6 tablespoons melted butter
¼ cup minced fresh parsley

1. Bring 2 large saucepans of water to boil. Cook red potatoes and sweet potatoes separately until fork-tender, about 30 minutes. Drain; cool slightly and peel. Push potatoes through a ricer into separate bowls or mash separately with a potato masher.

2. Heat oven to 350°F. Melt ¼ cup butter in a small skillet; add shallots. Cook, stirring often, until shallots are tender, about 5 minutes. Stir half of the shallot mixture into each potato mixture. Whisk sour cream into whipped cream. Fold half of cream mixture into each potato mixture.

3. Add ¼ teaspoon salt, ⅛ teaspoon white pepper, and 1/16 teaspoon nutmeg to each of the potato mixtures. Taste and adjust seasonings. Put half of the sweet potato mixture into a 2-quart baking or soufflé dish; top with half of the white potato mixture. Repeat layering. Swirl potatoes with a metal spatula to give a marbled effect.

4. To make topping, stir together bread crumbs, melted butter, and parsley in a small bowl. Sprinkle topping over potatoes. Bake until topping is golden and potatoes are heated through, 30 to 35 minutes.

❧ NOTE: *To freeze, complete recipe through step 3. Freeze well wrapped up to 2 months. Thaw in the refrigerator. Make topping as directed in step 4; sprinkle over potatoes. Bake as directed, adding time if necessary to be sure potatoes are heated through.*

NUTRITION INFORMATION PER SERVING:

442 calories	32 g fat	20 g saturated fat
63% calories from fat	92 mg cholesterol	347 mg sodium
37 g carbohydrate	5 g protein	3.3 g fiber

Michael Altenberg's Fingerling Potatoes

PREPARATION TIME: 5 minutes
COOKING TIME: 55 minutes
STANDING TIME: 15 minutes
YIELD: 4 servings

AFTER CHEF MICHAEL Altenberg of Campagnola restaurant in Evanston, Illinois, visited a local farmer's market, he was inspired to throw together this lovely dish of tiny fingerling potatoes with herbs and onions. Small new potatoes, quartered, can be substituted for fingerling potatoes.

1 head garlic, halved horizontally
2 teaspoons vegetable oil
1½ teaspoons balsamic vinegar
1 pound fingerling *or* other small potatoes, washed, skins on
1 teaspoon kosher salt

6 to 8 tarragon leaves, torn into small pieces
1 green onion, minced
Pinch crushed red pepper flakes
Salt
Freshly ground black pepper
3 tablespoons extra-virgin olive oil

1. Heat oven to 425°F. Place garlic on a piece of aluminum foil; drizzle lightly with vegetable oil and 1 teaspoon of the vinegar. Wrap in foil; bake until garlic is soft, about 45 minutes. Cool; squeeze pulp from skins. Set aside.

2. Cover potatoes with cold water in a small saucepan; add kosher salt. Heat to boil over high heat. Reduce heat; simmer until potatoes are just tender, about 10 minutes. Drain; cover with cold water to stop cooking. Drain. Place in a medium-sized bowl.

3. Combine 2 teaspoons or more to taste of the roasted garlic, tarragon, onion, remaining ½ teaspoon vinegar, red pepper flakes, and salt and black pepper to taste in a small bowl. Whisk in olive oil. Pour over potatoes; let stand 15 minutes before serving.

NUTRITION INFORMATION PER SERVING:

153 calories	12 g fat	2 g saturated fat
69% calories from fat	0 mg cholesterol	4 mg sodium
10 g carbohydrate	2 g protein	2 g fiber

Gorgonzola-Cheese Baked Potatoes

PREPARATION TIME: 5 minutes
MICROWAVE COOKING TIME: 14 minutes
YIELD: 4 servings

A FATHER'S DAY menu created by writer Pat Dailey included this hearty side dish of potatoes topped with a creamy blue cheese spread. The microwave oven is used for "baking" the potatoes, a strategy that saves time and keeps the kitchen from getting heated up.

4 medium-sized red potatoes, scrubbed	3 tablespoons crumbled Gorgonzola *or* blue cheese
½ cup sour cream	Freshly ground black pepper
	Snipped fresh chives, optional

1. Pierce potatoes in several places. Place on a microwave-safe plate; cook on high (100 percent power) until tender, 10 to 14 minutes, rotating the plate a quarter turn after 5 minutes. Let stand 2 minutes.

2. Stir together sour cream, cheese, and pepper to taste in a small bowl. Split potatoes in half; place a dollop of sour cream mixture on each. Sprinkle with chives if desired.

NUTRITION INFORMATION PER SERVING:

200 calories	8 g fat	5 g saturated fat
36% calories from fat	18 mg cholesterol	110 mg sodium
27 g carbohydrate	5 g protein	3 g fiber

Buttered New Potatoes and Peas with Watercress

PREPARATION TIME: 15 minutes
COOKING TIME: 20 minutes
YIELD: 4 servings

HARBINGERS OF SPRING—tiny new potatoes, fresh peas, and watercress—are teamed in this vegetable side dish. Serve with steamed fresh fish or chicken breasts.

1 pound small new potatoes	1 cup water
1 cup chicken broth	2 tablespoons olive oil

⅛ teaspoon salt

⅛ teaspoon freshly ground black
  pepper

1 cup fresh shelled *or* frozen peas

3 tablespoons unsalted butter

4 green onions, minced

2 cloves garlic, minced

¼ cup minced watercress leaves

2 tablespoons minced fresh parsley

1. Put potatoes, chicken broth, water, oil, salt, and pepper into a medium-sized saucepan. Heat to boil; reduce heat to medium. Simmer uncovered until potatoes are fork-tender, about 15 minutes. Remove potatoes with a slotted spoon to a bowl. Cut potatoes crosswise in half.

2. Drop peas into simmering potato cooking liquid. Simmer uncovered until peas are bright green and crisp-tender, about 2 minutes. Remove from heat.

3. Melt butter in a large skillet over medium heat. Add onions and garlic; cook, stirring frequently, until wilted, about 2 minutes. Stir in potatoes, peas, and cooking liquid. Cook, stirring often, until heated through, about 2 minutes. Stir in watercress and parsley.

NUTRITION INFORMATION PER SERVING:

281 calories	16 g fat	6 g saturated fat
50% calories from fat	23 mg cholesterol	280 mg sodium
30 g carbohydrate	6 g protein	5 g fiber

Glarner Stube's Roesti Potatoes

PREPARATION TIME: 20 minutes

CHILLING TIME: 8 to 12 hours

COOKING TIME: 40 minutes

YIELD: 6 servings

GLARNER STUBE IS a popular bar and restaurant in the Swiss-settled town of New Glarus, Wisconsin. These hash browns with Swiss cheese are one of its signature dishes. The recipe accompanied a story by Andy Badeker about cheese makers in that area of Wisconsin.

Salt

2 pounds russet potatoes

2 tablespoons butter

2 tablespoons vegetable oil

Freshly ground black pepper

1½ cups shredded Swiss cheese

Chopped fresh parsley

▶

1. Bring a large pot of water to boil; add salt. Cook potatoes until almost tender, about 25 minutes. Drain. Refrigerate potatoes 8 to 12 hours.

2. Peel potatoes. Using a large-hole grater, grate potatoes. Melt 1 tablespoon of the butter with 1 tablespoon of the oil in a large heavy skillet over medium-high heat. Sprinkle half of the potatoes in an even layer. Season with salt and pepper to taste. Sprinkle cheese evenly over potatoes. Sprinkle remaining potatoes over cheese. Season with salt and pepper to taste. Press lightly to compress.

3. Cook until bottom is browned, about 7 minutes. Remove skillet from heat. Place a large plate over the skillet. Using oven mitts, grasp skillet and plate; turn over, inverting potatoes onto the plate, browned side up. Return skillet to heat. Melt remaining butter with remaining oil in the skillet. Slide potatoes back into the skillet; cook until bottom is browned and cheese melts, about 7 minutes. Slide or turn potatoes onto the plate; sprinkle with parsley. Cut into wedges.

NUTRITION INFORMATION PER SERVING:

288 calories	16 g fat	8 g saturated fat
49% calories from fat	35 mg cholesterol	114 mg sodium
27 g carbohydrate	10 g protein	2.3 g fiber

Marjorie Biederman's Latkes

PREPARATION TIME: 20 minutes
COOKING TIME: 8 minutes per batch
YIELD: 50 latkes

HIGHLAND PARK, ILLINOIS, resident Marjorie Biederman revealed her secret for producing lots of latkes, the Jewish potato pancakes traditionally served at Hanukkah, in a 1998 "Good Eating" article. "I never make latkes at the last minute," she said. Instead, after draining them on brown paper bags until cool, she freezes them on a cookie sheet, then slides them off into freezer bags. "When I take them out," she continued, "I put them back on the cookie sheet and put them in the oven, as high as it will go, 500 degrees, until they're hot and crisp."

8 medium-sized baking potatoes, peeled and cubed	⅛ teaspoon baking powder
1 small onion, peeled and cubed	1 teaspoon salt
2 large eggs	1¾ cups vegetable shortening for frying
2 tablespoons all-purpose flour	Applesauce

1. Grate potatoes and onion in a food processor fitted with a grating blade; let mixture drain in colander about 10 minutes, pushing it occasionally to squeeze out liquid.

2. Combine potatoes, onion, eggs, flour, baking powder, and salt in a large bowl. Heat ¼ cup of the shortening in a large heavy skillet over high heat. Spoon mixture 1 tablespoon at a time into hot oil; do not crowd skillet. Cook in batches until brown and crisp, about 4 minutes per side. Add shortening as needed. Drain on brown paper bags or paper towels. Serve with applesauce.

NUTRITION INFORMATION PER LATKE:

85 calories	7 g fat	2 g saturated fat
77% calories from fat	9 mg cholesterol	25 mg sodium
5 g carbohydrate	7 g protein	0.3 g fiber

Curried Sweet Potato Latkes

PREPARATION TIME: 25 minutes
COOKING TIME: 8 minutes per batch
YIELD: 12 latkes

CHICAGO CHEF ERWIN Drechsler says he often experiments with adding herbs and root vegetables, including sweet potatoes, to his Hanukkah latkes, those traditional potato pancakes. But even Drechsler warns against too much experimentation. When it comes to a latke, "the simpler the better," he says.

⅔ cup all-purpose flour	½ teaspoon paprika
2¼ teaspoons curry powder	2 large eggs, beaten
2 teaspoons packed brown sugar	1 pound sweet potatoes, peeled and
1½ teaspoons granulated sugar	grated coarse
1¼ teaspoons baking powder	Salt
¾ teaspoon ground red pepper	Black pepper
¾ teaspoon ground cumin	¾ cup peanut oil for frying

1. Whisk together flour, curry powder, brown sugar, granulated sugar, baking powder, red pepper, cumin, and paprika in a large bowl. Stir eggs into dry ingredients to make thick batter. Add sweet potatoes and salt and black pepper to taste; mix well.

►

2. Heat oil in a large, heavy skillet over medium-high heat. Drop enough batter into hot oil to form 4-inch latkes when pressed down. Do not crowd skillet. Fry in batches until golden, about 4 minutes per side. Drain on paper towels.

NUTRITION INFORMATION PER LATKE:

115 calories	6 g fat	1.1 g saturated fat
43% calories from fat	35 mg cholesterol	50 mg sodium
15 g carbohydrate	3 g protein	2 g fiber

Herbed Sweet Potatoes

PREPARATION TIME: 15 minutes
BAKING TIME: 1 hour 10 minutes
YIELD: 6 servings

SWEET POTATOES ARE baked, scooped out, mixed with basil and dill, and then piped back into the potato shells for attractive, individual portions. Serve these for any holiday or dinner party with roast poultry or pork.

6 sweet potatoes	⅛ teaspoon salt
5 tablespoons half-and-half	⅛ teaspoon freshly ground black
3 tablespoons butter, softened	pepper
1 teaspoon dried basil	3 slices bacon, cooked, drained,
1 teaspoon dry mustard	and crumbled, optional
½ teaspoon dried dill weed	6 teaspoons butter, melted

1. Heat oven to 400°F. Bake sweet potatoes until tender, about 1 hour.

2. Cut off a long section from the top of each about ½ inch thick. Scoop out flesh to form a ¼-inch-thick shell.

3. Beat potato flesh, half-and-half, 3 tablespoons butter, basil, mustard, dill, salt, and pepper in the bowl of an electric mixer until light and fluffy. Stir in bacon if desired. Pipe mixture back into potato shells using a pastry bag fitted with ½-inch star tip, or spoon potato mixture back into shells. Drizzle each with 1 teaspoon melted butter.

4. Bake until tops are brown and potatoes are heated through, about 10 minutes.

❧ NOTE: *Always pierce any potato several times with a sharp knife when baking or microwaving. The slits allow steam to escape, preventing the potato from exploding.*

NUTRITION INFORMATION PER SERVING:

111 calories	6 g fat	3.4 g saturated fat
45% calories from fat	16 mg cholesterol	82 mg sodium
14 g carbohydrate	1.3 g protein	2 g fiber

Stir-Fried Gingery Snow Peas and Red Bell Peppers

PREPARATION TIME: 15 minutes

COOKING TIME: 5 minutes

YIELD: 4 servings

THIS COLORFUL MIX of vegetables, created for a "Fast Food" column, makes a nice accompaniment to grilled fish, especially salmon.

1 tablespoon Asian sesame oil
2 green onions, white part only, minced
1 1-inch piece gingerroot, peeled and minced

½ pound snow peas, trimmed and strings removed
1 large red bell pepper, seeded and diced fine
¼ teaspoon salt
Ground red pepper

1. Heat oil in a large nonstick skillet over high heat. Add green onions and gingerroot; cook, stirring constantly, until fragrant, 30 seconds.

2. Add snow peas and bell pepper; cook, stirring constantly, until peas are crisp-tender and bell pepper is beginning to brown at the edges, about 4 minutes. Add salt and ground red pepper to taste.

NUTRITION INFORMATION PER SERVING:

60 calories	4 g fat	1 g saturated fat
52% calories from fat	0 mg cholesterol	150 mg sodium
6 g carbohydrate	2 g protein	2 g fiber

Peas with Purple Basil and Shallots

PREPARATION TIME: 10 minutes

COOKING TIME: 5 minutes

YIELD: 8 servings

To GO WITH a story on growing herbs, former *Tribune* test kitchen cook Susie Goldstein developed this quick side dish to prepare with any type of basil from the garden. Fresh peas may be substituted for the frozen ones called for.

1 20-ounce bag frozen peas
3 tablespoons butter
2 shallots, minced

2 tablespoons minced purple *or* green basil
¼ teaspoon salt
Freshly ground black pepper

1. Heat a large pot of salted water to boil. Add peas; cook 3 minutes. Drain well.
2. Melt butter in a large skillet. Add shallots; cook until soft, about 3 minutes. Add peas and basil. Cook and stir until peas are coated with basil and heated through, 2 to 3 minutes. Add salt and pepper to taste.

NUTRITION INFORMATION PER SERVING:

93 calories
42% calories from fat
10 g carbohydrate

5 g fat
12 mg cholesterol
4 g protein

3 g saturated fat
175 mg sodium
4 g fiber

Spanakopita

PREPARATION TIME: 35 minutes

COOKING TIME: 45 minutes

YIELD: 10 servings

When the Field Museum in Chicago presented an exhibit on pastries called Pies Galore! Coming Together to Break Bread and More, this spanakopita was an example of one of the many ethnic pies featured. This Greek pastry combines fresh spinach with feta cheese. It's perfect for an entree or appetizer.

6 tablespoons olive oil
2 onions, chopped
2 bunches green onions, chopped
3 10-ounce bags fresh spinach,
    rinsed, drained, and chopped
½ cup chopped fresh parsley

½ cup chopped fresh dill
4 eggs
1½ cups crumbled feta cheese
1 cup ricotta cheese
¼ cup melted butter
1 box phyllo (about 20 sheets)

1. Heat 2 tablespoons of the oil in a large skillet or stockpot; cook onions and green onions until soft, about 5 minutes. Add spinach, parsley, and dill. Cook, stirring, for 3 minutes. Remove from heat; let cool. Beat eggs lightly in a bowl. Beat in feta cheese and ricotta cheese. Pour over spinach mixture in skillet; mix.

2. Heat oven to 350°F. Grease a 13″ × 9″ pan. Combine remaining 4 tablespoons oil with butter. Remove one sheet of phyllo dough; place in the center of the pan. Brush sheet with oil mixture. Continue with 9 more sheets of phyllo, brushing each with oil.

3. Pour in spinach mixture; fold overhanging edges of phyllo to enclose it. Top with remaining sheets of dough, brushing each with oil mixture. Tuck in overhanging edges. Bake until golden and crisp, about 45 minutes. Cut into 10 squares; serve.

NUTRITION INFORMATION PER SERVING:

384 calories	25 g fat	10 g saturated fat
58% calories from fat	130 mg cholesterol	580 mg sodium
27 g carbohydrate	14 g protein	3.1 g fiber

Andalusian Spinach

PREPARATION TIME: 20 minutes
COOKING TIME: 25 minutes
YIELD: 4 servings

CANNED BEANS ARE an easy alternative to soaking and cooking dried beans, particularly in recipes with aromatic, flavor-enhancing ingredients. Here is a crowd-pleasing example from Northfield chefs Rick Tramonto and Gale Gand, found in their book *American Brasserie*. Serve it as first course or as a side dish with ham or roast chicken.

2 pounds fresh spinach	⅛ teaspoon ground cumin
⅓ cup olive oil	1½ cups canned chickpeas
4 cloves garlic, peeled	(garbanzo beans), drained
4 slices bread, crusts removed and	Vinegar, preferably sherry vinegar
cut into triangles	Salt
1 teaspoon paprika	Freshly ground black pepper

1. Wash spinach; remove large stems. Do not dry. Transfer to a Dutch oven; cover and cook over medium heat, stirring several times, until spinach has wilted, about 5 minutes. Drain.

►

2. Heat oil in a medium-sized skillet over medium heat. Add garlic; cook until soft, stirring often, about 10 minutes. Remove cloves from oil; set aside. Add bread to oil; cook until browned on both sides, about 3 minutes. Drain on paper towels. Combine garlic and half of the toast triangles in a food processor fitted with a metal blade. Puree.

3. Return bread mixture to pan. Stir in paprika and cumin. Add spinach and chickpeas; cook over medium heat, stirring often, until heated through, about 5 minutes. Season with a few drops of vinegar and salt and pepper to taste. Add additional water if mixture becomes too dry. Garnish with remaining toast triangles.

NUTRITION INFORMATION PER SERVING:

379 calories	22 g fat	3.1 g saturated fat
49% calories from fat	1 mg cholesterol	277 mg sodium
38 g carbohydrate	13 g protein	10 g fiber

Spinach with Yogurt (Sag Paneer)

PREPARATION TIME: 25 minutes
COOKING TIME: 1 hour 10 minutes
YIELD: 6 servings

INDIAN COOKS BRING out the flavor of herbs and seeds by sautéing them in oil until the herbs emit a wonderful flavor, as demonstrated in this classic *sag paneer* from the now-defunct Chicago restaurant Gandhara. Look for fenugreek leaves in Indian food markets.

¼ cup vegetable oil	2 teaspoons fenugreek leaves
4 to 5 yellow onions, sliced	(*methi*), crushed, optional
4 large cloves garlic	16 ounces plain yogurt
1 ¾-inch-thick piece gingerroot	¼ cup (½ stick) butter
3 pounds fresh spinach, rinsed well	1 tablespoon paprika
½ teaspoon cumin seeds	1½ teaspoons ground cumin
1½ teaspoons turmeric	¼ teaspoon ground red pepper
1 teaspoon salt	

1. Heat oil in a heavy-bottomed Dutch oven over medium-high heat until very hot. Cook onions, stirring often, until light brown at edges, about 20 minutes.

2. Put garlic and gingerroot in a food processor fitted with a metal blade; process until chopped very fine. Remove and set aside. Cook spinach in boiling water just until tender, about 3 minutes. Drain well; puree in the food processor or in a blender. Set aside.

3. Add cumin seeds to onions; cook 30 seconds, stirring constantly, until golden and aromatic. Immediately add garlic mixture and turmeric. Cook and stir 5 minutes. Stir in spinach and salt. Cook, stirring often, 10 minutes. Add fenugreek leaves. Cook with pan mostly covered 15 minutes.

4. Stir in yogurt, butter, paprika, ground cumin, and red pepper. Cook partly covered, stirring often, over low heat until thickened and flavors are well blended, 15 to 20 minutes.

NUTRITION INFORMATION PER SERVING:

270 calories	20 g fat	8 g saturated fat
63% calories from fat	30 mg cholesterol	634 mg sodium
18 g carbohydrate	9 g protein	6 g fiber

Steamed Butternut Squash with Gingerroot

PREPARATION TIME: 15 minutes

MICROWAVE COOKING TIME: 8 minutes

YIELD: 6 servings

THE MICROWAVE OVEN is ideal for shortening the cooking time needed for butternut squash. Two pounds of squash cook in only eight minutes. In this recipe, they also absorb extra flavor from gingerroot.

2 pounds butternut squash, peeled and seeded	2 tablespoons butter
	Ground nutmeg
1 ¾-inch-thick piece gingerroot, peeled and minced	Salt
	Freshly ground black pepper
2 tablespoons water	

1. Cut squash into 1½-inch cubes. Put squash, gingerroot, and water in a 2-quart microwave-safe baking dish. Cover with plastic wrap; vent at one corner.

2. Microwave on high (100 percent power) until just tender, 6 to 8 minutes. Drain; add butter and nutmeg, salt, and pepper to taste. Stir until butter melts. Serve hot.

NUTRITION INFORMATION PER SERVING:

70 calories	3.9 g fat	2.4 g saturated fat
46% calories from fat	10 mg cholesterol	40 mg sodium
10 g carbohydrate	0.9 g protein	2.6 g fiber

Autumn Squash Stuffed with Carrot Couscous

PREPARATION TIME: 30 minutes
COOKING TIME: 20 minutes
YIELD: 4 servings

THE OCCASIONAL MEATLESS meal is a nice change from the usual, and this entree is a filling and pleasing alternative.

Squash
2 acorn *or* delicata squash
3 tablespoons whipping cream
3 tablespoons carrot juice (see Note)
1 tablespoon pure maple syrup
Salt
Ground red pepper

Carrot Couscous
¾ cup couscous
½ teaspoon ground gingerroot
½ teaspoon ground red pepper

Salt
1 cup carrot juice
1 tablespoon olive oil
1 leek, trimmed and sliced
1 red bell pepper, diced
3 tablespoons pine nuts
1 15-ounce can garbanzo beans, rinsed and drained well
1 cup fresh *or* frozen corn kernels
2 cups fresh spinach leaves, minced fine
1 tablespoon minced fresh mint

1. Halve squash crosswise; scoop out seeds. Cut a thin slice from bottom of each half so it stands upright. Arrange squash on a large microwave-proof plate. Combine whipping cream, carrot juice, maple syrup, salt, and ground red pepper in a small dish. Spoon into cavities of squash halves. Cover tightly with plastic wrap. Microwave on high (100 percent power) 6 minutes. Uncover; poke inside of squash several times with a fork. Replace plastic; return squash to microwave. Cook on high power until tender, 4 to 9 minutes longer. Let stand 2 minutes.

2. Meanwhile, to make carrot couscous, combine couscous, gingerroot, ground red pepper, and salt to taste in a medium-sized bowl. Bring carrot juice to a simmer. Pour hot carrot juice over couscous mixture; cover. Let stand 8 to 10 minutes. Heat oil in a large skillet over high heat. Add leek, bell pepper, and pine nuts. Cook, stirring, until vegetables are tender and begin to brown at edges, 6 to 7 minutes. Add garbanzo beans and corn; heat through. Remove from heat. Stir in spinach and mint; taste and adjust seasoning. Spoon couscous into squash halves, mounding generously.

❧ NOTE: *Fresh carrot juice is available in some supermarkets and natural food stores. Canned may be used in its place.*

NUTRITION INFORMATION PER SERVING:

580 calories	14 g fat	4 g saturated fat
20% calories from fat	15 mg cholesterol	86 mg sodium
102 g carbohydrate	19 g protein	16 g fiber

Turnip and Pear Puree

PREPARATION TIME: 15 minutes

COOKING TIME: 6 minutes

YIELD: 4 servings

"THE HUMBLEST OF vegetables becomes elegant when made into a puree," wrote *Tribune* staff writer R. C. Longworth. Here, the grainy texture of the pears teamed with the earthy flavor of turnips makes this an ideal match for roast duck or pork tenderloin.

1 pound turnips, peeled and cut into ½-inch cubes	2 tablespoons fresh lemon juice
1 pear, peeled, cored and cut into ½-inch cubes	1 tablespoon butter, melted
	¼ teaspoon salt
	Freshly ground black pepper

1. Boil turnips in salted water until tender, about 10 minutes. Drain.
2. Cook pears in lemon juice in a small nonstick skillet over low heat until pears are tender and most of juice is absorbed, about 5 minutes.
3. Puree turnips, pears, melted butter, salt, and black pepper to taste in a food processor fitted with a metal blade. Serve.

NUTRITION INFORMATION PER SERVING:

80 calories	3 g fat	1.8 g saturated fat
32% calories from fat	8 mg cholesterol	250 mg sodium
14 g carbohydrate	1.2 g protein	3 g fiber

Zucchini with Garlic and Cumin

PREPARATION TIME: 5 minutes

COOKING TIME: 5 minutes

YIELD: 4 servings

ZUCCHINI WITH GARLIC and cumin brings Middle Eastern flair to any meal. This makes a nice accompaniment to grilled or roasted chicken.

2 tablespoons olive oil	1 pound mixed zucchini and
1 small clove garlic, minced fine	summer squash, diced
¼ teaspoon ground cumin	Salt
¼ teaspoon ground coriander	Freshly ground black pepper

1. Heat oil in a large nonstick skillet over low heat. Add garlic; cook until fragrant, 45 seconds. Stir in cumin and coriander.
2. Increase heat to high; add zucchini and squash. Cook, shaking pan often, until squash begins to brown, 3 to 4 minutes. Add salt and pepper to taste.

NUTRITION INFORMATION PER SERVING:

76 calories	7 g fat	1 g saturated fat
77% calories from fat	0 mg cholesterol	3.2 mg sodium
4 g carboydrate	1 g protein	1.3 g fiber

Zucchini or Green Beans in Fresh Tarragon Marinade

PREPARATION TIME: 15 minutes

MARINATING TIME: 30 minutes to 2 hours

YIELD: 4 servings

WHEN SUMMER ZUCCHINI or green beans are at their peak, try mixing them with this light tarragon marinade. Small, light-colored zucchini usually will be sweeter than large, deep green ones. Serve this recipe as a vegetable or salad course, or toss it with chilled cooked pasta.

Vegetable	*Marinade*
1 pound small zucchini *or* fresh	4 green onions, minced
trimmed green beans	3 tablespoons olive oil
Salt	2 tablespoons vegetable oil

2 tablespoons white wine vinegar

2 to 3 teaspoons minced fresh
tarragon *or* 1 teaspoon dried

1 teaspoon Dijon mustard

¼ teaspoon sugar

¼ teaspoon salt

¼ teaspoon freshly ground black
pepper

1. To use zucchini, cut zucchini into thin slices. Sprinkle lightly with salt; let drain on a paper towel 20 minutes. Do not cook. To use green beans, boil water; drop beans into water. Cook until crisp-tender, 5 to 8 minutes. Drain; rinse under cold water to stop cooking.

2. To make marinade, mix green onions, olive oil, vegetable oil, wine vinegar, tarragon, mustard, sugar, salt, and pepper in a large bowl. Add zucchini. Refrigerate covered 30 minutes to 2 hours. Stir occasionally. Serve at room temperature.

NUTRITION INFORMATION PER SERVING:

174 calories	17 g fat	2.4 g saturated fat
85% calories from fat	0 mg cholesterol	183 mg sodium
5 g carbohydrate	2 g protein	2 g fiber

Vegetarian Stir-Fry with Pan-Seared Tofu in Citrus-Soy Broth

PREPARATION TIME: 35 minutes

COOKING TIME: 10 minutes

YIELD: 2 servings

THERE IS A profusion of fusion food in Chicago restaurants, according to a story by William Rice. Chef Mark Baker of Seasons restaurant demonstrates the trend with this blend of familiar vegetables and Asian flavors. *Mirin* (sweet Japanese rice wine), sake (Japanese rice wine), chili paste, and black sesame seeds are available in Japanese markets. Thai-style tofu is found in Thai markets.

Citrus-Soy Broth

Zest of 1 lemon

½ cup *mirin*

¼ cup sake

2 tablespoons unseasoned rice
vinegar

2 tablespoons soy sauce

½ teaspoon Asian chili paste

Vegetables

1 tablespoon plus 1 teaspoon
olive oil

1 carrot, peeled and cut diagonally
into 1-inch pieces

1 small rib celery, cut diagonally
into 1-inch pieces

▶

1 small zucchini, peeled and cut
　　diagonally into 1-inch pieces
1 yellow bell pepper, seeded and cut
　　into ½-inch strips
½ cup small broccoli florets
4 green onions, cut into ½-inch
　　pieces
½ pound shiitake mushrooms,
　　stems removed and quartered
1 8-ounce package baked *or*
　　marinated firm tofu, preferably
　　Thai-style
Black sesame seeds, optional

1. Stir together lemon zest, *mirin*, sake, rice vinegar, soy sauce, and chili paste in a small bowl. Set aside.

2. Heat a large skillet or wok over high heat; add 1 tablespoon of the oil. Add to skillet in 30-second intervals (in this order), stirring constantly, carrot, celery, zucchini, bell pepper, broccoli, green onions, and mushrooms. Add half of citrus-soy broth; cook, stirring constantly, until liquid is thickened and vegetables are just tender, about 2 minutes. Remove from heat; keep vegetables warm.

3. Heat remaining teaspoon oil in a nonstick skillet over medium-high heat until hot but not smoking. Sear tofu until heated through, 1 to 2 minutes on each side. Cut tofu crosswise into 10 slices.

4. Mound vegetables in the center of 2 large soup plates; pour in remaining broth. Fan tofu slices over vegetables. Garnish with sesame seeds.

NUTRITION INFORMATION PER SERVING:

444 calories	15 g fat	2 g saturated fat
29% calories from fat	0 mg cholesterol	1,116 mg sodium
51 g carbohydrate	17 g protein	9 g fiber

Grilled Vegetables with Rosemary Vinaigrette

PREPARATION TIME: 15 minutes

GRILLING TIME: 20 minutes

YIELD: 4 servings

ALMOST ALL VEGETABLES grill well. And with a little planning, tonight's dinner can become tomorrow's lunch. After grilling your steak or chicken for dinner, throw the vegetables on the grill to cook over fading coals. Basting vegetables with the vinaigrette as they cook also enhances flavor.

⅓ cup extra-virgin olive oil
¼ cup red wine vinegar

1 tablespoon Dijon mustard
¼ teaspoon salt

¼ teaspoon freshly ground black pepper

¼ to ½ teaspoon minced fresh *or* dried rosemary leaves

Assorted vegetables for grilling (see sidebar)

1. Put ⅓ cup oil, vinegar, mustard, salt, pepper, and ¼ teaspoon rosemary into a jar with a tight-fitting lid. Shake well to mix. Taste and adjust oil and rosemary.

2. Arrange vegetables in a baking pan. Pour over some of vinaigrette. Toss to coat. Grill until tender, occasionally basting with more of the vinaigrette. Serve grilled vegetables hot with any remaining vinaigrette.

NUTRITION INFORMATION PER SERVING:

69 calories	8 g fat	1.1 g saturated fat
98% calories from fat	0 mg cholesterol	97 mg sodium
0.2 g carbohydrate	0.1 g protein	0 g fiber

Vegetables for Grilling

To grill bell peppers: Place whole bell peppers 4 to 6 inches from hot coals. Grill, turning often, until skin is slightly charred and flesh is crisp-tender, 15 to 20 minutes. Remove from grill and put into a paper or plastic bag, close bag, and let sit 10 minutes. Remove bell peppers from the bag; discard charred skin, core, and seeds. Cut into slices.

To grill eggplant, zucchini, and yellow squash slices: Place slices 6 inches from hot coals. Grill, turning and brushing with vinaigrette until crisp-tender, 3 to 5 minutes.

To grill onions: Place green onions or medium-sized unpeeled white onions 6 inches from hot coals. Grill, turning often, until slightly charred and crisp-tender, 5 to 10 minutes. Remove peel before slicing and tossing with vinaigrette.

To grill green beans: Place beans on a sheet of heavy-duty aluminum foil. Brush with vinaigrette. Grill 6 inches from hot coals until crisp-tender, 5 to 10 minutes depending on thickness.

Vegetable Chili with Red Beans

PREPARATION TIME: 30 minutes

SOAKING TIME: 8 to 12 hours

COOKING TIME: 2 hours

YIELD: 6 servings

THIS CHILI—A second-helpings-for-everyone favorite in our test kitchen—is so hearty in texture and flavor that you won't miss the meat.

3 tablespoons olive oil

2 onions, chopped

2 cloves garlic, minced

½ pound mushrooms, sliced

1 28-ounce can crushed tomatoes in puree

1 16-ounce can red kidney beans, drained

1 15-ounce can tomato sauce

3 tablespoons tomato paste

2 tablespoons chili powder

2 small zucchini, sliced

2 red bell peppers, seeded and chopped

1 to 2 jalapeños, seeded and chopped

½ teaspoon salt

½ teaspoon freshly ground black pepper

1 10-ounce package frozen corn

1 10-ounce package frozen lima beans

Crushed red pepper flakes, optional

1. Heat olive oil in a large Dutch oven over medium heat. Add onions and garlic; cook, stirring often, 1 minute. Add mushrooms; cook until slightly browned. Stir in crushed tomatoes, beans, tomato sauce, tomato paste, and chili powder. Heat to boil over medium-high heat.

2. Reduce heat to medium-low. Add zucchini, bell peppers, jalapeños, salt, and black pepper. Simmer until vegetables are crisp-tender, about 30 minutes.

3. Stir in corn and lima beans; cook until heated through, 5 to 10 minutes. Taste and adjust seasonings. Serve with crushed red pepper flakes if desired.

NUTRITION INFORMATION PER SERVING:

359 calories	9 g fat	1.2 g saturated fat
20% calories from fat	0 mg cholesterol	908 mg sodium
62 g carbohydrate	16 g protein	19 g fiber

SALADS AND
SALAD DRESSINGS

Mixed Greens with Spiced Almonds and Chutney Dressing

PREPARATION TIME: 10 minutes
YIELD: 4 servings

"FAST FOOD" COLUMNIST Pat Dailey capitalized on the trend of Indian food that "has been quietly percolating on a back burner for the past year or so" with this spicy-sweet dressing. It takes advantage of bottled chutney, which is available in most supermarkets.

Dressing
3 tablespoons champagne vinegar
   or white wine vinegar
1 tablespoon mango chutney
¼ teaspoon dry mustard
⅛ teaspoon salt
¼ cup vegetable oil

Salad
3 tablespoons sliced almonds
¼ teaspoon ground red pepper
8 cups loosely packed torn mixed
   salad greens
1 small red bell pepper, seeded and
   chopped fine
Freshly ground black pepper

1. To make dressing, combine vinegar, chutney, mustard, and salt in a small bowl; whisk well. Whisk in oil.

2. To make salad, mix almonds with about 1 teaspoon of the dressing and ground red pepper; stir to evenly coat almonds. Spread on a small microwave-safe plate. Microwave on high (100 percent power) until lightly toasted, 45 to 60 seconds.

3. Toss together salad greens, bell pepper, and dressing. Divide evenly among 4 salad plates; top with almonds and freshly ground black pepper to taste.

➤

NUTRITION INFORMATION PER SERVING:

180 calories	17 g fat	2 g saturated fat
79% calories from fat	0 mg cholesterol	140 mg sodium
7 g carbohydrate	2.9 g protein	2.8 g fiber

Balsamic-Dressed Mixed Green Salad

PREPARATION TIME: 5 minutes

YIELD: 4 servings

"FAST FOOD" COLUMNIST Pat Dailey whisked together a simple balsamic vinaigrette enriched with whipping cream to dress a simple green salad. She served it with tagliatelle tossed with butter, cheese, and fresh oregano.

1 large clove garlic, halved	2 tablespoons balsamic vinegar
10 ounces mixed torn salad greens	1 tablespoon whipping cream
1 cup teardrop *or* cherry tomatoes, halved	Salt
⅓ cup extra-virgin olive oil	Freshly ground black pepper

1. Rub the inside of a large salad bowl with cut sides of garlic clove; discard garlic. Add salad greens and tomatoes; toss well.

2. Combine olive oil, vinegar, whipping cream, and salt and pepper to taste in a small bowl, whisking to combine. Add to greens.

NUTRITION INFORMATION PER SERVING:

195 calories	20 g fat	3.3 g saturated fat
86% calories from fat	5 mg cholesterol	25 mg sodium
5 g carbohydrate	1.6 g protein	1.6 g fiber

Autumn Salad with Goat Cheese

PREPARATION TIME: 25 minutes
YIELD: 8 servings

HARLAN "PETE" PETERSON gave up automotive design in the mid-1970s to pursue his passion, cooking. Today he owns Tapawingo, a gem of a restaurant in Ellsworth, Michigan, where he uses regional ingredients in his modern American cooking.

6 ounces goat cheese, preferably
    blue-veined
3 tablespoons cider vinegar
1 tablespoon Dijon mustard
½ cup olive oil
½ cup vegetable oil
Salt
Freshly ground black pepper
1 small head romaine, trimmed and
    torn into pieces

1 small head escarole, trimmed and
    torn into pieces
1 small head curly endive, trimmed
    and torn into pieces
1 small bulb fennel, julienned
½ small red cabbage, shredded thin
2 tablespoons chopped fresh chives

1. Put half of the goat cheese, vinegar, and mustard in a blender or food processor. Process until smooth. With machine running, add olive oil and vegetable oil in a slow, steady stream. Add salt and pepper to taste.

2. Mix romaine, escarole, endive, fennel, and cabbage in a large bowl. Add dressing; toss to mix. Arrange portions on plates. Crumble remaining cheese over greens. Sprinkle with chives.

NUTRITION INFORMATION PER SERVING:

350 calories
84% calories from fat
7 g carbohydrate

34 g fat
16 mg cholesterol
7 g protein

8 g saturated fat
180 mg sodium
3.2 g fiber

Caesar Salad

PREPARATION TIME: 20 minutes
CHILLING TIME: 2 to 12 hours
COOKING TIME: 18 minutes
YIELD: 4 servings

MORE INTERESTING THAN arguing over the origin of Caesar salad—that dish of romaine, garlic, croutons, and Parmesan cheese—is tossing one for friends. Leave the anchovies out if you must, or add them according to taste as did Caesar Cardini, a Mexican restaurant owner and the alleged creator of the salad back in the 1920s. The original Caesar salad dressing was made with a raw egg. Our dressing has been modified to cook the egg.

Croutons
1 tablespoon plus 2 teaspoons
    olive oil
3 cloves garlic, peeled and halved
3 cups French bread cubes
⅛ teaspoon salt

Dressing
1 large egg
2 anchovy fillets, chopped
2 tablespoons water
2 tablespoons lemon juice

¼ teaspoon Worcestershire sauce
¼ cup olive oil

Salad
1 head romaine lettuce, torn into
    bite-sized pieces and thick ribs
    removed
⅓ cup freshly grated Parmesan
    cheese
Freshly ground black pepper
6 anchovy fillets

1. To make croutons, heat olive oil in a 10-inch skillet over medium-high heat until hot. Add 2 of the halved garlic cloves; cook 1 minute. Add bread cubes in batches in a single layer. Toss well. Cook, tossing cubes occasionally, until lightly toasted on all sides, about 5 minutes. Remove garlic if it begins to burn. Repeat with remaining bread, using more oil if needed. Transfer croutons to paper towels; sprinkle lightly with salt.

2. To make dressing, combine egg, chopped anchovies, water, lemon juice, and Worcestershire in a blender; blend until smooth. Gradually pour ¼ cup olive oil through the feed tube with motor running. Pour dressing into a small saucepan. Heat over medium-low heat, stirring constantly, until an instant-reading thermometer reads 160°F, about 12 minutes. Chill at least 2 to 12 hours.

3. Rub remaining garlic halves over the insides of a large salad bowl; discard garlic. Add lettuce, Parmesan cheese, and black pepper to taste. Toss with dressing to mix; sprinkle with croutons. Garnish with anchovy fillets over the top.

NUTRITION INFORMATION PER SERVING:

305 calories	24 g fat	5 g saturated fat
69% calories from fat	60 mg cholesterol	440 mg sodium
15 g carbohydrate	9 g protein	2 g fiber

Grilled Tuscan Bread Salad

PREPARATION TIME: 20 minutes
GRILLING TIME: 5 minutes
STANDING TIME: 15 minutes
YIELD: 6 servings

BREAD AS A salad? On the grill? Yes, and this recipe offers a delicious take on the Italian *panzanella*: a bread shell—Boboli is a popular example—teams with fresh tomatoes and basil.

1 16-ounce Italian bread shell, such as Boboli	1 medium-sized red onion, diced fine
1¼ cups water or more as needed	¼ cup minced fresh basil leaves
4 tablespoons red wine vinegar	⅓ cup olive oil
1 pound cocktail tomatoes, chopped	1 anchovy, minced, optional
	Salt
2 ribs celery, diced fine	Freshly ground black pepper

1. Heat a charcoal grill. Grill bread shell 6 inches from medium-hot coals, turning once, until lightly toasted, about 5 minutes. Cut into 1-inch pieces; place in a bowl. Add water and 1 tablespoon of the vinegar. Let soak 15 minutes. Squeeze bread gently to remove excess moisture; place in a dry bowl.

2. Add tomatoes, celery, onion, and basil; toss lightly. Add remaining 3 tablespoons vinegar, oil, anchovy if desired, and salt and pepper to taste. Toss.

NUTRITION INFORMATION PER SERVING:

335 calories	15 g fat	2.3 g saturated fat
39% calories from fat	1 mg cholesterol	485 mg sodium
44 g carbohydrate	8 g protein	3.5 g fiber

Lyonnaise Salad

PREPARATION TIME: 30 minutes
COOKING TIME: 23 minutes
YIELD: 6 servings

RIB-STICKING SALADS with warm dressings on sautéed greens provide a middle ground between meat-and-potatoes entrees and the more usual chilly tossed salads. A traditional French *salade lyonnaise*, with frisé (curly endive), bacon, and poached egg, is a favorite at Mossant restaurant in Chicago.

5 slices thick-cut bacon	1 tablespoon fresh thyme
1 cup fresh French bread cubes	¼ teaspoon salt
1 clove garlic, minced	Freshly ground black pepper
1 tablespoon unsalted butter, melted	1 cup distilled vinegar
	8 cups water
3 tablespoons white wine vinegar	6 large eggs
1 tablespoon Dijon mustard	3 heads curly endive, torn into
½ cup canola oil	bite-sized pieces
½ cup chopped fresh parsley	Chopped parsley

1. Heat oven to 300°F. Cook bacon until crisp; keep warm. Toss bread cubes with garlic and melted butter. Bake cubes on a baking sheet until golden brown, turning once, about 5 minutes. Keep warm.

2. Whisk together white wine vinegar and mustard in a medium-sized bowl. Slowly whisk in oil; stir in parsley, thyme, salt, and pepper to taste. Set aside.

3. Pour distilled vinegar into a large saucepan with water; heat to boil over high heat. Reduce heat to low. Gently break eggs 1 at a time onto a small plate; slip each egg into simmering vinegar water. Cook 3 minutes each. Remove from water with a slotted spoon; keep warm.

4. Mix together endive, bacon, croutons, and vinaigrette. Divide among 6 plates; top each with 1 poached egg. Garnish with parsley.

NUTRITION INFORMATION PER SERVING:

345 calories	30 g fat	6 g saturated fat
78% calories from fat	225 mg cholesterol	420 mg sodium
8 g carbohydrate	11 g protein	1.6 g fiber

Spinach Salad with
Wilted Onions and Sesame Dressing

PREPARATION TIME: 10 minutes

COOKING TIME: 5 minutes

YIELD: 4 servings

BABY SPINACH IN a simple salad of onions tossed with a warm dressing goes well with ham sandwiches the day after Easter. If you have leftover hard-cooked eggs, try mincing one and sprinkling it over the top at serving time.

8 cups baby spinach leaves	3 knob onions *or* small sweet
Freshly ground black pepper	onions, peeled and sliced thin
3 tablespoons herb-flavored oil *or*	2 teaspoons sesame seeds
olive oil	3 tablespoons seasoned rice vinegar

1. Place spinach in a large serving bowl or divide among 4 salad plates. Sprinkle with pepper; set aside.

2. Heat oil in a medium-sized skillet. Add onions and cook, stirring occasionally, until softened slightly, 3 minutes. Add sesame seeds; cook until browned, 1 minute. Remove pan from heat. Carefully stir in vinegar; return to heat. Cook 30 seconds. Pour mixture over spinach.

NUTRITION INFORMATION PER SERVING:

130 calories	11 g fat	1.5 g saturated fat
72% calories from fat	0 mg cholesterol	50 mg sodium
7 g carbohydrate	2.6 g protein	2.4 g fiber

Spinach Salad with Orange-Chipotle Dressing

PREPARATION TIME: 20 minutes

YIELD: 4 servings

THE MEXICAN HOLIDAY Cinco de Mayo ("the fifth of May") provides a fine excuse for a Mexican inspired menu, including this sassy spinach salad. It gets a real kick from the chipotle chilies in the dressing. Use canned chipotle chilies packed in adobo sauce, available in the Mexican food aisle of some supermarkets. Remove a chili from the can and smash with the flat side of a knife. Add a small amount of sauce from the can and measure out for the dressing. The dressing can be made in advance and refrigerated up to two days.

Dressing
¼ cup fresh orange juice
2 tablespoons olive oil
1 tablespoon balsamic vinegar
1½ teaspoons minced chipotle chili
    with adobo sauce
½ teaspoon honey
Salt
Freshly ground black pepper

Salad
12 ounces salad spinach, rinsed and
    patted dry
½ small red onion, sliced
    paper-thin
1 navel orange, cut in segments
⅓ cup crumbled goat cheese
1 tablespoon plus 1½ teaspoons
    sesame seeds

1. To make dressing, combine orange juice, olive oil, vinegar, chipotle chili, honey, and salt and pepper to taste in a jar with a tight-fitting lid. Shake well.

2. To make salad, combine spinach, onion, and orange segments in a bowl; toss with dressing to taste. Divide among 4 salad plates; sprinkle with goat cheese and sesame seeds.

NUTRITION INFORMATION PER SERVING:

170 calories	13 g fat	3.9 g saturated fat
63% calories from fat	8 mg cholesterol	135 mg sodium
11 g carbohydrate	6 g protein	3 g fiber

Wilted Asian Greens with Toasted Sesame Seeds and Mango

PREPARATION TIME: 20 minutes

COOKING TIME: 3 minutes

YIELD: 6 servings

KRISTIN EDDY WROTE about the trend to serving warm salads at restaurants in 1998. Diners and home cooks got wise to the wealth of flavors in different greens, many of which are sturdy enough to stand up to hot toppings. This salad comes from chef Suzy Crofton, of Crofton on Wells in Chicago. Tamari, a mellow form of soy sauce, can be found in the Asian section of many grocery stores or at Asian markets.

¼ cup water

¼ cup tamari

2 tablespoons rice wine vinegar

2 tablespoons *mirin* (rice wine)

1 tablespoon sesame oil

1 teaspoon vegetable oil

1 clove garlic, minced

6 cups mixed torn Asian greens

1 mango, pitted, peeled, and julienned

¼ red onion, sliced thin

3 tablespoons toasted sesame seeds (see Note)

1. Whisk together water, tamari, vinegar, *mirin*, and sesame oil in a small bowl. Set aside.

2. Heat vegetable oil in a medium-sized saucepan over medium heat. Cook garlic 1 minute. Add vinaigrette mixture; heat 2 minutes.

3. Toss greens, mango, and onion in a large serving bowl. Pour warm dressing over salad; sprinkle with toasted sesame seeds.

❦ NOTE: *To toast sesame seeds, heat seeds in a small dry pan over medium heat, stirring often, until lightly browned. Immediately remove seeds from pan to stop cooking.*

NUTRITION INFORMATION PER SERVING:

65 calories

42% calories from fat

7 g carbohydrate

3.2 g fat

0 mg cholesterol

2.3 g protein

0.5 g saturated fat

685 mg sodium

1.4 g fiber

Arugula and Fennel Salad

PREPARATION TIME: 10 minutes
YIELD: 4 servings

"SOUP AND SALAD" is a favorite supper combo for "Fast Food" columnist Pat Dailey. This lemony fennel salad originally complemented a chard and white bean soup.

¼ cup olive oil
1 tablespoon white wine vinegar
1 tablespoon fresh lemon juice
¼ teaspoon minced fresh *or* dried rosemary
Salt

Freshly ground black pepper
1 medium-sized fennel bulb, stalks cut off
1 large bunch arugula (about 8 ounces)

1. Combine oil, vinegar, lemon juice, rosemary, and salt and pepper to taste in a small bowl; mix well.
2. Cut fennel in half lengthwise; core. Slice crosswise into paper-thin slices.
3. Combine arugula and fennel in a large bowl; toss with dressing. Divide among 4 plates; add additional black pepper.

NUTRITION INFORMATION PER SERVING:

155 calories
84% calories from fat
0.7 g carbohydrate

14 g fat
0 mg cholesterol
0.3 g protein

2 g saturated fat
50 mg sodium
2 g fiber

Beet and Mâche Salad with Walnuts

PREPARATION TIME: 20 minutes
COOKING TIME: 15 minutes
YIELD: 4 servings

FRESH BEETS ARE easily cooked by baking them with their skins on. Cook the beets just as you would a potato until tender. If the grocer is out of Belgian endive or price strikes it from the budget, substitute romaine. If you have walnut oil, substitute one to two tablespoons of it for that much of the safflower oil.

½ cup walnut halves
1½ tablespoons red wine vinegar
1 teaspoon Dijon mustard

¼ teaspoon freshly ground black pepper
5 tablespoons safflower oil

2 large heads Belgian endive (about ½ pound)

4 to 6 bunches (about ¼ pound) mâche (corn salad), rinsed and roots trimmed

2 cooked beets, peeled and diced fine

1. Heat oven to 350°F. Put walnuts on a baking sheet. Bake until toasted, being careful not to burn, about 10 minutes. Mix vinegar, mustard, and pepper in a small bowl. Whisk in oil in a slow, steady stream until smooth.

2. Pull off larger outside endive leaves and set aside. Cut smaller leaves on the diagonal into ¾-inch slices. Place in a bowl; add mâche and beets. Toss.

3. Place whole endive leaves on a serving plate with tips pointing out. Place endive mixture in the middle of plate. Garnish with toasted walnuts. Serve with dressing.

NUTRITION INFORMATION PER SERVING:

275 calories	25 g fat	2.3 g saturated fat
81% calories from fat	0 mg cholesterol	70 mg sodium
11 g carbohydrate	5 g protein	6 g fiber

Beet, Pea, and Avocado Salad with Balsamic Vinaigrette

PREPARATION TIME: 25 minutes

COOKING TIME: 18 minutes

YIELD: 4 servings

PERFECTLY RIPE AVOCADOS are crucial to the success of this salad—so is good balsamic vinegar. Not only does its flavor tie the ingredients of this salad together, but it also prevents the salad from tasting too sweet.

1 cup fresh *or* frozen peas

3 small fresh beets, stems trimmed

⅓ cup balsamic vinegar

3 tablespoons minced fresh chervil *or* Italian flat-leaf parsley

2 tablespoons peanut oil

2 tablespoons olive oil

2 tablespoons minced shallot *or* green onion

Pinch minced garlic

Pinch ground red pepper

Salt

Freshly ground black pepper

1 medium-sized cucumber, peeled and sliced

2 ripe avocados, peeled, seeded, and sliced

Juice of ½ lemon

►

1 bunch red leaf lettuce, rinsed and
shredded

1 bunch watercress, rinsed and
trimmed

1. Heat a medium-sized saucepan of water to boil; add peas. Cook just until bright green and crisp-tender, 2 to 3 minutes. Remove with a slotted spoon; rinse under cold water. Cook beets in the same pan of boiling water until crisp-tender, about 15 minutes. Drain; rinse under cold water. Peel. Cut into thin slices and put into a medium-sized bowl. Add peas.

2. Mix vinegar, chervil, peanut oil, olive oil, shallot, garlic, red pepper, and salt and black pepper to taste in a jar with a tight-fitting lid. Shake well. Pour a small amount of vinaigrette over beets and peas. Add cucumber; toss.

3. Sprinkle avocado with lemon juice. Arrange lettuce on 4 serving plates. Arrange avocado slices near lettuce. Arrange cucumber, peas, and beets around avocado. Garnish with watercress. Drizzle with remaining vinaigrette.

NUTRITION INFORMATION PER SERVING:

365 calories	29 g fat	4.5 g saturated fat
68% calories from fat	0 mg cholesterol	65 mg sodium
25 g carbohydrate	7 g protein	10 g fiber

Tomato and Onion Salad with Oregano Dressing

PREPARATION TIME: 10 minutes

YIELD: 4 servings

LOOKING FOR AN alternative to a plain tossed salad with a couple of tomato wedges to accompany pizza or pasta? The oregano dressing puts this recipe firmly in the Italian family. If tomatoes aren't in season, try using cocktail or cherry tomatoes, which often have good flavor.

2 tablespoons red wine vinegar
2 tablespoons extra-virgin olive oil
½ teaspoon dried oregano
Salt
Freshly ground black pepper
2 small ribs celery, sliced ¼ inch
thick

1 small sweet onion, quartered and
sliced ¼ inch thick
12 ounces tomatoes, cut into
wedges
Lettuce leaves

1. Whisk vinegar with olive oil, oregano, and salt and pepper to taste until blended.

2. Add celery and onion. Toss to coat. Stir in tomatoes. Serve on lettuce leaves.

NUTRITION INFORMATION PER SERVING:

90 calories	7 g fat	1 g saturated fat
68% calories from fat	0 mg cholesterol	25 mg sodium
6 g carbohydrate	1 g protein	1.6 g fiber

Santa Fe Vegetable Salad with Lime Cream Dressing

PREPARATION TIME: 20 minutes

YIELD: 4 servings

A corn and vegetable salad can do double duty at a party or other gathering: it's great with chips or served as a chilled salad.

Salad
1 9-ounce box frozen corn, thawed
   and patted dry
½ cup (2 ounces) cubed
   pepper-Jack cheese
2 green onions, sliced thin
1 small red bell pepper, diced fine
1 small zucchini, diced fine
1 small ripe avocado, peeled, pitted,
   and diced

1 serrano chili *or* jalapeño, seeded
   if desired and minced
½ cup minced cilantro

Dressing
2 tablespoons vegetable oil
1½ tablespoons fresh lime juice
1 tablespoon sour cream
1 to 2 teaspoons jalapeño jelly
½ teaspoon ground cumin
Salt

1. To make salad, combine corn, cheese, green onions, bell pepper, zucchini, avocado, serrano chili, and cilantro in a medium-sized bowl.

2. To make dressing, combine oil, lime juice, sour cream, jalapeño jelly, ground cumin, and salt to taste in another small bowl, mixing until smooth. Add to salad; toss well.

NUTRITION INFORMATION PER SERVING:

275 calories	20 g fat	5 g saturated fat
62% calories from fat	14 mg cholesterol	90 mg sodium
22 g carbohydrate	7 g protein	5 g fiber

Cucumber-Chili Salad with Yogurt-Cilantro Dressing

PREPARATION TIME: 10 minutes

YIELD: 4 servings

"FAST FOOD" COLUMNIST Pat Dailey came up with this cool and spicy salad as a partner for rotisserie chicken from the supermarket. Drain the yogurt if you have the time; it gives the dressing a nice, thick consistency. To do so, pour the yogurt into a strainer lined with a paper coffee filter and let stand several hours over a bowl in the refrigerator.

1 small onion, halved lengthwise and sliced

1 medium-sized cucumber, halved lengthwise and sliced

½ to 1 jalapeño, minced

3 tablespoons low-fat plain yogurt

3 tablespoons minced cilantro

Put onion, cucumber, jalapeño, yogurt, and cilantro in a bowl; toss to combine. Chill well and serve.

NUTRITION INFORMATION PER SERVING:

25 calories

8% calories from fat

5 g carbohydrate

0.3 g fat

1 mg cholesterol

1.7 g protein

0.1 g saturated fat

10 mg sodium

1 g fiber

Sesame, Broccoli, and Cauliflower Salad

PREPARATION TIME: 20 minutes

COOKING TIME: 10 minutes

YIELD: 4 servings

RESERVE SOME OF the sesame seeds called for to sprinkle over this salad before serving. Be stingy when measuring the sesame oil. It has a powerful flavor, and a little goes a long way.

1 pound broccoli, cut into 2-inch pieces

1 pound cauliflower, separated into florets

¼ cup chopped green onions

¼ cup soy sauce

1 tablespoon Asian sesame oil

1 tablespoon toasted sesame seeds (see Index)

1½ teaspoons honey

¼ teaspoon chili oil *or* pinch ground red pepper

⅛ teaspoon salt

Lettuce leaves

Tomato wedges

1. Bring 2 pans of water to boil. Cook broccoli and cauliflower separately until crisp-tender, about 10 minutes. Rinse under cold water to stop cooking; drain well. Place in a large serving bowl. Refrigerate until chilled.

2. Stir together green onions, soy sauce, sesame oil, sesame seeds, honey, chili oil, and salt. Taste and adjust seasonings. Pour dressing over broccoli and cauliflower; toss to coat. Serve on lettuce leaves. Garnish with tomato wedges.

NUTRITION INFORMATION PER SERVING:

125 calories	5 g fat	0.8 g saturated fat
33% calories from fat	0 mg cholesterol	1,165 mg sodium
17 g carbohydrate	7 g protein	7 g fiber

Broccolini Salad with Red Peppers and Onions

PREPARATION TIME: 5 minutes
COOKING TIME: 3 to 5 minutes
YIELD: 4 servings

A CROSS BETWEEN broccoli and Chinese kale, broccolini tastes like broccoli blended with asparagus. The entire stalk is edible, even when raw. You may substitute broccoli florets.

1 pound broccolini	2 tablespoons extra-virgin olive oil
½ small onion, diced fine	2 teaspoons balsamic vinegar
¼ cup diced roasted red bell pepper (see Index)	¼ teaspoon salt
	Freshly ground black pepper

1. Bring a pan of water to boil. Cook broccolini until tender, 4 to 5 minutes. Rinse under cold water until completely cool. Pat dry.

2. Arrange on a platter; sprinkle with onion and bell pepper. Whisk together oil, vinegar, salt, and ground pepper to taste. Pour over salad.

NUTRITION INFORMATION PER SERVING:

90 calories	1 g fat	0 g saturated fat
10% calories from fat	0 mg cholesterol	160 mg sodium
1.7 g carbohydrate	1.5 g protein	1.6 g fiber

Tomato, Mozzarella, and Basil Salad

PREPARATION TIME: 15 minutes
MARINATING TIME: 3 hours
YIELD: 4 servings

ITALY SPRINGS TO mind when preparing this salad—a standard on many restaurant menus. To capture the genuine flavor, buy fresh mozzarella (usually packed in water) and stick with fresh basil, not dried.

4 large tomatoes, sliced thin	½ pound fresh mozzarella cheese,
Salt	sliced thin
Freshly ground black pepper	1 cup fresh basil leaves, chopped
¼ cup extra-virgin olive oil	¼ cup pine nuts
2 tablespoons white wine vinegar	

1. Put tomato slices on a serving platter; sprinkle with salt and pepper to taste. Drizzle with some of the oil and vinegar.

2. Top with cheese slices. Sprinkle basil and pine nuts over all. Sprinkle again with salt, pepper, oil, and vinegar. Serve at room temperature.

❧ NOTE: *Toasting the pine nuts enhances their flavor. Place pine nuts in a dry skillet over medium heat. Cook, stirring frequently, until golden. Remove from pan immediately to stop the cooking process.*

NUTRITION INFORMATION PER SERVING:

365 calories	28 g fat	9 g saturated fat
67% calories from fat	30 mg cholesterol	315 mg sodium
12 g carbohydrate	19 g protein	2.8 g fiber

Holiday Cranberry Salad

PREPARATION TIME: 20 minutes

CHILLING TIME: 2 to 12 hours

YIELD: 8 servings

To ACCOMPANY A story on Thanksgiving disasters, freelance writer Joanne Trestrail convinced people to share their must-have family recipes. "Deciding whether this is a salad or a dessert is a fine subject for a mother-daughter debate," Trestrail wrote. It's from Holly Gerberding of Chicago.

1 cup whipping cream
1 cup confectioners' sugar
2 cups cranberries, chopped coarse
   in blender

1 8-ounce can crushed pineapple, drained
1 cup miniature marshmallows
2 to 3 bananas, sliced
⅔ cup chopped walnuts *or* pecans

1. Whip cream with confectioners' sugar. Mix cranberries, pineapple, and marshmallows in a medium-sized bowl. Fold in whipped cream.

2. Refrigerate 2 to 12 hours in a covered bowl. Before serving, fold in bananas and nuts.

NUTRITION INFORMATION PER SERVING:

280 calories	17 g fat	7 g saturated fat
52% calories from fat	40 mg cholesterol	15 mg sodium
32 g carbohydrate	4 g protein	2.7 g fiber

Tropical Bean Salad

PREPARATION TIME: 40 minutes

CHILLING TIME: 1 to 12 hours

YIELD: 10 servings

"POLYNESIAN RESTAURANTS ARE disappearing fast," *Tribune* staffer Renée Enna wrote in a story on Hawaiian food. "There was a time when pupu platters were as easy to find as an Elvis movie set in Hawaii. Today, only a few stalwarts remain afloat." Even if you don't share in the nostalgia for "tropikitsch," this bean salad, adapted from a recipe by Hawaiian chef Sam Choy, is a taste of paradise. To save time, you also can use a can of beans, drained, in place of the dried variety.

½ cup dried beans, such as navy, black, *and/or* pinto

2 mangoes, peeled, pitted, and diced

▶

2 papayas, peeled, pitted, and diced
2 litchis, peeled, pitted, and diced, optional
¼ fresh pineapple, peeled and diced, *or* 1 cup drained canned pineapple
2 plum tomatoes, seeded and diced
½ red bell pepper, seeded and diced

2 tablespoons cider vinegar
2 tablespoons chopped cilantro
½ teaspoon ground cumin
½ teaspoon salt
¼ teaspoon crushed red pepper flakes
¼ teaspoon white pepper

Cook dried beans according to package directions; cool. Stir together beans, mangoes, papayas, litchis if desired, pineapple, tomatoes, bell pepper, vinegar, cilantro, cumin, salt, red pepper flakes, and white pepper in a large bowl. Cover; chill at least 1 hour.

NUTRITION INFORMATION PER SERVING:

105 calories	0.5 g fat	0.1 g saturated fat
4% calories from fat	10 mg cholesterol	120 mg sodium
24 g carbohydrate	3.3 g protein	4.3 g fiber

Couscous Salad

PREPARATION TIME: 30 minutes
CHILLING TIME: 2 to 3 hours
YIELD: 8 servings

TRANSFORM THIS SALAD into a meal by adding shredded cooked chicken or thinly sliced strips of cooked lamb or beef. Almonds add crunch to the salad.

1½ cups instant couscous
2 cups warm beef broth
1 cup raisins
1 tablespoon butter
½ cup sliced almonds
3 ribs celery, chopped
1 Granny Smith apple, cored and diced

2 green onions, minced
1 tablespoon minced cilantro
1 teaspoon minced fresh mint
Zest and juice of 1 lemon
Salt
Freshly ground black pepper

1. Put couscous in a large bowl, add broth; stir to mix.

2. Put raisins in a small cup, add warm water to cover. Let stand until softened, about 10 minutes. Drain.

3. Melt butter in a small skillet over medium heat. Add almonds. Cook, stirring frequently, until almonds are golden. Remove from heat.

4. Add raisins, almonds, celery, apple, onion, cilantro, mint, lemon zest and juice, and salt and pepper to taste to couscous in the large bowl; toss to mix. Cover with plastic wrap. Refrigerate, tossing several times with a fork, until chilled, 2 to 3 hours. Taste and adjust seasoning. Serve chilled or at room temperature.

NUTRITION INFORMATION PER SERVING:

250 calories	5 g fat	1.3 g saturated fat
17% calories from fat	4 mg cholesterol	230 mg sodium
47 g carbohydrate	7 g protein	4 g fiber

Middle Eastern Tabbouleh Salad

PREPARATION TIME: 40 minutes
CHILLING TIME: 2 to 8 hours
YIELD: 4 servings

THIS TABBOULEH SALAD, from the late food columnist Roy Andries de Groot, can be stretched into a dinner salad by adding shredded cooked chicken or turkey. Or enjoy tabbouleh as a stuffing for pita bread sandwiches or a not-so-filling appetizer. Instead of bread, serve it on spears of crisp romaine lettuce.

1 cup uncooked bulgur (cracked wheat)
6 to 8 canned plum tomatoes, seeded, squeezed dry, and chopped, *or* 4 ripe tomatoes, chopped
Juice of up to 4 lemons
1 yellow onion, diced
1 large bunch green onions, including tops, diced

1¼ cups finely chopped Italian flat-leaf parsley
1 cup finely chopped fresh mint leaves
¼ to ½ cup extra-virgin olive oil
1 teaspoon kosher salt
½ teaspoon freshly ground black pepper

►

1. Place bulgur in a medium-sized bowl. Run under a stream of cold water, using your fingers to separate grains and break up lumps. Drain. Cover bulgur with fresh water to cover by at least 2 inches. Let soak according to package directions. (Time will vary from 10 minutes to several hours.)

2. Drain bulgur; squeeze out as much excess water as possible using your hands or twisting inside a clean towel. Place dry bulgur back in the medium-sized bowl. Stir in tomatoes, lemon juice, yellow onion, green onion, parsley, mint, olive oil, salt, and pepper. Refrigerate covered 2 to 8 hours. Taste and adjust seasonings.

NUTRITION INFORMATION PER SERVING:

320 calories	15 g fat	2 g saturated fat
37% calories from fat	0 mg cholesterol	855 mg sodium
47 g carbohydrate	8 g protein	11 g fiber

Tropical Fruit Platter with Honey-Lime Dressing

PREPARATION TIME: 25 minutes

COOKING TIME: 5 minutes

CHILLING TIME: 1 hour

YIELD: 8 servings

A HONEY-LIME dressing enlivens this refreshing fruit salad. The dressing is also delicious with fresh strawberries when they are in season.

1 large egg, beaten
⅓ cup honey
¼ cup fresh lime juice
⅛ teaspoon salt
1 tablespoon rum, optional
1 cup sour cream
Bibb *or* Boston lettuce leaves
1 Red Delicious apple, cored and sliced

1 Golden Delicious apple, cored and sliced
1 fresh pineapple, peeled and cut into spears
1 small honeydew melon, peeled, seeded, and cut into chunks
1 papaya, peeled, seeded, and sliced
1 banana, peeled and cut into chunks
½ cup chopped nuts

1. Combine egg, honey, lime juice, and salt in small saucepan. Cook, stirring often, over low heat until thickened, about 5 minutes. Do not boil. Remove from heat; stir in rum if using. Cool to room temperature. Fold in sour cream. Refrigerate until cold, about 1 hour or until ready to use.

2. Arrange lettuce leaves over large serving platter. Arrange fruits over lettuce. Spoon dressing over fruits. Sprinkle with nuts.

NUTRITION INFORMATION PER SERVING:

300 calories	12 g fat	4.5 g saturated fat
34% calories from fat	40 mg cholesterol	80 mg sodium
49 g carbohydrate	3.8 g protein	4.3 g fiber

Grilled Vegetables with Spicy Bean Salad

PREPARATION TIME: 30 minutes

CHILLING TIME: 1 hour

COOKING TIME: 25 minutes

YIELD: 8 servings

KEY TO THE success of this beautiful vegetable plate is vigilance. Adjust grilling times according to the thickness of each vegetable to preserve its texture, which is a big part of the appeal of the dish. For an added garnish, sprinkle the salad with chopped cilantro.

Bean Salad

2 15-ounce cans Great Northern
   beans
1 pint cherry tomatoes, halved
1 12-ounce jar salsa
¼ cup minced cilantro
1 small jalapeño, seeded and
   minced, optional
Salt
Freshly ground black pepper

Grilled Vegetables

6 medium-sized red, yellow, *and/or*
   green bell peppers
2 medium-sized eggplants, cut in
   1-inch slices
4 yellow squash, halved lengthwise
4 zucchini, halved lengthwise
Olive oil
Lettuce leaves

1. To make bean salad, drain and rinse beans. Put into a large bowl. Stir in cherry tomatoes, salsa, cilantro, and jalapeño. Add salt and pepper to taste. Mix well; refrigerate at least 1 hour. Let stand at room temperature 30 minutes before serving.

2. Prepare grill or heat broiler. Put bell peppers onto grill and cook, turning frequently, until skin is golden brown and flesh is crisp-tender, 10 to 15 minutes.

►

3. Put eggplant slices, squash, and zucchini onto grill. Cook, turning once and brushing with olive oil, until golden and crisp-tender, about 10 minutes.

4. Remove seeds and cores from bell peppers and cut into quarters. Put lettuce leaves onto the center of a large serving platter. Fill leaves with bean salad. Arrange grilled vegetables around bean salad. Drizzle vegetables with olive oil. Sprinkle with salt and pepper. Serve at room temperature.

NUTRITION INFORMATION PER SERVING:

150 calories	1 g fat	0.2 g saturated fat
5% calories from fat	0 mg cholesterol	605 mg sodium
35 g carbohydrate	9 g protein	12 g fiber

Early Herb Garden Coleslaw

PREPARATION TIME: 10 minutes

YIELD: 4 servings

CHIVES, MINT, PARSLEY, and with a little luck, cilantro are the earliest herbs to appear in gardens. Gather a big handful to add to this simple salad.

4 cups ready-to-use coleslaw mix
1 cup red cabbage slaw
1 small onion, chopped fine
¼ cup snipped mixed fresh herbs, such as chives, cilantro, and parsley
3 tablespoons cider vinegar

2 teaspoons sugar
Hot red pepper sauce
2 teaspoons vegetable oil
Salt
1 tablespoon regular *or* low-calorie mayonnaise

1. Combine coleslaw, red cabbage slaw, onion, and herbs in a large bowl.

2. Mix vinegar, sugar, hot pepper sauce, oil, and salt to taste in a small microwave-safe dish. Cook on high (100 percent power) until hot, 30 to 40 seconds, stirring once to dissolve sugar. Pour over slaw. Add mayonnaise; mix well. Let stand several minutes or overnight before serving.

NUTRITION INFORMATION PER SERVING:

85 calories	5 g fat	0.8 g saturate fat
52% calories from fat	2 mg cholesterol	35 mg sodium
9 g carbohydrate	2 g protein	2.3 g fiber

Sassy Slaw

PREPARATION TIME: 5 minutes

YIELD: 6 servings

ALREADY SHREDDED COLESLAW mix, bagged and ready to go at the supermarket, saves some time in the preparation of this spicy slaw from "Fast Food" columnist Pat Dailey.

¼ cup light *or* regular mayonnaise
2 tablespoons seasoned rice vinegar
1 tablespoon Creole mustard *or*
    country-style mustard
1 teaspoon hot green pepper sauce,
    such as green Tabasco

½ teaspoon sugar
¾ pound coleslaw, cabbage slaw, *or*
    broccoli slaw mix
½ cup minced cilantro

Combine mayonnaise, vinegar, mustard, hot sauce, and sugar in a large serving bowl; mix well. Add coleslaw mix and cilantro; mix to combine.

NUTRITION INFORMATION PER SERVING:

40 calories	3.4 g fat	0.3 g saturated fat
74% calories from fat	3 mg cholesterol	115 mg sodium
2.3 g carbohydrate	0.4 g protein	0.6 g fiber

Hot Red Cabbage Slaw
with Peppered Bacon and Chutney

PREPARATION TIME: 10 minutes

COOKING TIME: 15 minutes

YIELD: 4 servings

THIS HEARTY RED cabbage slaw is from "Fast Food" columnist Pat Dailey. She teamed it with an Indian squash soup for a light supper menu.

2 strips bacon, diced fine
½ teaspoon crushed black pepper
3 green onions, white part only,
    sliced thin
1 8-ounce package shredded red
    cabbage

1½ teaspoons seasoned rice vinegar
1½ teaspoons mango chutney
¼ teaspoon sugar
¼ teaspoon salt
¼ cup minced cilantro, optional

▶

1. Put bacon in a medium-sized skillet over medium heat; sprinkle with pepper. Cook over medium heat until crisp. Add green onions; cook until onions begin to soften, 1 minute.

2. Add cabbage, vinegar, chutney, sugar, and salt. Cook, stirring occasionally, until cabbage is crisp-tender, 3 to 4 minutes. Remove from heat; add cilantro if desired. Serve hot.

NUTRITION INFORMATION PER SERVING:

80 calories	5 g fat	1.7 g saturated fat
54% calories from fat	8 mg cholesterol	315 mg sodium
5 g carbohydrate	4 g protein	1.8 g fiber

Napa Slaw

PREPARATION TIME: 15 minutes

YIELD: 8 servings

"CABBAGE IS LIKE one of those great character actors in movies," said Mark Stanley, a chef-instructor at the Cooking and Hospitality Institute of Chicago. "You see them all the time, but they never are the stars." Stanley enjoys serving a colorful fusion slaw of shredded napa cabbage and radicchio tossed with a raspberry vinaigrette.

⅓ cup raspberry vinegar
2½ teaspoons sugar
⅔ cup vegetable oil
1 teaspoon kosher salt

Freshly ground black pepper
1 head napa cabbage
1 head radicchio, shredded

1. Whisk together vinegar and sugar in a small bowl. Let stand several minutes until sugar dissolves. Slowly whisk in oil; season with salt and black pepper to taste. Set aside.

2. Cut 1 inch off the bottom of the napa cabbage. Cut large leaves in half lengthwise; shred all leaves about ⅛ inch thick. Place in a large bowl with radicchio. Toss cabbage mixture with enough vinaigrette to coat. Taste and adjust seasoning. Serve soon after mixing to avoid excessive wilting.

NUTRITION INFORMATION PER SERVING:

185 calories	18 g fat	2.3 g saturated fat
86% calories from fat	0 mg cholesterol	250 mg sodium
5 g carbohydrate	1.5 g protein	0.2 g fiber

Bêtise's Summer Chicken Salad (page 370)

Photo by Bob Fila

Wilted Asian Greens with Toasted
Sesame Seeds and Mango (page 351)

Grilled Tuscan Bread Salad (page 347)

Southern Biscuits (page 409)

Seafood Salad with Warm Citrus Dressing (page 378)

Irish Soda Bread (page 408)

Chunky Apple Muffins (page 419)

Cool Strawberry Soup with Pound Cake Croutons (page 477)

Pineapple-Macadamia Scones (page 414)

Peaches and Cream Gelato, Honeydew Melon Sorbet, and
Pineapple-Ginger Sorbet (pages 468, 470, and 471)

Photo by Bob Fila

Strawberry-Rhubarb Lattice Pie (page 447)

Photo by Bob Fila

Strawberry Cream Tart (page 456)

Photo by Bob Fila

Mangrove Mama's Key Lime Pie (page 455)

Photo by Bob Fila

Java Brownies (page 498)

Orange Pecan Delights, Sour Cherry Rugelach, and
Fudgy Bittersweet Brownie Stars (pages 484, 492, and 496)

Photo by Bob Fila

Budapest Truffles (page 499)

Kohlrabi Slaw

PREPARATION TIME: 25 minutes
COOKING TIME: 2 minutes
CHILLING TIME: 2 hours
YIELD: 4 servings

CABBAGE'S COUSIN, KOHLRABI, could double for a pale green turnip in the looks department. What sets it apart is its unique nutlike flavor. This recipe is a variation on carrot slaw but with a Middle Eastern flavor from the ground cumin.

3 large kohlrabi, peeled and julienned	½ cup plain yogurt
2 large carrots, peeled and julienned	½ teaspoon ground cumin
	⅛ teaspoon ground red pepper
2 tablespoons white wine vinegar	Salt
⅓ cup vegetable oil	Freshly ground black pepper
	4 green onions, sliced

1. Cook kohlrabi and carrots in boiling water until crisp-tender, about 2 minutes. Drain; rinse under cold water until cool. Pat dry.

2. Place vinegar in a medium-sized bowl; whisk in oil in a slow stream until smooth. Whisk in yogurt, cumin, ground red pepper, salt, and black pepper. Taste and adjust seasonings. Add kohlrabi, carrots, and onions. Toss to coat. Refrigerate covered 2 hours; serve.

NUTRITION INFORMATION PER SERVING:

220 calories	19 g fat	2.7 g saturated fat
72% calories from fat	2 mg cholesterol	55 mg sodium
13 g carbohydrate	3.8 g protein	4.7 g fiber

Red Cabbage and Noodle Slaw

PREPARATION TIME: 25 minutes

STANDING TIME: 20 minutes

YIELD: 8 servings

WHEN THE *TRIBUNE* wrote about cabbage one March, the test kitchen created several recipes that raised the vegetable from humble origins to the realm of trendy and versatile. In this recipe, cabbage finds a niche with pasta and apples. Turn this into a heartier dish by adding two cans of water-packed tuna, drained well and flaked.

1 8-ounce box shell-shaped pasta
1 small head red cabbage, shredded
2 ribs celery, diced
5 green onions, sliced thin
1 large tart apple, peeled, cored,
    and diced

Dressing
1 cup plain yogurt
1 cup mayonnaise
2 tablespoons fresh lemon juice
½ teaspoon salt
½ teaspoon freshly ground black
    pepper

1. Cook pasta according to package directions; drain. Mix pasta, cabbage, celery, onions, and apple in a large bowl.

2. To make dressing, stir together yogurt, mayonnaise, lemon juice, salt, and pepper until smooth. Spoon over cabbage mixture; toss well. Let stand 20 minutes before serving.

NUTRITION INFORMATION PER SERVING:

350 calories	23 g fat	3.7 g saturated fat
58% calories from fat	18 mg cholesterol	355 mg sodium
31 g carbohydrate	7 g protein	4.3 g fiber

Garlic Potato Salad

PREPARATION TIME: 20 minutes
COOKING TIME: 10 minutes
STANDING TIME: 1 hour
YIELD: 4 servings

THE HEADY FLAVOR of garlic reigns in this delicious potato salad from Chicago's Café Ba-Ba-Reeba! Be sure to eat it with very close friends—or alone. Cut the richness of the mayonnaise if desired by adding a few dollops of plain yogurt.

15 small red potatoes	4 cloves garlic, minced
1 cup mayonnaise	½ teaspoon salt
¼ cup minced fresh parsley	Freshly ground white pepper

1. Cook potatoes in boiling water to cover until fork-tender, about 10 minutes. Drain; cool. Peel and halve potatoes.
2. Mix mayonnaise, parsley, garlic, salt, and white pepper in a large bowl. Add potatoes; toss gently. Let stand 1 hour before serving.

NUTRITION INFORMATION PER SERVING:

510 calories	44 g fat	7 g saturated fat
77% calories from fat	30 mg cholesterol	610 mg sodium
24 g carbohydrate	5 g protein	3.4 g fiber

Green Chili Potato Salad

PREPARATION TIME: 15 minutes
COOKING TIME: 12 minutes
YIELD: 6 servings

AMERICAN CLASSICS OFTEN are amenable to new flavors borrowed from the Pacific Rim. Take potato salad. It easily adapts to the flavors of Vietnam or Thailand, as the following recipe by "Fast Food" columnist Pat Dailey proves.

2 pounds small red potatoes	¼ cup plain low-fat yogurt
1 tablespoon vegetable oil	2 tablespoons coconut milk
1 stalk lemongrass, trimmed and minced	Salt
1 to 2 serrano chilies, minced	½ small sweet onion, diced fine
	⅓ cup minced cilantro

►

1. Put potatoes in a large saucepan with water to cover. Heat to boil over high heat; cook until potatoes are just tender, 8 to 10 minutes. Drain well; set potatoes aside. Wipe out pan.

2. Heat oil in the same pan over medium-high heat. Add lemongrass and serranos. Cook, stirring, until slightly softened, 1 minute. Remove from heat; transfer to a large bowl. Add yogurt, coconut milk, and salt to taste.

3. Quarter potatoes; add to bowl. Add onion and cilantro. Mix lightly. Serve at room temperature.

NUTRITION INFORMATION PER SERVING:

135 calories	3.6 g fat	1.3 g saturated fat
24% calories from fat	1 mg cholesterol	13 mg sodium
22 g carbohydrate	5 g protein	3 g fiber

Bêtise's Summer Chicken Salad

PREPARATION TIME: 25 minutes

YIELD: 4 servings

BRIAN SHRAGO HAS added this vibrant chicken salad to his summer menu at Bêtise, a bistro on the lake in Wilmette, Illinois. It's a great summer lunch or supper. Shrago suggests substituting diced tomato for the mango if desired. Herbes de Provence is a blend of dried herbs, including basil, fennel seed, lavender, marjoram, rosemary, sage, summer savory, and thyme, typically used in southern France. As a substitution, use a combination of any of these dried herbs you might have on hand.

Vinaigrette
1 clove garlic, minced
2 tablespoons plus 1½ teaspoons
    vegetable oil
1 tablespoon plus 1½ teaspoons
    sherry wine vinegar
1 tablespoon walnut *or* pumpkin
    seed oil
1 teaspoon dried herbes de
    Provence (see Index)

1 teaspoon fresh lemon juice
¼ teaspoon salt
Freshly ground black pepper

Salad
2 cups coarsely chopped skinless
    roasted chicken
1 ripe mango, peeled, pitted, and
    diced
6 cups torn mixed greens
1 avocado

1. To make vinaigrette, whisk together garlic, vegetable oil, vinegar, walnut oil, herbes de Provence, lemon juice, salt, and pepper to taste in a small bowl.

2. To make salad, toss together chicken and mango in a large bowl. Add all but 2 tablespoons vinaigrette to chicken mixture. Toss well. Taste and adjust seasoning. Add remaining vinaigrette to chilled greens. Toss until coated. Taste and adjust seasoning.

3. Peel, pit, and dice avocado. Divide greens among 4 chilled plates. Mound chicken salad on each. Garnish with avocado.

NUTRITION INFORMATION PER SERVING:

405 calories	29 g fat	5 g saturated fat
64% calories from fat	60 mg cholesterol	230 mg sodium
16 g carbohydrate	22 g protein	5 g fiber

Hotel Bel-Air's Cobb Salad

PREPARATION TIME: 40 minutes

COOKING TIME: 20 minutes

YIELD: 4 servings

ROBERT COBB, MANAGER of the Brown Derby restaurant in Hollywood in the 1920s, improvised the salad that would bear his name one night when he was raiding the restaurant icebox after a long day. As part of a "Good Eating" series, "American Originals," we explored the original recipe and variations for the Cobb salad, including this $20 version served at the exclusive Hotel Bel-Air in Los Angeles.

Salad

2 hearts of romaine lettuce, torn into bite-sized pieces

6 strips bacon, cooked and crumbled

2 skinless, boneless cooked chicken breast halves, chopped

2 plum tomatoes, seeded and chopped

1 ripe avocado, peeled, pitted, and sliced *or* chopped

½ cup crumbled blue cheese

Lemon Vinaigrette

1 small shallot, minced

¼ cup red wine vinegar

2 teaspoons Dijon mustard

1 teaspoon chopped chives

1 teaspoon chopped parsley

1 teaspoon sugar

¼ teaspoon salt

Freshly ground black pepper

¼ cup fresh lemon juice

1¼ cups peanut oil

1. To make salad, place romaine in a large salad bowl. Cover romaine with bacon, chicken, tomatoes, avocado, and blue cheese.

➤

2. To make dressing, cook shallot and vinegar in a small skillet over medium-high heat 2 minutes. Set aside to cool. Place mustard, chives, parsley, sugar, salt, and pepper to taste in a small bowl. Whisk to combine. Whisk together vinegar mixture, mustard mixture, and lemon juice. Slowly add oil, whisking constantly until blended. Toss salad at the table with lemon vinaigrette.

NUTRITION INFORMATION PER SERVING
OF SALAD WITH 2 TABLESPOONS VINAIGRETTE:

480 calories	41 g fat	11 g saturated fat
76% calories from fat	60 mg cholesterol	495 mg sodium
8 g carbohydrate	23 g protein	4 g fiber

Asian Chicken and Plum Salad

PREPARATION TIME: 30 minutes

YIELD: 4 servings

SWEET-TART PLUMS are the perfect foil for this Asian-influenced combination of chicken, pasta, and shredded bok choy. The salad can be served warm, at room temperature, or chilled.

¼ cup reduced-sodium chicken broth

3 tablespoons reduced-sodium soy sauce

2 tablespoons vegetable oil

2 tablespoons hoisin sauce

3 cloves garlic, minced

1 tablespoon minced fresh gingerroot

2 teaspoons sesame oil

1 teaspoon sugar

½ to 1 teaspoon crushed red pepper flakes

Salt

Freshly ground black pepper

4 ounces angel-hair pasta

4 skinless, boneless cooked chicken breast halves, cubed

3 ripe, firm red plums, pitted and cut into chunks

2 cups shredded bok choy

2 green onions, sliced

1 tablespoon toasted sesame seeds (see Index)

1. To make dressing, combine broth, soy sauce, vegetable oil, hoisin sauce, garlic, gingerroot, sesame oil, sugar, red pepper flakes, and salt and black pepper to taste in a blender container. Blend until mixed.

2. Cook pasta according to package directions. Drain; toss with 2 tablespoons of the dressing. Combine chicken, plums, and bok choy in a large bowl. Toss with remaining dressing.

3. Place pasta on a serving platter or individual plates. Top with chicken salad; garnish with green onions and sesame seeds.

NUTRITION INFORMATION PER SERVING:

415 calories	15 g fat	2.5 g saturated fat
32% calories from fat	75 mg cholesterol	625 mg sodium
38 g carbohydrate	20 g protein	3.4 g fiber

Cajun Chicken Salad with Honey-Jalapeño Dressing

PREPARATION TIME: 45 minutes

COOKING TIME: 10 minutes

YIELD: 4 servings

JIMMY BANNOS, CHEF-OWNER of the Heaven on Seven restaurants in Chicago, has had a long-running love affair with the cooking of Louisiana. He developed this main dish salad when his Loop restaurant was still called the Garland.

Chicken
1 cup all-purpose flour
1½ teaspoons Cajun seasoning for
   poultry, such as Paul
   Prudhomme's Poultry Magic
¾ teaspoon paprika
¼ teaspoon freshly ground black
   pepper
¼ teaspoon ground red pepper
¼ teaspoon salt
¼ teaspoon sugar
⅛ teaspoon celery salt
⅛ teaspoon garlic salt
⅛ teaspoon onion salt
⅛ teaspoon ground white pepper
Pinch cinnamon
Pinch ground nutmeg

4 boneless chicken breast halves
   (4 to 5 ounces each)
2 large eggs, beaten
Vegetable oil

Dressing
2 green onions, chopped fine
1 jalapeño, seeded and minced
1 cup mayonnaise
¾ cup whipping cream *or*
   half-and-half
2 tablespoons honey
½ teaspoon hot red pepper sauce
½ teaspoon Worcestershire sauce
⅛ teaspoon freshly ground black
   pepper
⅛ teaspoon ground red pepper

►

⅛ teaspoon ground white pepper
Assorted lettuces, such as iceberg, romaine, and green leaf
4 tomatoes, cut in wedges

8 cherry peppers
Black olives
½ pound fresh mushrooms, sliced
Alfalfa sprouts

1. To make chicken, combine flour, Cajun poultry seasoning, paprika, black pepper, red pepper, salt, sugar, celery salt, garlic salt, onion salt, white pepper, cinnamon, and nutmeg in a shallow bowl. Coat chicken breasts with spiced flour mixture. Dip in beaten egg; coat again with spiced flour mixture so chicken is well coated. Heat oil in a deep-fryer or saucepan to 350°F (use a deep-frying thermometer to check). Deep-fry chicken in two batches, turning often, until light brown, about 5 minutes per batch. Drain on paper towels.

2. To make dressing, whisk together onions, jalapeño, mayonnaise, whipping cream, honey, hot pepper sauce, Worcestershire sauce, black pepper, red pepper, and white pepper in a medium-sized bowl. Thin with additional whipping cream if desired. Refrigerate until serving.

3. Tear lettuces into bite-sized pieces; toss to mix. Place lettuce on 4 individual plates or in a serving bowl. Top with tomato wedges and cherry peppers. Garnish with black olives, mushrooms, and alfalfa sprouts if desired. Cut chicken into strips; place in the center of salad. Pour dressing on salad just before serving.

NUTRITION INFORMATION PER SERVING:

920 calories	76 g fat	20 g saturated fat
75% calories from fat	260 mg cholesterol	1,010 mg sodium
31 g carbohydrate	30 g protein	1.9 g fiber

Yellowfin Tuna Sashimi Salad

PREPARATION TIME: 25 minutes
YIELD: 4 servings

FRANCOIS KWAKU-DONGO, executive chef of Spago Chicago, is at ease with the French techniques, Asian flavors, and California vegetables and fruits that characterize the original Spago in Beverly Hills, California. "I do not do fusion," he says. "A dish remains true to the part of the world where it originated, but I may graft on some ingredients from outside the culture." In this sashimi salad, for example, he makes the *ponzu* (a Japanese dip) with lime juice and soy, plus French pickled shallots, pickled ginger, and rice wine vinegar, all topped with American caviar. Wasabi, *mizuna*, daikon sprouts, and nori are available at Japanese and some specialty markets.

Vinaigrette
¼ cup soy sauce
2 tablespoons lime juice
1 tablespoon minced wasabi *or* 1½ teaspoons prepared wasabi paste

Salad
1 cup baby *mizuna or* arugula
1 bunch daikon sprouts *or* radish sprouts
1 large ripe avocado, peeled, pitted, and cut into thin slices

8 ounces yellowfin *or* Ahi tuna, sushi grade, sliced thin (see Note)
1 small red onion, peeled and sliced paper-thin
½ cup pickled ginger
2 sheets nori (dried seaweed wrappers), cut into thin slices
2 tablespoons toasted sesame seeds
2 teaspoons whitefish caviar, optional

1. To make vinaigrette, stir together soy sauce, lime juice, and wasabi in a small bowl; set aside.

2. To make salad, place *mizuna* and daikon sprouts in the center of 4 salad plates. Fan avocado slices around half of salad. Place tuna slices around other half. Top tuna with onion slices; top avocado with pickled ginger. Sprinkle with dry nori and sesame seeds; spoon ½ teaspoon caviar on each portion if desired. Stir vinaigrette; drizzle over salad.

❧ NOTE: *Buy sushi-grade tuna from a reliable source; otherwise, fish may contain parasites. To kill possible parasites, freeze the fish for 24 hours.*

NUTRITION INFORMATION PER SERVING (INCLUDING CAVIAR):

250 calories	11 g fat	1.8 g saturated fat
40% calories from fat	150 mg cholesterol	1,795 mg sodium
16 g carbohydrate	22 g protein	6 g fiber

Poached Salmon Salad with Mustard Dressing

PREPARATION TIME: 30 minutes

COOKING TIME: 10 minutes

YIELD: 2 servings

NEED A REFRESHING entree for a sweltering day? Try this seafood salad, a cousin to salad Niçoise. Unlike France's classic salad, this one features boneless salmon fillets instead of tuna and a sassy mustard dressing with chervil and tarragon rather than the standard herb vinaigrette.

Mustard Dressing

¼ cup sherry *or* white wine vinegar

2 teaspoons Dijon mustard

2 teaspoons dried chervil

¼ teaspoon dried tarragon

⅛ teaspoon freshly ground black pepper

Pinch salt

⅓ to ½ cup extra-virgin olive oil

Salad

6 small new potatoes

¼ pound very thin green beans, ends trimmed

1 cup water

1 cup dry white wine

1 pound boneless salmon fillets

4 cups torn assorted lettuces

1 small cucumber, peeled, seeded, and sliced

1. To make mustard dressing, mix vinegar, mustard, chervil, tarragon, pepper, and salt in a jar with a tight-fitting lid. Add ⅓ cup of the oil; shake until well mixed. Taste and adjust seasonings. Add more oil as desired.

2. Cook potatoes in boiling water to cover until fork-tender, about 10 minutes. Drain. Cook green beans in boiling water uncovered until crisp-tender, about 3 minutes. Drain; rinse under cold water to stop cooking.

3. Heat water and wine to simmer in a medium-sized skillet over medium heat. Add fish fillets. Cover; simmer until fish barely flakes, 5 to 8 minutes. Immediately remove fish from water with a slotted spatula. Remove skin. Cool.

4. Arrange lettuces on 2 serving plates. Slice potatoes; toss with some of the dressing in a small bowl. Arrange potato slices over lettuce in a ring about 2 inches from the edge of the plates. Mix cucumber slices with some of the dressing in the same small bowl. Arrange cucumbers in the center of lettuce. Break salmon into large hunks; toss with some of the dressing. Arrange salmon over cucumbers. Toss green beans with some of the dressing. Arrange beans around salmon. Serve; pass any remaining dressing.

NUTRITION INFORMATION PER SERVING:

860 calories	55 g fat	8 g saturated fat
58% calories from fat	160 mg cholesterol	370 mg sodium
24 g carbohydrate	64 g protein	7 g fiber

Steamed Salmon and Caper Salad

PREPARATION TIME: 25 minutes
COOKING TIME: 6 minutes
YIELD: 4 servings

FOOD AND WINE columnist William Rice investigated the caper, the pickled flower bud of the desert shrub *Capparis spinosa*. "Cured capers are aromatic and contribute a lively bite to dishes but do not taste harsh," he wrote in the Sunday *Chicago Tribune Magazine*. "They also are a very useful weapon for cooks seeking to improvise a sauce or topping." Any size caper will work in this main course salad. Serve it with white wine such as sauvignon blanc or Riesling.

4 salmon steaks, cut ¾ inch thick	16 to 20 large drained capers,
⅓ cup water	chopped coarse
¼ teaspoon salt	1 shallot, chopped
Freshly ground black pepper	1½ teaspoons Dijon mustard
8 cups mixed greens, such as	½ teaspoon paprika
romaine, Boston lettuce,	1 tablespoon white wine vinegar
arugula, spinach, *or* mesclun,	¼ cup extra-virgin olive oil
torn into bite-sized pieces	¼ cup coarsely chopped fresh dill

1. Lightly oil a large skillet. Place salmon steaks in a single layer in the skillet. Add ⅓ cup water; cover. Heat water to boil over medium heat. Lower heat to medium-low; steam salmon 3 minutes. Turn steaks; season with half of the salt and pepper. Cover; steam just until cooked through, about 3 minutes. Set aside.

2. Combine greens in a large salad bowl. Combine capers, shallot, mustard, paprika, remaining salt, and pepper to taste in a small bowl. Whisk in vinegar and oil. Adjust seasoning; toss with salad.

3. Arrange salad on 4 plates. Cut skin from salmon steaks, remove bones, and place 1 steak on top of each portion of salad. Garnish with dill.

NUTRITION INFORMATION PER SERVING:

710 calories	39 g fat	6 g saturated fat
50% calories from fat	220 mg cholesterol	640 mg sodium
6 g carbohydrate	81 g protein	2.6 g fiber

Seafood Salad with Warm Citrus Dressing

PREPARATION TIME: 45 minutes

COOKING TIME: 5 minutes

YIELD: 4 servings

IN FALL AND winter, salads come in from the cold. A warm orange-lime dressing cozies up to scallops and shrimp in this recipe developed in the *Tribune* test kitchen.

½ cup sunflower oil

1 clove garlic, minced

1 ½-inch piece fresh gingerroot, minced

1 shallot, minced

Zest and juice of 1 lime

Zest and juice of ½ orange

1 tablespoon sugar

½ teaspoon salt

Freshly ground black pepper

6 cups torn assorted salad greens

¼ cup chopped cilantro

¼ cup chopped fresh mint

2 oranges, peeled and sectioned

½ pound scallops, cooked

½ pound peeled and deveined cooked shrimp

2 tablespoons sunflower seeds, toasted (see Note)

Edible flowers, optional

1. Heat 1 tablespoon of the oil in a medium-sized skillet over medium heat. Add garlic, gingerroot, and shallot; cook, stirring often, until tender, about 4 minutes. Stir in lime zest and juice, orange zest and juice, sugar, salt, and pepper to taste. Cook 1 minute. Slowly whisk in remaining oil.

2. Toss together greens, cilantro, and mint in a large serving bowl. Arrange orange sections, scallops, and shrimp on top of greens. Sprinkle with sunflower seeds and edible flowers if desired. Pour ¼ cup of the warm dressing over salad; toss to coat. Add additional dressing as needed.

❧ NOTE: *To toast sunflower seeds, heat them in a small dry pan over low heat, stirring often, until lightly browned. Immediately remove seeds from pan to stop cooking.*

NUTRITION INFORMATION PER SERVING:

460 calories	32 g fat	3.6 g saturated fat
62% calories from fat	130 mg cholesterol	675 mg sodium
20 g carbohydrate	25 g protein	4 g fiber

Vietnamese Beef and Mint Salad

PREPARATION TIME: 45 minutes
MARINATING TIME: 45 minutes
COOKING TIME: 15 minutes
YIELD: 6 servings

JEANMARIE BROWNSON, FORMER test kitchen director and writer of the "Curious Cook" column, bowled over tasters with this refreshing beef and fresh mint salad. Unsweetened coconut milk is available canned in many supermarkets and in Asian and Indian markets. If it is not available, try substituting plain yogurt. Rice stick noodles and fish sauce (*nam pla*) also are available in Asian markets.

1 pound boneless beef chuck *or* sirloin, trimmed
4 limes
½ cup unsweetened coconut milk
1 large clove garlic, minced
5 ounces rice stick noodles
1 head leaf lettuce, shredded
2 tablespoons fish sauce (*nam pla*) *or* 1½ tablespoons soy sauce
1 tablespoon sugar
1 serrano chili *or* jalapeño, seeded and minced
6 tablespoons peanut oil
3 green onions, minced
2 carrots, shredded fine
1 cucumber, peeled, halved, seeded, and sliced
2 cups fresh bean sprouts
½ cup fresh mint leaves
½ cup coarsely crushed dry-roasted unsalted peanuts

1. Slice meat as thin as possible in 3-inch pieces (see Note). Juice all of the limes, reserving the pulp of 3 of them. Mix meat, coconut milk, one-fourth of the lime juice, and garlic in a small nonaluminum bowl. Marinate 45 minutes at room temperature or up to 2 hours in refrigerator.

2. Soak rice stick noodles in a large amount of very hot water until softened, 20 to 30 minutes. Drain well. Line a large deep serving platter with shredded lettuce. Pile noodles in the center of the platter. Mix fish sauce, remaining lime juice, sugar, and minced serrano chili in a small bowl.

3. Drain meat well, reserving marinade. Heat a large skillet or wok until hot. Add oil; heat until hot. Add one-third of the meat; stir-fry until browned, about 3 minutes. Remove with a slotted spoon to a plate lined with paper towels. Repeat to fry all meat, adding more oil to pan if needed.

4. Add 1 more tablespoon oil to pan if needed. Add green onions, carrots, cucumber, and bean sprouts. Stir-fry 1 minute. Stir in reserved meat marinade and fish sauce mixture; stir-fry until heated through, about 1 minute. Stir in meat; stir-fry 1 minute.

➤

5. Spoon meat mixture and pan juices over noodles on platter. Sprinkle with mint leaves and crushed peanuts.

❧ NOTE: *Freeze the meat until almost frozen through; this will allow you to slice it thinner.*

NUTRITION INFORMATION PER SERVING:

425 calories	19 g fat	7 g saturated fat
39% calories from fat	50 mg cholesterol	530 mg sodium
39 g carbohydrate	28 g protein	5 g fiber

Avocado Dressing

PREPARATION TIME: 15 minutes

YIELD: 16 1-tablespoon servings

SMOOTH, COOL AVOCADO gets a jolt of hot chili in this dressing adapted from a recipe by Earth restaurant.

1½ ripe avocados, peeled and pitted
⅓ cup red wine vinegar
1 tablespoon Thai *or* other hot chili paste
1 teaspoon lime juice

1 cup safflower *or* other vegetable oil
3 tablespoons chopped fresh parsley
½ teaspoon salt
Freshly ground black pepper

1. Puree avocados, vinegar, chili paste, and lime juice in a blender. Slowly pour oil through feed tube, with motor running.

2. Pour dressing into a cruet or small bowl; stir in parsley, salt, and pepper to taste. Refrigerate or serve immediately.

NUTRITION INFORMATION PER SERVING:

95 calories	10 g fat	1 g saturated fat
97% calories from fat	0 mg cholesterol	50 mg sodium
1 g carbohydrate	0.3 g protein	0.7 g fiber

Mango Vinaigrette

PREPARATION TIME: 15 minutes
YIELD: 16 1-tablespoon servings

THE FOUNDATION OF the simplest vinaigrette consists of vinegar and oil. Any oil can be used, from corn, olive, or peanut to walnut or grapeseed. Here canola oil, a neutral-tasting oil, and champagne vinegar provide the base for a burst of mango flavor. This is adapted from a recipe from Cuisines restaurant in the Renaissance Hotel in Chicago. Try this over mixed greens with sliced avocados.

1 ripe mango, peeled, pitted, and chopped
⅓ cup champagne *or* white wine vinegar

1 cup canola oil
1 tablespoon chopped cilantro
¼ teaspoon kosher salt
Freshly ground white pepper

1. Puree mango and vinegar in a blender. Slowly pour oil through the feed tube with motor running; process until smooth.

2. Pour dressing into a cruet or small bowl. Stir in cilantro; season with salt and pepper to taste. Refrigerate or serve immediately.

NUTRITION INFORMATION PER SERVING:

85 calories	9 g fat	0.7 g saturated fat
95% calories from fat	0 mg cholesterol	19 mg sodium
1.7 g carbohydrate	0 g protein	0.2 g fiber

Chipotle-Honey Dressing

PREPARATION TIME: 10 minutes
YIELD: 16 1-tablespoon servings

THESE DAYS, YOU can easily shake trendy, tasty dressings out of a bottle. But it's nice once in a while to start from scratch, ending up with personalized flavors and textures. This spicy-sweet variation is from Salpicon restaurant in Chicago.

6 canned chipotle chilis
¼ cup balsamic vinegar
1 tablespoon Dijon mustard

¼ cup honey
¾ cup extra-virgin olive oil
½ teaspoon salt

1. Combine chipotles, vinegar, and mustard in a food processor fitted with a metal blade or in a blender; puree until almost smooth. Add honey and blend. Slowly pour oil through the feed tube with the motor running.

▶

2. Pour dressing into a cruet or small bowl; stir in salt. Refrigerate or serve immediately.

NUTRITION INFORMATION PER SERVING:

85 calories	8 g fat	1 g saturated fat
80% calories from fat	0 mg cholesterol	75 mg sodium
3.5 g carbohydrate	0 g protein	0 g fiber

Roasted Macadamia Nut Dressing

PREPARATION TIME: 15 minutes

YIELD: 16 1-tablespoon servings

DRESSINGS MADE WITH spices, upscale ingredients, and ethnic flavors are seasoning salads much more frequently. "Salad used to be served on the side," said Lynn Dornblaser, editorial director of *New Product News* magazine, quoted in a "Good Eating" article. "Now salad is your meal, with more ingredients, and they can take a dressing that's more assertive. Flavor is big." As an example, this Asian-influenced recipe comes from the Hudson Club in Chicago.

¼ cup balsamic vinegar
1 ¼-inch-thick piece gingerroot,
   peeled and minced
1 clove garlic, minced
1 teaspoon honey
1 teaspoon Thai fish sauce

1 teaspoon light soy sauce
⅔ cup peanut oil
1 tablespoon toasted sesame oil
¼ cup chopped macadamia nuts,
   toasted (see Note)

1. Combine vinegar, gingerroot, and garlic in a large mixing bowl. Stir in honey, fish sauce, and soy sauce. Gradually whisk in peanut oil. Whisk in sesame oil. Stir in nuts.

2. Refrigerate or serve immediately.

❧ NOTE: *Toast nuts in a small dry skillet, stirring occasionally, over low heat until lightly browned.*

NUTRITION INFORMATION PER SERVING:

100 calories	11 g fat	2 g saturated fat
99% calories from fat	0 mg cholesterol	45 mg sodium
0.9 g carbohydrate	0.2 g protein	0.2 g fiber

Warm Bacon and Shallot Dressing with Basil Shreds

PREPARATION TIME: 10 minutes
COOKING TIME: 10 minutes
YIELD: 5 2-tablespoon servings

FRESH GREENS AND warm salad dressing can make a wonderful combination. Prove it by trying this dressing, which combines the saltiness of bacon with the sweet-sour appeal of sugar and red wine vinegar. Use a variety of hearty, bitter greens such as endive, escarole, dandelion, flowering purple kale, and radicchio.

6 slices bacon, diced
2¼ teaspoons sugar
1 medium-sized shallot, minced
⅓ cup red wine vinegar
1 teaspoon Dijon mustard

⅛ teaspoon salt
Freshly ground black pepper
3 tablespoons shredded fresh basil
  leaves

1. Cook bacon in a large skillet over medium-high heat until crisp. Remove bacon with a slotted spoon. Drain on paper towels. Add sugar to bacon fat in the pan. Cook, stirring, until lightly browned.

2. Stir in shallots; cook, stirring often, until shallots are crisp-tender, about 2 minutes. Stir in vinegar, mustard, salt, and pepper to taste. Cook until sugar is dissolved. Remove from heat; stir in basil and bacon.

NUTRITION INFORMATION PER SERVING:

145 calories	11 g fat	4 g saturated fat
70% calories from fat	20 mg cholesterol	450 mg sodium
3.6 g carbohydrate	7 g protein	0.1 g fiber

Herb Mayonnaise

PREPARATION TIME: 10 minutes
YIELD: 16 1-tablespoon servings

USE THIS MAYONNAISE for cold fish, roast chicken, or beef or as a dip for vegetables. The handsome shade of pale green contrasts well with poached salmon. Experiment with different fresh herbs. You may store this mayonnaise in the refrigerator for up to one week.

1 cup mayonnaise
2 teaspoons minced fresh chives
2 teaspoons minced parsley

2 teaspoons minced watercress
1 to 2 teaspoons minced fresh basil

▶

Stir together mayonnaise, chives, parsley, watercress, and basil in a small bowl.

NUTRITION INFORMATION PER SERVING:

100 calories	11 g fat	1.6 g saturated fat
98% calories from fat	8 mg cholesterol	80 mg sodium
0.4 g carbohydrate	0.2 g protein	0 g fiber

Creamy Black Peppercorn Dressing

PREPARATION TIME: 10 minutes
CHILLING TIME: 30 minutes
YIELD: 24 2-tablespoon servings

THIS CREAMY SALAD dressing is delicious served over crisp romaine leaves or shredded cabbage. Freshly ground black pepper is a must here, but if you desire a less spicy dressing, use less. When buying peppercorns, look for those that are evenly shaped and colored and stored in tightly covered containers. Salad dressing will keep about two weeks in the refrigerator.

8 ounces plain yogurt	1 tablespoon coarsely crushed fresh
1 cup buttermilk	black pepper
1 cup mayonnaise	1 tablespoon dried basil
¼ cup minced fresh parsley	1 teaspoon dried tarragon
2 tablespoons minced fresh chives	¼ teaspoon dried leaf thyme
or green onion tops	¼ teaspoon salt
	Pinch paprika

1. Combine yogurt, buttermilk, and mayonnaise in a large jar. Add parsley, chives, black pepper, basil, tarragon, thyme, salt, and paprika. Shake well.
2. Refrigerate at least 30 minutes before using.
3. Taste and adjust seasonings.

NUTRITION INFORMATION PER SERVING:

80 calories	8 g fat	1.2 g saturated fat
86% calories from fat	6 mg cholesterol	95 mg sodium
1.8 g carbohydrate	1 g protein	0.2 g fiber

Creamy Cilantro Dressing

PREPARATION TIME: 10 minutes
YIELD: 16 2-tablespoon servings

THIS WONDERFUL DRESSING came from The Set, a former Chicago restaurant. The size of a bunch of cilantro can vary, so add more or less half-and-half and sour cream as needed to balance the flavor. For a little kick, add a dash of hot pepper sauce and a few drops of balsamic vinegar.

1 bunch fresh cilantro	¼ cup white wine vinegar
¾ cup half-and-half	⅛ teaspoon salt
¾ cup sour cream	Freshly ground white pepper

1. Puree cilantro and half-and-half in a blender or in a food processor fitted with a metal blade. Put puree in a small bowl.

2. Add sour cream and vinegar; whisk until blended. Add salt and black pepper to taste. Refrigerate or serve immediately.

NUTRITION INFORMATION PER SERVING:

40 calories	3.6 g fat	2.2 g saturated fat
80% calories from fat	9 mg cholesterol	30 mg sodium
1.3 g carbohydrate	0.8 g protein	0.2 g fiber

BREADS

Basic White Bread

PREPARATION TIME: 30 minutes
RISING TIME: 2 to 3 hours
COOKING TIME: 40 minutes
YIELD: 2 12-slice loaves

THIS BASIC WHITE bread recipe offers you the option of using several different mixing and kneading techniques. The bread can be prepared either in the food processor, using the electric mixer fitted with a dough hook, or by hand. Using a food processor to mix the dough is the fastest. You pick which method you want to use. These methods can be used for most of the breads in this chapter. Use this recipe as a guide.

6½ cups all-purpose flour	1¼ cups water
2 tablespoons sugar	1 cup plus 1 tablespoon milk
1 tablespoon salt	1 tablespoon butter
1 ¼-ounce package active dry yeast	1 large egg

1. Combine 5½ cups of the flour, sugar, salt, and yeast in one of the following:
   a. Food processor with a metal blade or dough blade.
   b. Large bowl of an electric mixer with a dough hook.
   c. Large bowl for making bread by hand.
2. Put water, 1 cup milk, and butter into a microwave-safe 1-quart glass measure or a medium-sized saucepan. Microwave on high (100 percent power) or cook over medium heat until mixture registers 130°F for active dry yeast (or 110°F for regular yeast) on an instant-reading thermometer.

➤

3. Mix using one of the following methods:

a. Food processor: pour heated milk mixture through the feed tube into the flour mixture with the machine running. Stop the machine when the mixture forms a ball and pulls away from the sides of the bowl, 1 to 2 minutes. If dough is sticky, add flour by tablespoons through the feed tube; pulse to mix.

b. Electric mixer with a dough hook: add heated milk mixture to flour mixture. Beat on low speed until blended, then on high until mixture pulls away from the sides of the bowl, about 10 minutes. If dough is sticky, add flour by tablespoons.

c. By hand: use a large spoon to beat heated milk mixture into flour mixture until dough is elastic, about 10 minutes. Lightly flour the work surface. Scrape dough from the bowl and put it on the work surface to knead.

To knead, grease hands lightly. Gather up dough and fold it over toward you. Then use the heel of your hand to press dough away from you. Rotate dough a quarter turn; knead again. Repeat until dough is smooth and elastic, 5 to 10 minutes, adding flour to work surface as needed. When dough is properly kneaded, it has a satiny surface and will no longer stick to the work surface.

4. For rising, grease a large bowl; put dough into the bowl. Turn dough over so the entire surface is lightly greased. Cover the bowl with a clean cloth. Put the bowl in a draft-free spot with a temperature of 75 to 85°F. Let rise until doubled in volume and an imprint from your fingertip remains in dough, 1 to 2 hours. At this point, use your fist to punch down dough; turn dough over. If you have time, allow dough to rise again until doubled in volume; it will have a finer grain.

5. To shape, punch down dough; divide it in half. Lightly flour the work surface. Use a rolling pin or your palms to press each half down evenly. Roll halves up jelly roll fashion; tuck in short ends. Put dough halves seam side down into 2 greased 9″ × 5″ loaf pans. Each end of the loaves should touch the pan sides to help support dough as it rises. Mix egg with 1 tablespoon milk. Brush the top of dough with egg mixture. Cover; let dough rise again until almost doubled in volume, about 1 hour.

6. To bake, heat oven to 450°F. Gently brush egg mixture over bread again. Bake 10 minutes. Reduce oven temperature to 350°F; bake until loaves have shrunk in from the sides of the pans and the bottoms sound hollow when tapped, about 30 minutes. Remove loaves from pans; cool completely on wire racks.

NUTRITION INFORMATION PER SLICE:

140 calories	1.2 g fat	0.6 g saturated fat
8% calories from fat	11 mg cholesterol	305 mg sodium
28 g carbohydrate	4 g protein	1 g fiber

Country Parmesan Herb Bread

PREPARATION TIME: 45 minutes
RISING TIME: 3½ hours
BAKING TIME: 20 to 25 minutes
YIELD: 3 loaves

IMPORTED PARMESAN CHEESE adds a robust flavor to this homemade country bread, says cookbook author Jane Freiman Schanberg. She adds that domestic cheese is a suitable and less expensive substitute. With the help of a food processor, it takes just two minutes to mix and knead the dough.

1⅓ cups warm water (105 to 115°F)
1 tablespoon sugar
1 ¼-ounce package active dry yeast
6 ounces imported Parmesan cheese, rind removed, cut into 1-inch chunks
3½ cups bread flour

2 tablespoons olive oil *or* vegetable oil
¾ teaspoon salt
1½ teaspoons dried oregano
¼ teaspoon freshly ground black pepper
Vegetable shortening
1 large egg white

1. Combine ⅔ cup of the water, sugar, and yeast in a small bowl; let stand until bubbly. Process Parmesan cheese in a food processor fitted with a metal blade until powdery. Measure ½ cup; set remainder aside.

2. Put flour, ½ cup of the cheese, oil, and salt in the food processor. Process, adding remaining ⅔ cup warm water in a thin stream within 15 seconds. Stir yeast mixture well. Process, adding yeast mixture in a thin stream within 15 seconds. Process until dough forms a soft, moist ball, about 45 seconds.

3. Rinse a large bowl with warm water; do not dry. Add dough. Cover with plastic wrap. Let rise in a warm place until tripled in volume, 1½ to 2 hours.

4. Remove dough from the bowl; divide into 3 equal pieces. Remove ⅓ cup of the dough from each piece; set aside. To shape each loaf, sprinkle 1 tablespoon Parmesan cheese on work surface. Roll out 1 large piece of dough to a 12″ × 8″ rectangle, turning to coat both sides evenly with cheese. Sprinkle 1½ tablespoons Parmesan cheese, ½ teaspoon oregano, and ⅛ teaspoon pepper evenly over the top of dough. Fold into thirds lengthwise to make a long, thin rectangle. Pinch the two long edges together tightly to form a cigar-shaped loaf. Repeat with 2 remaining dough portions.

➤

5. To make decorative dough strips, sprinkle work surface with 1 tablespoon Parmesan cheese. Roll out 1 ⅓-cup piece of dough to a 12″ × 4″ rectangle. Cut it in half lengthwise to form 2 long flat strips. With cheese side of dough strip facing the cigar-shaped loaf, wrap and stretch the strip diagonally around the loaf clockwise; pinch both ends firmly. Attach the second strip where the first ended and wrap it counterclockwise around the loaf to form a crisscross diamond pattern. Pinch dough strips at both ends to fasten securely. Repeat with other loaves.

6. Coat a curved metal French bread pan or baking sheet generously with shortening. Put each loaf seam side down in the pan. Sprinkle and gently press 1 tablespoon Parmesan cheese on top of each loaf. Cover with a lightweight towel. Let rise in a warm place until doubled in volume, about 1 hour.

7. Adjust oven rack to lowest position. Heat oven to 425°F. Wet a soft pastry brush and dip it into egg white. Brush tops with egg white. Bake until golden brown and bottoms sound hollow when tapped, 20 to 25 minutes. Loosen from bread pans; cool completely on wire racks.

NUTRITION INFORMATION PER ¼ LOAF:

215 calories	6 g fat	2.7 g saturated fat
27% calories from fat	10 mg cholesterol	380 mg sodium
30 g carbohydrate	9 g protein	1.2 g fiber

Whole Wheat Millet Bread

PREPARATION TIME: 45 minutes
RISING TIME: 3½ hours
BAKING TIME: 30 minutes
YIELD: 2 12-slice loaves or 4 6-slice loaves

THIS BREAD RECIPE, much asked for by readers, originated at the former Jerome's restaurant in Chicago. Millet, a tiny yet very nutritious grain, can be found at health food stores. Bulgur is a wheat that has been cracked, parched, steamed, and then dried. It, too, can be found at health food stores.

¾ cup honey	1 tablespoon salt
3 .6-ounce cakes compressed yeast (see Note)	1 cup millet
3 cups warm water (90 to 100°F)	⅓ cup bulgur (cracked wheat), optional
4½ cups whole wheat flour	2 to 3 cups all-purpose flour
¼ cup vegetable oil	1 large egg
	1 teaspoon milk

1. Dissolve honey and yeast in warm water in a large bowl. Let stand until bubbly, about 5 minutes. Stir in 3½ cups of the whole wheat flour, oil, and salt until smooth. Let rise covered in a warm place until doubled in volume, about 1 hour.

2. Stir in remaining 1 cup whole wheat flour, millet, and bulgur. Stir in all-purpose flour ½ cup at a time until stiff dough forms and pulls away from the sides of the bowl. Lightly flour the work surface. Knead dough until very stiff, smooth, and elastic, about 8 minutes.

3. Grease a bowl. Put dough into the bowl; turn dough to grease top. Let rise covered in a warm place until doubled, about 1 hour. Punch down dough. Turn dough over; cover and let rise in a warm place until doubled in volume.

4. Punch down dough; cut in half or quarters. Shape each piece into a round loaf. Grease baking sheets. Put loaves onto the baking sheets; cover. Let rise 20 minutes. Beat egg with milk. Brush loaves with egg mixture.

5. Heat oven to 350°F. Bake loaves until nicely browned and pan bottoms sound hollow when tapped, 30 to 45 minutes. Cool completely on wire racks.

❦ NOTE: *You may substitute 3 ¼-ounce packages active dry yeast for the compressed yeast; heat water to 105 to 115°F.*

NUTRITION INFORMATION PER SLICE:

245 calories	3.7 g fat	0.6 g saturated fat
13% calories from fat	9 mg cholesterol	295 mg sodium
48 g carbohydrate	7 g protein	4 g fiber

Five-Grain Bread

PREPARATION TIME: 20 minutes
RISING TIME: 2 hours
COOKING TIME: 35 minutes
YIELD: 1 18-slice loaf

WHOLE GRAINS SUCH AS oats, wheat, rye, barley, and triticale (a hybrid of wheat and rye) are rolled and sold as flakes. Any or all of the flaked grains can be used for this slightly sweet bread that was one of our favorite dozen recipes in 1990. Try it with ¼ cup each of the different grains, or use all of your favorite types.

1 ¼-ounce package active dry yeast	1¾ cups bread flour
3 tablespoons light brown sugar	¾ cup whole wheat flour or more
1⅓ cups warm water (105 to 115°F)	as needed

➤

1¼ cups rolled *or* flaked grains,
such as oats, wheat, rye, barley,
and/or triticale

¼ cup instant nonfat dry milk
powder
2 tablespoons vegetable oil
¾ teaspoon salt

1. Stir yeast and 1 teaspoon of the brown sugar into water; let stand until foamy, about 5 minutes.

2. Combine bread flour, wheat flour, rolled grains, milk powder, oil, salt, and remaining brown sugar in a food processor. Pour yeast mixture through the feed tube with the machine on; process until ingredients are mixed. Dough should be moist and slightly sticky but not wet. Add more flour if it is too wet or several drops more water if it is too dry. Process until dough is smooth and supple. Let rest 5 minutes; add more water if dough seems dry.

3. Oil a bowl. Transfer dough to bowl. Cover; let rise in a warm spot until doubled in bulk, about 1 hour. Punch dough down. With floured hands, shape into a ball. Oil a baking sheet. Place dough on the baking sheet; cover with a damp cloth. Let rise until doubled, 40 to 50 minutes.

4. Heat oven to 375°F. When dough has doubled, dust top lightly with flour. Use a sharp knife to make several shallow slits across the top of loaf. Bake until loaf is golden and sounds hollow when rapped on the bottom, about 35 minutes. Transfer loaf from the pan to a wire rack; cool completely.

NUTRITION INFORMATION PER SLICE:

110 calories	2.1 g fat	0.3 g saturated fat
17% calories from fat	0 mg cholesterol	105 mg sodium
20 g carbohydrate	3.3 g protein	1.6 g fiber

Black Pumpernickel Bread

PREPARATION TIME: 40 minutes
RISING TIME: 2 hours
BAKING TIME: 45 minutes
YIELD: 2 24-slice loaves

NICOLE'S BAKE SHOP in Chicago gave us this recipe for dense, rich pumpernickel bread. For the best texture, owner Nicole Bergere suggests using a medium-grind rye flour rather than fine-grind. She also uses quick-rise yeast to cut down on the rising time.

4 cups all-purpose flour

3½ cups medium-grind rye flour
(see Note)

2 ¼-ounce packages active dry
   yeast

2 cups uncooked oat bran hot
   cereal

2 tablespoons caraway seeds

1 tablespoon salt

1 tablespoon minced onion flakes

2 teaspoons Postum, optional
   (see Note)

1 ounce bitter *or* semisweet
   chocolate

⅓ cup dark molasses

¼ cup cider vinegar

¼ cup olive oil

2½ cups very warm water
   (120 to 130°F)

½ teaspoon cornstarch

¼ cup cold water

1. Mix 1 cup of the all-purpose flour, 1 cup of the rye flour, yeast, oat bran, caraway seeds, salt, onion flakes, and Postum in the bowl of an electric mixer. Combine chocolate, molasses, vinegar, and oil in a medium-sized saucepan. Cook, stirring frequently, over low heat until chocolate melts. Remove from heat. Add water; stir well.

2. Add chocolate mixture to dry ingredients. Beat on medium speed until well combined, 2 minutes (or by hand, 3 minutes). Slowly beat in 1½ cups of the rye flour. Flour the work surface. Turn dough out onto floured work surface. Knead, adding remaining 1 cup rye flour. Knead in remaining all-purpose flour a little at a time. Work dough after each addition until it's no longer sticky. Cover with towel; let rest 15 minutes.

3. Knead dough on lightly floured surface until smooth and elastic, about 6 minutes. Grease a large bowl. Put dough into the bowl. Turn to oil top. Cover tightly with plastic wrap; let rise in a warm place until doubled in volume, about 1 hour.

4. Punch down dough; divide in half. Shape each piece into an oblong or round shape. Grease 2 baking sheets. Put dough onto the baking sheets. Cover with 2 towels; let rise until doubled in volume, about 45 minutes.

5. Heat oven to 375°F. Bake until bottoms sound hollow when tapped, about 45 minutes. Remove loaves from sheets; cool on wire racks. Dissolve cornstarch in cold water. Cook cornstarch mixture in a small saucepan until it becomes clear. Paint loaves with mixture as soon as they are out of oven. Cool completely on wire racks.

❧ NOTE: *Medium-grind rye flour can be found in health food stores. Postum is a hot breakfast cereal.*

NUTRITION INFORMATION PER SLICE:

95 calories	1.9 g fat	0.4 g saturated fat
16% calories from fat	0 mg cholesterol	145 mg sodium
19 g carbohydrate	2.6 g protein	2.2 g fiber

Polish Sauerkraut Rye Bread

PREPARATION TIME: 20 minutes
RISING TIME: 3 hours
BAKING TIME: 30 to 40 minutes
YIELD: 2 24-slice loaves

THIS FLAVORFUL ETHNIC bread recipe came from Tuzik's bakery in Chicago. In the *Tribune* test kitchen, the recipe was adapted to a food processor.

5½ cups all-purpose flour	¾ cup well-drained sauerkraut
1 cup rye flour	2 cups warm water (105 to 115°F)
2 tablespoons butter	2 teaspoons cornmeal
1 tablespoon salt	1 egg yolk
1 tablespoon sugar	1 tablespoon milk
1 ¼-ounce package active dry yeast	2 teaspoons caraway seeds

1. Put 4½ cups of the all-purpose flour into a food processor fitted with a metal blade. Add rye flour, butter, salt, sugar, and yeast; process until mixed. Add sauerkraut; process until mixed. With machine running, slowly pour warm water through the feed tube. Add remaining flour by tablespoons until dough no longer sticks to the sides of the bowl and begins to gather into a ball.

2. Oil a large bowl. Put dough into the bowl. Turn once to oil top. Let rise covered in a warm place until doubled in volume, about 1 hour. Punch down dough. Let rise covered a second time until doubled, about 1 hour.

3. Punch down dough; divide in half. Roll each piece into a 1-inch-thick rectangle. Roll up jelly roll fashion; tuck in short ends. Grease large baking sheets; sprinkle with cornmeal. Put loaves onto baking sheets. Let rise covered until almost doubled in volume, about 1 hour.

4. Heat oven to 400°F. Mix egg yolk and milk; lightly brush over loaves. Sprinkle with caraway seeds. Cut 4 to 5 slashes on top of each loaf using a sharp knife. Bake 20 minutes. Reduce oven temperature to 350°F; continue baking until the bottoms are golden and sound hollow when tapped, 10 to 15 more minutes. Remove from baking sheet; cool completely on wire rack.

NUTRITION INFORMATION PER SLICE:

90 calories	1 g fat	0.5 g saturated fat
11% calories from fat	8 mg cholesterol	220 mg sodium
18 g carbohydrate	2.4 g protein	1.1 g fiber

Homemade Rye Buns

PREPARATION TIME: 25 minutes
RISING TIME: 1½ hours
BAKING TIME: 15 minutes
YIELD: 16 buns

RYE FLOUR, WITH its slightly bitter taste, is what makes these buns a special treat. Check health food stores or specialty food shops for availability. These buns can be made small to use as dinner rolls or made large to use for hamburger or sandwich buns.

¾ cup milk	¾ cup warm water (105 to 115°F)
⅓ cup unsalted butter	1 cup rye flour
¼ cup sugar	3 to 3½ cups all-purpose flour
1 teaspoon salt	Melted butter
2 ¼-ounce packages active dry yeast	Poppy seeds

1. Heat milk to simmer in a small saucepan over medium heat. Stir in butter, sugar, and salt; cook until sugar dissolves and butter melts. Transfer to a large bowl; cool to lukewarm. Dissolve yeast in warm water in a small bowl; let stand until bubbly. Stir into milk mixture.

2. Stir in rye flour. Stir in 1 cup of the all-purpose flour until smooth. Gradually stir in remaining flour to form stiff dough. Lightly flour the work surface. Knead dough until smooth and elastic, about 10 minutes.

3. Grease a bowl. Put dough into bowl; turn to grease top. Cover with a towel. Let rise in a warm place until doubled in volume, about 1 hour.

4. Punch down dough. Roll on lightly floured surface to ¾-inch thickness. Grease baking sheets. Cut dough into 16 rounds with a 3½-inch cookie cutter. Put onto baking sheets. Brush each bun with melted butter; sprinkle with poppy seeds. Let rise covered until doubled in volume, about 30 minutes.

5. Heat oven to 425°F. Bake until golden brown and bottoms sound hollow when tapped, 10 to 14 minutes. Cool completely on wire racks.

NUTRITION INFORMATION PER BUN:

160 calories	4.4 g fat	2.6 g saturated fat
24% calories from fat	11 mg cholesterol	150 mg sodium
27 g carbohydrate	3.7 g protein	1.8 g fiber

Dutch Oven Rosemary Potato Rolls

PREPARATION TIME: 35 minutes

RISING TIME: 1 hour 45 minutes

COOKING TIME: 20 minutes

YIELD: 16 rolls

YES, VIRGINIA, THERE is a World Championship Dutch Oven Cookoff, and in 1997 writer Eleanor Ostman filed a report from Logan, Utah, that included this recipe. It is adapted from one by Dale and Judith Hamaker of Hinckley, Utah. Incidentally, Dutch ovens got their name from itinerant German traders who traveled colonial America selling cast-iron cookware. Paul Revere is credited with developing a flat lid that would hold embers in place for top-browning cookery. These rolls also can be baked in a deep, round pan in a 350°F oven.

Dough

1 cup milk

¼ cup sugar

¼ cup olive oil

¼ cup hot mashed potatoes

1 teaspoon crushed fresh rosemary

¼ teaspoon salt

1 scant teaspoon active dry yeast

2 tablespoons warm water
    (105 to 115°F)

3½ cups all-purpose flour

1 egg, beaten

1 scant teaspoon baking powder

¼ teaspoon baking soda

Topping

¼ cup melted butter

¾ cup grated Parmesan cheese

Crushed fresh rosemary, optional

1. To make dough, scald milk; add sugar, oil, potatoes, rosemary, and salt. Let cool until warm. Soften yeast in warm water. Add to milk mixture. Stir in about 1 cup of the flour; add egg, baking powder, and baking soda. Stir in enough additional flour to make a soft dough. Knead 2 minutes until smooth and pliable. Grease a bowl. Put dough into the bowl. Cover with a towel; let rise until doubled in bulk, 45 to 60 minutes.

2. Punch down dough. Divide dough into 16 pieces. Roll each piece into a ball. Oil a 12-inch Dutch oven well. To add topping, dip each roll in melted butter; roll in Parmesan cheese. Put rolls into the Dutch oven. Continue until all dough is used. Sprinkle with crushed rosemary if desired. Let rise until about doubled in volume, about 1 hour.

3. Prepare a charcoal grill. Spread coals. Place the covered Dutch oven on about 9 coals; place 17 coals on the lid. Bake until rolls are golden brown, 20 to 30 minutes. Garnish with crushed rosemary if desired.

NUTRITION INFORMATION PER ROLL:

205 calories	9 g fat	3.5 g saturated fat
38% calories from fat	25 mg cholesterol	225 mg sodium
26 g carbohydrate	6 g protein	0.9 g fiber

Challah Bread

PREPARATION TIME: 15 minutes
RISING TIME: 2 to 3 hours
BAKING TIME: 30 minutes
YIELD: 2 18-slice loaves

A ROSH HASHANAH and Yom Kippur favorite, challah is a braided bread with a hint of sweetness to it. This recipe was contributed to our "You're the Cook" column by reader Agnes Ellegant. Leftover challah makes perfect breakfast toast.

1¾ cups warm water (105 to 115°F)	2 large eggs, beaten
2 ¼-ounce packages active dry yeast	2 teaspoons vanilla extract
	1 teaspoon salt
½ cup vegetable oil	6 to 7 cups sifted all-purpose flour
¼ cup sugar	1 large egg yolk, beaten

1. Dissolve yeast in ¼ cup of the water in a small bowl; let stand until bubbly, about 5 minutes.

2. Mix remaining 1½ cups water, oil, and sugar in a large bowl. Stir in 2 beaten eggs, vanilla, salt, and dissolved yeast. Gradually stir in flour to form a stiff dough. Lightly flour the work surface. Knead dough, adding more flour as needed, until smooth and elastic, about 10 minutes.

3. Grease a large bowl. Put dough into the bowl; turn to grease top. Cover loosely with a damp towel. Let rise in a warm place until doubled in volume, 1 to 1½ hours.

4. Punch down dough; divide in half. Divide half into 3 pieces; roll each piece into a long rope. Braid the 3 ropes together; tuck ends under. Grease 2 9″ × 5″ loaf pans and line bottoms and sides with waxed paper. Put loaf into a pan; brush with egg yolk. Repeat with other half of dough. Let rise covered until doubled in volume, 1 to 1½ hours.

➤

5. Heat oven to 350°F. Bake until golden and bottoms sound hollow when tapped, 30 to 35 minutes. Remove loaves from pans immediately; cool completely on wire racks.

NUTRITION INFORMATION PER SLICE:

115 calories	3.7 g fat	0.6 g saturated fat
29% calories from fat	18 mg cholesterol	70 mg sodium
18 g carbohydrate	2.7 g protein	0.6 g fiber

Russian Easter Bread (Kulich)

PREPARATION TIME: 45 minutes
RESTING TIME: 12 hours
RISING TIME: 4 hours
BAKING TIME: 27 to 37 minutes
YIELD: 3 12-slice loaves or 2 18-slice loaves

FOR PEOPLE OF the Russian Orthodox faith, the sweet, saffron scent of bread baking and other ritual food preparations signal the approach of Easter, their most important religious holiday. This unusual bread, adapted from a recipe by Marie Konon, is baked in coffee cans. You can use three 1-pound-10-ounce cans or two 3-pound cans. Make sure you remove all the coffee and wash them well. Saffron can be purchased in vials in some supermarket spice sections or at bulk food stores.

2 cups milk
½ teaspoon saffron threads
2 .6-ounce yeast cakes *or* 2
    tablespoons active dry yeast
7 cups all-purpose flour or more
    as needed
1 cup golden raisins
½ cup (1 stick) unsalted butter,
    melted and cooled

2 large eggs
3 egg yolks
1 tablespoon vanilla extract
1 teaspoon salt
Fine bread crumbs

Glaze
1 cup sifted confectioners' sugar
5 teaspoons lemon juice

1. Scald milk with saffron in a small saucepan over high heat. Remove from heat; cool to 105 to 115°F on an instant-reading thermometer. Add yeast; stir until dissolved. Pour into a large bowl. Stir in 3 cups of the flour; mix well. Cover loosely with waxed paper and a kitchen towel. Let rest at room temperature 12 hours.

2. Add raisins, butter, eggs, egg yolks, vanilla, and salt and enough of the remaining flour to form a soft, light dough. Allow to rise covered in warm place until doubled in size, 1½ to 2 hours.

3. Lightly flour the work surface. Punch dough down; turn out onto work surface. Knead, adding just enough flour to prevent sticking, until dough is smooth and elastic, 8 to 10 minutes. Divide dough into halves or thirds; grease coffee cans and sprinkle them with fine bread crumbs. Put dough into cans. Cover; allow to rise until more than doubled in size, about 2 hours.

4. Heat oven to 350°F. Bake bread 7 minutes. Reduce temperature to 300°F; continue baking until golden brown, 20 to 25 minutes for small cans and 30 to 35 minutes for large. Cool in cans 5 minutes; remove breads to cooling rack. To make glaze, combine confectioners' sugar and lemon juice. Spoon over cooled bread.

NUTRITION INFORMATION PER SLICE:

155 calories	3.8 g fat	2 g saturated fat
22% calories from fat	35 mg cholesterol	75 mg sodium
26 g carbohydrate	3.9 g protein	0.9 g fiber

Classic German Stollen

SOAKING TIME: 24 hours
PREPARATION TIME: 1½ hours
RISING TIME: About 6 hours
BAKING TIME: 30 minutes
STANDING TIME: 8 to 12 hours
YIELD: 3 12-slice loaves

LUTZ OLKIEWICZ PRESIDED over the Drake Hotel's pastries for twenty-five years, six days a week. The stollen he made there is legendary in Chicago. Its deep flavor comes from soaking the fruit in rum, using the very finest ingredients, and aging the stollen in the freezer. Even though you may be tempted to forego brushing the baked stollen with all that butter, don't. Not only does it add flavor and act as a preservative, but it is essential to the finished texture. You can eat the stollen immediately, but after storage in the refrigerator or freezer, it gets even better. It will keep up to a year if wrapped twice and stored in a heavy plastic freezer bag with a twister seal to secure.

Fruit Mixture
2¼ cups golden raisins
½ cup candied citron, chopped
½ cup candied orange rind, chopped
½ cup good-quality dark rum

Sponge
4 ¼-ounce packages active dry yeast
1½ cups milk, scalded, cooled to 105 to 115°F
1¾ cups bread flour

➤

Base Dough

2¾ cups (5½ sticks) unsalted
   butter, softened
½ cup sugar
1 teaspoon salt
1 teaspoon vanilla extract
½ teaspoon almond extract
Zest of 2 lemons, grated
6¾ cups bread flour
2½ cups sliced blanched almonds

Topping

2 cups (4 sticks) unsalted butter,
   melted, strained through
   cheesecloth
1 12-ounce jar apricot preserves
Vanilla extract
½ cup sugar
Confectioners' sugar

1. Put raisins, citron, orange rind, and rum into a large nonreactive bowl. Cover; let stand, stirring occasionally, up to 24 hours.

2. To make the sponge, put yeast in a large bowl. Add cooled milk; stir until smooth. Stir in 1¾ cups flour until smooth. Mixture should be about the consistency of thin mashed potatoes. Sprinkle the top with a little flour. Let rise in a warm place until 1½ times its original volume and flour on the surface develops tracks and cracks, 10 to 15 minutes. (If dough rises too much, it will collapse when touched on the top. If this happens, don't use it; the dough will have become too sour and strong.)

3. To make base dough, beat butter in a large mixer bowl until fluffy. Beat in sugar, salt, vanilla, almond extract, and lemon rind until creamy. Gradually beat in 6 cups of the flour. Add risen sponge to base dough, mixing well using your hands, a wooden spoon, or the paddle or dough hook of a heavy-duty electric mixer.

4. Flour the work surface; turn dough out onto it. Knead in remaining ¾ cup flour to form a soft dough. Knead dough about 8 times. Grease a large bowl; put dough into the bowl. Sprinkle top lightly with flour. Let rise covered in a warm place until doubled in volume, 2 to 3 hours.

5. Knead in fruit mixture and almonds on the lightly floured surface until well mixed. Put into a large bowl; cover. Let rise a second time until doubled in volume, 2 to 3 hours.

6. Punch down dough; divide into 3 pieces. Lightly press 1 piece on the floured surface into a thick rectangle. Repeat with 2 remaining pieces. Cover; let rest about 10 minutes. Make a lengthwise indentation down the center of 1 rectangle with your knuckles. Press a round stick of wood about the thickness of a broom handle and about 20 inches long into indentation. Remove; roll dough so it resembles a partly unrolled piece of paper, with a flat center and rolls on either side. One of the rolls should be twice as full as the other. Fold stollen in half so the two rolls are on top of each other. Repeat with 2 remaining pieces.

7. Lightly grease 3 baking sheets. Transfer each stollen to a baking sheet. Cover; let rise until 1½ times in volume, not more.

8. Heat oven to 375°F. Bake until golden and a wooden pick inserted in the center comes out dry, about 30 minutes. Let stollen sit on baking sheets on wire racks about 15 minutes. Remove and discard any burned raisins or nuts. Top 3 more baking sheets with parchment. Carefully transfer stollen to parchment-topped baking sheets. Liberally brush all surfaces of stollen 3 times with hot butter. Continue to coat stollen with butter until all of butter is used. Cover stollen tightly. Let rest 8 to 12 hours in a cool place.

9. Heat apricot preserves in a small saucepan to boil; push though a fine-mesh sieve into a small bowl. Lightly brush preserves over all surfaces of stollen. Cool. Put granulated sugar into a small bowl; sprinkle a few drops of vanilla extract over sugar. Work vanilla into sugar using your hands to a streusel-like consistency. Cover cooled stollen with sugar mixture; dust thickly with confectioners' sugar.

10. Store stollen in plastic bags in the refrigerator if you're using them within 1 week. If not, wrap stollen individually in plastic wrap; then wrap again in foil. Put stollen into plastic bags; seal. Freeze at least 1 week and up to 1 year (stollen improves with age).

NUTRITION INFORMATION PER SLICE:

460 calories	28 g fat	16 g saturated fat
54% calories from fat	65 mg cholesterol	90 mg sodium
48 g carbohydrate	6 g protein	2.3 g fiber

Cardamom Coffee Braid

PREPARATION TIME: 30 minutes
RISING TIME: 1 hour 30 minutes
COOKING TIME: 25 minutes
YIELD: 3 16-slice loaves

CECELIA LARSON OF Chicago sent a recipe for Cardamom Coffee Braid. Published in an October 1996 "You're the Cook" column, it became one of that year's top ten recipes.

6½ to 7 cups all-purpose flour	1 to 2 teaspoons ground cardamom
2 ¼-ounce packages instant dry yeast	2 cups milk
	1 cup (2 sticks) butter, softened
1 cup sugar	3 eggs
2 teaspoons salt	3 tablespoons sliced almonds
	or sugar

➤

1. Combine 2½ cups of the flour, yeast, sugar, salt, and cardamom in an electric mixer bowl. Heat milk and butter in a 1-quart saucepan until warm (120 to 130°F; butter does not have to be completely melted). Add to flour mixture.

2. Add 2 of the eggs; beat on low speed to moisten. Increase speed to medium; beat 3 minutes. Gradually stir in enough flour by hand to make a soft dough. Flour the work surface. Knead dough on the work surface until smooth and elastic, 5 to 8 minutes, adding flour as needed. Grease a bowl. Place dough in the bowl, turning to grease the top. Cover; let rise in a warm place until light and doubled in size, about 1 hour.

3. Punch dough down; cover. Allow dough to rest 10 minutes. Divide into thirds; divide each third into 3 equal-sized pieces. Roll each piece into a 16-inch rope on the lightly floured surface. Grease a cookie sheet; place pieces on the cookie sheet. Loosely braid 3 of the ropes starting from the center of the bread. Pinch ends; tuck under to seal. Repeat twice with remaining dough. Cover; let rise in warm place until almost doubled, 20 to 30 minutes.

4. Heat oven to 350°F. Lightly beat remaining egg. Gently brush braids with beaten egg; sprinkle with almonds or sugar. Bake until golden brown, 20 to 25 minutes. Transfer to racks to cool.

NUTRITION INFORMATION PER SLICE:

135 calories	4.7 g fat	2.7 g saturated fat
34% calories from fat	25 mg cholesterol	145 mg sodium
18 g carbohydrate	2.7 g protein	0.6 g fiber

Honey Nut Orange Bread

PREPARATION TIME: 35 minutes

COOKING TIME: 1 hour

YIELD: 1 10-inch, 16-slice loaf

KAREN REAGAN'S HONEY Nut Orange Bread was the grand champion recipe in the Illinois State Fair Blue Ribbon Culinary Contest in 1993. The Kinmundy, Illinois, resident created a light and fluffy breakfast bread that the "Good Eating" staff voted one of the best recipes of the year.

Bread
1 cup whole milk
¼ cup water

½ cup (1 stick) plus 2 tablespoons
  unsalted butter
4½ cups all-purpose flour or more
  as needed

2 ¼-ounce packages active dry
   yeast

¼ cup sugar

2 teaspoons salt

2 large eggs, lightly beaten

Honey Filling

½ cup honey plus more for top of
   bread

¼ cup sugar

Zest of 1 orange, grated

1 tablespoon orange juice

1 tablespoon melted unsalted butter

1 teaspoon cinnamon

⅓ cup finely chopped pecans *or*
   almonds

1. To make bread, heat milk, water, and ½ cup butter until very warm (125 to 130°F). Mix 4 cups flour, yeast, sugar, and salt in a large bowl. Stir milk mixture into flour mixture; add eggs. Mix well, adding enough flour to make a soft but manageable dough. Knead until smooth and elastic, 8 to 10 minutes. Cover dough; let rest 10 minutes. To make honey filling, mix ½ cup honey, sugar, orange zest, orange juice, butter, cinnamon, and pecans; set aside.

2. Divide dough in half; cover one half. Flour a board. Roll the uncovered half on the board into a 16″ × 12″ rectangle. Melt remaining 2 tablespoons butter. Brush top of dough with melted butter; spread with half of the honey filling. Repeat with remaining half. Roll each half in jelly roll fashion, starting at one long side; cut into 1-inch slices. Grease a 10-inch tube pan well. Make one layer of slices in the pan, placing the slices flat in the pan barely touching the slices. Add another layer, arranging slices so the spirals aren't directly on top of one another. Cover with a damp cloth; let rise in a warm spot until doubled, about 1 hour.

3. Heat oven to 350°F. If the pan has a removable bottom, wrap its base in aluminum foil. Bake bread until well browned, 50 to 60 minutes. Cool 5 minutes; loosen from sides of pan; transfer to a cooling rack. Brush top and sides lightly with honey; cool completely before serving.

NUTRITION INFORMATION PER SLICE:

295 calories	11 g fat	6 g saturated fat
34% calories from fat	50 mg cholesterol	310 mg sodium
44 g carbohydrate	6 g protein	1.5 g fiber

Giant Cinnamon Rolls

PREPARATION TIME: 45 minutes
RISING TIME: About 2 hours
BAKING TIME: 25 minutes
YIELD: 6 rolls

THESE ROLLS WILL certainly draw a crowd. They were created in the *Tribune* test kitchen to duplicate those sold at the popular cinnamon roll shops around town.

Dough
4 cups all-purpose flour or more as needed
1 ¼-ounce package active dry yeast
1¼ cups milk
¼ cup granulated sugar
¼ cup unsalted butter
1 teaspoon salt
1 large egg

Cinnamon Filling
¼ cup granulated sugar
2 tablespoons packed dark brown sugar
1 tablespoon cinnamon
5 tablespoons butter, melted

Glaze
1 cup confectioners' sugar, sifted
½ teaspoon vanilla extract
Half-and-half *or* milk

1. To make dough, mix 1½ cups of the flour and yeast in the large bowl of an electric mixer. Heat milk, ¼ cup sugar, ¼ cup butter, and salt in a small saucepan, stirring constantly, just until warm (115 to 120°F). Add to yeast mixture; add egg. Beat at low speed 30 seconds; scrape the sides of the bowl. Beat at high speed 3 minutes. Stir in enough remaining flour with a wooden spoon to form soft dough.

2. Lightly flour the work surface. Turn dough out onto the surface; knead until smooth and elastic, about 8 minutes. Shape into a ball. Lightly grease a bowl. Put dough into bowl; turn once to grease top. Let rise covered in a warm place until doubled in volume, 1½ to 2 hours. Punch dough down; turn out onto the floured surface. Cover; let rest 10 minutes.

3. To make cinnamon filling, mix granulated sugar, brown sugar, and cinnamon. Brush a 9-inch round cake pan at least 2 inches deep with 1 tablespoon of the melted butter.

4. Roll dough on a lightly floured surface into a thin 20″ × 12″ rectangle. Brush dough generously with melted butter. Sprinkle with cinnamon mixture. Roll up jelly roll fashion starting at one 12-inch end. You should end up with a fat log that is 12 inches in length.

5. Cut rolls at 2-inch intervals using a piece of thread placed under rolled dough and pulled up and around sides. Crisscross thread at the top, then pull quickly. Put rolls cut side up (so the cinnamon spiral shows) into the prepared cake pan. Drizzle any remaining melted butter over all. Let rise covered in a warm place 20 minutes.

6. Heat oven to 375°F. Bake until puffed and golden brown, 25 to 30 minutes. Cool in pan 10 minutes. Invert pan over a serving platter.

7. To make glaze, mix confectioners' sugar, vanilla extract, and enough half-and-half to make a medium-thick glaze. Drizzle rolls with glaze. Serve warm.

NUTRITION INFORMATION PER ROLL:

645 calories	20 g fat	12 g saturated fat
28% calories from fat	85 mg cholesterol	525 mg sodium
105 g carbohydrate	12 g protein	3.1 g fiber

Sticky Caramel Pecan Rolls

PREPARATION TIME: 1 hour
RISING TIME: 1½ plus 8 to 12 hours
BAKING TIME: 35 minutes
YIELD: 12 rolls

IF IT'S TOTALLY self-indulgent, incredibly rich, and unbelievably delicious breakfast rolls you want, then these caramel rolls from former test kitchen director JeanMarie Brownson are for you. For Sunday brunch, start the dough the night before so the rolls can be baked fresh the next morning. Or, skip the refrigerator rising time and make the rolls the same day. Simply punch the dough down after the first rising and let it rise a second time in a warm place until doubled in volume, about one hour. Then proceed as directed.

½ cup milk	1 whole large egg
¼ cup granulated sugar	1 large egg yolk
¾ teaspoon salt	4 cups sifted all-purpose flour
1 cup (2 sticks) unsalted butter	3 tablespoons water
½ cup warm water (105 to 115°F)	1 cup packed dark brown sugar
1 ¼-ounce package active dry yeast	1½ cups pecan halves

►

Filling   ½ cup chopped pecans
¼ cup melted butter   1 teaspoon cinnamon
½ cup packed dark brown sugar

1. Combine milk, granulated sugar, salt, and 6 tablespoons of the butter in a small saucepan. Cook until sugar dissolves, about 5 minutes. Remove from heat; cool to warm.

2. Put water and yeast into a large bowl. Let stand until bubbly. Stir in butter mixture, egg, egg yolk, and 2 cups of the flour until smooth. Stir in remaining flour as needed to form a soft dough. Lightly flour the work surface. Knead dough until smooth and elastic, about 10 minutes.

3. Butter a large bowl well. Put dough into bowl; turn once to butter top. Let rise covered in a warm place until doubled in volume, about 1 hour. Punch down dough. Refrigerate dough covered well 8 to 12 hours (overnight). Let dough sit in a warm place about 30 minutes before shaping.

4. Melt the remaining butter. Mix 1½ tablespoons water, 5 tablespoons of the melted butter, and ½ cup dark brown sugar in the bottom of a 9-inch round cake pan or cast-iron skillet. Sprinkle ¾ cup pecan halves over mixture. Repeat with a second cake pan.

5. Roll dough on a lightly floured surface into an 18″ × 12″ rectangle. To add filling, brush dough with ¼ cup melted butter. Sprinkle with ½ cup dark brown sugar, ½ cup chopped pecans, and 1 teaspoon cinnamon.

6. Roll up dough jelly roll fashion to end up with an 18-inch-long roll. Cut into 12 rolls using a piece of thread placed under the rolled dough and pulled up and around sides. Crisscross the thread at the top, then pull quickly. Put 6 rolls cut sides facing up and down in each prepared cake pan. Cover; let rise in a warm place until doubled in volume, about 30 minutes.

7. Heat oven to 350°F. Bake rolls until golden and puffed, 35 to 40 minutes. Let cool in pan 5 minutes. Then invert onto a serving platter. Cool to warm.

NUTRITION INFORMATION PER ROLL:

580 calories	33 g fat	13 g saturated fat
50% calories from fat	85 mg cholesterol	210 mg sodium
67 g carbohydrate	7 g protein	2.8 g fiber

Hot Cross Buns

PREPARATION TIME: 45 minutes
RISING TIME: About 3 hours
BAKING TIME: 15 to 20 minutes
YIELD: 20 buns

HERE'S A DELICIOUS recipe for hot cross buns, which were thought to have curative powers in pagan times. They are best served warm so the fruit and spice flavors come through.

¼ cup warm water (105 to 115°F)
1 ¼-ounce package active dry yeast
Pinch sugar
¾ cup plain yogurt, at room temperature
⅓ cup sugar
1 teaspoon salt
¼ cup (½ stick) butter, softened
2 large eggs
½ cup whole wheat flour
1 teaspoon cinnamon
½ teaspoon ground nutmeg

¼ teaspoon ground cardamom
3 cups all-purpose flour
½ cup currants
⅓ cup chopped crystallized ginger
¼ cup chopped pitted prunes
1 large egg yolk
2 tablespoons whipping cream
   or milk

Glaze
1½ cups confectioners' sugar
2 to 3 tablespoons fresh lemon juice

1. Stir together water, yeast, and pinch of sugar in a large bowl. Let stand until bubbly, about 5 minutes. Combine yogurt, ⅓ cup sugar, salt, butter, and eggs in a small bowl; mix well. Stir into yeast mixture.

2. Stir in whole wheat flour, cinnamon, nutmeg, and cardamom. Gradually stir in enough all-purpose flour to form a soft, slightly sticky dough. Lightly flour the work surface. Knead dough until smooth and elastic, about 10 minutes. Grease a large bowl. Put dough into the bowl. Turn once to oil top. Cover; let rise in a warm place until doubled in volume, about 1½ hours.

3. Punch down dough. Knead in currants, ginger, and prunes until evenly dispersed throughout. Return to bowl. Cover; let rise a second time until doubled in volume, about 1 hour.

4. Punch down dough; turn out onto the floured surface. Pat dough out to ½-inch thickness. Lightly flour a round cutter. Cut dough about 2½ inches in diameter. Grease baking sheets. Put buns onto baking sheets about 1 inch apart. Reroll and cut scraps. Let rise until doubled in volume, about 30 minutes.

►

5. Heat oven to 375°F. Flour scissors. Just before baking, use scissors to snip an X on top of each bun. Beat egg yolk and whipping cream together in a small bowl; brush lightly over bun tops. Bake until golden, about 15 minutes. Cool on wire racks until warm.

6. To make glaze, stir together confectioners' sugar and lemon juice in a small bowl to a thick consistency. Drizzle over each bun. Serve warm.

NUTRITION INFORMATION PER BUN:

185 calories	4 g fat	2.2 g saturated fat
19% calories from fat	40 mg cholesterol	155 mg sodium
34 g carbohydrate	4 g protein	1.4 g fiber

Irish Soda Bread

PREPARATION TIME: 20 minutes

BAKING TIME: 1 hour

YIELD: 2 round, 16-slice loaves

THIS IRISH RECIPE is an adaptation of one used at Winston's, a delightful butcher-grocery-bakery in Chicago that stocks a variety of British foodstuffs. Dark raisins can be substituted for golden raisins.

4 cups all-purpose flour plus more as needed	1 teaspoon salt
⅔ cup sugar	1½ cups golden raisins *or* currants
1 tablespoon baking powder	1¾ cups buttermilk
1 teaspoon baking soda	2 large eggs, beaten well
	2 tablespoons butter, melted

1. Heat oven to 350°F. Whisk together flour, sugar, baking powder, baking soda, and salt in a large bowl. Stir in raisins. Add buttermilk, eggs, and butter; mix just to moisten dry ingredients (dough will be sticky). Do not overmix.

2. Divide dough in half. Lightly flour the work surface. Shape each half into round loaves. Grease baking sheets; put loaves onto baking sheets. Cut an X on top of each; sprinkle with flour. Bake until a wooden pick inserted in the center comes out clean, about 1 hour. Cool completely on a wire rack.

NUTRITION INFORMATION PER SLICE:

225 calories	2.7 g fat	1.3 g saturated fat
10% calories from fat	31 mg cholesterol	370 mg sodium
46 g carbohydrate	5 g protein	1.5 g fiber

Southern Biscuits

PREPARATION TIME: 15 minutes
COOKING TIME: 20 minutes
YIELD: 14 biscuits

TENDER, FLAKY BISCUITS are the pride of Southern cooks. This recipe is from the Flying Biscuit Café in Atlanta, which goes through about 1,200 biscuits, hot from the oven, each weekend morning. The recipe is adapted from the *Flying Biscuit Cookbook* (Longstreet Press). Spread butter, honey, or a spoonful of sausage gravy over warm biscuits, or use them as the base for strawberry shortcake.

3 cups flour
3 tablespoons plus 1½ teaspoons sugar
1 tablespoon plus 1½ teaspoons baking powder
¾ teaspoon salt
6 tablespoons unsalted butter, cut into pieces
⅔ cup plus 2 tablespoons half-and-half
⅔ cup whipping cream

1. Heat oven to 375°F. Combine flour, 2 tablespoons plus 1½ teaspoons of the sugar, baking powder, and salt in a large bowl. Cut butter into flour mixture, using pastry blender or two knives, until it resembles coarse meal. Make well in center of flour; add ⅔ cup of the half-and-half and cream. Mix until dough just begins to form a ball.

2. Turn dough out onto lightly floured work surface; knead 2 or 3 times to form a ball. Do not overwork dough. Roll dough to ¾-inch thickness. Dip 2½-inch biscuit cutter in flour; cut out biscuits. Scraps can be gathered and rerolled one time.

3. Place biscuits on greased or parchment-lined baking sheet, leaving ¼-inch space. Brush tops with remaining 2 tablespoons half-and-half; sprinkle with remaining 1 tablespoon sugar. Bake until lightly browned, about 20 minutes.

NUTRITION INFORMATION PER BISCUIT:

210 calories
47% calories from fat
25 g carbohydrate
11 g fat
35 mg cholesterol
3.5 g protein
7 g saturated fat
290 mg sodium
1 g fiber

Southern-Style Corn Bread

PREPARATION TIME: 15 minutes

COOKING TIME: 20 minutes

YIELD: 6 servings

FREELANCE WRITER TRACY Poe traced the history of soul food in Chicago for a "Good Eating" article celebrating Black History Month. This was one of the traditional recipes included.

1 cup cornmeal
1 cup all-purpose flour
¼ cup sugar
2 teaspoons baking powder
1 teaspoon salt

¾ cup milk
¼ cup plus 1 tablespoon vegetable oil
2 large eggs, slightly beaten
Honey, softened butter, *or* molasses, optional

1. Heat oven to 450°F. Heat an 8-inch cast-iron skillet or a heavy ovenproof skillet in the oven.

2. Sift together cornmeal, flour, sugar, baking powder, and salt in a medium-sized bowl. Combine milk, ¼ cup of the oil, and eggs in a separate bowl. Add wet ingredients to dry; stir until just combined.

3. Add remaining tablespoon oil to the heated skillet; pour in batter. Bake until a wooden pick inserted in the center comes out clean, about 20 minutes.

4. Place skillet on a wire rack; cool 5 minutes. Run a knife around the edge to loosen. Place a large plate or a bread board on the top of the skillet; flip over quickly. Serve with honey, butter, or molasses if desired.

NUTRITION INFORMATION PER SERVING:

335 calories
38% calories from fat
44 g carbohydrate

14 g fat
75 mg cholesterol
7 g protein

2.4 g saturated fat
585 mg sodium
2.3 g fiber

Jalapeño Corn Muffins

PREPARATION TIME: 5 minutes
COOKING TIME: 15 minutes
YIELD: 20 mini muffins

THESE SPICY MUFFINS were presented as part of a "Fast Food" menu that featured Creole gumbo. The shortcut here is to use a packaged muffin mix and jazz it up.

1 7½-ounce package corn muffin
   mix (see Note)
½ cup cream-style corn

⅓ cup half-and-half
½ to 1 jalapeño, minced

1. Heat oven to 400°F. Line the cups of a 20–mini muffin tin with paper liners or oil the cups lightly.
2. Mix muffin mix, corn, half-and-half, and jalapeño in a medium-sized bowl. Spoon batter into muffin cups, filling them ¾ full. Bake until set, about 15 minutes.

❧ NOTE: *This recipe was developed using a muffin mix that calls only for adding milk or water. The muffins can also be baked in a regular muffin tin. Increase baking time to 20 minutes.*

NUTRITION INFORMATION PER MUFFIN:

55 calories	1.8 g fat	0.6 g saturated fat
29% calories from fat	2 mg cholesterol	140 mg sodium
9 g carbohydrate	1 g protein	0.8 g fiber

Cheddar-Onion Corn Muffins

PREPARATION TIME: 15 minutes
BAKING TIME: 30 minutes
YIELD: 18 muffins

SHARP CHEDDAR CHEESE and onion add interest and flavor to these basic corn muffins from chef Charlie Orr, owner of the Maple Tree Inn in Chicago. The muffins taste best when served warm with a little softened butter.

1½ cups flour
1 cup yellow cornmeal
1 tablespoon plus 1½ teaspoons
   baking powder
1 tablespoon sugar
½ teaspoon salt

1 cup shredded sharp cheddar
   cheese
1 medium-sized onion, chopped
2 large eggs, lightly beaten
1½ cups milk
¼ cup (½ stick) butter, melted

➤

1. Heat oven to 350°F. Stir together flour, cornmeal, baking powder, sugar, and salt in a large bowl. Add cheese and onion; mix well. Add eggs, milk, and butter; stir just until dry ingredients are moistened. Do not overmix.

2. Lightly grease the cups of muffin tins. Spoon into muffin tin cups, filling ⅔ full. Bake until puffed and golden, about 30 minutes. Cool on a wire rack.

NUTRITION INFORMATION PER MUFFIN:

138 calories	6 g fat	3.4 g saturated fat
38% calories from fat	40 mg cholesterol	270 mg sodium
17 g carbohydrate	4.8 g protein	1 g fiber

Sweet Potato Hush Puppies

PREPARATION TIME: 10 minutes

COOKING TIME: 3 minutes per batch

YIELD: 6 servings

FOR A FLAVORFUL twist on hush puppies, we add two cups of mashed sweet potatoes to the cornmeal batter of this recipe along with onions and seasonings. Use a light hand when stirring; overmixing will give the hush puppies a tough texture. Serve these with fried catfish.

3 large eggs, lightly beaten
1 cup buttermilk
2 large sweet potatoes, cooked, peeled, and mashed
2 green onions, chopped
1½ cups stone-ground yellow cornmeal

1½ cups all-purpose flour
1 tablespoon sugar
2 teaspoons baking powder
1 teaspoon salt
Vegetable oil

1. Whisk together eggs and buttermilk in a medium-sized bowl. Stir in sweet potatoes and onions.

2. Combine cornmeal, flour, sugar, baking powder, and salt in a large bowl. Make a well in the center of dry ingredients. Pour egg mixture into well. Stir with a fork just enough to moisten dry ingredients. Do not overmix.

3. Pour oil to a depth of about 2½ inches in a deep-fryer or Dutch oven. Heat oil to 350°F. Carefully drop batter by tablespoons into hot oil. Do not crowd. Fry, turning hush puppies with a slotted spoon, until dark golden brown on all sides and cooked through, about 3 minutes. Remove to a paper towel to drain. Cover lightly with foil to keep warm. Repeat with remaining batter.

NUTRITION INFORMATION PER SERVING:

445 calories	13 g fat	2.3 g saturated fat
26% calories from fat	105 mg cholesterol	635 mg sodium
70 g carbohydrate	12 g protein	5 g fiber

Rich Scones

PREPARATION TIME: 20 minutes

BAKING TIME: 15 minutes

YIELD: 12 scones

WHEN THE CARLTON Tower in London was selected in 1984 as the best British tea place, we had to have their recipe for scones. The secret for these rich biscuits is to use unsalted butter, not margarine. Do not overmix the ingredients or you'll be serving something similar to hockey pucks.

2 cups all-purpose flour	⅓ cup currants
⅓ cup sugar	2 large eggs
1½ teaspoons baking powder	½ cup milk
¼ cup (½ stick) chilled unsalted butter, cut into pieces	Unsalted butter, whipped cream, *or* jam

1. Heat oven to 450°F. Whisk together flour, sugar, and baking powder in a large bowl. Cut in butter using a pastry blender or two knives until mixture resembles coarse crumbs. Stir in currants. Whisk 1 egg and milk together in a small bowl. Stir egg mixture into flour mixture with a large fork just until soft dough forms.

2. Lightly flour the work surface and a biscuit cutter. Turn dough out onto the surface; pat into a ½-inch-thick circle. Cut dough into 2½-inch rounds using the floured biscuit cutter. Grease a baking sheet; put scones onto the baking sheet.

3. Beat remaining egg; brush over scones. Bake scones until they're puffed and tops are golden, about 15 minutes. Cool on a wire rack. Serve warm with unsalted butter, whipped cream, or jam.

➤

❧ NOTE: *As with most quick breads, try not to overmix the dough, which causes toughness. Just combine ingredients until free of lumps. Brush tops twice with eggs for a beautiful shine.*

NUTRITION INFORMATION PER SCONE:

151 calories	5 g fat	2.8 g saturated fat
30% calories from fat	47 mg cholesterol	78 mg sodium
23 g carbohydrate	4 g protein	0.7 g fiber

Pineapple-Macadamia Scones

PREPARATION TIME: 20 minutes

BAKING TIME: 15 to 18 minutes

YIELD: 8 scones

THESE SWEET HAWAIIAN scones are studded with candied pineapple and macadamia nuts. Instead of cutting them into rounds before baking, cut these into pie-shaped wedges.

1 3½-ounce jar macadamia nuts, chopped coarse
2 cups all-purpose flour
2 teaspoons sugar plus more for topping
1 teaspoon cream of tartar
1 teaspoon baking soda
½ teaspoon salt
½ cup (1 stick) cold unsalted butter, cut into pieces
¾ cup buttermilk
¼ cup dark rum
½ cup coarsely chopped candied pineapple
2 tablespoons milk

1. Heat oven to 400°F. Heat water in a small saucepan to a boil; add nuts. Cook 10 seconds. Drain; pat dry on paper towels.

2. Sift flour, 2 teaspoons of the sugar, cream of tartar, baking soda, and salt into a large bowl. Cut in butter using a pastry blender or two knives until the mixture resembles coarse crumbs. Stir in buttermilk and rum just until soft dough forms. Stir in nuts and candied pineapple. Do not overmix.

3. Lightly flour the work surface. Turn dough out onto the surface; divide in half. Pat each half into a ¾-inch-thick circle. Cut each half into quarters. Grease a baking sheet; put scones onto the baking sheet.

4. Brush tops with milk; sprinkle lightly with sugar. Bake until golden, 15 to 18 minutes. Cool on a wire rack. Serve warm.

NUTRITION INFORMATION PER SCONE:

340 calories	21 g fat	9 g saturated fat
55% calories from fat	32 mg cholesterol	332 mg sodium
33 g carbohydrate	5 g protein	2 g fiber

Apple Cider Doughnuts

PREPARATION TIME: 15 minutes
CHILLING TIME: 15 minutes
FRYING TIME: 15 minutes
YIELD: 10 doughnuts

LIGHT, SLIGHTLY SWEET and with a delicate taste of apple, these glazed, walnut-laden doughnuts won't hang around in the kitchen for long. Pay close attention to the temperature of the oil while frying. Oil that is too hot will result in undercooked doughnuts, and oil that is too cool will produce greasy ones.

Doughnuts
2 cups flour
3½ teaspoons baking powder
¾ teaspoon salt
½ teaspoon ground nutmeg
1 large egg
¼ cup vegetable shortening
¼ cup sugar

1¼ cups buttermilk
½ cup chopped walnuts
Oil for deep-frying

Apple Cider Glaze
1 pound confectioners' sugar, sifted
6 tablespoons unsweetened apple
    cider *or* juice

1. Whisk together flour, baking powder, salt, and nutmeg in large bowl. Beat egg, shortening, and sugar in the mixer bowl of an electric mixer until smooth. Alternately beat in flour mixture and buttermilk, beating well after each addition. Dough should be moderately stiff. Stir in walnuts by hand. Refrigerate dough about 15 minutes.

2. Heat oil in deep-fryer or large, deep saucepan to 375°F. Put dough into doughnut maker; press a few doughnuts at a time into hot oil. Cook, turning frequently, until golden brown, 3 to 5 minutes. Remove with slotted spoon. Drain on wire rack set over paper towels.

►

3. Mix confectioners' sugar with enough of the apple cider to make a thin smooth glaze. Dip one doughnut at a time into glaze; allow excess to drip off. Put onto rack set over baking sheet; let stand until glaze is set.

NUTRITION INFORMATION PER DOUGHNUT:

430 calories	14 g fat	2.5 g saturated fat
29% calories from fat	22 mg cholesterol	385 mg sodium
72 g carbohydrate	6 g protein	1 g fiber

Orange-Date Coffee Bread

PREPARATION TIME: 25 minutes
COOKING TIME: 40 minutes
YIELD: 12 servings

GOOD OR "PROTECTIVE" fats such as canola oil can improve health without necessarily trimming flavor or the fun of food. This healthful bread was developed in the *Tribune* test kitchen for a cover story on the good fats. Flaxseed, also a healthful addition here, is sold in natural food stores.

Bread
¾ cup orange juice
⅓ cup milled flaxseed
1½ cups all-purpose flour
1 teaspoon baking powder
1 teaspoon baking soda
¼ teaspoon salt
1 large egg
Zest of 1 orange

½ cup packed brown sugar
½ cup canola oil
2 teaspoons vanilla extract
1 8-ounce package chopped dates
½ cup chopped almonds

Syrup
¼ cup packed brown sugar
2 tablespoons orange juice

1. Heat oven to 325°F. To make bread, combine orange juice and flaxseed in a food processor fitted with a metal blade or in a blender. Process to a paste consistency, about 5 minutes; set aside.

2. Stir together flour, baking powder, baking soda, and salt in a large bowl. Set aside. Stir together egg, zest, sugar, oil, and vanilla in a medium-sized bowl. Add egg mixture and flaxseed mixture to flour mixture. Stir until moistened. Add dates and almonds; stir until well mixed.

3. Grease a 9-inch Bundt pan; transfer batter to the pan. Bake until a wooden pick inserted in the center comes out clean, about 40 minutes. Cool in pan 10 minutes; turn out onto a wire rack. Place rack over a shallow pan.

4. To make syrup, heat brown sugar and orange juice in a small saucepan over medium heat until sugar melts, about 5 minutes. Poke entire top of bread with a wooden pick; brush warm syrup over. Serve warm or at room temperature.

NUTRITION INFORMATION PER SERVING:

310 calories	14 g fat	1.1 g saturated fat
39% calories from fat	17 mg cholesterol	205 mg sodium
44 g carbohydrate	4.5 g protein	2.9 g fiber

Cranberry-Banana Nut Bread

PREPARATION TIME: 30 minutes
BAKING TIME: 1 hour 15 minutes
STANDING TIME: 8 to 12 hours
YIELD: 1 9-inch, 12-slice loaf

MRS. ANTON ZALESKY of Western Springs, Illinois, submitted this quick bread recipe, which successfully combines the tartness of cranberries with the mellow flavor of bananas. The bread slices and tastes best if made one day ahead.

2 cups all-purpose flour	1 cup fresh *or* frozen cranberries,
1 tablespoon baking powder	chopped coarse
½ teaspoon salt	1 teaspoon grated orange zest
½ teaspoon cinnamon	½ cup milk
¼ cup (½ stick) butter, softened	1 cup mashed ripe banana
1 cup sugar	1 cup chopped pecans
1 large egg	

1. Heat oven to 350°F. Whisk together flour, baking powder, salt, and cinnamon in a medium-sized bowl.

2. Cream butter and sugar in a large mixer bowl until light and fluffy. Beat in egg. Add cranberries and orange zest; mix well. Stir in milk; add banana. Stir in flour mixture and pecans by hand just until blended.

3. Grease a 9″ × 5″ loaf pan. Pour batter into the pan. Bake until a wooden pick inserted in the center comes out clean, about 1 hour 15 minutes. Cool on a wire rack 5 minutes. Invert on a wire rack; cool completely. Wrap in foil or waxed paper. Let stand 8 to 12 hours before slicing.

NUTRITION INFORMATION PER SLICE:

275 calories	11 g fat	3.3 g saturated fat
37% calories from fat	29 mg cholesterol	270 mg sodium
41 g carbohydrate	4 g protein	2.2 g fiber

Tasty Cranberry-Orange Bread

PREPARATION TIME: 15 minutes

COOKING TIME: 55 minutes

YIELD: 12 servings

LEE LEPINSKE OF Western Springs sent this delicious yet not too sweet cranberry-orange bread to the "You're the Cook" column in 1998. The oatmeal gives it a heartier texture than that of most quick breads. It also would make a wonderful gift for the holiday season.

2 cups all-purpose flour
1 cup quick-cooking oats
¾ cup sugar
2 teaspoons baking powder
½ teaspoon baking soda
½ teaspoon salt

2 large eggs
¾ cup orange juice
½ cup vegetable oil
1 tablespoon grated orange zest
¾ cup chopped fresh *or* dried
   cranberries
½ cup chopped nuts, optional

1. Heat oven to 350°F. Combine flour, oats, sugar, baking powder, baking soda, and salt in a large bowl. Mix thoroughly; set aside.

2. Stir together eggs, orange juice, oil, and orange zest in a medium-sized bowl. Add liquid to dry ingredients; mix just until moistened. Stir in cranberries and nuts if desired.

3. Oil and flour a 9″ × 5″ loaf pan. Spoon batter into pan. Bake until a wooden pick inserted in the center comes out clean, 55 to 65 minutes. Cool in the pan 10 minutes. Turn bread out onto a wire rack.

NUTRITION INFORMATION PER SERVING:

285 calories	14 g fat	1.8 g saturated fat
42% calories from fat	35 mg cholesterol	240 mg sodium
36 g carbohydrate	5.6 g protein	1.8 g fiber

Chunky Apple Muffins

PREPARATION TIME: 30 minutes
COOKING TIME: 22 minutes
YIELD: 15 muffins

READER BARBARA LAVELLE of Princeton, Illinois, asked for a recipe for apple muffins made with buttermilk and apples that didn't have to be peeled. Here's one from a 1995 column by Abby Mandel. These muffins can be frozen up to three months.

¾ cup sugar
3 tablespoons vegetable oil
½ cup buttermilk
1 large egg
2 large egg whites
1 teaspoon vanilla extract
1½ cups all-purpose flour

2 teaspoons baking powder
½ teaspoon baking soda
½ teaspoon cinnamon
¼ teaspoon salt
2 medium-sized Granny Smith
   apples, cored and cut into
   ⅓-inch dice

1. Heat oven to 375°F. Beat sugar and oil in the bowl of an electric mixer until smooth. Add buttermilk, egg, egg whites, and vanilla; beat until smooth. Add 1 cup of the flour, baking powder, baking soda, cinnamon, and salt; combine well.

2. Line the cups of muffin tins with paper cups or lightly grease them. Toss together apples and remaining ½ cup flour in a medium-sized bowl. Stir apples into batter by hand. Spoon batter into prepared muffin tin cups, filling each about two-thirds full.

3. Bake until golden brown and a wooden pick inserted in the center comes out clean, about 20 minutes. Cool in the tins on a wire rack 10 minutes. Remove from pan; serve warm or at room temperature.

NUTRITION INFORMATION PER MUFFIN:

130 calories	3.3 g fat	0.5 g saturated fat
23% calories from fat	14 mg cholesterol	165 mg sodium
23 g carbohydrate	2.5 g protein	0.7 g fiber

Date and Bacon Muffins

PREPARATION TIME: 10 minutes
BAKING TIME: 20 minutes
YIELD: 12 muffins

THIS MUFFIN RECIPE is from Chris Meier of Western Springs, Illinois, who was one of the winners in the Old Graue Mill Corn Meal Baking Contest. It also was selected as one of the *Tribune*'s top ten recipes of 1987.

¼ cup butter	5 teaspoons baking powder
2 tablespoons sugar	1 cup milk
1 egg	½ cup diced dates
1½ cups all-purpose flour	4 strips bacon, fried and crumbled
½ cup stone-ground cornmeal	Honey, optional

1. Heat oven to 400°F. Grease the cups of muffin tins. Cream butter and sugar. Add egg. Sift together flour, cornmeal, and baking powder; add alternately to butter mixture with milk. Fold in dates and bacon.

2. Bake in prepared muffin tins 20 to 25 minutes. Serve with honey if desired.

NUTRITION INFORMATION PER MUFFIN:

195 calories	8 g fat	3.9 g saturated fat
37% calories from fat	35 mg cholesterol	360 mg sodium
26 g carbohydrate	5 g protein	1.4 g fiber

Mixed Seed Crisp Bread

PREPARATION TIME: 10 minutes
COOKING TIME: 5 minutes
YIELD: 4 servings

THIS INDIAN-INSPIRED FLAT bread topped with three kinds of seeds was created by writer Pat Dailey for a "Fast Food" column. You can also add cumin and fennel seeds.

4 flour tortillas
4 teaspoons unsalted butter, softened
2 teaspoons crushed black pepper

2 teaspoons sesame seeds
2 teaspoons poppy seeds
¾ teaspoon caraway seeds
¼ teaspoon salt
3 tablespoons minced cilantro

1. Heat oven to 425°F. Spread each tortilla with 1 teaspoon butter. Combine pepper, sesame seeds, poppy seeds, caraway seeds, and salt in a small bowl; sprinkle evenly over tortillas.

2. Arrange on a baking sheet. Bake until crisp, 4 to 5 minutes. Sprinkle with cilantro. Serve hot.

NUTRITION INFORMATION PER SERVING:

215 calories	9 g fat	3.4 g saturated fat
37% calories from fat	10 mg cholesterol	380 mg sodium
29 g carbohydrate	5 g protein	2.4 g fiber

DESSERTS

Buttermilk Lemon Cake

PREPARATION TIME: 45 minutes
COOKING TIME: 1 hour 30 minutes
YIELD: 16 servings

THIS RECIPE BY Nancy Solomon is adapted from the 1983 book *Parker Cooks,* a collection from the alumni and friends of Francis W. Parker School in Chicago. This is delicious served with fresh raspberries or blackberries as a garnish, if you like.

Glaze
5 tablespoons lemon juice
1 tablespoon water
½ cup sugar

Cake
Fine bread crumbs
Zest of 2 large lemons, grated
3 tablespoons lemon juice

3 cups all-purpose flour, sifted
½ teaspoon baking soda
½ teaspoon salt
1 cup (2 sticks) unsalted butter,
    softened
3 cups sugar
5 large eggs
1 cup buttermilk

1. Heat oven to 350°F. To make glaze, mix lemon juice, water, and sugar in a small bowl; set aside. To make cake, line the bottom of a 10-inch tube pan with waxed paper. Butter pan and paper; dust completely with fine bread crumbs. Set aside.

2. Mix lemon zest and juice in a small bowl. Sift together flour, baking soda, and salt in a medium-sized bowl; set aside.

3. Beat butter in the bowl of an electric mixer until light, about 2 minutes. Gradually beat in sugar until light and fluffy, about 2 minutes. Beat in eggs one at a time, beating well after each addition. Beat 3 minutes.

▶

423

4. Alternately beat in dry ingredients and buttermilk, beginning and ending with dry ingredients. Stir in lemon zest and lemon juice. Pour batter into the prepared tube pan. Bake until a wooden pick inserted in the center comes out clean and cake has pulled away from the sides of the pan, about 1½ hours. Cool cake on a wire rack in the pan 5 minutes. Invert onto a platter; remove waxed paper. Apply glaze with a pastry brush until absorbed. Let stand until completely cool.

NUTRITION INFORMATION PER SERVING:

388 calories	13 g fat	8 g saturated fat
31% calories from fat	98 mg cholesterol	150 mg sodium
63 g carbohydrate	5 g protein	0.8 g fiber

Kentucky Butter Cake

PREPARATION TIME: 25 minutes
COOKING TIME: 1 hour
YIELD: 16 servings

GERTRUDE BAKER OF Crystal Lake, Illinois, submitted this recipe for Kentucky Butter Cake to our weekly "You're the Cook" column in 1998. Everyone fell in love with this very moist, very buttery cake that combines simple ingredients for extraordinary results. And yes, the cake really does use two tablespoons of vanilla extract.

Cake
3 cups all-purpose flour
1 teaspoon baking powder
1 teaspoon salt
½ teaspoon baking soda
2 cups sugar
1 cup (2 sticks) butter, softened
4 large eggs

1 cup buttermilk *or* sour cream
2 tablespoons vanilla extract

Sauce
1 cup sugar
½ cup (1 stick) butter
¼ cup water
1 tablespoon vanilla extract
Confectioners' sugar

1. To make cake, heat oven to 325°F. Sift together flour, baking powder, salt, and baking soda in a medium-sized bowl; set aside.

2. Beat sugar and butter in the bowl of an electric mixer until blended. Add eggs one at a time, beating well after each addition. Combine buttermilk with vanilla. Add buttermilk and flour mixtures alternately in thirds, ending with flour mixture, beating well after each addition.

3. Grease a tube pan; spoon batter into the pan. Bake until a wooden pick inserted in the center comes out clean, 1 hour to 1 hour 15 minutes.

4. Meanwhile, to make sauce, heat sugar, butter, water, and vanilla in a small saucepan over medium heat until sugar dissolves and butter has melted, about 10 minutes. Do not boil.

5. Prick cake with a wooden pick immediately after removing from oven. Pour hot sauce over cake; let stand until completely cool (cake is fragile when hot). Run a knife around the edge of the pan. Invert cake onto a serving plate; sprinkle with confectioners' sugar.

NUTRITION INFORMATION PER SERVING:

415 calories	19 g fat	11 g saturated fat
41% calories from fat	100 mg cholesterol	425 mg sodium
57 g carbohydrate	5 g protein	0.6 g fiber

Peach Cake Roll

PREPARATION TIME: 40 minutes

BAKING TIME: 12 to 15 minutes

YIELD: 12 servings

FRESH PEACHES, TEAMED with cream cheese and confectioners' sugar, star in this delicious cake roll sent to us by reader Ann Zorek of Chicago. As in most recipes for cake rolls, you have to "train" the cake—rolling the warm cake in a damp kitchen towel, then allowing it to cool completely—to prevent it from cracking when you fill it and reroll it.

Cake	*Peach Filling*
1 cup sifted cake flour	8 ounces cream cheese, softened
1 teaspoon baking powder	½ cup confectioners' sugar, sifted,
¼ teaspoon salt	plus more for dusting
3 large eggs	⅛ teaspoon almond extract
1 cup granulated sugar	1 cup pitted, finely diced fresh
⅓ cup water	peaches
1 teaspoon vanilla extract	
Confectioners' sugar	

1. Heat oven to 375°F. To make cake, sift together cake flour, baking powder, and salt in a small bowl; set aside.

➤

2. Beat eggs in the bowl of an electric mixer until thick and lemon colored, about 5 minutes. Gradually beat in granulated sugar. Add water and vanilla extract; beat on low speed. Gradually add dry ingredients, beating just until batter is smooth.

3. Grease waxed paper and line a 15″ × 10″ jelly roll pan with it. Spread batter evenly in pan. Bake until a wooden pick inserted in the center comes out clean, 12 to 15 minutes.

4. Sprinkle a clean, damp towel heavily with confectioners' sugar. Remove cake from the oven and loosen cake from the edges of the pan. Immediately invert cake onto the prepared towel. Carefully remove waxed paper. Trim off the stiff edges of cake if necessary. While cake is still hot, use the towel to roll cake, beginning with the narrow end. Let cake cool completely wrapped in the towel on a wire rack.

5. To make peach filling, beat cream cheese in another bowl of the electric mixer until light and fluffy, about 3 minutes. Beat in ½ cup sifted confectioners' sugar and almond extract; mix well. Add peaches; mix gently by hand.

6. Carefully unroll cake; spread with peach filling. Carefully roll cake up again. Sprinkle the outside with confectioners' sugar. Wrap loosely with the towel; store in refrigerator until serving.

NUTRITION INFORMATION PER SERVING:

202 calories	8 g fat	4.6 g saturated fat
35% calories from fat	74 mg cholesterol	161 mg sodium
29 g carbohydrate	3.7 g protein	0.4 g fiber

Fourth of July Apple Spice Cake

PREPARATION TIME: 30 minutes

COOKING TIME: 50 minutes

YIELD: 12 servings

THIS RECIPE COMES from Elizabeth Clark, a cooking teacher in Keokuk, Iowa. Clark grew up on a farm that had one hundred apple trees, and she vividly remembers the desserts her mother would make with the fresh apples—especially this spice cake flavored with applesauce and cocoa.

Cake Batter
1 cup pecans

½ cup (1 stick) butter, softened
1 cup sugar

2 large eggs
1 cup applesauce
2 cups all-purpose flour
½ cup cocoa
1½ teaspoons baking powder
1 teaspoon cinnamon
½ teaspoon baking soda
½ teaspoon ground cloves
½ teaspoon allspice
½ teaspoon ground ginger

½ teaspoon ground nutmeg
¼ teaspoon salt
½ cup buttermilk
½ cup raisins

Caramel Glaze
1 cup packed light brown sugar
¼ cup (½ stick) unsalted butter
½ cup milk
2 cups confectioners' sugar
1 teaspoon vanilla extract

1. Heat oven to 325°F. Toast pecans in the oven, stirring occasionally, until lightly browned, about 15 minutes. Cool and chop coarse. Meanwhile, beat butter and sugar in the bowl of an electric mixer until light and fluffy, about 3 minutes. Add eggs one at a time, beating well after each addition. Beat in applesauce. (The mixture will appear slightly curdled at this point.)

2. Whisk together flour, cocoa, baking powder, cinnamon, baking soda, cloves, allspice, ginger, nutmeg, and salt in a medium-sized bowl. Alternately fold dry ingredients and buttermilk into applesauce mixture beginning and ending with dry ingredients. Stir in pecans and raisins.

3. Grease and flour a 10-cup Bundt pan. Pour batter into pan; level the top with a spatula. Bake until a wooden pick inserted in the center of cake comes out clean, about 50 minutes. Cool cake in the pan 10 minutes. Turn cake out of the pan onto a wire rack; completely cool.

4. To make caramel glaze, heat brown sugar and butter to boil in a heavy-bottomed saucepan over medium heat. Remove the pan from heat; add milk, being careful to avoid spattering. Return pan to heat; heat milk to boil. Add confectioners' sugar; stir constantly until completely incorporated. Remove pan from heat; stir in vanilla extract.

5. Drizzle the top of cooled cake with caramel glaze.

NUTRITION INFORMATION PER SERVING:

504 calories	20 g fat	9 g saturated fat
35% calories from fat	68 mg cholesterol	277 mg sodium
80 g carbohydrate	6 g protein	3.2 g fiber

Pecan Meringue Cake (Dacquoise)

PREPARATION TIME: 1 hour 30 minutes

COOKING TIME: 45 to 50 minutes

COOLING TIME: 1 hour

YIELD: 14 servings

AT THE END of one summer, *Tribune* food writers decided to rejoice in the fact that bathing-suit, calorie-counting days were almost over, so we printed some of the most decadently rich dessert recipes available. This one comes from Fresh Start Bakery and Catering in Flossmoor, Illinois. It was, and is, an absolute favorite.

Meringue Layers (see Note)
8 large egg whites
⅛ teaspoon salt
1 cup sugar
½ cup finely ground pecans

Buttercream
3 cups sugar
1 cup water

5 large eggs, separated
4½ cups (9 sticks) unsalted butter, softened

Garnish
1 8-ounce package pecans, coarsely chopped
4 ounces bittersweet *or* semisweet chocolate, melted

1. Heat oven to 300°F. Cut parchment paper or brown paper to fit baking sheets. Trace 3 9-inch circles on paper. Set aside.

2. For meringue layers, beat egg whites and salt in the bowl of an electric mixer until soft peaks form. Gradually beat in sugar, until stiff peaks form. Fold in ground nuts. Fit large pastry bag with ½-inch round tip. Fill bag with some of the meringue mixture. Starting in center of circle on prepared paper, pipe out meringue in concentric circles to completely fill in traced circle.

3. Bake until golden and crisp, about 30 minutes. Reduce oven temperature to 225°F; continue baking until dry and crisp, 15 to 20 minutes. Turn off oven; let cool in oven, at least 1 hour to dry out meringue.

4. For buttercream, heat sugar and water to boil in a small, heavy saucepan. Cover; boil 2 minutes. Uncover, insert candy thermometer, and boil until candy thermometer registers 250 to 260°F.

5. Beat egg whites and egg yolks in the bowl of an electric mixer until light, about 2 minutes. Pour boiling sugar-water into eggs with motor running. Beat continuously until mixture is very light and cool to the touch, about 10 minutes. Gradually beat in butter until fluffy and of spreading consistency. (If buttercream begins to separate, set mixer bowl over a pan of simmering water; then beat until smooth again.)

6. To assemble, slip long metal spatula under meringue layers to loosen from paper. Put one layer onto serving platter. Spread generously with buttercream. Top with second meringue layer. Spread generously with buttercream. Top with remaining meringue layer. Frost top and sides of cake with remaining buttercream.

7. Press chopped pecans onto top and sides of cake. Drizzle melted chocolate in center of cake. Refrigerate until buttercream is firm, at least 1 hour. Slice with serrated knife.

❧ NOTE: *As with most meringue recipes, the cake layers are best made on a cool, dry day. If making in advance, be sure they are thoroughly dry and crisp; then store in a covered tin or in a closed, dark oven.*

If you do not own a pastry bag, cut one corner off a food storage bag. Fill bag with mixture; pipe onto traced circles.

NUTRITION INFORMATION PER SERVING:

956 calories	77 g fat	40 g saturated fat
70% calories from fat	236 mg cholesterol	84 mg sodium
66 g carbohydrate	7 g protein	2.1 g fiber

Almond Cake

PREPARATION TIME: 30 minutes
COOKING TIME: 30 minutes
YIELD: 10 servings

IN A 1998 article celebrating great food pairings, William Rice saluted the Spanish team of roasted almonds and dry sherry. Almonds and the grapes used for sherry grow in similar climates, he wrote. He suggested serving this rich cake with an oloroso-style sherry.

½ cup (1 stick) unsalted butter, softened
1 cup sugar
4 large eggs, at room temperature
Zest of 1 orange, grated
¼ teaspoon almond extract

¾ cup all-purpose flour
½ teaspoon baking soda
¼ teaspoon salt
¾ cup buttermilk, at room temperature
1½ cups ground almonds
Confectioners' sugar

►

1. Heat oven to 350°F. Beat together butter and sugar in the bowl of an electric mixer on medium speed until smooth and light, about 3 minutes. Reduce speed; add eggs one at a time, beating well after each addition. Add orange zest and almond extract; mix well.

2. Sift flour, baking soda, and salt together in a small bowl. Add to butter mixture, beating until smooth. Slowly beat in buttermilk. Add almonds, beating just until batter is smooth.

3. Grease a 9-inch round cake pan or 9-inch springform pan. Pour batter into pan. Bake until a wooden pick inserted in the center comes out clean, about 30 minutes. Cool in pan 20 minutes. Turn cake out onto a wire rack. Cool completely; sift confectioners' sugar over top of cake.

NUTRITION INFORMATION PER SERVING:

347 calories	22 g fat	7 g saturated fat
55% calories from fat	111 mg cholesterol	169 mg sodium
33 g carbohydrate	8 g protein	2.5 g fiber

Pineapple Macadamia Pound Cake

PREPARATION TIME: 20 minutes
COOKING TIME: 1 hour 30 minutes
YIELD: 12 servings

CAN'T GET TO Hawaii this year? How about a taste of it? Columnist Pat Dailey created this ultrarich pound cake to satisfy a reader's plea for a facsimile of a rich, mail-order pineapple cake.

⅔ cup dried pineapple pieces	1¼ cups sugar
⅔ cup boiling water	3 large eggs
1½ cups all-purpose flour	½ cup milk
½ teaspoon baking powder	1 tablespoon dark rum
¼ teaspoon salt	1 teaspoon vanilla extract
¾ cup (1½ sticks) unsalted butter, softened	¾ cup coarsely chopped macadamia nuts

1. Combine dried pineapple and boiling water in a small bowl; let stand 15 minutes. Drain thoroughly; blot dry. If pineapple pieces are large, cut into ½-inch pieces.

2. Heat oven to 325°F. Sift together flour, baking powder, and salt; set aside. Beat butter and sugar with an electric mixer on high speed until light, 3 minutes. Add eggs one at a time, mixing well after each addition. Reduce mixer to low speed; add milk, rum, and vanilla. Add flour mixture. Mix just until combined. Fold in pineapple and nuts with a spatula.

3. Grease and flour an 8½″ × 4½″ loaf pan. Transfer batter to pan. Bake until a wooden pick inserted in the center comes out clean, about 1½ hours. Cool in the pan 10 minutes. Loosen cake from the sides of the pan with a flexible knife; invert onto a wire rack. Cool before slicing.

NUTRITION INFORMATION PER SERVING:

354 calories	20 g fat	9 g saturated fat
49% calories from fat	85 mg cholesterol	94 mg sodium
41 g carbohydrate	4.5 g protein	1.2 g fiber

Deluxe Chocolate Zucchini Cake

PREPARATION TIME: 25 minutes
COOKING TIME: 1 hour
YIELD: 12 servings

How BIG DID you say that zucchini was in your garden? Everybody who grows zucchini knows they need lots of zucchini recipes, and here's one that combines that fast-growing vegetable with rich chocolate for a tasty, easy-to-make cake. If you don't have a garden, this cake even would be worth a stop at the vegetable stand.

2 cups all-purpose flour	3 ounces unsweetened chocolate,
1 cup whole wheat flour	melted and cooled
1¼ teaspoons baking powder	1½ teaspoons vanilla extract
1¼ teaspoons baking soda	½ teaspoon almond extract
1 teaspoon salt	1 cup chopped pecans *or* walnuts
⅛ teaspoon cinnamon	½ cup raisins *or* chopped dates
4 large eggs	3 cups coarsely shredded zucchini,
2 cups sugar	patted dry
1¼ cups vegetable oil	Confectioners' sugar

1. Heat oven to 350°F. Sift together all-purpose flour, whole wheat flour, baking powder, baking soda, salt, and cinnamon; set aside.

►

2. Beat eggs and sugar in the bowl of an electric mixer until thick and fluffy, about 3 minutes. Beat in oil, chocolate, vanilla extract, and almond extract. Fold in dry ingredients, nuts, and raisins by hand; fold in zucchini. Butter and flour a 12-cup Bundt pan. Spread batter evenly into pan.

3. Bake until a wooden pick inserted in the center comes out clean, about 1 hour. Let cool in pan 10 minutes; invert onto a wire rack. Cool completely. Sprinkle with confectioners' sugar.

NUTRITION INFORMATION PER SERVING:

595 calories	35 g fat	6 g saturated fat
52% calories from fat	71 mg cholesterol	401 mg sodium
67 g carbohydrate	8 g protein	4.3 g fiber

Chocolate Fudge–Peanut Butter Cake

PREPARATION TIME: 30 minutes
COOKING TIME: 40 to 50 minutes
YIELD: 10 servings

FUDGE! PEANUT BUTTER! These two classic treats make room for each other in this rich, indulgent cake recipe, developed in the *Tribune* test kitchen. A creamy chocolate frosting adds another layer to the indulgence theme.

Chocolate Batter
1 cup (2 sticks) unsalted butter, softened
2 cups sugar
2 teaspoons vanilla extract
4 large eggs
1½ cups all-purpose flour
¾ cup unsweetened Dutch-processed cocoa
1 teaspoon baking powder
½ cup peanut butter chips

Peanut Butter Batter
¾ cup creamy peanut butter

⅓ cup butter, softened
2 large eggs
⅓ cup sugar
2 tablespoons all-purpose flour
¾ teaspoon vanilla extract

Chocolate Frosting
3 ounces unsweetened chocolate
3 tablespoons butter
2⅔ cups confectioners' sugar, sifted
¾ teaspoon vanilla extract
¼ teaspoon salt
4 to 5 tablespoons water

1. Heat oven to 350°F. To make chocolate batter, beat butter and sugar in the bowl of an electric mixer until light and fluffy, about 3 minutes. Beat in vanilla. Add eggs one at a time, beating well after each addition. Beat in flour, cocoa, and baking powder until mixed. Stir in peanut butter chips by hand.

2. To make peanut butter batter, beat peanut butter and butter in the bowl of the electric mixer. Beat in eggs, sugar, flour, and vanilla until smooth.

3. Grease a 13″ × 9″ baking pan. Spread half of the chocolate batter over the bottom of the pan. Spread peanut butter batter over chocolate batter. Spread remaining chocolate batter over all. Swirl layers together with a spatula or table knife, creating a marbled effect.

4. Bake until top springs back when lightly touched, 40 to 50 minutes. Cool completely on a wire rack.

5. To make frosting, melt chocolate and butter in a small saucepan over medium-low heat. Remove from heat; stir in confectioners' sugar, vanilla, and salt. Stir in enough water to reach a spreading consistency. Frost the top of the cake. Let stand until frosting sets. Cut into bars.

NUTRITION INFORMATION PER SERVING:

869 calories	49 g fat	25 g saturated fat
48% calories from fat	203 mg cholesterol	359 mg sodium
103 g carbohydrate	15 g protein	6 g fiber

Chocolate Hazelnut Cake

PREPARATION TIME: 30 minutes

BAKING TIME: 1 hour

YIELD: 10 servings

THIS CHOCOLATE HAZELNUT cake from caterer Jean True is moist, dense, and full of hazelnuts. It is delicious plain or topped with a chocolate or vanilla frosting. The unfrosted cake freezes well.

8 ounces shelled hazelnuts
½ pound bittersweet chocolate
1 cup plus 1 teaspoon sugar
¾ cup all-purpose flour

1 cup (2 sticks) unsalted butter,
   softened
1½ teaspoons vanilla extract
7 large eggs, separated
Pinch salt

➤

1. Heat oven to 400°F. Put hazelnuts into a baking pan. Bake until nuts are golden and outer skins are loose, about 15 minutes. Immediately put nuts into a clean towel; rub together in the towel to remove skins. Let nuts cool. Pulse nuts in a food processor until finely ground and powdery. Place in a medium-sized bowl. Pulse chocolate with 1 teaspoon of the sugar in the food processor until finely grated. Mix ground nuts, grated chocolate, and flour in a bowl; set aside.

2. Reduce oven temperature to 300°F. Beat butter and sugar in the bowl of an electric mixer until light and fluffy, about 3 minutes. Beat in vanilla extract. Add egg yolks one at a time, beating well after each addition. Beat in chocolate mixture a few tablespoons at a time until smooth.

3. Put egg whites and salt in the clean bowl of the electric mixer. Beat until stiff peaks form. Gently stir one-fourth of the egg whites into batter to lighten; fold in remaining whites. Grease and flour a 13″ × 9″ baking pan. Spread batter evenly into the pan.

4. Bake until a wooden pick inserted in the center comes out clean, about 1 hour. Cool completely on a wire rack.

NUTRITION INFORMATION PER SERVING:

600 calories	44 g fat	18 g saturated fat
64% calories from fat	199 mg cholesterol	63 mg sodium
44 g carbohydrate	10 g protein	3.4 g fiber

Warm, Soft Chocolate Cake

PREPARATION TIME: 25 minutes

COOKING TIME: 12 minutes

YIELD: 4 servings

CHEF JEAN-GEORGES VONGERICHTEN, a native of Alsace, France, has garnered raves for the Thai-influenced menus he serves at his Vong restaurants in New York, London, Hong Kong, and Chicago. But here, the chef puts his classical training to work on an ultrarich chocolate dessert. You can prepare this recipe several hours ahead through step 2. Refrigerate batter and then bring to room temperature before baking.

½ cup (1 stick) unsalted butter	2 large egg yolks
4 ounces bittersweet chocolate	¼ cup sugar
2 large eggs	2 teaspoons all-purpose flour

1. Heat oven to 450°F. Melt butter and chocolate together in the top of a double boiler until almost melted; set aside. Beat together eggs, yolks, and sugar in the bowl of an electric mixer until light and thick, about 3 minutes.

2. Pour warm chocolate mixture into egg mixture; quickly fold in flour until just combined. Butter and flour 4 4-ounce molds, custard cups, or ramekins. Evenly pour batter into molds.

3. Bake molds on a baking sheet until the centers are slightly soft but sides are set, about 12 minutes. Invert each mold onto a plate; let sit about 10 seconds. Unmold by lifting up one corner of mold. Cake will fall out onto plate. Serve immediately.

NUTRITION INFORMATION PER SERVING:

455 calories	35 g fat	20 g saturated fat
67% calories from fat	275 mg cholesterol	45 mg sodium
33 g carbohydrate	6 g protein	0.3 g fiber

White Chocolate Coconut Cake

PREPARATION TIME: 1 hour
COOKING TIME: 35 minutes
CHILLING TIME: 2 hours
YIELD: 12 servings

WHITE CHOCOLATE HAS made a place for itself in the American heart and palate. This cake, with coconut in the frosting, looks like a yummy, giant snowflake.

Cake
⅓ pound white chocolate
½ cup water
1 cup (2 sticks) unsalted butter, softened
2 cups granulated sugar
4 large eggs, separated
2½ cups sifted cake flour
1½ teaspoons baking powder
½ teaspoon salt

1 cup buttermilk
1 teaspoon vanilla extract
1 cup chopped almonds *or* pecans
1 3½-ounce can flaked coconut

Frosting
2 cups whipping cream
2 tablespoons confectioners' sugar
2 teaspoons vanilla extract
1 cup flaked coconut

1. Heat oven to 350°F. Grease 3 9-inch round cake pans. Line bottoms with waxed paper. Grease paper.

►

2. Put white chocolate and water in top of a double boiler; cook, stirring often, over simmering water until melted. (Water should not touch bottom of top boiler.) Whisk until smooth; cool.

3. Beat butter and 1½ cups of the granulated sugar in the bowl of an electric mixer until light and fluffy, about 3 minutes. Add egg yolks, one at a time, beating well after each addition.

4. Sift flour with baking powder and salt. Add flour mixture to butter mixture in thirds, alternating with buttermilk, vanilla, and white chocolate mixture, beating until smooth after each addition.

5. Beat egg whites in the clean bowl of an electric mixer until soft peaks form. Gradually beat in remaining ½ cup granulated sugar; beat until stiff but not dry. Fold into batter; gently fold in nuts and coconut.

6. Transfer batter evenly into prepared pans. Bake until wooden pick inserted in center comes out clean, 30 to 35 minutes. Cool on wire racks 10 minutes. Remove from pans; cool completely on wire racks. Remove waxed paper.

7. For frosting, beat cream until frothy. Beat in confectioners' sugar and vanilla extract until soft peaks form. Fold in coconut. Put one cake layer onto serving platter; frost. Repeat layers. Frost top and sides of cake. Refrigerate up to 2 hours before serving.

NUTRITION INFORMATION PER SERVING:

714 calories	46 g fat	26 g saturated fat
57% calories from fat	170 mg cholesterol	268 mg sodium
69 g carbohydrate	9 g protein	2.1 g fiber

Frozen Chocolate Torte

PREPARATION TIME: 25 minutes
STANDING TIME: 45 minutes
CHILLING TIME: 2 to 12 hours
COOKING TIME: 45 minutes
YIELD: 8 servings

THIS DELICIOUS DESSERT, submitted by reader Mertis Stanley of Western Springs, Illinois, is a wonderful blend of meringue, chocolate, and whipping cream.

Shells
3 large egg whites
½ teaspoon cream of tartar
¾ cup sugar

¾ cup finely chopped pecans

Filling
1 pint whipping cream

¾ cup chocolate syrup   Chocolate curls, optional
1 teaspoon vanilla extract

1. To make the shells, heat oven to 375°F. Beat egg whites in the bowl of an electric mixer until frothy. Add cream of tartar; beat until soft peaks form, about 3 minutes. Gradually add sugar, beating on high speed until stiff peaks form, about 3 minutes. Fold in pecans.

2. Line two baking sheets with parchment or waxed paper; draw an 8-inch circle onto each. Evenly divide and spread meringue over circles to form flat discs. Bake 45 minutes. Turn off oven; leave shells in oven without opening door 45 minutes to 12 hours to dry.

3. To make filling, beat whipping cream on high speed until stiff peaks form. Fold in chocolate syrup and vanilla. Place one shell on a serving dish; spread with half of the whipped cream mixture. Top with second shell; spread with remaining whipped cream. Garnish with chocolate curls if desired. Cover; freeze until firm, at least 2 hours and up to 12 hours. Cut with a serrated knife to serve.

❧ NOTE: *Do not make this recipe on a humid day. The meringue will absorb moisture and become soft and sticky. The shells can be made the day before you add the filling, and the filling can be made the day before serving.*

NUTRITION INFORMATION PER SERVING:

420 calories	30 g fat	14 g saturated fat
64% calories from fat	80 mg cholesterol	70 mg sodium
39 g carbohydrate	4 g protein	1 g fiber

Mary Meade's White Fruitcake

PREPARATION TIME: 40 minutes
STANDING TIME: 8 to 12 hours
BAKING TIME: 3 hours
AGING TIME: 1 week or longer
YIELD: 4 12-piece cakes

LIKE BETTY CROCKER and Aunt Jemima, Mary Meade sprang full-blown from a *Tribune* editor's head in an era when it was customary to attribute recipes to a fictional name. The name is no longer used at the paper, but the rich, easy-to-make white fruitcake that still bears it is a longtime favorite. It stores well for months, and the flavor improves with age. If you wrap the fruitcake in plastic wrap, let the corn syrup dry first.

1 pound candied pineapple   1 pound candied cherries

➤

1 pound golden raisins

½ pound candied lemon rind

½ pound candied orange rind

½ pound candied citron

1½ cups orange-flavored liqueur *or*
     white wine

3 cups (6 sticks) unsalted butter,
     softened

2 cups sugar

12 large eggs

6 cups all-purpose flour

1½ teaspoons baking powder

1 teaspoon salt

1½ pounds pecan *or* walnut halves,
     chopped coarse

Light corn syrup

Whole candied cherries, pecan
     halves, *or* walnut halves

1. Cut pineapple in pieces of varying size. Slice cherries in half. Put pineapple, cherries, raisins, lemon rind, orange rind, and citron into a large bowl. Add liqueur; let stand covered overnight at room temperature.

2. Heat oven to 250°F. Beat butter and sugar in the bowl of an electric mixer until light and fluffy, about 3 minutes. Add eggs one at a time, beating well after each addition. Add flour, baking powder, and salt; mix well. Stir into fruit mixture. Add nuts. Blend until well mixed.

3. Grease 4 10″ × 3″ or 9″ × 5″ loaf pans. Line pans with heavy brown paper. Grease the paper. Spoon batter lightly into the pans. Put a shallow pan of water into the oven on the lowest rack. Bake cakes on the rack above until golden and pulling away from the sides of the pans, about 3 hours. Cool cakes in pans on wire racks 20 minutes. Unmold; remove paper. Cool completely on wire racks.

4. Brush with additional liqueur if desired. Store cakes wrapped in aluminum foil in a covered container 1 week or more. Brush cakes with light corn syrup, decorate them with fruit and nuts, and brush them again with corn syrup before serving.

NUTRITION INFORMATION PER PIECE:

442 calories	23 g fat	8 g saturated fat
45% calories from fat	84 mg cholesterol	97 mg sodium
58 g carbohydrate	4.9 g protein	1.9 g fiber

Eli's-Style Original Cheesecake

PREPARATION TIME: 20 minutes
COOKING TIME: 50 minutes
CHILLING TIME: 8 to 12 hours
YIELD: 12 servings

ELI'S CHEESECAKE, A Chicago culinary icon, is named for the late restaurateur Eli M. Schulman and his still-popular restaurant, Eli's the Place for Steak. The cheesecake made its first nonrestaurant appearance in 1980, at the first Taste of Chicago food festival; six thousand slices were sold. Today, Eli's Cheesecake World, located on the city's Northwest Side, bakes thousands of cheesecakes in dozens of varieties every day. This is the simple recipe that started everything. It's as easy as it is delicious.

Crust
1¾ cups finely crushed vanilla
    wafers
6 tablespoons butter, melted

Filling
4 8-ounce packages cream cheese,
    softened

1 cup sugar
2 tablespoons all-purpose flour
2 large eggs
1 large egg yolk
6 tablespoons sour cream
½ teaspoon vanilla extract

1. To make crust, butter a 9-inch springform pan. Mix vanilla wafer crumbs with butter. Press crust into pan.

2. Heat oven to 350°F. Beat cream cheese, sugar, and flour in the bowl of an electric mixer until light and creamy, about 3 minutes. Add eggs and yolk one at a time, beating well after each addition. Add sour cream and vanilla. Beat, scraping down sides of bowl, until smooth.

3. Pour mixture into prepared crust; place on a baking sheet. Bake until cake is firm around the edge and center barely jiggles when tapped, about 50 minutes. Refrigerate at least 8 hours.

NUTRITION INFORMATION PER SERVING:

494 calories	38 g fat	22 g saturated fat
67% calories from fat	156 mg cholesterol	352 mg sodium
33 g carbohydrate	8 g protein	0.3 g fiber

Chocolate Cheesecake

PREPARATION TIME: 35 minutes
COOKING TIME: 50 to 55 minutes
CHILLING TIME: Overnight
YIELD: 14 servings

THIS CHEESECAKE RECIPE, developed in the *Tribune* test kitchen, gives you fourteen servings of creamy chocolate flavor. A bit of rum is used instead of vanilla extract, but if you don't have any, the vanilla works well, too.

Crust
1 cup crushed chocolate wafers
¼ cup (½ stick) butter, melted
¼ cup chopped walnuts
¼ teaspoon ground cinnamon

Filling
3 8-ounce packages cream cheese, softened

1 cup sugar
3 large eggs
2 cups sour cream
2 teaspoons dark rum *or* vanilla extract
1 12-ounce package semisweet chocolate chips, melted
1 ounce unsweetened chocolate, melted

1. Heat oven to 350°F. Mix wafer crumbs, butter, walnuts, and cinnamon in a small bowl. Press mixture into bottom of a buttered 10-inch springform pan. Bake 10 minutes. Cool on wire rack. Line sides of springform pan with buttered wax paper.

2. Reduce oven temperature to 325°F. Beat cream cheese and sugar in the bowl of an electric mixer until light and fluffy, about 3 minutes. Add eggs, 1 at a time, beating well after each addition. Beat in sour cream and rum. Fold in chocolate by hand until smooth.

3. Pour batter over cooled crust. Bake until center is almost set, 40 to 45 minutes. Turn off oven. Prop oven door open a few inches. Let cake cool in oven 1 to 2 hours. Cool completely on wire rack. Refrigerate, covered, overnight.

NUTRITION INFORMATION PER SERVING:

519 calories	39 g fat	23 g saturated fat
65% calories from fat	123 mg cholesterol	261 mg sodium
40 g carbohydrate	8 g protein	2.2 g fiber

Mama T.'s Italian Cheesecake

PREPARATION TIME: 20 minutes
COOKING TIME: 1½ hours
CHILLING TIME: 4 hours
YIELD: 12 servings

THIS SIMPLE, RICH recipe came from Grace Tarantino and her restaurateur son, John. It substitutes creamy, low-fat ricotta cheese for cream cheese. Serve it topped with fresh fruit.

Crust
1½ cups graham cracker crumbs
¼ cup (½ stick) butter, softened
2 tablespoons sugar

Filling
1¼ cups sugar

¼ cup (½ stick) unsalted butter, softened
3 large egg yolks
3 tablespoons flour
2 teaspoons vanilla extract
2½ pounds ricotta cheese
2 cups sour cream

1. Heat oven to 325°F. For crust, combine all ingredients. Press into bottom and 1 inch up sides of a 9-inch springform pan. Bake until set, 10 minutes. Cool on wire rack.

2. For filling, mix sugar, butter, and egg yolks with electric mixer until well mixed. Mix in flour and vanilla. Add ricotta; mix until smooth, 4 to 5 minutes. Mix in sour cream.

3. Pour filling into crust. Bake until barely set in the center, 70 to 80 minutes. Cool to room temperature on wire rack. Refrigerate at least 4 hours before serving.

NUTRITION INFORMATION PER SERVING:

456 calories	26 g fat	15 g saturated fat
51% calories from fat	120 mg cholesterol	271 mg sodium
43 g carbohydrate	14 g protein	0.5 g fiber

Basic Pie Crust

PREPARATION TIME: 10 minutes
CHILLING TIME: 30 minutes
YIELD: 1 9-inch, 8-serving crust

IT'S THE CRUST—or rather, the fear of the crust—that keeps many cooks from attempting pie. All it takes is one mastered recipe, and the rest is as easy as, yes, apple pie. This recipe is literally taped to the cabinet in the *Tribune* test kitchen.

2 cups all-purpose *or* pastry flour	2 tablespoons chilled, unsalted
1 teaspoon salt	butter
⅔ cup chilled vegetable shortening	5 to 6 tablespoons ice water
or lard	

1. Mix flour and salt in a large bowl. Cut in shortening and butter with a pastry blender or 2 table knives until mixture resembles coarse crumbs. Stir in just enough water using a fork so mixture gathers easily into a ball. Shape into a ball; cover in plastic wrap. Refrigerate at least 30 minutes.

2. Lightly flour a board or pastry cloth. Roll the dough out with quick strokes of the rolling pin, working away from the center, to make a circle 3 inches larger than the pie pan and ⅛ inch thick.

3. Fold dough in half; lift it into the pie pan leaving a 1½-inch overhang. Trim the edges with a sharp knife if necessary. Double back overhanging edges so dough stands upright. Shape dough into fluted edges with your fingers.

4. Chill thoroughly, at least 30 minutes. Put in filling. Bake according to specific pie recipe directions.

❧ NOTE: *To make a **double-crust pie**, double the ingredients listed. Divide chilled dough into 2 portions, one slightly larger than the other. Chill larger portion until ready to roll out.*

To make bottom crust, roll out smaller dough portion as in steps 2 and 3, making a circle 1 inch larger than the pie pan and ⅛ inch thick. Fill. To make top crust, roll out larger portion of dough and then cut several slits near the center or pierce it with a fork to vent steam.

Brush the edge of bottom crust with water. Fit top crust over filling. Fold the edge of top crust over bottom crust. Press together lightly with your fingers or a fork. Bake according to specific pie recipe directions.

To bake a single **unfilled pie crust**, (or "blind," as the English would say), first pierce the bottom of crust with a fork. Chill thoroughly, at least 30 minutes. Line loosely with aluminum foil; fill with dried peas, dried beans, uncooked rice, or pie crust weights to keep crust from rising and bubbling. Bake in a preheated 450°F oven 8 minutes. Remove peas and foil. Put crust back in the oven to finish baking until lightly browned, about 2 minutes. Cool completely before filling.

NUTRITION INFORMATION PER SERVING:

289 calories	20 g fat	6 g saturated fat
63% calories from fat	8 mg cholesterol	292 mg sodium
24 g carbohydrate	3.3 g protein	0.8 g fiber

Pie Crust Tips

Chill the ingredients and utensils.

Use all-purpose or pastry flour.

Measure carefully. The correct proportions can make the difference between flaky and crumbly.

Butter has the finest flavor, but an all-butter crust can be hard and brittle.

Lard makes a fine, flaky crust but is best combined with butter for flavor. Such a pie usually tastes better when eaten warm.

Enough water is needed to make the dough hold together and easy to roll out. Too much will make the pastry tough.

Mix dough quickly. Overworking will make it tough.

In warm weather, refrigerate the flour-fat mixture for 1 hour before adding liquid.

Roll on a wooden board, if possible. A pastry cloth and rolling pin cover will keep the dough from sticking.

To prevent sticking and shrinking later, chill dough and avoid pressing down on it with the rolling pin or stretching it. Lift dough occasionally with a broad spatula and sprinkle the board or pastry cloth again with flour.

If patching is needed, cut a piece to fit. Moisten it with water. Press it into place.

If possible, hook the fluted edge over the edge of the pie plate to prevent shrinking.

To glaze the top crust, brush it with ice water, whipping cream, or beaten egg before baking.

Fast Food-Processor Pie Crust

PREPARATION TIME: 25 minutes
CHILLING TIME: 1 hour
BAKING TIME: 15 minutes
YIELD: 1 9-inch, 6-serving crust

MODERN CONVENIENCES CAN be put to work for any number of chores. Here, a food processor helps out with a pie crust.

1¼ cups all-purpose flour
½ cup cake flour
⅔ cup vegetable shortening

2 tablespoons sugar
½ teaspoon salt
¼ cup chilled milk plus more as needed

1. Put all-purpose flour, cake flour, shortening, sugar, and salt into a food processor fitted with a metal blade. Pulse until shortening disappears. Add milk through the feed tube with the motor running. Pulse until dough begins to clump. Gather dough into a ball; wrap in plastic wrap or waxed paper. Refrigerate 1 hour.

2. Heat oven to 350°F. Flour the work surface well. Roll out dough to a 13-inch circle. Loosen from work surface; carefully roll up on a rolling pin. Unroll over a 9-inch pie plate, working carefully, as dough is brittle. (If dough crumbles, add 1 to 2 tablespoons milk, reroll, and replace in the pie plate.)

3. Trim dough to ¼ inch beyond plate rim. Turn edges under, doubling dough along rim. Dough will crack; push together and flute the rim of the crust. Flatten bottom and sides gently against the pie plate. Pierce the bottom and rim of the crust with the tines of a fork. Refrigerate 10 minutes. Bake 15 minutes. Cool. Crust is partly baked and ready to fill.

NUTRITION INFORMATION PER SERVING:

344 calories	23 g fat	6 g saturated fat
60% calories from fat	1 mg cholesterol	200 mg sodium
31 g carbohydrate	3.7 g protein	0.8 g fiber

Classic Cherry Pie

PREPARATION TIME: 40 minutes
STANDING TIME: 15 minutes
COOKING TIME: 50 minutes
YIELD: 8 servings

HERE'S A TWO-CRUST cherry pie that George Washington might have been familiar with. If you like the taste of almonds, use a few drops of almond extract instead of the kirsch (cherry brandy).

Crust

2 cups all-purpose *or* pastry flour
1 teaspoon salt
⅔ cup chilled vegetable shortening
2 tablespoons chilled butter
4 to 5 tablespoons ice water

Filling

5 to 6 cups pitted fresh *or* frozen
    sour cherries, thawed
1⅓ cups sugar
¼ cup kirsch *or* other cherry brandy
2 tablespoons plus 2 teaspoons
    quick-cooking tapioca
1 teaspoon finely grated lemon zest
2 tablespoons butter, cut into pieces

1. To make pie crust, put flour and salt into a large bowl. Cut in shortening and butter with a pastry blender or 2 knives until mixture resembles coarse crumbs. Sprinkle in water 1 tablespoon at a time, mixing well with a fork until flour is moistened and a soft dough forms. Shape into 2 balls. Refrigerate 30 minutes.

2. Heat oven to 450°F. To make filling, combine cherries, sugar, kirsch, tapioca, and lemon zest in a large bowl. Let mixture stand 15 minutes.

3. Flour the work surface well. Roll out 1 ball of dough to fit a 9-inch pie pan; fit into pan. Roll out remaining dough ball for top crust.

4. Pour filling into pie pan; dot top with butter. Put top crust over filling. Seal; flute edges. Make 4 large slashes on top to vent steam.

5. Bake 10 minutes. Reduce oven temperature to 350°F; bake until crust is golden brown, about 40 minutes. Cool on a wire rack.

NUTRITION INFORMATION PER SERVING:

507 calories	23 g fat	8 g saturated fat
41% calories from fat	16 mg cholesterol	353 mg sodium
72 g carbohydrate	4.3 g protein	2.4 g fiber

Triple-Berry Lattice Pie

COOKING TIME: 1 hour
YIELD: 8 servings

"FRESH FRUIT PIES, with their homemade, flaky crusts and juicy, aromatic fillings, fill us with a deep nostalgia for a simpler life—the summers of childhood, perhaps," wrote JeanMarie Brownson in an article celebrating the fruits of summer. Blueberries, raspberries, and strawberries provide an ultrafruity filling for this pie, which Brownson developed. If you can, use fresh seasonal fruit, but frozen will work fine. A scoop of vanilla ice cream on top isn't a bad idea, either.

Dough for double Basic Pie Crust
　(see Index)
1 large egg
1 tablespoon milk
4 cups blueberries, stems removed
1 cup raspberries
1 cup hulled, sliced strawberries
1 to 1¼ cups sugar

1 tablespoon fresh lemon juice
⅛ teaspoon salt
⅛ teaspoon freshly ground nutmeg
¼ cup quick-cooking tapioca
2 tablespoons unsalted butter, cut
　into small bits
Sugar for sprinkling

1. Heat oven to 425°F. Roll out half of the pie dough; fit into a 9-inch pie pan. Beat egg with milk. Brush edge with egg mixture.

2. Mix 3 cups of the blueberries with raspberries, strawberries, sugar, lemon juice, salt, nutmeg, and tapioca in a large bowl. Transfer mixture to crust. Sprinkle remaining 1 cup blueberries over all. Dot top with butter. Refrigerate. Roll out and cut the remaining half of dough into ½-inch-wide strips for lattice top. Place lattice strips over pie.

3. Brush lattice strips and edge with remaining egg mixture. Sprinkle with sugar. Place pie on a baking sheet. Bake 15 minutes. Reduce oven temperature to 350°F; bake until crust is golden brown, 35 to 45 minutes longer.

NUTRITION INFORMATION PER SERVING:

366 calories	14 g fat	5 g saturated fat
34% calories from fat	34 mg cholesterol	254 mg sodium
59 g carbohydrate	3 g protein	3.9 g fiber

Strawberry-Rhubarb Lattice Pie

PREPARATION TIME: 45 minutes
CHILLING TIME: 1 hour
STANDING TIME: 30 minutes
COOKING TIME: 1 hour
YIELD: 8 servings

THE COMBINATION OF strawberries and rhubarb has become a classic. Here the two harbingers of spring are paired in a pie with a decorative lattice top.

Crust
2 cups all-purpose flour
¾ teaspoon salt
⅔ cup chilled vegetable shortening
    or lard
2 tablespoons chilled unsalted butter
4 to 5 tablespoons ice water

Filling
2 cups diced fresh rhubarb
¾ cup sugar

¼ teaspoon salt
1 tablespoon cornstarch
½ teaspoon grated lemon zest
1½ pints strawberries, hulled and
    halved
3 tablespoons finely crushed vanilla
    wafers
2 tablespoons whipping cream
Whipped cream

1. To make crust, stir together flour and salt in a large bowl. Cut in shortening and butter with a pastry blender or 2 knives until mixture resembles coarse crumbs. Sprinkle in water 1 tablespoon at a time, tossing with a fork until flour is moistened and a soft dough forms. Shape into 2 balls, one slightly larger than the other. Wrap in waxed paper or plastic wrap; refrigerate at least 30 minutes.

2. Lightly flour the work surface. Roll out larger half to ⅛ inch thickness. Fit into a 9-inch pie pan. Refrigerate while making filling.

3. To make filling, stir together rhubarb, sugar, and salt in a medium-sized bowl and let stand 30 minutes. Strain accumulated rhubarb liquid into a medium-sized saucepan. Add cornstarch and lemon zest. Cook, stirring constantly, over medium heat until smooth and thickened, about 5 minutes. Remove from heat. Stir in rhubarb and strawberries.

4. Heat oven to 450°F. Sprinkle vanilla wafer crumbs over bottom crust. Top with rhubarb mixture. Roll out remaining dough half on the lightly floured surface to ¼ inch thickness. Cut into ½-inch-wide strips. Arrange strips over pie in lattice fashion.

➤

5. Brush strips lightly with 2 tablespoons whipping cream. Place pie on a baking sheet; bake 15 minutes. Reduce oven temperature to 350°F. Bake until crust is crisp and brown and fruit is tender, about 35 minutes. Cool on wire rack. Serve warm with whipped cream.

NUTRITION INFORMATION PER SERVING:

415 calories	22 g fat	7 g saturated fat
47% calories from fat	13 mg cholesterol	312 mg sodium
52 g carbohydrate	4.2 g protein	2.9 g fiber

Ginger Apple Pie

PREPARATION TIME: 45 minutes

CHILLING TIME: 30 minutes

COOKING TIME: 1 hour

YIELD: 8 servings

FOR A SEPTEMBER story about the new varieties of apples coming out of Michigan, writer William Rice included this recipe from June Stover, whose fourth-generation family-owned Stover Orchards is one of the attractions along U.S. Highway 31 just outside Berrien Springs.

Crust

2¼ cups all-purpose flour

2 tablespoons sugar

1 teaspoon salt

½ cup (1 stick) plus 3 tablespoons chilled unsalted butter, cut into ¼-inch pieces

7 tablespoons chilled vegetable shortening

4 to 5 tablespoons ice water

Filling

5 cups peeled, cored, and sliced baking apples

1 pear, peeled, cored, and sliced

1 ⅛-inch-thick piece gingerroot, peeled and minced

½ teaspoon ground nutmeg

½ teaspoon cinnamon

¼ teaspoon salt

1 cup sugar

1 tablespoon all-purpose flour

¾ cup whipping cream

1. To make crust, mix flour, sugar, and salt in a food processor fitted with a metal blade or in a large bowl. Scatter butter pieces over flour mixture, tossing to coat butter with flour. Cut butter into flour with 5 1-second pulses of the food processor or with a pastry blender. Add shortening; pulse 4 times or until dough resembles coarse cornmeal. Turn mixture into a medium-sized bowl.

2. Sprinkle 3 tablespoons of the ice water over mixture. Lightly toss with a fork until dough begins to stick together, adding up to 2 tablespoons more ice water if needed. Divide dough in half; shape into 2 balls, one slightly larger than the other. Flatten balls into 4-inch-wide discs. Wrap in plastic wrap or waxed paper; refrigerate 30 minutes before rolling.

3. Heat oven to 425°F. To make filling, toss together apples, pear, gingerroot, nutmeg, cinnamon, and salt in a large bowl; set aside.

4. Lightly flour the work surface. Roll larger half of dough out to a 12-inch circle. Loosen dough from surface, fold it into quarters, and transfer it to a 9-inch pie pan. Unfold; gently ease dough into pan, being careful not to stretch it. Trim edge with a knife, leaving a 1-inch overhang. Patch any holes or tears with scraps of dough. Fill crust with apple mixture. Stir together sugar and flour in a small bowl; sprinkle over apples. Pour whipping cream over apples.

5. Roll out remaining dough ball. Place over filling. Lightly moisten the edge of bottom crust with water; press the edge of top crust down on bottom to seal. Crimp as desired; cut steam vents in top crust.

6. Place pie on a baking sheet. Bake 10 minutes. Reduce heat to 350°F; bake until crust is golden and apples are tender when pierced through vent holes with a sharp knife, 50 to 60 minutes. Cool on a wire rack.

NUTRITION INFORMATION PER SERVING:

610 calories	36 g fat	18 g saturated fat
52% calories from fat	75 mg cholesterol	375 mg sodium
71 g carbohydrate	5 g protein	3.4 g fiber

Apple Slices

PREPARATION TIME: 30 minutes
BAKING TIME: 50 minutes
YIELD: 12 servings

THIS FREQUENTLY REQUESTED recipe first ran in 1951. Originally it called for lard in the crust instead of vegetable shortening; either can be used.

Filling
1 cup water

1¼ cups sugar
1 teaspoon cinnamon

▶

¼ teaspoon salt

3 pounds tart cooking apples, such as Granny Smith, peeled, cored, and cut into eighths

2 tablespoons cornstarch

¼ cup cold water

Crust

2 cups all-purpose flour

½ teaspoon baking powder

½ teaspoon salt

¾ cup vegetable shortening *or* butter

2 large egg yolks, beaten

½ cup water

1 teaspoon lemon juice

Icing

1 cup confectioners' sugar

2 to 3 tablespoons fresh lemon juice *or* water

1. To make filling, heat water, sugar, cinnamon, and salt to boil in a large saucepan over medium-high heat. Add apples. Reduce heat to medium-low; simmer 10 minutes. Stir together cornstarch and ¼ cup cold water in a small bowl until smooth; add to apple mixture. Cook filling 5 minutes longer, stirring gently.

2. To make crust, sift flour, baking powder, and salt into a large bowl. Cut in shortening using a pastry blender or 2 knives until mixture resembles coarse crumbs. Stir together egg yolks, water, and lemon juice in a small bowl. Sprinkle over flour mixture 1 tablespoon at a time, mixing with a fork until flour is moistened and a soft dough forms. Divide into 2 parts, one slightly larger than the other.

3. Heat oven to 450°F. Roll out larger piece of dough to fit the bottom and up the sides of a 13″ × 9″ baking pan. Fill with filling. Roll the other half of dough to fit the top; crimp top and bottom edges together. Cut steam vents in top crust.

4. Bake 20 minutes. Reduce oven temperature to 350°F; bake until crust is golden, about 30 minutes. Cool slightly on a wire rack. To make icing, stir together confectioners' sugar and lemon juice in a small bowl. Spread over warm crust. Cut in 12 slices to serve.

NUTRITION INFORMATION PER SERVING:

368 calories	14 g fat	3.5 g saturated fat
33% calories from fat	35 mg cholesterol	170 mg sodium
61 g carbohydrate	3 g protein	2.8 g fiber

Ginger Peach Pie

PREPARATION TIME: 30 minutes
CHILLING TIME: 30 minutes
COOKING TIME: 1 hour
YIELD: 8 servings

THIS DEEP-DISH, double-crust peach pie would be a true American classic—except for the addition of a couple of simple ingredients: ginger and gingersnaps. The ginger adds to the flavor (not to mention the aroma), while the gingersnap crumbs absorb liquid that could otherwise make the lower crust soggy. Call it a neoclassic peach pie.

Crust
2 cups all-purpose flour
1 teaspoon salt
⅔ cup chilled vegetable
    shortening
2 tablespoons chilled unsalted
    butter
4 to 5 tablespoons ice water

Filling
7 cups peeled, sliced fresh peaches
    (about 12 medium-sized)

⅓ cup plus 1 tablespoon granulated
    sugar
⅓ cup packed light brown sugar
3 tablespoons cornstarch
1 teaspoon grated lemon zest
1 tablespoon fresh lemon juice
½ teaspoon ground ginger
¼ teaspoon cinnamon
¼ cup finely crushed gingersnaps
2 tablespoons whipping cream

1. To make crust, stir together flour and salt in a large bowl. Cut in shortening and butter using a pastry blender or 2 knives until mixture resembles coarse crumbs. Sprinkle in water 1 tablespoon at a time, tossing with a fork until flour is moistened and a soft dough forms. Shape into 2 balls; flatten into discs. Wrap each disc in waxed paper or plastic wrap. Refrigerate at least 30 minutes.

2. Heat oven to 425°F. To make filling, combine peaches, ⅓ cup of the granulated sugar, brown sugar, cornstarch, lemon zest, lemon juice, ginger, and cinnamon in a large bowl; toss to coat peaches.

3. Flour the work surface well. Roll out 1 dough disc to fit a deep, 9-inch pie pan. Fit dough onto the bottom and up the sides of the pan. Sprinkle the bottom with gingersnap crumbs. Add peach mixture. Roll out remaining dough disc for top crust. Put over filling. Seal and flute edges. Make 4 large slashes on top for steam vents.

►

4. Brush crust with whipping cream. Sprinkle with 1 tablespoon sugar. Put pie onto a baking sheet. Bake at 425°F 20 minutes. Reduce oven temperature to 350°F; bake until crust is golden brown, 30 to 40 minutes. Cool on a wire rack.

❧ NOTE: *To peel peaches with ease, drop them into boiling water for about 30 seconds. Test to see if skins come off easily; if not, repeat.*

NUTRITION INFORMATION PER SERVING:

461 calories	22 g fat	7 g saturated fat
42% calories from fat	13 mg cholesterol	332 mg sodium
63 g carbohydrate	4.5 g protein	3.5 g fiber

Pumpkin-Pecan Pie

PREPARATION TIME: 45 minutes
CHILLING TIME: 1 hour
COOKING TIME: 1 hour
YIELD: 8 servings

THE FILLING IS pumpkin, the topping is pecans, and the garnish is whipped cream. It's a classic fall and winter dessert from cookbook author Jane Freiman Schanberg.

Topping
¾ cup chopped pecans
3 tablespoons butter, slightly
    softened and cut in thirds
2 tablespoons dark brown sugar

Filling
2 cups solid-pack canned pumpkin
⅔ cup packed dark brown sugar
⅓ cup granulated sugar
2 teaspoons cinnamon

1 teaspoon ground ginger
½ teaspoon ground nutmeg
¼ teaspoon ground cloves
¼ teaspoon mace
3 large eggs
1 cup whipping cream
¼ cup milk
¼ cup bourbon *or* rum
1 partially baked Basic Pie Crust
    (see Index)
Whipped cream

1. Heat oven to 350°F. To make topping, combine pecans, butter, and sugar in a food processor fitted with a metal blade. Pulse until medium-sized crumbs form; refrigerate until ready to use.

2. To make filling, combine pumpkin, brown sugar, granulated sugar, cinnamon, ginger, nutmeg, cloves, and mace in a food processor. Process to mix 5 seconds; scrape down container sides. Add eggs, cream, milk, and bourbon. Process to mix. Pour filling into partially baked crust.

3. Bake 35 minutes. Remove pie from oven; spoon topping around rim. Return pie to oven; bake until a knife inserted in the center comes out clean, about 25 minutes. Cool completely on a wire rack. Serve with whipped cream.

NUTRITION INFORMATION PER SERVING:

467 calories	30 g fat	13 g saturated fat
57% calories from fat	133 mg cholesterol	341 mg sodium
46 g carbohydrate	5.5 g protein	3.2 g fiber

Sweet Potato Pie

PREPARATION TIME: 30 minutes

COOKING TIME: 35 minutes

YIELD: 2 9-inch, 8-serving pies

THIS RECIPE FOR sweet potato pie, a dessert mainstay for many Southern families, came from actor Brandon Hammond, one of the stars of the 1997 movie *Soul Food*.

4 medium-sized sweet potatoes, peeled and cubed	2 large eggs
1½ cups sugar	1 tablespoon baking powder
½ cup (1 stick) butter, softened	1 tablespoon vanilla extract
2 tablespoons all-purpose flour	1 teaspoon cinnamon
1 14-ounce can sweetened condensed milk	½ teaspoon nutmeg
	2 unbaked Basic Pie Crusts (see Index)

1. Heat oven to 425°F. Place sweet potatoes in a large saucepan; cover with water. Heat to boil over high heat. Boil until sweet potatoes are tender when pierced with a fork, 10 to 15 minutes. Drain.

2. Combine sweet potatoes, sugar, and butter in the bowl of an electric mixer. Beat until smooth. Add flour, condensed milk, eggs, baking powder, vanilla, cinnamon, and nutmeg. Beat until well mixed.

3. Pour mixture into unbaked pie crusts; place on baking sheets. Bake until crusts and tops are golden brown, 35 to 45 minutes. Let stand until filling sets.

NUTRITION INFORMATION PER SERVING:

330 calories	14 g fat	7 g saturated fat
37% calories from fat	51 mg cholesterol	294 mg sodium
48 g carbohydrate	4.1 g protein	1.1 g fiber

Caramel Chocolate Pecan Pie

PREPARATION TIME: 25 minutes
COOKING TIME: 20 minutes
CHILLING TIME: 4 hours
YIELD: 10 servings

WHEN A PHOTOGRAPH of this pie ran in the *Tribune*'s "Home" section, we were besieged with recipe requests. So we complied and printed the recipe, adapted from one that was used at the now-closed north suburban restaurant, Danny's.

Crust
2 cups chopped pecans
¼ cup granulated sugar
¼ cup (½ stick) unsalted butter, melted

Filling
1 pound caramel candies
⅓ cup whipping cream
1 cup coarsely chopped pecans

Topping
8 ounces semisweet chocolate
⅓ cup whipping cream
¼ cup confectioners' sugar

1. Heat oven to 350°F. For crust, process pecans and sugar in a food processor fitted with a metal blade until finely minced but not ground. Pulse in butter. Press mixture evenly into the bottom and up the sides of a 9-inch pie pan. Bake until lightly browned, 12 to 15 minutes. Cool before filling.

2. For filling, heat caramels and cream in top of a double boiler or in a bowl in a microwave oven, stirring often, until smooth. Cool to lukewarm; pour into crust. Sprinkle pecans evenly over top.

3. For topping, heat chocolate, cream, and sugar in top of the double boiler or in a bowl in the microwave oven, stirring often, until smooth. Pour over pie; smooth with spatula. Refrigerate at least 4 hours or up to 2 days before serving.

NUTRITION INFORMATION PER SERVING:

644 calories	47 g fat	16 g saturated fat
61% calories from fat	37 mg cholesterol	119 mg sodium
60 g carbohydrate	7 g protein	4 g fiber

Mangrove Mama's Key Lime Pie

PREPARATION TIME: 20 minutes
COOKING TIME: 23 minutes
CHILLING TIME: 4 hours or overnight
YIELD: 1 9-inch, 8-serving pie

WHERE ELSE CAN you get an authentic recipe for Key lime pie but the Florida Keys? Tom Daniels of Mangrove Mama's restaurant on Sugarloaf Key shared this recipe with food editor Carol Mighton Haddix for her article on Key lime pie. The story was part of our 1998–1999 series, "American Originals," which celebrated classic regional American dishes. When fresh Key limes are unavailable, Daniels uses bottled juice. But Persian limes—the ones typically found at the supermarket—can be used too.

Crust
¼ cup (½ stick) butter *or*
  margarine, melted
1 cup graham cracker crumbs
1 tablespoon sugar
1½ teaspoons cinnamon

Filling
5 large egg yolks
1 14-ounce can sweetened
  condensed milk
Juice from 6 to 8 Key limes
  (about ⅔ cup)
Whipped cream

1. Heat oven to 325°F. For crust, mix butter, graham crackers, sugar, and cinnamon in a medium bowl. Pat onto the bottom and up the sides of a 9-inch pie pan. Bake 8 minutes. Set aside; let cool completely.

2. For filling, beat yolks in a food processor fitted with a metal blade or with a hand mixer, about 2 minutes. Add condensed milk to yolks; process or beat until incorporated. Add lime juice. Process 2 minutes; pour into pie shell. Bake until set, 10 to 15 minutes. Remove from oven; cool on a wire rack 1 hour. Refrigerate, covered with plastic wrap set directly on top of filling, at least 4 hours or overnight. Top with fresh whipped cream.

✒ VARIATION: *Instead of whipped cream, you may top with meringue. Beat 5 egg whites until stiff but not dry. Add ¼ cup sugar, beating constantly until combined. Spread over baked filling; bake at 350°F until meringue starts to brown, about 5 minutes.*

NUTRITIONAL INFORMATION PER SERVING:

325 calories	14 g fat	8 g saturated fat
41% calories from fat	165 mg cholesterol	215 mg sodium
44 g carbohydrate	7 g protein	0.7 g fiber

Strawberry Cream Tart

PREPARATION TIME: 30 minutes
COOKING TIME: 30 minutes
CHILLING TIME: 3½ hours
YIELD: 10 servings

MOST STRAWBERRIES ARE bred less for taste than for sturdiness and uniformity, writer Kristin Eddy noted in a 1998 article. The best places to find the ripest, richest varieties are farmers markets, under signs designating local growers at the super-market, or from U-pick farms. And what better destination for a delicious bundle of fresh berries than a strawberry tart? This recipe, developed in the *Tribune* test kitchen, uses pastry cream—an egg- and flour-based custard—to complement the berries.

Crust
1 cup all-purpose flour
½ cup sugar
½ cup chopped almonds
¼ cup (½ stick) unsalted butter, softened
1 large egg
½ teaspoon salt
½ teaspoon vanilla extract
1 large egg white, slightly beaten

Cream
2½ cups whole milk
1 vanilla bean, split in half lengthwise
5 large egg yolks
½ cup sugar
2 tablespoons cornstarch
1 tablespoon all-purpose flour

Topping
1 pint strawberries, hulled

1. For crust, combine flour, sugar, almonds, butter, whole egg, salt, and vanilla in a large bowl. Stir together until well blended. Press onto the bottom and up the sides of a greased 10-inch tart pan with removable bottom; chill 30 minutes.

2. Heat oven to 400°F. Brush crust with beaten egg white. Bake crust until golden brown, about 15 minutes. Remove to a wire rack; cool completely.

3. For cream, heat milk and vanilla bean over medium heat in medium saucepan until just simmering, about 5 minutes. Remove from heat; let stand 30 minutes. Remove vanilla bean; scrape seeds from bean into milk. Discard bean.

4. Stir together yolks, sugar, cornstarch, and flour in a medium bowl. Heat milk back to boil over medium heat. Whisk about 1 cup of the milk into yolk mixture; pour back into pan. Cook until large bubbles break surface. Reduce heat to low; cook, stirring constantly, until thickened, about 4 minutes. Pour custard into cooled

tart shell. Place waxed paper directly onto custard surface. Chill until set, about 3 hours. Arrange strawberries on top of custard.

NUTRITION INFORMATION PER SERVING:

290 calories	13 g fat	5 g saturated fat
39% calories from fat	145 mg cholesterol	165 mg sodium
39 g carbohydrate	7 g protein	1.9 g fiber

Tangy Lemon-Plum Tart

PREPARATION TIME: 1 hour

STANDING TIME: 1 hour

BAKING TIME: 18 minutes

YIELD: 8 servings

NOTHING REPLACES THE fresh, deep flavors of fruits and vegetables in season. This lovely dessert, developed by former *Tribune* test kitchen director Alicia Tessling, puts seasonal plums to delicious advantage. The lemon curd filling in this tart . . . is quite tart! If you want a sweeter filling, increase the sugar used in the curd to ½ cup.

1¾ cups sugar	⅓ cup whipping cream
½ cup water	⅛ teaspoon salt
5 to 6 plums, pitted and cut into	⅔ cup plum preserves
¼-inch slices	1 baked, cooled Basic Pie Crust
Zest and juice of 2 lemons	(see Index)
2 large eggs	

1. Combine 1½ cups of the sugar and water in a medium-sized saucepan. Heat over low heat until sugar is dissolved. Increase heat to medium; heat to boil. Boil until syrup reaches soft ball stage, 238°F on a candy thermometer. Add plum slices; return to boil. Remove saucepan from heat. Let stand 1 hour.

2. Heat oven to 350°F. To make curd, combine lemon zest, lemon juice, eggs, and remaining ¼ cup sugar in the bowl of an electric mixer; beat until light. Add cream and salt; beat until smooth. Pour into cooled crust; bake until set, 18 to 22 minutes. Cool.

►

3. Remove plum slices from syrup; drain. Arrange on top of curd. Heat preserves in a small saucepan over medium heat. Pour through a fine-mesh sieve; discard plum pieces. Brush strained preserves juice over plum slices. Serve.

NUTRITION INFORMATION PER SERVING:

395 calories	10 g fat	4.3 g saturated fat
23% calories from fat	67 mg cholesterol	169 mg sodium
76 g carbohydrate	3.1 g protein	1.5 g fiber

Macadamia Nut Tart

PREPARATION TIME: 1 hour

CHILLING TIME: 20 to 30 minutes

COOKING TIME: 25 minutes

YIELD: 8 servings

THIS RICH AND delicious dessert from Fresh Start Bakery and Catering in Flossmoor, Illinois, showcases macadamia nuts. Yes, macadamia nuts are expensive. But what else matches their rich, buttery flavor and soft-crunchy texture? Because these nuts are high in fat, they can go rancid, writes Sharon Tyler Herbst in *Food Lover's Companion*, so store them in the refrigerator or freezer.

Crust

½ cup (1 stick) unsalted butter, softened

½ cup granulated sugar

2 large egg yolks

1 teaspoon vanilla extract

1½ cups all-purpose flour

Filling

1 cup packed light brown sugar

⅓ cup unsalted butter

3 tablespoons whipping cream

2 tablespoons plus 1 teaspoon pure maple syrup

2 tablespoons plus 1 teaspoon light corn syrup

¾ pound unsalted macadamia nut halves

Whipped cream

1. To make crust, beat butter and sugar in the bowl of an electric mixer until light and fluffy, about 2 minutes. Add egg yolks one at a time, beating well after each addition. Beat in vanilla. Stir in flour by hand just until dough forms.

2. Roll out dough between 2 sheets of waxed paper into a ½-inch-thick circle. Refrigerate on a baking sheet, 20 to 30 minutes.

3. Heat oven to 350°F. Remove one sheet of waxed paper. Grease a 10-inch tart pan with a removable bottom. Put dough paper side up into pan. Remove second sheet of waxed paper; gently press dough onto the bottom and up the sides of the pan. Do not stretch dough or the crust will pull away from the pan during baking. (Dough is very fragile; if dough cracks, simply press it together.)

4. Trim excess dough off the top with a sharp knife. Line bottom of crust with aluminum foil; fill with dried beans, uncooked rice, or pie weights. Bake until lightly browned, about 15 minutes. Remove foil and beans. Bake until golden, 5 to 10 minutes. Cool on a wire rack.

5. To make filling, put brown sugar, butter, whipping cream, maple syrup, and corn syrup in a medium-sized saucepan. Heat to boil over medium-high heat; boil until sugar is dissolved, about 1 minute.

6. Fill crust with nuts. Pour hot filling over nuts. Bake just until filling bubbles, 3 to 5 minutes. Cool completely on a wire rack. Remove the sides of pan. Garnish with whipped cream.

NUTRITION INFORMATION PER SERVING:

779 calories	55 g fat	19 g saturated fat
61% calories from fat	112 mg cholesterol	29 mg sodium
71 g carbohydrate	7 g protein	4.6 g fiber

Pear-Custard Kuchen

PREPARATION TIME: 25 minutes

BAKING TIME: 1 hour

YIELD: 8 servings

OLD-FASHIONED FLAVOR IS never out of style, but nothing says it can't get an update. A smooth custard adds another layer of flavor to sweet, cooked pears and a buttery, spicy crust in this kuchen recipe from Abby Mandel, the "Weekend Cook" columnist.

Crust
½ cup (1 stick) chilled unsalted
   butter, cut in 6 pieces
1¼ cups all-purpose flour
3 tablespoons sour cream

3 tablespoons packed light brown
   sugar
½ teaspoon ground ginger
¼ teaspoon grated nutmeg
¼ teaspoon salt

➤

Filling

3 large ripe Bartlett *or* Bosc pears, peeled, cored, and halved lengthwise

3 large egg yolks

1 cup granulated sugar

¼ cup all-purpose flour

⅓ cup sour cream

1 teaspoon vanilla extract

1.   Heat oven to 375°F. To make crust, combine butter, flour, sour cream, 1 tablespoon of the brown sugar, ginger, nutmeg, and salt in a food processor fitted with a metal blade or in a large bowl. Process or cut butter in with a pastry blender until butter is pea-sized. Reserve ½ cup of the crust mixture; press remaining crust mixture onto the bottom and up the sides of a 9-inch tart pan with a removable bottom. Stir remaining 2 tablespoons brown sugar into reserved crust mixture; refrigerate until ready to use.

2.   Bake bottom crust until it is very lightly browned, about 20 minutes. Remove from oven; reduce temperature to 350°F.

3.   To make filling, cut each pear half crosswise into ⅜-inch slices, keeping shape of pear intact. Use a metal spatula to transfer each sliced half to bottom crust, placing five pears along the edge with narrow tips pointing toward the center. Place the sixth half in the center.

4.   Beat egg yolks, granulated sugar, flour, sour cream, and vanilla in the bowl of an electric mixer until smooth; pour between pears. Sprinkle reserved crust mixture over the top. Bake until custard is set, 40 to 50 minutes, depending on how juicy pears are. Cool 10 minutes on a wire rack; remove sides from pan. Serve hot or at room temperature.

NUTRITION INFORMATION PER SERVING:

406 calories	17 g fat	10 g saturated fat
37% calories from fat	117 mg cholesterol	88 mg sodium
61 g carbohydrate	4.4 g protein	2.5 g fiber

Mixed Berry Cobbler

PREPARATION TIME: 30 minutes
BAKING TIME: 30 minutes
YIELD: 8 servings

THIS RECIPE WAS included in a food processor column by Jane Freiman Schanberg, who quite correctly commented that few desserts offer such delicious simplicity as old-fashioned cobblers filled with berries and topped with a thick, tender pastry crust. This cobbler can be made in the morning and then set aside until serving time. You can serve it with whipped cream, ice cream, custard sauce, or all by its wonderful self.

Dough
Zest strips of 1 medium-sized
   lemon
3 tablespoons sugar
1½ cups cake flour
2 teaspoons baking powder
⅛ teaspoon salt
¼ cup chilled unsalted butter
¼ cup chilled vegetable shortening
⅓ cup milk

Filling
1 pint blueberries
½ pint strawberries, hulled
½ pint raspberries
2 tablespoons cornstarch
3 tablespoons water
1 tablespoon fresh lemon juice
½ cup sugar
Whipped cream *or* vanilla ice
   cream, optional

1. To make dough, put lemon zest and sugar into a food processor fitted with a metal blade. Process until zest is minced, about 1 minute. Add cake flour, baking powder, and salt. Process 5 seconds to mix.

2. Cut butter into pieces; add butter and vegetable shortening to flour mixture. Pulse until butter and shortening disappear. Add milk; pulse until dough begins to clump. Wrap dough in waxed paper or plastic wrap. Refrigerate 20 minutes.

3. Heat oven to 350°F. To make filling, put berries in a large bowl. Dissolve cornstarch in water and lemon juice in a small bowl. Add sugar; toss to coat berries. Generously butter an 8-inch square baking dish. Transfer berry mixture to baking dish.

4. Lightly flour the work surface. Roll out dough. Transfer dough to the baking dish to completely cover filling. Bake until crust is golden and berries are tender, 30 to 35 minutes. Cool on a wire rack until warm. Serve warm, with whipped cream or ice cream if desired.

NUTRITION INFORMATION PER SERVING:

288 calories	13 g fat	5 g saturated fat
39% calories from fat	16 mg cholesterol	167 mg sodium
43 g carbohydrate	2.4 g protein	3 g fiber

Bourbon-Pecan-Pumpkin Pudding

PREPARATION TIME: 20 minutes

COOKING TIME: 35 minutes

YIELD: 10 servings

PUMPKIN PIE IS synonymous with the holiday season, but this moist pudding offers an alternative that's still close to the original. "A touch of bourbon along with chopped pecans gives this dessert a new flavor twist that makes it elegant enough for guests when it is served warm from the oven," wrote Paul Camp in a 1985 article that accompanied this recipe. You can serve this pudding hot or cold.

1¼ cups sugar

¼ cup (½ stick) unsalted butter, softened

6 large eggs

¼ teaspoon salt

¼ teaspoon cinnamon

¼ teaspoon ground cloves

¼ teaspoon ground nutmeg

2 cups pureed cooked fresh *or* solid-pack canned pumpkin

⅓ cup bourbon

½ teaspoon grated lemon zest

½ cup finely chopped pecans

1 cup whipping cream

Pecan halves

Whipped cream

1. Heat oven to 350°F. Generously butter a 2-quart soufflé or baking dish. Sprinkle dish with sugar; invert dish and tap out excess sugar.

2. Beat sugar and butter in the bowl of an electric mixer. Add eggs one at a time, beating well after each addition. Add salt, cinnamon, cloves, and nutmeg. Add pumpkin, bourbon, and lemon zest; beat until smooth. Stir in chopped pecans by hand.

3. Beat 1 cup whipping cream to form soft peaks in the bowl of the electric mixer. Fold into pumpkin mixture. Do not overmix.

4. Transfer to the prepared soufflé dish. Bake until a fork inserted into the center comes out clean, about 35 minutes. Cool on a wire rack. Top with pecan halves and whipped cream. Serve pudding warm, at room temperature, or chilled.

NUTRITION INFORMATION PER SERVING:

323 calories	21 g fat	10 g saturated fat
56% calories from fat	173 mg cholesterol	224 mg sodium
31 g carbohydrate	5.3 g protein	2 g fiber

Indiana-Style Persimmon Pudding

PREPARATION TIME: 15 minutes
COOKING TIME: 50 minutes
YIELD: 18 servings

WRITER KRISTIN EDDY traveled to southern Indiana in 1998 for a story on persimmon pudding, one of several articles that celebrated regional American food treasures. "The pudding—in the British sense of the word, more like a baked dessert—cooks into a purplish, shimmying custard that's shored up with just enough flour to keep the consistency from resembling crème brûlée," Eddy wrote. The recipe for this chewy, moist cake is adapted from one by Dymple Green of Mitchell, Indiana.

2 large eggs	1 teaspoon baking soda
2¼ cups all-purpose flour	1 teaspoon cinnamon
2 cups persimmon pulp	1 teaspoon ground allspice
1 cup buttermilk	½ teaspoon salt
1 cup granulated sugar	Sweetened whipped cream,
1 cup packed brown sugar	optional
1 tablespoon baking powder	

1.   Heat oven to 350°F. Stir together eggs, flour, persimmon, buttermilk, granulated sugar, brown sugar, baking powder, baking soda, cinnamon, allspice, and salt in a large bowl just until smooth. Grease 2 9″ × 9″ baking pans or 1 13″ × 9″ pan. Pour persimmon mixture into pans.

2.   Bake until a wooden pick inserted in the center comes out clean, about 50 minutes. Cool 15 minutes. Cut into squares; serve with whipped cream if desired.

❦ NOTE: *Native persimmons may be tough to find except at farm stands or certain orchards. Imported or California-grown Asian persimmons may be substituted for the native fruit in this recipe; they're sold at many supermarkets and ethnic stores. To turn fresh persimmons into pulp for recipes, pour boiling water over a bowl of stemmed fruit. Let stand about 2 minutes, then drain and run through a food mill.*

NUTRITION INFORMATION PER SERVING:

195 calories	1 g fat	0.3 g saturated fat
4% calories from fat	25 mg cholesterol	240 mg sodium
65 g carbohydrate	5 g protein	3.2 g fiber

Bread Pudding Soufflé

PREPARATION TIME: 1 hour 20 minutes
COOKING TIME: 45 minutes
YIELD: 8 servings

BREAD PUDDING HAS got to be the ultimate comfort food. This recipe from the famous Commander's Palace restaurant in New Orleans adds a sophisticated spin to this classic dessert by turning part of the bread pudding into a soufflé with a whiskey sauce. The remaining pudding can be chilled and reheated later.

Bread Pudding
10 slices dry white bread, torn in
    pieces
4 cups hot milk
1 cup whipping cream
4 large eggs
1 cup granulated sugar
¼ cup (½ stick) butter, melted
½ cup raisins
1 tablespoon vanilla extract
1 teaspoon cinnamon
½ teaspoon ground nutmeg

Sauce
1½ cups milk
½ cup granulated sugar
¼ cup water
1 tablespoon cornstarch
3 large egg yolks
3 tablespoons whiskey *or* brandy
1 teaspoon vanilla extract

Soufflé Mixture
6 large eggs, separated
½ cup granulated sugar
½ cup confectioners' sugar

1. Heat oven to 350°F. To make bread pudding, mix bread, milk, and whipping cream in a large bowl. Beat eggs in the bowl of an electric mixer. Add ½ cup of the sugar; mix well. Stir in bread mixture, butter, raisins, vanilla, cinnamon, and nutmeg by hand. Butter a 3-quart baking dish or casserole. Pour bread pudding into the casserole. Set casserole in a larger pan; fill with warm water about 1 inch deep.

2. Bake until a knife inserted in the center comes out clean, about 1 hour. Cool on a wire rack. Put 2½ cups of the bread pudding in a large bowl; set aside. (Remaining bread pudding can be served warm with maple syrup another time.)

3. To make sauce, put milk and sugar in the top of a double boiler over simmering water. Mix water and cornstarch until smooth. Stir into milk mixture. Cook over simmering water, stirring constantly, until thickened. Beat egg yolks in a small bowl. Stir some of the milk mixture into egg yolks. Pour egg yolk mixture back into remaining milk mixture. Cook, stirring constantly, until thickened, about 5 minutes. Do not boil. Remove from heat; stir in whiskey and vanilla. Cool.

4. To make soufflé mixture, butter and lightly sugar a 2-quart soufflé dish. Heat oven to 375°F. Mix 6 egg yolks and granulated sugar in the top of a double boiler over simmering water. Whisk yolks and sugar until frothy and shiny. Whisk into reserved bread pudding until smooth.

5. Beat 6 egg whites until frothy. Gradually beat in confectioners' sugar until whites are stiff but not dry. Fold into bread pudding mixture. Transfer soufflé mixture into the prepared dish. Wipe the edges clean. Bake until soufflé is puffed and golden, 30 to 45 minutes. Serve topped with sauce.

NUTRITION INFORMATION PER SERVING:

732 calories	30 g fat	16 g saturated fat
36% calories from fat	416 mg cholesterol	462 mg sodium
96 g carbohydrate	20 g protein	1.5 g fiber

Crème Caramel

PREPARATION TIME: 20 minutes
COOKING TIME: 50 minutes
CHILLING TIME: 30 minutes
YIELD: 4 servings

THIS RECIPE COMES from the now closed restaurant Jamin in Paris. The crème caramel couldn't be richer, but then it couldn't be better, either. This recipe can be made ahead through step 3 and refrigerated no more than one hour.

1 vanilla bean	1¼ cups whipping cream
3 large egg yolks	¼ cup milk
⅓ cup granulated sugar	4 teaspoons brown sugar

1. Heat oven to 325°F. Split vanilla bean in half lengthwise with a sharp knife. Scrape out and set aside small seeds from each half; discard shells. Put egg yolks into a medium-sized bowl. Whisk in granulated sugar and vanilla seeds until smooth. Gradually whisk in whipping cream and milk.

2. Fill 4 small, shallow oven-to-table custard cups or soufflé dishes with whipping cream mixture. Set cups in a large pan. Fill pan with hot water to halfway up the sides of the cups.

3. Bake until mixture is almost set but center still wiggles slightly, about 50 minutes. Remove cups from water; cool on a wire rack.

▶

4. Heat broiler. Sprinkle each cup with 1 teaspoon brown sugar. Broil until sugar is melted and golden, 30 to 60 seconds. Refrigerate at least 30 minutes before serving.

NUTRITION INFORMATION PER SERVING:

390 calories	32 g fat	18 g saturated fat
72% calories from fat	263 mg cholesterol	43 mg sodium
24 g carbohydrate	4.1 g protein	0 g fiber

Apricot Soufflé Filled with Whipped Cream

PREPARATION TIME: 20 minutes

COOKING TIME: 40 minutes

YIELD: 4 servings

THIS DESSERT SOUFFLÉ, created by former test kitchen director JeanMarie Brownson for the Sunday *Tribune Magazine*, stars apricots. Fresh apricots are hard to come by most of the year, but this dish bypasses that obstacle by using dried fruit and apricot brandy for a summery splurge any season of the year.

1 cup dried apricot halves (about 6 ounces)	Pinch salt
¾ cup unsweetened apple juice	5 tablespoons granulated sugar plus more for sprinkling
4 tablespoons apricot brandy	¼ teaspoon cream of tartar
1 tablespoon all-purpose flour	½ cup whipping cream
5 large egg whites	1 tablespoon confectioners' sugar

1. Heat apricots and apple juice to simmer in a small saucepan over medium heat. Simmer covered until apricots are soft, 15 to 20 minutes. Puree in a blender or in a food processor fitted with a metal blade. Add 3 tablespoons of the apricot brandy and flour; mix well. Transfer to a large bowl; cool completely.

2. Heat oven to 375°F. Butter a 3-inch-wide band of aluminum foil and 1 1-quart soufflé dish or 2 2-cup soufflé dishes well. Tie the foil band around the outside of the dish(es) to make a collar. Sprinkle foil and inside of dish heavily with granulated sugar to coat. Invert dish and tap out excess.

3. Beat egg whites and salt in the bowl of an electric mixer until foamy. Continue beating, slowly adding 5 tablespoons sugar and cream of tartar until stiff peaks form.

4. Stir one-fourth of the egg white mixture into apricot mixture to lighten. Carefully fold in remaining egg white mixture. Spoon mixture into prepared dish(es). Bake until puffed and golden, 20 to 30 minutes.

5. Beat whipping cream in the bowl of an electric mixer until soft peaks form. Beat in confectioners' sugar and remaining 1 tablespoon brandy until stiff peaks form. Carefully remove collar from soufflé just before serving. At the table, scoop off the top of the soufflé using a large spoon. Fill with whipped cream; replace soufflé top. Serve immediately.

NUTRITION INFORMATION PER SERVING:

336 calories	11 g fat	7 g saturated fat
30% calories from fat	41 mg cholesterol	119 mg sodium
52 g carbohydrate	7 g protein	2.3 g fiber

Superb Vanilla Custard Ice Cream

PREPARATION TIME: 5 minutes
COOKING TIME: 15 minutes
CHILLING TIME: 4 hours
FREEZING TIME: Variable
YIELD: 8 ½-cup servings

MAKING ICE CREAM at home is a bit more labor-intensive than making a trip to the supermarket, but one creamy spoonful of this vanilla custard ice cream will reward your efforts.

3 cups whipping cream	4 large egg yolks
1 cup half-and-half	1 vanilla bean
¾ cup sugar	

1. Heat whipping cream, half-and-half, and sugar in a medium-sized saucepan over medium heat. Cook, stirring occasionally, until sugar is dissolved and mixture is hot, about 5 minutes.

2. Whisk egg yolks in a medium-sized bowl. Stir in about 1 cup of the hot cream mixture; stir egg yolk mixture back into remaining cream mixture in the saucepan. Cut vanilla bean in half lengthwise. Scrape out seeds; add seeds and pod to mixture.

3. Cook, stirring constantly, over medium heat until mixture thickens and lightly coats the back of a spoon and temperature reads 180°F on an instant-reading thermometer. Do not boil. Strain mixture through a fine-mesh sieve into a large bowl. Refrigerate covered until well chilled, at least 4 hours.

►

4. Freeze in an ice-cream maker according to manufacturer's directions. Transfer to the freezer; freeze at least 15 minutes before serving.

NUTRITION INFORMATION PER SERVING:

450 calories	39 g fat	24 g saturated fat
77% calories from fat	240 mg cholesterol	50 mg sodium
23 g carbohydrate	4 g protein	0 g fiber

Peaches and Cream Gelato

PREPARATION TIME: 15 minutes

COOKING TIME: 5 minutes

CHILLING TIME: 1 hour

FREEZING TIME: Variable

YIELD: 8 servings

GELATO IS THE Italian word for ice cream. This seasonal treat was adapted from a recipe served at the now shuttered Sunset restaurant for a summer article on making ice cream at home.

1¼ cups milk	5 large egg yolks
1¼ cups whipping cream	2 large ripe peaches, peeled, pitted,
½ vanilla bean, split lengthwise	and diced
10 tablespoons sugar	½ teaspoon cinnamon

1. Heat milk, cream, vanilla bean, and 2 tablespoons of the sugar in a medium-sized saucepan over medium heat to just below boiling. Whisk together 6 tablespoons of the sugar and egg yolks in a medium-sized bowl. Slowly whisk into egg mixture about 1 cup of the hot milk mixture.

2. Return egg mixture to saucepan. Cook, stirring constantly, over low heat until slightly thickened, about 5 minutes. Strain mixture through a fine-mesh sieve into a medium-sized bowl. Place the bowl over a larger bowl filled with ice water. Stir mixture until cool to the touch, being careful not to get any water into the medium-sized bowl. Cover; refrigerate at least 1 hour or overnight.

3. Puree peaches with remaining 2 tablespoons sugar and cinnamon in a blender or in a food processor fitted with a metal blade until smooth. Stir into

chilled ice cream base. Transfer to ice-cream maker; freeze according to manufacturer's directions.

NUTRITION INFORMATION PER SERVING:

260 calories	18 g fat	10 g saturated fat
59% calories from fat	185 mg cholesterol	35 mg sodium
23 g carbohydrate	4 g protein	0.9 g fiber

Strawberry Margarita Sorbet with Fresh Fruits

PREPARATION TIME: 15 minutes

FREEZING TIME: Several hours

YIELD: 10 servings

THIS STRAWBERRY MARGARITA–FLAVORED ice takes a spirited approach to sorbet. Food and wine columnist William Rice, on a food tour of Phoenix, got this recipe from cooking teacher Barbara Fenzl. Serve it with seasonal fruits. You will need an ice-cream maker for this recipe.

2 cups water
1 cup sugar
2 pints hulled fresh *or* thawed
    frozen loose-pack strawberries
6 tablespoons fresh lime juice
6 tablespoons tequila

¼ cup orange liqueur, such as
    Triple Sec
Sliced fruit such as papaya, mango,
    pineapple, kiwi, and fresh
    strawberries
Mint sprigs

1. Heat water to boil in a medium-sized saucepan. Dissolve sugar in boiling water; cool. Puree strawberries in a blender or food processor. Mix in lime juice, tequila, and orange liqueur. Stir sugar syrup into berry mixture. Add more lime juice to taste if desired. Refrigerate until well chilled.

2. Process strawberry mixture in an ice-cream maker according to manufacturer's directions. Freeze in a covered container to mellow flavors. If sorbet becomes too solid, soften it in the refrigerator before serving.

3. To serve, arrange sliced fruit on dessert plates, leaving space in the center. Fill center with scoops of sorbet. Garnish with mint sprigs.

NUTRITION INFORMATION PER SERVING:

121 calories	0.3 g fat	0 g saturated fat
2% calories from fat	0 mg cholesterol	2 mg sodium
25 g carbohydrate	0.5 g protein	1.6 g fiber

Raspberry, Peach, and Passion Fruit Sorbet

PREPARATION TIME: 15 minutes
FREEZING TIME: 30 minutes or more
YIELD: 4 servings

THIS ICY, FRUITY—and nonfat—sorbet was created for a "Fast Food" column. Its distinctive blend of fruits is made possible with the new flavors of frozen juice concentrate, such as the passion fruit one used here. The technique for this recipe, using a food processor, is simple and can be applied to many varieties of fruit: Freeze bite-sized chunks of fruit until they are just shy of being rock-hard. Then, whirl them in the food processor until they whip up into a fluffy, smooth mass.

1 pint raspberries
2 to 3 large peaches, unpeeled, pitted and cut into 1-inch pieces

3 tablespoons frozen passion fruit juice concentrate

1. Line a jelly roll pan with plastic wrap. Spread raspberries and peach pieces in pan. Place pan in the freezer until fruit is almost solid.

2. Place semifrozen fruits in the bowl of a food processor fitted with a metal blade. Pulse until chopped fine. (If fruit is too frozen to process, wait several minutes and try again.) Add juice concentrate; continue to process until smooth and fluffy. Serve at once or return to the freezer. (If freezing, texture will be better if processed right before serving.)

NUTRITION INFORMATION PER SERVING:

77 calories
5% calories from fat
19 g carbohydrate

0.5 g fat
0 mg cholesterol
1.1 g protein

0 g saturated fat
1 mg sodium
5.8 g fiber

Honeydew Melon Sorbet

PREPARATION TIME: 15 minutes
COOKING TIME: 5 minutes
CHILLING TIME: 2 hours
FREEZING TIME: Variable
YIELD: 6 servings

THE RICH FLAVOR and creamy texture of this summery sorbet, adapted from chef Paul Bartolotta of Spiaggia, belies the fact that it is so low in fat and calories. And if that weren't enough, it is a breeze to make.

½ cup sugar

½ cup cold water

1 large honeydew melon, seeded,   Fresh lemon juice
    rind removed, and cubed

1. Chill a small bowl. Combine sugar and water in a small, heavy saucepan; heat to boil over medium-high heat. Cook until sugar is dissolved, about 5 minutes. Remove from heat, pour into the chilled bowl, and refrigerate until cold, at least 2 hours or overnight.

2. Puree melon and syrup in a blender until smooth; add lemon juice to taste. Strain mixture through a fine-mesh sieve.

3. Freeze mixture in an ice-cream maker according to manufacturer's directions until slushy. Place in the freezer until firm.

NUTRITION INFORMATION PER SERVING:

140 calories	0.2 g fat	0 g saturated fat
1% calories from fat	0 mg cholesterol	20 mg sodium
36 g carbohydrate	1 g protein	1.3 g fiber

Pineapple-Ginger Sorbet

PREPARATION TIME: 15 minutes
COOKING TIME: 5 minutes
CHILLING TIME: 2 hours
FREEZING TIME: Variable
YIELD: 8 servings

SURE, IT IS easy to buy ice cream and other frozen treats at the supermarket. But making them at home is worth the effort, Spago pastry chef Kim Stewart told writer Kristin Eddy in a 1999 article. "Freshly spun ice cream and sorbet is phenomenal compared to store-bought," Stewart said. "Both the texture and flavor are so velvety and fresh." This fruity-spicy sorbet is adapted from Stewart's recipe.

1 1-inch-thick piece gingerroot,   1½ cups water
    chopped coarse   1 large ripe pineapple, peeled,
1½ cups sugar   cored, and cubed

1. Combine gingerroot, sugar, and water in a heavy medium-sized saucepan. Heat to boil over medium-high heat; stir until sugar dissolves, about 5 minutes. Refrigerate until chilled, at least 2 hours or overnight.

▶

2.   Puree pineapple and ginger syrup in a blender until smooth. Strain through a fine-mesh strainer. Freeze mixture in an ice-cream machine according to manufacturer's directions until slushy. Place in the freezer until firm.

NUTRITION INFORMATION PER SERVING:

200 calories	0.5 g fat	0 g saturated fat
2% calories from fat	0 mg cholesterol	3 mg sodium
52 g carbohydrate	0.5 g protein	1.4 g fiber

Pear Lemon Ice

PREPARATION TIME: 10 minutes
COOKING TIME: 4 minutes
FREEZING TIME: 6 hours
YIELD: 8 servings

PEARS AND LEMONS team up for a delicious take on sorbet in a recipe that doesn't require an ice-cream maker—just a blender and freezer. Adding to this dessert's allure is the fact that the fruity ice is served in hollowed-out lemons and garnished with a mint sprig. Your guests will be most impressed!

1½ cups sugar	9 lemons
1½ cups water	Zest of 1 lemon
4 very ripe pears, peeled, cored, and quartered	1 pomegranate, optional
	Fresh mint leaves

1.   Heat sugar and water to boil in a large saucepan over high heat. Cook, stirring often, until sugar dissolves. Cover; cook 4 minutes. Set aside; cool to room temperature.

2.   Halve the lemons, juice them, and reserve 8 shells. Put pears, lemon zest, and 1 cup of the lemon juice in a food processor fitted with a metal blade or in a blender. Add 1 cup of the syrup; process until smooth. Taste and adjust sweetness, adding more syrup if needed. Pour into a large metal bowl; freeze until almost firm, about 2 hours.

3.   Clean out lemon shells. Cut a thin slice off each bottom so shells stand upright. Put frozen lemon mixture into the food processor or blender. Process until

smooth. Spoon into 8 lemon shells. Freeze until firm. Seed pomegranate and sprinkle seeds over ice if desired. Top with mint leaves.

NUTRITION INFORMATION PER SERVING:

212 calories	0.3 g fat	0 g saturated fat
1% calories from fat	0 mg cholesterol	2 mg sodium
56 g carbohydrate	0.6 g protein	2.4 g fiber

Frozen Mango Whip

PREPARATION TIME: 20 minutes

FREEZING TIME: 8 to 12 hours

YIELD: 6 servings

MANGOES CONTINUE TO gain popularity for their sweet and luscious flavor. Here, they're teamed with brandy and whipping cream for a tropical confection. Whips are light and airy desserts created by the addition of whipping cream or beaten egg whites. Serve them in pretty stemware, if you like.

4 to 5 mangoes	¼ cup brandy
½ cup sugar	Crystallized ginger *or* shredded
½ cup whipping cream	coconut, optional

1. Peel, seed, and cut mangoes into small chunks. Mix with sugar; freeze in a large metal bowl until firm.

2. Remove mixture from freezer. Spoon into a blender or into a food processor container fitted with a metal blade; process until light and smooth, about 1 minute. Add cream and brandy. Process until mixture is smooth and creamy. Put mixture in the large metal bowl. Cover; freeze 8 to 12 hours.

3. Soften slightly at room temperature. Put into the food processor or blender; process until smooth. Spoon into 6 dessert bowls or glasses. Top with ginger or coconut if desired.

NUTRITION INFORMATION PER SERVING:

238 calories	8 g fat	4.7 g saturated fat
29% calories from fat	27 mg cholesterol	10 mg sodium
41 g carbohydrate	1.1 g protein	2.5 g fiber

Blueberry–Passion Fruit Compote

COOKING TIME: 2 minutes

PREPARATION TIME: 5 minutes

YIELD: 4 servings

COMPOTES—SWEET SAUCES that star fresh fruit—add panache to many kinds of dishes. This example, from a "Fast Food" column by Pat Dailey, teams fresh blueberries with the more exotic flavor of passion fruit. This recipe uses frozen passion fruit concentrate and frozen unsweetened blueberries so you can make it year-round. Use this compote to top pancakes for an extra special weekend breakfast or brunch.

2 cups fresh *or* frozen blueberries

2 tablespoons frozen passion fruit juice concentrate

1 tablespoon sugar

2 teaspoons fresh lemon juice

½ cup black raspberries, optional

1. Combine 1 cup of the blueberries, passion fruit juice concentrate, sugar, and lemon juice in a small saucepan. Cook, stirring often, over medium heat just until berries begin to pop, 1 to 2 minutes (most should be soft but still hold their shape).

2. Transfer blueberry mixture to a medium-sized bowl; gently fold together with remaining blueberries and black raspberries if desired. Serve warm.

NUTRITION INFORMATION PER SERVING:

78 calories

6% calories from fat

19 g carbohydrate

0.6 g fat

0 mg cholesterol

0.8 g protein

0 g saturated fat

5 mg sodium

2 g fiber

Apricot-Cherry Compote

PREPARATION TIME: 10 minutes

COOKING TIME: 2 minutes 15 seconds

YIELD: 4 servings

A FRESH AND appealing dessert doesn't have to be demanding. This recipe from a "Fast Food" column stars seasonal apricots and cherries in a compote that cooks up quickly in the microwave. A sugar-honey crumble adds crunchy texture. Pour the compote over vanilla ice cream or frozen yogurt for a sweet finale to lunch or supper. We've also added a version you can make on the stovetop.

1 tablespoon unsalted butter

1 tablespoon sugar

2 teaspoons fresh lime juice, preferably Key lime

1 teaspoon honey

5 apricots, pitted and cut into eighths

¾ cup pitted sweet cherries

1.   Combine butter, sugar, lime juice, and honey in a shallow, 4-cup microwave-safe casserole or bowl. Microwave uncovered on high (100 percent power) until bubbly, about 1 minute 15 seconds, stirring once halfway through.

2.   Stir in apricots and cherries; return compote to the microwave and cook on high until fruit is hot, about 1 minute. Serve warm.

❦ VARIATION: *To make compote on the stove top, combine butter, sugar, lime juice, and honey in a medium-sized saucepan. Heat over medium heat, stirring often, until bubbly, about 2 minutes. Add apricots and cherries; cook until heated through, about 2 minutes.*

NUTRITION INFORMATION PER SERVING:

84 calories	3.3 g fat	1.9 g saturated fat
33% calories from fat	8 mg cholesterol	1 mg sodium
14 g carbohydrate	1 g protein	1.7 g fiber

Kiwi and Strawberry Compote with Ginger-Mint Syrup

PREPARATION TIME: 15 minutes

COOKING TIME: 5 minutes

YIELD: 4 servings

THIS COMPOTE ADDS a light, fruity finale to any meal, but it is especially suited to Asian ones. It accompanied an Asian stir-fry menu from a "Fast Food" column. Adding to its allure, there's very little fat and the calorie count is low. Look for crystallized ginger in the spice aisle of some supermarkets.

⅓ cup water

¼ cup sugar

1 tablespoon crystallized ginger

2 sprigs mint

2 cups hulled and quartered strawberries

3 kiwis, peeled, halved, and cut in thirds

1.   Combine water, sugar, ginger, and mint in a small saucepan. Heat to boil over medium heat; boil 3 minutes. Remove from heat; remove mint sprigs.

➤

2. Place strawberries and kiwi in a medium-sized bowl. Pour hot syrup over.

NUTRITION INFORMATION PER SERVING:

114 calories	0.5 g fat	0 g saturated fat
4% calories from fat	0 mg cholesterol	6 mg sodium
29 g carbohydrate	1 g protein	3.6 g fiber

Fresh Figs and Raspberries with Cream

PREPARATION TIME: 10 minutes

YIELD: 4 servings

WHY GET IN a dessert rut when your supermarket's ever-expanding produce section gives you so many opportunities to experiment? This easy dessert, developed for a "Fast Food" menu with an Italian theme, combines fresh figs and raspberries with whipping cream and sour cream. Fresh figs are most widely available in summer and fall.

8 fresh ripe figs	2 tablespoons sour cream, well
½ pint raspberries	chilled
¼ cup whipping cream, well	2 to 3 teaspoons light brown sugar
chilled	¼ teaspoon anise seed

1. Cut figs in half; divide among 4 shallow dessert plates or compote dishes. Add an equal-sized portion of raspberries to each.

2. Stir together whipping cream, sour cream, and brown sugar. Spoon over fruit. Rub anise seed between fingers to crush; sprinkle a bit over each portion.

NUTRITION INFORMATION PER SERVING:

165 calories	8 g fat	4.4 g saturated fat
38% calories from fat	24 mg cholesterol	11 mg sodium
26 g carbohydrate	1.6 g protein	5 g fiber

Cool Strawberry Soup with Pound Cake Croutons

PREPARATION TIME: 25 minutes
CHILLING TIME: 1 hour
COOKING TIME: 4 minutes
YIELD: 6 1-cup servings

WHEN STRAWBERRIES ARE in season, serve this dessert soup to chill out on a warm summer night. It was developed in the *Tribune* test kitchen.

2 pints strawberries, hulled and
  sliced
1 banana, sliced
¾ cup half-and-half
¾ cup sour cream
½ cup orange juice

⅓ cup sugar
2 tablespoons raspberry-flavored
  liqueur, such as Chambord
½ prepared pound cake, cut into
  1-inch cubes
Mint sprigs

1. Combine strawberries, banana, half-and-half, sour cream, orange juice, sugar, and raspberry liqueur in a food processor fitted with a metal blade or in a blender. Process or blend until smooth. Pour into a medium-sized bowl. Cover; refrigerate at least 1 hour or until ready to serve.

2. Heat broiler. Spread pound cake cubes in a single layer on a baking sheet. Broil until lightly browned, 1 to 2 minutes. Turn cubes over; broil until lightly browned, 1 to 2 minutes.

3. Serve soup in 6 dessert bowls or parfait glasses. Top with pound cake croutons and mint sprigs.

NUTRITION INFORMATION PER SERVING:

320 calories	16 g fat	9 g saturated fat
44% calories from fat	85 mg cholesterol	145 mg sodium
44 g carbohydrate	4.4 g protein	3.2 g fiber

Passion Fruit Soup

PREPARATION TIME: 25 minutes
COOKING TIME: 3 minutes
CHILLING TIME: 3 hours
YIELD: 4 servings

CHICAGO-AREA PASTRY CHEF Gale Gand devised this refreshing, fruit-filled dessert that is served in a soup bowl. Just don't let the word *soup* throw you off. One taste and you'll know: it's definitely a dessert.

Soup
½ teaspoon unflavored gelatin
½ cup passion fruit puree (see Note)
⅓ cup sugar
½ cup whipping cream

Citrus Juice
½ cup fresh orange juice
1 tablespoon fresh lemon juice
1 tablespoon passion fruit puree

Garnish
½ pint citrus sorbet, such as
    orange *or* lemon
Assorted fresh fruits such as
    peeled, sliced kiwi and papaya
    and blueberries, raspberries,
    and strawberries

1. Sprinkle gelatin over passion fruit puree in a small saucepan; let stand until soft, about 5 minutes. Add sugar. Heat over medium heat, stirring often, until gelatin dissolves, 2 to 3 minutes. Transfer to a large bowl. Cool to room temperature.

2. Beat whipping cream in the bowl of an electric mixer until soft peaks form. Fold ¼ of the whipped cream into cooled gelatin. Gently fold gelatin mixture into remaining cream. Pour into 4 individual soup bowls. Cover with plastic wrap; refrigerate until firm, about 3 hours.

3. To make citrus juice, stir together orange juice, lemon juice, and passion fruit puree in a small bowl. Pour juice mixture evenly over each soup bowl. Garnish with a scoop of sorbet and assorted prepared fruits.

❧ NOTE: *Make passion fruit puree by scooping out the pulp from fresh passion fruit and pushing it through a fine-mesh sieve. Or substitute passion fruit juice or frozen concentrate, available at specialty food stores and some supermarkets.*

NUTRITION INFORMATION PER SERVING:

261 calories	11 g fat	7 g saturated fat
38% calories from fat	41 mg cholesterol	26 mg sodium
40 g carbohydrate	2 g protein	3.6 g fiber

Chocolate Cognac Sauce

PREPARATION TIME: 5 minutes
YIELD: 2 servings

ON VALENTINE'S DAY, even kitchen-shy novices find themselves seriously considering a culinary extravaganza—multiple courses, complicated recipes, wine—all the things that make the day special. But columnist Pat Dailey wrote that a little romance shouldn't be stymied by a meal that takes too much time and effort. She came up with a menu that included this dessert sauce, which can be made well ahead of time. Serve it over coffee-flavored or vanilla ice cream with fresh raspberries. Also serve it over more elaborate desserts such as raspberry tartlets or chocolate cake, either homemade or store-bought.

¼ cup good-quality chocolate
  sauce
1 tablespoon Cognac *or* brandy

1 teaspoon vanilla extract
¼ teaspoon finely grated
  orange zest

1. Heat chocolate sauce in a microwave oven or small saucepan just until hot.
2. Remove from heat; stir in Cognac, vanilla, and orange zest.

NUTRITION INFORMATION PER SERVING:

50 calories	1 g fat	0.7 g saturated fat
18% calories from fat	4 mg cholesterol	20 mg sodium
4.5 g carbohydrate	1.1 g protein	0.1 g fiber

Spiced Applesauce

PREPARATION TIME: 25 minutes
COOKING TIME: 30 minutes
YIELD: 5 ½-cup servings

THE APPLE HARVEST brings with it a promise of lots of old-fashioned, home-baked goodies—pies, crisps, and applesauce. Here, cinnamon, ginger, cloves, and allspice spice up this easy-to-make applesauce. Serve this with waffles, French toast, or potato pancakes. If you make the applesauce ahead, cool it and refrigerate it in covered containers up to one week, or freeze it up to two months.

1½ pounds cooking apples, such as
  Winesap *or* Jonathan, cored,
  peeled, and chopped coarse

2 tablespoons water
½ cup sugar
2 tablespoons unsalted butter

►

1 tablespoon fresh lemon juice	½ teaspoon ground ginger
½ teaspoon grated lemon zest	⅛ teaspoon ground cloves
½ teaspoon cinnamon	⅛ teaspoon allspice

1. Put apples into a large nonreactive saucepan with a tight-fitting lid. Add water; cook covered, stirring often, over low heat until apples are tender, about 20 minutes. Drain excess water.

2. Put apples into a blender or into a food processor fitted with a metal blade. Process until smooth. Stir in sugar, butter, lemon juice, lemon zest, cinnamon, ginger, cloves, and allspice.

3. Return apple mixture to the saucepan. Heat to boil; reduce heat to medium. Cook, stirring often, until slightly thickened, 5 to 10 minutes. Serve warm or chilled.

NUTRITION INFORMATION PER SERVING:

200 calories	5 g fat	2.9 g saturated fat
22% calories from fat	12 mg cholesterol	1 mg sodium
41 g carbohydrate	0.3 g protein	2.8 g fiber

COOKIES AND CANDIES

Lemon Shortbread Cookies

PREPARATION TIME: 20 minutes
CHILLING TIME: 2 hours
COOKING TIME: 15 minutes per batch
YIELD: 60 cookies

A STORY BY William Rice on the future of brunch predicted that the meal will go a lot further than chafing dishes of eggs and bacon. Jean True of True Cuisine, a catering firm in Glen Ellyn, Illinois, contributed this recipe for a sweet ending to a weekend gathering.

2 cups (4 sticks) unsalted butter, softened	Pinch salt
	Zest of 2 lemons, grated fine
1½ cups packed brown sugar	1 large egg
4 cups all-purpose flour	2 teaspoons water

1. Beat butter and brown sugar in the bowl of an electric mixer until smooth and fluffy. Gradually beat in flour and salt to make fairly stiff dough. Stir in lemon zest. Shape into 2 flattened discs; wrap in plastic wrap or waxed paper. Refrigerate at least 2 hours.

2. Heat oven to 350°F. Lightly flour the work surface. Line baking sheets with parchment paper. Roll out dough to ½ inch thick. Cut dough with assorted 1½- to 2-inch cookie cutters. Place cookies on baking sheets.

3. Beat egg and water together in a small bowl. Brush cookies lightly with egg mixture. Bake until light golden brown, 15 to 20 minutes per batch. Cool 5 minutes on baking sheet; remove to cooling rack. Store in an airtight container.

NUTRITION INFORMATION PER COOKIE:

107 calories	6 g fat	4 g saturated fat
53% calories from fat	20 mg cholesterol	7 mg sodium
12 g carbohydrate	1 g protein	0.3 g fiber

Coriander Shortbread Cookies

PREPARATION TIME: 15 minutes
COOKING TIME: 20 to 25 minutes
YIELD: 48 cookies

FORMER *TRIBUNE* TEST kitchen director JeanMarie Brownson created this recipe that infuses classic, buttery shortbread cookies with the unusual flavor and aroma of coriander seed. They are great served warm with hot tea.

2 teaspoons coriander seeds
1 cup (2 sticks) unsalted butter, softened
½ cup confectioners' sugar, sifted
1 teaspoon vanilla extract
⅛ teaspoon salt
1¾ cups all-purpose flour

1. Heat coriander seeds in a small skillet over medium heat until aromatic and lightly toasted. Immediately remove from pan to a paper towel; cool. Grind cooled seeds to a very fine powder in a spice grinder. (There will be about 1 teaspoon powder.)

2. Beat butter in the bowl of an electric mixer until light and fluffy, about 2 minutes. Beat in sugar, vanilla, salt, and coriander powder until light and fluffy, about 3 minutes.

3. Heat oven to 350°F. Lightly flour the work surface and a knife. Stir in 1¾ cups flour by hand until mixed. Do not overmix. Turn dough out onto floured surface. Press dough into a ½-inch-thick rectangle. Cut dough into 1-inch squares using the floured knife. Put squares onto an ungreased baking sheet about ½ inch apart. Bake until golden and crisp, 20 to 25 minutes. Cool on wire racks.

❧ NOTE: *You can substitute toasted and ground coriander seeds in recipes calling for cardamom; the coriander seeds are less expensive and give a similar sweet flavor and aroma to baked goods.*

NUTRITION INFORMATION PER COOKIE:

55 calories
63% calories from fat
5 g carbohydrate
4 g fat
10 mg cholesterol
1 g protein
2.4 g saturated fat
7 mg sodium
0.2 g fiber

Jam-Filled Butter Cookies

PREPARATION TIME: 45 minutes
COOKING TIME: 7 minutes per batch
YIELD: 36 cookies

THESE JAM-FILLED BUTTER cookies were a third-place winner in the 1998 Holiday Cookie Contest for Caroline St. Clair of Skokie, Illinois. The festive and buttery sandwich confections evoke memories of her late grandmother, who, she wrote, "had so much patience and love for baking that she probably had given a name to each and every cookie she made."

5 cups all-purpose flour	2 large eggs
1 cup sugar	1 tablespoon vanilla extract
2 cups (4 sticks) chilled butter	Decorative sprinkles
4 large egg yolks	½ cup of your favorite jam

1. Heat oven to 350°F. Stir together flour and sugar in a large bowl. Cut butter into flour mixture using a pastry blender or 2 knives until crumbs the size of very small peas form. Add egg yolks, 1 of the whole eggs, and vanilla; stir well.

2. Lightly flour the work surface. Lightly grease a baking sheet. Roll out dough in batches to ⅛ inch thickness. Cut out dough with a 2-inch cookie cutter. To make cookie tops, cut a ½-inch circle from the center of half of the cookies using the end of a small pastry tip or thimble. Place cookie tops and bottoms on the baking sheet. Lightly beat remaining egg. Brush over cookie tops; decorate tops with sprinkles.

3. Bake cookies until dough is set and glaze is slightly golden, 7 to 9 minutes. Cool completely on a wire rack. Place ½ teaspoon jam in the center of bottom cookies; spread slightly. Place top cookies over each bottom; press down lightly.

NUTRITION INFORMATION PER COOKIE:

200 calories	11 g fat	7 g saturated fat
50% calories from fat	65 mg cholesterol	110 mg sodium
23 g carbohydrate	3 g protein	1 g fiber

Orange Pecan Delights

PREPARATION TIME: 25 minutes
COOKING TIME: 10 minutes
YIELD: 60 cookies

JULIE FORAN OF Glenview, Illinois, made a hit at the 1997 Holiday Cookie Contest with her orange pecan delights: pillow-soft cookies frosted with orange-scented icing and topped with a pecan half. These inviting cookies are the result of years of cookie preparation with her much-missed grandmother, with whom Foran figures she made about thirty-five hundred Christmas cookies over the years.

Cookies
3 cups all-purpose flour
2 teaspoons baking powder
½ teaspoon baking soda
½ teaspoon salt
¾ cup unsalted butter, softened
1 cup brown sugar
½ cup granulated sugar
2 eggs

½ cup sour cream
1 tablespoon grated orange zest
1 cup chopped pecans

Frosting
2 cups confectioners' sugar, sifted
2 teaspoons grated orange zest
⅛ teaspoon salt
3 tablespoons fresh orange juice
Pecan halves

1. Heat oven to 375°F. To make cookies, sift together flour, baking powder, baking soda, and salt into a large mixing bowl.

2. Cream together butter, brown sugar, and granulated sugar in the bowl of an electric mixer. Beat in eggs one at a time. Add sour cream, orange zest, and chopped nuts; mix together. Stir into flour mixture until smooth. Grease cookie sheets. Drop dough by teaspoons onto cookie sheets; bake 10 to 14 minutes or until golden.

3. To make frosting, stir together confectioners' sugar, orange zest, salt, and orange juice. Spread frosting on warm, not hot, cookies. Top each cookie with a pecan half.

NUTRITION INFORMATION PER COOKIE:

97 calories
39% calories from fat
14 g carbohydrate

4.3 g fat
14 mg cholesterol
1.1 g protein

2 g saturated fat
56 mg sodium
0.3 g fiber

Brown Butter Maple Spritz

PREPARATION TIME: 1 hour
CHILLING TIME: 30 minutes or longer
COOKING TIME: 16 to 18 minutes per batch
YIELD: 30 cookies

SARAH FRUDDEN OF Chicago was a prize winner in the annual "Good Eating" Holiday Cookie Contest with her Brown Butter Maple Spritz. Her Wisconsin dairyland heritage clearly shines through in this indulgent ode to butter. Frudden's Swedish spritz recipe is based on an old family favorite that she has updated with maple syrup and a rich filling.

1¼ cups (2½ sticks) unsalted butter	2 large egg yolks
1 cup confectioners' sugar	2¼ cups all-purpose flour
2 teaspoons vanilla extract	½ cup pure maple syrup
1¼ teaspoons salt	Milk *or* whipping cream
1 large egg	

1. Melt butter in a small, heavy saucepan over low heat; increase heat to medium when it's fully melted. Cook, stirring constantly, until butter turns medium brown and smells nutty. Measure out 1 cup for cookies; reserve the rest for filling. Refrigerate until firm but not solid, about 30 minutes.

2. Heat oven to 325°F. Beat 1 cup of the brown butter, ½ cup of the confectioners' sugar, vanilla, and salt in the bowl of an electric mixer until creamy. Add egg and egg yolks; mix to combine. Add flour; mix on low speed just until flour disappears. Transfer dough to a cookie press; press onto ungreased baking sheet in desired shapes, spacing cookies 1½ inches apart. Bake until set, 16 to 18 minutes. Transfer to a wire rack to cool.

3. Cook maple syrup in a heavy 2-quart saucepan over medium heat 5 minutes to thicken. Cool to lukewarm; stir in remaining ½ cup confectioners' sugar. Beat reserved brown butter in the small bowl of an electric mixer until light. Add syrup mixture; beat until smooth. If filling is too thick, add a small amount of milk or whipping cream until it's spreadable.

4. Spread about ½ teaspoon of the filling on the flat side of half the cookies. Sandwich each with another cookie.

NUTRITION INFORMATION PER COOKIE:

136 calories	8 g fat	5 g saturated fat
54% calories from fat	42 mg cholesterol	101 mg sodium
14 g carbohydrate	1.4 g protein	0.3 g fiber

Rumprint Cookies

PREPARATION TIME: 1 hour 30 minutes
CHILLING TIME: 1 hour 15 minutes
COOKING TIME: 12 minutes per batch
YIELD: 36 cookies

THIS WINNING RECIPE from the 1994 Holiday Cookie Contest, a petite, buttery cookie flavored with rum extract and fresh nutmeg, is the result of weekends of marathon cookie baking. Rebecca Gottfred of Arlington Heights, Illinois, and her sister, Priscilla Metzger of St. Louis, Missouri, bake together more than two thousand cookies each year to share with friends and give as gifts. Gottfred says this recipe doubles and triples easily and the baked cookies freeze well.

Cookies	*Filling*
⅔ cup unsalted butter, softened	¼ cup (½ stick) unsalted butter, softened
⅓ cup granulated sugar	
1 large egg	1 cup sifted confectioners' sugar
1 teaspoon vanilla extract	½ teaspoon rum extract
¼ teaspoon salt	Freshly ground nutmeg
1¾ cups all-purpose flour	
¼ teaspoon freshly ground nutmeg	

1. To make cookies, beat butter in the large bowl of an electric mixer until light; beat in sugar until fluffy, about 3 minutes. Beat in egg, vanilla, and salt; beat well. Stir in flour and nutmeg by hand until well mixed. Cover; refrigerate dough 1 hour.

2. Heat oven to 350°F. Shape dough into 1-inch balls. Place 2 inches apart on ungreased baking sheets. Press down centers with your thumb. Bake until barely golden, about 12 minutes. Cool on wire racks.

3. To make filling, beat butter in the bowl of an electric mixer until light, about 2 minutes. Add confectioners' sugar; beat until fluffy, 2 to 3 minutes. Add rum extract to taste. Beat well. Fill a pastry bag fitted with a medium-sized star tip with filling. Pipe a star into the center of each cookie. Sprinkle with nutmeg. Chill until filling is firm, about 15 minutes.

NUTRITION INFORMATION PER COOKIE:

62 calories	4 g fat	2.1 g saturated fat
52% calories from fat	15 mg cholesterol	19 mg sodium
7 g carbohydrate	1 g protein	0.2 g fiber

Best Gingerbread Cookies

PREPARATION TIME: 25 minutes
CHILLING TIME: 8 to 12 hours
BAKING TIME: 7 to 10 minutes per batch
YIELD: 144 cookies

FOR YEARS, THE *Tribune* received hundreds of entries for its annual Holiday Cookie Contest. In 1988, Gloria Heeter's recipe for gingerbread cookies took third-place honors. Heeter noted that she personalizes the Christmas cookies for friends and family but added that gingerbread is "truly a cookie for all seasons"—she once made them for her golden retriever's first birthday party. "We invited the neighborhood kids in for punch and cookies—cookies shaped like dog bones."

1 cup (2 sticks) corn oil margarine, softened
1 cup sugar
1 cup molasses
1 large egg
4 cups all-purpose flour
1 tablespoon cinnamon
2 teaspoons baking powder
2 teaspoons ground cloves
2 teaspoons ground ginger
1 teaspoon baking soda

1 teaspoon ground nutmeg
1 large egg yolk
1 teaspoon water
Currants
Raisins
Decorating candies

Icing
1 cup sifted confectioners' sugar
Water
Food coloring, optional

1. Cream margarine, sugar, and molasses in the bowl of an electric mixer until light and fluffy, about 3 minutes. Beat in egg. Stir flour, cinnamon, baking powder, cloves, ginger, baking soda, and nutmeg into mixture by hand.

2. Divide dough into 4 equal portions. Wrap each piece in plastic wrap or waxed paper; shape into flat disc about 1 inch thick. Refrigerate until firm, about 8 hours (or up to 3 days).

3. Heat oven to 350°F. Flour the work surface well. Roll out one piece of the dough to ⅛ inch thickness. (Dough is soft and can be difficult to work with, so work quickly and use plenty of flour.) Dip cookie cutters into flour; cut dough into desired shapes. Put cookies 1 inch apart on ungreased baking sheets. Mix egg yolk with water in a small bowl. Paint cookies with egg yolk mixture. Decorate with currants, raisins, or candy for eyes or buttons if desired. Bake until lightly puffed, 7 to 10 minutes. Cool on wire racks.

➤

4. To make icing, mix confectioners' sugar with a small amount of water until thick and spreadable. Stir in food coloring if desired. Put icing into a small plastic bag. Cut a small hole in one corner; drizzle icing onto cookies.

NUTRITION INFORMATION PER COOKIE:

39 calories	1.4 g fat	0.2 g saturated fat
31% calories from fat	3 mg cholesterol	32 mg sodium
6 g carbohydrate	0.4 g protein	0.1 g fiber

Walnut Refrigerator Cookies

PREPARATION TIME: 20 minutes

CHILLING TIME: 8 to 12 hours

BAKING TIME: 10 to 12 minutes per batch

YIELD: 60 cookies

THESE COOKIES ARE to be commended for two reasons. One, they taste great. Two, the dough keeps in the refrigerator for weeks.

2 large eggs, well beaten
2 cups packed brown sugar
¾ cup (1½ sticks) butter, melted
    and cooled
3 cups all-purpose flour

2 teaspoons baking powder
1 teaspoon salt
1 cup chopped walnuts
1 teaspoon vanilla extract

1. Beat eggs in the bowl of an electric mixer until light, about 2 minutes. Beat in sugar until smooth. Add melted butter; blend thoroughly.

2. Mix together flour, baking powder, and salt in a medium-sized bowl. Add to butter mixture; beat until combined. Add nuts and vanilla; blend thoroughly. Dough will be thick but not firm.

3. Lightly flour the work surface. Turn dough out onto the surface; shape dough into 3 logs about 2 inches in diameter. Wrap in plastic wrap or waxed paper. Refrigerate 8 to 12 hours or longer.

4. Heat oven to 375°F. Grease baking sheets well. Slice logs into ⅛-inch-thick slices. Put onto baking sheets. Bake until golden, 10 to 12 minutes. Remove immediately to wire racks. Cool completely.

NUTRITION INFORMATION PER COOKIE:

86 calories	4 g fat	2 g saturated fat
38% calories from fat	13 mg cholesterol	84 mg sodium
12 g carbohydrate	1.4 g protein	0.3 g fiber

Zucchini-Walnut Cookies

PREPARATION TIME: 20 minutes
COOKING TIME: 12 minutes per batch
YIELD: 36 cookies

RAFFAELLO LAMANTIA OF Chicago shared this cookie recipe with the *Tribune* for the "You're the Cook" column. The cookies are thick and chewy, and they freeze beautifully in airtight containers. Leave them plain or spread them with a cream cheese frosting. LaMantia sometimes substitutes dried cranberries for the walnuts.

½ cup (1 stick) butter, softened	1 teaspoon baking soda
1 cup sugar	1 teaspoon cinnamon
1 large egg	½ teaspoon baking powder
1 cup shredded zucchini	½ teaspoon salt
1 cup chopped walnuts	½ teaspoon ground nutmeg
2 cups all-purpose flour	¼ teaspoon ground cloves

1. Heat oven to 375°F. Beat together butter and sugar in the bowl of an electric mixer on medium-high speed until light and fluffy, about 3 minutes. Add egg; beat well. Stir in zucchini and walnuts by hand. Set aside.

2. Whisk together flour, baking soda, cinnamon, baking powder, salt, nutmeg, and cloves in a large bowl. Add zucchini mixture; stir until completely mixed.

3. Grease baking sheets. Drop rounded teaspoons of batter onto baking sheets. Bake until golden brown, 12 to 15 minutes. Cool on sheet 2 minutes; remove to a wire rack to cool completely.

NUTRITION INFORMATION PER COOKIE:

95 calories	5 g fat	2 g saturated fat
45% calories from fat	13 mg cholesterol	100 mg sodium
11 g carbohydrate	2 g protein	1 g fiber

Praline Cookies

PREPARATION TIME: 25 minutes
COOKING TIME: 10 to 12 minutes per batch
YIELD: 24 cookies

WHEN READER JEAN McGREE entered this recipe in one of our Holiday Cookie Contests, she recalled growing up in the South, where the pecan trees in her grandmother's yard in South Carolina provided work—plucking, sorting, and shelling—as well as pleasure. This was one of the winning recipes.

½ cup (1 stick) butter, softened	1½ cups all-purpose flour
1 large egg	1 cup chopped pecans
1½ cups packed brown sugar	1 teaspoon vanilla extract

1. Heat oven to 350°F. Beat butter, egg, and sugar in the bowl of an electric mixer until light and fluffy, about 3 minutes. Stir in flour, pecans, and vanilla by hand.
2. Grease baking sheets. Shape dough into walnut-sized balls. Put onto baking sheets; flatten to about ⅛ inch thick. Bake until bottoms are browned, 10 to 12 minutes. Remove to a wire rack; cool completely.

NUTRITION INFORMATION PER COOKIE:

151 calories	8 g fat	3 g saturated fat
43% calories from fat	19 mg cholesterol	47 mg sodium
20 g carbohydrate	1.5 g protein	1 g fiber

Crescent Cookies

PREPARATION TIME: 35 minutes
CHILLING TIME: 2 to 12 hours
COOKING TIME: 15 minutes per batch
YIELD: 60 cookies

ANNE MARIE REBAND of New Lenox, Illinois, won second place in one annual Holiday Cookie Contest for her grandmother's crescent cookies. "A couple of weeks before Christmas," she wrote with her entry, "I was looking for a recipe in my file box. My heart stopped—there was Grandma's recipe for crescent cookies! I didn't even know it was in there. I baked the cookies, fearful that somehow they wouldn't taste quite the same. On Christmas Eve, the verdict came in. Everyone agreed they tasted exactly like Grandma's. Of course, now I bake them every year. It just wouldn't be Christmas without them."

½ cup (1 stick) butter, softened	½ cup solid shortening

⅓ cup granulated sugar
⅔ cup finely chopped walnuts
1⅔ cups all-purpose flour
¼ teaspoon salt

1 cup confectioners' sugar plus
 more for sprinkling
1 teaspoon cinnamon

1. Beat butter, shortening, and granulated sugar in the bowl of an electric mixer until light and fluffy, about 3 minutes. Beat in nuts. Add flour and salt; beat on low until combined. Wrap dough in plastic wrap; refrigerate 2 to 12 hours.

2. Heat oven to 325°F. Roll dough into a ½-inch-thick rope; cut into 2-inch lengths. Form dough into crescents; place on an ungreased baking sheet. Bake until set but not browned, 14 to 16 minutes. Cool 5 minutes on the baking sheet; remove to a wire rack. Sift together confectioners' sugar and cinnamon. Dip cookies into sugar mixture while still warm; cool completely. Sprinkle with additional confectioners' sugar before serving to taste.

NUTRITION INFORMATION PER COOKIE:

60 calories	4 g fat	2 g saturated fat
59% calories from fat	4 mg cholesterol	25 mg sodium
6 g carbohydrate	1 g protein	0.2 g fiber

Kolachy

PREPARATION TIME: 40 minutes
CHILLING TIME: 4 to 12 hours
COOKING TIME: 15 minutes per batch
YIELD: 25 cookies

THE RECIPE FOR these tender cookies, from chef Suzy Crofton of Crofton on Wells restaurant in Chicago, ran with a story on the joys of real butter. Mascarpone cheese is an Italian double- or triple-cream cheese with a rich buttery taste and texture. If it is unavailable, substitute regular cream cheese.

1 cup (2 sticks) unsalted butter,
 softened
4 ounces mascarpone *or* cream
 cheese, softened
1½ cups all-purpose flour

⅛ teaspoon salt
⅛ teaspoon sugar
½ cup of your favorite preserves
Confectioners' sugar

▶

1. Put butter in the bowl of an electric mixer. Beat on medium speed until butter is light and fluffy, about 2 minutes. Add mascarpone; beat until smooth and well incorporated, about 2 minutes. Beat in flour, salt, and sugar just until most of flour is combined. Stir by hand until all flour is incorporated. (Do not overbeat or kolachy will be tough.) Flatten dough into a disc; wrap in plastic wrap. Chill 4 to 12 hours.

2. Heat oven to 350°F. Divide dough in half; return one half to refrigerator. Lightly flour the work surface. Roll dough out to about ⅛ inch thick. Cut dough into 3-inch squares with a sharp knife. Put squares on an ungreased cookie sheet; place 1 teaspoon preserves in the center of each square. Fold each corner to center of square, pressing dough lightly into preserves. Repeat with remaining dough.

3. Bake in batches until very lightly browned, about 14 to 16 minutes. Let sit on cookie sheet 5 minutes. Remove cookies to a wire rack. Generously sprinkle with confectioners' sugar while still warm and again when cool to taste.

NUTRITION INFORMATION PER COOKIE:

125 calories	9 g fat	6 g saturated fat
65% calories from fat	25 mg cholesterol	30 mg sodium
10 g carbohydrate	1 g protein	0.3 g fiber

Sour Cherry Rugelach

PREPARATION TIME: 30 minutes

CHILLING TIME: 1 hour

COOKING TIME: 20 minutes

YIELD: 64 cookies

THE "GOOD EATING" staff loved these crescent cookies from Jean Linsner of Chicago, first-place winner of the 1997 Holiday Cookie Contest. The tender cookies are not too sweet, so you can eat several without overdosing on holiday cheer. If you can't find dried cherries, substitute dried cranberries.

Dough

1 cup (2 sticks) unsalted butter, at room temperature

1 8-ounce package light cream cheese, at room temperature

½ cup sugar

2¾ cups all-purpose flour

1 teaspoon salt

Filling
¾ cup sugar
1 3.5-ounce package (⅔ cup) dried
  sour cherries, chopped fine
  (see Note)
⅔ cup finely chopped toasted
  walnuts

½ cup (1 stick) unsalted butter,
  melted
2 teaspoons cinnamon
1 teaspoon ground allspice
⅛ teaspoon salt

Glaze
1 large egg, beaten
Granulated sugar

1. To make dough, beat butter and cream cheese in the large bowl of an electric mixer until light. Add sugar; beat until fluffy. Mix in flour and salt. Gather dough into a ball; gently knead until smooth and flour is incorporated. Divide dough into 8 equal-sized pieces. Flatten into discs; wrap in plastic wrap. Refrigerate at least 1 hour.

2. To make filling, mix sugar, cherries, walnuts, melted butter, cinnamon, allspice, and salt in a medium-sized bowl. Set aside. Heat oven to 350°F.

3. Lightly flour the work surface. Unwrap dough discs; roll each into an 8-inch round. Spread 3 tablespoons of filling on the center of the dough, leaving about a ½-inch border. Use a pizza cutter or other straight blade to cut the circle into 8 wedges.

4. Starting at the wide end of each wedge, roll up each cookie tight. Place cookies tip side down on ungreased cookie sheets; bend into crescents. Repeat from step 3 with 7 remaining dough discs. Brush each crescent with beaten egg; sprinkle with sugar. Bake 20 minutes or until rugelach are golden brown. Cool on wire racks.

❦ NOTE: *Nuts and cherries are easily chopped (separately) in a food processor. To keep cherries from sticking to the blade, chop with about 1 tablespoon of the sugar.*

NUTRITION INFORMATION PER COOKIE:

93 calories	6 g fat	3 g saturated fat
53% calories from fat	16 mg cholesterol	56 mg sodium
8 g carbohydrate	2 g protein	0.3 g fiber

Pecan–Toasted Coconut Mandelbrot

PREPARATION TIME: 30 minutes
CHILLING TIME: 3 hours
COOKING TIME: 55 minutes
YIELD: 48 cookies

EVELYN BAUMANN'S CRISP, pecan-studded *mandelbrot* won over a kitchen full of fussy tasters at the 1998 Holiday Cookie Contest. The family recipe, passed on to Baumann by her mother, was never written down. "When pressed by me for specific ingredients her reply was, 'a little of this and a bit of that,'" she wrote. *Mandelbrot* comes from the German, meaning "almond bread."

3 cups all-purpose flour	1 teaspoon vanilla extract
1½ teaspoons baking powder	1 teaspoon almond extract
⅛ teaspoon salt	½ teaspoon grated lemon zest
3 large eggs	¾ cup chopped pecans
1 cup sugar	½ cup unsweetened coconut,
1 cup vegetable oil	toasted

1. Whisk together flour, baking powder, and salt in a medium-sized bowl; set aside. Beat eggs, sugar, and oil in the bowl of an electric mixer until light in color, about 5 minutes. Beat in vanilla extract, almond extract, and lemon zest. Add a quarter of the flour mixture, pecans, and coconut. Mix by hand after each addition until smooth. Wrap dough in plastic wrap; refrigerate at least 3 hours.

2. Heat oven to 350°F. Divide dough into 4 equal-sized pieces. Shape dough into 1½-inch-thick logs; place logs on an ungreased baking sheet about 2 inches apart. Bake until lightly browned, about 25 minutes. Cool on a wire rack.

3. Reduce heat in oven to 300°F. Slice each log diagonally into ½-inch-thick slices with a serrated bread knife. Place back on the baking sheet cut side up. Bake until light golden brown, about 15 minutes; turn each over. Bake 15 more minutes. Cool completely on the wire rack.

NUTRITION INFORMATION PER COOKIE:

105 calories	6 g fat	1 g saturated fat
55% calories from fat	13 mg cholesterol	25 mg sodium
11 g carbohydrate	1.4 g protein	0.4 g fiber

Chocolate Peanut Butter Cookies

PREPARATION TIME: 20 minutes
COOKING TIME: 10 to 12 minutes
YIELD: 36 cookies

A COVER STORY, "How they crumble: A crash course on chemistry for cookie lovers," produced this addictive cookie in the *Tribune* test kitchen. It was a staff favorite in 1990.

8 ounces semisweet chocolate	2 eggs
½ cup (1 stick) unsalted butter	¾ cup sugar
1½ cups all-purpose flour	½ teaspoon vanilla extract
½ teaspoon baking powder	8 Reese's *or* other peanut butter
½ teaspoon salt	cups, cut in chunks

1. Heat oven to 350°F. Melt chocolate with butter in a bowl in the microwave oven or in the top of a double boiler over simmering water. Set aside to cool slightly. Stir flour, baking powder, and salt together in a small bowl.

2. Beat eggs, sugar, and vanilla with an electric mixer in a large bowl until light and fluffy. Add cooled chocolate and mix well. Add dry ingredients; mix just until combined. Fold in peanut butter cups.

3. Drop batter by large spoonfuls onto baking sheets. Bake until set, 10 to 12 minutes. Cool on baking sheets 1 minute; transfer to a wire rack to cool completely.

NUTRITION INFORMATION PER COOKIE:

152 calories	9 g fat	4.3 g saturated fat
50% calories from fat	19 mg cholesterol	78 mg sodium
17 g carbohydrate	3 g protein	1 g fiber

Fudgy Bittersweet Brownie Stars

PREPARATION TIME: 20 minutes
COOKING TIME: 20 to 25 minutes
YIELD: 24 brownies

JEAN CUMMINGS OF Mokena, Illinois, takes off two weeks each December to do her holiday baking, which includes these brownie stars. The Cummings's cookie elf, as she is known at home, used twenty-five pounds of butter for cookies alone one holiday season.

¾ cup all-purpose flour
¼ teaspoon baking powder
¼ teaspoon salt
½ cup (1 stick) unsalted butter
3 ounces unsweetened baking
    chocolate

1 cup granulated sugar
1 teaspoon vanilla extract
2 large eggs, at room temperature
½ cup semisweet chocolate chips
Colored sugar, sprinkles, *or*
    frosting, optional

1. Heat oven to 350°F. Line the bottom and sides of a 13″ × 9″ pan with foil, leaving a 2-inch overhang at each end. Butter the foil, including sides and bottom; set aside.

2. Sift together flour, baking powder, and salt; set aside. Melt butter in a 3-quart pan over medium heat. Add unsweetened chocolate; stir until melted. Remove from heat. Stir in sugar and vanilla; mix well. Stir in eggs, mixing well. Stir in flour mixture and chocolate chips.

3. Spread batter evenly in the prepared pan. Bake 20 to 25 minutes, until the tops of brownies are firm when gently touched. Cool completely on a wire rack; lift foil and brownies from the pan. Cut brownies with a 2-inch star-shaped or other cookie cutter. Decorate with colored sugar, sprinkles, or frosting if desired.

NUTRITION INFORMATION PER BROWNIE:

122 calories
50% calories from fat
15 g carbohydrate

7 g fat
28 mg cholesterol
1.4 g protein

4.3 g saturated fat
36 mg sodium
1 g fiber

Cream Cheese Swirl Brownies

PREPARATION TIME: 25 minutes
COOKING TIME: 35 minutes
YIELD: 16 brownies

FREELANCE WRITER JOANNE Trestrail's article on the search for brownie nirvana led to this recipe, for those who hanker for brownie variation and a mild chocolate flavor.

4 ounces sweet baking chocolate
5 tablespoons butter, softened
1 3-ounce package cream cheese, softened
1 cup sugar
3 large eggs

½ cup plus 1 tablespoon all-purpose flour
1½ teaspoons vanilla extract
½ teaspoon baking powder
¼ teaspoon salt

1. Heat oven to 350°F. Melt chocolate and 3 tablespoons of the butter over very low heat, stirring occasionally. Set aside to cool.

2. Combine remaining 2 tablespoons butter with cream cheese in a small bowl. Add ¼ cup of the sugar, beating well. Blend in 1 egg, 1 tablespoon of the flour, and ½ teaspoon of the vanilla. Set aside.

3. Beat 2 remaining eggs until thick and light, about 2 minutes. Gradually add remaining ¾ cup sugar, beating until thickened. Add baking powder, salt, and remaining ½ cup flour. Blend in cooled chocolate mixture and remaining 1 teaspoon of the vanilla.

4. Butter an 8-inch square pan. Spread half the chocolate mixture in the pan. Top with cream cheese mixture, spreading evenly. Add remaining chocolate mixture by dropping in spoonfuls. Cut through batter in a zigzag pattern with a knife to make swirls. Bake until a wooden pick inserted in the center comes out clean, about 35 minutes. Cool before cutting.

NUTRITION INFORMATION PER BROWNIE:

164 calories	9 g fat	5 g saturated fat
48% calories from fat	55 mg cholesterol	116 mg sodium
20 g carbohydrate	3 g protein	0.3 g fiber

Java Brownies

PREPARATION TIME: 15 minutes
COOKING TIME: 40 minutes
YIELD: 16 brownies

THIS RECIPE COMBINES the best elements of fudgy and cakey with the drawbacks of neither. The coffee adds an earthy taste; serve the brownies with coffee ice cream, of course. The recipe is from freelance writer Joanne Trestrail.

4 ounces (4 squares) unsweetened chocolate
1 cup (2 sticks) butter
1 cup granulated sugar
¾ cup brown sugar
1 teaspoon vanilla extract

1 cup all-purpose flour
½ teaspoon baking powder
1 tablespoon espresso powder *or* 2 tablespoons very finely ground dark coffee beans
3 large eggs

1. Heat oven to 350°F. Melt chocolate and butter in a medium-sized pan over very low heat. Stir together; remove from heat. Add granulated sugar, brown sugar, vanilla, flour, baking powder, and espresso powder; stir thoroughly. Add eggs; mix.

2. Butter an 8-inch square pan. Spread mixture in the pan. Bake until a wooden pick inserted in the center comes out clean, 40 minutes. Cool before cutting.

NUTRITION INFORMATION PER BROWNIE:

271 calories
52% calories from fat
31 g carbohydrate

16 g fat
71 mg cholesterol
3 g protein

10 g saturated fat
150 mg sodium
1.3 g fiber

Frango Chocolate Brownies

PREPARATION TIME: 15 minutes
COOKING TIME: 25 minutes
YIELD: 9 brownies

ONE OF THE *Tribune*'s most requested recipes is the one for Marshall Field's Frango brownies, a recipe that canonizes the company's popular mint-flavored chocolate candy. The texture should be fudgy, not cakelike, and the top shiny. These brownies can be made up to two days in advance.

½ cup (1 stick) unsalted butter
2 ounces unsweetened chocolate, chopped fine

2 large eggs, room temperature
1 cup sugar
1 teaspoon vanilla extract

½ cup all-purpose flour
¼ teaspoon salt
½ cup coarsely chopped pecans

8 Frango mints *or* other flavor
(dark) chocolates, chopped fine
(about ½ cup)

1. Heat oven to 350°F. Melt butter in a medium-sized saucepan over low heat. Remove from heat, add unsweetened chocolate; stir until chocolate is melted. Let mixture stand until lukewarm.

2. Beat eggs in the bowl of an electric mixer until light and fluffy, about 2 minutes. Gradually beat in sugar; beat 1 minute. Add melted chocolate mixture and vanilla. Beat until incorporated. Fold in flour and salt. Fold in pecans and chopped Frango chocolates. Butter an 8-inch square baking pan. Spread batter evenly in the pan.

3. Bake until a wooden pick inserted halfway between center and the edge comes out with moist crumbs, about 25 minutes. Do not overbake; brownies should be moist. Cool completely on a wire rack. Cut into 9 squares. Store in an airtight container at room temperature.

NUTRITION INFORMATION PER BROWNIE:

308 calories	20 g fat	9 g saturated fat
55% calories from fat	77 mg cholesterol	90 mg sodium
32 g carbohydrate	4 g protein	2 g fiber

Budapest Truffles

PREPARATION TIME: 25 minutes

CHILLING TIME: 15 minutes

YIELD: 20 truffles

CHOCOLATE AND PAPRIKA? You'll be surprised at how well the combination works with these delectable truffles. Bittersweet chocolate and fresh cream are blended together, then dusted with—honest—sweet Hungarian paprika. The recipe comes from chocolatier Katrina Markoff of Vosges Chocolates in Chicago's Bucktown neighborhood. Incidentally, most supermarkets sell only American paprika; look for Hungarian paprika at specialty or spice markets.

6 ounces bittersweet chocolate
¼ cup whipping cream
½ vanilla bean
1 tablespoon sugar

2 teaspoons light corn syrup
1 tablespoon butter, softened
1 cup sweet Hungarian paprika

►

1. Break up chocolate; place in a medium-sized metal bowl. Melt chocolate in a bowl over a saucepan or bowl filled with hot water. Heat whipping cream, vanilla bean, and sugar to boil in a small saucepan over medium heat. Pour over chocolate; stir to combine. Cool to room temperature. Stir in corn syrup; mix well. Stir in butter; do not overmix. Remove and discard vanilla bean.

2. Line a baking sheet with parchment or waxed paper. Pour chocolate mixture onto the baking sheet. Chill until firm, about 15 minutes. Form into ¾-inch balls. Roll in paprika; chill until ready to serve.

٭ NOTE: *If the chocolate mixture sticks to your hands when you're rolling it into balls, coat your hands with paprika.*

NUTRITION INFORMATION PER TRUFFLE:

65 calories	4.3 g fat	3 g saturated fat
60% calories from fat	6 mg cholesterol	4 mg sodium
7 g carbohydrate	1 g protein	0.2 g fiber

Brittle Breakup

PREPARATION TIME: 10 minutes

COOKING TIME: 15 minutes

YIELD: 16 servings

THIS RECIPE—AN easy version of English toffee—is a favorite of the food staff. When it comes time for a candy fix or a holiday gift idea, the call goes out, "Make an extra copy of the brittle recipe for me!" Store the candy in a covered glass jar or tin box at room temperature.

1 cup (2 sticks) butter	1 tablespoon light corn syrup
1 cup sugar	1 cup semisweet chocolate chips
2 tablespoons water	⅔ cup finely chopped nuts

1. Grease a baking sheet. Melt butter in a medium-sized saucepan over low heat. Add sugar; cook, stirring often, until melted, 3 to 4 minutes. Add water and corn syrup. Cook without stirring until a small amount of syrup dropped into cold water becomes brittle (300°F on a candy thermometer), 15 to 20 minutes. Do not undercook. Remove from heat. Immediately pour onto the greased baking sheet. Cool until hardened.

2. Melt chocolate in the top of a double boiler over simmering water. Spread chocolate over cooled candy base. Sprinkle nuts over chocolate; press gently. Cool; break into pieces.

NUTRITION INFORMATION PER SERVING:

235 calories	18 g fat	9 g saturated fat
64% calories from fat	31 mg cholesterol	120 mg sodium
21 g carbohydrate	2 g protein	1 g fiber

Oven Caramel Corn

PREPARATION TIME: 25 minutes

BAKING TIME: 1 hour

YIELD: 12 servings

NEITHER ADULTS NOR children can resist buttery rich caramel corn. This version, from the *Tribune* test kitchen, requires some patience while the glazed corn bakes, but it's well worth the wait. Store popcorn in an airtight container.

6 quarts popped popcorn (about 2 cups raw)	2 cups packed light brown sugar
1 cup chopped nuts, optional	½ cup light corn syrup
1 cup (2 sticks) unsalted butter	1 teaspoon salt
	1 teaspoon baking soda

1. Heat oven to 200°F. Carefully remove all unpopped kernels from popcorn. Grease a very large baking pan. Mix popcorn and nuts if desired in the baking pan; set aside.

2. Heat butter, sugar, syrup, and salt to boil in a medium-sized saucepan; boil uncovered 5 minutes. Remove from heat; stir in baking soda.

3. Gradually but quickly pour caramel mixture over popcorn, tossing popcorn with 2 large wooden spoons to coat evenly.

4. Bake popcorn, stirring every 15 minutes, until crisp, about 1 hour. Cool on a wire rack.

NUTRITION INFORMATION PER SERVING:

485 calories	27 g fat	11 g saturated fat
49% calories from fat	41 mg cholesterol	526 mg sodium
60 g carbohydrate	5 g protein	3 g fiber

INDEX